The Propp Family History

פּרָאפּ

1760 - 2015

Henry W. Propp
David-Hillel Ruben

Published 2015

www.arimapublishing.co.uk

ISBN 978 1 84549 653 1

arima publishing
ASK House, Northgate Avenue
Bury St Edmunds, Suffolk IP32 6BB
t: (+44) 01284 700321

THE PROPP FAMILY HISTORY

פּרָאפּ

1760 - 2015

By HENRY W. PROPP & DAVID-HILLEL RUBEN

SECOND EDITION

2015

פּרָאף

This book is dedicated to all of our Family,
Our Ancestors and to all those who perished in the Shoah

(Of Blessed Memory)

Preface

The old, distinguished, Propp family currently dates back to the eighteenth century in Shkudvil, Lithuania and earlier elsewhere, without the surname, Prop (p). The members of the family are now spread through out the world. The family history and tree has been kept for well over one hundred and twenty years. It was first complied by Louis Arne (Lazer Aronovich) of Shkudvil, Kovno Guberniya, Russia, Calumet, Michigan and South Milwaukee, Wisconsin, later by Dr. Jerome Sachs of Chicago, Illinois, President Emeritus of Northeastern Illinois University. I have used past family trees compiled by various family members plus my own research to get where we are today. Louis Arne, who passed away in 1939, compiled the most comprehensive older family tree in 1938. Louis was a very bright and intelligent gentleman and he used the information his parents and grandparents had told him while he lived in Shkudvil. I have also gained additional and/or confirming information from family trees done by Isadore and Leo Propp of Peoria, Illinois, one compiled by Morris Propp, one by Seymour Propp, both of New York City and one that Dr. Leif Jacobsen of Stockholm, Sweden provided. Dr. Stanley Ruttenberg provided a family tree, one from Bill Berton (Berlowitz), Esq. of Saginaw, Michigan and finally the 1816 and 1847 reviskie skazki, box and candle taxes and Rabbi Elector lists. In addition to the United States Federal censuses, draft cards, Social Security information and cemetery Information.

The family descendants chart is presented in generational order starting with the oldest known generation, The next generation, Shimel Girshevich Probnovich (Shimon Prop) is −1 generation and his children each having a separate sections, this is the number 2- generation. Each subsequent generation(s) then are numbered from the number 1- generation, such as 3-, 4- or 5-, etc. We are currently into the 12th generation from Hirsh Probnovich. (Probnovich was most likely used only by the Russians and not the within the Jewish Community. There it most likely was still Prop - or maybe Propn, (Both mean cork or plug in Russian and Yiddish! But read on.)

I have had confirming through vital documents, which are in Kaunas archives for Shkudvil. These documents are dated 1816. They are reviskie skazki (census), also called revision lists. The documents were designed for taxation and conscription purposes of the Jews begun by the czarist authorities in the 1795 during the third partition and established of the "Pale of the Settlements". The 1816 reviskie skazki lists Shimel Girshevich Probnovich with sons Avram, Efraim and Hirsch which matches family historic name of Shimon Prop, his date of birth is listed as 1765, he came from abroad, meaning from outside the immediate area of Shkudvil, Vilna Guberniya, Russia (Lithuania).

Six areas of research need to be continued and will waiting for a new researcher: (1) Holocaust Information and the impact on our family; (2) Attempt to document the source of the name, Propp, i.e. Probn, Probnovich, Propkovich and Prop; (3) Trace the family back further than 1730; (4) Add historical information concerning Shkudvil, Lithuania and/or other areas the family has lived; (5) Continue to identify all family members and (6) To gain additional historical individual and/or family information.

This second edition of The Propp Family History is dedicated to our extraordinary family historian, Henry Propp, through whose efforts and expenditure of time and money all of this was made possible. All of what follows is his work, not mine, and I only had the nerve to put my name to it in order to be able to write this dedication to him and to thank him, in the name of all the Propp Family, for all that he has done.

One caveat. The first edition of the book was a private publication, without an ISBN, and circulated only to family members. Since this was the case, Henry wrote the historical and genealogical material in the early pages using sources that he acknowledged but without direct quotation marks around those parts of their texts that he used. Rather than rewriting those pages, Henry and I agreed that this general message would suffice, in order to acknowledge the fact that such use was made of those sources.

David-Hillel Ruben, London January 2015

Table of Contents

פֿראָפּ
Prop, our name

With the fall of the Roman Empire, surnames virtually disappeared. They did not reappear to any large extent until the late middle Ages and did not develop in England until after the Norman Conquest in 1066. They started to become generally used only during the Renaissance. In 1563 the Council of Trent speeded the adoption of surnames by establishing baptismal registers, which required the surname as well as the given name-also Called baptismal or Christian name.

Family names originated in a variety of ways. In England it became common to give surnames based on occupation. There were so many Johns, Roberts, and Thomases, with nothing to tell them apart, for example, that people began to refer to them as John the smith, Robert the miller, or Thomas the baker. Gradually these distinguishing names became fixed as family names, or surnames.

Other surnames that come from occupations include Carpenter, Taylor, Wright, Turner, Clark (clerk), Cook, Carter, and Gardiner. The reason there are so many surnames of Smith today is that during the Middle Ages the name was used for all metalworkers, or smiters, which means "to beat." These included blacksmiths, who worked in iron; whitesmiths, who worked in tin; locksmiths, silversmiths, and goldsmiths. Another common way of forming surnames came from the given name of the father. Such names are called patronymic meaning "father names." Johnson is "John's son." Jones and Jennings are modified forms of the same name. Williams, Williamson, and Wilson all mean "the son of William."

In Spain the men of many cultured families also use the metronomic, or "mother's name." The man's surname begins with the patronymic, which is then joined by the Spanish word y, meaning "and," to the metronomic. An example is the Spanish philosopher Jose Ortega y Gasset.

Modern Jewish Surnames

Because the Jewish people in Europe usually lived in compact, segregated communities, they did not need the identification of surnames. As they grew in number, however, various nations made laws compelling the Jews to adopt surnames. Austria led the way in 1787, France followed in 1808, and Prussia and Russia in 1812. In the Pale although the Jewish families were ordered in 1812 to take surnames but they were not commonly used until after 1840. Some Jewish families took their surnames from personal names such as Jacobs, Levy, and Moses. Others formed surnames from place-names such as Hamburg, Frankfurt, and Speyer. The noted Rothschild family took its name from the red shield (rothen Schilde) used as a sign over their shop in Frankfurt (See Rothschild Family). Many Jewish families took poetical or colorful names such as Rosenberg (Rose Mountain), Gluckstein (luck stone), Rubenstein (ruby), and Goldenkranz (golden wreath). Animal names were also popular-for example, Adler (eagle) and Hirsch (deer).

The Russian suffix -ovich means "son." The Russian name Ivanovich, or son of Ivan (John), corresponds to the English Johnson. The Swedish suffix is -son; Danish and Norwegian, -sen, in Modern Greek, -opoulos, the Yiddish people used. "vitz" (a.k.a. "vichy "vic", "witz", etc.) Just means "son of', and is usually appended to the father's name, in the case of a male. (Whereas "ova" and its variants would be used for a woman, meaning "daughter of'.) Say in this case, the father's name would have been "Yosel", the diminutive of "Yossi" or "Yosef", which happens to be the common Yiddish diminutive ending, so many Yiddish names end that way. There is also the suffix sky, ski which mean "from the location or town of, a place-name".

Compton's Encyclopedia

Propp Surname

There is a small ancient village named Propoisk (פּראָפּאָסק) Propojsk, Propoysk) just south-west of the fortress city of Smolensk, which means place of Prop and Prop is the way our name was spelled in Yiddish, פּראָפּ and in Hebrew, פּרופּ. A map of the Grand Duchy of Lithuania; Propoisk (see map) was listed on, is dated 1733. This town has existed since well before the first partition of the Polish-Lithuanian Common-wealth, which occurred in 1773. The name of the settlement remained Propoisk until 1945, when it was changed to Slavgorod. During the time of 1790 to 1820, the Prop family moved to Shkudvil. This was a period of general conflict and upheaval in the Propoisk area. The conflicts between Russia, Prussia and the Polish/Lithuania Empire were causing major changes to occur. Napoleon's armies marched through this area in 1812 on the way to Moscow. After the third partition of the Polish/Lithuania Empire in 1795, the extremely anti-Semitic Czarina, Catherine the Great, ordered all of the Jewish people to move to the "Pale of the Settlements" from locations inside Russia, and even some of the borderlands around Propojsk. Further, there were even more acute religious conflicts between different Jewish factions, Mitnagdim and Hasidim, which could force families to relocate because of a herem (excommunication), pronounced against them. These conflicts were especially turbulent in this area of medinat rusiya (Land of Russia) because of the Governmental support given to the Kahal there. Source: *Russia's First Modern Jews, The Jews of Shklov* by David E. Fishman.

• Prop, פּראָפּ, (Rossieny Area; Kovno Guberniya, Russia; Lithuania; The Pale of Settlement), Adjective, Noun: from Propn, פּראָפּן, (Yiddish) cork, plug, fool (figuratively). Source: *A Dictionary of Jewish Surnames from the Russian Empire* by Alexander Beider.

10

- Propes, Town: see Propishchanskij, Source: *A Dictionary of Jewish Surnames from the Russian Empire* by Alexander Beider.

- Propishchanskij, (Poltava Guberniya) Town: from the townlet Propojsk{Propes, Prupes, Prupis, Prupas} Source: *A Dictionary of Jewish Surnames From the Russian Empire* by Alexander Beider.

- From a town (fishing village). Max Propp of Vancouver said his father, Arthur Propp, used to say that his father, Max or Meyer, told him that the Propps took their name from a fishing village. Location Unknown. 1/8/94.

- The following information came from a document in Yad Vashem. Shkudviler, born October 5, 1907 gave this testimony. It was taken at the Displaced Persons Camp, Feldafing, West Germany on July 19, 1947. It is most likely, the original source for much which is written about Shkudvil in many other books. I will only quote the first two paragraphs here:

"Shkudvil, located in Tavrig region, was a small shtetl of two hundred Jewish families. Jewish people lived in Shkudvil for the past two hundred years. It was a bit far from a railroad station, however, it was astride the highway from East Prussia to Riga.

At its inception it consisted of two taverns on each side of the highway. Later on many villagers from the surrounding areas settled in Shkudvil. "Every new settler was called by the name of his original shtetl..."

"The village of Shkudvil was established by young Jewish settlers from other areas dating back to 1790 - 1800. It was fully developed by 1820". (Source *Yiddish Article from YIVO/94*)

From 1816 reviskie skazki, Rossieny Uyezd, Kovno Guberniya, Empire of Russia the original Shimon Propp with his family is listed as Shimel Girshevich Probnovich with Girshevich being the patronymic for his father, Hirsh and Probnovich would be his giving name and surname in Russia.

In the 14th century the Jews of Poland and Lithuania already received a charter of liberties and enjoyed the protection from King Casmir the Great. They were escaping from the persecutions of Western Europe, as well as all the major expulsions by England, France, Germany, and Spain of the 13th, 14th, 15th and 16th centuries. The Cossack Insurrection was in 1648. Vilnius (Wilno) was the capital of Lithuania in 1323. (*Border Lands of Western Civilization* by Dr. Oscar Halecki).

- **Slavgorod** (פּראָפּאיסק, **Propoisk**, Propoysk, Propojsk) the name changed in 1945 from Propoisk to Slavgorod. Its location is 53° 35' north, 31° 27' East 67. It is about 20-30 kilometers south-south west of Smolensk. A city and administrative center of Slavgorod, Mogilev Oblast, Belarus.

It is a landing at the inflow of the Pronia River into the Sozh River. It is 58 km from the Krickev railroad junction. The rail lines go Mogilev, Orsha, Vorozhba, and Roslavl.

The city has a vegetable drying plant, a Creamery and a concrete plant. (Could have easily been a fishing village, at one time because of the two rivers meeting there.)

This town was originally settled sometime in about the 14th century where the area was part of the Polish/Lithuanian Commonwealth. These governments welcomed Jews into their areas and gave them autonomy to run their parallel governments to the Polish-Lithuanian governments or regimes. The town became part of Czarist Russia during the first partition of Poland in 1773. As the second partition took place in 1793 and the third and final partition of Poland in 1795 caused this area to be in upheaval, change and disruption. If one adds to these facts the movements of Napoleon's armies through this area on there way to Moscow and all fighting which took place around Smolensk just 20 km to the north, one can understand why anyone might want to leave the area. *Historical Atlas of Russia, 1951.*

During the period of the Polish-Lithuania Commonwealth, Propoisk belonged to the Wojewodztwo of Minsk, and in the year 1766, there were 148 Jews living there. In 1847, there were 521 Jews living in Propoisk. As of 1897, when there was an all-Russian census, Propoisk was in the Mogilev Guberniya, Bykhov uyezd and it had a Jewish population of 2,304 out of a total population of 4,351 or 53 percent. *Russian-Jewish evreiskaia entsiklopediia, Published in St. Petersburg, Russia, c: 1915.*

During the first years of the nineteenth century the Jews of the German States were ordered to acquire surnames. This timing seemed to cross borders because the French also ordered the Jews and Christians to take surnames for census purposes. Since France controlled the Netherlands at this time, they too were ordered to take surnames. Jewish historiography has not succeeded in clarifying satisfactorily how and why the largest Jewish population known in history came into being in Eastern Europe. From *East to West* by Moses A. Shulvass.

- In a letter from a Christian named Propp, he said that he had found a town named Propp, north of Hussenbach by Saratov (Volgograd), Russia. This area was a homesteaded for Germans in the 18th and 19th centuries and this is where his family came from. He was a German Lutheran. On July 22, 1763, Catherine the Great of Russia issued a manifesto to invite Europeans (Germans) to develop the empty steppe region along the Volga River. By 1768, 27,000 Germans responded to the call. About three miles north of Hussenbach (Linevo-Osero) is the village of Propp, population under 100. Hussenbach was developed as a town in 1776. The date Propp was developed as a village is unknown. The German village names were changed back to Russian in the 1930's. I do not believe this village had anything to do with the Jewish Propp family from Lithuania as all Europeans were invited with the specific exception of Jews as outlined in the manifesto. Some records at the LDS date German Christian Propps back into 1660's in the Duchy of Mecklenburg (Northern Germany). I have enclosed a map of the region showing the village of Propp. (Ref.: *The Volga Germans* by Fred Koch - ISBN 0-271-01236-6). These Russian Germans immigrated into the United States about the same time as Eastern

European Jews were immigrating into this country, 1880-1920. They mostly settled in the mid-west and western states and were farmers there.

- All through the latter part of the 17th and 18th centuries in Carmin, Mecklenberg-Scherwin there was Christian Propps living there. These Propps most likely would predate any Jewish Propps. The records show births, marriages, and deaths dating from about 1666 through the 1800's. (Source: LDS records) Some Jews took their surnames from Christians in the area. Below is a listing of some the Christian Propps from Northern Germany:

Name	Date of Event	Place
Propp, Jochim	Marriage, 10/29/1666 to Maria Kaisers	Carmin, Mecklenburg-Schwerin Germany
Propp, Anna	Birth, 6/6/1668 F: Jochim Propp M: Maria Kaisers	Carmin, Mecklenburg-Schwerin Germany

This is only a small sample of Christian Propps from the Mecklenburg area. There was Christian Propps also in Königsberg in Neumark, Prussia; Stargard, Pommern, Prussia and Evangelisch Lutherische, Westpreussen, Prussia.

Conclusion

- In the preceding paragraphs I have included all the information I have collected relative to our name Prop(p). I have done this to allow each person to make his or her own mind up as to where our name came from. I have had several convictions about our name over the past five or six years. My opinion now is that the name, Propp, was derived from the word: Propn, פּראָפּן (Yiddish), in Yiddish, and is equal to Probn, Пробн in (Russian), it translates to cork or plug in both language. In the 1816 Shkudvil census our name is listed as Probnovich and in Russian as Пробнович. The census was made for Russian authorities and written in Russian by a Jew who is certified as taking the census. He most likely knew everyone in the village of Shkudvil. Therefore, Shimel was most likely known within his Yiddish community as; Propn, פּראָפּן and sometime during the next forty years the "n" or nun was dropped from the end of the name, if it was ever used within the Jewish Community and we ended up with a very unique surname of Prop and in English, Propp. The implication that the name means "fool" is only given in the dictionary: *Stutchkoff, N. Der oytser fun der yidisher shprakh, YIVO Institute for Jewish Research, 1950.* This is the listed reference for the name, Prop, used by Beider in his book, *A Dictionary of Jewish Surnames from the Russian Empire* by Alexander Beider.

I can find no connection between the German Propp family and our Jewish Propp family. I do not believe that either family had converts, which created the second or other Propp family. This is not to say that there may not have been converts both ways.

13

Also I can not trace any member of our family back to Byelorussia and the village of Propoisk. Although this is true, I do not know where Shimel Girshevich Probnovich came from except that he was not born in Shkudvil.

You might also want to see "Economic Origins of anti-Semitism" by Hillel Levine (Yale Univ. Press), especially Chapter 4 and a bit in the Introduction. Incidentally, he cites estimates that 75% of the "rural" Jewish population were principally in the alcohol trade, known as the "Propinacja" (small-scale production, transport, and inns often all together). Usually when vital records use the term "leaseholder" (arrender) this involves inn keeping and the alcohol trade. It is a common (and often not necessarily flattering) image of the rural Jew in Polish literature and art. Some of my oldest known ancestors were innkeepers and original Jewish settlers in Skaudvile, Lithuania about 1790 CE. The original Jews there operated roadside inns according to Skaudvile historical documents. Dr. Beider's "Dictionary of Jewish Surnames of the Russia Empire", gives our surname as: *PROP (N)* meaning "cork, plug or fool." It is a unique surname; all *PROP* or *PROPP*s throughout the world are decedents of Shimel and originally lived in Skaudvile. The Skaudvile's 1816 Revision List lists my oldest known ancestor, as Shimel Girshevich *PROBNOVICH* and Dr. Beider must have taken that to mean Propn in Yiddish, which means the aforementioned. (I have never fully accepted this meaning and I keep searching)

I have spelled the Propp's name as they appear in the contemporary census of the periods. In earliest census available in 1816, the family was listed as Probnovich; remember these are Russian censuses, so the Russian patronymics were being used all through the various censuses from 1816 through 1912. A Lithuanian personal name, like in most European cultures, consists of two main elements: the given name (*vardas*) followed by family name (*pavardė*). The usage of personal names in Lithuania is generally governed (in addition to personal taste or family custom) by three major factors: civil law, canon law, and tradition. Lithuanian names always follow the rules of the Lithuanian language. Lithuanian male names, as well as the rest of words, have preserved the Indo-European masculine endings (*-as; -is*), that make them look similar to Greek names. Further the Propp's also used Lithuanian surnames such Propas or Proppas for the males, and females use ienė indicating married at the end of their own surname such Propienė, or Proppienė. If the female is single they use the follow listed suffix to surname aitė such as Propaite or Proppaitė.

There is a word: Propinacja and I note the similarity with our surname. I have to wonder if our surname could have been an occupation rather than a noun? And if it was derived from "PROPINACJA" to PROPN then shortened to PROP. The surname PROP was firmly established by the 1847 Revision List of Skaudvile, Lithuania. I would ask anyone who wishes to either reply in private to my email address or in public i.e. LitvakSIG to give whatever input they would wish to.

1. The Jews were in the alcohol trade for two main reasons aside from the economics:

   a) They anyway made their own wine and liquors for the festivals and especially Pesach, and these had to be very carefully processed in order to conform to the requirements of Kashrus.

   b) The Catholic Church forbade Christians from manufacturing liquor and so that opened the trade to the Jews almost exclusively.

I would imagine that the type of liquor produced vary from area to area, depending on the fruit or corn grown there. For example, again my family town, Zagare was famous for its cherries and so there was an industry there for manufacturing a Cherry Brandy called Zagersk, which is still produced there. I should not be at all surprised if my family started that industry. Yes they made Vodka, and Schnapps and of course wines which were largely for their own use.

I should also differentiate between a Kretchma and a Tavern or Shenk, as it was known in Yiddish. I have already described the Kretchma, which was far from being a drinking place. However the Jews also owned most of the Taverns, which were usually set in and around the market squares of the shtetls. The peasants came into town and sold their wares and then proceeded to the taverns to spend their hard earned money and invariably got drunk. This often ended in violence and destruction. It must have been a very lucrative trade for the Jews to take these risks.

2. Names: The edict requiring Jews to take family names was issued in 1808 and by 1825 pretty well all the Jews had family names. It is possible to divide these names into two rough groupings:

   a) Universal names, like Kagan, Levy, Katz, Segal, Zaks etc. these names appear all over Lithuania and other areas in Pale of Settlement.

   b) Regional names, I call them regional for want of a better word. The Jews took names at random from their trades, physical features, patronymics, places of origin or domicile and so on. Because there was not a great deal of movement of population within Lithuania in the 19th century, these names were often confined to the original areas in which they were taken. Beider based his work on the 1895 All Russia census and the 1907 electoral Lists and from these he drew his conclusions, mostly if not always correct as to the geographical origins of the names. The names in themselves were static in the sense that they were not connected to trade or other movement going on around them. The Jews took no pride in these names, which were forced upon them by the authorities; only their synagogue names had any meaning for them. If you look at the Revision Lists you will notice that nearly all the first names were variations firstly of their Yiddish name, diminutives of their Hebrew names etc. but the full Hebrew name in the Holy Tongue never appears. By the way Beider does not and cannot know the origins of all the names so you must take his information with limited credentials. To give you one example my paternal grandmother's name was Elion, to which he tries to give Hebrew connotations. The name is the corruption of a Sephardic place name, Ayllon but he could not know this. Likewise the geographical origin was Kraziai, but he has Vilna. The reason being that they were a family of Rabbis and as such moved around looking for Rabbinical Office and apparently the biggest concentration of them was in the Vilna area at the time those two lists appeared.

I have been doing research for more than 30 years now, in fact since my retirement I have begun to work professionally. Much of my accumulated knowledge came from examining the facts and events in the field as well as reading much of the Hebrew and Yiddish literature on the subject. There is in fact very little in English although a good book for background of the period is: "*Life is with People* by Mark Zborowski and Elizabeth Herzog."

You might find my article in *Avotaynu Vol.10 No.3 of 1999*; "*Tackling the Lack of Surnames in 18th-Century Russian Records*" for some further elucidation. I do hope that helps a little.

I would add that to the best of my knowledge the 1795 census for Skaudvile does not exist. The Western movement of the Jews began in earnest in the 1880s. Until then there was a considerable movement from Lithuania into the Kurland and Livonian Guberniya in the North, mostly illicit. I have yet to find any record Shimel Girshevich Probnovich prior to 1816. There are censuses in the eighteenth century, one 1789 and one in 1767. Since the Jewish people of the Duchy of Lithuania-Poland did not have surnames prior to about 1805, identifying the family who difficult, however more Jewish Kahal lists of the Jewish people are become available, most are written in Polish which was the official language of the Duchy prior to the Russian second and third partitions.

A History of Lithuanian Jewry

Lite (Lithuania in Yiddish) was historical territory of ethnical Lithuania and Byelorussia, i.e. Historical territory of the Dukedom of Lithuania, for about 650 years has been heart of Yiddish-speaking Jews-Litvaks, and since the middle of the 19th c. Center of the East European Haskala, Jewish Enlightenment. On this territory the non-assimilated part of the Jewish Ashkenazi culture survived right up to the Holocaust.

These Lithuanian Jews shared the fate of all Eight million pre-war Yiddish speaking Ashkenazi Jews of Central and Eastern Europe: they were almost entirely annihilated in Holocaust. Their distinctive culture also came to an end. The people, however, left an indelible mark on the social, economic, and intellectual landscape of Europe.

The first Jews are supposed to have come in Lithuania in the 12th c. as refugees from the atrocity of the crusaders. First compact settlements appeared in the early 14th century, when many Jews came among artisans from Western Europe. 1388 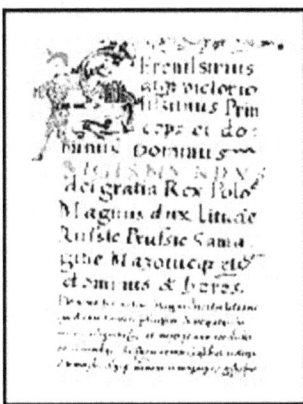 and 1389 Duke Vytautas (Witold) the Great granted the privilege to the Jews approving equality of their religious and civil rights and exempting synagogue and cemetery land from taxes. Lite served for centuries as an asylum for Jews from all over Europe, where they sought and found refuge from persecution and hostility, For several centuries prior to its destruction, the Jewish community in Eastern Europe was the most important in the world. The life of the Eastern European Jews, in the tradition of the Ashkenazi, who, driven out of the Rhineland in the Middle Ages, had settled in Eastern Europe, is illustrated by the history of Jewish Vilnius, Yerushalayim de Lite ("Lithuanian Jerusalem"), between 1830 and 1930. Vilnius was the center opposed to Chassidism, a religious revival movement that emerged in the second half of the 18th century and, particularly popular among the poor, represented a kind of social revolutionary movement.

The Chassidism, born in Ukraine, spread from Poland and Byelorussia. Its theological grounds were pantheistic; its moral and social grounds were love and social equality. This was based on specific interpretations of Torah and Talmud. Those who opposed Chassidism considered the Chassidic interpretations to be wrong. One of the strongest opponents of the Chassidism was Reb Eliyahu Kremer (1720-1797), the famous Gaon of Vilnius, who is said to be the last representative of traditional Talmud scholastics in Europe. During all his life he elucidated original meaning of Talmud texts using dialectical logic.

The rise of German Jewish Enlightenment in the 1760s intensified the eventual decline of Yiddish in Western and parts of Central Europe. At the same time Eastern Europe rapidly rose to prominence as the new center of Yiddishkeit, where by the end of the 19th century it underwent swift and vigorous process of modernization. Under the influence of Mendelssohnian Enlightenment spread from Germany, the Haskala, the East-European Jewish Enlightenment, began in the 19th century among the Jews of Poland/Lithuania and Russia. Its spiritual father was Isaac Baer Levinson. 1828 saw the publication in Vilnius of his book Teuda Beisrael ("A testimony in Israel"), the manifesto of the Jewish Enlightenment in Eastern Europe. Thus Vilnius became center of the late Jewish Enlightenment.

The "Pale of Settlement" was created in the late 18th century, when the right bank Ukraine, Byelorussia and Lithuania, all with large Jewish populations, were surrendered to Russia as a result of the Partitions of Poland. Only "local Jews" were permitted to live in Courland Province, the Caucasus and Middle Asia.

At the beginning of this period there were 1,044,000 Jews in the fifteen Guberniya of the Pale of Settlement (in 1847) and 468,000 in the ten Guberniya of Poland (in 1856), which were annexed by Russia in 1815, making a total of 1,512,000. From 1831 on, the annexed territory was called "The Congress Poland." In 1870 there were 2,688,000 Jews in the Pale, Poland and the thirty-five Guberniya of the interior. In 1881 there were a total of 2,835,000[1]. The only census of the whole population took place in 1897, when the Pale had 3,558,060 Jews, Poland 1,306,576, the rest of Russia 314,765, a total of 5,179,401. Thus only six percent of Russian Jewry lived outside the Pale. In 1917 a reasonable estimate of the total number of Jews is six million. To this should be added 1,200,000 who emigrated to the United States, 185,000 to other countries and 80,000, who were said to have converted to Christianity, making the total number of Jews approximately seven and half million, which represents more than a five fold biological increase in the seventy years of this period. In Russia, Jews constituted about four percent of the general population of Russia, in Poland, fourteen percent and eleven percent in the Pale

The fifteen Guberniya of the Pale were Bessarabia, Chernigov, Ekaterinoslav, Grodno, Kherson, Kiev, Kovno, Kurland, Mogilev, Podolia, Poltava, Tavrida, Vilna, Vitebsk and Volyn. The ten Polish Guberniya were Kalish, Kelets, Lomzha, Lublin, Petrokov, Plotsk, Radon Sedlets, Suvalki and Warsaw. The thirty-five other Guberniya of European Russia include St. Petersburg and the Caucasus, where few Jews lived.

The period started with the most ominous proposition by Tzar Nicholas' I government. They conceived the concept of razbor (selection) of the Jewish population into productive and non productive groups in the 1840s. The law was designed to press into the army three fold of the unproductive, such as small storekeepers, and to expel them from villages. Administrators largely disregarded this, since it would have meant ruin for the major part of the Jewish population. Still, the threat remained suspended as a Damocles sword over the heads of the Jews for fifteen years.

---

[1] *All these figures are approximate.*

18

With the abolition of the *Kahal* many of the former powers of the community over the individual were eliminated. To name a few: community taxes on consumer goods, river tolls, postal charges, market supervision. In addition, debts to Christian monasteries were also canceled. A number of economic practices, however, were perpetuated, such as *hazukuh*, rentals from stores, issuance of passports, *korobka*, candle tax and assessment of taxes.

However, the greatest transformations were a result of events in the Western World of which industrialization, the development of railroads and the growth of a proletariat were the most important. In Russia the changes among the Jews were cataclysmic: secularization, a move from hevrah to trade unions, mutual aid associations, national and world organizations for economic rehabilitation, government regulations of association, development of proletarian consciousness and mass revolution.

In Russia, merchant corporations are known to have existed as early as the 12th century. In the 16th and 17th centuries there existed privileged corporations of the richest merchants (gosti), clothiers (torgovye liudi sykonnoi sotni), and companies of traveling traders (gostinye sotni). Within the corporations, merchants were divided according to property into three ranks – first, middle, and third. The term guild is first mentioned in 1719 in the regulation of Chief Magistracy, the creation of guilds in all cities was declared compulsory. The population of the posad (merchants' and artisans' quarter) was to be divided into regular and irregular citizens. The first group in turn was divided into two guilds: the first included bankers, notable merchants, doctors, pharmacists and several categories of craftsmen (such its gold and silver masters). The second included petty tradesman and craftsman (with the formation of shop, tradesmen and craftsmen in 1722, some of the craftsmen were not included in the guild division). The remaining population, including unskilled workmen and those for hire, was included among the irregular citizens.

In practice, from the 1720's to the 1770's, the posad population designated as merchants continued to be divided according to property into three ranks or guilds, among which there was no substantial difference in class character. The situation changed in the 1770's and 1780's. By the manifesto of March 17, 1775, the merchants were divided into the privileged guild merchants (three guilds) and the meshcane (lower urban groups).

The Privileged Guild included merchants having capital of 500 rubles or more, the three guilds of which were, according to the edict of May 25, 1775, the Third Guild (500-1,000 rubles of capital), the Second Guild (from 1,000 to 10,000) and the First Guild (10,000 and above). The remaining citizens were classified as meshcane. The Guild Merchants were freed from poll tax payments and from military service obligations, which were replaced by monetary payment. The rights and obligations of the Guild Merchant class were defined in the Charter of Cities of 1785. At that time, the largest merchants (with capital of over 50,000 rubles), bankers (capital of 100.000 200,000), and various other urban dwellers were designated its "Distinguished Citizens".

Merchants of the First Guild and Distinguished Citizens received the preferential right to carry on foreign trade. Distinguished Citizens and Merchants of the first two Guilds were exempted from corporal punishment. Jews of the first two Guilds and the descendants of these persons had the right to reside outside the Pale, and when the Third Guild was abolished in 1863, all Jewish merchants gained that right too. In 1861 another proclamation followed permitting Jews with university degree (doctors included) the same right, and in 1879 pharmacists, dentists and midwives were added.

In the late 18th and early 19th centuries, there was a gradual decline of the Guild Merchants. A major reason for this was the widespread competition of serfs engaged in commerce. With the development of capitalism the role of the guilds declined. In 1863 the Third Guild was abolished. After 1898 Guild licenses, were acquired voluntarily only by persons who wanted merchant class rights.

There were five razriady (classes) among Jews: merchants, peasants, artisans, settled commoners and those with no definite occupation. A small number belonged to the nobility, or after thirty years of membership in a Merchant Guild he became an Honored Citizens, a status which was also hereditary. There were also raznochintsy (professionals, such as educators and dentists).

The following table provides an overview of the Jews in there various vocations.

Thus seventy-five percent of the Jews were small traders and artisans. The nobility alone could own land and taverns and were exempt front taxes. Some Jews did, nevertheless, obtain leases on land and others sold liquor at lower prices than the nobility. When the state took over the monopoly on the production of liquor in 1891, some Jews became very wealthy and others became rich in many new manufacturing ventures. Every town had some wealthy Jews; however, with a few exceptions, they did not control sufficient capital to launch large business enterprises. Burghers were taxed more heavily than merchants, though they were of a lower class. However, despite the various restrictions, the Jews advanced in many fields.

The cruelty of the government destined the greatest majority of Jews to a life of poverty and oppression. The recurrent expulsions and various other restrictions filled the highways with itinerant paupers bearing their *talith* and *tfillin* and the growth of the factory did not improve their circumstances in any way. The Pahlen Commission testified that "Jews are a most desperate proletariat, there is none like them in all of Russia or anywhere else in Europe."

In the course of Russian educational reform under Czar Nicholas I, a Russian-language rabbinical academy, which included a secondary school, was established in Vilnius in 1847. For a long time this academy was the intellectual center of the East-European Judaism. On the other hand, the library founded by Matityahu Strashun. Vilnius in the late 19th century became an intellectual center in its turn, since a copy of every single book in Hebrew or Yiddish that was published in Eastern Europe had to be collected there. In addition, Vilnius was the main printing center for the Yiddish literature in Eastern Europe. The most renowned printing works belonged to the Romm printing house.

[Table 4. Occupations of Jews in Russia, 1897]

Group	Men	Women	Dependents	Percent of Jews
Commerce	408,330	66,650	1,956,852	38.65
Artisans	467,890	87,339	1,793,937	35.43
Messengers Day Labors				
Privileged Employees	62,012	113,738	334,817	0.61
Unproductive				
Uncertain Professions	68,583	47,755	278,095	5.49
Public Service	66,874	5,040	264,683	5.22
Transport	45,493	465	201,027	3.98
Agriculture	32,993	4,380	1,79,400	3.55
Military	53,195		54,277	1.07
	1,205,370	325,367	5,063,098	100.00

Towards the end of the 19th century, its traditional use in the study of the Talmud and interpretative literature and above all its subsequent use by religious and educational innovators (in Chassidism and Haskala) as well as by the nascent workers' movement (Jewish socialist mass organization called Bund), and the increasing prominence of Yiddish in the press, theatre and education gradually assured the Yiddish language of its function as a comprehensive means of communication in every social sphere. Yiddish developed into a fully-fledged literary language in the wake of the national-cultural emancipation movements in Eastern Europe.

Yiddish literature has produced significant works: Isaac Baer Levinson (1788-1860) is regarded as the "Moses Mendelssohn of the Russian Jews". His writings were to become the program of Enlightenment for Eastern European Jewry in the process of emancipating itself under the influence of Haskala. The most outstanding writers of the Haskala were Mendel Moykher Sforim (1836-1917), Yitshok Libya Perets (1851-1915) and Sholem Aleykhem (1859-1916). Mathias Strashun (1817-1885), who combined an immense Talmudic knowledge with a command of modern languages and sciences, fought for the ideals of the Jewish Enlightenment throughout his life. One of his great achievements was setting up an extensive library in Vilnius, which soon became one of the most important libraries in Eastern Europe. Samuel Joseph Finn (1820-1890) was among the many authors, mostly from Lithuania, who had a strong influence on the Yiddish language and laid the foundations for the historiography of Jewish literature in Yiddish. Their spadework served as the basis for "The History of Jewish Literature", which was written in Yiddish by the historian Israel Zinber and published in Vilnius in 1927-1937. It was republished in English in the 1970s. Another notable writer and expert on Talmudic scholarship and Jewish pedagogy was Eysik Meir Dick (1807-1893), who taught at the first state-maintained Jewish school in Vilnius and led Yiddish belles letters to its heyday.

Great works of Yiddish theatre were produced in Eastern Europe too: in addition to the dramas of Abraham Goldfaden (1840-1908), Der Dibbuk, a work written in Yiddish by An-sky, was to become the most significant Yiddish stage play in Eastern Europe. This play was not premiered until 1920, after Ansky's death, in Warsaw. It was performed by the 'Vilnius Company', the most renowned Yiddish theatre in Europe at the time.

The "shtetl", i.e. an East European Jewish settlement, was the hearth of the Yiddish culture before the Holocaust. This term connotes the diversity of the Yiddish language, literature, music and traditions, though it also specifically refers to the place and time of the decisive stages in the evolution of Yiddish. The shtetl is vividly documented in early 20th-century art, in the works of Yankel Adler, Issachar Ryback and Marc Chagall for example. Yiddish culture also finds particular expression in its music, which draws from two sources: religious culture and folklore. The oldest folkloric Yiddish musicians are the Klesmorim, whose only instrument was initially the violin. Without being able to read or write music, they composed melodies, which were strongly influenced by regional folklore.

In 1925, a Yiddish Scientific Institute (YIVO) was founded in Berlin. The YIVO soon moved its head office to Vilnius and became a worldwide magnet for the study of the East-European Jewry. It was relocated to New York at the beginning of the World War II (besides the YIVO, there are many institutions academically researching Yiddish in the USA now, e.g. the public organization Arbeyter Ring or Center far Yiddishe Bikher in Massachusetts, many periodicals in Yiddish etc.).

It is estimated that in the late 1930s the numbers of native Yiddish speakers were well in excess of 11.000.000 worldwide. Some 8.000.000 in Europe (3.3 million in Poland, 3 million in the Soviet Union, 800.000 in Rumania, 250.000 in Hungary, 180.000 in Lithuania and others in England, France, Germany, Latvia, Belgium, Switzerland) and the rest in North and South America, South Africa and Australia. As for the Yiddish press the most updated bibliography of Yiddish periodicals in inter-war Poland lists more than 1.700 titles. The number of books and pamphlets printed at that time in the Soviet Union were in excess of 7.500 titles. A survey of 364 Yiddish books published in 1923 showed that 24.4% were belles-lettres, 13.5% for young readers, 11% - textbooks, 8.5% - poetry, 8.8% - dramas; of these surveyed books 25 titles were translated from other languages; as for the place of the publication, over 70% were published in Poland, 13% - in Germany, 6% - in the U.S.A. and 6% - in the USSR Nowadays, after the extermination of a large part of the Yiddish-speaking community in the Holocaust, Yiddish is represented with an estimated 2 million speakers (C.J.Hutterer, Die germanischen Sprachen. Budapest: Akademiai Kiad, p. 350), chiefly in the U.S.A. and Israel, though also in Eastern and Western Europe, who are fluent in it at least as a second language.

Lietuvos Jeruzale, the only Jewish newspaper is still published in Vilnius, is printed there in Yiddish, Lithuanian, English and Russian.

The modern situation of the Yiddish language and culture is a result of their extermination by Nazis on the one hand and by communist totalitarian regimes on the other hand, as well as of the restitution of the Israel State in 1948 where the single Ivrit language is state-supported.

Eastern Europe as traditional hearth of Yiddish has given its place mainly to the U.S.A., where the sphere of Yiddish is constantly diminishing (cf. dynamics of publishing 1200 Yiddish books in the U.S.A. and Canada between 1945 and 1984: 500 books in 1945 - 1954, 370 books in 1955 - 1964, 200 books in 1965 - 1974, and 80 books in 1975 - 1984 as according to J.Baumgarten & coll., Mille ans de cultures Ashkenazi's. Paris 1994, p. 588). Only 10 % of the Yiddish speaking Litvaks of Lithuania and Byelorussia escaped the Holocaust, most of them having moved to Israel after World War II. Therefore, there are only about 15000 Jews in Lithuania now, most of them being post-war migrants from Soviet Russia and Soviet Ukraine. A large part of them are Russian speaking with no knowledge of Yiddish and of the Jewish culture in general. The only centers of the Yiddish culture in Vilnius are The Jewish State Museum of Lithuania and editorial board of the newspaper 'Lietuvos Jeruzale', published in Yiddish, Lithuanian, English and Russian.

Yiddish Folklore is represented by the Yiddish Folklore Theatre, directed by E. Khersonsky, and by Yiddish Song Group, directed by J. Magid. Hard economic situation of the restituted Lithuanian Republic restricts possibilities of the State support. There are practically no more Yiddish cultural workers or scholars in Lithuania. Besides, the material heritage of the 600 year-old Litvakian Yiddish culture, forming basis for bringing up young generations, has been fully annihilated and costly collections disembodied. The beginning was made already in 1940 by Soviet communist invaders in Lithuania and Polish Western Byelorussia. Then followed systematic and total plunderage by the Nazis. First it was carried out by Mr. Pohl, scientific fellow of the Oriental Museum of Frankfurt/Main, who while fulfilling the instructions of Reichsleiter A. Rosenberg sent to Frankfurt 84 chests of values mostly containing more than 20000 rare books, 4 incunabulas and other ancient costly Jewish collections from M. Strashun's library. At the same time other 80,000 books of this and other Jewish libraries were sold to a paper-mill as waste paper. On the way 6 of 84 chests sent by Mr. Pohl to Germany were used for sending pork by Mr. Sporket, a German warrant officer, who threw values and the books out and sold about 500 leather backs to a shoe factory. According to the order of the German Education Office (Ausbildungsamt) No 1608 of January 24, 1942, works of any kind by Jewish authors had to be withdrawn from the libraries. Jewish periodicals were burnt on the spot. In May 1942 were sent to paper-mill 5 lorry Jewish books from the Kaunas Old City Library as well as collections of the Kaunas Jewish libraries of Abraham Balosher and Abraham Mapu, and 14120 Jewish books and periodicals from the Kaunas Central Library were destroyed in October. Lithuania having being robbed of independence up to 1991, most of those cultural values that had been sent to Germany have emerged as illegitimate property in the U.S.A. after 1945. Finally, in 1948 all Jewish cultural institutions were closed by the Soviets including the restituted (1946) Jewish Museum in Vilnius, the Jewish section of the Soviet Lithuanian Writers' Union, all-Jewish orphanages, kindergartens, Jewish first forms in primary schools. It was also the time of Soviet repression when the Yiddish writer Hirsh Oserovitch was arrested. After its destruction by the Nazis and by the Communists, the famous Yiddish culture of Europe is strongly endangered. Traditional ethnical zones of non-assimilated Jewry in Central and Eastern Europe do not exist any more since World War II, the Yiddish language becoming one of languages of disappearing dispersed minorities.

Mindful of the tragedy of the Holocaust and the destroyed Yiddish culture, every means possible must be used to gather, record, and preserve whatever remains, in memory and text, of the Lithuanian Yiddish heritage. This is the main aim of the activities of the Lithuanian State Jewish Museum.

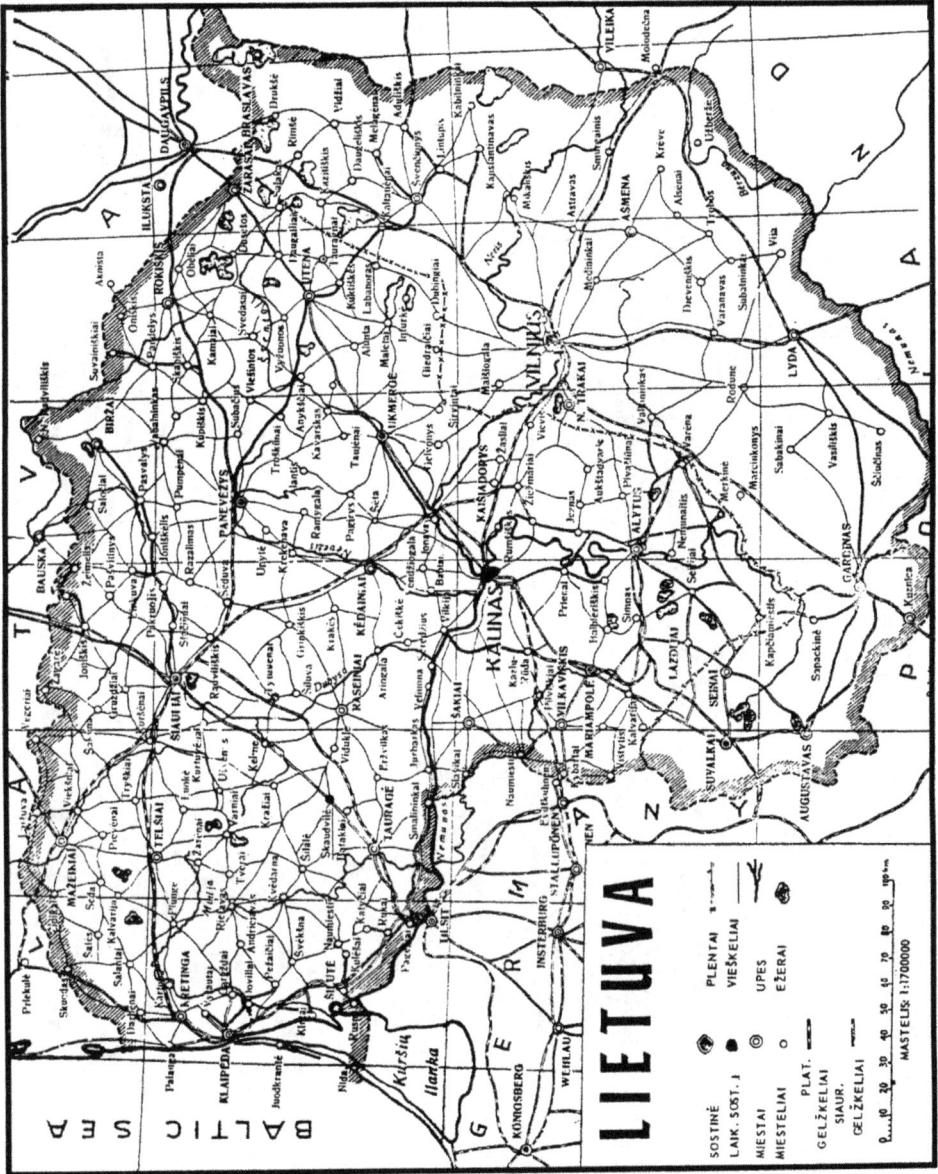

LIETUVA

SOSTINĖ
LAIK. SOST. J
MIESTAI
MIESTELIAI

PLENTAI
VIEŠKELIAI
UPĖS
EŽERAI

GELŽKELIAI PLAT.
SIAUR. GELŽKELIAI

0 10 20 30 40 50 60 70 80 90 100 km

MASTELIS 1:1700000

BALTIC SEA

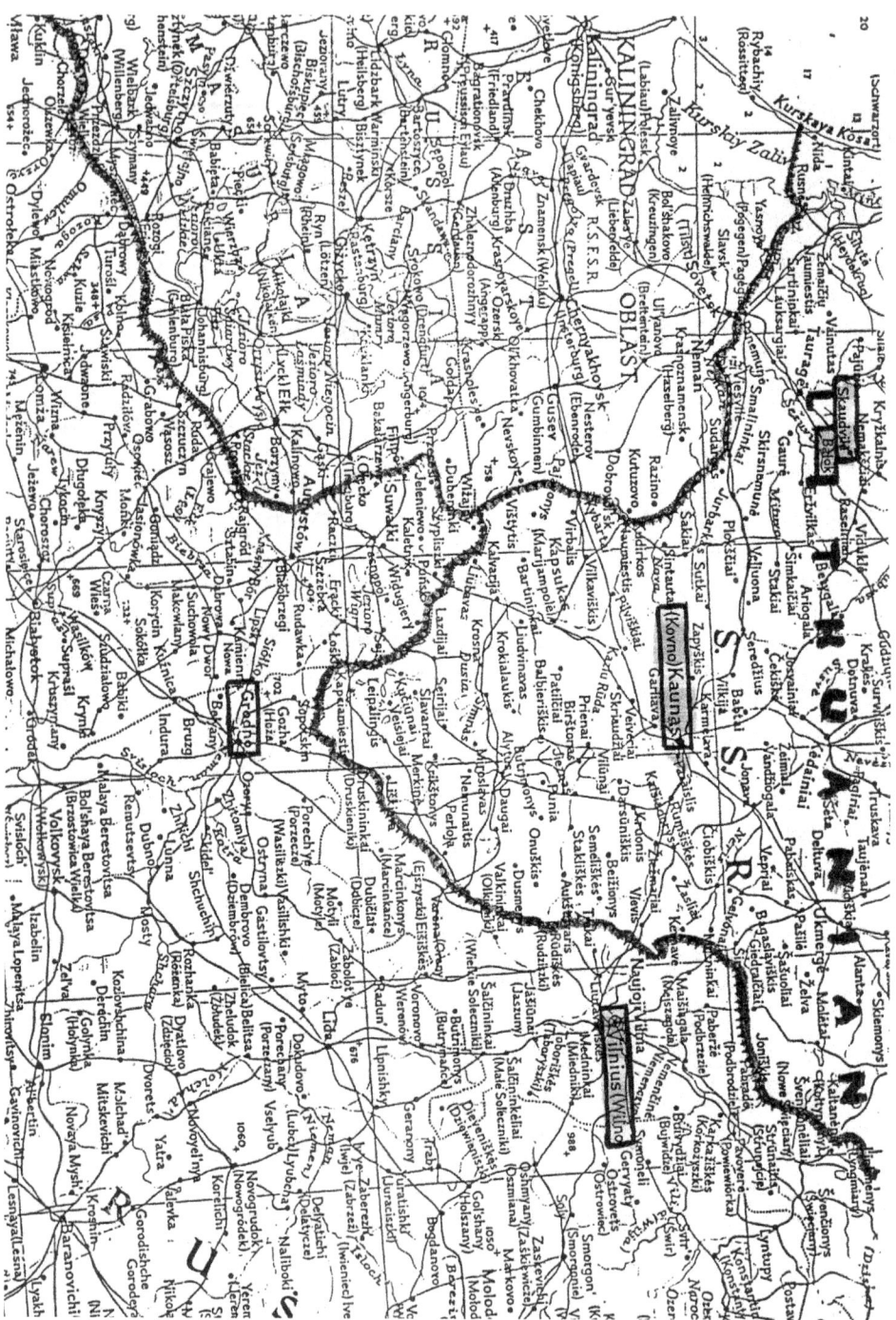

A Horse and Dresgah - Shkudvil, circa 1917

Wooden Shule, later a Cheader - Shkudvil

*The Stone Shule in Shkudvil, circa 1880,
currently a dairy processing plant in 1997*

The 9th Fort Memorial,
Kovno, Kaunas, Lithuania

The old Jewish Cemetery
in Shkudvil

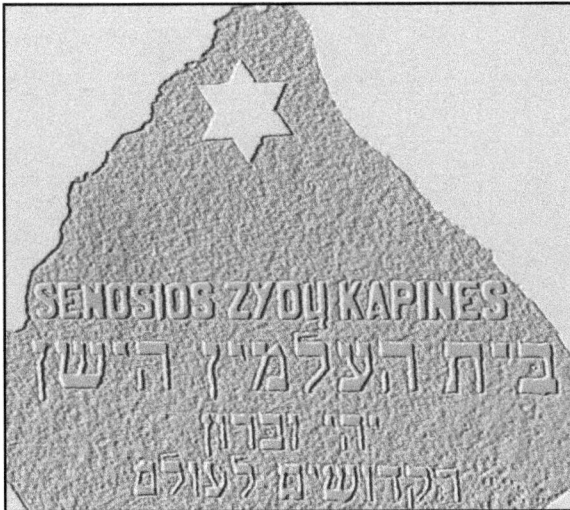

SENOSIOS ZYDY KAPINES

בית העלמין הישן

יהי זכרון

הקדושים לעולם

June 20th 1997

The Old Cemetery may the Memory of the Sacred be Forever

A stylized representation of the broken monument in
the center of the old Jewish Cemetery in Shkudvil

29

Tauroggen, Lithuania

The Last Jew of Radauti

פּראָפּ
Propp
Ancestral Shtetl in Lithuania

שקודוויל
Shkudvil
(1916-1940) Tavrig District - Lithuania)
(1847-1916) Kovno Guberniya - Russia)
(1797-1847) Vilna Guberniya - Russia)

The following information is about our family's shtetl of Shkudvil, Lithuania. From about 1790, our family's forefathers and mothers for many generations raised their children there, prior to the general departure and emigration to other countries. This emigration occurred from about 1882 until 1940. Of course there was ongoing small-scale emigration, where individual Propp families left the Shkudvil area for one reason or another. This emigration went on right from the first and second generations of Propp's who had settled in the village. The early departures were generally relocations in Lithuania to other cities such as Kovno, Vilna or small shtetlach, such as Smalininkai, Jurburg, Kelm or Tavrig. These Propp's also relocated to Russia and Sweden since they were in close proximity to Lithuania. The first Propp to depart Shkudvil for the United States was Sleime Propp, son of Betzalel Propp. It was 1870 and the entire Propp family of Shkudvil came out to say good-by and wish Sleime well. Louis Arne who was there that day in Shkudvil wrote on July 7th, 1938 the following:

> "The year 1870 marks the beginning of the immigration to America, although, previously some settled in Scandinavian countries and various parts of Russia and across the border into Prussia.
>
> As stated, in 1870 Sleime Propp left Skaudville for America. He was the son of Betzalel (Tzalel), the son of Hirsh, the son of Shimel (Shimon). "I still remember that when he left our town of Skaudville for America, and at the parting, many tears were shed and I did not realize the cause of it, so I asked my mother, who was his sister, why they were weeping. She replied, Your Uncle Sleime is going far far away to the other side of the world and we will never never see him again."[2]

In general there was a remarkable amount of religious freedom in Lithuania. Lithuania developed as a center for Jewish religion, education and scholarship, however there was also religious intolerance and fierce anti-Semitism there too. During most of the last two hundred years Lithuania was under Russian control, first under the Czars and then under communism. The Russian governments implemented many pogroms, which persecuted the entire Jewish population of the Russian Empire, most of who were living in the Cherta, Pale of the Settlements. There was also the fear of conscription (1827 to

---

[1] Written by Louis Arne, June 1938.

1867) in the Russian army for the young Jewish men and boys (12 years old). The duty in the army would be very severe and could last up to twenty-five years or sometimes-even more. Each Jewish community through the Kahal was given quotas to meet. Even boys of eight or nine years old were at times kidnapped by snatchers (Khapers) who were employed by the Kahal for purpose of filling their quotas. The assignments were made to distant points in Russia and many of the young men never saw their families and loved ones again. During their time in the Russia service tremendous pressures were brought to bear on these young men to convert to the Russian Orthodox Religion. When Czar Alexander II came to power he relaxed the conscription laws and provided some support to Jewish people of Russia. When his son, Czar Alexander III, came to the Russian throne in 1881, all of the anti-Semitism, pogroms, and mistreatment of the Jewish population greatly intensified and finally forced a large-scale emigration from Lithuania. However, there remained in Lithuania a large part of the Propp family and 240,000 other Jewish people right up until World War II. During the latter periods of the nineteenth century and into the twentieth century the Propp family was much more spread more broadly, throughout Lithuania, Sweden, South Africa, Germany, Russia and the United States rather than all living in the Shkudvil area as in previous times.

Shkudvil is 22-km northeast of Tavrig in western Lithuania. It is located on the road from Kaliningrad (Königsberg) to Saint Petersburg, Russia and is situated along the Ancia River. It has a population today of about 3000 Lithuanians and not a single Jewish person lives there.

The town of Shkudvil began as a site for some roadside inns. At the very end of the eighteenth century, younger Jewish settlers were attracted to the area, where they established a small village. Every new Jewish settler was called by the name of his original shtetl. The Jewish community immediately began to develop and was fully organized by 1820. After several years, a small yeshiva (religious university) began to draw people to it from the settlements. Some families would come to the area to seek bridegrooms for their daughters from the yeshiva. A large Jewish community grew and flourished in Shkudvil. In the following listed years. All during the period of the Yeshivot, the Jewish families had okhel tag or food days where students from other shtetlach would eat at the homes of Jews in Shkudvil.

In 1847, the Jewish population of Shkudvil was 204 and in 1897 it was 1012 or seventy two percent of the total village population. Just before the Holocaust there were 1590 Jews or sixty percent of the population. The town burned down in 1922, 1931, and 1937 and it was rebuilt in 1938-39. Today it serves as a township seat with two houses of worship: Roman Catholic, and Evangelical Lutheran. There is a hospital and secondary school there. There were buildings in Shkudvil, which predated the period of Jewish settlement and were built, in the very early part of the eighteenth century. The oldest building is a Catholic Church, which dates back to 1726. The Shule, which is no longer, used because they're no longer any Jews who live in Skaudvile. The building that was used as the synagogue is now a rooming house and diary processing plant.

32

The shtetl is described in The Books of Rabbi S. I. Scheinfeld. "Shkudvil like countless other shtetlach was a poor community with a few shops and the usual assortment of small trades people and artisans, and a large proportion of men who spent most of their days studying the Talmud or teaching, while their wives often scraped up the family income." The village became known throughout Europe as village of Torah scholars primarily of the Musar movement, which was popular in this part of Lithuania as well as knowledgeable people of secular subjects, Maskilam! The mood and attitude of the shtetl is further amplified in the "forward' written by Rabbi Shlapobersky and the story concerning the life of his brother, Rabbi Mordechai Shlapobersky.

Note, in the 1915 picture of Shkudvil, the large white building in the center is the stone Shule and the Jewish school is just to the synagogue's right (The old wooden Shule). The large house on the main road was the home of Naftali Propp and wife's, Rivka's, home. Note; the three German soldiers walking down the street.

In 1995 a large group of Russian documents were found in the state archives in both Kaunas and Vilnius, Lithuania. They are called *reviskie shazki*. These are lists of revision lists were published by Avotaynu Monograph of "Jewish Vital Records, Revision Lists, and other Jewish Holdings in the Lithuanian Archives. These are a series of ten early Russian censuses of the Jews living in the Pale of the Settlements. Czarist authorities in the late part of the 18th century began them. The lists start in 1795 in eastern Lithuania and were organized by family and listed by name and age. The Russians for conscription in the Russian army and taxing the Jewish subjects used these revision lists. The lists are not necessarily very accurate for the obvious reasons, but they are useful tools for researched for additional information about our family in Shkudvil. They list some of the Jewish population in many of the villages of what is now Lithuania. We have obtained three of these lists for 1816, 1851 and 1912. The lists are actually two pages one page for male head of the household and any other males residing within the household and a second page listing all of the females of the same household. The lists are of limited use. This is because they only list changes made after the main census, thus the name reviskie, meaning in English: revision.

In the August 14, 1816, *Reviskie Shazki*, there is listed a *"Shimel Girshevich Probnovich aka Shimon Prop"* born 1765 listed with his sons: Efraim, Hirsh and Abram and on the female side with a wife, Ruch'l, and one daughter which can not be read from the original document. These members lived in one household. The information passed down from Louis Arne's grandparents that the first Propp in Shkudvil was Shimon Propp and he had three sons: Efraim, Hirsh and Abe, along with four daughters. Louis also said he only had information on four of the seven children: Hirsh, Abe, Sara and Rivka. The 1816 Reviskie Shazki lists that Efraim departed Shkudvil in 1812 at the age of 24 years old. These reviskie shazki are a primary vital record confirming that Shimon or Shimel Propp did come to Shkudvil before 1811, the year of the previous census. The 1816 census indicates that Shimel was in Shkudvil during the previous census. Shimel is very common nickname for Shimon. It is very likely that Shimel was an one of the original Jews who operated an Inn/Tavern in 1795.

In 1857, under Czar Nicholas 1, the Russian government announced that all of the Jews who lived less than 50 versts (approximately 33 miles) from the Prussian border should leave the area. The Russian government also told them to go to an established area further inside Russia. They gave the Jewish people the opportunity to choose where they wanted to go. Nineteen small communities of Jews in the area met and decided they were not going to leave the area. The people of Shkudvil were one of these communities. As it worked out the Russia Government under the Czar also relented on the requirement for Jews to move only because it was not considered in their best interest. The Jewish people there were rabbi's, teachers, merchants, small store owners, tradesmen and a few farmers who raised corn, rice, grains, cows, horses, and chickens. One of the principal commodities was the small and sturdy Samogitian horse breed, well suited for work in the coal mines.

Tuesday was market day and it was thought that it was one of the largest markets in the Zhamot (northwestern) region. In 1871 in Lithuania, there was a terrible famine, where the Jewish people suffered much worse than the general population of Lithuanians.

On Shavuoth Holiday of 1932 a big fire consumed half the homes in Shkudvil. After that a purely Jewish fireman's group was organized not only for fighting fires but also to protect the Jewish population from the Lithuanian gangs and hooligans. Later on, the Firemen's group became the shtetl's selbstshutz (self-protection group). In 1936 a blood libel again broke out against the Jewish people in nearby Tavrig (Taurage).

Shkudvil is listed in *Where Once We Walked*, A guide to the Jewish communities destroyed in the holocaust, and *The Shtetl Finder Gazetteer*. There is a plaque for Shkudvil in the Chamber of the Holocaust, Mount Zion, Jerusalem, Israel and a Memorial Window in the United States Holocaust Memorial Museum in Washington, DC. It is also listed in *Yahadut Lita*. Lithuanian Jewry. In the book, *Lithuania Jewish Communities*, lists the Yizkor Dates (Nazi Massacres) for Shkudvil as 26 Tammuz 5701 (July 21, 1941) and 23 Elul 5701 (September 15, 1941). it is also mentioned in a document which is only known as "A Schkudviler", name unknown, at the central archives, Yad Vashem in *Volume III in the Guide to Unpublished Materials*.

The Nazi's developed a new type of "unit" just prior to its invasion of the Russian borders on the eastern front. The units were called Einsatzgruppen; these were the first of the Nazi "mobile killing units", in the German Planning sessions for Operation Barbarossa in March, 1941, Hilter declared, "That the Jewish Bolshevik intelligentsia would have to be eliminated and that these tasks could not be entrusted to the army." Einsatzgruppen A was assigned to Army Group North. The Einsatzgruppen was then broke down into smaller operational units called Einsatzkommando. These units operated independently but under guidelines of the Einsatzgruppen mission, which was to murder all the Jewish people who lived in the overrun areas. The Einsatzkommando Three (3) assigned to Lithuania and were augmented in the field by indigenous groups of Lithuanians, Estonians, Latvians and Ukrainians in the form of auxiliary police. To reach as many villages and cities as fast as possible, the Einsatzgruppen moved closely on the heels of the advancing German armies, entrapping the large Jewish population centers before the victims had a chance to discover their fate. It should be noted that the Lithuanian's took such willingness and displayed so much passion in the murdering of heir fellow Jewish countrymen, that the Nazi's used Lithuanians throughout the killings of the Jews in all the overrun areas of Russia.

In 1940 the Jews of Lithuania were listening very closely to their radios. They listened to the hate, the Jew baiting, and how they were being blamed for everything that was wrong with Germany and the world. They were listening to what the Nazis were doing in other parts of Europe. The Jewish people of Shkudvil and Lithuania were terribly frightened and scared. In May of 1940, the Russians occupied Lithuania and reinforced the front lines between Lithuania and Germany. There were miles and miles of trucks with Russian soldiers, tanks, and big guns, which drove right through Shkudvil to the border. The Jews there were very impressed with the awesome power of the Russian government. They felt safer and most were glad to see the Russians for that reason. The Jewish people in Lithuania at this time had many restrictions imposed by the Lithuanians. The Russians lifted some of the restrictions, and made many Jewish people government employees. The Lithuanians intensely resented these changes and this may have contributed to the later brutalities committed by some Lithuanians, but there had been years of Anti-Semitism and hate. The Jewish people had already lost most of their rights granted in 1920 when Lithuania constituted its new government.

On Sunday morning, June 22, 1941 the German government implemented "Operation Barbarossa", the invasion of the Soviet Union along the Eastern front. The German Army Group, North, crossed the borders of Lithuania at Tilsit, East Prussia and drove the 65 Kilometers to Shkudvil, Lithuania arriving there in the afternoon of June 22, 1941 (according to one eyewitness the date was June 24, 1941). The Russian army did not in any meaningful way oppose the Germans. Most just surrendered or quickly retreated. The people of Shkudvil and the occupying Germans lived in a relatively peaceful coexistence for the next two or three weeks. Then on July 16th, 1941 the Lithuanian Government, through some of its Lithuanian auxiliary police in conjunction with the occupying German army and Einsatzkommando called ail the people in Shkudvil together at the center of the town for a very important announcement. This included the Jewish and non-Jewish men, women, and children of the village. The Lithuanian paramilitary organization, and the German Einsatzkommando, then separated Jews and non-Jews into two groups. The non-Jews were all told to go home, leaving only the Jewish people of Shkudvil standing there in the center of the village. While there the Jews were harassed and tortured by many of the Lithuanians. They ripped the beard from a Rabbi and then killed Reb Hillel Zilberg with a shotgun. The famous Gaon Rabbi Abraham Yitzchak Pearlman was dragged out of his home that Friday, and after being tortured was brutally murdered. The Jewish men were then separated from the women and children. The Lithuanians had to use a great deal of force to make this final separation and many of the people were kicked and beaten. Finally, after many assurances were given to the people that men were only to form work details. That they would be treated well and given kosher food. The Jewish men were separated from their wives and their mothers and their children, then they were walked two kilometers south into the Puzai forest. It was not until 4:00 AM the next morning when the remaining women and children heard the shots and yells coming from the Puzai Forest. Almost all of the three hundred Jewish men and older boys of Shkudvil were murdered that day, only a very few were able to escape. The dead men and boys lay in an open grave for weeks until the remaining Jewish women and children could at least cover their rotting bodies. Later on July 21st, some of the communal leaders, Reb Moshe Baruch Braude, Benyamin Stein, Shmuel Eli Brett and Ya'akov Dorfman were taken to the cemetery of Upyna and brutally murdered together with Upyner Jews including their Rabbi Yitzchak Yoffe. These same procedures were used in 180 villages throughout Lithuania where Lithuanian Jewry was totally decimated. It was also used throughout the rest of the Pale for the mass annihilation of the Jewish population. In 1941, many of the Propp family who had remained in Europe, lived in village of Taurage (Tavrig) and cities of Kaunas (Kovno), Lithuania and Königsberg, Germany.

A few days after the men were taken to the Puzai Forest and murdered; a long row of empty wagons entered Shkudvil and stopped next to or in front of every Jewish home in the village. The older people, the women and the children, who were Jewish, were loaded on to the wagons along with what meager belongings they could bring with them. The long line of wagons took them to the train station in Batakiai (Batok). All during this period the Germans and Lithuanians were still hunting down the few Jewish men who had escaped and were in hiding. Most of the men were caught and taken to the village of Upyna and killed.

The elderly Jewish people, the women and children, were kept prisoners for some time at Batok. The stronger ones were made to work for Lithuanian farmers in the area. They were guarded by the Lithuanian auxiliary police and were constantly being harassed by Lithuanian gangs. Feige Schertz, sister of Leon Brett and Rivka Propp the wife of Naftali Propp, and Mrs. Braude (This is the daughter-in-law to Moshe and Rochel (Propp) gave birth while there, without any medical assistance. In the early part of September, some of the Lithuanian guards told the prisoners there, that they too were to be killed soon. Many of the women tried to run and escape, but only a very few succeeded; most were either recaptured or shot. Some did manage to escape. On September 15, 1941, the remaining 1800 Jews were taken to the Gryblaukis forest, twenty-two kilometers north east of Tavrig, and murdered in a most hideous and cruel manner. In the darkness of that cold night in the forest one could hear the moaning and cries of Shima Yisro'el from the throats of the dying and martyred woman and children.

There were less than ten survivors of those who were in Shkudvil, Lithuania at the time when the German army entered the village. All the rest were massacred and are buried in the following listed mass graves.

At least two Propps were fortunate to either not be in Shkudvil at the time or escaped. First, Itzig Propp, son of Chone Propp, who was about thirty five years old and lived with an uncle, Naftali Propp and his wife Rivka. Naftali and his brother, Yehiel Moshe Propp, owned a dry goods store and a book company in Shkudvil. Naftali had a large house on the square in Shkudvil. Itzig met Leon Brett outside of Shkudvil on June 22, 1941. Leon Brett had a new English bicycle and was riding it towards Russia to escape the invading Germans. They traveled together for sometime heading northeast toward Russia. One night as they approached the village of Kelm, Lithuania they stopped and hid in what looked like an empty barn. The barn was full of Jewish people who were huddled together and were trying to hide from the Germans. The next day Itzig wanted to continue and Leon felt more secure in the barn with all the other people. After another day, Leon Brett felt lonely and left the barn to catch up with Itzig. All the people in that barn were found by the Lithuanians and murdered. Itzig and Leon arrived in Shavli (Siauliai), Lithuania that is about 75 kilometers north east of Shkudvil. Leon Brett was captured and for two years he was a prisoner in the Shavli Ghetto that was established there. Leon finally escaped and joined the Jewish partisan forces in Lithuania and fought the Germans. Itzig Propp went on to Russia. Itzig came back to Shkudvil and lived there until 1994. Yankel Propp, who was an esteemed scholar and teacher, was not in Shkudvil at this time but was in a town south of Kovno teaching at the university there and was able to flee into Russia. Yankel Propp was a very ardent Zionist and a leader in the Zionist Movement before the war. In 1958 Yankel made his way from Russia through Poland to Israel. Itzig Propp passed away in Tavrig, Lithuania in 1994 and Yankel Propp is still living in Jerusalem, Israel and I visited with him there in 1997.

The Mass Burial Sites for the Jews of Shkudvil, Lithuania

1. City of Upyna, one one-half kilometers southeast of the Upyna, there are one hundred victims buried there. These included the village leaders of Shkudvil and the Jews of Upyna. They were murdered in June of 1941.

2. Puzai Forest, four kilometers from Shkudvil. Three hundred men are buried here. They were murdered in July 21st, 1941.

3. Batakiai, in the Gryblaukis Forest, twenty-two kilometers northeast of Tavrig off the Tavrig Shkudvil road. Eighteen Hundred Elderly, Women, Children and babies are buried here. They were murdered September 15th of 1941.

There was a ghetto formed in Siauliai (Shavli). These Jewish people were send to Dachau, Germany and other Nazi death camps from this Ghetto.

* Included are first hand accounts by Mr. Leon Brett A Shkudvilian and Holocaust Survivor, who now lives in this country.

In Avraham Tory's book Surviving the Holocaust, The Kovno Ghetto Diary, it is mentioned that in August of 1942: "Two sisters had arrived in the Ghetto from Shkudvil. They were saved by a miracle. Until now they had been hiding in peasant houses."

That was about one year after Shkudvil and those Jewish people left had been destroyed, by the Nazi's. Very few Jews escaped the annihilation of Shkudvil or Lithuania. Only 6,000 to 7,000 survived out of the over 160,000 Jewish people who lived in Lithuania before the war.

These two sisters from Shkudvil were Luba and Freda Friedman and this is the story of their miraculous escape from the Nazi and Lithuanian's. While researching the shtetl of Shkudvil at the United States Holocaust Museum archives in Washington, DC, I discovered one tiny article concerning Shkudvil. Freda Karpul wrote this article. I later found out it was limited to four double spaced pages and it along with a video and audio taping of a holocaust survivor, Mrs. Freda Karpul, was part of Steven Splieberg's Holocaust project. This is the story that Freda Friedman Karpul told me in 1996 when I visited with her in her apartment in West Rogers Park, Chicago, Illinois:

"Freda Friedman lived with her father and mother and her two sisters in Shkudvil in 1941. On June 21st, Freda attended a dance that Saturday evening. She had fun, frolicking, dancing and enjoying the festivities. On the way home, she was accompanied by Leib (Leon) Brett, who was a few years older than she. Freda was skipping and running getting her shoes and stockings very wet. Leon took the stockings and put them in his back pocket and laughing, he said: "I will give these back to you tomorrow, Freda". The next day was Sunday, June 22, 1941 and about noon, the Germany army entered and occupied Shkudvil as the start of the German offensive against Russia in World War Two.

In mid July of the same year all of the Jews of Shkudvil were brought to the center of the village for a very important announcement. The Jewish men and women were separated. Although the separation was made very difficult because of the great fears of the Jews. The separation was finally made by both force and by assuring everyone there that the men were to form a work detail and would be properly cared for with good housing and Kosher food. These assurances calmed some of the fears of the villagers. The men were marched off towards the Puzai Forest and the elderly, the women and the children were told to return home and not to worry about their sons, husbands, fathers and grandfathers they would be well taken care of. Then while still in sight of their love ones, they were made to dig long ditches between the bushes and trees. Shortly, the women and children could hear noises of gunshots and the moans of their men, the women all feared for the worse. These men were never seen again. The few that were able to escape were later caught and shot.

Then a short time later the rest of the Jews who remained alive were rounded up. The people were told to give up all of their possessions to the Lithuanians and Nazis or be shot. Most did give up everything they owned of any value. The Jews were taken by wagon a few kilometers to the railroad station at Batok where they were imprisoned for about a month until mid-August.

In August of 1941 most of the remaining Jewish people from Shkudvil and a few from Upyna were gathered together. This included Freda, her mother and her sisters, Luba and the youngest, Zebra, who was about nine years old. Their father had already been murdered with rest of the men of Shkudvil in the Puzai Forest massacre. They were all taken to a small deserted building beside the railroad tracks. They had seen the Lithuanians rigging explosives through out the building, under and around the building, so the Jewish women knew full well what was in store for them. They were told to go into the building or they would be immediately shot to death on the spot. They remained in this building for over six hours, just waiting, while the Lithuanians attempted many times to "explode all of them into eternity". They were then surprisingly removed and returned to their prison. They later found out that the Nazis had stopped the explosion, because they feared it might damage the railroad tracks where German soldiers were being move back and forth from the front lines. Also it would spread the body parts of the Jews all over the area and be very difficult to clean up.

The women, children, and the elderly were held until September 16, 1941. When they were marched to the Gryblaukis forest where the Lithuanians were ready to shoot them. Freda's mother yelled in Yiddish "run, run, my children, run". The family had previously planned to all run in different direction when their mother told them to. Freda ran and ran, but did look back to see her mother and Zebra being shot and falling to the ground.

Freda Friedman continued to run through the rest of the day and late into night. The nights were cold and damp in Lithuania in September. She finally found a Lithuanian farmhouse that she knew. Her father and this farmer did business together before the war. They gave her warm food and dry clothing and hid her. A few days later, her sister, Luba, turned up there too. The farmer and his wife were very frighten that these Jews would be found in their home and they and their family would be shot with Freda and Luba, so the sisters had to leave.

They slept during the nights in the cold forest, receiving some food and once in a while, they were allowed to sleep in a farmer's barn. Both, Freda and Luba, were sick, cold, and felt that it was hopeless to continue. They talked and talked about what had happened, that their mother and father had been killed along with their younger sister, their village was gone, all the people they had known and relatives were gone, they knew they would be shot if found by either the Germans or Lithuanian forces. They felt hopeless and very helpless, so their talk turned to suicide. For days they thought that this was the only way to escape from the suffering. Freda was given pork to eat most of the time from the Lithuanians who did help them but because of her up bringing, it caused her to vomit and become sick. The two girls finally decided to go out on to the Neiman River and they planned to lay on the ice until they froze to death. Luba went to quickly to sleep while Freda waited to freeze. As the sun started to rise she saw Luba's lips and face turning blue, but Freda could not sleep. After a while Freda became frightened because she thought she would not die and be all-alone, which frightened her much more than death with her sister. As Freda's fear grew she start trying to wake her sister up so they could be together. She shook Luba and the more she did, this activity provided Freda with additional warmth. She was finally able to get her sister fully awake. Freda and Luba sat there on the river ice until they spotted a small light on a hill in the distance. Both started walking toward the light, which was a few miles away. When they arrived, it turned out to a very small *farmhouse with very large dog, about the size of a calf. At first the dog was very vicious and barked and growled loudly, which almost caused the sisters to run. All of sudden the dog stopped growling and pushed the front gate open and backed into the house pushing the front door open.*

The Lithuanian family, the father and mother with their daughters, were eating breakfast. When the farmer saw what had happened he made the sign of the cross, because this was a miracle. He told Freda and Luba that the dog had never done anything like this and would attack anyone he did not know. The Friedman girls were giving food and warm clothing and they slept in the house with the farmer's children for a few days. Then they had to move on, because again the farmer and his wife became worried about their own safety and their children's welfare.

This now was in the late winter of 1942, and Freda became very sick. She stopped eating and had a fever. It was very hard for her to sleep. Another Lithuanian friend told them they had to go to the Kovno Ghetto so Freda could receive medical treatment or she would die in a few days. So the two sisters were smuggled into the Kovno Ghetto, which in its self seems strange because while they were sneaking in, many were attempting to escape the ghetto. Freda was treated by Jewish doctors there and got well over a period of several months. She had had typhus. Months later, the sisters escaped from the Kovno Ghetto and again hid in the forest until the Russian Army arrived and liberated them. It was now 1944 and the war in Europe was almost over.

After the war Freda married Abram Karpul and had a daughter. They lived in Kovno, Lithuanian until 1980. She and her husband, Abram, moved to Chicago, Illinois with their daughter, Sophie, and their son-in-law and granddaughter. Her sister, Luba, is married and now lives in Khar-Saba, Israel. Both are well and alive in 1996. They are two of only five survivors from the Shtetl of Shkudvil who are still alive today. One of the other survivors is Yaakov (Yankel) Prop who lives in Israel and is very elderly now."

Prior to the war, eighty percent of the youth were affiliated with Zionist organizations. Many joined pioneer training and made Aliyah to Eretz Yisrael. Others immigrated to the United States, Sweden, Norway, South Africa, South America Russia and many other countries. Almost every member of the community belonged to a society for Torah study, such as Mishnayot, Chayei Adam, Menorot Hamaor, Tiferot Bachurim, or Shas, led by Leibchik, the clock maker, Yosef Yavetz and Benyamin Stein. There was also a "Daf" (daily-page) for scholars, led by Hirsh Lifshitz, Moshe-Baruch Braude and Leizer Fein.

There was a Jewish Peoples Bank, which was administered by Meir Krom and there was a Beit Midrash, founded in 5626/1866. The charitable organizations included Chevra Kadisha, Lechem Aniim, and Bikur Holim.

Some of the earliest Rabbis in the village of Shkudvil were Rabbi Moshe Lurie; he served between 1820 and 1830. Lurie died about 1835. He was the son of Rabbi Todres Ben Orvom Lurie. Rabbi Todres Lurie passed away in 1818. Rabbi Moshe Ben Lazer who died in 1889. His son Rabbi Eliyahu-Ber came to Shkudvil by 1913.

Before this, he was in Yanashouk. Between the two World Wars, when Lithuania was an independent country, there were two small Yeshivas in Shkudvil. Rabbi Shmuel Shach, Rabbi Eliyahu-Dovid Katz, and Rabbi Ya'akov Levy supervised them. Later Rabbi Perlman also supervised the Yeshiva.

A few of the better-known natives of Shkudvil are the late Gaon Rabbi Michel Shlapobersky, Rosh Yeshiva Tiferet Zvi in Jerusalem, and patriarch of a large rabbinical family in Israel. Rabbi Shlapobersky's mother was Hinda Rivka Propp, daughter of Reb Shimon Propp and Gitel Propp. Rabbi Yitzchak Katz - Head of a Kollel in Petach Tikva; Dr. Moshe Zilberg, who was born in 1900 and late became the Chief Judge of the High Court of Jerusalem. Dr. Zilberg was a lecturer at the Hebrew University and he was also an author. He wrote in the Jerusalem press about the justice system. Simon Fishman was born in 1878. Simon came to the United States at the age of 13 in 1892 and stayed with his brother, Max or Meir Fishman in Trenton, Tennessee. This family took their mother's surname rather than their father's, which was Aronovich. Their paternal grandmother was Rivka Propp, daughter of Shimon Propp. Simon started from Tennessee as a peddler at a very young age and traveled to Oklahoma and Texas selling his wares such as pins and needles from a donkey's back. He later moved to Sidney, Nebraska and opened a mercantile store. He served as Mayor of Sidney. Simon Fishman then moved to Tribune, Kansas and became a world famous agriculturist, who introduced wheat farming to western Kansas. Mr. Fishman built the first grain elevator in Tribune, Kansas and in 1926 shipped one million tons of wheat from there, when ten years prior not one grain of wheat was shipped from western Kansas. In 1933 he became a State Senator for Kansas. He was important in establishing the AAA under the President Franklin D. Roosevelt administration during the great depression of the 1930's and he was a good friend of Herbert Wallace and Will Rogers. Simon Fishman passed away in Denver, Colorado in 1956. Rabbi Shard-Feul Shapiro was born in 1900. He attended and taught in a Yeshiva in Belgium. He also studied at Telz and other Yeshivas throughout Lithuania. Rabbi Shapiro was murdered in a Nazi concentration camp in 1940. Rabbi Chaim Mayer Greenberg was a renowned Talmud scholar. He taught in Yeshivas throughout Lithuania. His father, Moshe-Zvi, said that he was the "Shkudvilian of the time" on Jewish matters. Shmuel Yitzchak (Solomon Isaac) Sheinfeld was born in 1860. In 1891 he immigrated to the United States. A few years later he became a Rabbi in Louisville, Kentucky. He then moved to Milwaukee, Wisconsin and worked there for over 40 years. He was descended from a family that has contributed many scholars and spiritual leaders to the world. His father, Aaron Scheinfeld was a Talmudic scholar, and the Governmental Rabbi of Shkudvil, Lithuania. Some of the duties of the Governmental Rabbi were to record births, weddings, deaths, and other legal documents. Another of Rabbi Sheinfeld's ancestors was the distinguished Rabbi of the seventeenth century, Zvi Hirsh Ashkenazi better known as Chacham Zvi. Rabbi Sheinfeld passed away in Milwaukee in 1943. Rabbi Abraham Yitzchak Perlman was born in 1913 in Telz, a small village in Lithuania. Later Rabbi Perlman became a very elite scholar and writer. He was thirteen, when he remarkably wrote a Torah, in 1926 at the distinguished Slabodka Yeshiva located in a suburb of Kovno, (Kaunas), Lithuania. The Telz Yeshiva was founded in 1881.

It remained open until World War II, when the surviving faculty founded the Telzah Rabbinical College in Cleveland, Ohio. Gaon Rabbi Chaim Stein from Shkudvil became a Mashgiach there. Rabbi Stein still lives in Cleveland and in 1991 he visited Lithuania and Shkudvil.

Today, as of 1997, Shkudvil, Lithuania is a very small and very poor village with no industry and high unemployment. There is the paved highway, the road from Tavrig to Shavli, which still runs through the center of town. As the old stone Shule is now a small diary processing plant and the very poor Lithuanians live in all the houses, which most, were previously build and owned by Jews. You could still see when the Mezuzahs were torn from the outside doorframes. The Jewish cemetery has been preserved, but almost all the gravestones have been removed. We do not know for sure what happened to the gravestones, however one Lithuanian Jew who was acting as our guide told us that they were taken and used again by the Lithuanians. Two of the three mass gravesites were maintained, if not in good condition, at least in a satisfactory state. However the gravesite of the three hundred murdered men in Puzai Forest had no road marker to find it, the path you have to take is a couple of miles long through a dark overgrown roadway and the memorial site is completely overgrown and in a very sad state of disrepair. We hope that all these very sad items will be corrected in future. They have an open-air market in Skaudvile on Sundays ever week. One of the most prevalent items noted at the new market is used clothing.

See the 1915 picture of Shkudvil. The three men walking down the middle of the main street look as if they are wearing Germany Army uniforms.

A list of the contributors from 1913 and 1914, which were members of the Agudat, a Jewish relief organization follows. This list accounts for about thirty-five percent or slightly more of the families of the total Jewish population at that time.

A list of 1913

Rabbi Abram Yitzchak Perlman, Reb Moshe Baruch Braude, Rabbi Eli-Dovid Katz, Chaim-Zvi Lifshitz, Zal-Kind-Reichl, Hillel Zilberg, Note Zaks, Esale Osherovitz, Yisrael Moshe Friedman, Mordechai Maram, Zev Krom, Bentzion Lurie, Betzalel Zinger, Yosef Becker, Dov Lurie, Markahy Millner, Achern Aaron, Shmuel Zaks, Rabbi Shmuel Kateznellenbogan, Aaron Grollman, Rabbi Yosef Yedall, Zev Millner, Eli-Yudl Segal, Aron Gleek, Chaim-Itzig Liberman, Ben-Zven Klynovitz, Yosef Berman, Yisrael Ravayovitz, Yisrael Tarlovah, Shulman Yolovitz, Aron Yued Romberg, Yaakov Katz.

A list of 1914

Betzalel Friedman, Abram Shapiro, Chaim Milner, Shulman Lurie, Menhokem Lyzevovitz, Zvi-Yaakov Toobe, Betzalel Beker, Yosef Yevitz, Kalman Kaplan, Moshe Lurie, Yankel Dorfman, Joshua Friedman, Shmuel Krom, Abram-Menhockam Blume, Abram Nachman Friedman, Eli-Reuven Shine, Betzalel Fite, Freidal Duk, Yisheihen Friedman, Baruch Reichl, Benjamin Shine, Neisen Kurzner, Eli Beker, Yockem Layeb Lurie, Todres Prop, Zvi Klein, Yudel Shuve Yidelsack, Moshe Duk, Rude Tunn, Hirsh-Zvi Prop, Elikum Godin, Moshe Leib Sharfalts, Moshe Itzig Segal, Zelig

Duk, Itzig Lazer, Moshe Zaks, Itzig Shlomo, Rabbi Abram Yitzchak Perlman, Moshe Baruch Braude, Eli Zilberg, Chaim-Zvi Lifshitz, Zev Krom, Kalman-Meier Braude, Mordechai Maram, Zalkind Ribel, Moshe Lurie, Shmuel Maram, Mikhel Kushefsky, Yudel Osherovitz, Rabbi Shmuel Zaks, Samuel Lurie, Yankel Grobey, Menhokem Lyzevovitz, Yosef Kashin, Shmuel Krom, Betzalel Zinger, Yankel Shine, Yankel Pak, Zvi Nocmokest, Abram Shnieder, Henry Foglkin, Sheva Greenberg, Yankel Shemash, Menhokem Itzig Friedman, and Hirsh-Zvi Lifshitz.

This information was compiled from various books, magazines and papers from Hebrew, Yiddish, English, and Lithuanian sources. Also from first hand written and spoken commentary of three of the four remaining survivors who were alive in 1995:

1. *Encyclopedia Judaic, 1971, s.v. Lithuania.*

2. *Where Once we Walked Gary Mokotoff and Sallyann Amdur Sack, (Teaneck, NJ: Avotaynu, Inc., 1991), 315.*

3. *Great Soviet Encyclopedia, 3rd Ed., 1979, s.v. @ Shkudvil."*

4. *Encyclopedia Lithuania, Simas Suziedelis and Antanas Kucas, eds., (Boston: Juozas Kapocius, 1976), s. v. Shkudvil. "*

5. *Shtetl Finder, Chester G. Cohen, (Los Angeles: Periday Co., 1980), 93.*

6. *The Shtetl Book, Diane K. Roskies and David G. Roskies, (Hoboken: KTAV Publishing House, Inc., 1975) 7. Yahadut Lita, Volume 3 (Tel Aviv: Association of Lithuanian Jews in Israel, 1951), 368. (Translated from Hebrew by Avrum Anton, Milwaukee, Wisconsin, August 1990.)*

7. *The Books of Rabbi S. I. Scheinfeld, Rabbi Scheinfeld, translated from Hebrew by Dr. David Kuselwitz with an introduction by Amram Scheinfeld, (Chicago: The Scheinfeld Foundation, 1977)*

8. *The Jewish Community Blue Book of Milwaukee and Wisconsin (Milwaukee: The Wisconsin Jewish Chronicle, 1924), 49.*

9. *Schkudviler," name unknown, document number M-1/E1235/1201, at The Central Archives, Yad Vashem, Jerusalem, Israel. (Translated from Yiddish for the author by Leo Kram, Flushing, New York, August 1991.) Reference to the document is contained in the "Guide to Unpublished Materials of the Holocaust Period, n Volume III, Jerusalem: Yad Vashem, 1975, 341.*

10. *Yahadut Lita, Volume 4 (Tel Aviv; Association of Lithuanian Jews in Israel, 1951), 372. (Translated from Hebrew by Avrum Anton, Milwaukee, Wisconsin, August 1990.)*

11. *"Lita" (Lithuania), Volume 1, ed. Dr. Mendel Sudarsky, et al., New York: Jewish-Lithuanian Cultural Society, 1951, 1861. (Translated from Yiddish by Leo Kram, Flushing, New York, July 1991.)*

12. *The Destruction of the European Jews, Raul Hilberg, (Holmes and Meier, New York, New York, 1985)*

13. *The Jews of Lithuania, Marsha Greenbaum, (Gefen Publishing House Ltd., Jerusalem, Israel, 1995,)*

14. *The Annihilation of Lithuanian Jewry, Rabbi Ephraim Oshry (The Judaic Press, Brooklyn, New York, 1995)*

Shkudvil, Lithuania Circa 1917

Family Holocaust Victims

Evil does not prevail until it is given power
Rabbi Eleizer
The Zoha

Name	Location	Date
Matilde Feinberg	Kovno Ghetto, Lithuania	1942
Libali Hirsch	Kovno Ghetto, Lithuania	1942
Sira (Prop) Abramovitch	Auschwitz, Poland	Mar, 1942
Solomon Isaac Abramovitch	Kovno Ghetto, Lithuania	26 Mar, 1942
Max Abramovitch	Camp Port Kunda, Estonia	1944
Boris Abramovitch	Camp Port Kunda, Estonia	1944
Reuvem Abramovitch	Kovno, Lithuania	1944
Boris Abramovitch	Stutthof Camp, Germany	1944
Benno Abramovitch	Shavli Ghetto, Lithuania	Jul, 1941
Rivka Griliches, Dr.	Kovno Ghetto, Lithuania	21 Jan, 1945
Note Stolov, Dr.	Kovno Ghetto, Lithuania	Oct, 1941
Goldie (Prop) Kaplan	Kovno Ghetto, Lithuania	4 Oct, 1941
Zalman Kaplan	Stutthof Camp, Germany	4 Oct, 1941
Rivka Kaplan	Kovno Ghetto, Lithuania	4 Oct, 1941
Sara (Prop) Flaks	Latvia	1944
Rivka (Prop) Shlapobersky	Latvia	1944
Tamar Shlapobersky Aran	Kovno Ghetto, Lithuania	1944
Etta Shlapobersky Helphan	Kovno Ghetto, Lithuania	1944
Hinda (Prop) Shlapobersky	Kovno Ghetto, Lithuania	1944
Rochel Shlapobersky	Shkudvil, Lithuania	1943
Leiba Shlapobersky	Batakiai, Lithuania	1943
Moshe Baruch Braude	Theresienstadt, Germany	21 Jul, 1941
Rochel (Prop) Braude	Theresienstadt, Germany	19 Sep, 1941
Julies Berlowitz	Auschwitz, Poland	19 Sep, 1941
Hinde-Esther Kupferberg	Riga, Latvia	22 Apr, 1943
Hertha Berlowitz	Auschwitz, Poland	30 Jan, 1944
Lotte Berlowitz	Theresienstadt, Germany	
Elsa Propp	Auschwitz, Poland	

Trude Berlowitz	Auschwitz, Poland	1943
Sigmund Basch	Unknown	Sep, 1943
Heinz Basch	Auschwitz, Poland	
Steffie Cohn	Theresienstadt, Germany	
Fritz Podschubski	Smalininkai, Germany	
Alfred Kann	Theresienstadt, Germany	
Benjamin Berlowitz	Switzerland	
Arno Berlowitz	Smalininkai, Germany	
Herman Feinstein	Estonia	Jul, 1941
Siegfried Berlowitz	Sveksne, Lithuania	28 Nov, 1942
Meta Berlowitz	Sveksne, Lithuania	1944
Miriam Zvi	Shkudvil, Lithuania	1941
Minda Zvi	Batakiai, Lithuania	21 Jul, 1941
Yosel Prop	Batakiai, Lithuania	19 Sep, 1941
Aydeh Prop	Shukdvil, Lithuania	19 Sep, 1941
Ester Prop	Batakiai, Lithuania	21 Jul, 1941
Naftali Prop	Batakiai, Lithuania	19 Sep, 1941
Rivka Prop	Batakiai, Lithuania	19 Sep, 1941
Ari Prop	Batakiai, Lithuania	19 Sep, 1941
Shayne (Prop) Zaks	Shukdvil, Lithuania	19 Sep, 1941
Sonya (Prop) Markov	Shukdvil, Lithuania	19 Sep, 1941
Itzig Markov	Shukdvil, Lithuania	21 Jul, 1941

EVERYTHING IS JAKE
A Paean to Poppa by Seymour, Son # 2
January 1993

Possibly because of certain genes still not isolated but clamoring for identification, most Americans somehow seem to love their fathers. Of course, the degree of affection varies considerably. Please read on as I tell you about my sire. My father, Jacob Samuel Propp, was my hero, my pal, my buddy, someone whom I admired, loved, and still sorely miss him so many years after his death.

He came to America as a twelve-year old, and never looked back at his Russian birthplace.

Although we spent countless hours discussing trivia as well as world politics, Poppa never had anything but spoken and implicit praise for America. He respected and totally accepted its laws and institutions, its mores, and especially, its unparalleled opportunities for individual education and eventual personal affluence.

This seeming difference towards our legal system did not extend toward the presidents, judges, police commissioners, and other major office holders enjoying generous salaries and varied perks. Poppa vociferously denigrated, although always with a laugh, folks such as Mayor Jimmy Walker and his girlfriend, President Herbert Hoover and his chicken in every pot, and all local Republicans.

Poppa's flower shop was a place of refuge for me. Whenever I entered his store, he greeted me with a big smile; a tight hug and a loud deafening kiss right over the eardrum. Strong coffee in a thick white cup, stolen by a local gofer, Tommy Logan, from the Horn and Hardart Cafeteria on 42nd Street and Third Avenue, always followed. Then came jokes and laughter and unspoken affirmation that life was good and our family members all were great. With due respect to Jehovah, someone like Poppa similarly must rave helped build up David's confidence just before he went out to tackle Goliath.

The Depression years came to Poppa as shock and total denial of his family's ordained shining future. In retrospect, it seems that Poppa felt responsible for not having anticipated and taken effective measures to head off the Depression.

Shaken badly, he operated his flower hop for another dozen or so years of blurred horizons, and loss of confidence in himself. He no longer greeted panhandlers with a buck and a word of encouragement. Instead, he'd say, "Keep walking, buddy—there's nothing here for you."

What didn't change at all, however, was the warmth and love for his family. His cute little jig and fast shuffle lingered on, as did the hot coffee he always proffered whenever I visited his shop.

In ultimate review, Poppa builds no towers to the sun; but, he left behind everlasting memories of a splendid man who hoped and tried his utmost to provide for and guide his family members towards happy, and fruitful lives.

Starting at the End

Incredibly, I'm now older than Poppa was when he died. I have a faint sense of guilt about that, more than matched by a stronger sense of regret that so many of his dreams never were fulfilled. Among his dreams that were fulfilled, was making it to America (he arrived here twice, which I'll explain later), marrying Dina, earning a big buck (he did for more than two decades), and begetting four children whom he adored. However much it might wound Josie and Teddy, though they probably already concede it, there was one child closest to Poppa's heart. It was Sidney, born on April 21, 1914; a few years after a never-named premature daughter unexpectedly died three days after birth.

Nearly every late November, Momma would remember, and softly cry for her beautiful lost baby, who was "perfect and pretty." Momma never got a clear or even muddled explanation of why the baby died. Poppa never spoke about it. Momma, who had not been lactating properly, theorized at first, and later came firmly to believe that the nurse somehow carelessly must have poisoned the infant by introducing a deleterious substance into its formula. Perhaps the fact that gestation was a month short of full term played a role... Anyway, after that bitter loss, when Sidney arrived and thrived, Poppa was more ecstatic than Kunta Kinte's kin were when the black infant wailed for the first time. A special, "above and beyond" love affair blossomed and endured for 44 years until Sidney died in June of 1958.

After a year of steady deterioration, the removal of one lung by a renowned chest surgeon, and finally, experimental oncology by an infamous "last chance" quack, Sidney died of lung cancer. Sid's siblings shielded his fatal affliction from his elderly parents on the tiny chance that he might beat the long odds against him. Hence his "sudden heart attack" when we had to break the news of his death to Dina and Jake.

Josie, Ted, and I had been worried and afraid that Momma might be crushed totally to learn that Sidney had died of an invented "sudden heart attack".... But it was Poppa who succumbed. Two weeks after Sidney's death, Poppa collapsed outside the East End Synagogue where he had just finished saying Kaddish for his son. As a neighbor tried to help him to his feet, thoroughly Americanized Poppa rasped out, "Je-Je Jesus Christ, I can hardly speak." He died one week later. Momma lived a full, socially active life for more than 22 years after suffering the double loss of both her husband and son a scant three weeks apart.

Leaving the Old Country

I never learned, or else I knew and forgot, whether Poppa's family emigrated from Russia en masse, or as was most common, in erratically spaced phases that were determined by the availability of pooled family rubles to finance the arduous two stage hegira. Cousin Mary Rose (nee Propp) believes Jake's oldest brother, Marcus, served as point man for his family. The first leg of the trip to America, the fabulous "*Goldene Medina*," usually was via rail to Hamburg, with small bribes en route to any loud-speaking uniformed person who held out his hand. Next, there was a ghastly sea voyage in steerage, where previously unimaginable indignities became accepted as part of the daily routine. It is fascinating to note here that Uncle Yael Cantor, Momma's oldest brother, left Russia via an entirely different first-leg journey. Yael (Joe) was on the verge of being called up to serve in the Czar's army... but not as a soldier. In the 1890's Jews weren't allowed to become arms-bearing grunts. They were drafted into quasi-military service as servants for officers, as stablemen, or as cobblers. Although subject to military codes and regulations, the sons of Abraham neither earned the honor of wearing a full uniform, nor the meager full pay of a private. But worst of all, they had to eat "*trayf*." In effect this meant that they no longer were Jews, understandably a grievous loss to the family. In many households so cursed, Kaddish was said in traditional remembrance of the recently deceased. To avoid Yael's de facto excommunication and religious death, his parents, Mary and Joseph, gave him the entire contents of every family *pushka* and *knippel*, plus whatever they could borrow from nearby relatives. After tearful good-byes and rabbinical blessings, Yael departed his shtetl before sunrise one day, hidden in a wagon under sacks of potatoes. Periodically on empty stretches of the road, the driver would; top to water his horse and call to Yael that it vas safe to emerge to take care of his bodily needs. In late afternoon of the second day came the most perilous part of the journey - crossing the border into eastern Poland. (Yael, who later boasted, "*Itch hatt vergonvit der grenetz*" (literally, "I stole the border") was very lucky. Many such would-be escapees were beaten, robbed of their money, and kicked off the wagon. If they could still walk, and not be arrested en route back to their *shtetl*, typically they would arrive in pitiful shape, only once again to face imminent induction into the army.

At the end of the nineteenth century, Russia had a fairly large naval fleet, but none if the tales I heard ever mentioned forced induction of Jews into the navy. Everyone knows that navy personnel always complain about cramped quarters... and who would want to sleep, dress, and eat side-by-side with a Jew?

Jake at School

Unlike Momma, who regaled her children with wondrous tales about her early years in Byelorussia on farmland near "*Minsk* in the *Guberniya*" (mountains), Poppa's stories rarely dealt with his childhood in Russia. Instead, he focused his anecdotes on life in Manhattan from about 1895 on. Poppa arrived here a little before his twelfth birthday. He was adept at quickly learning languages that included English and really first class cussing. The Propp family took up residence in East Harlem, and little Jake soon was enrolled in the public school on East 125th Street.

Starting out in the fifth grade, after only two days Poppa was promoted to the sixth grade for two reasons. He was older than the other fifth graders and more important, the combination desk-chairs in the classroom were too small, and his teacher felt sorry that Jake had to sit sidesaddle at his desk. After two months as a sixth grader, Jake was promoted to the seventh. This was a merit promotion. Amazingly, he spoke English with almost no foreign accent. And his grasp of history and geography far exceeded that of any of his classmates. Daily weekday classes began at 8:30 a.m., and at 10:30 a.m. there was a half-hour recess. During this break the faculty sipped coffee, while all students had a choice of reading in the auditorium, or playing various games in the schoolyard. Jake usually had a dozen or so classmates grouped around him in the yard, avidly listening to his on-the-spot improvised stories of life in the wilds of Borneo, where Jake supposedly was born and raised by his massively strong and quick-witted friend, a ten-foot tall version of today's Arnie Schwarzenegger. Poppa steadfastly maintained that his giant pal, John Ugon, actually existed. Some of Jake's less perceptive schoolyard chums occasionally entered into raucous debate as to whether or not John Ugon was real. Shades of, "Is There A Santa Claus?"!!!

Poppa was given to many sly pranks at school, one of which vividly stands out in my Emory. Every so often, kids who took the 10:30 a.m. break outdoors would forget and gave their brown-bagged lunches behind on the pavement. At about 11:15 a.m. a monitor from the eighth grade would make a sweep of the schoolyard and pick up any lunches or books left behind and bring them to the principal's office. At 12:30 p.m., the start of the regular lunch period, students who discovered their losses would repair to the principal's office to claim their lunches and/or books. Frequently, several lunches weren't claimed. In such instances, the principal would open the bags and divide the contents among the very poor kids whose parents couldn't afford to provide them lunches. On a whim, early one morning Jake scooped up horse manure from the street, carefully slid it into a brown bag, placed the brown bag into a shoe box, and then secured the package with string. He took the neat package to school. Towards the end of the 10:30 a.m. break, Jake left his present against the wall of the schoolyard and returned to his classroom. Later that afternoon Jake's imaginative efforts were rewarded. The principal, who obviously had opened the package of turds, summoned Jake to his office and sternly questioned him about his culpability in the prank. Poppa, of course, denied any involvement. Accepting reality, the principal terminated the arraignment with, 'Propp", I can't prove it, but this is your kind of work. I'll be watching you carefully from now on." Poppa didn't laugh until he got home several hours later and recounted his deed to brothers Harry and Dave.

Poppa Goes to Work

After he graduated, exactly what Poppa did, and in what sequence, escapes me. I know that for a while he continued delivering newspapers early each morning to several hundred families resident in the local tenements. Freed of the daily hours devoted to obtaining his brief formal education, Poppa now took on a milk delivery route which he coordinated with his newspaper route. This required his getting up at 4 a.m. to insure that milk at 10 cents a quart, and newspapers at one cent weekdays and five cents on Sunday, were received before the breadwinners among his customers left home for their jobs. During these getting-to-know-you years, America didn't provide gold in the streets, or full stomachs for the Propp family. Poppa was hungry and undernourished most of the time. In 1897 homogenized milk hadn't yet been invented. The cream in each quart bottle of Borden's collected at the narrow neck of the bottle, and extended downwards for about two inches. In cold winter weather the milk in the bottles stacked on the delivery wagon froze and expanded, pushing the cream and the bottle cap up about one or two inches above the top of the glass bottle. Poppa seized on this climatic vagary to steal sweet sustenance. Just before effecting delivery, he'd carefully remove the protruding caps from several bottles, take a large tablespoon from his pocket, cut off an inch of the frozen sweet cream protrusions on each bottle, swallow the treat, and then replace the round cardboard bottle caps. Jake's arctic thievery never was discovered.

In 1897 many, if not most, of the Jewish families in Western Russia hoped for a chance to immigrate to urban America, the land of the Golden Medina where, rumor had it, the streets were paved with gold. Unfortunately, Sutter's Mill was on the other side of the continent, gold had been discovered there in 1848, not 1897, and none of the paved streets of nearby San Francisco shone golden yellow unless a diarrheic horse recently had passed by.

The economy in New York City was somewhat out of kilter, and it was difficult for recent immigrants to get even the poorest paying jobs. Jake's fluency in English helped him somewhat. After suffering some painful dental problems, Jake decided he'd like to become a dentist. He realized that this took a lot of money. He somehow established a friendship with a local politician known as the "Hustler," who alleged that he had an important role in deciding who was granted the franchise to operate a newsstand under the steps at each side of the city owned Third Avenue Elevated Railway at 125th Street and Third Avenue. To better his chances, Poppa added an incentive: he offered the politician a 15% cut of the profits. The then-current operator was an elderly gentleman who seemed sick most of the time. Poppa figured that while he was in dental school, Harry and Dave would run the newspaper business for him, taking reasonable salaries for themselves, and that sufficient profits would be left over to pay for his dental school expenses. For almost two years, Poppa was a gofer and somewhat abused manservant or the Hustler. When the elderly guy who had been operating the targeted newsstands died suddenly, Jake spoke up to his professed sponsor and asked for the franchise that had been promised to him. Mr. hustler back-pedaled rapidly and told Jake that someone higher up in the Tammany Hall hierarchy previously had pledged the franchise to another guy.

Many of Poppa's dreams faded away, as he learned that politicians' promises were made and destined from the start to be broken.

Poppa had cousins in London, England, and he decided to try his luck there. He signed on as cabin boy on an ancient rusty ship that ferried sheep to England. Despite rough weather and his lowly position, the trip cross the Atlantic was not all unpleasant for Jake. He became a friend of the second mate, and enjoyed the company of the crew who worked, drank, and sang, just as several Warner Brothers films of the 1920's portrayed them. Although Poppa weighed only 125 pounds, he participated with other members of the crew in wrestling on the deck. Despite being the smallest contestant, Jake evaded being pinned by all except the second mate and the cook.

Job opportunities and the scale of living in London turned out to be even worse than in New York City. After four months, Poppa took a similar job on a similar ship going back to New York. He landed near South Ferry with only his meager pay of fourteen dollars in his pocket. Rather than spend come of the gelt on trolley fare to 125th street, he walked north all the way to 125th street, and bought two oranges for his chronically sick sister, Rosie.

Shortly after the turn of the century, Jake developed a friendship with Harry Braverman whose family lived on the same block in East Harlem. Harry was a painter, proud of his status as a union member. He urged Jake to become an apprentice because, once in the union, there were many side benefits. Jake agreed to a tryout on the job. The foreman assigned Harry and Jake to work together on a scaffold and paint the brick sides of three nearby tenements. For most of two hot summer days Jake was up on the scaffold, alongside Harry, wielding the brush, and sweating profusely. The third day of his apprenticeship was a scorcher. Jake began painting at eight in the morning, and by eleven, sweat was running into his eyes and down his back. He put the paint brush down for a moment so he could get a cloth out of his pocket to do some mopping. Just then the foreman came by, looked up, and bellowed, "Propp, you're a bum. You're not going to make it if you don't keep working." Poppa made Harry assist him in lowering the scaffold. When he reached the ground, he strode up to the foreman and hit him in the face with the wet paintbrush. This, of course, terminated Poppa's brief career as the poor man's Van Gogh. Years later, by coincidence, Harry Braverman and family took up residence on Boynton Avenue in the Bronx, just one block from the Propp mansion on Elder Avenue. Ted Propp and Harry's younger son, Saul, became a good friend during their school days. Sidney and Saul's older brother, Irving also developed a happy friendship, and both shared the summer of 1926 at Camp Kee-yo-no on Fourth Lake of the Fulton chain of twelve lakes in the Adirondacks.

Poppa's Brothers and Sisters. et al,

From 1908 to 1910, Poppa worked at Goldfarb's on East 34th Street. Reputedly, this was then the largest retail flower shop in the USA, as it actually was in 1936 when I worked for Goldfarb's (My Florist, Inc.) at its shop on 83rd Street and Broadway. Poppa's new vocation was rather unique, considering that almost all Minsk area expatriates, proudly self-described as "Litvaks," entered into one or another aspect of the garment industry. That certainly was true of Momma's brothers, Yael, Jake, Abram, and Alex who became either garment cutters or pressers. Come to think of it, atypically, none of Poppa's brothers found employment in the garment industry. Marcus, 17 years older than Jake, was into some odd-ball aspect of "General Merchandise. "He's buried in Washington

Cemetery in Brooklyn, as is his father... who may or may not be the same person as Jake's father. In late 19th century Russia, a spouse's early death often created a widow with children who subsequently would marry a widower with his own children. Then they produced a third crop of half and full brothers and sisters. That's the situation with Poppa's parents, and I don't know exactly who the offspring of which parent was. I'm named "Shimen," supposedly after Poppa's dad. In recent conversation with Cousin Mary Rose, a lovely lady, she confirmed the status of Marcus as the eldest. He was followed by Rosie, whom I never met (she died very young), then Dora, David, Katy, Harry, Jake, Leah, and Anna. I'm a bit confused about one point. If Poppa's Hebrew name is Yaakov ben Shlomo, where does the Shimen (my name) come in?

Dora married a mid-level executive in the Postal Service, Ben Kantrowitz, and bore two sons who didn't care to maintain contact with the rest of the Propps. David, a half-brother of Jake, opened a business in 1922 in which he had little prior experience. He did it with a small cash down payment and a plethora of notes. Via a distress sale, he took over a retail coal delivery business that boasted four trucks and five employees. The company's service area covered most of the Bronx and northern Manhattan. Uncle David worked on low mark-up and minimal expenses. By 1925, he owned, before encumbrances, about 40 trucks conspicuously marked on each side with placards reading, "DAVID PROPP COAL." Almost without warning, this nascent empire collapsed. Family legend has it that David developed cancer and died shortly after diagnosis was made. The business, loaded with debt, wasn't salable and only a few months after David's demise, everything was liquidated. This left his two Orthodox, nubile daughters, Mary and Lillian, with vastly reduced chances of marrying well. Orphaned Jewish daughters, sans even the proverbial pot for a dowry, didn't have nearly as much mating appeal as the daughters of a coal tycoon with 40 trucks. Nonetheless, Mary married Cantor Abe Rose, who sang at my wedding, and later became an Orthodox rabbi in the wealthy Chicago suburb of Elgin. He officiated at the funeral of Mike Todd, and sired two sons, Emanuel and David, who, "*auf tzu loches*", became Reform rabbis with congregations, one in Oregon, and one in North Carolina.

Lillian married Bernie Weinstein, a genial, hardworking man. For about twenty years he operated a Manhattan luncheonette on 39th Street and Sixth Avenue, before retiring to Florida. During his years on Sixth Avenue, he earned the sobriquet of "The Egg Cream King." Customers averred that his - concoctions had that certain a "*Je ne says quolfft*" element that set his drink above all competition.

Next to last in rank by age, but first when rated by good looks came Leah, followed by Anna did not bare any children. Leah, a stunning beauty, married Randolph Baremore, a Protestant advertising executive. Vivacious Anna became a star on the Loew's and RKO-Keith vaudeville and musical comedy circuits. In 1925, Poppa took the family, sans infant Ted, to Loew's Miner's, a vaudeville-only theater on 149th Street, just west of Third Avenue in the Bronx. l was thrilled to read on the marquee, "ANNA PROPP AND HER 16 BEAUTIES." Many years later when her husband, John McNamara (an even bigger musical comedy star than Anna) had passed on, she came to visit us at Josie's home on Shore Road in Long Beach, New York. Anna was a complete show by herself. All four feet ten inches of her delighted us with her charm, giggles, and reminiscences. Poppa never spoke to me about the double shanda of two girls from one Jewish family marrying Goyim. Evidently, they were ahead of their time in this respect, and both enjoyed long and happy marriages. The Propp brothers apparently accepted the inter-marriages without rancor or prejudice. It seems as though marrying a Christian was less frowned upon than marrying a Galitziana. (Author's note: I married a Galitz and she's been generous, gracious and loving all during our years together.)

Now for thumbnails of Harry and Katy

The song goes, "Into Each Life Some Rain Must Fall…," and apparently into each family one member must evolve so as to earn the appellation "Black Sheep." Little Harry - he barely was more than a bantamweight - and never held a full-time job in his life. During the college football season (there was no pro football then), he sold flannel pennants, flags, souvenir pins, and other "*chazerel*" at Baker's Field, Columbia University's home stadium on the northern tip of Manhattan. I don't know if Uncle Harry had any other regular or intermittent source of income. For many years Harry, homeless, slept on a shelf attached to the back of the icebox in Jake's store. He had a key to the premises, and would let himself in after the store was closed for the day. On occasion, Harry would run errands for his brother, or deliver a small floral piece to a nearby address. Poppa, understandably, always paid him several times the going rate for such chores. When by chance I'd meet Harry at the shop, almost invariably he'd comment, hey kid, you don't know it, but you're sitting on top of the world." I found Uncle Harry to be a gentle, forlorn loser, pathetically unable to adapt to the American culture. The last ten years of his life, Uncle Harry upgraded his living quarters from the icebox shelf to a furnished bedroom on Boynton Avenue in the Bronx. Although living only a block from Jake's residence on Elder Avenue, Harry rarely visited, or made his presence known. When his landlady found him dead in his bed one late spring day in 1955, she immediately phoned Momma. This was after she prudently had searched through Harry's pockets and dresser drawers; she told Momma that she had found $550 hidden in a sock. she was afraid that the cops, whom she summoned an hour later, would steal the cash cache. It was decided that I'd handle the legal, funeral and financial aspects of Harry's death. Going by the book, I ascertained I would have to get releases from his next of kin so that the money could be used to provide Harry with a grave, coffin, and funeral. This was accomplished expeditiously, and Harry now rests in a fine New Jersey cemetery in a grave only several hundred feet from the Cantor family plot.

Finally, we get to Poppa's half-sister, Katy. She already was married to Yael Cantor, Momma's brother, when Dina at age 18 landed at Ellis Island in 1904. Jake, the by-now suave man-about-New-York-Town, often traveled down to Cherry Street on the lower East Side to visit Katy and Yael. There he encountered Yael's beautiful greenhorn sister and instantly fell in love. No shodken (professional matchmaker) was needed. The phenomenon of Dina's brother married to Jake's sister, and Jake marrying Yael's sister, created what we called "double first cousins." Though genetically very similar, Yael and Jake's offspring didn't look alike, think alike, or get similar education's Perhaps Dina's forceful drive made some difference with respect to her children's education and world outlook. As far as I know, Momma didn't tamper with the genes.

Jake the Entrepreneur

Jake and Dina were married on January 8, 1911 at a catering hall on East Broadway. Their honeymoon lasted only a day and a half, because he had to go back to work at Goldfarb's. Over some 40-plus years, I suppose the couple had a bit more than the usual quota of spousal quarrels. But their love for each other always was there. As a matter of fact, Jake's last known words were to Dina from his bed in Long Beach Memorial Hospital when he whispered to her a few hours before he died, "Dina, I love you."

Several months before their wedding, Poppa bought out an established florist, a Mr. Brock, whose shop was located in an almost purely Irish neighborhood on Second Avenue between 36th and 37th Streets. The purchase price was $600. In 1955 Poppa sold his shop, by now relocated three blocks north on Second Avenue, for $1,000. Subsequently, I would tease ever-denigrating Momma by praising Poppa as a very astute businessman who cleverly had managed to sell his business at a whopping net gain of over 66 percent.

When Irish Eyes Are Smiling

"May you never forget what is worth remembering
or remember what is best forgotten"
(An Old Irish blessing)

From 1910 until 1935, Jacob Samuel Propp (Shloymo Yaakov) operated Propp's Flower Shop at 697 Second Avenue. Here he prospered, became "The White Jew" to his mostly Irish clientele and was so highly respected and admired, that a friend in Tammany Hall had him appointed Democratic County Committeeman for his election district. Jake used this position to good business advantage. He donated bouquets and appropriate floral pieces to local churches and organizations on special occasions and holidays. Insofar as a source for the purchase of flowers was concerned, Jake figuratively "owned" St. Gabriel's and its parishioners. The church was headquartered from 1870 until the mid 1930's on East 35th Street between First and Second avenues. Ever-increasing automobile and truck traffic racing into Manhattan each a.m., and racing out again each p.m. resulted in the demise of St. Gabriel's. The entire block of buildings was demolished coincident with the construction of the Queens Midtown Tunnel and its approaches. In the 1990's, vehicles no longer race into, or later in the day, out of Manhattan. Despite Robert Moses' far fetched" advance planning, cars now creep into and out of the smallest borough in daily near-total gridlock. Tommy Hogan's wife, Mary, sobbed loudly when she learned that St. Gabriel's was Thurman as equal partner and shop manager, even though Bernie put up no money. Bernie had a German father and an Irish mother. Her brother was a famous monsignor in the Catholic hierarchy in the Big City. He had heard about Jake's dealings with St. Gabriel's, and he thought he could suggest teamwork that would get his sister and unemployed nephew off his ecclesiastical back. Jake bought the deal when he got specific sacerdotal assurances of acceptance into the community. Jake's partnership role was played down. Bernie signed the lease, and on opening day his uncle graced the shop with his revered presence, augmented with two kegs of beer for free distribution. Over the next decade, the shop prospered and Jake's role became increasingly evident. The local embargo on "furriners" gradually lifted. The newly relocated Madison Square Garden arena at Eighth Avenue and 50th Street brought people of diverse backgrounds into the area. These newcomers included Italian and Greek restaurateurs whose exotic bills of fare drew many tourists to the area. The taboo on outsiders conclusively was shattered when Mayor Hylan hosted Jack Dempsey at a much-publicized dinner at the grand opening of a posh Italian restaurant on 46th Street just west of Eighth Avenue, scheduled for demolition. "Why don't they dig the friggin' tunnel up on 45th Street? Nobody but a couple of Eyetalians and a bunch of lousy atheists live up there...." Each week from about 1918 to 1930 Poppa donated a basket of groceries to a needy family that worshipped at St. Gabriel's. On Sunday the priest had the unenviable task of selecting the recipient family of the week. Every so often, a really hard-up family that had qualified for Jake's largesse the previous creek still was desperately hungry. In such stases, the head of the family was counseled quietly to seek out Jake on the chance that another gift for the pantry was possible. poppa usually met the situation with a second, somewhat smaller handout. This beneficence earned him lavish thanks from he families so assisted, along with ever increasing popularity and respect in the community as "one Jew almost as decent as Christ himself." By 1914 Jake's business and profits had grown substantially. Spurred on by Dina's urgings, he opened another flower shop on the East Side of Tenth Avenue, between 48th and 49th Streets. I specify the East Side of the avenue because at the time there existed an unofficial but generally respected proscription against anyone not of Irish ancestry operating a retail business or establishing residency in a sharply defined demesne. This Hibernian enclave, known as Hell's Kitchen, extended from West 45th Street to and including 49th Street and from the East Side of Tenth Avenue all the way east to Eighth Avenue. Allow me to explain how Jake was permitted to operate in this forbidden territory. He installed Bernie Thurman as equal partner and shop manager, even though Bernie put up no money. Bernie had a German father and an Irish mother. Her brother was a famous monsignor in the Catholic hierarchy in the Big City. He had heard about Jake's dealings with St. Gabriel's, and he thought he could suggest teamwork that would get his sister and unemployed nephew off his ecclesiastical back. Jake bought the deal when he got specific sacerdotal assurances of acceptance into the community. Jake's partnership role was played down. Bernie signed the lease, and on opening day his uncle graced the shop with his revered presence, augmented with two kegs of beer for free distribution. Over the next decade, the shop prospered and Jake's role became increasingly evident. The local embargo on "furriners" gradually lifted. The newly relocated Madison Square Garden arena at Eighth Avenue and 50th Street brought people of diverse backgrounds into the area. These newcomers included Italian and Greek restaurateurs whose exotic bills of fare drew many tourists to the area. The taboo on outsiders conclusively was shattered when Mayor Hylan hosted Jack Dempsey at a much-publicized dinner at the grand opening of a posh Italian restaurant on 46th Street just west of Eighth Avenue.

Bernie and Jake remained partners and good friends until the advent of the Great Depression. Bernie had been drawing a modest salary before splitting profits with Jake. But when for almost a year there were no profits left to be shared after Bernie's salary, the partners decided it was time to abandon ship. Subsequently, Bernie drove a Checker cab, and then became a numbers runner. Just in time, as his health began to fail, he inherited a small farm and relocated to upstate New York.

Next door to Poppa's shop at 697 Second Avenue, was a poolroom owned by a one-of-a-kind eponymous slob I thought was named John de Louis. Only after several years did I learn that John's appellation was quite different: it was "John the Loose." John was ugly, foul-mouthed and resembled the late actor Wallace Berry with a major case of Bell's palsy. Almost every other word John gravel voiced out was foul, and as he spoke to you, chewing tobacco juice often would dribble from his mouth onto his shirt. Almost unbelievably, many fastidious locals patronized John's joint, seeming to enjoy a brief descent into a lower world. Once or twice, John the Loose was written up in the pages of the Daily News as entertainingly unique in his grossness and someone to meet and then relish leaving shortly thereafter. John once accidentally did Poppa a favor. In the twenties and thirties there was a tough local cop named Johnny Broderick. Jack Dempsey had called him the best rough-and-tumble fighter in the world." Broderick had gained considerable fame by scaring the homicidal Two Gun Crowley" into surrendering to him after Crowley had broken out of his jail cell in the old Tombs pokey. Johnny also had beaten up the notorious Jack "Legs" Diamond, and had single handedly destroyed several hoods in a Coney Island Mafia hangout

The New York City Police Department was searching for a fugitive felon named Pasta Pete, who on this day was in John's poolroom. Pete saw Broderick enter the front door at almost the same time Broderick spied him. Pete dashed out the back door of the poolroom, vaulted a fence and then entered the back room of Poppa's shop. Here, his feet got entangled in several empty flower pots on the floor, and he toppled, just before Broderick caught up with him, kicked him in the face, and then put on the cuffs. Broderick mistakenly thanked Poppa profusely for tackling Pete and helping nab him. Actually, Poppa was frightened and almost frozen into immobility during the several minutes the action took place. Poppa feared possible retaliation by Pasta Pete's friends. But nothing untoward happened, and Pasta Pete was remanded to upstate Clinton prison for five to seven years.

Meanwhile, Jake's hitherto ever expanding world had collapsed. His Second Avenue daily average "take" that had numbered in the hundreds of dollars, now was reduced to twenty and thirty dollar grosses gleaned from picky posy purchasers. Poppa stopped all donations to all causes. He had weighed 125 pounds when he married Dina (Josie has pictures so attesting), but when things became real tough, somehow he ballooned up to 205 pounds on the same 63 inches tall corpus.

Just before the repeal of prohibition, a still grateful John Broderick offered Poppa a chance to make a lot of money in an enterprise that clearly was illegal. Broderick planned to set up, with Jake as a 25% partner, three "whiskey flats" in mid Manhattan, to sell freshly made bathtub gin" and a two-day-old liquor that masqueraded as imported bootleg Scotch. All Poppa had to do was visit each location once a week, check things out, and then deliver the take to Broderick's cousin. Jake's florist business now was off about 75%, due to the maturing of the Depression. At first, Poppa agreed to the proposed set-up, in which he wasn't required to invest any money. He visited the three sites and met the three retired cops who each would run a shop. After initially accepting the deal, and profusely thanking Broderick, Poppa didn't sleep for a week. He backed out, and someone else replaced him as the supervisor and collector of weekly receipts. Broderick wasn't angry. He merely said something to the effect that "Some Jews always want to play it extra safe."

Wait there's still another reprise involving Broderick.

About six months after Repeal, a recently retired middleweight Italian professional boxer, known as Bobby Lyons, approached Jake with a legal enterprise. He said Broderick had suggested that he speak to Poppa about opening a saloon next door to the flower shop at 693 Second Avenue. Once again, Jake was to become a partner with no investment required. He would draw no salary until after Bobby Lyons got back his investment, then they'd split, 60% for Bobby and 40% for Jake. Friendly city and state officials quickly granted an operating license for the saloon (now they're called bars), and within less than three months, poor Poppa was working 18 hours a day, up from the 13 daily hours he averaged in his flower shop. About 8 to 10 times a day, Jake was scheduled to walk next door to the saloon, check things out, listen to the bartender's complaints and suggestions, mollify loud drunks, cheerfully greet the "regulars," and occasionally give them a free drink on the house.

Beers were only 5 and 10 cents per glass, and best selling rye whiskey cost 25 cents for a 1 /2-ounce shot. The saloon operated from about 11:00 a.m. to 3:00 a.m., and had several dozen or so regulars. It was usually crowded from 5:30 p.m. to 7:00 p.m. each weekday afternoon with workers who stopped at the spa before going home to Ma, the kids, and supper. Jake's friendship with the nearby St. Gabriel's parishioners drew most of the regulars.

After eight months of operations, Jake was euphoric. Soon, Bobby's investment would be entirely repaid, and he'd start sharing in the profits.

At 10:00 one weekday morning, Poppa got a call from a police sergeant friend directing him not to go next door to the saloon, and that "all hell was about to break loose." About an hour later, two trucks parked outside the saloon, and burly men armed with hammers and crowbars proceeded to bust apart the mirrors and fixtures in the saloon. Then they carried out all the booze bottles and cuspidors.

At about 4:00 p.m., a local precinct plainclothes cop told Jake the reason for the destruction of the saloon. It seems that Bobby Lyons was a big bettor on the horses and on baseball games. He had had a long losing streak and owed certain Mob connected bookies a large amount of moola. Bobby had made several promises to pay, but had failed to produce or even offer an explanation. This finally resulted in the destruction of the saloon and more of Poppa's dreams. Bobby Lyons never apologized to Poppa.

Jake learned that a West Side tenement Bobby owned in his wife's name was used to square things with the bookies. Poppa never again spoke to Bobby, although they'd meet on occasion at funerals and parish parties.

Funeral work always was the principal part of the flower shop's volume and profits. Although Poppa wasn't manually adroit (Sidney used to allege that his old man, armed with a four-pound hammer, still couldn't drive a nail into a cork plank). He was a speed demon at constructing elegant floral wreaths, bleeding hearts, crosses, and every so often, a magnificent blanket designed to be laid across an entire coffin. It's not reasonable to believe that the neighborhood death rate sharply declined in 1930 and 1931. Nonetheless, Jake's funeral business declined about 85%. If twenty million people were unemployed nationwide, it seemed to Jake that over half of them lived within a ten block radius from his shop. Murray Hill resident's by-and-larye needed whatever money they had to buy, in preference to flowers, groceries and other vital necessities such as tobacco, and/or a pint of bootleg rye.

Expensive sentimental floral farewells to departed kin and friends no longer were in vogue. Of the decently "showy" funerals that did take place, strings frequently were attached. It was the custom to have enough life insurance, not for the education of children and grandchildren as commonly obtains today, but to provide sufficient funds for a respectable wake and send-off to Valhalla. In the 1930's there were no such things as unemployment insurance or other entitlements. If a death occurred in a family whose wage earner was unemployed, a seemly funeral followed, nonetheless. Typically, undertakers took charge of everything and provided funeral and all related services "on-the-cuff," hoping to receive payment when life insurance proceeds actually were received by the beneficiaries. This extension of credit encompassed the florist, the church, and even the gravediggers. Everybody had to wait for the Metropolitan Life or Prudential check to arrive at the home of the recently deceased. The term "recently deceased," however, often became somewhat inappropriate. Some checks arrived at the beneficiary's home more than two years after the interment. Perhaps such delays, with Metropolitan and Prudential earning interest on the undistributed funds, in part help explain their phenomenal growth in the early decades of this century. Jake's best customer, by far, was the undertaking establishment of skeet and Larney, located on 30th Street, just west of Second Avenue. More than a third of all his income during his salad days derived from that establishment. Jake and Larney both suffered when Old Man Skelly died. Jake feared for the hitherto mutually beneficial concord between S & L and himself. Larney suddenly realized that, despite his many years in the business, his knowledge of it was limited in certain key areas. He confided to Jake that he somehow had assumed that Skelly never would die. Larney took over and promptly ran into a financial snag. He extended liberal credit to bereaved families who had asserted there was ample life insurance to cover all funeral costs. Unfortunately, too often there was no insurance at all, or a policy had lapsed. Although Skelly always had verified insurance coverage, hapless Larney didn't bother to check until mounting unpaid bills forced him to realize the error of his ways. After a year under Larney's sole ownership, the firm owed Jake the not inconsiderable amount of $2600 for the flowers and potted palms provided for seven funerals where Larney had acted in the role of a general contractor. Jake never learned whether or not Larney received the proceeds of any of the seven putative life insurance policies, nor did he ascertain whether the priest or cemetery workers ever were paid. He, however, did learn that Larney, a childless widower, suddenly had folded the shop and gone back to Ireland to live with a nephew. Some years later, Jake received a letter from Larney advising that he was an appointed representative for the Irish Sweepstakes and was authorized to sell tickets via the mails to Americans. Although such gambling activity was contrary to domestic law, and despite Larney's tarnished record, Jake bought four tickets each year, one for each of his children, mailing the money to Larney in Limerick, Ireland. Poppa never won anything except the cheers of Sidney and myself, and the jeers of Dina. She felt he was throwing away twenty dollars each year in a quixotic endeavor.

Over the years, Poppa had several assistants in the retail flower business. The most notable and valuable was Katy's son, Irving. He was tall, fair, and handsome, with a John Barrymore profile. As did his aunt Dora, Irv somehow acquired a William Buckley manner of speech. This served to fascinate and attract customers, particularly on-the-make society ladies of all ages. After learning the basics of the trade at Jake's, Irving moved on to Goldfarb's main shop at 57th Street and Third Avenue. A few years later, owner Morty Goldfarb installed Irving, now known as Eddie Canter, as manager of the sparkling new shop at 63rd Street and Madison Avenue. Here, Eddie took up fairly serious drinking at Cerutti's, a fashionable nearby high-society spa. He proved to be an irresistible magnet for tall, well-educated, affluent women, whether married or single, who eagerly sought his companionship and favor. When Irving married Rosaline Tillman, all this gallivanting abruptly ended, at least insofar as womanizing was concerned. His ongoing affair with booze continued at a somewhat lesser level until his death.

Irving's younger brother, Morris, succeeded him as Poppa's aide. Although a quick learner, Morris' career in the trade ended after three years when he secured a New York City Civil Service position. Poppa's Sidney, who always had hung out at the shop for years on end, became the proprietor of The Gramercy Park Florist in 1939 and ran it until his induction into the U.S. Army in 1943. Curiously, Momma's sister, Libba, had two sons who became florists without first working for Poppa. I, Jake's second son (after graduating from CCNY in 1936), briefly worked at Goldfarb's shop at Broadway and 83rd Street. l left that employ to sample and quickly reject a profession as a veterinarian.

Of course whoever has read this far most certainly is aware that Jake's third son, Ted, survived Townsend Harris Hall, City College, the Army Air Force in WW 11, and Harvard Law to become a successful CPA, tax lawyer, estate planner, and grandfather. However, lest Ted become too haughty let me hereby remind him that Momma often referred to her fourth child as "Potscrebbicull," which translates into "scrapings of the pot."

Working with Jake for years was the powerful Roger Noonan. He drove the shop's light truck delivering his boss' creations throughout Manhattan. Roger had the largest paws I ever saw on a human. When he squeezed your hand, even your toes felt compressed. It wasn't his exceptional strength, however, that marked Roger as It one-of-a-kind. The self-starter on automobiles first appeared on Detroit's products in the early twenties. Up until then, a car was started via a steel crank that was inserted into a notch in the front of the vehicle and then forcefully turned until the motor caught. As the crank was turned, considerable resistance developed; sometimes, if the crank hadn't been inserted all the way, it would slip out and spin dangerously. In 1919 such a crank slipped its notch and slammed into Roger's face, horribly disfiguring him. After many surgeries, he still resembled a monster. Behind his back, Roger became known as "No Nose Noonan." But his name-callers needn't have feared being caught. Despite his awesome strength and fierce visage, Roger was a gentle soul, whom I never saw angry enough to threaten anyone with physical force. The building housing Poppa's shop was torn down in 1935 so that a large apartment house could be built on the site. Poppa relocated to 777 Second Avenue between 41st and 42nd Streets.

Visiting Royalty

Poppa closely followed the boxing game. He was thrilled when Jackie Fields, a great Jewish welterweight champion, visited him at his shop. Jackie was in the same army medical unit as 1. We bunked together and became lifelong friends. Jackie, who owned 2% of the Riviera Hotel and Casino in Las Vegas, invited Poppa to spend a week there as his guest. Poppa had to decline, but the aura of Jackie's visit lingered on for many days.

When I was honorably discharged from the Army in 1946, Poppa asked me to visit him wearing my Captain's uniform. Poppa took me on a tour of several local saloons. He proudly introduced me to his friends and customers, many of whom had served in World War I as members of the Fighting Sixty-ninth" Regiment. You may remember a movie of that name that starred James Cagney and Pat O'Brien.

Not Totally Obliterated Footprints in The Sands of Time

In the early twenties, Poppa would close his shop early on Sundays and arrive home on Wheeler Avenue in the Bronx at about 3:30 p.m. Sidney and I watched to spot Poppa's arrival, and then we'd run to greet him. Often we ran into him at top speed, trying to climb up his chest, and often we got hurt. But such shtick delighted Poppa and made his day, if not his week.

More Footprints

Poppa once bet $1,000 on heavyweight boxing champion yet-to-be Jack Dempsey. Jack was fighting with an opponent whose name I can't recall. Poppa won his bet but the guy who owed him the $1,000 was acutely short of gent. He made Poppa an offer: "Give me $1,000, cancel the $1,0001 owe you, and I'll transfer to you my White Limousine (valued between a Caddy and a Rolls), plus my 'colored' chauffeur, 'Doc.'" Poppa bought the deal and it paid him rich dividends for about six years. Every couple of months on a Sunday, Doc would arrive with the limo at our Wheeler Avenue home, and then drive us to visit Momma's mother who lived with Jacob Cantor, Mom's brother, in a very poor Bronx neighborhood. Sid and I delighted in picking up the car's microphone and talking to Doc, whose front area was sealed in heavy glass. En route, we also made sure we enjoyed a soda kept cold in a small icebox in the vehicle.

Epilogue (1996)

Jacob Propp's name was passed, somewhat modified, to his son Theodore's second son, the brilliant mathematician James Propp, who is "Jimmy" to his family and friends, not "Jake."

Jake's genes now have spread to a fifth generation, where they are diluted (to one sixteenth if I correctly remember my 1935 course in genetics) to a minor role in the Genome (chromosomal complex) of each descendant.

It is hoped, nonetheless, that this narration of Poppa's life in America, his Victories and losses, will equally serve as a tough philosophic guide to all his descendants. Implicit in the foregoing tale is Jake's simple credo,

"BEFORE ALL ELSE, THE FAMILY COMES FIRST."

Editors Note: This story, in part, is about Shimon Propp's family. Shimon was born in Shkudvil, Lithuania and was the son of Todres and Leah Prop. Nine of his children are described in this article. Jacob Propp, who this article was actually written about. Jake was born about 1884. The author is Jake's son, Seymour Propp. Seymour passed away in 2001.

The Reminiscences of Charlotte Sachs Lazerwith

Introduction

This is the story of "The Reminiscences of Charlotte Sachs Lazerwith", who was born in 1912 in Chicago, Illinois and died in 1993 in Portland, Oregon. Charlotte was the daughter of Leon Sachs, whose mother was Marjasha Propp, and father was Yankel Sachs. Charlotte's mother was Ella Propp, daughter of Tzvi-Hirsh (Henry Propp) and Sarah (Sora Frum) Propp. Charlotte was an excellent writer and historian with a marvelous memory for unique and historically important family situations. Charlotte also wrote the history in 1940 of the Propp's Cousin Club of Chicago, Illinois, *which has not been found*. Her reminiscences were tape recorded in 1992 by her daughter, Myra Gevurtz, and edited by her brother, Dr. Jerry Sachs.

Forward

The following bits and pieces of family memorabilia are transcribed from tapes recorded by my sister, Charlotte Lazerwith, assisted by her daughter Myra. They were recorded as Charlotte, who had a remarkable memory, recalled separate incidents and hence they lack a time line. In only a very few instances was I able to combine parts of separate taping because they represented different phases of the same event. Even if I had been able to reorganize all of these memories into a chronology order, much would have been lost. There would have been a little less choppiness and repetition, but the spontaneity would have been destroyed. The only intrusion I have made in Charlotte's story is in the explanatory footnote on Milk Leg.

This then is not a family history but a series of vignettes obviously incomplete partly due to Charlotte's untimely death but mostly because they were intended as snapshots rather than as a continuous story.

Jerry Sachs -- July 9, 1993

Dates for some of the people mentioned in the reminiscences:

Charlotte (Sachs) Lazerwith	(1912 - 1993)
Jerry Sachs	(1916 - 2012)
Henry (Hirsh) Propp	(1859 - 1918)
Sarah (Frum) Propp	(1861 - 1910)
Louis Arne	(1864 - 1939)
Celia (Ruttenberg) Arne	(1876 - 1957)
Leon Sachs	(1878 - 1953)
Ella (Propp) Sachs	(1888 - 1964)
Lillian (Propp) Ruttenberg	(1894 - 1977)
Ted Propp	(1892 - 1974)
Jessie Propp	(1895 - 1987)
Lydia (Propp) Imber	(1897 - 1994)
Hinde (Sachs) Gordon	(1874 - 1966)
Sarah (Arne) Leviton	(1897 - 1981)
Edith (Gordon) Melman	(1906 - 1983)
Louis Gordon	(1907 - 1991)
Manja (Propp) Littwin	(1872 - 1950)
Morris Propp	(1884 - 1933)

Lydia Propp, Lillian Propp, Sarah Propp, Ella Propp, Hirsh Propp, Ted Propp

Ted and Jess Propp

Hirsh (Henry) Propp

The Propp Sisters, Lill, Ella, Lydia and Charlotte

The Reminiscences of Charlotte Sachs Lazerwith

When I was a little girl my father had a horse named Harry. I wish I could say that I remembered the horse but I don't believe I ever saw him. My mother told me that my father used to say, when I was the only child before my brother was born, "Come on Harry, let's go home to Honey." Honey was my nickname then. He used the horse and buggy in his business. He was a jewelry salesman, men's jewelry mainly. He must have kept Harry and the buggy in a stable close to our house. Shortly after I was born my father bought his first car; it was early times to own an automobile. I don't know what kind of car it was. I recall that the last car he had was a "Star" and he had this when I became engaged to Sam Lazerwith because Sam began driving it. The first car was an open car with four doors as I remember it. My mother loved to take rides. When it rained or the weather was inclement in any way my father would hand us leather and isinglass curtains which snapped on to close in the car. The isinglass was like a see-through plastic though it wasn't completely clear. One day we were on a country road, most of the roads were of that sort then. The skies got rather gray. and my father decided to put on the isinglass windows. We were snapping these on from the inside and no one noticed that a cow had come ambling along the road until she stuck her head into the car. It was quite scary and we all screamed. Imagine sitting in a car and suddenly finding yourself face to face with a huge cow!

Jerry and I had only one grandparent we knew. He was our Grandpa Harry, our mother's father, who lived with us. His real name was Henry but everyone called him Harry. Our mother's mother, Grandma Sarah, I am named after her, died before our mother was married. She was quite young, about 48 when she died. I was told that she had what was called Milk Leg, probably something simple which could be cured now. My father's name was Leon Aaron Sachs. My paternal grandfather, Jacob Sachs, Yankel in Yiddish, died in Lithuania at a young age. Jerry is named after him. Yankel Sachs had what we would call a ranch and raised horses for the Russian Army. Harry Benet, who was born in Lithuania, once said to me that on Jacob's land and you could ride from dawn to sundown and not come to the end of it. My paternal grandmother was named Marjasha.

After Marjasha was widowed she came to America with Hinde and father's little brother, Charley. Charley died in childhood. Leon was in Hebrew School and did not come with them. There were many relatives in the east and it seems to me that I recall my father saying that his mother lived in Wilkes-Barre, Pennsylvania. She opened a shop; it may have been a millinery shop. When business warranted it she sent passage money for her son to come and join the family. Some relative called Aunt Ray I don't know where she fits in the family though I think she was a sister of Bessie, wife of Big John Sachs of Chicago - took the passage money and came to America herself. When Marjasha realized that Leon was not going to be able to join her in America she closed up her shop and returned to Lithuania.

Marjasha then followed tradition and married her widower brother-in-law, Shaya-Mendel Aronovich. Mark Alan Lazerwith is named for Marjasha whose name in English would have been Marianne. Shaya-Mendel had been married to Marjasha's older sister, Sora, the grandmother of Sarah Leviton who was her namesake.

When Shaya-Mendel's sons came to America they shortened Aronovich to Arne. My father told me that his stepfather was fanatically orthodox. The family consisted of Marjasha, Shaya-Mendel, Shaya-Mendel's two sons, Louis and Benjamin, father and his sister Hinde. If Shaya-Mendel had daughters they were not mentioned. Shaya-Mendel was so orthodox that respecting the Sabbath was an obsession with him. After sundown on Fridays the boys were not allowed out of the house for fear that they might break a twig or do something equally sinful and thus break the Sabbath. In the long winters in Lithuania sundown might occur as early as three or four in the afternoon so the youngsters had long tiring hours in which prayer was the only activity allowed. My father went to Hebrew School in a different town. I do not know if Shkudvil was a shtetl or how big it was. Since he has been gone I think of many questions I wish I had asked him. There were no dormitories in his school. The boys slept in the classroom on the benches. The older boys frightened the newcomers by telling them that there was a meshugener (crazy man) in the attic and at night he came down to torment the students. This did not help the young ones to sleep. There were no cooking facilities in the school so the good people of the town would offer to provide meals. For example one family might say that Leib (Yiddish for Leon) can come to dinner twice a week.

My father was a thin-skinned person, easily offended, and also a very picky eater. His stepfather could have well afforded to pay for his meals but this was not done. Then after accepting the invitations a student had to come in at back doors and express appreciation even if the meal consisted mainly of black, unappetizing soup covered with fat. This kind of treatment was probably one of the first steps in the development of my father's negative attitude towards religion in general and orthodoxy in particular. This attitude applied to Judaism or any other formal religion.

My father was not fond of animals. Most of the farmers in the area had big dogs and when he walked along the country roads the dogs would rush to the fences, bark loudly and try to get out. This scared him when he was small and he never got over his distaste for animals.

Young Jewish men, age sixteen or seventeen, had to leave Lithuania, which was ruled over by the Russian Tzar, to avoid conscription into the army. Once in the army a conscript could be sent anywhere, even Siberia, and could be kept in for indefinite periods, sometimes for life. This was particularly true for Jewish boys since the Russians were notoriously Anti-Semitic. There were three places to go. One was the United States, one was South America, and one was South Africa. The choice was South Africa because the family had landsmanschaften (people from the same town or area) there in Durban, South Africa. Durban is east of the Cape of Good Hope on the Indian Ocean. Father was well supplied with money. It was a sad parting; he did not know if he would ever see his family again. About the same time his stepbrother Louis Aronovich (Arne) and perhaps also Leon's older stepbrother, Ben, chose to go to America and settled in the upper peninsula of Michigan, an area called the Copper Country. My father was very attached to Louis who was both his cousin and his stepbrother. Before my father left his stepfather gave him the benefit of much advice mostly dealing with the dangers of deviating from strict orthodox practices. My father recalls that he was told that if he ever ate trayf, non-kosher food, the ceiling would fall on his head. The family put him on the train probably with a supply of kosher food to see him through the first stage of his journey. The train took him to Amsterdam where he stayed a few days. He was impressed with Holland and told me that it was a country where people were able to follow their beliefs, religious and secular, without persecution or discrimination. I remembered this when I visited Amsterdam many years later. From there he went to the port of Rotterdam. He sailed from Rotterdam to Tenerife in the Canary Islands. He was proud that he had not traveled steerage. He could not afford first class accommodations but I think he traveled cabin class due to the generosity of his stepfather. The first night at sea he went to the dining room and was handed a menu in English, which he could not read. He was rather fluent in several languages, German and perhaps Lithuanian as well as Yiddish and Hebrew but knew no English. Not knowing what to do, he glanced around and saw someone eating a dish which looked appetizing. He pointed at it and the waiter brought him his dinner. As he was eating it he recalled what Shaya-Mendel had told him and being sure that whatever he was eating was not kosher he looked up at the ceiling, which seemed to be solid and in one piece. He then said to himself, "The old man didn't know what he was talking about!" He stayed a few days in Tenerife, the port where Columbus had mended his ships on his voyage to the New World. He boarded another ship and took the long voyage down the West Coast of Africa, around the Cape of Good Hope and up the East Coast of Africa to Durban. Durban was a resort town and the climate was warm. When he came to the United States some years later, my mother said that his skin was very brown. The plans for my father were that he would be apprenticed to a jeweler and learn watch making. Durban was near the diamond country so his stepfather, who was apparently a bright man, thought he could become an expert on diamonds. When he arrived found lodging with landsmanschaften on a farm near Durban. There were several other Jewish boys from Shkudvil living here also although my father had not known them at home. He asked them how long they had been there. One of them said over a year and another said nine months. They spoke no English and I do not know where they worked. This was not at all what my father had in mind. He knew the British Empire was admired the world over and he intended to become a British citizen and certainly wanted to learn English. He made his excuses to the Shkudvil people with whom he was living and moved into the city. He took a room "on the square" as he put it. It must have been a rooming house. No meals were provided. He still had problems ordering food in restaurants. He taught himself by listening and watching. A woman ordered eggs and he waited until they were brought to the table and he would say to himself, Eggs, that's eiyre." He put what he heard together with what he learned from the newspapers and he began to learn English. His skill with the language improved over the years and he had practically no accent. (In America he frequently used British expressions. When annoyed he might say, "Dash it all!" to which my mother would remark with devilish relish, you mean damn it all!") He became apprenticed to a jeweler. Later on he opened his own store. He stayed in South Africa about ten years and did become a British citizen.

When he opened his own store, he hired a young native boy as a porter to clean the store. This porter also made tea for my father. My father was very fond of tea. He had enjoyed drinking it at home in Lithuania and of course it was the standard British drink. The porter started calling my father "Mr. Cup-of-tea." My father made friends and belonged to a club called The Ivy Club. The club motto was "I cling to thee." This was a club of mixed (Jewish and non-Jewish) membership. It was a social club with dancing included among its activities though its members would do some charitable work and visit people who were ill. The grapevine carried the word back to Shkudvil that father was going with a non-Jewish girl. His mother, a real smart cookie if there ever was one, wrote him. She knew her son and she did not express disapproval of his dating. She wrote, "You have been in South Africa long enough. The climate isn't so good and there are better opportunities in America where we have many relatives." He was probably not deeply in love and though he did like the warm climate he took his mother's advice, sold his store and made plans to come to the United States. I remember when I was a child and told my friends that my father had lived in South Africa, the astonishment was usually followed by a question like, "What did he do there, shoot lions?" My answer, "No, he had a jewelry store," it was quite a letdown.

When he left Durban, my father did not go directly to the United States. He went to Berlin. He had arranged a rendezvous there to see his mother who brought his sister Hinde, called Hindely by her brother, with her. The most popular tune of the times was The Merry Widow Waltz and they danced to the tune in the beer gardens of Berlin before their sad farewells.

Shaya-Mendel Aronovich came to America to attend the wedding of his younger son, Ben Arne, in the copper country of the Michigan Upper Peninsula. Marjasha did not accompany him on this trip. He probably took a train to one of the major ports and then a ship to New York. From New York he went to the wedding in Calumet, Michigan and after a short stay came to Chicago where he stayed at the Sherman Hotel. He was apparently a man of importance in his part of Lithuania. He was visited by relatives and landsmanschaften. He was related to the Propp family and there were quite a number of Propps in this area, in Centralia, Illinois, in Kouts, Indiana and Michigan City, Indiana. The word got around that Shaya- Mendel Aronovich was in Chicago and he "held court at the Sherman Hotel for his admirers who came to see him. On his way to America he passed through Germany. The Germans were widely admired as skillful artisans and made unusual toys. Shaya- Mendel purchased a doll for his only grandchild, Sarah Arne (Leviton). The doll was as big as a two-year-old child. The head was made of China. He brought this magnificent doll across the Atlantic and delivered it in Calumet, Michigan. I saw that doll many years later when Sarah was an elderly lady. I visited her apartment in Hollywood Park, a neighborhood in northwestern Chicago. The doll was named Charlene. It had its own rocking chair and was well taken care of, carefully repaired when anything went wrong. This beautiful doll was cherished and enjoyed not only by Sarah but also by her daughter and granddaughters. I am sure that her daughter, Joyce Hammer, still has it in a place of honor).

During the First World War, Shaya-Mendel lost almost all of his money, which he had kept in the Bank of Moscow. Nevertheless he managed to follow the dream of so many orthodox Jews, "Next year in Jerusalem," and left Lithuania for Palestine accompanied by Marjasha. My father was in America by then and his sister Hinde was married and living in Lithuania but not in Shkudvil. I can recall my father being worried because he had not heard from his mother. My father would say to my mother "I don't hear from her; something must be wrong." One day a box came from Lithuania. In it was the heavy gold bracelet he had made for his mother in Africa, some raw coral, a beautiful little bible with wooden carved cover, which I still have, and a lulif and esrog. (I think esrog is like a lemon of some kind.) My father knew she was gone. She had died in Jerusalem much earlier. Shaya-Mendel survived her for only a short time. When I was in Israel I asked a Rabbi if it was possible to locate, my grandmother's grave. Of course what is now Israel had been part of occupied territory for many years and some of the cemeteries had been desecrated? Though I was able to give her name and some details he told me it would take years to go through all the records, even those still in existence. Her death must have occurred sometime about 1918. Her grave could be found given the details I knew but I was there for only a few days so I was unable to follow up.

There is more I should tell about my father's family. My father knew when he landed in New York in 1909, that he had a cousin named Manja Littwin living in Brooklyn. He contacted her and she arranged for all of the local relatives to meet him. He came to her house on a Saturday afternoon from wherever he was staying, and he was smoking a cigarette. Manja kissed him and said, Cousin, I am honored to have you here but it is Shabbas and if you don't put out that cigarette I cannot let you stay. It was not his intention to offend anyone but he had lived in a mixed community in South Africa and orthodoxy had become foreign to him. He went outside and got rid of the cigarette. The relatives greeted him warmly and everyone had a good time. I don't know how long he stayed in New York but soon he started for the Upper Peninsula of Michigan, stopping first in Chicago.

The Arne brothers in Michigan were my father's cousins who had become his stepbrothers through the marriage of Marjasha and Shaya-Mendel Aronovich. Louis Arne and my father were very close. By then Louis was married to Celia and they had at least the one child, Sarah. When my Aunt Lydia Propp was about 15 years old she had a growth spurt. She grew quite tall in a very short time and was not at all well. She might have had tuberculosis. Louis Arne's wife Celia, the dearest, most loving and caring person in the world, found out about Lydia's health from my mother, either by phone or letter. She told my mother," Send Lydia to me. I'll fatten her up. I'll feed her wine and eggs and bring her back to health." Lydia went up and spent the summer with the Arnes. They called her L.P., a nickname made up of her initials. She was a lively handsome girl, dark haired with very white teeth and seemed to have an attractive personality at that time.

Later when the Arne children were grown Louis and Celia moved to South Milwaukee Wisconsin so that Sarah, Phillip, Rosalie, Charlie and Lilly would have Jewish friends and could find Jewish mates in the larger Jewish community around Milwaukee. There was another reason for the move. The copper mines were closing and business at Louis Arne's general store had dropped off drastically. I think the Ben Arne family also came to Wisconsin at this time. In South Milwaukee the Louis Arnes had an apartment over their small town, department store. They may have owned the building. They lived well. They had a great deal of help. I recall that when Lydia and I became friendly with Sarah again and had dinner at her house, Lydia said to me, Sarah is just like Aunt Celia. She puts a lace tablecloth on her dining room table and serves beautifully." In both the Copper Country and Wisconsin Jewish salesman could count on having a good meal at the Arne household.

My father and Aunt Lydia told me how the relatives lived in the Copper country. Louis and his family lived in Calumet. Ben and his family lived in Houghton or Hancock. They were the Jewish merchants of those towns. There were a few Jewish families in that area and quite a number of Welsh working in the mines. Albert Ruttenberg, I am not sure whether he was a relative or not, married a Welsh girl named Carrie; these were Uncle Nate's parents. Louis Arne had what amounted to a small town department store in Calumet. I don't know what Ben Arne did but it seems he was rather prosperous.

He may have had the same type of store as his brother Louis but in another town. My father found the climate of the Upper Peninsula shocking. The long severe winters with heavy snowfalls were in stark contrast to the mild semi-tropical climate of Durban. In addition Durban was a cosmopolitan community and Calumet was far from that. My father found the climate unbearable and the lack of activities boring. The only leisure activity was card playing. They played cards every night. This probably accounts for my father's antipathy to card playing. Louis was very religious; the family owned a Torah. My father, who was looking for a permanent place to settle down, he had opened up a shoe store in Calumet but when he found the climate and lack of social life unacceptable he left and went to Cincinnati. About one year in the cold north was all he could stand.

Papa had relatives in Cincinnati, aunts and many cousins. My paternal grandfather, Jacob Sachs, had brothers John and Hymen and sisters Sadie and Ida. My father's aunt, Sadie Price, lived in Cincinnati as did his uncle, Hymen Sachs, and his aunt, Ida Benet. I don't know if there were any other aunts and uncles. Father's Aunt Sadie wanted him to marry her daughter Jean. (My mother always called her Jenny but she had changed her name to Jean.) The fact that they were first cousins apparently did not bother Aunt Sadie. However Jean did not appeal to my father and he decided that the best course was to leave for Chicago where his Uncle John and his family were located.

Before going on with the saga of my father's adventures in Chicago I want to reminisce a little about what I recall of visits to the Arne Family in South Milwaukee. We made such visits at least once a year and always had a good time. They had a big wooden house filled with lively people. Everyone played the piano a little. We would spend some time at the store. Sarah would choose some material and make me a dress. Sometimes we stayed with them more often than once a year. I looked forward to these trips because I always enjoyed myself.

Going back to father's departure from Cincinnati, he went from there to Chicago and stayed with the family of his Uncle, John Sachs, for a few months until he opened a store. John Sachs owned saloons. He was a very religious and very generous man. Any drunk who would cry on his shoulder was sure of getting money. John Sachs and his wife, Bessie, had five children, Sadie, Mamie who changed her name to May, Hymen, Harry and Leah. Hymen became head of the English Department at Louisiana Polytech in Ruston, Louisiana. In Ruston he was known as Tony Sachs. He co-authored an English textbook. I have a copy tucked away somewhere. At this time Sadie, whose married name is Glass is the only survivor. My mother told me that Big John Sachs rode a horse at the Levee, which was an area of Chicago near the river. Wearing his usual white cowboy hat he must have made an impressive figure. I remember seeing him when he was quite old and thinking that he didn't look so big to me. He used to call my mother by the pet name of Ellis. John and his beautiful Bessie had a big house on the West Side, servants and a carriage. They lived in style.

My parents were married in the home of Bessie and John. My maternal grandmother had died not too long before the wedding. My grandfather insisted on providing the food. Big John provided the liquid refreshments with a huge well-stocked bar. At the time of the wedding my father had lived with his aunt and uncle for about six months. He loved his cousins and they loved him.

The family in Cincinnati had a wonderful reputation. They were rather orthodox. Aunt Sadie Price's children were Jean (Jennie), Lillian, Pauline and Harry. Pauline, whose married name, was Glazer, moved to Anderson Indiana. Lillian's married name was Miller. Harry was a prominent architect in the city and there is a section called Price Hill named after him. When I was first married and lived in Cincinnati I lived on Beatrice Drive a street named after Beatrice Price, Harry's wife. Other cousins like Will and Faye Sachs were in the real estate business and some were in the furniture business. Lillian Miller had an engaging personality and I loved her. she had no children and always lived in her mother's house. Her husband, Mitchell Miller, a very affable man, was a pharmacist. Aunt Sadie was a domineering woman, sure of herself and very bossy. All of the cousins were bright but listened to the advice, generally good, dished out by the matriarch.

Sadie Glass recalled the happy times when my father lived with the Sachs family in Chicago. He was older than his cousins and played imaginative games with them. one of his variations on Hide and Seek was to hide their maid in a cupboard and ask the children to find her. Sadie recalls that he had a marvelous sense of humor. When my father died, May, who was a few years older than Sadie, hung over the casket murmuring, "What an aristocrat: So…Handsome" Harry Sachs had a tour of duty in the Navy when quite young. Once he flirted with me on an El train, not aware of whom I was. I told my friend, Ruth, which he was a cousin and went over to him. When I said," Harry, don't you recognize me? I'm Charlotte Sachs, Leon's daughter," he was embarrassed. Harry always had an eye for a pretty girl. He told me a story, which showed the generous nature of his father. When he was a boy, Harry was invited by a friend to come home with him. "Home" turned out to be some small shabby rooms back of a store shared by quite a number of family members. The head of the family was without a job. That night Harry told his father about the visit. His own home was comfortable and large. His father listened sympathetically and then said," If I give them money it will be gone in a week and then they will be no better off than they are now. I'll get this man a good line of goods to sell. Then he will earn his own living and the family will be able to afford a better place to live."

John Sachs and his wife Bessie were very religious orthodox Jews. Harry married young and brought his beautiful bride Edith home; he had no job and no money. Edith was not Jewish. Aunt Bessie accepted her without question and told her other children they were to treat her as though she was their sister. Aunt Bessie was a wonderful woman loved by my father who visited her often. After John Sachs died, Bessie lived with her daughter May. John Sachs had purchased a set of beautiful intricately carved chairs and each daughter kept at least one of these in her home. I saw the one in home of

Sadie Glass. Sadie is the only one of the children of Bessie and John surviving in this year 1992. She is in her nineties and in full possession of all of her faculties. I have visited her in the past few years. Sadie was a piano teacher and an accomplished pianist. Her husband was a violin teacher. They had three daughters. Jerry and I were never enthusiastic when our mother told us we were to visit the Glasses. The three daughters were younger than we were and must have learned piano in the cradle. We had been taking lessons for some years but the lessons did not take. David Glass would, after a short exchange of greetings and news inevitably ask, well Leon, how is the music education of the children progressing? "I generally knew one piece like Anitra's Dance but the Glass children had extensive repertoires and played like professionals. I don't think Jerry was forced to perform after the first few times but I always felt intimidated and embarrassed when I had to compete with the talented daughters of David and Sadie. June Glass died fairly recently. Beverly Glass (Kolodny) still plays the piano and in addition has a beautiful singing voice.

Shifting over from papa's recollections and his family, my mother was in kindergarten during the Columbian Exposition of 1893 so she must have been born in 1888 or 1889. Our maternal grandfather Hirsh Propp, he took the name, Henry, in the USA and was called Harry. Henry came from Shkudvil and our maternal grandmother, Sarah Frum, came from the seaport town of Memel in what was then Germany. The marriage might have been arranged but our grandfather adored our grandmother. She was a lovely woman with a gracious and engaging personality. My father told me that everyone loved her including her neighbors, Jewish, Irish or whatever. Henry Propp came to Chicago from Shkudvil to establish himself so that he could bring his family. He was an accountant in Lithuania but apparently those skills were not transferable. He had relatives in Chicago named Levinson. Their father was an old man with a beard who called me "Hansal the Getch." Some of the Levinsons were cigar makers. For a time they lived in Whiting, Indiana. My mother remembered digging in the sand on the beach in Whiting. My grandfather tried his hand at rolling cigars but being asthmatic he found this a far from ideal occupation for him. Shortly after he came to America he sent for his wife and daughter. My mother recalled that coming over in steerage her mother was seasick for the entire voyage. My mother who was about four years old remembers having a little tin plate which was filled through the generosity of other passengers since her mother was too sick to take care of her. My mother was named Anna or Annie Propp but there were too many Annie Propps so, being an individualist even at an early age, she changed her name to Ella. It seems likely that she came to Chicago in 1890 since she recalled going to the Columbian Exposition of 1893.

The family lived for a while in Whiting but as the cigar business was a health hazard for Grandpa so they moved to Chicago, probably somewhere on the West Side, and Henry opened a grocery store. Both Sarah and Henry worked in the store. Their second child, Lakah (Lillian) was born in Chicago as were Lipke (Lydia) and Todres (Theodore). Theodore, called Teddy or Ted later was nicknamed, Freddy, as a child. My mother changed her own name when she was ten or eleven years old in later years she told me that if she had known of the name she would have called herself, Ellen, which she thought was prettier than Ella. She was also responsible for picking the Americanized names Lillian, Lydia and Theodore for her sisters and brother. Ella was an excellent student, bright, quick and very interested in learning. Her thirst for knowledge remained with her throughout her life. Her friends like Jennie Kadison, Florence Teplitz and Flora Rosenbaum came into her life at various times as she grew up. I am not aware of exactly when. She was not happy at having to drag Lydia or Teddy along frequently when she went out with her friends. She attended the Garfield School. Once or perhaps more than once an impressed teacher wrote on a paper written by Ella "TO THE GRAMMARIAN OF THE GARFIELD SCHOOL!" She was an omnivorous reader and told me once that she was in the schoolyard reading a book, which she felt her teacher would not approve of. It may have been something risqué or controversial in some way. Rather than take it into class she hid it under the wooden sidewalk near the entrance. When she left school to return home she found the book exactly where she had left it. I was impressed by both the idea of wooden sidewalks and my mother's daring in reading books considered beyond the pale.

There was a sad ending to my mother's school career. She had finished eighth grade with distinction and was looking forward to the graduation ceremony. There was no money to buy her a dress for graduation. Her mother took an old dress of hers and remodeled it for Ella to wear. At that time the children dressed up for graduation. (When I graduated from grammar school, all the girls wore middy blouses and navy blue skirts.) In my mother's class was a girl named Schiff whose father was a banker. His daughter came to graduation looking like a bride. My mother did not want to hurt Grandma's feelings but she knew that she could not wear the inappropriate makeshift dress to graduation. Instead Ella walked around the school, crying, but did not go in for the ceremony. She never told her parents and they did not know because working foreign parents did not often go to graduations. In later years my mother told me that out of this disappointment came the firm determination that Lillian, Lydia and Theodore would have the appropriate clothes when they graduated from school. She would earn the money to provide these.

The next-door neighbors, the Beckers, became friends of the family. Mrs. Becker died young leaving a number of children. I recall the names of Isadore, Mildred and Rose. there may have been others. Mr. Becker brought over his single sister, Sarah, from Latvia to help raise his children. The sister had been a seamstress in Latvia. She spoke no English; she did not know how to cook. My grandmother taught her cooking and my mother taught her to speak English. The families became very close. Isadore Becker and Ted Propp became best friends. Ted admired Isadore immensely. Isadore became a prominent attorney in Chicago. Lydia Propp and Mildred Becker were good friends. At Mildred's wedding Lydia was a bridesmaid and recalls seeing her wearing a big picture hat. (We must have lived in several places on the West Side but the only one I am sure of was on 12th place near Roosevelt Road and Kedzie Avenue.) After helping to raise her brother's children, Sarah Becker married a man named Goldberg. Years later one

Sunday my mother said, "I would like to visit Sarah Goldberg in Momence. (I think she wanted to see Momence at least as much as she wanted to see Sarah because she loved to go to new places and the idea of living in a small town interested her.) The Goldberg children were Jean, nicknamed Goldie, Naomi, Ruth, Alex and Max. I stayed overnight with Jean and we became fast friends. We corresponded for a while but Jean was several years older than I was, I was about fourteen at the time and we lost contact as our interests diverged. Years later I saw her at a Pioneer Women's meeting and recognized her. Her married name was Jean Mandel. The mention of the Pioneer women sparks my memory of another encounter with a relative. The youngest daughter of Sadie Sachs Glass, Beverly Kolodny, was very active in Pioneer Women at he time when Jean Mandel was a member. Beverly often sang at meetings. Sometimes her mother served as her accompanist I did lot attend meetings regularly and had not seen them together. I did see Beverly in passing but did not make the connection. One meeting we came face-to-face and there was instant recognition on both sides. She said," I think you are Charlotte Sachs," and I answered, "And I think you are Beverly Glass." It was strange to have this mutual recognition since we had not been together since we grew up though we were second cousins.

After my mother finished grammar school she got a job in a hat factory, she must have been about fourteen years old. she also worked at Mandel Brothers, a large department store in downtown Chicago. I am not sure of the chronology here. At Christmas time at Mandels Brothers the employees were given the broken toys, which could not be sold. Mother got a doll perhaps without an arm or without a leg that she gave to her sister, Lillian. Mama told me that Lill loved that doll she named her Jerusha. Lill made up a song about her beloved doll. she would sing, "Jerusha came to live with me at Christmas time!" Lillian had a good voice. When mother worked at the hat factory the girls would sit around a table and each one would have a simple task to perform. One would put a bit of ribbon on the hat form; another would add a feather. It was an elementary production line. Mama had done this for a very short time when she said to herself, "This job has no future!" She did not think of moving from the ribbon girl spot to the feather girl spot as a promotion. Mama promptly quit the job. she did not tell her parents but continued to take a lunch and go out for the day. Mother was never at a loss for things to do. She went to the Art Institute, she wandered around Lincoln Park, she haunted the library, and she gazed at the mansions on Michigan Avenue and imagined what life would be like if she lived there. Her father realized what was happening and after a few days said to her: "Ellinke, I don't think you are working any more. " Mama admitted it and her father was most sympathetic. She got a job as a cashier in what was called an Italian Production Store on the near West Side. In this job she met a young attorney and his wife who shopped at the store. These were the Clearance Darrows. This was long before he became a famous lawyer. When she told her father that she was going to work as a cashier, he gave her this advice, "Don't think of the things you handle as money; think of them as worthless pieces of wood." This was grandpa's way of saying that his beloved daughter should not be tempted to test her honesty. Knowing my mother as I came to know her, this advice, well meaning as it was, was unnecessary.

Mother was a woman of character; integrity was inherent in her soul. Probably the last job Mother had before she got married was as a cashier in a store on Blue Island Avenue. It was an early version of a Ten Cent Store. She may have applied for the job in answer to an advertisement in a newspaper. A Scotsman named Stark owned the store. The customers in the Store were mostly immigrants, many of them Polish. Mr. Stark often found it difficult to understand them and would call to my mother, 'Ella come down and wait on these people. I can't tell what they want." Mother was apparently good at communicating with those who had little or no English. Mother started making suggestions to Mr. Stark when he was going to the wholesale house to replenish his stock. For instance she suggested before Easter that he buy some artificial flowers so that the customers could trim their hats. Her ideas, and she had many of them, proved to be successful and Mr. Stark made her his buyer.

Mother was a compulsive reader. She said once that she had read her way through the library as a girl and young woman I believe this to be close to the truth at least in the arts, literature and the humanities in general. I suppose the statement did not apply to science. When I was going to college I found my mother amazingly knowledgeable in most areas in which I took courses, able to hold a discussion and to make intelligent and informed comments in a wide variety of subjects.

At this point I just want to include what my mother told me about her attitude towards early rising. She detested getting up early and told me that when she was working she often finished dressing on the streetcar on her way to her job. This must have required great ingenuity since streetcars did not have private booths. Ella belonged to the Young Peoples Socialist Club, a group of young intellectuals who explored the city as well as exploring ideas and ideals. She went out with a young man named Harry Finder, a law student, whom she liked very much. She grew up in a kosher household but when Harry said to her, "You Know Ella in restaurants there are many interesting things to eat. You don't need to order a cheese sandwich every time." Her eyes were opened to new food possibilities. She was not afraid to try new things but until then had followed the customs of her family. Once she started experimenting there were few limits. She found that she loved shrimps for example. In itself this was not very important but it demonstrates an attitude that was and is important. Taboos were to be questioned. New ideas were exciting rather than frightening. Old ideas were not necessarily bad because they were old. New ideas were not necessarily good because they were new. All ideas, new and old, were subject to examination, discussion and evaluation. When the group met at the Propp home Ella raided the fancy goods shelves of the family store and was making a crabmeat salad for her friends. Her mother came into the kitchen, looked suspiciously at what her daughter was mixing up and asked, "Vos is dos?" My mother answered; Salmon salad." She was sure that her mother didn't believe her but grandma did not pursue the matter. My mother's social group attended lectures and went to see plays. The top actors and actresses appeared on the Chicago stage and mother was entranced by Shakespeare and Shaw and thoroughly enjoyed the rich theatrical fare, which was available.

At this point Isadore Becker was finishing high school and was applying for entrance to the University of Michigan. As part of his application he had to submit an essay under the title: "Patriotism and Its Development Through the Ages." Isadore was a very good student in many ways but writing was not his strong suit. He looked for someone to help him, if possible someone to write the essay for him. Of all the people available to him he chose Ella Propp who had not gone beyond the eighth grade. Isadore knew how well mother could speak and write. We have copies of the essay and it was very logically crafted and beautifully written[1]. Isadore was accepted at Michigan, finished Law School there and as previously mentioned, became a successful and very prominent lawyer.

Returning to the saga of my father who, after arriving in Chicago, stayed with his Uncle John and Aunt Bessie. His first cousins loved him. They were quite a bit younger and Papa was very popular with them. It was touching at his funeral when all of them told us how they adored Leon. Papa opened a jewelry store on Blue Island Avenue; I don't know the exact location. He was then a man in his late twenties. Papa enjoyed seeking and finding relatives. He began with those most closely related and eventually found Henry Propp's family. Henry was a rather distant cousin. My father's mother, Marjasha, was a Propp. My grandmother, Sarah Propp was rather impressed by her husband's family and liked Papa. Papa had his eye on Mama from the first. she was beautiful, spunky, interested in everything and had a sparkling, unusual, colorful personality. When Papa came to visit, her mother would say, "Sachs kumt." (Sachs is coming.) Mama would then say, "I'm going!" and Papa did not impress her. He seemed very foreign to her. He wore high button shoes and still had a trace of an accent. Then Grandma Sarah died of what mother called Milk Leg[2].

Grandma Sarah was an endearing person. She was generous to a fault; giving tender loving care to her family and having a friendly smile and a helping hand for the entire world. The man who delivered bread to the Propp store, an Irishman who liked Grandma said," I can't believe she is gone!" Pointing to the tree outside the store he added, "I thought Mrs. Propp was as strong as that tree. Papa was very considerate and helpful during this stressful period. He even helped in the grocery store during the period of Shiva. Mama adored her mother and she was terribly affected by this unexpected loss.

After all Sarah Propp was only in her forties and maybe in her early forties. It was a dreadful summer for my mother. She told me that she was so run-down that she was always cold and wore a winter coat through much of the summer. She went to a doctor who gave her a tonic to "remake the sun shine for you again." Father was very supportive. When the mourning period was over Mother said that she considered herself engaged. This was a great change for Mother. She had been a bookkeeper and was now a buyer, a successful businesswoman for her time. she had an active social life

---

[1] A copy of the essay is appended at the end of these recollections.

[2] Milk Leg is a deep iliofemoral thrombophlebitis. In this condition blood clots develop first in the small veins of the leg. The clots enlarge and move upward to obstruct the main vein returning blood to the heart.

with her liberal friends and was accustomed to fine places like the College Inn, a fine restaurant with an orchestra and good entertainment located in the Sherman House in the Chicago Loop. Mother, now felt responsible for the entire family. Her siblings were not small children. Lillian was a year or two younger than Ella and Ted a few years younger than Lillian. The baby Lydia must have been at least fourteen years old. Mother also felt a responsibility for her father who was asthmatic and generally not in the best of health.

Mother said that she could not marry Father unless the entire family could live together. Her own father objected. He told her that this was not the way for newlyweds to live. He said, we'll rent a flat near you and you can have us over to dinner once in a while. There was a note of optimism in this suggestion! My mother had never cooked anything in her life. Over her father's objections and with my father's agreement, Ella had her way. My father really did not mind. He had been living alone for so long that having a close family around him seemed attractive.

As I mentioned before Mother and Father were married at the home of Uncle John Sachs. Henry Propp supplied the food for the wedding and John Sachs supplied the liquor. The newlyweds went to Milwaukee for their honeymoon. They took an apartment on the West Side of Chicago. I believe the second apartment was where they lived when I was born. This was rented from a family named O'Leary. It was a two-flat building near Homan or St. Louis and Roosevelt Road, probably on 12th Place. Papa was teaching Ted the jewelry business. Ted was a student at Crane Technical High School. Papa was very energetic and perhaps demanding. Ted was a teenager, probably no more attentive than most teenagers and sparks flew occasionally. Once when Papa was very angry because Ted had not brought him his lunch until it was almost time for dinner, they were engaged in a shouting match. A downstairs window opened and Mrs. O'Leary asked my mother what was happening. My mother told her, My husband and my brother are fighting." Mrs. O'Leary said, in her thick Irish brogue, "Sure and let them kill each other. Bring the kids down and I'll make coffee." We lived on the second floor and the O'Learys lived on the first floor although they did a great deal of their daily livings cooking and socializing in the basement. The parlor on the first floor was kept for occasions such as the visit of the priest. Mr. O'Leary was a policeman and the daughters were teachers. They were a warm friendly family. I'll have a story of an encounter with one of the daughters when I was in high school a little later.

When Ella was first married she teamed up with her father to experiment in trying to make the dishes her mother Sarah had made. Between the two of them they were able to reproduce some of the wonderful dishes they recalled, particularly baked goods. The apple raisin kuchen and the poppy-seed kuchen, even if they were not exact copies of Sarah's, were mouthwatering and filled the house with heavenly scents. On Friday Momma made pans and pans of kuchen. It had butter in it; before she put it in the oven she would brush the outside with melted butter and when I ate it I would slather it with more sweet butter. No one knew or worried about cholesterol in those days! Later when I was a school child I would come home on Fridays to find the house filled with

78

delightful odors. Heading for the kitchen I would butter a huge piece of kuchen with the intention of sitting on the sofa in the living room eating as I read a book. Alas the apartment had the long hall so common in those days and by the time I reached the living room the kuchen had been eaten and I would have to go back for more. There was also tempting coffee cake with a streusel top and sometimes cheese filled kuchen as well.

Back to the O'Leary daughters for a moment. One of them was a Physical Education Teacher in the Chicago High Schools. After we had moved to the North Side and then to the South Side I graduated from elementary school and enrolled in Englewood High School. As freshmen girls we were seated on one side of the gymnasium while several Physical Education Teachers sat at a table on the other side. When they called out a name, the girl called was to cross to the table and give the teachers such information as they requested. My name was called and as I started across Marie O'Leary who was one of the teachers shouted, "Honey Sachs, you come here!" I felt the kind of embarrassment that only a teen can suffer not only because of the nickname but because of being singled out for attention. My Aunt Lydia once said that they called me Honey because I was honey colored. I had light hair, a fair complexion and blue eyes. I was called Honey by everyone in the family-so much so that when I had first started school I wasn't sure whether my real name was Charlotte or Honey.

After the family moved from the West Side we lived on Burling Street in the Lincoln Park Area Aunt Lill got a job at Butler Brothers, a big wholesale supplier to stores. She became a star saleslady with buyers from the stores in small towns lined up to wait for her. She dressed stylishly and always wore a rose fastened to her lapel. When Aunt Lydia got old enough she worked in the hosiery department at Mandel Brothers Department Store. Ted, after what was probably a very short apprenticeship with Papa in his jewelry store, got a job as a salesman with the Parker Pen Company. He was very successful and later was given the territory centered at Pittsburgh for Parker.

Lydia was devoted to her father She would go for walks with him and give him the attention which Ella could not after the birth of her children. I have a lovely photograph of Lydia with Grandpa taken on one of their outings together. Grandpa suffered a great deal from his asthma. Mother said that he coughed so much that it finally affected his heart. When he was taken to the hospital he objected, I don't want to leave my babies!" Jerry and I did not know any of the other three grandparents but Henry Propp was a loving and demonstrative grandfather. He was buried in Waldheim Cemetery but it was apparently not possible to buy a gravesite next to that of Grandma Sarah. Years later Aunt Lydia quietly managed to have her father's grave moved so that he and his beloved Sarah were side by side. she was both pleased and proud that she could make this sentimental gesture on behalf of her beloved parents.

Uncle Ted was very prosperous in his days with Parker Pen. He lived well and was exceedingly generous to his sisters and to Jerry and me. Ted took us to the theater and to the best restaurants. I recall seeing The Follies and almost every other musical show, which came to town. Uncle Ted would take my mother and me. I am sure that some of these shows were daring for their times but I enjoyed all of them. Later on Jerry was included although he tells me that the only show he recalls was Topsy and Eva. In that show I was entranced by Eva who sat at the edge of the stage wearing a beautiful wig of blond curls, swinging her legs out over the orchestra pit and singing, "Memories." I wanted to meet her. Uncle Ted took us to stage door and told the custodian, "My kids want to meet the Duncan Sisters," and we were ushered in. They were very nice and friendly but I was shocked. The stage Eva did not look young and beautiful close up. The heavy cake makeup was obvious. This must have been about 1923 so I would have been eleven years old. Almost every Saturday Jerry and I were taken downtown to offices where people made a big fuss over us. We were taken by Uncle Ted, Aunt Lill and Papa, who for some time was a wholesale jewelry salesman, and worked out of an office in the Mailers Building at Wabash and Madison. He was associated with a man named Maltz.

Uncle Ted married Aunt Jess but did not tell anyone in the family. I suppose that this was because she was not Jewish and he anticipated some less than pleasant reactions from some family members. The family heard about this through the grapevine and even saw the two together when driving somewhere. Everyone tried to get a good look at Jess from the moving car. Aunt Jess had a very good job with Bartlett Real Estate. Ted in his dating had been highly critical of the average Jewish girl. My mother once talked him into taking his sister Lillian to a dance given by the Shriners. He was a member of that organization. Afterwards he told my mother, "Don't ever do that to me again! She is so affected; she can't speak or act naturally."

Aunt Jess, Jessie Elizabeth Amanda McCutcheon, was from southern Indiana. She was related to the famous cartoonist John McCutcheon, the artist who drew the 'Indian Summer" cartoon, which the Tribune reprinted year after year. The family knew that Jess and Ted were married. At that time we lived at 3709 Rokeby Street in Lance View. By then Lydia was married to Louis Imber and she invited the family over for dinner. Everyone expected Ted to announce that he was married. Every time he started to say something all attention was focused on him. Finally he did say," I guess you know that I am married." At that the three sisters, the weeping willows, all began to cry. I used to refer to the sisters as The Three Graces. That is what I called them when I came out of the anesthetic, after my appendix was removed and found all three of them hovering tearfully over my bed.

For a few years after the marriage of Jess and Ted, he continued to work for the Parker Pen Company. Jess and Ted lived in Detroit; they had a beautifully furnished apartment in a good building in a desirable neighbor-hood. Ted had a big Locomobile. It was a half block long." A two door elegant sports car with a rumble seat and all of the appointments available at that time. We visited Detroit when I was about sixteen. Uncle Lou Imber accompanied by my father escorted us as far as the Indiana line and Jerry drove us to Detroit. He was not quite fourteen years old but he was a good driver. Illinois. They did not have driver licenses in those days and no one thought it odd that a small boy was driving a big car. My mother and I were wondering how to approach our new relative. We were very comfortable with our loving Ted but what kind of a relationship would we have with our new sister-in-law and aunt? We considered what we should say and how we should say it and came to no conclusion. In the end my mother solved the problem. She was subject to what must have been migraine headaches. She would see light flashes in, her eyes and become violently sick to her stomach. Perhaps the combination of the long ride, the exhaust fumes and her tension brought on the attack. At one point we had to stop the car near a grassy patch and let her lie down. We were very close to Detroit by then and Jerry found a phone nearby and called Ted who came to the rescue. He put mother in his car and Jess drove ours. Mother had solved the problem of how to make an entrance in a very uncomfortable way.

Jess was gracious and warm and made us feel at home immediately. I recall that she was always beautifully dressed. She had the car most days and took us across to Canada and showed us all the sights in the area. Jess told us that she was so glad to find out that Jerry and I were normal youngsters. Ted had raved so much about us that she did not know what to expect. They lived in Detroit for some time. One summer Jenny and I spent three weekends in Detroit. We would go by bus and a salesman who worked for Ted and came into Chicago frequently would drive us back. The last visit we made was when I was a little more than seventeen and had completed one semester at Northwestern University. I think Jerry was with me in Detroit but I was going on to New York alone to visit the Gordons. Aunt Jesse took me to Hudsons, the best department store in Detroit - equivalent to Marshall Fields in Chicago - and bought me a beautiful black velvet dinner dress. It was a long dress with long sleeves, a square neck and artificial gardenias as trim. She also bought me an Empress Eugenie hat, a small hat with a feather worn tipped on the head. When those hats were in vogue there was a popular rhyme about them, "The Empress Eugenie she must have been a meany to wear such teeny weeny little hats." I have a snapshot taken with Louis Gordon in New York in which I was wearing that hat. Jess and Ted lived graciously and were wonderful to Jerry and me. Ted was a remarkably successful sales representative and the older Mr. Parker was very fond of him. After the older Mr. Parker died the atmosphere changed. Ted was the only Jew working for Parker Pen and young Parker was openly anti Semitic. When he made a vicious remark in Ted's presence, Ted told him, "You know what you can do with your job. You can shove it." Jerry is sure that Ted was quite specific about where Parker could shove it.

At the end of that last visit to Detroit I went on to New York by bus. It took most of two days. I had a wonderful time in New York and I stayed a month or perhaps more. The Gordon Family lived in Brooklyn and Louis who was somewhat older than I was, took me everywhere. I had relatives, first cousins of my mother who lived in Newark. Their mother and my maternal grandfather were brother and sister. These relatives were overwhelmingly hospitable. They loved me before they met me because I was a relative. When I visited them they could not do enough for me there were two younger girls in the family, Jewel Mandy and Myra whose last name I do not recall. The family did not want me to leave and after a few days I was anxious to get back to Brooklyn and the exciting round of activities with my cousin Louis. Finally I went for a walk one day and called Louis. I told him that he had to come and get me or I would never get away. The cousins in Newark were warm and loving people who adored anyone related to them. Louis did come for me so I was able to return with him to Brooklyn. Years later Sam and I visited them. They lived in South Orange then. We spent some time with them and then told them that we had to drive to Mount Vernon to have dinner with Sam's sister Dorothy. They were very disappointed as they wanted us to have dinner with them. As a compromise they suggested that if we couldn't stay for dinner we must at least break bread with them and promptly plied us with hot dogs, all the trimmings, dessert, coffee and candy. They coaxed us to eat more and more. These people had such strong family feelings that they were sure that all relatives were automatically wonderful and lovable. I think they would have smothered a horse thief or bank robber with attention if he was related. When we finally got away that afternoon we were an hour and a half late in getting to Dorothy's house and much too full to be interested in dinner. One of the female cousins (*Anna Propp*) in New Jersey married a man named McNamara who was some kind of a VIP in show business. He used to get the Chicago relatives passes for all the shows, which came to Chicago. I remember Lou Imber telling about going up to the box office at the Blackstone Theater and asking for tickets for McNamara. He said that he held one hand over his nose as he did so because no one looking at his big nose would believe his name was McNamara.

I recall that Sarah Leviton came to Chicago from the Copper Country after she had graduated from high school. She wanted to attend a school to learn millinery and corsetry. She stayed for a short time with other relatives on the South Side but she was not happy there. It was apparently not a house with a large family or an active social life so Sarah felt lonely. My mother told her to find some excuse for leaving and come and stay with us. We lived on Burling Street near Diversey. There were plenty of people in our house and a great deal of activity. Our household consisted of my mother and father, my grandfather, Aunt Lillian, Uncle Ted, Aunt Lydia, Jerry and me. I must have been about six-years old and Susie, a Lithuanian girl who was our live-in maid. I will talk more about Susie shortly. Susie made the tenth. Imagine all of these people in a three-bedroom apartment! It was a large apartment but non-the-less that was a crowd. Sarah was a pleasure to have around. We all adored her. Sarah would do and try anything. We had just moved into this apartment and my mother bought some material for drapes. Sarah whipped them up in no time flat. They might have been less than perfect, a little crooked perhaps, but done quickly and enthusiastically. Sarah had a great stock of nursery rhymes and stories and kept Jerry and me entertained. Jerry was crazy about her. He called her Taya, as close as he could come to Sarah; she was a spirited eighteen years old with an engaging personality. Lydia was a year or two older but Sarah and Lydia were already friends from Lydia's stay in the Copper Country and they cemented that friendship during the year Sarah stayed with us.

After Jerry was born my mother needed steady help. She had a woman to do the washing and a woman to do the cleaning. The washwoman whose name was Hattie Ellis. I remember that she chewed tobacco. Hattie would spend all one day in the basement using a boiler, a wringer and other primitive equipment washing for ten people. The next day she would spend the whole day ironing. At the end of this day Poppa's white shirts were immaculate, starched and ironed to his satisfaction and he was very fussy about his appearance. My father went to an agency to hire someone to live with us and help my mother with the children. My mother would use my father saying, "He did not look for someone experienced; he picked the youngest and prettiest shikse in the place!" Susie had first come to America. She had never even Ben a carpet sweeper before but she justified fly father's judgment. She learned quickly and became very proficient. She turned down the beds at night; she made strudel; she did exquisite embroidery, making a hat and dresses for me. she lived with us a long time. She, Sarah Arne, finished her course and returned to Calumet she went into business. he opened Milady's Shoppe stocking corsets, intimate apparel and hats.

When I was about thirteen my father's sister, Hinde, and her younger son, Jack, came to America from Lithuania to join her husband, Morris Gordon, her daughter, Edith, and older son, Louis. Morris and his older son had come over first and were given jobs by Morris Propp, a very well to do relative who manufactured electrical devices like Christmas tree lights. Morris Propp owned Noma Electric Company and was a very successful and thereby very wealthy man. He wore black silk suits and had an almost Chinese cast of features. He really looked Oriental. Morris was more closely related to my father than to my mother in spite of having the same name as my mother's family. Edith followed her father and brother, coming over on a student visa sponsored by my father. She came to live with us in Chicago rather than staying in Brooklyn with her father and brother. I will have more to say about Edith and her visit shortly. In 1926, after Edith's mother and younger brother had come to America our family drove to New York to see the Gordons. An automobile trip of that length was a great adventure in those days. Aunt Lydia had been married only a short time but could not resist the temptation to share in this adventure. She regretted her decision almost immediately and missed her husband a great deal. Lydia and I shared sleeping quarters throughout the trip. She decided that if we left very early each day we would get to New York more quickly and she would return to her beloved Lou faster. At six in the morning she would wake me and say, "Sissy, let's get up!" Sissy was another nickname for me. Mother used to say to Jerry when he was just learning to talk, "This is sister; say Sissy," and the nickname stuck. In the car I sat in the back with my mother and Lydia and Jerry sat in the front with my father. Jerry would always claim afterwards that our father was the world's worst driver. Driving was not really much of a challenge. There were few cars on the road and perhaps the greatest handicap was the lack of road signs. My mother was in her element. I did not start elementary school until I was eight years old because my mother, with her children, would accompany my dad on his business trips in the Chicago Area. He did not go far afield but we visited places like Joliet and Niles Center and our mother instilled in us a love of travel. She knew a great deal about all the places we visited, probably reading about them beforehand. I recall her saying once, Look children, this is the beautiful Rock River," and going on to tell us a great deal about the history and geography of the area. We would sometimes stay overnight if my dad had several customers to visit in the vicinity. At this time my father had a line of jewelry, which he sold, to retail stores. He worked for a large wholesaler. At other times he had his own business and his last big stores were in Jefferson Park at Lawrence and Milwaukee Avenues and on 75th Street near Kingston in South Shore. In these last ventures Emanuel Maltz backed him. Matte was a wholesaler and he and my father had been in business together earlier.

My mother thoroughly enjoyed the trip east although she and Lydia were terrified by driving in the mountains. There was a considerable amount of screaming from the two ladies who did not help the driver who was pretty nervous himself. Jerry and I laughed until we cried at some of the antics. Approaching Wheeling, West Virginia we climbed a steep slope and drove into a gas station at the top. The attendant promptly put wooden blocks behind the wheels, a common practice in hilly country at that time My mother, as usual eager for information, asked the attendant, "What mountain is this?" He snorted and replied, "Lady, this ain't no mountain; this is a little old hill! The mountains are ahead of you." This information did little to reassure our nervous Nellies. We went to Washington D.C. and stayed at a famous hotel which had been open when Lincoln was President and had just been completely redone. I think it was the Willard. Despite Aunt Lydia's protests we stayed in Washington five or six days and saw everything it was possible to see. Naturally my mother supplied a great deal of historical background. There were some tensions on the trip most of which seem comical in retrospect. My father had a penchant for losing his way. When convinced that he was not on track he would stop the car and say in funereal tones, "Ella, I'm lost!" He would annoy my mother when he asked directions of a policeman. He would begin, almost pleadingly, officer please, can you tell me..?" My mother objected to the tone more than the question. She would bristle," Leon you are not in Lithuania talking to a Cossack. You are in the United States and you are a citizen with rights and as good as any policeman! Don't beg, just ask!" Papa did all the driving and it must have been very tiring.

In the days before super highways, fast food stops and motels, you had to find eating and sleeping accommodations in the towns and cities. There were none along the empty stretches of road. When Papa decided it was time to get food he would stop in a town, pull over and call to the nearest passer-by, "Hey buddy, do you know of a good restaurant?" Frequently my mother would mutter," He's asking a bum who hasn't had a good meal in his whole life!" Papa got himself into trouble in Philadelphia by turning the wrong way into one-way streets. These were the first he had encountered; I do not think there were any in Chicago at that time. His nervous reactions probably accounted for Jerry's evaluation of his driving. My mother undoubtedly overreacted to his idiosyncrasies. My mother wanted good clean accommodations and first rate food. Though my father would become irritated when my mother had refused many of his suggestions she generally got her own way. Sometimes the deciding comment would be, it's a Greek restaurant!" In our family at least this was the kiss of death. It is difficult to say why this was true but Greek restaurants had a bad reputation for cleanliness and quality. In later years all of us loved the Greek food we tasted at the Petrakis household and enjoyed eating in the restaurants on Halsted Street. Somehow, despite many calls for Maryland fried chicken we managed to cross he state of Maryland without tasting any.

My father tired of the stops my mother kept insisting upon to visit historical monuments find, at one point declared," I refuse to stop at any more cemeteries." When we were driving through the Appalachians we saw a great number of white crosses along the steep mountain roads. When we stopped at a gas station my mother said to the attendant, "I am surprised that the KKK is active this far north and has the effrontery to erect crosses at so many places along the road." He answered, "Lady, that has nothing to do with the Klan. Each cross marks a place where a car went off the road and the occupants were killed when it crashed into the rocks below. This may have made mama feel better about the Klan but it did nothing to make her less apprehensive about mountain roads. Jerry and I laughed and made jokes when Mama and Lydia screamed in terror. Neither reaction helped to calm our nervous father.

When we arrived in New York we were put up in a house in Brooklyn belonging to some relative who had gone to the mountains for the summer. The furniture had all been covered and we did not find this the most comfortable of quarters. I have already told a good deal about how we were received by the New York Area cousins. From New York City we went upstate and stopped at Niagara Falls. We crossed to the Canadian side and found rural Canada dull and lacking in good food and accommodations. We came into the United States through Windsor and Detroit and then drove back to Chicago.

My father had definite ideas about children participating in sports. He took us to the park and taught us to play tennis. He had played lawn tennis in South Africa and Uncle Ted had a tennis net, rackets and balls but I do not know if he ever played. We made good use of the equipment. Papa was not really athletic and in a short time both Jerry and I could beat him in tennis. He took us to the beach and taught us to swim. He held us up as we learned to ice-skate on the frozen lagoon in Washington Park. We lived very close to Washington Park. I can recall, in the days before air-conditioning, the whole family taking blankets and spending a hot night or part of it sleeping under the trees in nature's air cooling. This was a different age and people were not afraid to venture deep into the park at night. Though there were robberies, especially of stores and businesses, shootings were rare. Seldom was a victim shot to prevent identification as happens so often today.

We took farm vacations frequently in Wisconsin or Michigan. We would go on the Fourth of July, generally to a place with a big farmhouse. There would be a few other families with children. Each family would have one big bedroom. Papa would return to Chicago and spend every weekend and his two week vacation with us. We would stay until Labor Day. This would cost about eight dollars per week. Mother would make preparations months in advance getting her dressmaker, Mrs. Higgins, busy to provide clothes including the dress-up clothes worn on Sundays for herself and for me. We would go downtown and pick out the material for Mrs. Higgins to work on. Made to order clothes were not for boys so Jerry was not included. Mrs. Higgins would then take over our dining room for about a week for her cutting and sewing while we ate in the kitchen. I remember that she was deaf as a post and we had to shout to make her understand. A little later a cousin of my Dad, a man who was in the dress business, came to Chicago to display and sells his line to the buyers of local stores. We would visit with him and my mother would pick out pretty things for herself and for me.

We enjoyed the farm vacations very much. Somehow it seemed that there was always a girl about my age and a boy for Jerry to play with. They were either the farm children or from other boarding families. The farm I remember best and I suppose it was typical of the others was Robinson's Farm just outside Lake Geneva, Wisconsin. Mrs. Robinson was a former school teacher and she and my mother hit it off extremely well. I recall that when a crew came in for about a week to harvest the crops, I think they were called threshers, Mama worked with Mrs. Robinson in the kitchen and the men were treated to her peach cake and her other bakery goods. As city kids we found the farm fascinating. There was no running water in the house. We had to go outside to pump water. Our washing facilities in our room consisted of a large bowl and a pitcher which we filled at the pump. The one drawback was the lack of plumbing. Toilet facilities consisted of an outhouse. Mother would make our beds and clean our room. There was no maid service but clean linens and towels were provided. I enjoyed the farm atmosphere and loved the walks into a nearby village. Mr. Robinson would load all of the boarders into his farm truck and take them to the beach in Lake Geneva. He would return for us a few hours later. He did this every day or two so we had swimming as well as farm life. The farm food was superb and served home style. The only part of the food I disliked was the milk which was warm and smelled of cows since it was brought in directly from the barn when the cows were milked. My mother wanted us to drink large quantities of it because she thought it was very healthy just as she wanted us to spend much of our time outdoors seeing what farm life was like. Papa came out each weekend and on Sundays we dressed up. I just adored one of the dresses Mrs. Higgins had made for me. It was white silk with red dots and had red binding in front. After the dress was made I was downtown with my mother in Carsons or Fields and I saw the perfect hat to go with the dress. We wore hats when we were dressed up. This hat went down in front and up in back and was decorated with triangles of white leather and red silk. I really felt dressed up in that dress and hat!

After several years of farm vacations we branched out somewhat. We went to the Wisconsin Dells and to Starved Rock. I must have been eleven or twelve years old when we went to the Jensens in Deep Lake, Illinois. This was also a huge house but it was built as a resort. or a country hotel. It had indoor plumbing and steps going down to a small private beach on the lake. Here I had a wonderful time. My closest friend at the time was Louise Ramis. Her parents never took vacations of that kind but were happy to pay Louise's way. Louise and I shared a room. We were there all summer. The

Jensens were Danish and the food was excellent. Sarah Arne came and stayed a week and I believe many members of the family did also. That was the last of the all summer vacations. It was there that I wrote my first poem, "Ode to Deep Lake". The next year or perhaps the one following that was the summer of the trip to Washington and New York. My first poem stirred my interest in writing. Years later when I was at Hyde Park High School there was an organization called Story Scribblers. To be admitted a student had to submit a piece of original writing, an essay, a short story or a poem. Admission was granted only if the submission was judged to be of high quality. I wrote The Spirit of Industry, a poem about the steel mills which we passed when we drove into Indiana and when we returned from Indiana. I was thrilled that this poem was accepted and I was admitted to Story Scribblers.

After living on Burling Street we moved to Roke, by now renamed Fremont, and when I was about eight years old we moved to Washington Park. The neighborhood on the southeast side of Chicago was quite near the University of Chicago. It was just south of the park itself, running from 60th Street to 63rd Street and from Cottage Grove Avenue to South Park Avenue, now Martin Luther King Drive. We moved to the south side because my father had closed his store was selling jewelry to stores in such cities as Indiana Harbor and Whiting. Living on the North Side would have meant a great deal of unnecessary travel. There was one other place we lived. During World War I we lost the apartment on Burling Street and moved temporarily into a two flat on West End Avenue. In Washington Park we lived first in an apartment on Chaplain Avenue across the street from the school. Then we lived in two different apartments on Eberhart Avenue, a few blocks west When Papa brought a two flat across the street on the same block the Petrakis Family rented the upstairs apartment and we formed lasting friendships with them. Tasula and I were best friends. Mike and Jerry were in the same small group and we knew Dan, Barbara, Harry and Irene. Harry Petrakis became a well-known author publishing many novels and short stories. A short time back Harry remarked to my brother, that the greatest compliment paid to him came from a famous author Isaac Bashevis Singer who wrote about Jewish people as Harry wrote about Greek people. Singer told Harry that the reason he loved Harry's stories was because they were so Yiddish. If you change the Greek names to Jewish names the stories make sense. I guess this says something about the universality of the immigrant experience. When Papa sold the two flat we moved a block east to Rhodes Avenue. When Papa opened the store in Jefferson Park we moved northwest and lived on Eastwood Avenue and Leland Avenue in Albany Park. When Papa opened the South Shore store we moved to 76th and Kingston.

Coming back to Edith Gordon's stay in Chicago. Edith must have been about nineteen and I was about thirteen. She had stayed for a short visit with her father and brother in New York City and then took the train to Chicago. We all went to the station to meet her. My parents after an emotional greeting tried to talk to Edith in Yiddish. She told them," No Auntie, No Uncle, I studied English in Lithuania and if you talk to me in English I will learn more." A week or so later she had a crying spell and was almost hysterical as she told us that though she had studied English for some time she did not understand most of what we had been saying to her. The idioms escaped her entirely. Speaking a language with native speakers who talk fast and use slang and idiomatic expressions is a very difficult task and takes time and patience. Sometime later when she was more comfortable with English we went to see the movie "Speakeasy" together. Edith seemed to understand and enjoy it. she was laughing in the right places so she understood the humor. Afterwards I asked. "Did you enjoy the movie?" Edith answered, "Oh yes, it was very good. but I don't understand why they called it Easy To Speak." Since Edith was here on a student visa she had to attend school. She registered at Lewis Institute, which was located at Damen and Madison. She was bright and caught on to our ways very quickly.

Edith and I shared a room. We got along well though once I really took advantage of her. I belonged to an organization called Infants Aid devoted to doing charitable work. The members were rehearsing a play to be given at the Stevens Hotel. Our mothers were invited. In this play I had the role of a suburban matron. Although I had a much more extensive wardrobe than Edith she had a new silk suit which in my mind was the ideal costume for the part I was to play. Edith was coming with my mother. She had told me she was not going to wear the new suit. I went early for a dress rehearsal and without asking and took the suit with me. Edith was slender and rather bony and I was big boned. When I came out on the stage in her suit she said to my mother, "Auntie, I am going to kill her! Every seam in my new suit will come apart!" My action was childish, nervy and selfish but Edith, though very angry, was quick to forgive me. Edith worked part-time at various jobs when she lived in Chicago. Louis Gordon came to Chicago and stayed with us for a while to explore the job market here. My mother felt that since Hinde and Leon had been separated for so many years that the Gordons should live in Chicago. However the job opportunities with the Propps in New York who owned Noma Electric were so much better and my father certainly could not support the entire Gordon family. Morris Gordon had a rather minor position with Noma but Louis gradually worked himself up to a position of importance. Hinde did come to Chicago to visit. We met her at the train and Papa exclaimed, "Hindele, you got so gray!" His own hair had started turning gray when he was in his twenties. Morris Gordon came from a well-to-do family in Lithuania and was a quiet dignified man. I imagined that he looked like an Austrian Duke.

He spoke little English so I found it hard to hold a conversation with him. He was a very sweet natured man and Hinde who was a strong character directed him in a very bossy manner. Hinde and Leon had very similar facial features. Both had light blue eyes, fair skin and high cheek bones. They had a Tartar look about them, almost oriental. My brother Jerry inherited that same look. When Edith was living with us she would frequent the International House on the campus of the University of Chicago. She had friends from India, Russia and Lithuania. Edith and I became good friends. I have already mentioned the one action in which I incurred her righteous anger but in general we got along very well. When I visited them in New York I remember Jackie, who was just a small boy, calling excitedly to a friend, "My cousin from Chicago is here!" Edith, Louis and Jack quickly adjusted to the American scene and lost all traces of foreign accents.

Louis, who was very bright, did not get a chance at college because the family needed his income. Edith had attended Lewis Institute and Jackie went to Brooklyn College, a good school that was part of the City University of New York. Edith Gordon's married name was Melman. Jack married another Edith and they had a son named Mark. Neither Edith Melman nor Louis Gordon had children.

Jack and Louis were both in the army during World War II. They were not in the same unit but both were in the African Campaign. Both outfits were sent to Italy after the Allies invaded that country and the brothers bumped into one another in a small Italian town. This was a remarkable coincidence considering the number of American servicemen in the European Theater. They had lost touch with one another and neither knew where the other was before they met. I corresponded with both of them. Jackie remarked later, "Charlotte's letters all began with an apology for not writing sooner and all ended with a promise to write again more promptly." When Jack got out of service he came to visit us in Chicago. We lived on Langley Avenue in Chatam at that time. Mark was a little boy and Jackie bought him a tricycle. He was a very loving person.

My mother was an early feminist long before the Feminist Movement got started. When I was a senior in high school my father said to my mother, "We'll find a good secretarial school for Charlotte so she can get a job before she gets married. We have to send Jerry to college so that he can get an education for a profession. My mother was adamant, "that's not the way it's going to be. Charlotte is as smart as Jerry is and either both of them go to college or neither one of them goes to college!" As usual Ella P. got her way and I started at Northwestern University when I graduated from Hyde Park High School.

89

PATRIOTISM AND ITS PROGRESS 'THROUGH 'THE AGES
Written by Ella Propp for Isadore Becker

"Breathes there a man with soul so dead who never to himself has said,
This is my own, my native land."

No that is not so, that nature in a human being would not be true to itself somewhere, be it here in this country or in a foreign land, each human being holds some spot dear as his native land. Bereft of patriotism the heart of a nation would be sordid and cold. It is the virtue, which gives to paganism its luster, to barbarianism its redeeming trait. It throbs in the bosom of all nations not always for the right or what would be best for humanity at large. Be it a nation of Christians, pagans or barbarians still that love of country, that same willingness to live or die for it can be found. Staunch and true the words of Brutes in telling the Romans why Caesar was dead, "Not that loved Caesar less but that I loved Rome more." Patriots have-died for their countries throughout history.

In our own country patriotism was always an ideal reality. Well has it been the watchword of America for breath there a man, woman or child in this great land whose heart does not beat faster at the sight of our Star Spangles Banner? What country has produced another Washington? What a man and what a spirit of love and justice! It seems to me that he saw beyond his time. Perhaps as in a mirage he saw this land of forest and savage disappear and in its place arise a beautiful, fertile land peopled by a strong and mighty nation and swayed with a spirit of patriotism almost equal to his own. Again when our nation was almost severed Lincoln's love of country led him to turn against slavery. He saw that its practice brought a blight of shame over the land and that it could not truly be called the land of the free when some were masters and some were slaves. Generous men and great patriots we are now enjoying the fruit of your great deeds, Liberty and Unity. Your names shall live forever in the hearts of all true Americans.

Now, in what is called a practical age, it is said that we are becoming commonplace and less patriotic. It is not so? Our liberty was dearly bought and we of the present know its cost and story from our warriors of the past. That is why we cherish peace Columbus seeking a passage to India found a wilderness which is now a garden peopled t by new and beautiful ideals, arts, inventions everything they can be called progress. Our men of letters, our thinkers and students of human life and nature, each in his own way says to his fellow men, "We wish to work together in mighty harmony for we have a singleness of purpose." They love their country well but are striving, yearning for the good of the world at large.

That is the spirit of our leaders of today and we say that they are great patriots whose hearts echo the hope of humanity. Oh let it not be in future ages as in the past. Let the grandeur of man be discerned not in bloody victories or in ravenous conquests but in the blessings he has secured, in the good we have accomplished and in the triumph of justice and benevolence in the establishment of perpetual peace over the whole world.

November, 1938 in Königsberg

By Arthur Propp

Arthur Propp (1890-1965) was a prosperous lumber merchant in Königsberg, the principality of East Prussia. After Kristallnacht he immigrated via England to Bolivia and following the war he moved to Canada. In his later years Arthur Propp wrote a large number of manuscripts in Germany (currently in the possession of the Leo Baeck Institute of New York city) that recount various aspects of his life - his service as a German soldier in the First World War, his experiences under Weimar Republic and the Third Reich, and his life after emigration. Possibly the most significant of these manuscripts is the one presented here, which describes Mr. Propp's experiences during and just after Kristallnacht. The text, abridged from the original version, was edited and translated by Christopher R. Friedrichs of the University of British Columbia, Canada.

It was November, 1938. You could sense that Hitler planned a new strike against the Jews. After the assassination of the Nazi diplomat von Rath by a young Jew in Paris, this feeling of dread grew stronger.

The night that von Rath died, I went to my friend, Jim von Simkowitz. Jim was a Hungarian; he had been a Hapsburg officer. He now worked in a Königsberg shipping agency. I had known him for many years. He had a small apartment, not far from mine, and I spent the night there.

The next day around ten, I went back out into the street. The sun was shining. The sky was blue. All the fears I had felt the night before drifted away like spider webs in the wind. But suddenly Dora Wolff spotted me. "For God's sake, what are you doing here? Hide, fast. Don't you know what's going on?" Then Frau Jacobsohn came and grabbed my hand, saying "Quick, quick, before anyone sees you..." and took me to her home. Both women told me, through their tears, that the synagogue had been burned down, along with the Jewish orphanage and the cemetery; all the Jewish males had been picked up during the night by the SS and the SA and were probably in jail and nobody knew what was happening to them. I felt suddenly as if the earth was quaking. Something was happening, something the human mind could not absorb: the orphanage... the cemetery...

But here I was in the home of Frau Jacobsohn, where I had never been before. "Where is your husband?" I asked. She held her hands before her eyes.

The telephone? Was it still working? Yes. I called home. A voice stammered out, "Good God, its Herr Propp." It was Glinka, my housekeeper. First I heard nothing but sobs. Then she started to talk. They had come at five in the morning. A friend was at my place; he had come to see me in the evening, after I left, and decided to stay. They took him along. They had interrogated her about my whereabouts, but she did not know.

93

I called my neighbor, a trusted friend. He came with his car and brought me to his place. But a few hours latter he got nervous. "They have their eye on me, you know." I knew that - he was a well-known anti-Nazi. "My wife and children would not say anything," he said. "If it were just for them, I could hide you. But the maid has seen you. She knows who you are, she knows what is going on."

I decided to try anything to get across the border. I thought of friends who already escaped to Lithuania, who would be waiting for me there.

I called my secretary Fräulein Mey, who had worked for me for 20 years. I asked her to bring me 3,000 marks from my Office. I called Jim and told him where I was. Frauen Mey never came with the money.

But Jim came, right away. From him I began to earn the full extent of the catastrophe: Jews all over Germany had been arrested; many of them had been carried off to concentration camps. All over Germany, synagogues lay in ashes. Jewish stores had been plundered, Jewish homes ransacked, cemeteries desecrated. It was all over for the Jews. But low to get out? How could one save oneself? How could one get over a border?

'It will be hard," Jim said. "The main roads will be under surveillance for escaping Jews. The only chance is at night, when they are tired and think they have caught all of them.

Then I had an idea: there was a man named Schneidereit, a big good-natured, trustworthy man who used to drive the (mostly Jewish) cattle merchants across the countryside in his big old Ford. I had also driven with him a lot. Jews were his livelihood.

"I want to get to Tilsit," I told him by phone. "Tonight. Do you have time?"

"I don't know, does it have to be tonight? Can't it be tomorrow morning?"

"No," I said, "tonight."

"Very well," he replied. "Come around eleven. I'll be ready. I have to get gas." He knew that I owned a sawmill in Tilsit. He had often driven me there.

It was shortly before eleven when I left with Jim in his little car. I had nothing but my coat. Schneidereit lived outside the city, in remote settlement. His car was not there. His wife told me to wait; her husband had just gone to get gas. Schneidereit did not return. A motorcyclist in uniform drove up, stopped, drove on - a police station was nearby. In the neighboring house, lights were still on. It seemed that someone was keeping an eye on Schneidereit house.

"Let's drive back to town," Jim said. "Something's wrong. It's taking too long."

We were almost in the city, about to cross a bridge. Suddenly we hear beeping. A big black car raced past us, stopped and blocked our way. Four SS men jumped out, revolvers in hand. "Stop! you Jewish scum," they shouted. "So you thought you could get to Tilsit and disappear across the border? We knew about that. Schneidereit reported everything."

It was midnight when we were delivered to the police presidium, the headquarters of the Gestapo. The four SS men were half drunk. In the Gestapo once there were only two or three men. They asked a few questions.

"Bring the Jew Propp into the main cell. see that you run him down the stairs fast; maybe he'll break his neck." A small winding staircase led five floors down to the cellar. But before I was too far down I could still hear the sound of a man being punched, and I heard someone shouting: "But you aren't even Jewish - you are Catholic -and here you were helping a Jew get over the border - and you imagine you can say that you don't think there is anything wrong with 'helping a friend'? You, who get 400 marks salary in the shipping agency, you can be sure that that will stop."

The winding steps ended in a little guard's office. An old police guard awaited me. "Hey, don't be so excited... you can bring all your stuff with you, just come with me, Herr Propp, the main thing is to calm down."

I followed him over a little stairway to the cellar, down a long corridor, at the end of which was a heavy iron door with huge iron bars and a lock of the kind I had seen in old castles. He unbarred the door. I heard the door close behind me and heard the bars being put back into place and the door being locked.

It was a vault, almost dark. Somewhere high up there must have been a small oil lamp. Slowly my eyes began to adjust to the darkness. There were bare walls, and plain black benches - with people on them. People covered entirely with coats and with hats over their faces, only the feet sticking out. In the middle of the chamber was a pair An old man was sitting on it.

A sudden wave of joy and relief swept over me. There were other people here, other Jews. I went from bench to bench, lifting the hats that covered each face. Some woke up "Propp," they said and went back to sleep. I knew most of them, There were 13, including the man on the pail. In one corner a man was sitting up against the wall, not sleeping. He made some room for me on his bench. I stretched out and fell asleep. One can sleep on a wooden plank, or anything, after a day like that.

When I woke up it was already light. My neighbor was still sitting up against the wall. He was staring at the wall as if it was not there.

"Who are you?" I said. "I know almost everyone here, but not you.

"I am a teacher." "And what do you teach?

"Ancient languages... University."

"You have a family?"

"Yes. My wife; she is Christian. And two daughters. They both belong to the Hitler Youth. I had a son too, but he died a year ago. He was 20. You know, this is the first time in my life that I am together with Jews. My parents lived in Munich. They were rich, from my mother's side. My father did not really work. All the important people who came to Munich came to our house.

When I was growing up I never heard anything about Jews, I have never set foot inside a synagogue - but I did pay my dues to the Jewish community. I don't know why. I guess I thought one doesn't lose one's connection with one's own people, even if one has nothing to do with them. But of course they found my name on some list of the Jewish community. So here I am.

"But why can't you sleep?" I asked. 'Why do you keep staring at the wall?"

"I have been thinking," he said, "all night, and now I know why the Jews of the middle ages, at the time of the Crusades, preferred to take their lives rather than have dealings with Christians. It was not because they were Jews, it had nothing to do with religion - it was sheer disgust. They preferred to kill themselves than to submit to the brute force of people they considered barbarians. That was the reason. From this cell the road goes right to the funeral pyres of the middle ages. Nothing has changed."

"And you?" I said, "What would you do, today, if...?"

"Me?" he replied. "There is no question. I would kill myself without a thought rather than abase myself before the Nazis."

Suddenly, the cell was full of light. Or so it seemed to me.

My first morning in prison was a time of total confusion. Obviously not one of us had ever been in prison before, we had no idea what to do. But the old guard, Wachtmeister Soult, helped us.

First we had to pile up our coats. Then it was time to get washed. The great door opened and we were allowed to walk up and down the corridor and wash ourselves. Then we got breakfast: a tin can with hot dark, chicory-flavored water - it was far from coffee, but at least it was hot - and some bread, even some marmalade. We were hungry and it tasted good. There were no leftovers. But now what? What would happen to us? What would they do with us? Work camp, concentration camp - or even worse? Would we ever see our families again? Or, our possessions? The thoughts plagued us like insects.

Obviously we had to keep busy if we were not to give way to despair. By now we were 12 - two had been taken away, nobody knew where. I was chosen as leader and we decided to spend our time teaching each other things. We called it our "adult education program. Maas, the teacher, gave English. Jim gave instruction in various forms of boxing and jujitsu. Falkenstein was especially versatile. He was a glazier, so he lectured about the history of glass, and about how it was made. But Falkenstein, who was about sixty, was also in charge of entertainment. He draped some cloth around himself and demonstrated how the dancing girls had performed, 40 years earlier, in the first cabarets. He copied their suggestive movements so flawlessly we forgot ourselves in laughter.

An auto mechanic taught us how motors and automobiles were assembled. A stamp dealer spoke about rare stamps. I myself had to lecture about lumber. I was also in charge of exercises we did every morning and evening.

There was a pair of young brothers in the cell, good boys, about 20 years old. They were musical. Every evening when we lay down on the benches, they sang and whistled duets and soothed us to sleep.

The others, who had no special contributions to make, were in charge of keeping the cell clean. Our rules were strict: the floors and benches had to be scrubbed, the blankets, once we got some, had to be cleaned off, the latrine pails had to be kept as clean as cutlery.

In a week we were quite used to each other. Word had also gotten around where we were. Food packages arrived. Everything was shared. Everyone tried to make sure nobody would lose spirit. Nobody let himself show what he was feeling. Yet despite the appearance of calm, as we lay on the benches cloud upon us. I contemplated what the best I could hope for might be. I tended to assume that the concentration camps were too far from East Prussia, and already too full, for me to be sent there. I recalled how, during the war, Russian soldiers had been used as forced laborers in agriculture. Perhaps I would be sent as a laborer to the Samland nearby, where some people knew me. It was the best I dared to hope for. If that were my fate, at least I would not starve or freeze to death, and maybe I'd even have a proper bed.

There were two men who seemed to be disturbed by nothing. One was Maas, the teacher. He made himself quite at home in prison; he was one of those high intellects who are little affected by their external surroundings. He ate with a hearty appetite whatever was put before him or whatever some of the others had left in his cup or on his plate, as if he had never eaten anything but prison food all his life.

The only other person whose mood never soured was the old guard, Wachtmeister Soult. Gradually he let us spend more time in the corridor than in the cell. The corridor was bright and had windows; through the bars we could look into the outside world. This small corridor, onto which many cells opened, seemed to us a wonderful place compared to the cell.

"You know," the guard said to me once, "I've been a Nazi since 1925. My sons, too. So in 1933 I was put in charge of setting up the camp at Quedenau. I did my duty, I did what had to be done. But we didn't beat the people. I've always had a heart. If we could spare some underwear or collect some, I'd give it to the prisoners. I'll tell you - just between you and me - there is something about all this I don't understand. I'm a good National Socialist, you know and a good German too— but this stuff about the Jews, I can't see it. I was a guard for years in the suburb where lots of Jews live. They never did anyone any harm. A lot of them were soldiers in the war, none of them ever swindled anyone. They were good citizens."

"Herr Wachtmeister," I said abruptly, "can't we get some cigars or cigarettes?"

"No," he said, "provisionally forbidden for your group." But he pulled out a big black cigar, lit it and smoked it. Someone called and he went into his office, leaving the cigar behind in an ashtray. The 12 of us finished it off.

One morning Jim was summoned. He came back after 10 hours. He looked so pale and broken that nobody dared to ask him any questions. He flung himself into a corner of the cell. There was a deadly silence.

At night he talked to me. "They know everything. It is amazing how much they know. Three men interrogated me. Everything from the time I was born. They know that I fought for Bela Kun back in Budapest, during the Communist revolution. They know what I did in Russia. If they get into my house now, they will find pictures of Stalin. They think I'm a spy, they think that's why I got a job in the shipping agency."

The next day Wachtmeister Soult told me: "It's definite now. You are getting out of here soon.

But not your friend Jim. He's never coming out of this place."

We sat gloomily in the cell as the door creaked open. Four S.A. men were there. Young men, faces of stone.

"Jew Propp - come here."

I followed them. They took me outside to a scar. I got in nobody talked. The car headed in the direction of the Brown house. That was where Jews and non-Jews were tortured to death. We turned in another direction. A sudden thought: this is even worse - the cemetery: short "trial," right next to the open grave.

But no. Another turn, to an office building. Into the building. Offices with people in and out of uniform. But offices - thank God for offices! Better that the other places.

Suddenly I saw Fräulein Mey, my old trusted Fräulein Mey. There were other people there, polite people. They were the local leaders of the Nazis. The new County Leader was there. He came from Tilsit, and knew me. Also there, in uniform, was notary Wolff, a friend of my brother's. I breathed more easily.

"Herr Propp," he said, "here is Fräulein Mey. She informs us that you have promised to transfer ownership of the property at Hinterrossgarten 40 to her, in recognition of her many years of devoted service. Is that true?"

Fräulein Mey was sitting next to me. she nudged me with her foot. Suddenly I thought: she wants to rescue the property for me, by letting it be transferred to her. Otherwise it might just be seized outright.

"It is true," I said.

The County Leader said firmly, "You are under no pressure here. Nobody is forcing you to transfer the property, I repeat: nobody."

Only later did I find out that the whole episode was a trick, arranged in advance. Perhaps at first she had really wanted to help. But eventually greed took over. Still what is a piece of property, once one has been driven past the brown house - and the cemetery? I was relieved to be returned to my cell. All the others breathed more easily too when they saw me.

The next day Jim was summoned again by the Gestapo. He came back after only a few hours.

This time he did not seem so beaten down.

"So...?" I asked.

He stretched out on the bench and murmured. "Free ticket out of here - who cares about anything else? Anyway, I had no choice.

I did not understand what he was talking about. I did not want to ask.

Soult fetched me and brought me up to the police office. In the room stood a gorgeous woman who looked at me in a friendly way. I froze: I had never seen her in my life. But obviously she was going to report me. And an accusation of Rassenchande - Sexual relations between Jews and non-Jews - would be the end for me. But instead she said, quite casually, "I am Frau Dzubba. You must know that my husband is the right-hand man of Gauleiter Koch. I heard that you are thinking of selling your villa on Kronprinenstrasse. I am sure you will have no objection if I purchased it."

Well, I thought, losing a house is better than Rassenschande.

"Certainly," I replied, "it would be a pleasure. soon after this came the end of my stay in prison. But first there was one more visit to the police office. There were a police captain and three men in suits. One was the District Economic Advisor of the party.

"We understand, Herr Propp, that you have been wanting to dispose of your real property?"

"Oh yes. For a long time."

For a long time actually, Herr Schultze-Roever had been interested in my property. This was a nice turn of events for him, to get it for free.

"Do you attach any importance, Captain, to keeping Herr Propp any longer in prison?"

"Depends entirely on you," the captain said.

In exchange for my property, I was no longer "Jew Propp," but "Herr."

I returned with mixed feelings to the cell. All of my cellmates looked at me, but asked nothing. Nothing was asked in the cell: one waited until someone wanted to say something.

"I can go," I said slowly and told what had happened. All were quiet. Each thought, " Why you and not me?"

But they helped me collect my things, the handful of things that my housekeeper Glinka had brought for me. Then each one came, singly: "Can you visit my mother?" "Can you visit my wife?" "Can you...?" "Can you...?" I had a notebook, and took down all the addresses. I promised each one I would do what he asked. Especially Jim - Jim who was in the cell with us Jews, because he had tried to help me get over the border, Jim who would probably lose his position on my account. God only knew what would happen to him.

As I came out into the day, around noon, my eyes were blinded by the light. It was Saturday. People were leaving their work to go home. Across from the prison people were coming and going, the streets were swarming with people.

I stood and stared. Right now, hundreds of thousands of Jewish people were sitting in concentration camps, being robbed of their family's lifetime earnings, being beaten, being killed - and here people were coming and going and laughing and living as if the Jews justice, with human decency. A sudden wave of hared swept over me.

I did not take the train home. I did not want to mingle with these people. Instead I walked quickly to the Lithuanian consulate. That was where Jim's girlfriend, Fräulein Markow, worked. "Message from Jim," I said. "He wants you to go to his apartment and take everything out that would not look good. you have the key." "I did it all ready," she said. "Half an hour after his arrest. The Gestapo came too late."

I went home. I took a bath to wash off the prison filth. The house seemed strange to me. Then I went to Consul Haslinger, head of the shipping firm in which Jim work. I told him what Jim had said. "I'm glad you came," he said. "But as for Jim... I'm not sure I can do anything for him. He certainly can't work for me any longer. Anyway, he was getting a bit strange. Maybe later on I can judge better what we can do about Jim."

My next stop was at an old house in Sackheim. There was a dark apartment in which three women sat, desperate about a 16-year-old boy from Riga, their nephew, who had been one of my cellmates. From them I heard a strange story. When all the Jewish males were being arrested, in their anxiety the three women told the boy to report to the nearest police station. He went, and the police told him to go home and wait till he was picked up. But nobody came. The women got more and more nervous. So they sent him to a SA post. The SA finally took him. Only later did they hear that some Jewish males had been left free. Now they were bitterly reproaching themselves. I could only urge them to be brave. The fact that the boy was still alive was some consolation to them.

Soon it was Monday, my first workday after the prison. There was dead silence in my office as I entered. Only Frau Zimmermann cried. She was the bookkeeper and in charge of the money. Fräulein Mey says nothing but Frau Zimmermann cries. She must be more devoted to me than I realized. I stood by her and tried to calm her down, but she kept saying the same thing: "I have not slept a single night, not a single night, I can't get over it."

'Well," I thought, "at least some people...."

intermittently, in her sobs, I could make out the word "sister"

What sister?" I thought. I did not know she had a sister.

"Your sister." she said. "Remember that business with your sister? When she came from Paris to Berlin for the operation? You had me make out a check for 500 marks. But your sister lives in Paris. So that counted as an exchange transfer, didn't it? And you know One needs permission for that. It was two years ago, and I haven't had a good night's sleep since then. After all, I signed the check, I will be held responsible too. I have to report it before they find out. Unless I get 5,000 marks, I just have to report it."

I called Bottke, the accountant. He negotiated with Frau Zimmermann. In the end she got 3,000 marks.

Freudenreich turned up. He had been with me or 18 years, most recently in charge of the Sawmill in Juditten. There had been a problem; the cash balance at the sawmill had been 1,800 marks. But the cash box was empty. Freudenreich had not taken any money for himself, he explained. He had needed it for his family. The children had been sick. Freudenreich," I had said, "You can pay it off in installments."

I had gone to Damm, the lumber dealer, and Arranged for Freudenreich to get a new job. Her new job paid better, and he would have nothing to do with the money. I thought things had gotten better for him and his wife. But now he turned up and said, "of course I am very grateful to you, but you know, I worked for you so many years, perhaps you could give me a little help before you leave Germany. I do have a big family.

You are a young man, you have your family," I told him, "you have a good job, a good future. Now I have to leave Germany almost empty handed. Has the thought ever occurred to you that perhaps I should be allowed to hang on to something for myself, instead of losing the last of what I might be able to take with me?" He Smiled weakly and disappeared.

I sold the house I owned in Berlin. The purchaser had years earlier been assistant to he socialist leader, Hugo Hassse. "You can count on me the purchaser said. I am still Social Democrat, through and through. "The payment never came. Finally, even my good old housekeeper Glinka came to see me. "Now that everybody else has gotten something," she said. "I alone have been good and true to you. Should I be left quite empty handed?" She was pleased to get 1,000 marks, and did not even pack the fur coat and the Brussels lace I had offered her.

By now the others had all been released from prison - including Jim. I went back to Consul Haslinger, about Jim. "Don't worry about him," he said. "He won't need you anymore, or me. He refused to say more. I had no idea what he meant. Then Jim came in to see me; he had been to Berlin.

"I am getting married tomorrow," he said, "to Fräulein Markow. At the Hotel Berliner Hof. Just a small group of friends." He said nothing about inviting me. I remained silent. "I have gotten a job," he said. "Head of a shipping agency in Budapest. It's being completely reorganized for me." Then he went to a telephone. "Gestapo?" he said. "I would like to speak to Oberregierungsrat Fixon." Fixon was the head of the Gestapo in Königsberg. "Simkowitz here. I'll be there around twelve. Will you be in?"

Now, at last, I understood. There was a long silence between us. Then he began to talk. "I had no choice," he said. "It was a free ticket out, or else. Even that was just due to an accident. You see, one of Himmler's top men was at one time here in Königsberg. He had a girlfriend here, and he had a child with her. Fräulein Markow and I knew the woman. He knew me, too. So because of that they put me in touch with him. What happened then, well, you can see for yourself." On the day before my departure from Germany, I visited Wachmeister Soult. He lived in a small, rather dilapidated house near Metgethen. It was easy to locate him. "So," he said as I handed him a parcel with cloths for his current prisoners, " you have not forgotten. Try not to think too ill of Germany," he said. "I hope everything goes well for you. Good luck. But do me one favor - don't write to me."

Every year on the tenth of November, in my thoughts I find myself again in the prison cell. And I ask myself, what happened to my 12 cellmates? In some cases I know: Mass made it to England. Lowenstein's family went to Brazil. And one day in November 1953 I received a letter from the daughter of Falkenstein, the glazier. Her father, who had lived with her in Zurich, had just died. Often, she wrote, he had spoken of our association in prison.

How often I think of Falkenstein! Here were 12 Jews together for the first time in prison. They had been torn from their beds by the Nazis, their homes destroyed, their synagogues buried, their cemeteries desecrated - and yet, a man in his sixties danced. In a dark cell, with death before each eye, 12 Jews laughed, forgetting everything around them and ahead of them. What a will to live! Perhaps that is why despite everything that has happened; there are still Jews in the world.

Propp, Arthur. "November, 1938, Königsberg," Midstream Feb. 1987: 49 - 54. Copyright © 1987 Christopher R. Friedrichs and Daniel Propp.

The Gaon Rabbi Michel Dovid Shlapobersky
(Of Blessed Memory)
Rosh Yeshiva "Tiferet Tzvi"

He was Kelmer! *The people who knew him told me this!*

They ask me to recount a thorough story about the life of Rabbi Michel Shlapobersky, s more involved and more comprehensive than any that has been written or told of him. His daily manners, his complete order, his punctuality in all his regular activities, were in fact the great and lengthy story of his life His heart beat according to the clock-like rhythm of Kelm. The Kelm on which he was nourished in his youth, whose symbols were carved deeply within him, and thus for decades he managed his life according to the same pattern. His measured and thoughtful steps became his nature and his essence, reasoning and stability were his entire being, and like you see the sun rise every morning, then one expected to see Rabbi Michel in his set ways. Within that same "routine of life" there opened a window between the rocks of his solid personality, and through this window were seen pictures that could tell, for those who did not know him, how great were his deeds, how much love of the Torah and fear of Heaven was contained within him. How he integrated them into the path of life so that they were all dedicated to G-d. Perhaps it would be more appropriate to say "Telz" since it was there he studied in the Yeshiva, and grew to be one of its brightest students and was taken under the wing of its head, Zetzokal.

Indeed during his youth, Rabbi Michel Shlapobersky studied in the small Yeshiva that was founded by the Gaon Rabbi Eliyahu Lapian (Of Blessed Memory) in Kelm. Before he had reached the age If 13, he received the honorary title: "Kelmer." He had the special privilege: to pray during the High Holy days in the Talmud Torah of Kelm. He absorbed and was nourished by its special Atmosphere. Indeed Kelm deeply engraved its mark upon him. The Gaon Rabbi Michel was a man who in all his ways and through all the events of his life was a living example of Kelm and everything, which that implies. He was a man, who sustained his power from deep roots, distant and ancient, which grew in fertile ground that was tended the great people of the world and by spiritual giants. Impressions of Kelmian existence were topic conversation on various opportunities. He painted his images of Kelm with a bright brush and he viewed them with great affection. An example this is Rabbi Michel's introduction to the book, "Lev-Eliyahu," of his teacher and Rabbi, Gaon Rabbi Eliyahu Lapian (Of Blessed Memory).

This article radiates the light of truth to the reader, a light that clarifies images of Rabbi Eliyahu Lapian and those of additional figures who dwelt in the "East of Kelm". In this article he told of the marvelous and prominent Gaon Rabbi Mordechai Pogramansky (Of Blessed Memory), whom Rabbi Eliyahu saved and redeemed and who gave to the world his book of the living Torah. Rabbi Eliyahu, who saw his brilliant potential, arranged for him, living quarters with older students who would help him prepare for his lessons. One of them was Rabbi Michel, himself, who studied Chumash and introductory Gemara with him. This memory filled his entire being with joy over the great privileges which had come his way. It should be pointed out that in the book he edited and wrote an introduction to, Rabbi Michel did not mention the part he had played in the education of the Gaon Rabbi Mordechai Pogramansky, (Of Blessed Memory), iluyim of Tavrig. This is certainly additional testimony to his great modesty and humility. The strong ties between Rabbi Michel and Rabbi Eliyahu can be learned from the following story, all of which gives a living illustration of true friendship.

When Rabbi Eliyahu Lapian was making Aliyah to the Holy Ark (*Aron Kodesh*) he visited the Gaon Rabbi Yehezkel Serna (Of Blessed Memory), the head of the Hebron Yeshiva, in his home in Jerusalem. When Rabbi Michel heard that this prominent Rabbi was in the home of the head of the Hebron Yeshiva, he immediately went to greet him, and while Rabbi Eliyahu Lapian and Rabbi Yechezkel Serna were there at the Yeshiva. Rabbi Michel, who was already a Rosh Yeshiva, entered and greeted them warmly with "Shalom Aleichem," and Rabbi Eliyahu returned a joyous "Shalom." After settled in, Rabbi Eliyahu asked for permission to kiss Rabbi Michel, after receiving his permission he got up and kissed him on the head... In addition, the Tzadik Rabbi Shlomo Bloch (Of Blessed Memory) who was one of the glorious figures of Kelm was recalled by Rabbi Michel as an example and symbol of persistence. He told them that he remembered him studying upright all day while he was covered with Tallit and Tfillin.

Shkudvil, the town of his birth, was filled with love of the Torah and reverence. There he studied in the Yeshiva for youths that was founded by the Gaon Rabbi Abraham Yitzchak Perlman (Of Blessed Memory). He would recall Shach Salita who studied there in the Yeshiva in Kelm, and even ate at Rabbi Michel's parents home once a week. Later Rabbi Michel moved to a small Yeshiva in Kelm. When the First World War broke out he returned home. After the war, the Gaon Rabbi Lapian (Of Blessed Memory) traveled through various towns in order to encourage and hearten the children of Israel and collect students for his Yeshiva. The Gaon Rabbi Lapian found Rabbi Michel at his parent's home and opened a discussion with him on Gaon Rabbi Shelomoh Yitzchak (Rashi) "Rashi's Commentary" on Leviticus regarding the verse and the soul who offers a sacrifice of 'Mincha'. It does not say 'soul' in every sacrifice of 'Nedeva', only at 'Mincha.' Because who will give 'Mincha' sacrifices? The poor. Then G-d said: "I will give him credit as if he had sacrificed his own soul." Rabbi Eliyahu Lapian concluded that "even in our time the Torah requires devout devotion to study. The students of Torah are few, and they cling to the Torah as if they were sacrificing their own soul," thus Rabbi Michel Shlapobersky returned to the Yeshiva.

In Kelm, he possessed spiritual properties, noble qualities, and the way of Musar. His manners were always the same. One never saw him run or walk hastily, he always walked in a peaceful way, calm, with serenity of mind from his youth until the end of his days. In a list of sayings he wrote: "let each hour of the day be in order with you, and above all live according to resolute principals." Even his prayers were special and exemplary.

He would stand while praying like a slave before his master, he would utter the words from his mouth like counting money while considering the prayer, with intonations corresponding to the depths of his intention. Thus he prayed for many many years with the same rhythm and the same movements, with the examination of the content of the prayer and with a completely devoted and holy heart. On the proverb of our great Rabbis (Chazal) "And you should worship with all your heard—which worship is in the heart?" It is a prayer, he would say: whoever prays without meaning and without attentiveness is like he who puts on the Tefilin on the wrong part of the body. The place of the prayer is in the heart!

The four years that he studied in Kelm were enough to form his whole personality. From there he was already prepared to move on to the great Yeshiva in Telz and to huddle in the shadow of the wings of the great Gaonim, the spiritual giants, the Rabbi Bloch (Of Blessed Memory), Gaon Rabbi Rabinovitz (Of Blessed Memory) and the Rabbi Chaim Telzer (Of Blessed Memory).

In Telz, he acquired a method of studying Torah and was one of the most special and sublime students in the Yeshiva. He was numbered among the first committee of the members of the board who wrote the lessons of Rabbi Chaim Telzer, printed and disseminated them in "stencil" from time to time, and thanks to them we have these important lessons today. While he was in Telz, he was called by the Gaon Rabbi Bloch to deliver a lesson to the Yeshiva for youths. Against his will, he accepted the Rabbi's orders and began to instruct the youth of this flock in the basics of study. This was the first step for Rabbi Michel Shlapobersky in teaching the knowledge of the Torah to young yeshiva students and he was just 22 years old. The students received him with great affection.

After seven years of studying and teaching in Telz, it was determined by the leaders that Rabbi Michel would have to leave his country of Lithuania and emigrate to Eretz Yisrael. It was the time when he was about to be drafted into the army. His uncle, Gaon Reb Moshe Baruch Braude, who was married to Rochel Propp Braude, the sister of his mother, Hinda-Rivka Propp Shlapobersky, lent him 500-trot sterling. This made it possible for him to emigrate to the Holy Land as a capitalist, and thus he arrived in the summer of 1925 in Hebron, fortified with outstanding recommendations from the Gaon Rabbi Bloch (Of Blessed Memory) and the Gaon Rabbi Telzer (Of Blessed Memory). From here he continued to correspond with his teachers in Telz regarding profound issues of the Torah.

The "Hebron" Yeshiva, located in the city of our fathers, was the "royal crown" in the kingdom of the Torah. There they studied and were perpetually and profoundly diligent under the leadership of the Gaon Rabbi Epstein (Of Blessed Memory). The holy Yeshiva acquired the reputation of a good name thanks to the superb students who came from it. The spiritual direction was managed by the Righteous Gaon Rabbi Nosson Tzvi ben Moses Finkel (Of Blessed Memory), the "Alter of Slobodka", who placed his imprint upon the entire Yeshiva. His conversations and sayings were a source of spring, filled with wisdom, and his students drew from him a way of life. Even the silences of the "Alter" were very educational, insofar as he added no words over and above what needed to be said, and when he said whatever he had to say, everyone knew that his words were the fruit of thought. Behold one day Rabbi Nosson Tzvi Finkel turned to his student, Rabbi Uri Braude, and asked him, "have you met the Shkudviler?" This expression implied that there was something inside and something worth knowing in Rabbi Michel Shlapobersky. Rabbi Uri approached Rabbi Michel and asked him what the "Alter of Slobodka" had spoken with him about, and Rabbi Michel answered that he knew of nothing in particular that he had told him, and so he tried over and over to uncover what the Gaon Rabbi Finkel was conveying with such a special expression that only a few were worthy of it. Until it became clear that Rabbi Michel had organized a moral framework that accounted for the difficulty of why the Torah needed to warn us "thou shall not murder", a thing that was directly understood by logic and even the nations of the world comprehend, and surely it was understood by Israel? He explained this question in different ways. One way through the system of Kelm, another way through the system of Telz, a third way by the system of Slobodka, and one extra way which he had added himself. When all this got back to the Rabbi Nosson Tzvi Finkel, he was deeply impressed and that is why he had expressed himself as he had. As a result of this event, Rabbi Michel's name became well known and the appreciation of him grew and he was considered one of the "Select of the Yeshiva."

1928 he married the daughter of the Rabbi Abraham Yochanan Blumenthal (Of Blessed Emory). One of the most important men in Jerusalem, at the time, and a disciple of the Gaon Rabbi Maharil Diskin, the "Angel from Brisk" (Of Blessed Memory). Nechama, Rabbi Michel's wife, stood by his side all his life she did this, so that he could entirely devote himself to his studies without any disturbances. They built their house in the holy City of Jerusalem and thus, with the grace of heaven, he was saved from the infamous Arab Massacre that struck the students of the Hebron Yeshiva in 1929. After this terrible slaughter, the holy Yeshiva at Hebron was relocated to Jerusalem.

It was decided to open a preparatory Yeshiva for We famous Hebron Yeshiva and they discussed who was to head it. The Gaon Rabbi Shapira (Of Blessed Memory) said at that point: has not Rabbi Michel's teaching experience in Telz made him appropriate for this position? He was chosen by the Gaon Rabbi Chasman to head the small Yeshiva. Rabbi Michel accepted the burden of founding that Yeshiva and was 29 years old when he took over lie famous "Tiferet-Tzvi" Yeshiva. At first the Yeshiva was located next to a small synagogue in me center of Jerusalem. Later on it moved to the synagogue "Fraternity" (Achava) it was there for a long time, until it moved to its present location. The Yeshiva gathered the best students and acquired a reputation as a Yeshiva that builds its students and guides them into the world of the Torah through love of the Torah and fear of heaven. Rabbi Michel's special imprint was stamped on the students and the reputation of the Yeshiva continued to grow. Rabbi Michel would deliver the lessons himself. He taught what he was taught by his teachers, with understanding and attentiveness to the questions of le Gemara, commentary on the Mishnah, in a clear and eye opening manner. Many of his students justified that he taught them to read a page of the Gemara in a extraordinary style. It was said of his technique, that when he explained an interpretation, with great clarity and honesty, his students were as joyful as if they had received the words from Sinai.

The organization of the "Teferet-Tzvi" Yeshiva was symbol and example for many Yeshivot that were funded afterward. The fruit of this Yeshiva, who later went on to the "Hebron" Yeshiva and became the backbone of "Hebron". They grew to be the greatest of the Yeshiva heads and the most intelligent students in their generation. They testified themselves that Rabbi Michel Shlapobersky was the angel who electrified them and called to them: "Become Great!" He did this through encouragement and a moral sense. Sometimes he would publicize throughout the entire Yeshiva news of a student in order to elevate him and make him noteworthy, Rabbi Shlapobersky would be as delighted about this as if it were news about himself. Sometimes he would also give out an honored. Award, until the students. Felt, each one in his own way that Rabbi Michel's true hope was to see each of them develop and succeed in their studies. His total dedication to his students was the secret of his success.

When the children of Tehran and other refugees arrived in Eretz Yisrael, Rabbi Michel took some young men and placed them in the Yeshiva. The Yeshiva didn't have a dormitory and those students didn't have any place to go after the day's studies. Rabbi Michel took them home with him, he put. Mattresses on the floor in other rooms, the members of the household crowded together and they made room for the "guests". They were, for a long time, like his own children. He took care of all their needs, material and spiritual, and got them on their own two feet.

A scholar studying at the "Porat-Yosef" Yeshiva. During his Shivah, this important young scholar who was very intelligent, came home seeking solace. One day he just left the Yeshiva and returned home, wandering around without any direction. The young man's father, who was very worried about the situation and was concerned about his son's future, approached Rabbi Shlapobersky and spoke to him of his son's predicament. Rabbi Michel told the father that he should bring the young man to him, and he will make sure that he gets integrated into the Teferet-Tzvi Yeshiva. The young man arrived and Rabbi Michel received him with warmth and became very close to him, matching him with an older student who taught and helped him to develop. Rabbi Michel also acquired for him Valuable awards and influenced him through his great goodness and even invited him to his home, until the young man felt like a member of the family. Today, that young man, whose has since gained great fame, could testify that the profound affection of Rabbi Michel Shlapobersky was what enabled him to continue in the Yeshiva.

Other testimony to his dedication and the level of his commitment: since the founding of the Yeshiva and its great financial difficulties. The Gaon Rabbi Yehezkel Pratzovitz (Of Blessed Memory) one of the Yeshiva heads, traveled throughout the Mediterranean countries to raise money. During such times, the heads of the Yeshiva went without any salary. The situation got so difficult that Rabbi Michel and his family didn't even have a piece of bread to eat. During that period, Rabbi Michel received an offer from the Gaon Rabbi Michel Tukotzinski (Of Blessed Memory), head of the Tree of Life" Yeshiva, to serve at his Yeshiva as an instructor. His friends, acquaintances and relatives urged Rabbi Michel to accept the position but he refused, reasoning that it was precisely during this period that the Yeshiva depended upon him most, and he wasn't willing to destroy the Yeshiva even though he had no bread in the house. Such dedication sustained him, and he managed to elevate the Yeshiva to its present glory.

"Kollel!" An idea so simple and accepted in our time. The younger generation is already born within a "Kollel" environment, which extends throughout the Holy Land. But forty years ago, the situation was completely different. The Kollels that existed grew from within the great Yeshivot. The scholars studied together in the Yeshiva. However, groups of scholars, which studied alone, each under a separate structure, were a new phenomenon in his time and the fruit of the thinking of the Gaon Rabbi Michel Shlapobersky (Of Blessed Memory).

It was in the year 1956, when he suggested, to his already important son-in-law, the Gaon Rabbi Raphael Riechman, to develop a special structure for scholars. He even outlined for him the academic programs, and encouraged him to open a "Kollel." His son-in-law, who was already known for some time as a distinguished young scholar took the mission upon himself and right after his "seven blessings" he opened the Kollel "Ateret Shlomo". In Elul of 1956, a new idea was created in the world of Torah, a new form, new perspectives and even greater supports. This Kollel was in effect, the model for the many Kollels that were founded afterward.

Rabbi Michel Shlapobersky, himself, when well along in years, rapidly regained his youthful vitality and founded a Kollel for outstanding young scholars called "Ner Yehuda" after his teacher and Rabbi, The Gaon Rabbi Tasman, (Of Blessed Memory). There he delivered lessons and discussions on Musar on a regular basis despite his advanced age. That Kollel was a source of great satisfaction to him. Because his happiness and spiritual satisfaction were derived from the glorification of the Torah and its teaching. It is interesting to note that both the preparatory Yeshiva for youngsters and the construction of Kollels, which are so accepted in our time, were in fact, the results of the thoughts of the Great Gaon Rabbi Michel Shlapobersky.

Thus all of his days were a single string of Torah and good qualities. A continuous process of teaching the Torah and spreading its meaning to the many. Even during the period of his illness, in his last year of life, he didn't cease his individual routine according to the way of Kelm. As long as there remained within him strength, he would reflect upon and discuss issues of the Torah, because that was the ardent desire and the joy of his life. When he grew weak, his image appeared still but remained glorious. While he remained in full possession of his exceptional faculties; he bore his suffering in silence and took care not to disturb anyone. Even in that condition, he would think carefully about every movement. A single fact can exemplify his thoughtful behavior. It was when he was already on his deathbed and he needed to be helped by his family. It was amazing to witness his special virtuous consideration of others. It was when one of his grandsons prepared a cup of tea for him and offered it to him to drink. Rabbi Michel was not able at that time to drink. Then when he (the first grandson) got up to leave and another grandson again tried to offer him the cup of tea, Rabbi Michel insisted that the grandson who prepared the tea should be the one to give it to him to drink, because after all he had prepared it... The best way to describe his personality would be to quote the saying of Our Great Rabbis (Hazal): "if Rabbi Michel Shlapobersky is similar to an Angel of G-d, seek out the Torah from his mouth." The pageant of Rabbi Michel's life with his singular leadership and his elevated acts are encapsulated in this saying. As all of the angel's essence is a mission, then Rabbi Michel felt like a faithful messenger who was wholly devoted to his holy task of teaching the Torah and education of the "fear of G-d." He clung to this mission for over seventy years of his life. Like an Angel who is known as "steadfast", thus it is known of Rabbi Michel Shlapobersky that from the first until the last of his days he maintained the same deliberate pace and tranquility of spirit without being influenced by mood swings or distress over time. Being an elevated soul possessed of such rare qualities. Indeed there exists the end of the saying of our Great Rabbis: they (his students) bought, they owned and learned from him and they still sought the Torah from his mouth, indeed many of the best students of the Torah, today teach his Torah and his mode of education and so do their students throughout the Holy Land.

His pure soul was raised to heaven this year, 1995, on Yom Kippur, and laid to rest after midnight on the 12th of Tishri. Delivering the eulogy, one of his students. The Gaon Rabbi Shmuel Yakov Bernstein said, "the sun came in at noon, even though he was advanced in his old age, to the generation for which he became a holy symbol, his absence will be thought of as the Absence of The Sun at Noon."

May His Soul Rest in Peace

Translated by Dalit and Adam Katz
Syracuse, New York, 1996

Mordechai's Shroud

Innovations and Explication in Talmudic Issues,
the Rambam and the Six Books of the Mishnah
(and the Booklet of Essays concerning Musar and Knowledge)

By the Great Rabbi Mordechai Slapobersky
The Rabbi Der Zernoga and Member of the Rabbinate at Rehovot

Formerly a Teacher and Member
of the Rabbinate of Kovno and Lithuania

Published by the Author's Brothers:

Rabbi Michel D. Slapobersky, 24 Malachi., Jerusalem

Rabbi Ari Lieb Slapobersky, 5 Tel Chai St., Petach Tivka

Rabbi Yosef Slapobersky, 8 Yehoshua Ben-Gamla St., Jerusalem

Translated by
Dalit Katz, Syracuse, New York
and
Sylvia Brilliant, Tel Aviv, Israel
1997

Forward

By Rabbi Michel David Slapobersky
Rosh Yeshiva Tiferet Zvi
Jerusalem
(Brother of the Author)

People of the Book

In preparing to publish our brother's (Of Blessed Memory) book, we wanted to erect here a monument to his memory, because no one is left alive of his honored family, all of whom were annihilated in the terrible Shoah, and this book will be for him and in his memory, and his lips will speak from the grave.

This book was probably ready for publication in his lifetime, and it was only necessary to organize it and edit some parts. We tried with the help of G-d to organize and edit it and publish it as a finished work, and with the pleasing elegance befitting the honor of the brilliant author (Of Blessed Memory) and his book. The title of the book was determined by the author himself.

It is necessary to point out that due to his enormous modesty, it being like him to conceal his abilities - he didn't reveal over all this time the excellent treasure that he possessed, and only near the end of his life did he hint at the matter of publishing it, but to our regret he didn't succeed in acting upon that while alive. And here we discovered in front of us a tool full of wonder and wealth, containing deep and wide systematic investigations on all religious inquiries and innovations and explanations on fundamental and eternal questions, and even some profound inquiries into halachic opinions and decisions.

This book is also altogether unique, because most of the inquiries were renewed and written by the author after he had endured years of hardships and suffering in the Kovno Ghetto and death camps. Hardships such as no one could imagine, which had the power to oppress the human soul until the ultimate suppression of the spirit. Even if there are sufferings accepted lovingly that don't negate the Torah, nevertheless terrible sufferings - physical and spiritual - such as those endured by the author have the power not only to negate all thoughts of the Torah, but also to blur the human image, to obscure the divine image which is in man and bring about the "canceling of the existence" of his Individuality.

Is it not a wonder that after all this there still remained in this man enough of the divine spark of the fire of the Torah, so that there rose from within him a flame which became a blazing torch of light - the Light of the Torah. This is not thanks to the strong and sturdy spiritual foundations that created a golden rode in the spine and backbone that could remain erect even after all the shocking humiliations. Then the sufferings that like the sayings of the Chazal (Brachot 5) on the verse "and these are the things of the covenant", that they polish men like a covenant of salt, and keep him upright. And thus the book that stands before us.

His Chronicles

In order to search for the roots of this marvel, it is necessary to take a look at his life story, his roots and childhood. The author was born in the year 1905, in the City of Shkudvil, in Tavrig District, Kovno Guberniya, Russia (*Lithuania*), to our parents Rabbi Moshe Yitzchak Slapobersky and his wife, Rivka Hinda, (Of Blessed Memory). Our father (Of Blessed Memory) came from Vilna, his father, the Rabbi Michel David (Of Blessed Memory) was a famous person and among the leading proof readers in the famous Ram Printing firm. He studied in the "Group of Men" with the city's Rabbis as was the norm in Lithuania. Then he studied for some time in the Slobodka Yeshiva. Living afterward with his uncle the brilliant and righteous famous Great Rabbi Yehoshua Leib Stein, the Rabbi of Dauphina near to Shkudvil, (Who was the father-in-law of the great genius Ginzburg who is known as the Rabbi Dinuva in the book" The Origins of Blessing"). From there he took as his wife,

Rivka Hinda Propp, our mother, and the daughter of Reb Shimon Propp (Of Blessed Memory), who was among the most honored and important men of Shkudvil. Our mother was a modest and pious woman, well educated in the fear of the Lord, and also learned according to the ideas of the time and gracious and good hearted.

While our brother, the author (Of Blessed Memory) was still of a tender age, our father (Of Blessed Memory) traveled to America before the first World War, and stayed there until the War was over. He returned from America, broken and crushed because he was cut off from his family during the entire war, and was concerned about their situation, since they remained without support. He fell sick and never recovered so it was difficult for our brother to receive a fatherly education. Still, our righteous and moral mother took care of the education of her sons. Guiding them in the way of Torah and piety. Our mother, with the aid and devotion of our righteous Uncle Moshe Baruch Brodie(a long time student in the Talmud Torah of Kelm), she saw to the dedication of the older brothers in the Yeshiva of Telz and Kelm in their education as Torah devotees. Despite the fact that the times were miserable, and there were constant worries about keeping afloat, and things were very tight in the house, she took care to send food packages to her sons in the Yeshiva so that they were able to continue studying. Little Mordechai'le stayed home during that time under our mother's teaching. She took care to send him to the appropriate teachers. Her dedication and love for the Torah influenced the soul of her delicate and tender child, directly and indirectly, and planted in him an exalted spiritual treasures.

We still remember well the atmosphere of the house, especially on the Holy Shabbat, when it was the custom that Shabbat afternoon our mother would read the weekly portion "Tzeena and Reena" but not just for herself. Rather, there were gathered many women in our house every Holy Shabbat to hear the weekly portion from our mother. She knew how to read fluently, and with intonation which would emphasize every nuance of the portion and the Haftorah, and

in the necessary place would give a deep sigh "akractes", or another reaction appropriate for the issue. After that would come the "Mincha" prayer read out loud and the women would repeat after her word by word. She would recite Pirkey Avot (Ethics of the Fathers) in the summer days (this celebration had the character of a "Shabbat party" because it did not lack the honoring of guests with a cup of hot tea, etc.). Her children would sit on the side listening carefully to all the Torah stories and the Agadah from "Ze'ena and Ur'ena". Engraved in our memories are the sayings of "our living Rabbis" and "our pillars" that are quoted there and which were referred to in good taste. All this affected and ploughed deeply in the furrows of our tender hearts and left powerful impressions and feelings.

As was already mentioned, he, our brother (Of Blessed Memory), received a fair portion of all this, his being in the house more than anyone, and he spent all the days of his childhood and youth. In this atmosphere, and in addition to his natural noble characteristics he was further refined by the influence of the house and by delicate feelings and good judgment, with great love to study the Torah. He became a nice and pleasant flower and was loved by all. When he reached the age of his Bar Mitzvah he was already developed in his understanding of his studies. He prepared the sermon for his Bar Mitzvah by himself from the book, Shaga, without the help of others, and as was mentioned before our father (Of Blessed Memory) was still in America, and he astonished his listeners with his understanding of the issues.

The Influence of our City Shkudvil

While we are discussing influences, it is impossible to forget the Torah atmosphere that prevailed in the city named "Shkudvil," which despite being one of the smaller towns of Lithuania was filled with learned men and writers, of different kinds. There was the "ba'ab" circle, lovers of Torah, and observant Jews, with fixed time for studying Torah. They formed the society of the synagogues and the houses of Torah in the city, from Shas (The Six Orders of the

Talmud-Mishna) to the association "Ch'a", and the "Ein Yaakov" after "Shacharit" Prayers and between "Mincha" and "Ma'ariv" Prayers.

The second circle from the Yeshivot and Prayer Houses that, together with their business in trade - among them storekeepers and even qualified druggists and educated men - was organized especially for regular Torah study in a special arrangement. Among them were those that were not satisfied just with the study of the page with the group but also arranged to study with another group at set times before morning prayers or late at night after they finished work. From these "study groups" arose the great and famous Yeshivot like Telz, Slobodka, Mir and Kelm. Even in the daytime they arranged their studies in the Beit Midrash, in spite of their being busy supporting their families. They continued to promote the atmosphere of the Yeshiva even when in the city, through study, and others also in the determination to study Musar (Standards, Morals, Ethics). Most of them being from Musar Yeshivot. In the High Holy days some of them traveled to the "Talmud Torah" Yeshiva in Kelm next to Shkudvil, and they would bring to there "fortifying" improvements and administrators for all times of the year. Among them were some amazing and precious ones, men exalted in Torah, and in performing deeds of righteousness and grace for the community and private persons. Some of them should be noted as an example for the memory of future generations: like Rabbi Hillel Zilberg. It is possible to define Rabbi Zilberg as a man whose "Torah was his faith" because we always saw him sitting in the Beit Midrash involved in the Torah, and his being of the Musar school, he also fixed a time to study ethics. But in addition he was an excellent dealer, and all the municipal responsibilities connected to religion and the strengthening of Torah were delegated to him, from the collection of Synagogue dues, in Talmud Torah, to Mikvas and the Kaddish community. And when he founded a small Yeshiva in town he took responsibility for its reconstruction, which was also done in a disciplined and orderly manner. He was from his outward appearance - a short man - a simple man, walking with his head bent without looking up like one of the world's poor. Indeed he carried out his public activities without fanfare. They were carried out quietly and modestly, demure by his nature, quick in his work, and all with clean hands and not in order to receive any reward, and just out of responsibility for all the issues concerning religion and charity. Rabbi Zilberg intention was only for G-d's sake. Even though he was treasurer in the Synagogue in the High Holy days his place continued to exist in the Beit Talmud Torah in Kelm from year to year.

The second of those engaged in public works was Rabbi Eli Bar Katatz (Of Blessed Memory) also from the prayer houses of the Musar masters in Kelm, a man elevated from the midst of the simple folk, storekeepers and workers, students in Mishnah, Halacha and Agadah groups. He hearkened at their own level and led them in the fear of G-d, captivating in his Aggadic sayings and sermons. He was warmly devoted to all who suffer and are depressed. A helper in body and soul to all who are in need. Caretaker of the sick and concerned about their needs (he immigrated to Eretz Israel with his family, settled in Ra'anana, and managed there a farm and lived there all the time struggling to adjust to the country and there he died.

Here before our eyes stands the marvelous image of our uncle, the righteous Moshe Baruch Braude, who came from the city of Kelm. An exemplary representative of the school of Kelm. On the one hand a stable and successful shopkeeper, and on the other hand, his behavior and demeanor was that of a Yeshiva student. In his disciplined schedule of studying several hours a day in the Beit Midrash, and during the hours of study he would not stop for any profane reason (to urgent matters he would answer only by hinting). In those hours he would leave his place of business and rely upon his companion, his exemplary wife, and our aunt, Rochel (Propp) Braude. On market days in Shkudvil, he would change his schedule as was needed. At a fixed hour every day he would study the Musar as an unbreakable principle. In his youth he studied in the Telz Yeshiva, in the time of the mighty Gaon Rabbi Eliezer Gordon, and after that he was educated at the Beit Talmud Torah in Kelm, and stayed devoted and committed to that place all his life. During the month of Elul each year, he would leave his home and his business and travel to Kelm, beginning the first evening of Elul, and stayed there until after Yom Kippur. There, Reb Moshe Brodieentered every section of the place in study and ethics, and he was involved with the Torah and the work of G-d. For periods of abstinence for day and half day long fasts.

Thus Reb Brodieinsisted upon the education of his sons in the way of the Torah and taught them with extra rigor. He paid attention as well to their education of his relatives - who were as close to him as sons. He also insisted upon preserving education in Shkudvil and would inspect classes in the Talmud Torah from time to time, as one who feared and trembled at G-d's word. He responded forcefully to every breach that was liable to blaspheme against religion and Judaism in the town. He participated in the Mitzvah of joining in weddings and was the greatest celebrant, and was famous with his clever and wise sayings for every celebration and party. At Simchat Torah Reb Moshe Braude was among the first celebrants in honor of the Torah. He played a big role in everything concerning charity and righteousness in the city for the community and individuals, and he used to give on a regular basis to charity.

Here and there were other exalted people, masters of Torah and piety. Masters of devotion and good deeds in our city, but we don't have the space to go into any more details. Therefore it is no wonder that, in accord with the warm Torah and pious atmosphere, the charity and righteousness, which prevailed in our town. The town of Shkudvil was famous in the world of Yeshivas with the great number of students in every Yeshiva, large and small, and the gathering of all the Yeshiva students for holidays gave the very recognizable impression of a Yeshiva brigade throughout the town. The parents were full of pride for their sons, and the inhabitants of the city were proud of their great sons, and honored them.

Shkudvil was also famous with its great Rabbis. The last who served the Rabbinate was the famous genius Rabbi Abraham Yitzchak Perlman, author of the book "The Pnai Avraham," which was well known in the Yeshivot. He was known in his time, in the world of the Yeshivot, by the name Rabbi "Abraham Yitzchak Talzer," the outstanding student of the Gaons Rabbi Eleizer Talzer, Rabbi Shimon Shakof and Rabbi Haim Rabinovitz (Of Blessed Memory), and afterward as a student in the Slobodka Yeshiva. He was immersed every day in the deep study of the Torah and contributed greatly to the renewal of the Yeshiva's vitality, and in his essence and through his learning he influenced, not a little, the spirit of the students of Shkudvil. Out of his desire to teach the Torah he founded a Yeshiva for the youth of the city, selecting from among talented people, and he himself recited to them the lessons. Among those chosen ones was our younger brother (the author) who was privileged to receive the Torah from him and to rise quickly to the heights of understanding in his studies, relative to his age. Even after the Yeshiva closed, for various reasons, he remained there with a few students from among the most excellent and engaged them in Torah study and entertained them. Our brother especially was his prized student and he placed on him great hopes that he would be a genius and source of pride.

After he had already acquired a high level of understanding in his studies, our brother moved to the Yeshiva of Telz. There he was accepted as an advanced, excellent and talented student, with a quick and easy grasp of the material, and logical rigor. He grew and rose from level to level. Even though the extreme enthusiasm for the Torah, as was the style in Telz, did not conform to his nature, as he comported himself with special moderation and calm and yet he was known as one of those who grasped the main point of the lesson. He knew how to repeat before his colleagues the entire lesson in all of its aspects rapidly and accurately, and he also knew how to summarize in writing the lesson in an easy and apt way. It was customary in the Yeshiva that the lessons would be prepared by the students and printed by a special editorial board established to disseminate them among the students. Our brother said that the younger Bloch told him one time that his father, Rabbi Bloch, saw a passage from a lesson that was taught in the Yeshiva which was arranged by our brother. The great Rabbi Bloch was deeply impressed by it, that a youth in the Yeshiva knew how to descend to the depth of the issues, that were expressed with explanatory logic and precision, to find the essence, and get to the point and in a marvelous style and formulation. He was indeed influenced by the method of study of the Rabbi Rabinowitz, (Of Blessed Memory) from Telz in his understanding and depth.

Our brother was also influenced by the great Rabbi Abraham Yitzchak Bloch, head of the Yeshiva and the last great master of Telz, and these are his remarks and impression of the aforementioned Rabbis:

"He was like a hero of the Torah, with profound sensitivities and elevated thoughts. With an elevated spirit, his eyes always filled with soulful excitement. On the one hand goodhearted and soft as buffer, and, on the other hand, he managed with a strong and uplifted iron hand not to move from his viewpoint or behavior on any issue. The standards of his father and his teacher, and the one aim that was always before him was to make holy the name of heaven in the world, and out of this during great and holy sufferings with (Kiddush Hashem) on his lips his soul departed in purity."

And thus he grew and ascended by his diligence to become one of the select among the students in the great Yeshiva. He was known by his deep knowledge of the Torah and his expertise. In addition he developed in knowledge and morality, and was influenced by the mode of thought of Rabbi Yitzchak Bloch (Of Blessed Memory) drawn from his discussions on knowledge and morality. While still in his youth he copied the pamphlet "The Way of the Torah in Telz Yeshiva," that was edited by Rabbi Bloch (Of Blessed Memory), taken from the

content and essence of the lessons on knowledge of the Rabbi.

Visits to the Beit Talmud Torah in Kelm

From Telz he went to visit the Beit Talmud Torah in Kelm that was under the management and influence of the profoundly wise and among the greatest of wise men of the Musar in his generation, Rabbi Daniyel Movshovitz (Of Blessed Memory).

Thus he described the greatness of the Rabbi Daniyel (Of Blessed Memory). "A man without official post, modest, and an adorable man whose entire being expressed honor and respect. With sharp eyes, a pleasant face, a modest attitude toward the other and he raised his fellow above himself, along with deep philosophical ideas with faith and knowledge of G-d. He speaks of morality and reproach with simplicity and cordiality. When one sat near him one forgot about bad things, because he was all good, and when he entered the house of the Talmud it felt like a breeze from the Garden of Eden had entered with him."

There, our brother, rose as a master of the Torah, and was perfected in ethics and other qualities. He was very popular there and beloved by the people and the managers of that great house until he became part of management and accepted the function of arranging the study of the Torah, and for this he was given special rights and privileges. Thanks to his talents and fine qualities he absorbed within himself all kinds of study. Through education and thought, and mixed within himself, acquired all the good and beauty that the schools of Telz and Kelm had between them, and he became a fruitful tree, great in Torah and knowledge, and perfect in his qualities and in his practices.

His Portrait as a Member of the Rabbinate in Kovno

From Kelm he took another honor and marrying the daughter of the great Rabbi Gershon Gutman (Of Blessed Memory). The righteous judge and teacher in Kovno. There he continued to study in the kolel of Kovno, in an easy and apt way. It was customary in the Yeshiva that the lessons would be prepared by the students and printed by a special editorial board established to disseminate them among the students. Our brother said that the younger Bloch told him one time that his father, Rabbi Bloch, saw a passage from a lesson that was taught in the Yeshiva which was arranged by our brother. The great Rabbi Bloch was deeply impressed by it, that a youth in the Yeshiva knew how to descend to the depth of the issues, that were expressed with explanatory logic and precision, to find the essence, and get to the point and in a marvelous style and formulation. He was indeed influenced by the method of study of the Rabbi Rabinowitz, (Of Blessed Memory) from Telz in his understanding and depth.

Our brother was also influenced by the great Rabbi Abraham Yitzchak Bloch, head of the Yeshiva and the last great master of Telz, and these are his remarks and impression of the aforementioned Rabbis:

"He was like a hero of the Torah, with profound sensitivities and elevated thoughts. With an elevated spirit, his eyes always filled with soulful excitement. On the one hand goodhearted and soft as buffer, and, on the other hand, he managed with a strong and uplifted iron hand not to move from his viewpoint or behavior on any issue. The standards of his father and his teacher, and the one aim that was always before him was to make holy the name of heaven in the world, and out of this during great and holy sufferings with (Kiddush Hashem) on his lips his soul departed in purity."

And thus he grew and ascended by his diligence to become one of the select among the students in the great Yeshiva. He was known by his deep knowledge of the Torah and his expertise. In addition he developed in knowledge and morality, and was influenced by the mode of thought of Rabbi Yitzchak Bloch (Of Blessed Memory) drawn from his discussions on knowledge and morality. While still in his youth he copied the pamphlet "The Way of the Torah in Telz Yeshiva," that was edited by Rabbi Bloch (Of Blessed Memory), taken from the content and essence of the lessons on knowledge of the Rabbi.

Visits to the Beit Talmud Torah in Kelm

From Telz he went to visit the Beit Talmud Torah in Kelm that was under the management and influence of the profoundly wise and among the greatest of wise men of the Musar in his generation, Rabbi Daniyel Movshovitz (Of Blessed Memory).

Thus he described the greatness of the Rabbi Daniyel (Of Blessed Memory). "A man without official post, modest, and an adorable man whose entire being expressed honor and respect. With sharp eyes, a pleasant face, a modest attitude toward the other and he raised his fellow above himself, along with deep philosophical ideas with faith and knowledge of G-d. He speaks of morality and reproach with simplicity and cordiality. When one sat near him one forgot about bad things, because he was all good, and when he entered the house of the Talmud it felt like a breeze from the Garden of Eden had entered with him."

There, our brother, rose as a master of the Torah, and was perfected in ethics and other qualities. He was very popular there and beloved by the people and the managers of that great house until he became part of management and accepted the function of arranging the study of the Torah, and for this he was given special rights and privileges. Thanks to his talents and fine qualities he absorbed within himself all kinds of study. Through education and thought, and mixed within himself, acquired all the good and beauty that the schools of Telz and Kelm had between them, and he became a fruitful tree, great in Torah and knowledge, and perfect in his qualities and in his practices.

His Portrait as a Member of the Rabbinate in Kovno

From Kelm he took another honor and marrying the daughter of the great Rabbi Gershon Gutman (Of Blessed Memory). The righteous judge and teacher in Kovno. There he continued to study in the kolel of Kovno,

The Miracle of the Escape from Kovno

On that same bitter day that the Germans entered the city (Tamuz, 5201). The first thought came to "flee," and spontaneously, without accounting and without a destination he put his two daughters in a children's' wagon with a few light belongings and "one bottle of water" and they ran across the road leading from Kovno to Jonava. They didn't have a car, and they fled by foot with the children in the wagon, to the village next to the city of Kovno, a place where some of his family members lived. But when they arrived there the town was abandoned and in the hands of the Goyim who didn't allow them to enter. They ran away with the Russian army, which retreated from Kovno along that road. It was very hot, and the children drank thirstily from the bottle that they had with them, but the water was finished quickly, and along the way it was impossible to obtain water because of the fear of poisoned wells. The villagers along the way were afraid to give any shelter or help to the Jews due to the threats of the Lithuanian partisans, and thus they continued on their way in hunger and thirst with the children crying out for water.

In the evening they were forced to turn to the Forest to rest from their exhaustion and lack of "food and sleep." The thunder of cannons and machine guns, from German planes, of the retreating army didn't allow them to get much sleep even in the forest. With the morning light, they again continued on the way to Jonava. Here it happened miraculously that along the way they met with some of their family from the village. Instead of water they found milk, from the cows that their family members took with them from the village, and they had milk for food and drink like Manna in the desert. This revived their spirits and those of their children. Behold they also had a carriage already and continued along their way with the feeling that their redemption was close by. But upon their arrival near Jonava, there arrived an order from the Russian army that all civilians must leave the road, because they were interfering with the rapid retreat, and they directed everyone to the adjacent villages. Those villages received them with

food and drink but absolutely refused to allow them to stay in the village, so without any choice they were forced to return to Kovno and fall into the lair of the terrible lion. On their arrival close to the city of Kovno, the villagers warned them not to enter the city yet because the Nazis and Lithuanians had already in the first few days carried out pogroms against the Jews of Kovno and Slobodka. They were forced to delay again in the middle of the way and also to sleep outdoors with the children.

It was here they received the first terrible information of the pogrom in Slobodka that they had killed by the sword the Rabbi Zalman Aushobeski and his son, the Rabbi Feivel Alekshater and other Torah greats and Yeshiva members. The Righteous Rabbi Elchanan Wasserman they took to the seventh fortress for execution. Here they found themselves between the fire of both sides without any way out, but the situation forced them to enter the city again. Already they could not enter their house because the wicked Lithuanian was afraid to allow Jews to stay on his territory, and they found shelter with family members. Thus it was made known to him that a miracle had occurred to them in that they fled the city. Because the Lithuanian partisans looked for the Rabbi Slapobersky in his home on the day that they carried out the mass murderers in Slobodka and Kovno, and since they had fled the city they were saved.

The Ghetto Decree and the Yellow Star

To go out on the road for a man like him dressed as a Rabbi was already very dangerous. Because when they caught them and sent the Rabbis for extermination or work, both led to the same end. Only members of the household allowed themselves to pass on the road, and that also only with the sign of the yellow star, made in the form of the "Magen Dovid". Jews were forbidden to go in the middle of the roads and were only allowed on the side. They were beginning to feel the oppression and the humiliation of being Jews, and then came the decree requiring their concentration in the ghetto. There went out an order that by a certain date - and very soon - all those Jews living in the city about forty thousand people, had to move into the Ghetto of Slobodka. They permitted them to take with them all the possessions and the portables from their home. (this was done on purpose so that the concentration could afterward make it easy for them to collect the spoils). The panic over obtaining living quarter began until it was that five neighbors would with difficulty be squeezed into one tiny room with an adjoining kitchen. The territory of the ghetto as marked off by a metal fence and one could not leave or enter. Meanwhile the food they brought with them from the city was completely exhausted. There began the black market with the Gentiles outside of the Ghetto. In exchange for silver and gold jewelry and furniture, they threw them food over the metal fence of the ghetto. This posed a mortal danger from the guards who shot whomever they caught in this terrible sin, and indeed many victims fell daily as a result of this trading, and with the shortage of food began an epidemic of deaths by starvation.

Decree followed decree. One day an order went out, to bring all the silver that they had left, while they were permitted to keep just a mall sum. Another day an order to bring silver and gold jewelry and good household furniture, and all of this accompanied by the threat that in case of anything remained hidden in the house the Germans would blow up the whole street. In order to facilitate the work they organized a Jewish police force, "Yiddishe Polizei," and they helped them against their will to repute all the these decrees.

The Decree on Books

After they robbed and plundered all the property of the Jews in silver and gold and the rest, they suddenly issued an order to bring to them all the books everybody had, both religious and secular. This too under the threat of capital punishment against those who refused. Due to their fear they had to bring all of their books. Some, to whom their books were worth more to them than their money endangered themselves and did not bring them. Others proceeded in hiding them. Our brother (Of Blessed Memory) endangered himself and hid all of his books

in different warehouses. He also hid the holy books that were left in the warehouse. The Gaon of Law Courts of Kovno, who had a treasure greater to him than thousands of metals and valuables was unable to hide his books, and he was forced to his great sorrow to deliver to them all of his wealth. They brought from Germany, a scholarly expert who also knew the Talmud, to sort out and classify the books. They packed them in boxes and shipped them to Germany, while the torn ones they sent to a paper factory, and the purpose of this looting remained unknown. But they got better those evil ones, in that they returned the Sidurim and Machzorim "Gebet Biher" to the Ghetto.

The Beginning of the "Akztions"

And here began the primary goal of the slow extermination of the Jewish population of the Ghetto, and they used all the possible means and inventions toward this end. Here and there they would catch Jews in the street and bring them to the ninth fortress by Slobodka. They would grab the Jews from the street as if for "work". One time they deceitfully announced the need for a few hundred well dressed "intelligent men," because, they were needed for work, and about a hundred gathered innocently, and those elegantly dressed people were taken straight to ninth fortress and exterminated there without pity or hesitation.

Healthier people would be assembled for crushing labor in building an extended airport next to the Alkshott. Every day they had to walk from Slobodka to Alkshott to do this hard work and this was done under the command of the Nazi soldiers who would beat them viciously at every pause and breath taken during the work.

The Big Aktzion and the
Miraculous Rescue

After a while they began the systematic liquidation of the people of the Ghetto. It was announced to all of the thirty thousand people living in the Ghetto that the next day at six in the morning they were to present themselves in the Ghetto Square, men and women, elderly and children. The people began to speculate on the purpose of this, but in the morning the purpose of the gathering became clear to them. In the middle of the Square stood the German commanders and the Lithuanian commandos and they began the Aktzion, distinguishing and dividing all the Jews there into two categories of people. On the right side they sent the aged, the weak, and families with children; to the left young healthy people still capable of working. This kind of division enabled everyone to understand the purpose of the separation, Separation between husband and wife, parents from children, these on one side and those on the other, the cries and screams from those who had been separated tore the air and ripped into the hearts. To our brother (Of Blessed Memory) the criterion was simple and clear. to them belonged all the qualities those selected for the right side...A middle-aged Rabbi, head of a family with nail children-and here they stood completely depressed and desperate, waiting for their bitter fate, in the middle of at great tumult of 30,000 people. Suddenly there appeared like a redeeming angel from the heavens, their devoted Brother-in-law Reb Koppel Gutman (Of Blessed Memory). He was decorated with a tape of the Jewish police on his arm, and he tells them that he had been looking for them all day in order to rescue them and he did not find them. Without waiting a moment, he grabbed the children's stroller in his arm, and he told them to follow him through the masses of people. Thus they somehow evaded the murderer's eyes and he pushed them to the left side. He endangered himself with this act, but they are already among the saved and breathed sigh of relief. The next day they saw and heard of the fate of those who were on the other side. They took thousands of men, women and children that same day to ninth fortress where there were already pits prepared for them and they were buried alive in them, and from then on everyone was taken with fear and terror, depression and desperation, and their lives dangled in front them.

His Existence in the Cave of Prayer

After the partial annihilation of the Ghetto. Those "living" in the Ghetto had rested a bit they received terrifying news from the towns of the surrounding area. Of all that those vicious mass murderers had done to the Jews, from the destruction of the Torah centers in the towns of Lithuania, including the destruction of Telz, Kelm, and Ponibz. The Gentiles outside the Ghetto passed on rumors to the Ghetto that every first and fifteenth of the month they would carry out an "Aktzion". and it was not long before there was whispering in the Ghetto that they were again planning some Aktzion. This time for relocation to work in Riga and these rumors plucked at one's nerves, and after the rumor followed the deed. There came the day of the order to gather in the square in the morning and line up. They chose a few hundred people and put them on trucks without anyone knowing to this day where they disappeared to, but this time not everybody believed them that the destination was "work," and they began to devise ideas of how to conceal themselves in hiding places and secret bunkers. Our brother (Of Blessed Memory) and other neighbors found themselves in a small, narrow and dark warehouse. They were crowded in there, in great fear and terror, and the prayer in their hearts was the "wisdom that came to David when he was in the cave"... Until they received the news that the transport had already left, and they were miraculously saved from the danger of separation.

Change for the Better and Mortal Sickness

For a few days the commander of the guards at the Ghetto was changed, and instead of the evil and cruel commander there came another in his place who was a little more yielding, who allowed for food to enter from the outside by way of the Ghetto gate. He received some work in the city with the Germans arranging their affairs, and in this way it was possible to come into secret contact with the Gentiles to buy food in exchange for the possessions they still had. There was a little boost in the economy and the children who suffered physically all the time from the lack of food and nutrition now received a bit.

The time of the Passover holiday approached, and they procured Matzo flour, and they were able to prepare Matzo for Passover and other holiday necessities. They arranged everything for the first Seder in their narrow room, with the four questions asked by the children (and in addition an adult asked; "what has changed"?). The Seder night passed without drawing the attention of anyone around them. But the next day came a serious attack of lung disease, and in addition he got an infection of the spinal cord. Medicines and injections were not available in the ghetto, but the famous Dr. Elchanon Elkes, the head of the Jewish Council of the Kovno Ghetto) cared for him devotedly. His dear brother-in-law, Mr. Koppel, devoted is soul to him and tried secretly to get some medicines from the town, but his illness grew worse and his sufferings were hard to bear. The doctor had already despaired of saving his life, and in this situation he laid there for about five months in mortal sickness and shivered is his misery. There was no bread winner in the house. His wife was in a postnatal condition (their third daughter was born while they were already in the Ghetto the birth in the Ghetto was a whole story in itself, and a very distressing one). Here the gnawing thoughts that maybe there will suddenly arrive a decree to leave the ghetto for another place as often happened how could they move from there in such a critical situation. The Holy One blessed and had mercy on him and sent his healing power from heaven and he began to slowly emerge from his sickness. However, it was necessary for him to get well, because there was no one in the house to work. Since he was still not capable due to his weakness. Their situation was very sad, until his valorous and devoted wife took it upon herself to work instead of him, and he took care of the children all day.

The Murder of their dear Brother-in-Law Mr. Koppel Gutman

As we said before, their exemplary brother-in-law, Koppel, stood by them like a redeeming angel, who at every difficult moment put his own life in danger in order to rescue them. However, with the growing ease with which food could enter the Ghetto gates, there developed a trade in food that was a bit wider than was permitted, and he was drawn into this trade along with other people. One time, while he was passing with a wagon filled with flour he was stopped at the gate by the Commandant himself, and he immediately sentenced him to death by shooting. This ended the rich and energetic life of a young man filled with fervor and devotion to saving the lives of others, and the family lost a savior and redeemer in all times of trouble and misery.

The Period of Easing in the Ghetto a Breath of Material and Spiritual Respite

With the sense of easiness and relief they began to arrange for work in the area. They arranged work stations which produced for local needs, and for the Germans. This involved industrial works of various kinds. Those without work in the city, worked at some other job. Since to be accepted on the list to work in the factory one needed work qualifications. Our brothers professions as a Rabbi made him foreign to any other kind of work. His talents and adaptability made it possible for him to train himself. A friend taught him how to make wooden shoes. He acquired expertise in that area quickly. The Rabbi became an expert shoemaker and a craftsman. In this way he was saved from working outside and was instead able to work in his own home. This "craftsmanship" also helped him a great deal in the Dachau camp. There he also managed to get accepted to the shoe workshop of the camp and in this way was saved from going to the arduous jobs in the forests and on the roads, in the cold and heat.

There was also a spiritual awakening among people along with the stabilization of the situation. Up until now the children still wandered around without education and without anyone to take care of their studies. However, at this point, rooms and study centers were arranged for their education, and indeed a study schedule for adults was set up in the Prayer House as well as a communal youth center for the young.

Encouragement and Reinforcement
by the Rabbi Grodzensky

The remainder of the members of the Rabbinic Yeshiva centered around the house and influence of Rabbi Abraham Grodzensky (Of Blessed Memory), the spiritual leader of the Slobodka Yeshiva. On the Sabbaths they would gather in his house for prayer, for study, and for the spiritual awakening for those who during the weekdays found no vehicle for spiritual expression due to the hard work and spiritual degradation. The Rabbi Grodzensky presented moral lectures to them. This is to be noted the same lectures that he gave in the Yeshiva when it existed, on charity and justice and other topics, and in the same style and with his special pleasantness. Even in gloomy days joy did not fade from him. They received from this spiritual strength a reason to live, and they felt on that day: "the meaning of life" "and on that day the children of Israel rested from work."

Another Spirit comes upon the
Ghetto from the Appointment
of a Famous Murderer

Now they began to hear from "Radio London" that there would be a new leader appointed to the Kovno Ghetto, named "Gaka," Who was known by the title "Sadist with the White Glove." This was a Premonition of another spirit, and it was the beginning of the fall of the Germans on the Russian front and their rapid withdrawal, which became crucial to their situation in the Ghetto, freedom or extermination? But in this new appointment of the expert murderer to the task of liquidating the Ghettos in Provintz, they saw the signs of rapid extermination. Indeed after a few days le began his work. He demanded a list of thirty thousand people for work and with deceptive calm claimed that this was just for preparation and not implementation. Suddenly the next day came the order that the people were to present themselves within four hours. With the help of the Ukrainian murderers they were gathered and snatched and sent to Austland were they disappeared from the world.

The mood in the Ghetto became sad and distressed, because they could see his system of rapid extermination, so they began to occupy themselves with hiding and began to build bunkers. The Slobodka Yeshiva students built a well prepared, carefully concealed and well camouflaged bunker with remarkable ingenuity, arranged with water, food and light. They also took care to listen to the news on the radio because it was urgent to them to know the situation of the war. They would hide there until the Russians would pass through and free them. Everyone found themselves some hiding place. To their sorrow there arrived In order to transfer the location of the ghetto to another place populated by Lithuanians. So all their work and toil was for nothing. But they nevertheless took a chance and stayed in the bunkers underneath the noses of the Lithuanians in the expectation that in a little while the saving deliverance would come. In the new place they also built hiding places and didn't despair because this was their only possibility of being saved.

The information of the liquidation of the Vilna Ghetto arrived. That hell. Since the system was to exterminate the elderly and children in particular, the elderly disguised themselves as younger by coloring their hair. Hiding places were arranged for the children, and others prepared for their delivery to the protection of Gentiles in the city and village. The priests were ready to receive children and hide them, and there arose a difficult question of Halacha in this case.

The SS begins the "Kinder Aktzion"

One cloudy day there came upon them the abduction from the Ghetto of the elderly and the small children. They went from house to house, and they took each and every elderly person, and they gathered every small child and threw them into the truck without mercy. This was done without paying attention to any of the shattering screams of the mothers and fathers regarding their small children, and the screams of the children regarding their parents.

122

Others managed to obtain information of this abduction. They were able hide their children inside the bunkers they had prepared. In our brother's house they didn't have a well hidden bunker because the window opened onto the street. Having no other choice at the moment they threw the three children into the basement. They filling them with "Limonal" to put them to sleep so the Nazis wouldn't hear the sound of their crying, and in this way they were able to save them this time from the hands of the murderers. But the murderers didn't stop as long as they knew that there remained other children in hiding, and they used all their means, their efforts and attack dogs to find the hidden places. In this situation, our brother's family, decided to move the children to a more securely hidden place. Even though this move necessitated great danger, they were compelled to take the risk and move. They put each child in a sack, so as to put the little one on their shoulder as if carrying a package and to move her successfully, and then the second after her. But with the third and oldest child, who was about six years old, His wife and daughter suddenly ended up in the middle of gangs of abductors and there was no escape! She miraculously managed to turn down an alley and disappear from their eyes. She returned to the house with the daughter to the temporary bunker. In this way his family was separated in the two bunkers, he stayed with the two children in the new bunker, and his wife with the oldest child in old bunker in the house.

The new bunker it happened that the Germans sniffed the place out and looked at entrance, and suddenly the little girl woke crying and screaming. He held her in his arms but could not calm her by any means. The danger was great that through the sound of the crying they would discover the hiding place. In order to avoid any other danger to the rest of the children and the people that filled the bunker from end to end they decided that they had to silence her by choking her. But he did not accept that verdict and still tried somehow to calm her. But to his sorrow he did not succeed. Someone approached and gave her a strong squeeze on the neck and silenced her and her breath stopped... He was deeply shocked and continued to hold the lifeless child in his arms. He was overcome by depression and desperation, but suddenly, he felt signs of life and movement from her. She slowly woke up and opened her eyes. He saw before his own eyes the resurrection of the dead. But meanwhile the "Bandas" found the opening of the bunker and broke in with axes. They opening it and saw everyone. They ordered that everyone was to come up and if not they would throw a grenade inside and blow them up together. Of course they got out immediately from there one by one with the children. The men of the "Banda" fell immediately on the children like beasts of prey and brutally removed the children from their hands. They brought them over to the cars which were ready for them. The small children trembled and shivered in the vulgar arms of the murderers, screaming tearfully and begging their fathers "Abaleh, Abaleh," take us home with you! And the cries tore their hearts, and the father stood frozen in the distance unable to rescue them.

This horrifying scene of the final separation of his two daughters, the dearest things in the world to him. That they were taken, in front of his eyes, to be victims to the Ninth Fortress. This left deep wounds in his heart, and the echo of the children's entreaties resound in the parent's ears for a long time and these wounds do not ever heal. Thus they succeeded in eliminating almost all the children in the Ghetto along with the elderly. They still found some consolation in their oldest daughter who survived in the bunker in their house, but their hearts trembled within them all the time from fear of the future, and they looked at her with pity, Who knows? Who knows? What will happen.

The Awakening to Repentance by the Rabbinate and the Rabbi Grodzensky

The depression that prevailed after this in the Ghetto, and the fear of the immediate future, motivated them to search for some means of rescue. The Rabbis called for a day of fasting, prayer and repentance, with prayers, tears and begging and with broken hearts, they accepted "Kabbalah" like those who make a vow in a troubled time. In the house of Rabbi Abraham Grodzensky (Of Blessed

Memory) the members of the Yeshiva gathered, including the scholars, the prominent men and the geniuses, and the Rabbi called for repentance, and offered them twelve "Kabbalot" and everyone agreed to observe them if they survived. (The "Kabbalot" were printed for the last time in the introduction to the book "The Torah of Abraham," on page 17). Also, they came with tactical advice and tricks of how to save themselves from the final decree: that of the liquidation of the Ghetto, whether to hide or flee to the forest, etc.

The Arrival of Zero Hour to the Liquidation of the Ghetto

On the 15th of Tamuz, different rumors and guesses circulated in the Ghetto heralding the liquidation of the Ghetto in the coming days. But without revealing the form or method. There were those who imagined they would be transported to work camps, and others who imagined that this was the final extermination. A great disturbance arose in the camp, and thus began the search for counsel and deception with which to rescue themselves. They went down to the bunkers they had prepared earlier, and those who hadn't manage to prepare for themselves such places, crowded in with those who had. The crowding was unbearable, in a bunker of two by two meters about forty people were crowded in without air to breath, and there were choking victims from the stifling heat and lack of air. His wife also fainted in the bunker and he had great difficulties in getting her out.

On the 20th of Tamuz came the order to leave the Ghetto. Those who had not managed to hide gathered at the designated area outside of the city, and throughout the rest of the day they brought the rest of the people whose hiding places had been discovered. They set the Ghetto hospital on fire with the people in it, and they were killed along with the Holy Rabbi Abraham Grodzensky. Finally there came the order to walk to the train station, where there were already cattle cars ready. They crowded everyone inside the cars and the train began to move. There was a heavy guard on them, but they were not told where they were being taken. And thus they traveled on and on without knowing the destination, with all the different guesses and speculations, until they arrived at the train station of Shtuthoffen, Germany, and stood there. And here arrived the fatal hour: the Nazis ordered the women and children to get down from the cars, and the men to stay in the train. With brutality and cruelty they hurried the women down from the train, and those of the men who came down to join their families were shot on the spot.

The Hour of the Final Separation

Now came the time of the separation of families. The screams and cries from both sides were terrible. From the windows they saw how the women and children wailed with heartbreaking cries, and they didn't even manage to say good-bye to one another. The guards explained to them that the women with children would be brought to a certain place which was known to them by its furnaces (the crematorium). That the single women who were able to work would be brought to a labor camp. The men, would travel on until they arrived at the "labor camp" of Dachau.

In the Labor Camp of Dachau

In this labor camp began a new "life," which was sensed immediately with the warm *reception* they receives from the evil and cruel German authorities. Including beatings and humiliations, with the participation of the Jewish Kapos that were ready there and suited to their function... They immediately received due notification that they were to behave according to the discipline of the "Arbeit Lager" with all its harsh and cruel laws. The daily schedule included difficult work in the forest and paving roads. Every day, from morning to evening, with a tiny portion of food, just enough to keep them alive, "housing" in tents and in tunnels under the earth, humiliating and repressive treatment and the domination exercised over them by the authorities. Many were broken under the yoke of the backbreaking work. They dropped from exhaustion, sick, without energy, and were sent to the furnace.

For our brother there appeared some glimmer of salvation when he was transferred from the most oppressive labor to a job within a factory producing wooden shoes, the "profession" in which he had already specialized in the Kovno Ghetto. They lived a life of suffering and oppression, slavery and degradation, and there remained of them only the skeleton of men, broken and crushed in body and soul. This was their fate until liberation came with the occupation by the American army.

The Liberation

With the occupation by the American army they were liberated, but this salvation was tenuous and still involved great dangers, because the Germans still did not leave them alone even in their retreat and flight. They had to run a few miles from the camp to a certain place. Some of them fell from exhaustion and those who made it were taken under the protection of the Americans. But there still lay before them trials and danger. When the Americans opened in front of those freed prisoners the German's food supplies. The starving people pounced upon the supplies and "filled themselves," and since their digestive organs were already shrunken after all this time, most of them were overcome by dysentery and other diseases, and many died from "plenty." It took some time before they arrived at some place of rest and some order.

The Rabbi is Joined with the Remaining Refugees in Paldafing

In Munich and Paldafing, and other surrounding cities the remnants were organized in refugee camps. Our brother (Of Blessed Memory) was placed in the city of Paldafing and was assigned as the Rabbi of the community of people from Lithuania. He was also ordained as a member of the Munich Rabbanite. He stayed there a while among the few of the rescued ones who remained refugees.

The First Signs of Life through a Letter to his Brother in Eretz Israel

We, who lived in Eretz Israel, did not hear from our brother and did not know of his survival even after the liberation, until we received a sign that he survived through a letter that he sent through an American Rabbi. This is the letter:

To my dear brother; Rabbi Michel in Jerusalem,

With trembling hands and a torn heart and tearful eyes I am notifying you that I am, with G-d's help, among the living, and that G-d brought me out of the iron furnace and from the mouth of the lions. And here I am now in the Dachau camp in Ashkenaz (Germany), under American rule. But what am I and what is my life now that I remain the only one left of my entire family? My wife and older daughter were taken prisoner, and I have heard nothing from them My two remaining daughters were burned by the torch of Amalek (the crematorium). Of all the Jews of Lithuania, not even one percent survived, of all the Rabbis of Lithuania not even one remains. Solitary, I remain and alone I stay, and my only goal is to meet with my brother who is in our Holy Land. I look for my brother, and I hope for G-d's help, G-d, who guided me unto this day, that he will deliver me successfully along the paved road. Here is not the place to go on at length about all the tribulations that I have undergone, because the space is not sufficient and it is not humanly possible to convey it on paper. When we see each other face to face I will tell you all and you will certainly not believe me. For now, the Americans support us, and thanks to that, from the dry bones we were left with having developed flesh and skin, and our condition has improved somewhat. But we still remain within the borders of Amalek and under special guard and we don't have real freedom. The days pass by without spiritual activity, because we haven't here any Holy books, but lately the American Rabbi brought us some study portion and I was very happy. We wait unto someone from the outside will come to help us, because the prisoner does not release himself from prison (Thank G-d), and give us a helping hand. Unto now, there has not been any outside help for us. If it is possible for you to work for me and help me leave here, I would appreciate your doing whatever is in your power. There are other Jews here from different countries, but only a few. And G-d who gave strength to me and will comfort me in the way of the truth.

How are you and how is all our family? Write your answer to the address sent you under the name of the American Jewish soldier, because we have no other way of sending letters. I have already placed my name on many lists sent to the newspaper to publish. Now it is time to say good-bye...

From Your Brother,
Mordechai Slapobersky

His Arrival in Israel

We managed to acquire a certificate for him, which allowed him to make Aliyah, and he was received by us, his brothers, with joy at finding their lost brother. He was established temporarily as a Rabbi in a Synagogue in Petach Tikva. After that he was accepted as the Rabbi in Zernoga near Rehovot, a place where new immigrants from Hungary and Romania settled. Here also he went through the difficulties of integration and the sorrows of Eretz Israel. He married again, to the Rabbanit Chaja, who was also a survivor of the camps. She became very sick, and he traveled with her to the United States for an operation. The disease got worse and she died. He remained again a widower, and he married for a third time. Following the annexation of the settlement of Zergona to Rehovot he joined the Rabbinate of Rehovot. Here he found ample space to express his abilities in Holy work as a Rabbi and teacher. With the experience he gained as a member of the Kovno Rabbinate, his trenchant style and capacity for rapid evaluation, he laid down judgments with good sense and knowledge. The Rabbis,

judges, wise men, students and residents of the city of Rehovot

knew how to esteem the Rabbi like a wise and brilliant student. A Halachic judge with a wide range, a remover of obstacles with great generosity, and an amazingly proficient problem solver. A innovator in the Torah, like of the great Rabbis", (from the evaluation n the newspaper after his death) and he was considered the pillar of the Rabbinate.

Until that bitter and emotional day, early in the morning of the first of Nisan, 5727, (April 11th, 1967) this great scholar collapsed in the yard of the synagogue when his sick and grieving heart stopped, after a glowing and passionate sermon on the honor of the Torah and the Rabbinate. That was his final and "farewell" sermon. His righteous and worthy soul soared in a rage to heaven.

As we have mentioned, he left another book of memoirs written by hand that besides the descriptions of the horrors of the Ghetto and camps also includes a lot of information and impressions of the men of Torah in Lithuania that were annihilated, the Torah centers that were destroyed. Those, in an abbreviated form, were included in the introduction to this book. We pray for him that the purification of his soul is complete by all the kinds of hellish sufferings that he had to endure on this earth. The light of his Torah will be a credit to him in the Garden of Eden with the righteous who sit and enjoy of the Divine Spirit. May his soul in peace.

Written in sadness and in honor and memory of our brother (Of Blessed Memory)

Michel David Slapobersky
The Brother of the Author

Gaon Rabbi Michel Dovid Slapobersky passed away after Yom Kippur on October 6, 1995 / 12 Tishri 5756. He was 95 years old. At the time of his death he did not need eye glasses or a cane for support when walking. He lived alone and took care of himself. His mind was clear and acute and when he retold of his young years in Cheader, in Yeshiva, and in the Kollel it was so vividly described you could almost feel it happening. He remembered Shirurim he had hear his Rebbes in the holy Yeshivos in Kelm, Telz and Slobodka (Lithuania) and would relate them as if he had just heard them

His funeral was attended by thousands, many of were his students and others liked and revered Rabbi Michel Slapobersky. He was eulogized by his students, the Chief Rabbi of Jerusalem and Gedolei Roshe Yeshivos.

יהי דכרו בוך

MAY HIS MEMORY BE BLESSED

Rabbi Eliezer Rakowsky
son-in-law

The Baker Family of Clarksdale, Mississippi and Shudvil, Russia - Circa 1920
left to right: Harry, Fannie, Frank and Morris

An Interview between a Reporter and Mr. Ora Baker

By
Julia Baker Glassman

This Interview takes place on August 1ˢᵗ, 1916 in a village in what is now Lithuania. At the time the village of Skaudvil. was located near the border between East Prussia and Lithuania. R is for Reporter and MR. B is for Mr. Ora Baker.

R- Good morning, Mr. Ora Baker. I am a reporter for the JCC News in Memphis, Tennessee

MR. B- Come in Kinderla. I was in Memphis each time I went to America. First my wife wants to serve some refreshments.

R- Tell me about your life before you took your trips to America, Mr. Baker

MR. B- I was a buyer of horses for the Czar of Russia and I traveled to a lot of different places. But first I must tell you, I have been married twice and I have three sons and four daughters. My youngest son died very young. When I was on a boat to Africa, I met two very nice young men and I took than back to Skaudvile with me. I introduced them to my two older daughters and we had two weddings. One daughter, Edie, and her husband went to South Africa and settled in Johannesburg. Fanny, the other daughter, and her husband went to America and now live in Pennsylvania. What was the question? Oh, yes, you asked me about my life before I went to America. My wife has a bakery. You probably noticed the large outdoor oven in the yard as you walked up to the front door. When I wasn't traveling for the Czar I helped her in the bakery.

R- When did you take your first trip to the USA and did any of your children go with you?

> ### RELIGION
>
> *When a little Jewish boy of Eastern Europe had to walk in deep snow for several miles to be tutored by his Rebbe. When he watches his parents daven daily.*
>
> *That's Religion*
>
> *Later when the boy is grown and living in America and has a family of own, he and his wife make sure their children get a good Jewish education*
>
> *When the father says the blessing for his family on holidays and goes with his family to shul.*
>
> *That's Religion*
>
> *When I open my curtains in the morning and look out at the rising sun.*
>
> *And at night when I look at the moon and stars before closing the curtains*
>
> *That's Religion*
>
> *Julia B. Glassman, 12/92*

MR. B- Yes, my oldest son, Frank, and I went before 1900. At my age I can't remember exact dates but I am sure it was the late 1800s - After we went through Ellis Island and had all of our papers in order, we went to New Jersey where my wife had two brothers. Since we wanted to go to Mississippi to contact a distance cousin, and since we were low on money, we went to the Jewish Welfare offices. There they gave each of us a pack of merchandise to sell as we traveled across the USA. When our merchandise got low, we took jobs with the Railroad Company laying ties. This was much better than peddling. We had transportation and made more money while working.

R- How long did you stay in Mississippi?

MR. B- Just long enough to make sure my son had a comfortable place to stay and he had a Job. After all I had other children to think about. I told you I had been in Memphis several times. We stopped there before going to Clarksdale, Mississippi.

R- Where did you stay in Memphis and while in Mississippi? I know you are a religious man.

MR. B- Oh, we had no Problem. Every place we went we found nice Jewish people who were very gracious to us, they gave us lodging and fed us and took us to Shul too.

R- Tell me about your other children, Mr. Baker. How many more of them went to America, too?

MR. B- My second son Harry, went by himself. After he stayed with his uncles in New Jersey several months, be aim vent to Mississippi. He and his brother moved to a very small town out of Clarksdale and went in business. Later they also farmed and traded cattle including horses. I taught them well don't you think?

R- Yes, it seems you did. Tell as about your third son.

MR. B- Morris left home when he was almost 16. We hated to see him leave, but you know about the soldiers and how the Czar would send them to a family's home and conscript the sons for the army? We did not want that to happen to our Morris. He also went to New Jersey and he celebrated his 16th birthday there.

R- Did he go to Mississippi too?

MR. B- Yes he did. He was 20 years younger than Harry, so by the time he got to Mississippi his brothers were doing good financially and had children of their own.

R- Was this the time you went back to America?

MR. B- Let me think a minute -- I'm an old man now and my memory is not very clear. Oh, yes, now I remember! I went in February of this year. What's wrong with me it was so recent I should remember that.

R- Was Morris married when you went back?

MR. B- Yes, and he was living in Dublin. The town had grown a lot by then and Harry and Frank had moved to Clarksdale and opened stores of their own.

R- What about your daughters here in Skaudvile?

MR. B- All of my daughters are married now and my wife, Rivka, and I are living alone. We have this comfortable home and we still have the bakery. Is there anything else you would like to know Kinderla?

R- No, Mr. Baker, I think I have enough information for my newspaper. I want to thank you and your wife for your hospitality. And I especially want to thank both of you for the very-very delicious strudel and Russian tea made in your samava. You have certainly made my long trip from America worthwhile, and it has been a pleasure meeting you and your wife. Thank you.

(R- The people, places and information in this report are true. None of the names have been changed.) ❏

130

An Article Appearing the Jerusalem of Lithuania Newspaper[1]
by
Vladas Dautartas[2], Writer

I am connected with both books[3]: I was involved in the publication of one, and the other, published by the Museum, contains a portrait of my mother and the girl she saved. I am connected to the Jewish nation right from childhood, because my father fished in the Nemunas and Nevezys rivers. The Jews, Notke and Abke bought his fish from him, and they often slept over at our place. It was very interesting for me to watch them: how they eat, how they speak. As a child, I and the others used to especially wait for when they would bring matzos. We knew that was the name for their unleavened bread. We'd wait very impatiently. And when those terrible times of annihilation of people and of an entire nation came around, our family's position was already clear.

The Jews from the ghetto were building an embankment. As was his custom, my father fished, and he helped those Jews as much as he could he'd give them fish. He got to know the family of Dr. Abramovicius[4]; one day they ran away from the Ghetto[5], and came to us. In the beginning we hid them in the cellar, where they stayed for a few weeks; in the meantime my father was preparing a new hiding place. I won't give you all the details, because they are very sad memories. I remember that my father prayed for two weeks. We kept their two year old daughter, Aviva[6], who was covered in boils. It looked as if she wouldn't make it. My father knew something about medicinal herbs, and he prepared various decoctions, cordials, and baths for her. It seemed like the child was ready to expire. Mother and father had already lit the candles. But she survived, she escaped the clutches of death. And that left a deep impression in my memory and my heart. Such a tiny little girl, with such a desire to live.

I recall another moment: quite often the Germans would drive over from the next village. As the youngest, I'd be told to take the girl, whom my parents christened Brone, and to row her over to the other shore, into the reeds, so that no one would see her. But the interesting thing was that when I'd lay her down in the bottom of the boat, cover her up with a jacket, and say: "Aviva, don't move", she'd seem to understand. and she wouldn't move until we reached the other side.

I've written more than one story on the theme of this terrible Jewish tragedy. One of them is called "The train of the living, the train of the dead". It was wonderfully translated by G.Kanovicius, and we hoped to have it published in Moscow, but didn't succeed. All of it really upset me and the Lithuanian intellectuals, especially those they call the "bread growers."

One more important detail: in our village there was a fellow who literally shot Jews at the Ninth Fort. He'd always bring home various things that had belonged to those who were killed: clothing, etc. Our homestead had the only well, from which the entire hamlet drew their water. After they found out where those things were from, my father would close the gates when the killer's mother would come for water. I think that says all there is to say about him.

---

[1] From Jerusalem in Lithuania, Nr. 1-2(77-78) January-March 1998
[2] Vladas Dovtort
[3] The Hands of Sorrow and Hands Bringing Life and Bread
[4] Dr. Yankel Abramovich
[5] The Kovno Ghetto
[6] Ariela (Aviva) Abramovich, today Ariela Abramovich-Sef

The Berlowitz Family of Smalininkai, East Prussia

By Bill Berton

Mr. William Berton of Saginaw, Michigan provided almost all of what has been written about the Berlowitz family history. He has done extensive research in areas that the family lived in. The Propp's have at least had two marriages (Yenta and Rochel) with the Berlowitz family and possibly more. Further, two other male Propps, Sleime and Joseph, changed their name to Berlowitz to help leave Russia. The two family villages, Shkudvil and Smalininkai, were located only few miles from each other. The Berlowitz family had been in this area of East Prussia/Lithuania for a much longer period (at least 100 years more) than the Propps. Therefore may have been a larger family there, but I think we can safely assume from the aforementioned relationships that the two families were close and respected each another, because of the inter-family marriages. A good place to start with, is the Berlowitz family is with the story about Pincas Isakowitz (also spelled Izakowitz), he is the earliest know ancestor of the Berlowitz's, which simply means Pincas, the son of Isaak. Research documentation references are available for all the information concerning the Berlowitz family.

(W. Berton/H. Propp)

As far as we know, the earliest mention of his name in an official German record is in a "Petition for Permission to Settle" in the Kreis Ragnit of East Prussia. Our ancestor and one Mosis Jonoszowitz, dated Berlin jointly signed this petition, April 8, 1707. The petition states that they are now living in Jurenburg also known as Georgenburg and Jurbarkas in Lithuania with their families, only two (Prussian) miles from the Prussian border. They further state that they have been fortunate in that G-d has blessed them with substantial fortunes, but, due to increasing Muscovite (Russian) influence in the area, they are faced with absolute ruin unless their petition is granted. Furthermore, they indicate that the chief of the Kreis Ragnit, the Count (Burggraf and Graf) Von Dohna, knows their families, as well as the surrounding circumstances. They further petition that they be permitted to build an inn and a small brewery on an abandoned parcel of land. On April 11, 1707, the Berlin government, over the signature of King Frederick, requests a report from the local government in regards to the Petition. The report is promptly written, signed by a Count, whose name cannot be deciphered. The handwriting of the report leaves a lot to be desired. There s some indication that our ancestor was an 'Arrendator" in Jurburg, generally an influential and rewarding position. The 'Ruin" to which Pincas refers in his petition may be a fear of loss of this rewarding appointment. On May 30, 1707, the head of the Ragnit district is ordered to admit the two petitioners and our family petitioner probably moved to Prussia sometime in 1707. Nothing further could be found about the other petitioner, Mosis Jonoszowitz.

Unfortunately, the petition does not contain any particular information about our ancestor, when and where he was born, or the names and ages of his wife and children. From what we learn about him subsequently, it would seem that he was born about 1660 to 1670, although it is impossible to say whether he was born in this area. The

Petition also indicates that he had a wife and children at that time. Thus far, despite greater openness in Eastern Europe, the writer has been unable to find any documents that might have some additional information.

A family tradition; has it that our ancestors Here given special permission to settle in the area because they helped someone of importance flee across the border during the thirty Year War. As the Thirty Year War ended in 1648, the family member who extended that help would have to be born by about 1630, and consequently would be 78 I/ears old at the time the license was granted. This essentially rules out Pincas Isakowitz, who emerges as a much younger man from the remaining documents, and, to date, nothing has come to light that refers to an ancestor of Pincas, which would substantiate this tradition.

Another tradition tells us that; it was the son of the Great Elector (Grosse Kurfuerst) of Brandenburg who was saved by our ancestor while he was fleeing from the Russians, possibly during the Nordic Wars. His son, Frederick (1657-1713) had himself crowned in 1701 in the city of Königsberg as King Frederick 1st in Prussia and the coronation ceremony was the occasion when our ancestor received his reward/award.

Actually, the admission of Pincas Isacowitz to Prussia was in line with then current policy. As a consequence of previous wars, the area was economically depressed and the authorities authorized and encouraged the immigration of a limited number of Jews who were willing to settle in the small towns or in the countryside and who possessed capital and/or needed skills which would be beneficial to the economic developments. Pincas easily fits into this category, because at that time he was a man of means and he probably possessed certain business skills, which were in demand, and, therefore, we do not need a story or some extraordinary feat to explain his admittance to Prussia.

What was unusual, however, was the fact that he was given permission to buy a parcel of land, with "Koelmisch" rights, because Jewish land ownership in the countryside with those rights was, at that time, exceedingly rare. A possible explanation for the unusual land ownership might be found in Pincas' relationship to the district chief, the Count von Dohna. As a practical matter, he gave the Count as a character reference when he applied in Berlin for permission to settle in the Ragnit area. We may, therefore, surmise that he had discussed this with the Count, and had the Count's permission, and was fairly sure what kind of endorsement he would receive from the Count. This seems to indicate that there had been some prior dealings between the parties, which could have been of a commercial nature, since Pincas was an influential businessman on the Lithuanian side of the border. Or, Pincas may indeed have helped either the Count or a friend or relative of the Count to flee across the border as family tradition has it, and was rewarded later with permission to buy the parcel of land for the inn. The absence of corroborating archival material can be explained by the lesser importance of the Count as compared to the Elector's son.

In any event, Pincas received permission in 1708 to build an inn in Schmalleningien. He paid for the property out of his own means, although loans were available for that purpose. He was extensively engaged in the import trade and, in addition, in 1710, he bought the inn in Schillehnen, on the other side of the Memel River. For reasons that are not clear, he suffered a number of financial setbacks, and, by the year 1720, he seemed to be barely holding his own. At the time of his death, which occurred, either late in 1722 or early in 1723, he was in debt to creditors in Tilsit and Königsberg and, at the very least, his estate had liquidity problems.

Pincas' immediate family consisted of his Wife, who, incidentally, survives him by about 25 years, and his children. His wife, and later widow, is mentioned quite often in the Berman records, but only as "wife" or, after his death, as "the widow of the deceased Jew, Pincas". There are two exceptions. The "General Tabelle" (Osfol 15361) mentions a *Chaya Pincassin* as owning the two inns. While ending -in can denote widow of', it is more generally used to denote "daughter of' and, therefore, it is not clear whether Chaya is the widow, or the daughter as some have thought. However, in a tabulation of inns with "koelmisch rights" (Osfol 15183-Koelmische-Kruege, p.226)). This matter is cleared up by the statement the Jewess, Chaya Pincassin, innkeeper, with koelmisch rights in *Schmalleningien*, Jurisdiction *Kasigiehmen*, received her inn license due to an agreement negotiated by the district chief of Ragnit, the Count von Dohna, and her deceased husband Pincas Isakowitz".

It is even more difficult to establish the number, names, and ages of the children. In the early 18th century, the authorities were only interested in the number of children at home at the time the count was taken, and how many were under and over he age of 12. In the case of Pincas, it is a fair assumption that he had no sons, or at least none that survived to adulthood, because his inns passed subsequently to his son-in-law. Also, since various documents speak of children, we may assume that he was blessed with at least some daughters. One daughter is identified in a 1750 list as Feige Pincas, and she and her husband take over the Schmalleningien Inn. A 1768 sales contract mentions Pincas and Lewin Schlomocka, the grandchildren of Pincas Isakowitz, which leads us to believe that there was a second daughter who married Mr. Schlomocka. Pincas might have had other children, some who died at a tender age, but nothing was found in the records.

We further know that another Isakowitz, possibly Pincas' brother, lived for a while in Schmalleningien, but had left the area by 1720. The social life of the family must have been rather bleak by modern standards. From 1708 until 1720, they were essentially the only Jewish family in the area. A second family moved into a neighboring village just a short time before the 1720 report was written. The Prussian side of the border was lacking facilities. Jewish religious services were unavailable, in part because there were insufficient adult Jews available to form a minyan, and in part because the inn license forbade, specifically, the holding of religious services at the inn. This is surprising because the patents of several Jews gave them permission to hold private services within their homes, unless in this instance it was feared that it would attract coreligionists' from across the border. Therefore, Pincas and his family had to attend services on the Lithuanian side, and, since a head tax had to be paid on the occasion of a border crossing, it was not only inconvenient, but also expensive. The immediate area also lacked a burial ground, and the dead had to be taken to Lithuania for burial, namely to Jurbarkas.

Schooling was also unavailable and Pincas' children had to attend school in Jurbarkas or Wilkowischken. Later on (1734), a private tutor resided at the inn, possibly for the grandchildren. The 1720 report indicates that by 1720 Pincas' children were still attending school, and that, as yet, none of them was married, which seems to indicate that Pincas was probably born after 1670. He also was a protected Jew, although his "Schutzbrieff" (letter of protection) could not be located in the archives.

As was pointed out earlier, the 70 questions in this questionnaire were of a standard format, and the local authorities were required to answer them. The tenor of the questions was strongly influenced by the experience the Prussian government had with the <i>Königsberg Jewish community</i>. That community was split into various factions who quarreled often and violently and it was not unusual for the police to be called to the synagogue to break up fisticuffs, and restore order. From the answers, it emerges that Pincas never gave rise to complaints by his Christian neighbors, nor did he fight and quarrel with other Jews, because, as the answers indicate, there were none.

Now, to his business ventures, the best Cemented of which is the inn in *Schmalleningien*. Application for this license probably sometime in 1707. The Surliest document mentioned, of which we so have no copy, is a "Rescript" dated Königsberg, February, 10 1708, wherein the Royal Court directs the Königsberg officials to enter into a contract with Pincas Isakowitz pertaining to the construction and aeration of the inn. A "Rescript" is an order from one level of government to a lower level government, frequently used within the East Prussian administration. This contract AS subsequently drafted by government Vials and signed on March 13, 1708, on behalf of the government, by the Count Fredrick Christoph von Dohna.

The contract grants to Pincas an abandoned parcel of land with "koelmisch" rights. Koelmisch" rights were those rights granted a landowner, which were granted under e legal code of the city of Kulm, which de was adopted subsequently in East Prussia, and was the law of the land there for about two centuries. The code of Kulm was patterned after the legal code of the city of Magdeburg, and essentially gave a perpetual lease to the grantee, his heirs and assigns, as long as the agreed upon lease, money is paid. The heirs, as well as any buyers, stand, so to speak, "in the shoes" of the original grantee, and have the same rights and duties. According to a searcher, who located most of the documents in the East Prussian archives, is the only case known to him, where Jews were granted real estate with koelmisch rights.

The contract then lists two other inns, which are in the area, and also states that the owner of these inns has no objections to the granting of this license. The agreed upon lease money is 60 Thalers per year, payable semiannually in September and March. The payment of this lease money, however, exempts him from paying several other taxes, which are listed by name in the contract. Pincas is authorized to build on this parcel the inn proper, as well as any other buildings which are necessary in the conduct of the business, such as a brew house and storage sheds. Besides the operation of the inn, he is authorized, pursuant to the contract, to brew beer and to engage in the costermonger {Hoeker} trade. The contract also places several restrictions on the operation. Namely, he may not deal in stolen goods, nor may he give shelter to Polish refugees, and he is forbidden to conduct any other business which is not specifically authorized in the contract. Two restrictions, which are not business related, prohibit the use of the inn as an assembly place for other Jews, and for the conduct of public religious services. Violations of any of the above restrictions could have resulted in the loss of the license. The above contract was then forwarded to the Royal Court in Berlin for approval (Konfirmation). The Royal Court, over the signature of King Frederick I, approved the contract as of April 25, 1708, repeating briefly the main provisions of the contract, but reserving specifically the right to make changes in the contract provisions. The approval took place only six weeks after the contract was submitted by the Königsberg office, and, when we consider that the contract traveled by horse and wagon for about 350 miles to Berlin, the time compares very favorably with today's pace.

Pincas Isakowitz was also engaged in the export-import trade in a substantial way as evidenced by a blanket receipt given him for the customs, due to the Grand Duchy of Lithuania. The receipt, dated December 1708, in Jorbork was executed by one Miccel Staislaw Suzin, the superintendent of customs for the Grand Duchy, and certifies that Pincas Isakowitz had paid the customs owed for the past year. The receipt was written in Polish. A receipt of this type indicates that Pincas was an important man.

Two years later, in 1710, Pincas acquired the inn in Schillehnen, which is located on the opposite (southern) bank of the Memel River. Traffic across the river was by ferry and during his life theme was one ferry daily. The parcel of land, on which the Schillehnen was located, was by the king to Johann Bulbeck, the licensee, for 150 Thalers, on November 24, 1708, who in turn erected the inn, and other buildings thereon, and sold it all, including unused lumber still on the site. The contract contains what is basically a warranty clause, similar to the ones found in English real estate deeds. The inn was apparently built on a parcel of 6 Morgen (3.8 acres) because an excerpt of the Land Kataster (real estate register) of 1748 indicates that the heirs of Pincas own that amount of land.

The next official mention of Pincas known to us is the aforementioned 1720 Judenliste (Jews List). By now, the business affairs seem to have taken a turn for the worst, rough the reason is not clear. According this document, his involvement in any kind trade is quite limited now and the officials indicate that he has only limited funds at his disposal. He still owns the two inns and he employs an unspecified number of Polish nationals to assist in the brewing of beer and distillation of brandy. Permission for the operation of a still was locally granted and, therefore, not mentioned in the original contracts

The year is now 1723 and Pincas is dead. He passes either towards the end of 1722 or the beginning of 1723. He leaves a widow and at least two children behind, along with the two aforementioned inns, and a sizable indebtedness, which must have been a source of serious concern to his family and placed them into a difficult situation. We might note that it is difficult to determine how bad his situation was in 1720, and again in 1723. A tax levied from Jews in those days was oppressive and, therefore, incentive to minimize one's income and assets. The indebtedness precipitated a legal and administrative proceeding and our knowledge of the facts were obtained from the documentation of these proceedings.

It appears that Pincas' estate was liquid, her than insolvent. That is, his assets exceeded his liabilities, but there was sufficient cash on hand to pay off his creditors. The creditors, who were Christian businessmen from Tilsit and Königsberg, petition King Frederick Wilhelm 1st, son of Frederick 1st, who granted the original license and died in 1713, stating that the widow owes them sizable but unspecified amount money, and their chances of being paid are doubtful. That the Inn in Schmalleningien should be foreclosed in satisfaction of the debts. However, they also state that the widow and the heirs have been very diligent in the operation, attracting additional business from amongst the travelers. That there is a reasonable chance that they will be paid over a period of time. We should note that the petitioners do ask for foreclosure of the inn in Schillehnen as additional security for the repayment, and, since they also have a few good words to say about the inn's operation, it is possible that foreclosure at this time was their real objective. Most likely this petition was required to preserve their rights in case the installment payment of the debt did not proceed as planned by making an official record of the debts owed. It is also possible that the petition was used to establish a superior lien on the property, in case there were other creditors as yet still unidentified. This petition was filed on March 28, 1723, in Tilsit. The widow filed her answer to this petition, which is rather lengthy, and seeks a variety of relief, on March 30, 1723, in Königsberg. It deals with several matters, which we shall discuss, in more detail:

The King had issued an edict the year before, in 1722, expelling all the Jews from the province:

Chaya pleads to be exempted from the edict because:
- *She already lives very close to the border.*
- *She was under the impression that this only applies to Jews who, because of their personal or business conduct, had been the subject of complaints of the Christian neighbors.*
- *Her husband has a considerable investment in the inns and abandoning them would constitute a considerable hardship.*
- *Regardless of economic conditions or other misfortunes, her late husband has regularly paid his lease money of 60 Thalers without fail.*
- *Her late husband's conduct was always exemplary.*

The creditors allege that Pincas Isakowitz owes them a sizable amount of money, and that the inn should be taken from the heirs, although the creditors concede that the present management is good, and there is a chance that they will ultimately be paid.

The widow concedes that the debts are owed, but argues that loss of the inn would constitute an extreme hardship for her and her family. She implies that this can be avoided and the creditors satisfied, if the inn is left to her and she is permitted to pay in installments.

Chaya also asks for interim relief for herself and her family, while the two petitions are under consideration by the authorities. It seems that shortly after her husband's death, the Sheriff (Wachtmeister) from Ragnit and several soldiers (Heiducken) paid visit to her inn, and, after partaking of considerable quantities of food and drink without payment, took several of her possessions with them to Ragnit, impounded the remainder of possessions. They then chased her and her family across the border into Lithuania. It is not clear whether this action was done pursuant to the king's edict or pursuant to the creditor's petition. We are o in the dark as to how she managed to enter Prussia.

She asks the king to have this matter investigated, so that the king can see that her story is not unfounded, and that his civil servants misbehaved. However, along more practical lines, she asks that she be permitted to stay at the inn while the whole matter is being investigated and considered, since Passover, which lasts eight days starts the next Shabbat. Furthermore, she asks that her articles be returned to her, those impounded on her premises, as well as those that have been removed.

She receives temporary permission on April 1723 from the Königsberg authorities to remain at the inn and, on April 23, 1723, from Potsdam, the Königsberg office forwards both petitions to Berlin on April 25, together with a letter asking for instructions to how the matter should be decided. The final decision was given in early 1724, however it could not be found in the archives.

Chaya apparently manages to pay off the indebtedness because she remains in control of the inns for about a quarter of a century. She is not listed in the 1748 tabulation, so we may assume that she died early 1748 or in late 1747. In the 1730's I 1740's, she is occasionally mentioned in connection with the inns. In the 1734 - 1740 period, the list indicates, besides Chaya there was in the inn, a hired hand, a maid, a Jewish school teacher, and one Schmuel Anschelowitz with his wife and a child over 12 years of age. In the 1739 "Generaltabelle", she is mentioned as owning both inns with a valid license for Schmalleningien and an invalid license for Schilleknen. The 1742 tax tables show, at the Schmalleningken Inn, besides Chaya, two children under twelve, possibly grandchildren, two maids, a school teacher and a shepherd. In the 1736 - 1747 period, a Samuel Schlomocka from Königsberg operated a tannery in Schmalleningien, and we will discuss our relationship with the Schlomockas in the later chapter.

Chaya seems to have been a remarkable person. Faced with a rather dismal financial situation at the time of her husband's death. Responsible for the well being of two or more children, who at the time were either adolescents or young adults, she did not despair, but took energetic action to solve her problems and was ultimately successful.

Pincus' next child was a son, Israel Pincus, born December 7, 1817 in Schmalleningien. Nothing is known about his youth or schooling. It is quite likely that he helped his father with the operation of the Schmalleningien Inn. In 1850, he is listed as a "Krugpaechter" (inn lessee) on the birth certificate of one of his sons. In a "Gewerbesteuerrolle" (tradesmen's tax list) for the year 1855 (Osfol 15832), he is listed as an innkeeper, and the volume of his business is described as "recht bedeutend" (quite significant). The same trades list also indicates that he was engaged in the "Hoeker" (costermonger) trade, the business volume being described as "mitten (medium), and we saw in previous generations that these occupations always went hand in hand.

Another source of information about Israel is the partially surviving synagogue records, and, from those, we learn that he and several others signed a petition to hire a full-time religious teacher, (Rep. 12, Abt. II NR 232). He also signed the petition to form a regional (Kreis) synagogue on February 1, 1855, and he is one of the members invited to the first congregational meeting on March 6, 1856, and is elected to the board of Governors on February 7, 1857.

In 1858, according to the "Praestationstabellen" (tax tables), he signs the inn over to Baer Isaak Berlowitz, from another branch of the family, and we assume that he leaves Schmalleningien then. We further assume that he moves directly to Goldap (Kreis Goldap), where two and possibly three of his children are born. An 1864 wedding license of one of his daughters gives his residence as Goldap, and lists his occupation as merchant, however there is no indication what kind of merchandise he dealt in, and how successful his business was. He subsequently moved to the City of Memel, the year is unknown, where his two oldest sons lived. He died there February 15, 1881. How he earned his living there is also unknown.

A direct descendent of Pincas Isakowitz, an Israel Pincas Berlowitz, who was born in December of 1817 in Smalininkai, married Jenta who was from Shkudvil, Kovno Guberniya, Russia, which is about 35 kilometers from Smalininkai and across the Lithuanian (Russian) boarder. Israel and Jenta had twelve children. Israel and Jenta also operated the same inn in Smalininkai, East Prussia as Pincas Isakowitz originally purchased in the previous century.

Israel was married and there is conflicting evidence as to the correct name of his wife. In the birth certificate of one of his sons, her name is listed as Jante Hirsch. A picture taken a few years before her death is inscribed as "Jante, daughter of Zalman (Salomon)". The notes of the late Hirsch Berlowitz give her name as Jente, while, in the extensive notes of one of her granddaughters, she appears as Henriette Propp, and, last, but not least, the inscription on her tombstone reads "Henriette Berlowitz nee Salomon". I would be inclined to say at her real name was Jente Hirsch, that she assumed the names of Johanna and Henriette unofficially as secular names, as she moved from place to place, and became more assimilated (in another branch we have the transformation of Feige to Fanny to Fay). Her father's name probably was Salomon or some variant thereof. Her mother's name incidentally was Chaya and a daughter was named after her. Since none her sons were named after him, we may, assume that he was still alive when his grandchildren were born. I have no explanation why the name Propp* appears in this context. After Jenta's husband's death, she moved from Memel to Elbing to live with one of her sons and she died there on January 7, 1903. Israel and Jante had 12 children!

In the Propp original family tree written by Louis Arne who was born in Shkudvil in 1864, the information contained was a Jenta Propp, daughter of Hirsch and Chaya Propp married a Berlowitz from Smalininkai, East Prussia." It showed three children all of which were parts of the twelve that shown on the Berlowitz family tree. Jente was born on December 15, 1817 in Shkudvil, which is the Kowno or Kovno Guberniya. When we combined, Mr. Berton's information and the information from the Propp family tree the relationships and a name becomes clear.

Note: Concerning German Jews:

In the 18th century, there was an economic revival but most Jews remained quite poor. Most of them lived in what is now called Germany and was then divided into small Kingdoms. (about 300, 000 Jews)

The Jews became an important part in this revival, because of their experiences in business. Those Jew's, who were involved in this role, were given special standing and were called "Schutzjuden" (protected Jew's). For which they had to pay a so-called Schutzgeld. The amount of this would differ, depending how many Jews were needed or wanted in the Kingdom. Their rights though differed too. Every kingdom (about 300) had their own dictum):

- *The right could be only for the individual*
- *The right could be for a group.*
- *It could be hereditary.*

And here it comes, it could be only given to the oldest son. In this case, it meant that the rest had to leave the kingdom. For instance, In Schwetzingen the following rule existed. Married children were allowed to live another year with their parents. After that they could become a "Schutzjude" if the oldest son owned, a certain wealth. The others have to own twice or triple as much as the oldest son to be able to a come a "Schutzjude". Of course most did not have this and had to leave. This was exactly what the king or prince wanted. These rules were explicitly to prevent too many Jews of settling in a kingdom.

The aforementioned history of the Berlowitz and even though it only tangentially affects the Propp family is included to point out not only the difficulty in genealogy work, but some of the great strides that it is possible to make. This is an excellent example of genealogical research.

David and Rochel (Propp) Berlowitz Family - Smalininkai, East Prussia, C: 1897
Back Row: Bessel, Selma, Arno, Max, Martha (Propp) Berlowitz, Adolph, Anna
Front Row: Clara Propp, Rochel (Propp) Berlowitz, Anna Propp, David Berlowitz

Martha Berlowitz Propp

*Max (Meir) Propp,
son of Itzig*

Circa 1850, East Prussia

ELBING.
Neuer Wall str 13

Jenta bat Hirsh Prop Berlowitz

The Adventurer, an Autobiography of Yankel Propp of Shkudvil

In fact, I was not born in Shkudvil, but actually in Raseiniai, as in Shkudvil there was no professional midwife, and also because my mother did not want to live in a small town, but rather in the city. And so, after she gave birth to me she remained in Raseiniai for six years, at her parent's house. By the way, she didn't like my father's family, especially his arrogant and dominating mother, who came from the famous family of Ha'Gra, (descendants of the Vilna Gaon), and also my father's brother, Naftel (Naftali), who was a stiff and very formal man. My father had promised her they would leave Shkudvil but he didn't keep his promise. In Raseiniai, I began studying in Cheder at the age of 4 or 5. I remember how I amazed the Jewish community with my "Epicuros" Question: "If God is all powerful and created the world, and that with just one word; why did "He" get tired and need a whole day, the seventh, to rest?" I arrived at Shkudvil at the age of six. There I studied in the elementary Hebrew school (as the law demanded) and in the afternoon also in a Cheder, and then, when a little older in "The Little Yeshiva". At the same Yeshiva, before my time, also studied the Shlapobersky's and Rav Shakh had studied there.. (By the way do you know that Michel Shlapobersky died, of old age, last Rosh Ha'Shana?). When I reached the age of Bar

Mitzvah, the Head of the Yeshiva announced, that the Yeshiva had done all it could for me and that I had to move on to higher Yeshiva. However, I was an only son and my mother was very worried about me, and she wouldn't agree that I move away, in her view, so "far" from the house, to either Telz or to Slobodka. So I was sent to Raseiniai, where there was the Hebrew Gymnasium, "Tarbut" ("culture") and there, as they say, "I came under some bad influence."

There, in Raseiniai, I also participated in the Jewish Scouts movement, that in time became a leading educational institution in the Zionist movement, which aimed at the realization of Zionism, at Aliyah and towards an honest and cooperative life and was known as the "Ha-Shomar Ha-Tzair" movement.

In 1930, I completed, with honors, my studies at the Gymnasium and was faced with the question: what next? This was a dilemma. Like all Jewish mothers in Eastern Europe, my mother wanted me to be a doctor, but the Lithuanian University in Kovno placed quotas on the number of Jews who could go to medical school. Places were set aside for graduates of public schools, that is, the Lithuanians, and the Gymnasium was considered a private school, and so its graduates had to register in another department and then transfer after a year to medicine, or go abroad to study medicine.

A number of factors helped me to solve this problem, among them being the sickness and death of my parents. There was also the objections of the leadership of the Movement to medical studies, which would have required a complete personal commitment, and meant I would have had to spend all of my time at the University. While there were departments where one didn't even have to attend the lectures, because students took notes in shorthand and wrote every single word the professor said (including his jokes...), had them copied and sold them. Thus ended my medical career and began my activities in the Movement, a broad beginning that centered in Shkudvil and then spread to all of Lithuania, and in 1935 I left Shkudvil for good. Along with my activities in the Movement I continued my studies at the University and over the next ten years, I completed studies in Law, Economics, Philosophy, and halfway through Education. During my university years I was the General Secretary of Ha-Shomer Ha-Tzair. I also served as a foreign correspondent for the Daily Worker Newspaper. I wrote under different names as if I was located in London rather than in Kaunus where I actually lived. I lived in Kovno, on a commune near the head leadership.

It is said, there is nothing stranger than reality itself. I took upon myself learning halfway through the Education course for Kibbutz life in Israel, since I considered that my three other professions would be worthless in Israel, (except perhaps for accounting). However, when the Soviets pounced on Lithuania in 1940, Zionist activities were discouraged as being anti-Soviet. Education turned out to be for me, the one job I was needed for, or be unemployed (since the Soviet government was the only employer, and I, as a Zionist, was not exactly "beloved" by them). I got, unexpectedly, a position as a teacher in a Government Gymnasium, (Lithuanian, as they had disbanded the Hebrew Gymnasiums) in the city of Vilkovisk. (There, also my wife also found a job and taught sewing in the vocational government school, previously of the "Ort" chain.) I also became a lecturer in Law at the national university. And that's it, in spite of my Zionism: the Jewish saying "when you need a thief you bring him from the hanging tree" came true with me.

A combination of fortunate causes, opportunities properly exploited, initiative dexterity and a bit of luck: On the second day after the war between Nazi Germany and the USSR broke out, we got on a train from Vilkovisk to the Kovno station, exactly a half an hour before the last train pulled out. Six days later we arrived a few hundred kilometers away in east Moscow. We were saved. But the Nazi army went from strength to strength and arrived at the gates of Moscow. Although I had never studied military strategy, I thought that Hitler could not occupy Moscow but would only circle it and go on toward the east to the Ural Mountain area where the Soviet military industrial complex was concentrated. Their army could have executed that maneuver easily with the help of the local population, who did not hide their desire for the arrival of the Germans, thinking, "they'll undo the Kholkozes (collective farms) and open the Churches." But the German Army was obsessed with their own power and ignorance. They probably had never read Tolstoy's "War and Peace" on the 1812 campaign of Napoleon. They waited outside Moscow to receive the army at the Kremlin, but the army of Ponpilov disappointed them. We, of course, did not witness the foolishness of Hitler's General Staff and decided to precede the arrival of the Nazis and leave the city and Russia and to travel to Soviet Asia, Uzbekistan. There, it seemed, we would be further away from and more secure from the German dangers. This was actually an illusion, because if the Nazis had succeeded in getting through to the Caucasus, the danger would have been very close. I also harbored the hope that from there, there would be a better chance to arrive at my final destination: the Land of Israel, (this too was an illusion).

Along the way we paid a very heavy price, our first child, a daughter, who was born in the Ural Mountain city of Ulyanovisk (Now Simbirsk, the city of Lenin's birth which bore his original name), died from the difficulty of the journey and from hunger when we arrived in Uzbekistan. All the time she cried softly and her crying remains with me until now, in my innermost thoughts and will never leave me until I draw my last breath.

While there, in east Moscow, the limits, and the worthlessness of my diplomas became clear, due to the unusual circumstances and especially my lack of knowledge of Russian, and I had to engage in unskilled physical labor, which was physically very tough. On the other hand the importance of having a craft increased: my wife managed to find work quickly in her profession (sewing). We got to Uzbekistan, after not a few hardships along the way, at the beginning of January 1942, and by chance we came upon a tungsten mine. Here also, as far as my occupation went, the situation was the same, hard physical labor (here even harder than before), half of it underground, and under near starvation conditions. (I thought that if not for my "exercise" on the Commune in Kovno, it is doubtful whether I would have survived). Also perhaps, thanks to a break I got when I became an assistant coachman, another respectable profession, easier physically, which I tried. This made things better. Here I need to clarify: it is taken for granted that horses are stupid, but "my" horses were "smart" enough. Because their coachman was not so experienced they didn't have to obey him! When I would pull the reins hard and command them to walk, they wouldn't move, and vice versa-they would go despite my orders: when I would urge them to go faster they would slow down, and vice versa. Other than that, I owe them thanks: they overturned my wagon with hay and I injured my leg and had to lay in the hospital in the nearby town where I read books that I had previously read in Hebrew or Yiddish but now, of course, I read them in Russian. In addition there were Russian patients lying next to me and in this way I became fluent in Russian.

With my return to the mine from such an excellent "school" for learning Russian I took my first steps towards progressing in my career in the mine. I began as a statistician and was quickly appointed manager of the economic management department and won such recognition in that position that after the war, I was promoted to the upper management of the corporation ('trust' in Russian) of all the tungsten and colored and precious metal mines in Uzbekistan. However, not for long: not because I failed at that job, but on the contrary, I was promoted to a higher position to salvage from chronic failure, the third largest tungsten mine in the entire Soviet Union.

That mine was opened just before the war and in those days they didn't calculate how much tungsten they mined or how much it cost, since it was crucial for hardening the steel. After the war the need for tungsten did not decrease. It was necessary to rebuild and replace war equipment that had deteriorated or been destroyed. There was also a great need for money to invest in repairing the destruction of the war, and it was impossible to accept that such a big and important mine would not continue to operate on a large scale, since the loss of ceasing production would run in the millions. They sent a new manager to the mine along with the "Three Musketeers". (By the way, all of us; Zamora, Marshak, and I were Jewish). I understood quickly that the weak point was in organization and management of personnel according to the traditional Soviet routine that was viewed by Stalin as a "sacred cow" (the Stakhovist methods, within

147

strict norms, etc). It was necessary to "slaughter" these sacred cows and change to other methods of organization that were more rational, but I knew that there is nothing more difficult or more dangerous than to harm the "sacred cows" in a totalitarian regime. So I decided to go at it in a Jewish way, that is "With God's Help" (in Hebrew or "with help of the Name") to keep the old (Soviet) names, but give them a new content... Fortunately, my friends on the team understood this "trick" and cooperated completely with me, and the results were outstanding.

As it turned out, that year of my management position brought about the stabilization of production, and over the next years even an increase in production and substantial profits of millions of rubles. Although the profits did not belong to us personally, we did enjoy a good life; as they say in Yiddish, "we had wealth and honor." Still, after eight years, despite the success of the mines and the financial rewards and my being treated well by colleagues, local institutions, and even higher authorities, I felt distressed as if I were performing "idol worship," and losing my worldview to move to a Kibbutz in Eretz Israel, and was very concerned about the future of my children in the face of assimilation. I waited for the day when I could leave all that (the "Shmatz-Grove," as the Jewish head doctor of the firm defined it, and who called me the "adventurer" when he found out I was leaving).

And this day came in the form of the Soviet-Polish agreement (Gomulka) on the rights of Polish citizens still in the Soviet Union to return home. We weren't among them, but by paying money we became one of them... In August 1957 we crossed over the Polish border. At the station on the Polish side I filled out a questionnaire and said that Moshe Propp, (Son of Todres Propp), an Israeli, was my father, in order to expedite our Aliyah to Israel through "Family Reunion." But this gentleman refused to issue me a confirmation and an invitation to the Polish immigration officials, and thus we ended up spending more than a year in Poland, and finally arrived in Eretz Israel in October 1958. At the Haifa port, a taxi from one of the largest Kibbutzim, "Afikim," was waiting for us, and we were absorbed there happily, even though we were over the age limit for joining the Kibbutz. Unfortunately, especially for the children, who loved the kibbutz, we had to leave because of my wife's health. We continued to be welcome guests at the kibbutz, but we moved to Jerusalem. For seven years I worked in the Labor Department, and for nineteen years at the Ministry of Health as Manager of Internal Inspections. At the same time, from 1967 to 1988, I had a radio program dealing with economic issues in Hebrew and Yiddish. I also published columns in the following newspapers: the Dvar, Revaon LaCalcala, Min-Hayasod and Beshaar. They were economic articles.

If you are interested, I have a son, born in 1945, and his name is Victor. As a child, there, Vic wanted to be a geologist, but here in Eretz Israel, there are no mineral deposits, (except for a few in Timna) and so that was not a profession which is much in demand, and since he isn't much inclined toward office work, he studied surveying. He now lives in a rented apartment right across from me; he ha left his home and wife and is now in the process of getting a divorce. He has a son and a daughter, and he Hebraized his family name to Ramon. In his marriage he repeated my mistake, but in reverse. I married a simple, uneducated seamstress who didn't even finish high school, not out of a lack of talent for studying, but because she was born into a poor family, and not out of youth loves, in every respect there were differences. With my son, his wife was more educated than he and also it turned out, she didn't love him.

I have a daughter, born in 1951, named Aliza, divorced, she is a nurse and lives in Rishon Le-Tzion, on 17 Vinik Street, under her married name Shavli (which she keeps for the sake of her two daughters). As you can see, marriage didn't agree with my family members; as for my marriage, it was a chapter unto itself, and an experienced and gifted writer could use it as material for a best selling tragic-comic novel, I won't bother going into details.

I received your book but I can't study it due to my health and lack of understanding of English. It is clear that you have spent a great deal of time and effort investigating the Propps, and this is very praiseworthy, but no list of human deeds can be complete. Regarding Naftali's wife, Rivka, who was the daughter of the Rabbi of Memel, it seems to me that I wrote you that they also had a son, named Ari, who died in the Holocaust. If I am not mistaken, he was 13 years old. I do not remember if I mentioned him to you. In Shkudvil there was also a family by the name of Ya'abetz whose son Tzvi was Teddy Leib's father's partner in South Africa. I don't recall the name of the oldest daughter, but the younger one, a little older than me, was named Aida. She lives here in Jerusalem, I have her phone number, however I can't read it, my grandson wrote it down in big numbers, but another man answered, and said that this was always his number. You might try Teddy who has contact with Aida or maybe he can tell you what happened to her (if Aida is still alive she is close to 88 years old).

You asked about Itzig Propp, there was nothing really exciting about him. What he did after the war I do not know, since I did not return to Lithuania. Instead I traveled directly from Uzbekistan to Poland and then to Israel.

By the way, your list totally neglects, it seems to me, the Tavrig branch of the (extended) family. To my regret, I also know little. I just know of two families: Dr. Ussim (Yosef) Shapira, whose wife that was from the Propp family, named Helena, they had two daughters. The older one was married to a wealthy businessman, Bat Brig, and she graduated from the conservatory in Berlin, (I don't remember her name). The second and younger one married a well-known tycoon, the Soviet oil importer, Plakovsky; the husband's name of the older sister was Berkovitz.

The second family was Dr. Stolov I don't remember his first name since I rarely visited them. He was a dentist and an enthusiastic communist. There were always arguments between us and I didn't need dental care since I was still young. His wife was also part of the Propp family and they had two daughters. The older one completed her studies and the second one, completed dentistry studies. The older daughter married an electricity engineer (he studied in Liege, Belgium). The Germans killed their father. The women, by chance, survived, and eventually immigrated in the 1930's to Biro-Bizan and then to Moscow. The husband of the older daughter, was a Rabinovitz. He was an excellent engineer, because he was promoted to manager of an electricity station in Moscow. In 1956, after some time, I visited Rivka several times. In 1957 on the way to Poland we had to pass through Moscow and I wanted my wife and children to get to know this city. Since the Rabinovitz's were away at Krim they let us stay in their apartment. When the war broke out the mother was visiting her daughters and stayed alive.

And now I have arrived at the tenth and last page of this letter, which, if I am not mistaken, one can say is more than a letter, it is almost an abbreviated autobiography of one of the Propps. And maybe, even, it is a text of separation from the adventure, which all of us are thrown into, unintentionally, and that is at times wonderful and at times frightening and that is called life... Now seems to be a time, perhaps too early, of separation, but indeed in a few days on March 15th, I will turn 85 and certainly my time will come, as does that of every living creature, so you can see this letter as a kind of "advance". And in this connection, a request if, of course, you are willing and able: commission a copy of my letter, but without the many mistakes and the repetitions and confusions, and type it in the computer. Previously, when I would type on the typewriter, I would correct the mistakes and the spelling and also the style and other things with white out, but now, to my regret, I can't read what is written.

Listening to the reading of the list of the Propp's, with its different origins and branches for example, you, myself, the Shlapobersky's, etc. I have the feeling that a tiny tribe of the Propp's exists, and if one adds those who probably were not counted I came up with the incredible idea. Indeed, not so easy to realize, to propose that we organize in Israel a meeting of this tribe in order to bring all the Propps together. This way we can all become acquainted with one another, and especially to deepen the relation among the young generation and its offspring to their roots in order that the tribe. not become extinct.

I was happy to receive your last two letters; especially the story of Lybka (or Leon, as you would call him) Bret, regarding his trip to Kelm, along with Itzig (Yitzchak) Propp, that resulted in the two of them being rescued from Hitler's murderers and their nationalist Lithuanian helpers. First of all let me clear up your doubt, the "Yankel" of whom Lybka-Leon speaks, is indeed I; Yankel is me! Yankel is Yaakov in Hebrew just as Itzig is Yitzchak in Hebrew, Chana -Alchanan, Le'ev- Arieh, Yosel - Yosef, Wolf - Ze'ev, and Tevya-Tuvia. From my generation in Shkudvil as far as I remember there was one other Yankel who was known as "Yanketzka". He was the town butcher and was probably also slain with other Jews who lived in Shkudvil.

Yaakov (Yankel) Prop, Jerusalem
The last Propp to live in Skaudville, Lithuania
Written in 1996, Israel

In 1996, in Israel Yankel Propp was still living. He was very old and almost completely blind but you still feel his intellect, he was kind and a humble man who suffer greatly. He remained proud to be a member of the Propp family and I was very honored to able visit with him.

Hank Propp

The Morris Propp Family

Morris Propp, was a manufacturer and philanthropist, in the United States. The son of Ephraim Propp and Rebecca Rose (Nachenson) Propp. He was born at Tobolsk, Russia, May 22, 1884. His father, Ephraim, was well-known Jewish religious teacher, who was born in Shkudvil, (Lithuania) Russia.

Morris Propp, at his son Mortimer's request, wrote the following: "I was born the sixth day of "Sivan" or about May 22, 1884 in the city of Ishim, in the province of Tobolsk (Tobolsk Guberniya). My father was a "shochet" and Rabbi. When I was about two years old, we moved to a little village near Wekolowa called Zavod where there was a vodka distillery owned by a Jewish firm named Murapolsky. Because they employed about a dozen Jews as help, who worked in the office, my father took a position there as a distiller, a shochet, and rabbi of the small Jewish community of the village. Although my Mother had told me that I was less than five years old when we moved from Zavod, she was wondering how I remembered the various things that occurred there. Some of the things I reminded her happened when I was only two years old. The things of which I reminded her of were: "Wekolowa was the nearest village to Zavod where we could buy provisions and other things needed for our household. This village was about five miles away from Zavod. So when we needed anything, my oldest brother, Isaac, who was about fifteen years old would hitch up the horse and buggy and we would drive to Wekolowa. One day he took me along and as he stopped on the way to pick some flowers, the horse became frightened and galloped away with me in the wagon. Poor Isaac ran after us yelling for me to pull the reins. I heard him yell, but did not understand; the horse ran so fast that soon Isaac was out of sight. I was crying bitterly."

The family came to the United States in 1893 and Morris attended public schools in South Norfolk, Connecticut, and in New York City. At the age of fifteen in 1901, he went to work in his sister, Anna Propp Glasgow's, store in New York City, and working from 6:00 A.M. to 11:00 P.M. daily. He then went into business for himself as a house-to-house peddler of various articles, finally making Welsbach gas mantles his chief stock in trade.

Because of his hard work and close economy he accumulated enough money to open a small store of his own at 92 East Broadway, New York City, in 1902. The store sold Welsbach mantles and other lighting accessories and fixtures. Morris developed a considerable trade with peddlers and small merchants who resold merchandise and his business grew steadily, with the increasing use of electrical illumination. Electrical light fixtures and other electrical appliances were quickly added to his line of business. Morris began to manufacture electrical specialties. As a result of his intelligent and extensive advertising, Propp products soon acquired an established reputation of high quality in the electrical appliance's field.

In 1913 Louis Propp, a younger brother of Morris, who had been employed by him for about six years, became a partner in the business, which operated under the name of the M. Propp Company. The brothers, then added to their line of manufactured goods, high grade Christmas tree lighting outfits. This branch of the business then developed to such proportions that the M. Propp Company became the largest producers in the country of equipment for the decoration of Christmas trees with miniature electric lights and for use on other festive occasions. Morris Propp, more than any other person, popularized the practice of displaying electric lighting on Christmas trees and in doing so, created an important new element in decorative arts. Besides the new electrical lights contributing to greatly to improved safety by fire prevention which further popularized these wonderful and beautiful lighting systems.

In 1929, Morris sold his business to the Noma Electric Corporation, previously organized by many of his leading competitors in the industry, the M. Propp Company becoming a subsidiary of Noma Electric Corporation. Noma Electric Corporation became the dominating factor in this industry, doing at one time 80 percent of the country's Christmas tree lighting business and distributing 90 per cent of the miniature Mazda lamps. He had previously been a large Noma stockholder and as a result of the merger, the brothers acquired another large block of shares in the Noma Electric Corporation. With these holdings and other stock purchased in the open market they eventually held the controlling interest in the Noma Electric Corporation. Morris Propp became Noma Corporation's President in 1931, serving as in that position until the time of his death. He was also President of the 524 Broadway Corp. and the Ephraim Realty Corp.

Morris made a comfortable fortune upon which he freely gave for contributions to charitable, religious and other worthy causes. For years his donations for benevolent purposes equaled or exceeded a fifth of his total income. In 1930, Morris established the Propp Foundation to "aid and assist charitable and religious corporations, religious schools, institutions that aided and supported orphans, the aged, the sick, and the poor." The foundation has maintained scholarships and student aid funds in schools of orthodox and secular collegiate learning and gave aid to hundreds of different causes, among which is the publication of several masterpieces of religious compilation.

Morris Propp had a winning personality and enjoyed the highest reputation for character, ability and moral character. His career from an immigrant boy to the leader of an important industry added an absorbing chapter to the romance of American business. At the same time he created a decorative art form with electric lights.

Morris was married Nov. 29, 1908, to Anna, daughter of Leo Cohen, of New York City, and had three sons: Mortimer J., Seymour and Ephraim Propp. Morris passed away in New York City on February 22, 1933. Mortimer Propp served as the treasurer and a director for the Noma Electrical Company. Morris' son's divested their interests in the Noma Electric Corporation in 1939. They then invested in the Quincy Mining Company and joined the board of directors of that Company in 1946. Seymour

Propp served as vice president and treasurer from 1949 to 1976. He became Quincy's President in 1977, shortly after the death of its previous President, W. Parsons Todd, the late Mayor of Morristown, New Jersey.

Around 1982, the Propp family became founding shareholders of Peninsula Copper Industries of Hubbell Michigan, a leading supplier of cupric oxide. Quincy Mining was dissolved in 1986. Under their leadership, the company diversified successfully first into real estate and then into securities. As private investors, they backed numerous Broadway musicals and dramas, including "Gypsy" and "Dolly."

During World War II, Mortimer was with the War Department, Seymour served in US Army and Ephraim work within the industrial complex concerned with the design of aircraft.

In 1947, Mortimer Propp who had just purchased a home in Mamaroneck was approached by Rabbi David Golovensky about the necessity for an uncompromising Orthodox Jewish school where Jewish children could receive a first class education in secular and as well as religious studies. Rabbi Golovensky introduced a group of supporters to Mortimer Propp, a real estate investor, who was well known for his interest in Jewish causes. He located a property the Weatherbee Estate, which was adjacent to his own home. Mortimer found additional supporters to pledge the funds to purchase the estate with its buildings and 26 acres of land. The Westchester Religious Institute was established and Mortimer became its first president. The primary task at hand was to find a suitable principal. Mortimer and his wife, Eugenie, knew a friend who had just hired a principle for a school in Hyde Park, New York and still had the resumes of the candidates. After reading the resume of S. Maurice Plotnick, Mortimer called him and setup an interview. Mr. Plotnick was interviewed and immediately hired by the founders of the school. In September 1948, the Westchester Day School opened with fifty students. Today in 1998, the school now has more than 500 students. Mortimer and Eugenie are also active with the United Jewish Appeal of New York City and various other organizations and charities. He is an advisor to the New York Board of Rabbi's.

Morris Propp's youngest son, Ephraim Propp, owns and operates Propp and Company, a stock brokerage firm and is a member of the New York Stock Exchange.

The brothers have continued to be active in Jewish causes. Mortimer Propp acts as the President of the W. Parsons Todd Foundation, founded by W. Parson Todd and is involved in the Real Estate Business in New York City.

Rev Ephraim Propp, his wife Rivka, and his family came to the United States in 1893. Morris as a child, attended schools both in South Norfolk, Connecticut and New York City. In 1901, when he was seventeen years of age, Morris went to work for his sister, Anna Propp Glasgow, at her store in New York City. A hard and diligent worker despite his youth, he toiled horribly long hours, usually working from 6:00 A.M. until 11:00 P.M. every day.

Due to his hard work, Morris was able to save enough money to seek employment on his own later that same year. A devout Jew, he went into business for himself as it was hard to find a job which allowed him to honor the Sabbath on Saturdays when working for others. He became a door-to-door peddler of assorted merchandise, but soon was specializing in the sale of Welsbach gas mantles. These mantles were chemically treated so that when heated with a gas flame, they would incandesce, greatly increasing the light output of the flame. Extremely popular for both home and streetlamp use, mantles quite similar to the ones Morris sol are still in use today. The picture to the left is a circa 1908 Welsbach advertising tray, which shows the various mantles the company offered pictured around the rim.

Amazingly, Morris Propp was only 18 when, in 1902, he had saved enough money from peddling to open a tiny store of his own, located at 92 East Broadway in New York City. His savings of $250, a substantial amount of money in those days, allowed for payment of first month's rent of $45, twelve empty wooden cases at 25 cents each that he made into shelves, and a used countertop for $6. The remaining funds were used to buy stock to sell. He continued to sell the popular Welsbach mantles, and other gas lighting parts and accessories. Soon he was able to add lighting fixtures to his inventory, and not long after had developed an impressive trade with door-to-door peddlers and other merchants who re-sold his wares. Pictured on the right is a 1910 gas lantern using a Welsbach mantle, similar to what Morris sold.

During these early days of the century, Morris demonstrated his wonderful aptitude for business by quickly capitalizing on the growing public interest in electrical illumination. He soon added electrical accessories and fixtures to his line of wares, and it was not long after that he was actually manufacturing and selling electrical accessories of his own! In 1907, Morris' brother Louis joined him to work in the business. In 1910, Morris married Anna Cohen. 1913 was a pivotal year for both Morris and Louis, for it was then that Louis became a partner in his brother's business, and together they operated the business under the name of the M. Propp Company. It was during this time that the Propp brothers also added a selection of very high quality electric Christmas lights to their line of manufactured goods, the humble beginnings of what was soon to become the largest manufacturing company of electrical Christmas decorations in the world.

Once again Morris Propp's business skills would be called into play. As the first decade of the century faded into the second, public awareness of electrical Christmas decorations was heightened by a judicious but extensive advertising campaign sponsored by Morris' company. Propp electrical accessories were in widespread use by this time, with their line of Christmas lights leading the way. Almost all of the popular women's magazines of the day included Propp ads for Christmas lights during the season, as well as many trade publications and scientific journals. Here is an example of one such ad:

Wisely, all of the Propp Christmas light sets from the early 1920s and onward included the "One-4-All" connectors, allowing their use with just about any other company's brand of attachments. This allowed Morris' sets to be instantly compatible with those offered by his competitors, and sales increased even more.

The safety of Propp sets was loudly touted in the advertisements as well, for many people were still afraid of electricity, despite the more obvious dangers of using candles on their trees. The sets were approved for safety by the infant Underwriters Laboratories, and many advertisements proclaimed that Propp outfits were "Approved by Santa Claus and the Underwriters!" What more could anyone ask for?

By the time the ad pictured above ran in the November 1921 issue of *The Electrical Record*, the Propp brothers were in offices at 524-528 Broadway in New York City. The greatly expanded offices and manufacturing facilities were the fruit of Morris' extensive advertising campaign, and by now the Company was indeed the largest manufacturer of Christmas lighting outfits the world had ever known. It was hard to imagine that little more than a decade had passed since Morris Propp was running his small gas light fixture operation...

Here is the classic offering from the Propp brothers, and is circa 1924 Santa Claus himself is pictured prominently on the front cover of the box, proclaiming "FOR SAFETY SAKE, DEMAND PROPP ELECTRICAL DECORATIVE SETS." The safety warnings were more against the use of "unapproved" electrical outfits rather than candles, but it is still interesting to note that even by this time, electrical illumination was far from universal in the United States. Electrical mishaps were almost as common as were accidents caused by open flame illumination, and those manufacturers who really wanted to sell their electrical wares were wise to conform to the Underwriter's standards for manufacturing and safety. The M. Propp Company was the first to produce *only* Underwriter's approved outfits.

Morris proudly employed family members in his business, and, along with his brother, many cousins and other family members immigrating to the United States were given good, solid starts through employment within his Company. One family member, writing of her father's sister and her immigration to the US from Lithuania, described Morris as a "very well to do relative who manufactured electrical devices like Christmas tree lights." The woman was most appreciative of the kind help that Morris extended to the family. She went on to say that Morris was "very successful", and "wore black silk suits, and had an almost Chinese cast of features..." The sister's son, Louis Gordon, became quite involved in the day-to-day operation of the Propp Company.

In the early 1920s, many small companies sought to capitalize on Morris Propp's successes in the Christmas light market, and there were many offerings of these sets, most of them quite similar to each other. Here are some 1921 advertisements from just a few of the competing companies:

As you can see from the ads, most of the companies had their own forms of "interconnecting" devices, which allowed multiple strings of lights to be connected together. But only Morris Propp's sets had the "universal" connectors, which would work with anyone's light sets. And again, the Propp outfits were *always* "approved by the Underwriters," while the majority of the sets from the competition were not.

In 1925, many of the smaller decorative lighting companies, eleven in all, formed a trade association specifically designed to compete against Morris Propp and his hugely successful company. Called NOMA, the name stood for the National Outfit Manufacturer's Association. The association members were hopeful that in joining together, they could pool advertising resources and purchasing power, thereby proving to be an effective competitor to Morris and his Company. All of these companies licensed manufacturing rights for the newly patented "Tachon" connector. This connector was basically a bladed wall plug of the type still in use today, but in its earliest form it was intended only to facilitate the interconnection of two or more strings of Christmas lights. As Propp's strings were already compatible with the bladed connector, patent rights and issues came to the legal forefront. The situation was a bit complicated, as before the 1924 patent on the Tachon, most electrical companies then producing Christmas lights were using similar forms of the connector freely and without having to purchase manufacturing rights to it.

It is unclear why the United States Patent and Trademark Office allowed a patent on a device that had been in use for more than seven years, and one that was made in almost identical form by several independent companies. A careful reading of the full text of the patent will reveal that it even covers the bladed forms of attaching connectors, as well as the screw in types, in what appears to be a blatant attempt to capitalize of the inventions of others. Nonetheless, the patent was granted to "inventor" Lester Haft, an employee of the C.D. Wood Company, which were one of Morris Propp's biggest competitors and a member of the new NOMA group of companies. At this point, Morris had no choice but to pay for licensing rights to a device, which he himself essentially both invented and improved upon. It was quite a strange situation indeed. The name "One-4-All Connector" was trademarked, but the device it described apparently was not patented.

In July of 1925, the same year of the formation of NOMA, Morris applied for a patent for what he called a "current tap fitting", an in-line type of add on connector that accepted a bladed plug, and a variation on the Tachons. The patent was not granted until March of 1930, quite a delay. The whole situation with the patents and inventions concerning the interconnectability of Christmas light strings is quite confusing, and more research is needed to discern what events actually occurred. I believe it is safe to say at this point that these devices were the turning point in the competitive war regarding Christmas lighting strings, and the battle lines had been drawn between the NOMA group and Morris Propp and his company.

The year 1925 was quite a successful one for the NOMA consortium, and in 1926 the National Outfit Manufacturers Association officially incorporated to form the NOMA Electric Corporation. Below is pictured a lighting outfit from their first year of operation as that new company:

Although NOMA Electric was now technically a bigger operation than was the M. Propp Company, the Propp name was still forefront in the public's mind when it came to quality electric Christmas lighting outfits. The NOMA brand was now only two years old, and during their first years of operation the company was selling out of the stock of the 11 smaller businesses that were involved in its formation. As a result, both the quality and consistency of NOMA products was questionable, although the few sets that they made new during 1926 were approved by the Underwriters. In fact, these first year sets were extremely close in both quality and appearance to Morris Propp's outfits.

Starting in 1926, Morris again showed his shrewd business savvy by quietly buying large amounts of NOMA stock on the open market. His brother Louis did the same, and they continued to operate their company, increasing their advertising and holding their own against NOMA Electric. But as time progressed, it became obvious that the bigger company would soon be able to sell their light sets at a lower cost than could the Propp brothers. In 1928, Morris and Louis Propp agreed to merge with NOMA Electric, virtually assuring the success of both companies. NOMA Electric had the buying power and advertising resources, and Morris Prop had the uncanny ability for making incredibly smart business decisions. The brothers received a huge block of NOMA stock in the merger, and combined with their previous holdings, now owned controlling interest in the company that was formed with the intention of putting them out of business. Morris Propp became the President of NOMA Electric in 1929, and held that position until his death.

Morris Propp was not only a most effective businessman, but was a devout Jew and philanthropist as well. Besides helping many of his family members as they immigrated to America for a more promising life, he established foundations "to aid and assist charitable and religious causes, and religious schools and institutions that aid and support the sick and the poor." These foundations continue today some eighty years later still under the direction of the family.

Both Morris and Louis Propp were well respected by their large family and by the community. It has been written that Morris "enjoyed the highest reputation for character and integrity" and of his brother, Louis, which "he spent a lifetime of concern and unselfish contributions for his fellow man..."

Two of Rav Ephraim and Rivka Propp's Children
C: 1915

Ida "Propp" Brilliant
Brooklyn, New York

Morris Propp
New York City

Ephraim Propp Family - New York City, Circa 1915
Top Row: Morris, Ida, Louis   Bottom Row: Anna, Ephraim, Rebecca, Manja

New York, Circa 1950s
From Left to Right: Celia Propp, Anna Gordon Propp, Frieda Reiss Propp,
Helen Stern Propp, Isaac L. Propp and Sophie

Isaac and Granddaughter, Gloria Propp
Under the Portrait of Isaac's father
Rav Ephraim Propp

Dr. Kalman Davidson ben Peretz Davidson

Vainutas, Russia to Boston, Massachusetts

Beth Israel Hospital

The Townsend Street property was in a pleasant, residential neighborhood. The population had been largely Irish, but in recent years many Jewish families had moved there from the West End, the North End, and East Boston. Many Jewish doctors had opened offices in the area, usually in their homes; Humboldt Avenue and Warren Street, only a few blocks from the site, were popular locations. The estate had many favorable features. This section of Roxbury, once called Boston Highlands, was a healthy one, with abundant sunshine and fresh air. These considerations had been important when the new buildings of the New England Hospital for Women and Children had opened nearby in 1872. The Dennison grounds, rising from the street, were spacious, with shade trees and arbors. Public transportation was good: from Copley Square, one took a Huntington Avenue car to Dudley Street, changed to an Egleston Square car that went out Washington Street, got off at Townsend Street, and walked up a short distance to number 45. Furthermore, the elevated system along Washington Street opened in 1901 and extended to this area in 1909, provided rapid transit to and from Boston.

Title to the property was not secured until early in December, just after the Massachusetts State Board of Charity granted a charter of incorporation to the association on December 6. Two hundred and thirty one people were listed as charter members two hundred and two women and twenty nine men. Officers, directors and an executive board of directors were elected. The corporation was for the purpose "of establishing, supporting, and managing an institution to be known as the Beth Israel Hospital, and the affording of medical and surgical aid and nursing to sick or disabled persons of any creed or nationality. The wording of this objective was almost exactly the same as that of the Mount Sinai Hospital Society. Subsequently, the bylaws of the association included the statements that the religious services of the hospital shall be conducted in conformity with the doctrines and forms of the Jewish faith, and the Jewish dietary laws shall be strictly observed. Nothing herewith contained shall preclude the attendance (on the solicitation of a patron) of a clergyman of any faith.

The year 1916 was a busy one for the association. Successful fund raising aimed at redemption of the mortgage, culminated in a "mortgage burning" celebration in March. The auxiliaries added a Cambridge branch and expected that the total membership of about 4,000 would soon double. The directors planned to remodel the buildings. As an economical approach, national authorities were recommending such conversion of an old building into a hospital, especially in view of wartime scarcities. Myer Dana, a member of the executive committee of the board and chairman of the building committee, supervised the work. He was helped by Drs. Davidson and Ehrenfried. The cost of alterations, which exceeded the original estimate of $40,000, created a financial problem for the association. Mr. Dana gave his personal warranty for $40,000, and a new mortgage was placed for $10,000. The organization started a campaign for $100,000 in April, but by October pledges had been obtained for only about $20,000.

In October 1916, although the remodeling was not yet completed, the public was invited to week long exercises to dedicate the new hospital and to celebrate the fifth anniversary of the association. First, there was a parade on Sunday, October. Townsend Street and nearby streets were closed to traffic and as many as five thousand people were said to have marched. Starting at Temple Adath Jeshurun on Blue Hill Avenue near Brunswick Street, the route was circuitous: Blue Hill Avenue, Quincy Street, Humboldt Avenue, Crawford Street, and then Walnut Avenue to the hospital grounds. The parade, led by a military band, featured two floats prepared by the auxiliaries. One float had a hospital bed with three people representing a patient, a doctor and a nurse; the other had people representing Uncle Sam, Liberty, Zion, and justice. After the parade, with twenty five thousand people reported as present, exercises were held on a large stage in front of the hospital. Prominent red, white, and blue electric lights displayed the Star of David on the stage. Simon Swig, treasurer of the association and a representative in the state legislature, was master of ceremonies. Speakers included the mayor of Boston, James M. Curley; State Treasurer Burrill; and Messrs. Danzig and Dana. Mayor Curley addressed the financial problem of maintaining the hospital, and he announced his own contribution of $100 toward a fund for this purpose. On Sunday evening there was a concert, and the celebration then continued all week. On Monday the hospital was open to the 5,000 members of the association; there were morning and afternoon speakers, and another concert in the evening. Tuesday was Out of Town Day; Wednesday, Organization Day for lodge and society members; Thursday, Professional Day and Friday, Children's Day. On Saturday rabbis of leading congregations offered prayers, and as the final event on Sunday evening, October 29, a banquet was held in Roxbury's Brunswick Hall

In connection with this celebration, an *Advocate* editorial summarized the history of the Jewish hospital movement in Boston:

The dedication of the first Jewish hospital in Boston is unquestionably an event in communal history, the more so that only recently the Mount Sinai Hospital Dispensary had to be closed owing to lack of funds. The hospital movement has been popular from the start; the dispensary was regarded as a makeshift, for indeed, it was started as a means to founding a hospital. Indeed the Jewish Advocate owes its direct origin to the publication of the Mount Sinai Monthly as a means to finance a hospital propaganda campaign.

The hospital then is the realization of a dozen years of hoping, and at least five years of patient activity. We congratulate all concerned. If special mention be in order, the compliment belongs to Mr. Hyman Danzig, who has agitated and labored to this end unceasingly. The question now before the community is the support of the institution. It should be forthcoming because the hospital is a first class necessity. But it will take an earnest and deliberately planned campaign to place the hospital in a position where it can be of first class service. Let us hope that it will prove a permanent pride [as an addition to] the still few possessions of Boston Jewry.

During the summer and fall of 1916, a "Medical Advisory Board" of twelve physicians organized and selected a medical staff. Seven members of the board were chosen by the Beth Israel directors and five by the Greater Boston Medical Association. This association, soon known as the Greater Boston Medical Society, had been incorporated on November 4, 1915, "for the purpose of improving the economic conditions and to elevate the standard and to promote social and friendly intercourse among its members. Dr. Abraham J. Hurwitz was president of the new society, and Dr. Philip Castleman was secretary and treasurer. By this time, the earlier Boston Medical Society, incorporated in 1897, had become inactive.

Beth Israel Hospital, Townsend Street, 1916:
right foreground, Platform with six pointed star for dedication;
left background, nurses' home

The chairman of the advisory board was Dr. Kalman M. Davidson; a strong supporter of Mr. Danzig's efforts since 1911, he was a member of Beth Israel's Executive Board and the only physician director. The secretary of the advisory group was Dr. Philip Castleman. The advisory board drew up bylaws, and rules and regulations for the medical staff. Numerous sections, such as those dealing with the responsibilities of department heads, with attendance, and with periodic reports by individual staff members and department heads, were copied verbatim from Mount Sinai Hospital documents. In a major difference from the Mount Sinai staff organization, however, the advisory board did not provide for an executive committee of the staff to be responsible for the general conduct of professional affairs. Instead, the board gave responsibility to "each physician in charge of a department. Selection of the surgical staff raised problems. Dr. Ehrenfried accepted one of the three top positions, and four non Jewish surgeons from the Boston City Hospital were considered for the other two positions:

Drs. Frederic J. Cotton, LeRoi G. Crandon, Frank H. Lahey, and David D. Scannell. Disagreement among members of the advisory board could not be resolved even after numerous meetings, and the choices were finally made by a secret vote. Drs. Crandon and Scannell were each appointed "Visiting Surgeon in Chief. At the same time, Dr. Ehrenfried resigned from the advisory board and from the staff, over the issue "as to whether the Staff of the Hospital was to be selected by the representative committee appointed for this purpose, or was to be dictated by outside influences. Two doctors were each appointed "Visiting Physician in Chief": Dr. Kalman M. Davidson, and Dr. Harry W. Goodall who had trained at the Massachusetts General Hospital and was on the staff of the Peter Bent Brigham Hospital. Twenty two doctors recommended by the advisory board were appointed and Dr. Scannell was elected president of the staff.

By early 1917 alterations were completed. The main building had a basement, three floors each with a porch and a half story attic. There was room for about forty five beds: two large wards, each with about twelve beds, several smaller rooms, each with three to five beds, and one private room. The kitchen, for kosher food, was in the basement, and a modem operating room was on the third floor. Rooms for other hospital activities were also crowded into the building, and an elevator ran from the basement to the third floor. A motto, "Where There's Life There's Hope," was displayed on an inside wall near the entrance The building higher on the hill, formerly a stable, was converted into the nurses' home. Vigorous auxiliary work continued. On January 13, Leo Lyons presided at a large and enthusiastic meeting of the junior auxiliary, and three days later the United Auxiliaries celebrated with a ball at Mechanics Building on Huntington Avenue. Hyman Danzig was elected superintendent. He was succeeded as president of the association by Simon Swig, who was succeeded as treasurer by Philip S. Aronson. Dr. E. Louis Friederman was appointed house physician, and Miss Anna Steinberg, head nurse."

On Sunday, February 4, 1917, Mrs. Fannie Levine, of 60 Chambers Street in the West End, was admitted, as Beth Israel's first patient.

Shaya-Mendel Aronovich
and his youngest brother,
Dr. Kalman Meyer Davidson

L to R
Margaret (Gitel) Davidson,
Kalman Meyer Davidson,
Rochel Greenberg

Anna Davidson Graduation Radcliffe College. Her Mother was a special student at Radcliffe And her Daughter, Margaret, who graduated in 1933 was the first 3rd Generation Radcliffe Student.

Circa: 1898 Boston
Meyer ben Avram "Prop" Greenberg
1837 - 1916
Shkudvil, Russia, Sweden and
Boston, Massachusetts

Anna Propp of the New York Theater
A Collection of Newspaper articles of the Period

Anna Propp was born in New York City in 1896, she was the youngest daughter of Shimon Propp of Shkudvil, Lithuania. She was later married to Frank McNamara, who was also a star in show business. The following are newspaper excerpts about Anna Propp and some of her stage career:

TINIEST GIRL ON BURLESQUE STAGE:

Look who's here a sweet dimpled little bunch of femininity that fits in the Buckingham's "Follies of the Day" company like a chocolate drop in a box of candy. This is Miss Anna Propp, No, she is not a schoolgirl. She has passed the "sweet sixteen" mark and is now eighteen years of age. Even at that she is young to be so clever a performer and so skillful a votary of terpsichore. She is only four feet tall, and weighs eighty-four pounds, being the smallest girl in burlesque. She has been on the stage three seasons in dancing specialty. She whirls, kicks, jumps, "splits" and does everything that a genuine burlesque dancer should do.

No, that is not a "nightie" she has on. it is her stage costume, in which she appears when singing a special, "bugaboo": song. - *February 5, 1914*

CORINTHIAN THEATER

Fun, fast and furious, holds the stage at the Corinthian this week from the first bar of the overture to the grand finale. "The Follies of the Day" has a cast of principles whose business is to provide comedy and sing lively musical numbers, and, to do it well. George F. Murphy in his role of August Furst, the hot-dog man, and Chester Nelson as a rube kept yesterday's audiences laughing for a good part of two and a half hours. Gertrude Hayes and Anna Propp kept the house busy appreciating their dancing and singing. Enough vim and vivaciousness are stored in Miss Propp's diminutive form to stock an entire chorus. The first part of

the show is called "Hot Dog, fir What Does the Public Want" and it answers its oven question, judging from the applause yesterday. Musical numbers that fire especially catchy are "Sixty Mile an Hour baby," "Ragtime Lullaby," and "Saving, Saving, Saving." The second part is in three scenes, - all well staged, show in a burlesque on David Belasco's play, "The Boomerang," and on "Three Weeks." another scene, "The Taxi Station," brings out many novelties that were well liked Yesterday. - *October, 3, 1916*

BERCHEL THEATER

Good and continuous entertainment without any particular outstanding feature aside from he Temple quartet specialty is provided by Barney Gerard's "Follies or the Day," which opened a four day engagement at the Berchel theater yesterday matinee.

Chester Nelson and Frank Mackey are the two fun makers, and they with Gertrude Hayes, are generally able to carry the show alone when the chorus is taking off or putting on a little more colored clothes. The chorus too, is a hard working, fair looking crowd of girls with voices good enough to make the ensembles sound something like a real opera chorus.

The show is a round of burlesque on such plays — or parts of them — as "Experience," "Uncle Tom's Cabin, "Railroad Jack" and "The Easiest Way," during the first act switches to a satirical skit in "Spies" in the second act and then goes to a burlesque of "The Wanderer," the latter giving opportunity for a colorful scenic set with an oriental flavor and smoking incense that smelled like the burning of Ninth street.

A distinct hit of the show was little Anna Propp, a diminutive miss with vim and pep enough for a girl three times her size. Her Sixty-Mile-an-Hour Baby" at the opening performances, sung with the chorus girls, resulted in a dozen insistent encores. Again in the second act, Miss Propp's "I Want to Ride on Sammy's Gee-Gee," Sung with eight ponies proved a popular number with burlesque fans.

As comedians Nelson and Mackey do as much as their parts allow, Nelson carrying off the honors for Clowning comedy. Mackey is a good yodeler but doesn't yodel enough to suit those who like that class of song. The Temple quartet offers excellent harmony.

Two dozen good musical numbers throughout the performances with several Specialties, a round of comedy skits, plenty of show by the chorus and a pretentious spectacular effort in the second act help the show to score. - *March 15, 1918*

The Theater

Perhaps there is something in the name Gerard. James was a wise diplomat in Germany. Barney is a wise showman in burlesque. The latter's "Follies of the Day" came into the Gayety Sunday a piece with no desultory moment. fast, clean clever

Neither does it pursue a selfish route. It hammers away at the benefits of Liberty bonds and does other things of patriotic flavor quite more valuable than and superior to cladding the women in khaki and breaking out an American flag. Art and loyalty to government enterprises therefore go in hand in hand in skillful mixture.

Moreover the Follies is studded with features. A syncopated grand opera closing for the first act is given with a great and mellifluous volume of voices and in the second act the Temple quartet quite stopped the show.

Chester Nelson, Frank McKay and Gertrude Hayes retain all their old knack of getting laughs and the supporting company is excellent Anna Propp is an attractive midget soubrette and Lulu Beeson is a first-class song-leader. Nelson's familiar guitar specialty also is a nice spot.

The chorus is long on good looks and out of the ordinary track. It is se stage pictures interrupt the burlesque but the oriental set of the last act did that Sundays.

The Follies of the Day ought to do big business. - *April 29, 1918*

AMUSEMENTS
Empire Theater
"Follies of the Day."

If Barney Gerard had organized his "Follies of the Day" Into a corporation and passed out the dividend-paying shares to every member of the company. There couldn't be any more individual effort or a better balanced show that Mr. Gerard opened yesterday afternoon at the Empire for a twice-a-day stand until the end of the week. If the audience had Its way with encores the show would last about four hours.

Like most good burlesque shows of the day the "Follies" has dropped what semblance of plot and story it ever had and all that holds it together is the personalities of its people. And that's quite enough. It is just one amusing situation after another. Full of specialties and every minute up to the standard that makes it possible for men to forget their club pals and enjoy a good show and a smoke in the company of their wives.

Also the show is new in everything except its cast, and if you don't believe press agents can be truthful take it from the writer who isn't paid for advertising the show. Mr. Gerard has done a make-over job as big as the automobile manufacturer who jumped from a six to a 12-cylinder motor in one season.

The lithographs indicate that George Murphy, Gertrude Hayes and Chester Nelson are the stars. Billboards aren't: large enough to tell the whole story. Murphy is the same old hot dog man. with his act improved and Miss Hayes surely puts ginger in the show. Likewise Nelson pulls off that rube stuff to a feather-edge finish. There is also a Miss Anna Propp just about large enough to live on hospital rations, who sings And dances about once every five minutes.

Miss Elsa May the young woman who dignifies the stage always in street length cloths has a voice which is a real treat. Her "Romany" is one of the delights of the show. With a six-foot-six girl, Miss Edith Malvore. and the assistance of some good men singers. Miss May also does some excellent operatic songs.- *October 24, 1916*

"GIRLS DE LOOKS"
SHOULD GET MONEY
IN EVERY TOWN

Barney Gerard's "Girls de Looks" has never failed to please and this season lives up to its past reputation as a great comedy, scenic and costumed offering. It's a whirl-wind laughing show and more than pleased a packed house at the Columbia Monday afternoon.

The name of the book is Bankers and Brokers a satire on Wall street and tells a story of a stolen stock certificate taken from an office in New York and finally found in the Hawaiian Islands. The books by Gerard and Jos. K. Watts. Victor Hyde staged the dancing numbers which are worth seeing. Watts a finished performer in the line of comedy stands out in the show. He has an individuality of his own and is uproariously funny. Never have we seen him to such a good advantage. He is witty, clever and does not depend on any make-up to get laughs. In fact he uses none. He is a neat dresser a fast worker and kept his audience constantly amused all through the performance. He is a credit to burlesque.

Sam Greene, a wonderful straight man assisted materially in the comedy by the way he fed the comedians. He knows how to work up a scene with a comedian and does it. He is a neat dresser and has a fine stage presence.

Jack Thomas, is doing an eccentric comedy role and is amusing. He is a tall slender chap uses a funny make-up and is a dandy dancer. Georgie Stone, a young juvenile fits in nicely. He is a corking good hoofer a natty little fellow and a neat dresser.

Fred Evans does an old man character and William Kao shows up well in bits.

Momi Kalama, an attractive looking brunette with a pleasing personality did nicely with her numbers and in the scenes.

Anna Propp, a wee bit of a soubrette and very snappy is an artist of exceptional merit in the art of dancing. She sure can dance and all her endeavors were well received.

Miss Propp is a lively little girl and worrisome dresses just suited to her style. She put her numbers over well and in a way that showed undoubted ability of a quality that should carry her far along the road of success.

Betty Evans a rather graceful person of a brunette style of beauty was successful in all her numbers. She also reads lines well. Her wardrobe is pleasing to the eye. Eddie Simp, a colored performer, did well as a porter and bellhop.

The opening scene a broker's office was a reproduction of what it was intended to be. It had a stock board ticker and a dozen or so telephones, such as one would see in any stock broker s office in lower New York.

Stone and Miss Propp did well in this scene with their singing and dancing specialty. A pretty telephone number was given by Miss Propp and Miss Evans assisted by eight girls.

There was plenty of comedy in this - scene the comedians proving capable of holding it at high speed. Momi Kalama and William Kao offered a dandy Hawaiian act in one in front of a special drop. Kao played the ukulele and guitar, while Miss Kalama offered a very graceful Hawaiian dance. The act was well received.

In the ship scene Simp put over a corking good dancing specialty

Anna Propp cleaned up in her dancing specialty in which she offered a fine Russian
Dance of many difficult steps

Watts was a decided hit in his comedy. He works in front of a plush drop. He has fine material and best of all knows how to deliver. He had the audience laughing from the start to the finish of his act and it was after 4:30 when he walked off stage.

In the cabaret scene which closed the show several specialties were offered which started off with Stone and Miss Propp both in dress suits offering a real fast dancing act that was well done. Thomas followed in a "rube" make-up and dress doing a corking good eccentric dance that went over big.

Kao pleased with his ukulele specialty which was next. Gerard has a show in the "Girls de Looks" that stands up with the best we have seen at the Columbia this season. should do big everywhere. *SID - December 23, 1920.*

Smallest Burlesque Star in Empire Show Theater News

The question as to who is the smallest star in burlesque has been settled. She is little Miss Anna Propp, twinkling soubrette with Step Lively Girls at the Empire this week. Anna rises to the majestic height of 52 inches from the tips of her slippers to the upper most curl on her pretty head. But Anna is a perfectly formed young person not in any sense a Lilliputian. She is shorter by Four inches than- Marguerite Clark and Nazimova by "building up" her hair is able to tower seven inches above the tiny burlesque queen. *–February 28, 1919* ❐

Anna Propp, daughter of Shimon Propp, and of the New York Theatre New York City, 1914 - 1920

170

New York City Burlesque and Vaudeville Information
Circa 1910 to 1920

<u>NYC Theaters Anna Propp played:</u>

Buckingham Theater

Corinthian Theater

Gayety Theater (A Marc Klaw & A. L. Erlanger Theater in which George M. Cohan had an interest in)

Empire Theater - (across from the Metropolitan Opera House - 1893 - demolished in 1953 - for many years it was the oldest and most prestigious playhouse in New York -Declassee 1919 (257),

<u>Some of the actors, Anna Propp-Burlesque Queen, Singer and Dancer, played with</u>

George F. Murphy-Singer	Elsa May-Singer
Gertrude Hayes-Singer	Edith Malvore-Singer
David Belasco-Playwright	Sam Greene-Comedian
Chester Nelson and Frank Mackey-Comedians	Jack Thomas-Comedian
Barney Gerard-Director	Momi Kalama-Actress
George Murphy	Georgie Stone-Actor

Variety, New York Office
245 West 17th Street
New York, NY 10011
Tel: 212 645 0067
Fax: 212 337 6977

Actors Equity, Eastern Regional Office
Carol Waaser, Eastern Regional Director
165 West 46th Street
15th Floor
New York, New York 10036
(212) 869-8530; FAX (212) 719-9815

No map shows a location for Tin Pan Alley. It is simply a nickname for the New York City neighborhood that once hosted several music publishers. On West 28th Street near Fifth Avenue, many songwriters once plied their craft (the important William Morris Talent Agency was here, as was vaudeville's trade journal, The New York Clipper). Journalist and songwriter Monroe H. Rosenfeld is credited for coining the term. Harry Von Tilzer told the colorful tale of Rosenfeld visiting him on West 28th Street and exclaiming, "It sounds like a tin pan." He was referring to the sound of Von Tilzer's piano, which had been muted with paper. Or perhaps Rosenfeld was referring to a combination of Von Tilzer's instrument along with competing pianos in that building and in neighboring buildings. In any case, Rosenfeld soon afterwards gave the title "Tin Pan Alley" to one of his newspaper articles, and the name stuck by 1903. By the 1920s most music publishers had moved uptown, to 42nd Street and elsewhere (the famous Brill Building was built in 1931 at 1619 Broadway at 49th Street), but though publishers moved from 28th Street, the term "Tin Pan Alley" stuck as a nickname.

New York, Circa 1910
Anna Propp in
"Step Lively Girls"

Anna Propp youngest daughter
of Reb Shimon Propp, New York City
Anna was Vaudeville Headliner
from 1909 into the 1930s

The Ruttenberg's of Saint Paul, Minnesota

by Stanley Ruttenberg

Great Grandfather Benesh (Benjamin) Ruttenberg, Ed's grandfather, evidently was an itinerant, perhaps traveling to escape the Czar's conscription into the Russian Army. We think he was Russian, but Ruttenberg may not have been his original family name. At least Grandmother Goldie Ruttenberg, Ed's mother, and Ed's sisters seemed to think that that was the case. In any event, Benjamin ended up in Skaudville, Prussia (now Lithuania), where he met Marjasha (Miriam), daughter of Abraham Propp, and married her. Herb thinks he remembers hearing that Benjamin knew and worked for Napoleon III. Benjamin had been married before, but we have no details; family legend has it that he had two sons by his first wife; the sons migrated to South America and came to their end there without leaving any progeny.

Great Grandfather Benjamin and Miriam had ten children; most of them came to the USA in the 1880s or so. Simon, Ed's father, came to St. Paul in the late 1860s or 1870s, where, among other things, he evidently worked as part of a Jewish organization helping resettle immigrants. In this capacity, he met Goldie Masavich.

Several of Grandfather Simon's older brothers, including Nathan, moved to Ishpeming, in the Michigan Upper Peninsula, following the iron rush. Benjamin and Miriam went there also, and ran a boarding house with their youngest daughter Celia. Nathan operated a mercantile store, remnants of which are incorporated in a renovated building. Stan and Pat visited in 1990 and chatted with the latest owner, who operates a variety store there, and who knew nothing of the older history.

Using the Polk City Directories in the Ishpeming and Marquette libraries. Stan found the addresses and photographed all but one of the many houses occupied by the various Ruttenbergs, who lived there from the mid 1880s to the early 1900s; the one missing house burned and the site is still empty.

Great Aunt Celia later moved to Chicago, as did Benjamin and Miriam, and married Louis Arne, a distant cousin on the Propp side. Her daughter, Sarah Arne, was a close cousin of the St. Paul Ruttenberg's. The only survivor of that line is Joyce Arne (married name unknown). Joyce's younger brother Ted died in about 1980 of ALS, the Lou Gehrig disease, and is survived by his wife Joyce, niece of Abe Saperstein, developer of the Harlem Globe Trotters, and two daughters; Joyce was fond of telling of her flamboyant uncle and trips with the Globe Trotters. Stan was in touch with Ted and visited him several times during his illness. The last time was not long before he died when he could only move his eyelids but could still communicate this way with Joyce. Now contact is temporarily lost with Ted's family and sister.

Ben and Miriam are buried in a Jewish cemetery in Chicago, whereabouts unknown at this time. In Skokie, Illinois, lives a lady who is a Ruttenberg descendent, and who has compiled a list of several thousand Ruttenberg's globally. Her earliest entries come from Poland and Germany not too far from Shkudvil, and date from about the time of Benjamin. We cannot establish that Benjamin is a member of that Ruttenberg clan, in as much as we have no information on his brothers or uncles, if any, or if indeed he really was a Ruttenberg. The search for earlier Ruttenberg roots continues.

Goldie Masavich was born sometime in Russia in the 1860s and reared around Odessa, Russia. Young Jewish girls living in the small villages evidently were not schooled and Grandmother Goldie remained illiterate (in the 1930s she did go to night school in Philadelphia, but it proved too late and difficult). Herb recalls that she told that as a little girl she would sneak into the park in Odessa. This is where the rich people would have tea in their one outfit, and brass bands would play in the pavilion. She said that she watched a parade where the Czar of Russia came by in a carriage. She lived in Russia when an attempt was made on his life—apparently a bomb was thrown at his carriage. Grandmother Goldie told of the severe pogroms when, usually at Easter time, the Cossacks would come into the villages to kill the Jews. When the Russian government decided to draft all eligible men into the army

Her family left Russia by sneaking out. Grandmother Goldie explained to Herb that all the men dressed as women, acquired a cart and the family simply walked out. They had to swim some rivers to get to Austria. There, Goldie recalled, she was overwhelmed by the beauty and especially by the rich pastries in the windows. In Vienna they were directed by a relocation center to London. From London the family immigrated to the USA where she thought that the streets would be paved in gold.

Grandmother Goldie landed in St. Paul—we do not know why—and was probably placed as a servant girl in a home. She was frightened in St. Paul because there were Indians on the street and the Indian wars were still in progress. Goldie could not remember the year, but she said that not long after she arrived in the USA a president was assassinated; Garfield was assassinated in 1881, and Grandmother Goldie was about fifteen or sixteen years old. That helps us place her birth in the mid 1860s. It is family legend that Simon Ruttenberg helped place her in a job. As one can see, she was a strikingly beautiful young lady of some sixteen years, and Simon, then about forty, thought that she would be a fine wife. They married and had many children; survivors born in St. Paul were Abbot, Sara, Frances and Bessie (AKA Betty). They then followed (Stan's conjecture) some of Simon's brothers to the iron country, Ishpeming, Michigan, where Ed was born (perhaps Arnold also). Simon was a peddler (spelled peddler in one of the Polk directories), and also lived in a nearby town, Negaunie. Evidently, there were many Swedes in St. Paul, and maybe also Ishpeming. At any rate, Grandmother Goldie used to say that she learned Swedish as her second language, before English. Sara and Frances remembered their uncles who were, they used to say, from the old country. Unfortunately, we never interrogated our aunts thoroughly and can only surmise some of the family history. Betty, when she could still remember, only a few years ago, did remember that Great Uncle Oscar (Ed's youngest Ruttenberg Uncle) "sold shirts." Indeed, Oscar had a men's store in Calumet, Michigan. Oscar's daughter Miriam, is still alive, living in Marquette, Ml. Stan and Pat visited her and her children in 1990; she knew very little of the family, having been raised, for some reason she could not explain, in another family. Betty also remembered "Old Ish," a statue of an Indian in the Ishpeming town square, sell standing. Simon moved his family back to St. Paul in Yearly 1900s, where Harold was born. Simon apparently was an asthmatic, and died when Harold was young. Ed left fourth grade to go to work! Goldie took in boarders.

Abbot was the oldest of the Ruttenberg Children and was a very bright youngster who graduated high school at fifteen; he was offered a scholarship at a college in Michigan. His father, Simon, however, refused to let him go because he needed Abbot's help with Simon's work, which was basically dealing in junk. Probably Abbot never forgave his father or that. Abbot was a gifted musician, playing he flute and violin. He and Ed, who played drums, used to play in a band. Abbot returned to St. Paul after W.W.I, but it was sometime in the late 1920s (Stan remembers him) went to Canada and has not been heard from since.

Sara was artistic and talented, but girls were not educated in those days - they married and reared families. Sara married Bill Harris and lad one daughter, Marcelle, who died in the early 1930s. Stan remembers her. One of Marcelle's admirers, Irving Green, was left bereft at her death. He had no close family of his own and lived with Sara and Bill during their St. Paul years. He later lived in Beverly Hills.

Francis, the third of the children was a good student, she always said that she was good in math and worked most of her life in St. Paul or the Great Northern railroad. When she retired she moved to St. Paul in the late 1940s, where she re-encountered and married Art Brash, who had been interested in her when she had lived in Chicago. Art himself was quite an adventurer, having been in Pershing's army Chasing Pancho Via before W.W.I. He also flayed for the Chicago "Black Socks" as a Utility infielder—the White Socks were known as the Black Socks" during a particular year when there was some sandal attached to the team. Stan worked for Art in Los Angeles making special brushes to clean Venetian blinds.

Betty married Dan Hacker, who had emigrated o the USA from England. Dan died in the late 1980s, about a year after a very happy and lively 90th birthday party, but Betty is still going at the Sherman Oaks at the ripe age of ninety-one, hard to tell her exact age). Her mind sometimes comes back into focus and she can remember a few things. Arnold also served in W.W.I overseas. He never returned and there is no information as to if he had been killed or MIA or had simply stayed in Europe.

Edward Harold enlisted in the Army in 1917, and was sent for training to Camp Benning, Georgia. He gradually was promoted to made Corporal and then Sergeant. Then he was demoted to Buck Private for slugging an officer. He never saw overseas duty but from his stories it is evident that he certainly enjoyed the southern belles in

Georgia. He was a successful amateur boxer in the Army. When he returned to St. Paul after the Armistice, he decided to become a professional boxer. He trained and had one professional fight. He was knocked silly and that was the end of his professional boxing career. He also worked on a surveyor's crew, and also had a job testing liquor that had to be "100 Proof" in order to be bonded. Ed worked in St. Paul for Sam Fisher, inventor of Salted-in-the-Shell Peanuts. Later, in Philadelphia, Ed was very active in the local American Legion Post; somehow, even though he had never served overseas, Ed managed to become a member of the 40 & Eight, an elite group of the Legion the members of which had to have seen service in France.

Ed played snare drum in the Post's marching band. Harold Edward, the youngest of the clan, went to night law school and eventually became a partner in a major St. Paul firm. Harold was an excellent sportsman and outdoorsman. He took his mother and Francis on many camping trips. He played piano well, and was the idol of his sisters and mother. Perhaps that is the reason why, when he married, he and his new wife remained distant from the rest of the family too much competition from adoring and smothering females. Harold was unbeatable at tennis; he had a strange sidestroke that had much spin and was very accurate. Stan fished with him many times and never caught a fish while Harold reeled them in one after the other. Harold's daughter, Marty, moved to Los Angeles with a young family; Herb and Diane saw much of them in the 1950s, but they disappeared and we haven't had much contact since. Stan and Herb did visit with Harold once in LA. His wife, Blanche, was apparently an invalid, and Marly had been divorced, so Harold was still working in his mid 80s, serving as a trial consultant to a legal firm. He moved in about 1991 with no forwarding address and we have not been able to trace him.

Using the Polk City directory as a guide, Stan was able to locate the house where Simon and family lived circa 1898-99, still standing but probably considerably renovated. Nearby is the little house where Ben, Miriam and Celia took in boarders. It was an interesting and nostalgic event to visit this town where so many Ruttenbergs lived.

Ishpeming, Michigan C: 1897
Benjamin and Mary (Miryam Propp) Ruttenberg

Milwaukee, 1956
Back Row: Charles Arne, Ellie Arne, Mary Arne, Lois Schwartz, Bertha Arne, Ted Leviton
Middle Row: Lillian Arne, Leif Jacobsen (Cousin from Sweden), Celia Arne, Philip Arne, Albert Ruttenberg
Front Row: Sadie Ruttenberg, Rosalie Arne Schwartz, Betty Ruttenberg, Annette Arne

The Propps of Tupper Lake, New York
by Richard Propp, MD

My grandfather, Peter Propp, came from Königsberg, East Prussia, about 1890, and married his childhood sweetheart, Anna Rockoff, in Baltimore. I presume his brother, Barnatt, came over about the same time, as the picture shows them both in Baltimore at that time. Barnatt settled in Ogdensberg in northern New York State with his wife, Betsy Singer Propp, but moved to Tupper Lake, New York when the railroads came into this new lumbering region. He opened a clothing store in that village, which is west of Lake Placid and Saranac Lake. He later was elected and served as Mayor of Tupper Lake.

Peter worked for the Baltimore railroad, winning a commendation from that company. My father, Elihu, was born there in 1893, in Baltimore, as were his brother, Jesse, and sister, Leah. Hazel was born in Flemingsberg, Kentucky where the family moved and traded in furs and horses until Barnatt called them to Tupper Lake, because of the booming mercantile opportunities. Abram and Simon were born in Tupper Lake. The family had a beer and soda bottling business until prohibition, and then established a profitable feed and coal business. Peter was on the school board, chaired the drive to build Mercy Hospital, and with Elihu was active in Free Masonry.

Elihu graduated from Eastman School of Business and worked with his father. Elihu then took his fortune to New York City and managed to lose it in the development of sound records for movies, but he did meet a lovely secretary at Universal Studio from Gloversville, New York named Sara Rockovitz. They married in 1929, moved to Albany, New York and bought a mail advertising business called the Albany Letter Shop. Which he operated until 1980, one year before his death.

His son, Larry, continues the business and with his wife, Mancia, and has 3 children. David, a physician in Philadelphia, receiving management degree from Wharton in May, 1995; Jonathon, is in the computer business in Helsinki, Finland and with his wife Tina Suzanna are the proud parents of a Maxwell bias on April 23, 1995, and Laura, a physical therapist in Atlanta.

My wife, Vera, and I have two children: Peter, is with IBM in White Plains marketing on the Internet, and he and his wife, Susan, are expecting a new addition to he family in May, 1995. Elizabeth works in New York City as Project Manager for finance for the new Pennsylvania Station. After practicing internal medicine in Albany for twenty-six years, I recently joined the New York State Health Department Hospital program as a physician surveyor.

Leah married Frank Siegal from Tupper Lake, an avid sportsman, who ran a plumbing and hardware store. They had two children, Adele, who married Dr. Sam Reiter and moved to Long Beach, California and Ted, recently deceased, who had a career in electronics for Bendix. Ted and Naomi Siegal's son, Frank, is a busy trial lawyer in Atlanta.

Jesse Propp ran the Sonny Boy Bakery in Tupper Lake, retiring to Santa Monica California in the 60's where he and his wife, Shirley, spent their final years. Jessie and Shirley had three daughters. Their oldest daughter, Joan Propp Potter, is an author and publisher in Westchester and Elizabethtown, New York. Joan has four children; Alison Munoz is a graphic designer, Katherine Richardson is a children's book illustrator, Stephen is a computer graphics person, and Jonathan is a cabinetmaker. Joan's sister, The next oldest is Abby Propp Schlesinger, she is a librarian with the Ojai, California Public Library. Abby has four children: Joseph is the Department head and Instructional designer for PAC, Lauren is a fabric designer for Esprit Clothing and a free-lance artist, Juliane is a Spanish instructor for Cate Private Preparatory School and Nicholas is a Creative writing student, songwriter and musician. Jessie and Shirley's youngest daughter is Linda Propp, she is a retired librarian for Gavilan Community College. She has three children: David is an independent contractor for desktop publishing training, he is married to Elaine and they have a daughter, Nicole Marie; Leslie is a Certified Paralegal/Notary for B. T. Mangan Law Offices in San Jose, California and is the mother of Matthew Jessie; Kirsten is a Journalism major at the University of Nevada, Las Vegas.

Hazel studied piano at the New England Conservatory of Music in Boston, then moving back to Tupper Lake. She married Victor Sohmer later in life. They lived in New York City, where she still lives and is sharp at 95.

Simon went on to the University of Pennsylvania and its medical school, and had a general practice in Albany after internship at Philadelphia General Hospital. He then studied hematology at Pennsylvania State University and practiced internal medicine and hematology during five years in the Navy, during WWII in the states, and in the war campaigns of North Africa and Italy. After the war he developed the new Division of hematology at Albany Medical College. He is actively retired in Longboat Key, Florida. He and his late wife, Mary Francis Stern, have three children: Paula Goldsmith, lives in Connecticut with her husband, Irv, who is with IBM; Julie, a psychologist lives in New Jersey with her husband Eric Martin; and Marilyn Propp Jones, an artist, who lives in Chicago with her husband David. Paula has two children, Bruce married Riko, and Jeffrey married to Jacqui, and Julie has two children, Meg and Drew.

Several thematic elements of Tupper Lake Proppiana may be of interest, including tragedy, humor, religion, art, and modesty.

The untimely deaths of Abram Propp, Naomi Seigel and her son, Peter, represent one type of tragedy that touches all families. The side effects of World War II and intra-family alienation also need to be noted and mourned.

A capacity for boisterous Tupper Lake humor marked our family, and perhaps is typified by the following experience: During an early morning fishing trip on Big Tupper as a child with Uncle Jesse, I was perched precariously on a seat in a rocking boat answering the call of nature. Suddenly, Jesse yelled a loud "Hello!" right next to my ear. Startled and embarrassed that observers were nearby, I fell into the lake. Clambering back aboard I saw no one around except Jesse, collapsed in laughter in the bottom of the boat.

Peter Propp helped found Beth Joseph Synagogue in 1905 at Tupper Lake. It is now on the National Historic Registry. Today it operates year round as a cultural center and, in the summer holds Erev Shabbat services every Friday night. My grandfather Joseph Rockovitz helped found Kenesseth Israel in Gloversville in 1910. I helped found Congregation B'nai Sholomi in Albany in 1971.

Jesse and Leah Propp were fine artists, as is Marilyn Propp Jones. Hazel Propp and Adele Siegal were excellent pianists. Joan Potter is an accomplished author, Mancia Propp has contributed to various articles and my wife, Vera, is negotiating on her first book, a children's story about the Holocaust.

It appears to be a family characteristic to take care of people silently. Hazel and Leah Were eating at Lindy's in New York City in the 1950's. A waitress recognized them and told them that Peter Propp kept her family in Food and clothing during the depression. They had never known about this activity.

The Propps I know and hear about seem to possess a strong will and ability to work effectively for themselves and their communities in the spirit of ethical monotheism. *(6/30/97)*

Circa: 1885, Baltimore, Maryland

Peter and Barnett Propp

Betsy Singer Propp and Barnatt Propp

Circa: 1900, Flemingsberg, Kentucky

Peter Propp

Anna Rockoff Propp

PROPPIANA: Travels with Cousin Henry, The Drushka from Syracuse to Shkudvil

by Richard Propp

It is perhaps too soon or too late to write this story, which, as you will see, is somewhat difficult. Still, we must write our stories when we can to continue the tradition of legends and lore that gives a group its history. This story begins in 1993. Until then, you see, I did not know that I had any other Propp relatives besides those from Tupper Lake and some distant ones in New York City who for some reason I had never met. But I got a telephone call at that time from a Henry Propp who lives near Syracuse. He was trying to track down some Propps he had heard about who were from Tupper Lake in upstate New York. Was I a part of that family? Yes, I was. Where did he come from? Well, Henry was born in Chicago and has been working on the Propp family genealogy for about three years, and he thinks our families are connected somehow. Where did my grandfather come from? I believed at that time that my grandfather Peter (Pesach) Propp came from Königsberg in East Prussia about 1885.

And we talked some more, and eventually met each other in Albany and Jamesville. Gradually Henry pieced in more of the picture working from new information and from old scrolls developed by his late Cousin Louis Arne and later his cousin Jerry Sachs. Last year I learned that my grandfather's other brother, Todres, had a grandson Ted who had emigrated from South Africa to Israel in 1955. So I had a second cousin I never knew about before, I must meet this person. Henry and I decided about February of 1996 to take a trip to meet our relatives in Europe and Israel, and to visit Shkudvil, our family shtetl in Lithuania, not far from Königsberg, now named Kaliningrad.

Now Henry, as all people, has his own ideas about traveling. One must take along a quantity of clothes suitable for formal and informal affairs, and there should be a quantity sufficient to last for two weeks without washing or dry cleaning. While I suggested, on more than one occasion I might add, that my way of traveling, two carry ons, one with rollers, and clothes enough only for three days, all washable, would be preferable, Henry was not to be dissuaded. He would take three large bags and a rack with wheels. It is this rack I have dubbed the "Drushka".

You know the story of the Drushka that went from Minsk to Pinsk? No? I will tell it once more. It is a metaphor for some of our current life. You see, this lady from Minsk wanted to go to Pinsk to visit relatives during the nineteenth century. A Druschka was to leave that day during those years when horses pulled carts for transportation. So, off they went on the Druschka until they came to a hill. "Everybody off, said the Drushka driver to the travelers." The horse is not strong enough to pull everyone up this hill." So off they got until the top of the hill when they re-boarded. Along the level, they traveled for awhile, until they came to a downward hill. "Everybody off, said the driver. " The horse is not strong enough to hold back the Drushka with everyone on it. " This kept repeating itself at every hill until they arrived at Pinsk. When they got there, this lady asked the driver; "I know why you, the driver, had to go to Pinsk, and I know why I had to go to Pinsk", said the lady; "but why did the horse have to go?"

I first saw the Druschka when I met Henry at the United Airlines area at Kennedy Airport in New York. Already it was hard to keep the three huge bags on it. When we got out of the tube at Russell square in London and tried to take it up the stairs, things were failing all over the place, and one lady gallantly carried the lower end up the stairs behind Henry.

London

In London we stayed for three days with a cousin, Dr. Louise Abrams, and her husband, George Browning, who is a lawyer. George's family left Berlin in the thirties. Louise' father is Arno, and his mother was Shira Propp from Tavrig, a short distance from where my grandfather probably actually lived, Shkudvil. We met Arno and had a long talk with him. He was born in 1898.

That Friday night we attended services with another cousin, David Hillel Ruben, born in Chicago, Illinois, who teaches philosophy at the London School of Economics. We walked to his Orthodox synagogue in Hendon. It was a lovely, joyous musical service. The girls came outside the synagogue to meet the boys after the service.

We had an elegant dinner prepared by Louise and George the next night. In attendance were Arno Abrams, Alice Propp Rodwell, who told us her story, as well as Solomon Abramovitch, Arno's nephew from Kaunus or, as it is known in Yiddish, Kovno, Lithuania, who is also a physician. His father had been a physician in the Kovno ghetto and survived to practice after the war. The next night there was a dinner at Solomon's house with Roslyn Flashman, granddaughter of Joseph Propp, and Michael Flashman from Brighton as well as the Rubens and their children Simon and Anna, and Solomon's sister Ariela Sef of Paris.

Arno had been taken from Taurage by the Germans to work in the mines in Tilsit in 1913 and had numerous adventures and escapes during his life. He finally made his way to England from Berlin in 1936 through persistence and intelligence. His is an illuminating story which I recorded.

Ariela was placed as an infant in a Christian orphanage in 1941. When it looked like she was going to be found out, her father brought her in a bag to a fisherman who took care of her during the war. When she was returned to her parents who were among the few people to survive the Kovno Ghetto, she did not believe they were her parents. Ariela states that "One cannot live in the past and must live in the present and plan for the future." It was a moving and joyful evening.

We also heard the intricate stories of Alice Propp Rodwell from Germany, and her husband Henry Rodwell. When Henry, born in Germany, came to enter the British army, he changed his name from Heinz Rosenthal so that if he were captured he would be safer. There are now about 300,000 English Jews out of a population of about sixty million. That percentage is apparently stable but not increasing. It is hard to prognosticate about the future of that community.

Stockholm

We next took the Drushka to Stockholm where we met and stayed for three days with the family of Leif and Birthe Jacobsen, Leif is a dentist who had been born in Norway whose great-grandmother was a Propp, who had moved from Russia with her husband. He had been an observant Jew in Norway. When the Nazis came in the Norwegian police put them in prison. He was eventually taken to a German prison in Norway and beaten severely for days. Eventually he and his family were to be sent by train to Auschwitz but for some reason the train was delayed, and he was able to get to Sweden. There he was in the army and later was able to study dentistry and still practices at the age of 72. We stayed at his office. He and Birthe met at a Jewish youth convention. She was originally from Denmark, and she told us of her family's escape from that country in 1941. A son , Per, is 26, is finishing medical school, and a daughter, Ann, is studying dentistry.

There is only a small Jewish community in Sweden, and apparently not much choice of how to practice one's Judaism. The secular life appears to be very an attractive alternative in Sweden. There is significant anti Semitism. Per feels that Judaism is not being well "marketed" in Sweden. There are presently about 15,000 Swedish Jews out of a population of ten million. One fears for the survival of that community as it is presently constructed.

Lithuania

Our next three days were in Lithuania. We flew into Vilnius (Vilna) late at night, and were met at the airport by a driver courtesy of the Hotel Villon. Ariela had made reservations for us there instead of allowing us to travel to Kovno at night, which she thought unwise. This hotel was a magnificent five star resort hotel.

The next morning we were met by our guide, Chaim Bargman, whom Henry had found on the Internet. He was born to a survivor of the Kovno ghetto in 1951, and was educated in Lithuania. He became interested in Judaism as a young man during the Soviet period when religion was being taken away from the Jews and presumably others. They formed an underground group to study Judaism and Hebrew. Eventually he was able to study in Israel and decided to leave the engineering profession and become a full time guide. He speaks Hebrew, Yiddish, English, Russian, and Lithuanian.

He and his driver took us first to the public library in Kovno where he talked his way into the library without a card. We copied a 1991 historical article about Shkudvil which included stories about the Propps. We then drove about an hour and had a nice lunch in a restaurant in Raseinia. About one half hour later we were in Shkudvil. There were a few newer houses but mainly there were old wooden houses that had belonged to the Lithuanian Jews before the war and now were being lived in and apparently belonged to the Lithuanian Christians. One can go back and reclaim one's house if you then live in it. In Shkudvil, Chaim found some older people who knew Naftali Prop and Itzig Prop. Naftali had a general store near the square. He and his wife, Rivka and their child, Ari, were killed along with the rest of the Jews of Shkudvil in the following manner, according to Oshry:

- *"The Jewish population in 1939 was 1,017 (total population: 2,000). Shkudvil was unique in that the whole town studied Torah, it was one big yeshiva. When you walked into a shop you could engage the shopkeeper   whether Leibchik the watchmaker, or Moshe Rivkin, or Lifshitz   in a Torah discussion and be amazed by his scholarship, particularly his understanding of the Talmud. Three Talmud shiurim were given daily for the public. The town rabbi taught one shiur for the older men. Binyomin Stein and Leibchik taught the younger men. And another Talmud shiur was taught by the town's scholars In rotation.*

- *Shkudvil's Tiferes Bachurim was an extraordinary chapter of that organization. Their rebbi was Reb Moshe Rivkin, who had a great Influence on his students. There was also a Chevra Kinyan Torah, where every day they studied Mishnayos and Chayey Odom.*

- *When I visited Shkudvil in 1939, 1 found almost every Jew of the town in the synagogue Friday night studying Torah. It is therefore no wonder that Shkudvil's rabbis were major Torah scholars. Their roster includes the Gaon and Tziddok Rav Eliyahu Yissochor Yoffe and his son in law, Rav Avrohom Y. Perlman.*

- *On June 22, 1941, the Germans entered Shkudvil. Almost no one managed to escape. The details were provided me by Rav Chaim Stein, Rosh yeshiva of Telz Yeshiva in Wickliffe, Ohio.*

- *On July 16, 1941, an announcement was made that all the town's citizens, Jews as well as Lithuanians, should gather at the marketplace. The Jews, however, were immediately encircled by Lithuanian partisans who chased the women away, and herded all the men they could catch into a building a mile away from town. On July 18th they were murdered by SS men.*

- *Three days later, on 26 Tamuz, the Lithuanians began to search for the men who had evaded the first Akzion. Some of the older men caught then were Moshe Baruch Broida, Binyomin Stein, Shmuel Eliyahu Bret, and Yaakov Dorfman. They were taken to the Jewish cemetery in Upina where they were murdered together with the rabbi of Upina, Rav Yitzchak Yoffe.*

- *That same day the Lithuanians, with the approval of the German commandant, issued an order that all women and children from Shkudvil must leave their homes. Some 800 women and children from Shkudvil were taken to a place not far from the town of Batok, and locked into a roofless barracks. They were kept there, under horrifying conditions of hunger and filth, for seven weeks. A number of children were born without any medical assistance. On the night of September 15, the surviving women and children were killed by the Lithuanians and buried in a mass grave. "*

We went to find the mass graves. There were no directions or signs. Chaim found a farmer who knew where the closest mass gravesite was. We drove off the main highway towards a woods. About half a mile in we came upon another side road with a faded sign; saying that this was the site of the shooting of the Jews. We drove in a bit but it was impassible. We got out and walked for about twenty five minutes through mud and woods in the Puzai forest. In my black "Rockports" I imagined that I was walking along the same path that the men were taken on from a holding building to this mass grave site, which we eventually reached. It was overgrown with weeds and in poor repair. We said an emotional Kaddish and came out of the woods somewhat stunned. We declined to see the holding building. We then found the two other mass graves in nearby villages, said Kaddish, and found a hotel in Taurage to stay in. It was somewhat Soviet style and not well maintained. We found a lovely restaurant where we had an elegant dinner for four, with music, it came to thirty dollars.

The next day we were able to find the young mayor of Shkudvil and had an hour meeting with him about the gravesite and the signs and road. He promised he would take better care of the gravesite but we would have to contact the regional government or the central government about the signage and a better road to the mass grave.

We then drove to Kovno and stopped first at the Ninth Fort. Have *you* heard of Ninth Fort 9, No? Not many people have. Kovno was a fort city, one of a series of cities built by the Russians in the 1800's to prevent the Germans and Prussians from invading, and they were about as successful as the Maginot line was in protecting the French. The cities were ringed with forts to be manned by artillery and soldiers. The forts later became prisons, and Ninth Fort was one of these. During the war it held Jews transported from all over Europe, including France. On a cell wall I saw the inscription, "Jules Herskovitz, Janvers 18, 5, 1994, de Monaco via Drancy Paris, Kaunus."

On October 28, 1941, The "Black Day" for Kovno Jewry, ten thousand people were selected from the Kovno ghetto by Helmut Rauca, Commandant of the Gestapo security police. They were marched to Ninth Fort where they were machine gunned by the Germans and their Lithuanian helpers. The corpses were later exhumed and burned by the Germans. Forty thousand Jews from all over Europe were killed at this fort during the Holocaust.

In 1943, a group of 64 Jews were in this prison. They were prisoners of war who were suspected of being Jewish, members of the Kovno ghetto underground military organization, and members of the ghetto prisoners brigade. They realized they must get out. Alexandr Podolski led the development of an escape plan which included an unused tunnel, keys made for the cell doors, and the hand drilling of 300 small holes in the exit door to the tunnel that they were able to push through on the night of December 25th. Most were eventually recaptured, but the members of the Kovno ghetto underground managed to reach the ghetto where they were hidden and drew up a document that told posterity the villainous acts committed in the Ninth Fort.

Lithuania before the war contained some 2.5 million people, of which ten percent were Jews. The Lithuanian Communist party contained some 1000 people, of whom half were Jews. A Lithuanian anti Semite told the Lithuanian Christians who had worked with the Russians that if they killed one Jew they would be welcome into the Lithuanian Nazi party. The man who made that statement was "Skirpa", and today there is a street named for him in Kaunas. One excuse for the Lithuanians to butcher their Jewish neighbors was because they were communists. This is obviously mathematically impossible and untrue. Another excuse was that the Jews looked down on the Lithuanian Christians. That is a perception that may have been based on their mutual apartness. That bears some thought and study. In my opinion the real reason for the killing and collaboration is the same as it has always been for the past two thousand years, institutionally preached and driven Christian anti Semitism.

We next visited the only synagogue left in Kovno, there were many before the war. They do have a minyan and are led by two Gabbis who survived the concentration camps. There are very few young people in Kovno. We also saw the street named in honor of the Nazi, Skirpa.

At three the next morning we left the Hotel Villon and were driven to the airport. When speaking with the lady at the airline desk, I forgot to tell her to check our bags through to Tel Aviv and she did not ask my ultimate destination. That led to us sitting practically outside the airport for an hour at Istanbul while they tried to figure out what to do with us. I asked Henry if he knew any good lawyers in Istanbul. Eventually we were reunited with our luggage and the Drushka in the VIP lounge and had a lovely flight to Israel on Air Turkey. The young lady next to me worked for a cardiac electrophysiology company in Brussels and was going to work with some new equipment in an Israeli hospital.

Israel

We were met at the airport by our fourth cousins, Sylvia Brilliant and Grace Berlow, and a second cousin, Ted Propp, who had made Aliyah from South Africa in 1955. Sylvia's late husband, Moshe, was a prominent journalist and writer. They had witnessed the birth and development of modern Israel and were friends with the country's leadership from Ben Grunion on. Ted and Sylvia had never met before. The way in from the airport revealed a bustling and burgeoning city that was typical of Jerusalem as well. There were many cars and cellular phones.

There are many picturesque walks to take in Tel Aviv. To be sure there were MacDonalds and other American imports. But there was much that was distinctly Israeli and Middle Eastern. We spent practically an entire day at the Museum of the Diaspora and I noted many exhibits not there on my last trip in 1989. It was hot, humid, and balmy in Tel Aviv, and the traffic was constant. I Joined a group of women demonstrating in front of MacDonalds. I thought it might be against carnivorism, but it turned out they were from "Peace Now" and were demonstrating against Netanyahu.

Next day we took the bus to Jerusalem. After praying at the Kotel and leaving some money in some Old City shops, we interviewed two families. The first was of Yankel Propp, age 85 and fragile. He had been a secular Jew, teaching constitutional law at the university at Kovno. The day he heard the Germans were coming he went home, grabbed his wife, and got on the next train to Moscow. He knew no Russian but was able to get work in a tungsten mine near Moscow. At the end of one year he had learned Russian and had become assistant manager of the mine. After the war he reached Israel. A son and his family live across the hall from him, and a daughter works as a nurse.

We then took a taxi to Geula near Mea Sharim where we met with the Slapobersky rabbinical family. An Uncle was in the Kovno ghetto and wrote a memoir of its horrors. There are now two daughters and a son all with very large families. While Henry frantically copied all their names, I fell asleep on the couch. We insisted on taking the taxi back to Tel Aviv despite Sylvia's wish to take the bus. Next day we had breakfast with Sylvia's and her son, Yehoshua, who is a journalist in Tel Aviv. He belongs to a small but growing conservative synagogue there. It was a pleasure to get his view of the accomplishments and challenges of Israel.

Next day we went with Ted Prop back to Jerusalem to see some special views of the city near where Ted had fought against the Jordanians in the '67 war, and to see a non descript land area called Har Homar which is within Jerusalem. I visited a friend at the Ministry of Health to try to set up an exchange on hospital quality management. A radiologist in Israel told me that they don't have quality assurance in Israel, they have quality assertion. I said I have seen that too in New York State in some hospitals.

Before leaving Jerusalem we needed to buy some tsatskes at the stores. Ted told us he was confused because in Hebrew that means loose women. I said it was also a Yiddish word with eight meanings according to Leo Rosten, and I was using one to mean inexpensive toys. So we got some souvenirs and headed out of the most beautiful city in the world.

That night at Ted Propp's Moshav outside of Rehovat we met his five children, their spouses and girlfriends and grandchildren, his wife Mazal, and his sister, Aviva. Slowly there gathered Propps who had never met before. And since they are from different branches of Judaism, including secular, modern orthodox and ultraorthodox, who don't talk often to each other, the fact that they did talk was very moving. Regretfully we left for the airport at 11:00 P.M. and wended our way back to New York, Albany, Syracuse.

Now what do make out of these confusing histories, stories, and encounters? This would appear to be only a romantic trip, full of emotion but not meaning. After all, these terrible events are in the past, not subject to change. On the other hand, if we do not learn something from them, they will, like the facts of "King Lear" be only a sad story of history. If we can learn something from them, then it can at least be elevated to the level of tragedy.

It so happened that without their knowing it, Lithuania was being organized for the mass murder of the Jews with the aid of their very neighbors. There is Information on this in the Encyclopedia Britannica and in other books on the Jewish Holocaust. How do you plan for the annihilation of the Jews of 47 towns and several large cities? Does that take weeks, or months, or years of planning? Do you plan with only Germans, or do you also plan with Lithuanian Christians and Russians? If we can learn how that happened, we will perhaps be able to understand a little better how we should conduct ourselves now around the world. There are continuing problems of anti Semitism and racism. My own belief is that anti Semitism will die the same day racism does, which is to say, never.

So we must know what is going on. How is this to be done? We are told that anti Semitism is present but marginalized in the United States, Canada, and England, but less so in Argentina and elsewhere. That must be worked on. How? By supporting our Jewish organizations that are on the forefront of this action such as B'nai B'rith. It is vitally important that we support and have dialogue with Israel via AIPAC, Hadassah, and other organizations. And at the same time we do this, we can reconnect up with our brethren in other lands. We must have a world view. How about a million Jewish people meeting in Buenos Aires to protest that country's handling of the bombings investigation? And if we can marginalize anti Semitism, then we can also manage to marginalize the forces that would disunite the Jewish people. We need to belong to and support our synagogues and federations. We must continue to develop our synagogues and our youth and adult programs into positive experiences. Federation is beginning to have a role here. And if we can unite the Jewish people we will have accomplished, as on Ted Propp's Moshav, at least one element of Tikkun Olam.

I have kidded my cousin, Henry, about his Druschka. But the fact is that by studying our family, its history, and world history, Henry was able to develop a very significant data base. It was also very meaningful to be personally in contact with all these relatives. By so doing, he not only brought people together physically in several countries, but also he restored and developed new emotional ties between family members that could lead to fence mending and family projects, like the one he is organizing for proper access to the mass grave site near Shkudvil in the Puzai forest. I remember saying a few kind words about Henry at Ted Propp's Moshav. He answered, "I would just like all the Propps to love one another." People like Henry are to be congratulated for study, for prayer, and for deeds of loving kindness. I am personally very grateful for the opportunity he provided during this Lithuanian genealogical odyssey.

PROPP COUSINS CLUB NEWS

VOLUME I   JUNE 1939   NUMBER 1

"THE STICK-TO-GETHER FAMILIES"
by
Edgar A. Guest.

The finest of conventions ever
held beneath the sun,
Is a real family gathering when
the busy day is done.
It's the stick-together family
that wins the joys of earth,
That hears the sweetest music,
that finds the finest mirth;
To each and every one of you,
if contentment you would win,
Come you back unto the circle
and be comrade with your kin.

*   *   *

JUNE MEETING

Hotel Chicagoan

67 West Madison Street

Parlor "M" and "N"

7:30 P.M. sharp

As this will be the last meeting of the season, let's all try and be present
to help plan for the summer.

Edyth Morton will be the hostess for the June Meeting.

The meeting is to be held in the large double parlor which is AIR CONDITIONED.

REMINISCING

Something's in the air! Taint music! Taint Gossip! Taint something that can be eaten or drunk, but it sure can be felt. It's that Mothers' Day meeting that we had at the Hotel Chicagoan.

As we look back and remember the evening, we can think of nothing nicer than the events as they followed their normal procedure during the evening. First came the short business meeting, then followed the program which everyone seemed to enjoy.

Praises cannot be sung loud enuff for the manner in which the Blumenthal girls entertained us with the violin and piano accompaniment. Such talent, and right in our own midst, and they were so gracious in offering their services. Many thanks, girls, from the Propps.

Then came Doctor William Bishop who started in by saying he did not know what to say, but ended up with all of us glad he didn't know what to say because he said so many entertaining things. Thanks to you, Doctor Bishop. Then followed the "Tone Poems" given by Mr. Charles Edgar Salmon and his pianist, Miss Marion Elizabeth Smale. Their selections were certainly befitting the occasion, and so many congratulated them for their kind assistance and entertainment. We thank you, too, Mr. Salmon and Miss Smale.

As we look around the room, what fun everyone seemed to be having. In one corner sat the boys. Let's see, there were Charlie Berlow from South Bend, Max, Ted, Earl, Elliott and Mike Propp, Ben Twery and Nimsy, and several others too numerous to mention. Oh yes, Dave Rice whom incidentally we let win at cards this time, because we want to take him for bigger stakes next time, and we were certainly pleased to have with us Mrs. Dave Rice, who brought along her four charming daughters,

(continued - page 2 column 1)

COMMITTEES

Picnic.
General Chairman
    Mike Propp
Co-Chairman
    Earl Propp

Let's give them all the cooperation they ask for.

Transportation
    Ben Twery

It's Ben's job to see to it that all who can't arrange for any other transportation are transported safely to and from the picnic grounds.

See, call or write Ben for full particulars.

Games, Prizes and Awards

    Mike Propp
    Elliott Propp
    Earl Propp
    Edyth Morton
    Sam Lazerwith
    Bud Ruben

Location and Grounds

    Sam Blumenthal
    Mike Propp
    Earl Propp

- - - - - - -

HISTORIAN

We're going to write a history of the Propp Cousin's Club organization since the time it was an Idea up to the present date, and from there on we will carry a continuous history for future generations.

Cousin Charlotte Lazerwith, is the first appointee for historian, and Edyth Morton associate historian.

Give them every support you can, and any information that you may have that will help make the story of the Cousin's club interesting and good reading.

PICNIC

Of course, the big event for the summer is going to be the second annual picnic. We naturally hope to make it bigger and better in every way than last year (if possible) and we want everyone's cooperation in this direction.

The date has been definitely set for JULY 9th, the second Sunday in July - the place, MARQUETTE PARK at Miller, Indiana, where we held it last year, and we are going to try very hard to hold it in one of the more shaded and secluded spots.

A committee will be appointed to be on the grounds real early that day to see that all arrangements are made for your enjoyment, comfort, and convenience. Plan now to get there real early and stay late, and we will plan for you a truly enjoyable outing.

Games, contests, prizes, refreshments for everybody. There is no cost, but bring plenty of your own food because that good fresh Indiana air is going to make you awfully hungry and you are going to be out all day long Plan and arrange right now if you possibly can for your transportation. Maybe you can get one of the Cousins or some of your friends to drive out with you. For those who have no transportation facilities, we are arranging for a special chartered bus that will stop at convenient places along the route to pick up and discharge passengers, and for which the total cost of the round trip will be only $1.00. If you can't arrange any other transportation, arrange to ride on the bus. It's going to be a lot of fun, and all those that rode on the bus last year had a very enjoyable trip. You

(continued - page 2 column 3)

Continued - REMINISCING

Marion (Mrs. Harry Balaban), Caroline (Mrs. Al Marks), Ethel (Mrs. Ben Gordon) and Shirley Rose. Harry Balaban was unable to attend this meeting, but we hope to see him at some of the others -- Caroline brought along her husband, Albert, whom we were glad to welcome, and Ethel brought the doctor with her, (it is always good to have a doctor in the house).

Some of those that came the longest distance were there first. We must say that Celia and Charlie Berlow who come all the way from South Bend always get there early - congratulations.

Someone had a happy thought when it was remembered that it was Dave Rice's birthday, and at the last moment we all sang "Happy Birthday to Dave".

Edith Morton's husband, Herman, drove several hundred miles to be with us. We were glad to have his mother and father with us -- not to forget to mention the fact that Mr. and Mrs. Albert Given were with us, whom of course we all know is Gertrude Blumenthal's mother and dad. They were able to give several of us a slant as to what is happening at the San Francisco Fair.

Let's hold our August meeting at the San Francisco Fair.

There was so much going on; have we missed anyone? We hope not, because everybody had such a good time.

Oh, yes, we mustn't forget Nate Ruttenberg; it isn't every meeting he can attend.

Bert Ruben also makes quite a sacrifice to get in from out of town to be with us. He is a very gracious fellow, isn't he, and after all he is the father of our secretary.

NEWS ITEMS

Confirmation of Lucyle Blumenthal on May 21st - at East Chicago. It was a galla event. Congratulations to the Samuel Blumenthals.

* * *

Confirmation of Barbara Propp on May 28th in South Bend. Reports from this party tell us it was a very happy affair. Congratulations to the C. H. Propp family.

* * *

Confirmation of Phyllis Propp on May 28th in Chicago. What a gathering. People and more people - food and more food - need we say anymore? Congratulations to the Mike Propps.

* * *

Our sympathies to Celia Propp on the loss of her father Phillip Mendelsohn.

* * *

Lou and Ann Smith and Hirdie Propp just returned from a vacation in Memphis, Tennessee, where they visited with their family.

* * *

Uncle Louis Arne of Milwaukee tells us he enjoys receiving our announcements so much. Some of us that have been up to see him are so pleased to find him recovering rapidly.

* * *

Word comes that Blanche Leviton is ill. Best wishes for a speedy recovery.

* * *

Esther Nimz and son David are vacationing with grandma and grandpa Charnoff in Boston, Massachusetts. Hurry back, Esther.

'PICNIC Continued

will have to buy your bus ticket at our June meeting, so make up your mind definitely how you're coming out so that we can arrange for the bus charter.

Remember, Marquette Park is right on the lake so be sure to bring your bathing togs. There are plenty of lockers and the beach has every possible comfort and facility. Umbrellas can be rented for very little money for use out on the beach. We want everyone's suggestions on the picnic so here's your chance to make suggestions at the June meeting. We want to again remind you that we rented the air-conditioned parlors for the June meeting at which time all of the details for the picnic will be carefully discussed and we want your presence and we want your suggestions.

AUGUST ? ? ?

Also, we may have time to discuss our plans for the August outing. We will not have a meeting in August but we would like to have someone suggest a nice boat trip, say to St. Joe. Here's a good idea. Let's hold our meeting in St. Joe - we'll all take a boat ride, get off at St. Joe and have our meeting at Silver Beach, and go back by return trip by evening. We'll try to have full information for you at our June meeting for the July picnic and the August boat outing, unless someone has a better idea for the August outing, and ideas are welcome. In fact, that's what we want more of. Every member who has any kind of an idea should stand up at the meeting and express his views on any subject.

* * *

193

PROPP COUSINS CLUB NEWS

VOLUME 1   OCTOBER 1939   NUMBER 2

"When the Frost is on the Punkin"

They's something kind O'harty-like
     about the atmusfere,
When the heat of summer's over
     and the coolin' fall is here
Of course we miss the flowers,
     and the blossums on the trees,
and the mumble of the hummin' birds
     and the buzzin of the bees;
But the air's so appetizin;
     and the landscape through the haze
of a crisp and sunny morning of
     the airly auturmn days,
Is a pictur' that no painter has
     the colorin' to mock
When the frost is on the punkin
     and the fodder's in the shock.

DEDICATION

Sunday, October 15th at 2 P.M.

Western Star Cemetery
Waldheim

Rabbi Lassen,
S.S. Hebrew Congregation

MEETING

Sunday, October 15th at 7:30 P.M.

Brevoort Hotel
"Lincoln Room"

Sarah Romain, will be
hostess for the meeting.

OCTOBER
M E E T I N G

Please note that the Dedication
and the October Meeting will be
held on the same day.

Also please note that the place
of meeting has been changed to
the BREVOORT HOTEL
     120 W. Madison Street.
     "Lincoln Room"
The "Lincoln Room" has just
been freshly decorated and will
make an ideal meeting place for
us.

BE PROMPT ! !   BE PRESENT ! !

IN MEMORIAM

It is with profound sorrow that we must advise you of the passing of Uncle Louis Arne. He passed away on Sunday morning, September 18th at 6:00 A.M. Final rites were held at Weinstein's Chapel in Chicago on Monday September 18th at 2:00 P.M. Services were conducted by Rabbi Lassen of B'nai Zion. His final resting place being P.O.W. Cemetery, Waldheim. He lived to be 73 years of age and all that knew him loved him. He leaves behind his immediate family, his widow Celia, and the children Phillip, Charles, Sarah, Lillian and Rosalie. Genealogy was his hobby, and when the Propp Cousins Club was started it was his very complete record of the family and all of its branches that was used. This record traces the family back to 1806. He was the only one that knew the different branches of the family and their origin. In his passing the family feels the loss of a good and true friend.

The Propp Cousins Club in its entirety extend to the members of the Arne Family their heart-felt sympathy.

- - - - - - - -

Our sympathies go to: Gertrude Blumenthal - and Mr. and Mrs. Givens, in the loss of Nancy Givens, the daughter of Mr. and Mrs. Eugene Givens, who passed away September 6th very suddenly.

- - - - - - -

For those who are not aware of it, Mrs. Lillian Propp has been very ill for a considerable time, but is now reported that she is recovering, and will be with us again very shortly. We miss her smiling face and cheerfulness at our meetings and hope that she will not have to miss any more of them.

-- Hurry back, Lillian --

DEDICATION
DAVID and ETTA PLOTKE STONE

Mike Propp, our chairman of the Dedication Committee reports that the stone has been set and all is in readiness for the dedication. It will be held on October 15th at 2:00 P.M. at the Western Star Cemetery, Waldheim. Rabbi Morris Teller of the South Side Hebrew Congregation will officiate. As this has been sponsored by the Club, we hope that all of you will make it a point to be there.

Let's have 100% representation.

- - - - - - - -

HISTORIAN

Charlotte Lazerwith reports that the outline for the history of the club has been made, and soon she will collaborate with Edith Morton and they in turn will have something to tell us.

- - - - - -

INCORPORATION

According to the report from Mr. Sam Lazerwith, the Propp Cousins Club is now properly incorporated under the laws of the State of Illinois.

- - - - - -

CONSTITUTION

The Constitution has been re-written in accordance with changes that were suggested and voted on, and will be placed on file with the Secretary.

- - - - - -

DECEMBER 10th, 1939
C A R D   P A R T Y

Resolve now to reserve the date, December 10th, 1939, for the second annual Propp Cousins Club CARD PARTY. We have reserved the entire second floor of the Brevoort Hotel for this occasion. For those that attended last year you will remember the hundreds of Door Prizes that

SUMMER CLUB ACTIVITIES

The second annual picnic of the Propp Cousins Club was held on July 9th at Marquette Park and, as usual, a great success. There were over 100 at the picnic and from all that we hear, everyone really had a good time.

Popcorn, candy, peanuts, chewing gum, balloons, etc. for everyone and for those of you who could not be there can you picture anything nicer than to stand and view this great group of Propp Cousins scattered over this hill, that was our place at the park, at dinner time. It wasn't a lot of little groups but one large group with everybody eating something from everyone elses lunch basket...food and food and what food !...We are sure that it was an occasion that everyone will long remember.

- - - - - - -

THE AUGUST GET-TOGETHER

There are many of you who will never forget the Propp Cousins Club trip, which was held on Sunday, August 13th, 1939. Thanks to Mr. and Mrs. Nate Ruttenberg, and Mrs. Celia Propp it was a financial success. It was a beautiful day and a fine trip, and all of those who took the trip enjoyed every minute of it.

- - - - - - - -

were given, as well as prizes for each table. Refreshments will be served.

More details later; in the meantime, remember the date

Sunday, December 10th, 1939

GOLD ROOM - BREVOORT HOTEL

195

WHERE HAVE YOU BEEN ? ?

As summer has come to a close, and the fall and winter season has begun, we are thinking about where the PROPPS spent their summer. Your "Inquiring Reporter" has found that the activities have been many and varied.

Sometime in late June Mr. and Mrs. Jerome Sachs took a river boat trip up the St. Lawrence and Saguenay Rivers with stop-overs in Montreal and Quebec. They are willing to recommend it to anyone, as they say it was the most wonderful trip they had ever taken. (No wonder, it was their "honeymoon").

Mr. and Mrs. Gordon Berlow spent a lovely three weeks in California, visiting with cousins Pete and Dora Berlow - as well as taking in the San Francisco Fair and other sights.

Edith Morton is just bubbling over with news regarding the California relatives and her extended vacation this summer to the Coast. Edith left early in the summer and Herman and Lester and Milton Sisken followed by car later on and brought her back. They visited several of the National Parks on the way home.

Mr. and Mrs. Morrie Berlow had a cottage at Paddock Lake.

Rose and Ben Twery had a cottage at Round Lake.

Mr. and Mrs. Sam Lazerwith spent several wonderful week ends in Aurora with friends.

Mr. and Mrs. Nate Ruttenberg took several week-end trips.

Miss Zerna Rubin started her vacation by visiting with relatives in South Bend, and as yet we have not heard what the balance of her vacation consisted of - although we understand she had a very lovely time.

Congratulations ! to Mr. and Mrs. Jerome Sachs on their wedding which took place on June 23rd. On June 22nd a betrothal dinner was held for the family at Del Prado Hotel in the evening - and on the following day the ceremony was held at 1:00 P.M. in the study of Rabbi Berman at Temple Isiah. Following the ceremony the bridal party was invited to the home of the groom's parents, Mr. and Mrs. Leon Sachs, where a buffet luncheon was served. The bride was stunning in a white sharkskin suit with a lovely orchid shoulder corsage. -- It was a lovely wedding.--

On September 10th, at the Country Club Hotel, our Ruth Blumenthal became Mrs. Edward Gradman. A very large attendance was noted -- it was a beautiful service. The bridge wore a lovely net wedding gown and a very beautiful veil. We could go on and on, telling about how stunning the bride's mother looked -- not to forget her sister Ceil, who was a member of the wedding party. They have just returned from their honeymoon, and their "at home" address will be announced later.

- - - - - -

We are happy to report that Carol Givens, daughter of Mr. and Mrs. Eugene Givens is well on the road to recovery.

- - - - -

Mrs. Ben Gordan has had quite a siege of sickness this summer, but is okay now, and we hope she will attend some of our meetings.

Harold Nimz says he hopes that the meetings will start soon, as he misses the little side-money he gets from "Mike". (That ain't the story that Mike tells us).

Ceil and Phyllis Propp also vacationed in South Bend, and we believe Mike spent some time there with them.

Leon Sachs spent ten days visiting with his sister, Hinde Gordon, and family in New York; also attended the Fair.

Esther Nimz spent the summer with her mother in Boston.

The Harry Balabans had a summer place in Winnetka.

Mr. and Mrs. Al Marks vacationed at the Grand Hotel in Mackinac.

Mrs. Givens reports that for a real rest, you must go to the Hotel "Witcomb" in St. Joe.

Lill Perlman and friend hubby can tell us all about Madison in the summer.

Lill Arne motored to Twin Cities in the early summer.

Mr. Charles Berlow and Mr. Charles Propp toured the copper country up and around Calumet.

Mr. and Mrs. Phil Arne also spent some time in the Calumet region.

Mr. and Mrs. Charles Berlow of South Bend, and Sophie and Bubbles Propp spent some time in Chicao this summer. They are always welcome guests.

Lou and Anne Smith - and the Max Propps had their summer home in Michigan City open this summer.

The Lou Imbers had a lovely vacation in New York City, at which time they visited with some of the New Jersey relatives.

* * * * *

The Propp Cousin Club of Chicago, Illinois
Marquette Park, Indiana 1939

Top Row (L to R) Buddy Ruben, Lou Imber, Harry Berlow

*3rd Row (L to R) Julius Propp, Leo Propp, Phyllis Propp, Roy Propp, --, Earle Propp, Ruth Propp, Lillian (Propp) Ruttenberg,
Sophie Propp, Lydia (Propp) Imber, Ella (Propp) Sachs, Sarah (Berlow) Romain, Anna Propp, Harold Blumenthal, Jake Shapiro, Mike Propp,*

*2nd Row (L to R) Mrs. Givens, Sam Blumenthal, Celia Propp, Lillian (Propp) Ruben, Gert Blumenthal,
Mary Blumenthal, Celia (Ruttenberg) Arne, Moshe Berlow/Irene Berlow, Evelyn Berlow, Leon Sachs, Lillian Arne, Ida Shapiro
Bottom Row (L to R) Essie Greenberg (Not a Relative), Zerna Ruben, Bert Ruben, Anna Shapiro, Arthur Blumenthal, --, Henry Propp, Mark Lazerwith*

197

The Propp Cousin Club of Chicago, Illinois
Lincoln Park, Chicago, Illinois 1940

Buddy Ruben
——, Esther Charnoff Nimz, ——,

Harry Berlow
Ruth, Cel and Mary Blumenthal, Celia Berlow, Annie Shapiro,
——

Arthur Blumenthal   *Ivan Charoff,*   *Leo Propp,*   *Roy Propp,*   *Irving Charoff*

198

Joseph (Propp) Berlow's Family, Chicago, Illinois - 1917

back row: Charles, Abe, Harry, Irving, Peter and Maurice
front row: Gordon, Sarah, Rochel, Joseph and Rose

This photograph of Harry's son, Richard (Dick) and his wife Kathi Balaban was taken in the mid-1990s. (Photograph courtesy of Richard Balaban)

This photograph of Harry and Marion Balaban was taken in the mid-1980s. (Photograph courtesy of Richard Balaban)

This is the same Balaban family of Chicago, Illinois who owned all the movie theaters in Chicago and Paramount Films in Hollywood during the 1930s and 1940s and are still in the theater business. Harry was a brother of Barney Balaban of New York. All were born in Chicago on the near west side.

Shkudvil, Russia, 1880
Yankel Prop

London, England, 1903
Joe Propp, son of Yankel,
and his wife, Annie

1904, Tavrig, Russia - Dov-Ber ben Itsik Prop

Back: Dora (Propp) and Note Stolov, Julius Propp, Sira (Propp) and Solomon Abramovitch, Sol Propp Front: Dov-Ber (Bertzik) Propp Sarah Propp Zlata (Shrage) Propp

1948, Peoria, Illinois
Back: Wanda (Dubriner) Propp, Fred Propp, Zava Baicovitz, Julius Propp, Jenny (Propp) and Jacob Baicovitz Front: Roy Propp and Isadore Propp

Back Row: *Sira, Devorah, Goldie*
Middle Row: *Bertzig, Ella, Rivka*
Front Row: *Sarah, Chaim, Meier*

Shira Propp Abramovich

Tavrig
Sara and Jenny Propp C: 1899

Shira's son Arno Abrams, London, England - 1996

Alice Propp Rodwell, London, England - 1943

Sira Prop Abramovich in the Kovno Ghetto

Последние дни бабушки Сиры
в гетто 1944
с мешок в руках
Сохраните не уничтожайте!

Sira and her husband
Solomon Abramovich
were murdered in the
Kovno ghetto during a
Nazi action to murder
women, children and
old people. This was on
March 6, 1944.

Kovno, Lithuania

Sira Prop and her Husband, Solomon-Itzik Abramovich with Some of the grandchildren;
Boyra (first left) and Boris who perished in the ghetto and concentration camps. Rivochka,
Miriam and Josef (standing) survived the concentration camps. The photograph was taken
before the war in 1936.

Max and Simon Fishman, the sons of Shmuel and Jenta - circa 1920

Memoir: The Holocaust Recalled

By Miriam Abramovitch Reich

My experiences are not unique, not even original. They are similar to those of hundreds of thousands of other men, women, and children who came face to face with unprecedented evil, the systematic annihilation of a people, the Holocaust. No, my story is not original, but because it is mine, the task in front of me is daunting.

I have waited a long time to tell my tale, battling an invisible wall of resistance, saying to myself that it's all been said before, feeling inadequate to the task, and wondering where I'll find words for the ineffable. Moreover, revealing myself never came easily to me. I always found more "interesting" things to talk about.

I have been very protective of my past. I feared that the scars were too tender to the touch of others as well as to my own memories of how they came to be. I kept these memories like a genie in a bottle since I did not know what to expect of them once I let them loose. Lately, they appear less threatening, more friend than foe, coaxing me to action, and are becoming increasingly more impatient with my procrastination. Perhaps it is the approaching Fiftieth Anniversary of my liberation from Bergen-Belsen, a symbolic milestone, or the gentle urging of family and friends to tell my story, or both, that finally compel me to undertake this very difficult task. To bear witness to human suffering is tough; how much tougher it is when it's your own.

Some time ago, as I was walking along the beach on Siesta Key, I reminded myself how lucky I was to have the freedom to do the things I was doing and to be at peace with my surroundings. It has not always been that way. A scene flashed through my mind. My mother and I were on a train travelling through Germany, being transported from a concentration camp in Estonia, a place that was becoming threatened by the Red Army, to a camp in Germany. Through the few slats of the box car in which we were riding, I saw many villages and small towns dotting the landscape. There were cottages surrounded by neat picket fences, animals grazing, people going about their business, children playing, and dogs running and barking. It is impossible for me even today to describe the feeling of despair and sadness I experienced watching these scenes of daily normal life. How I wished to be one of those children, or even a dog.

It all started in June, 1940, as I was celebrating my tenth birthday. The party table was set outdoors in the gazebo of our garden. My mother, father, and my brother Boria (Boris) who was two-and-a-half years older than I, were having strawberries with whipped cream, my traditional birthday fare (June was strawberry time in Lithuania too). Suddenly we heard a commotion in the street, which was not visible to us from where we were. Our property was surrounded by a tall concrete fence with a heavy wooden gate for an entrance. We ran to the street. It turned out to be the arrival of a convoy of the Red Army. The Soviet Union had invaded Lithuania

On March 23, 1939, Germany annexed Memel (Klaipeda), a city on the Baltic Sea which was inhabited mainly by Germans, but whose control was given to Lithuania at the end of World War I and had a special status as an autonomous territory. The Nazi--Soviet Pact placed Lithuania in the Soviet sphere of influence, and on October 10 of that year, Lithuania was compelled to permit the establishment of Soviet bases on its territory. Vilnius (Vilna), a Lithuanian city, but given to Poland in 1918, was restored to Lithuania, and on June 15th, 1940, the Soviet Army assumed control of Lithuania.

I vividly remember the great welcome the arrival of the Red Army received from the local citizens as they were passing through our street. There was a lot of waving and cheering. The Lithuanian army offered no resistance. The contest was between an elephant and a flea. While I found out later that there were pockets of resistance by the Lithuanian national army, on the surface it appeared like a friendly invasion. There was no fighting and no visible destruction. My family, however, had nothing to cheer about. We were the bourgeoisie, the wrong class, and therefore the enemy of the proletariat. That day changed our lives forever.

My father Ruvim (Reuven) Abramovitch was a businessman. It was a family textile business, owned by my father and his brothers. They imported cloth first from Germany, then Great Britain. They were wholesalers and had a large warehouse on Daukshos Street, not too far from our home. During World War I, my father was taken prisoner of war by the Germans who invaded Lithuania on their way to Russia. In the 1920's he visited Palestine, and in the 1930's he made several business trips to England. My mother, Bassia, was a housewife. She had a Ph.D. in economics but did not practice her profession. Whether it was by choice or lack of opportunity, I don't know.

We lived in the old part of town on Janovos Street, on a very large properly that belonged to my maternal grandparents. It was a white washed bungalow overgrown with ivy, next to my grandparents' house. Our home consisted of a kitchen with a wood stove, two bedrooms and a living-dining room. When we were younger, my brother and I shared a nursery. As I got older, I slept in my parents' bedroom. The maid had a small room off the kitchen. For as long as I can remember we always had live-in help. Housework was not easy in those days. The laundry had to be washed by hand with the aid of a ribbed washboard and then boiled. It was followed by bluing, starching, and ironing. Wash and wear clothes did not exist. The Persian carpets had to be taken outside, hung on a line, and beaten to remove the dust. The daily chores were hard and time consuming.

Shopping for food was a daily expedition. Bread was bought fresh daily, before breakfast, of course. So was milk, for it could not be stored for long without modern refrigeration, particularly in the summer. The milk had to be boiled since it was not pasteurized. The fine skin that would form on the surface of the milk after it was scalded was the bane of my life. No matter how carefully it was removed, some of it would remain floating, making me gag as I drank it. Neither was the milk homogenized. The cream would rise to the top, thick and yellow (no 2% milk then), and would be partially removed to be used in coffee or made into whipped cream. We used to make our own cottage cheese, and as a special treat the cream would be whipped into butter. It was the most delicious butter I ever tasted.

We had no central heating. Every two rooms shared a thick wall that was partially tiled. This tiled section of the wall contained a wood burning heater. The tiles on the outside of the heater formed part of the walls. The tiles would become warm, retain the heat, and in turn heat the rooms. We had a modern bathroom, telephone, but no refrigerator. There was a cellar underneath the kitchen floor and an attic with well worn, shaky stairs on the outside of the house leading to it. The attic was a mysterious and fascinating place for my brother and me to browse in. The stairs, which I considered very dangerous (I was scared of heights), presented a real challenge, and in turn contributed to the excitement of this exploit. We also had an outdoor cold storage area for storing perishable food in the summer. It looked like an earth covered igloo with a wooden door at the entrance. It was a large, shallow walk-in area that was lined with blocks of ice and protected from the summer heat by saw dust and earth. The ice was cut in the winter from the river Neris (Viliya), which bordered our property. That river also caused us a lot of worry in the springtime. There was always danger of flooding, and every couple of years it did. On several occasions we had a foot or two of water inside our house, and we had to navigate to and from the house by row boat. On those occasions my brother and I were sent to stay with Aunt Rosa, Ida Rogovin's mother, and her family, in an apartment downtown on Laisves Aleya. This was the main street of Kaunas, both residential and commercial. My aunt was very hospitable, and what I remember best were the wonderful chocolates and candies that we ate there.

Our property was subdivided into several sections. The two homes faced a large garden. Whatever knowledge and love of gardening I have today goes back to those days. We grew some vegetables and had beautiful flower beds. The irises were particularly plentiful, and to this day when I smell the lemon-like scent of iris, I associate it with our garden of long ago. We also had fruit trees, and in the fall the grounds were covered with chestnuts from a couple of very large chestnut trees. A bit further on there was a saw mill that was no longer used. Further still was a commercial area that bordered the street, and on the opposite side, our property ran along the river, separated from it by a tall, mesh fence. My brother and I used to roam the grounds by foot or bicycle exploring all the nooks and crannies of which there were many. There were no other children to play with, though. The only girl my age on the grounds was the watchman's daughter, Birute. She and her parents lived in a cottage that was located inside the entrance to our property, next to the gate. At night our grounds were protected not only by a tall fence and locked gate, but also by a vicious hound that was let loose past a certain hour. My grandparents' house was larger than ours since my widowed uncle, Boris, a doctor, and his two young adult children, university students, lived there too. My uncle also had his office there.

My grandmother, Chana Strassbourg (Camber) was a tall, rather austere, dignified, no nonsense lady who had an excellent head for business. My grandfather, Israel was a very warm and charming man. He had more time for us children than my grandmother since she was preoccupied with the day to day business activities related to the property. He was an ardent Zionist and scholar. Both grandparents left for Palestine in 1938. My grandmother could not adjust to the harshness of the new environment. She returned home to Kaunas before World War II broke out and died a natural death soon after. My grandfather died in Palestine the day the war broke out. Whether they meant to remain apart, I have no idea.

My paternal grandparents, Shira (Propp) and Solomon Abramovitch, lived downtown on Gednias Street. It was a twenty-five minute walk from our place. We used to visit with them frequently, often taking a caleche in the summer or horse drawn sleigh in the winter to get there. This was a common means of transportation, equivalent to the taxi of today. My grandmother, a real beauty in her youth, was very affectionate and extremely hospitable. My grandfather used to discuss business and politics with my father, but had time for his grandchildren too. They both lost their lives subsequent to our departure from the ghetto in one of the Selections.

Summers we used to go to a datcha (summer cottage) in Kolotovo, a village not too far from the city, a place that we often shared with my paternal grandparents. We used to get there by horse and buggy, loaded with all kinds of provisions such as bedding and kitchen items that we needed to see us through the summer. The cottage was located in a wooded pine tree area not too far from a river where we used to go bathing. It was rather Spartan inside, but cool and comfortable. Built of knotted pine, it looked very clean and smelled of new wood. There was no electricity, no running water, but a well and an outhouse close by. This was standard for the countryside since only a few of the larger cities in Lithuania had electricity and indoor plumbing. Some summers we would go to Klaipeda (Memel) on the Baltic seashore to the beach. From a child's perspective, life was on an even keel.

Having said all this, I still wonder why my parents chose to remain in Lithuania. I remember my father listening to the radio very frequently, particularly to speeches broadcast from England. Politics were discussed often at home, and I remember the names of Hitler and Chamberlain being mentioned. Surely, they knew the vulnerability of our geographic location, caught between Germany and Russia, each vying for supremacy, and Russia wanting an outlet to the Baltic Sea. Also, the Lithuanian past checkerboard history, as well as the families, should have provided them with a clue to the future. Both of my parents had been abroad. My mother had graduated from the University of Giessen in Germany. Many of my aunts and uncles lived abroad. Was it complacency or a conscious choice to remain where they were? It's hard to leave behind aged parents (fathers), a business, and property. Visas to other countries were difficult to obtain. The fate of an immigrant is unpredictable - so many reasons not to leave home. Who could have imagined the insanity that was to follow. And yet, the question lingers on. It's a subject on which I still dwell.

With the Soviet invasion our life changed immediately for the worse. My father's business was confiscated, our house was deemed too large for a family of four and we were made to share it with another family. Whatever silver and gold we had, and all items of any value were taken from us. Shvabes Gymnasium, the Hebrew school that I had attended for three years was closed, and I had to switch to a Russian school. All the Jewish institutions were forced to disband, and in June 1941, mass deportation of the "enemies of the people" took place. We lived in constant fear.

Whatever Hebrew I know today dates back mainly to those three years at Shvabes Gymnasium. I never attended kindergarten since that year my brother came down with whooping cough and missed a school year. My parents had engaged a governess to teach us both at home. We spoke Yiddish and Russian at home, and Lithuanian with the local population. Lithuanian was only a subject at school since the rest of the subjects were taught in Hebrew. Among the Jews in Lithuania, Russian and Yiddish were spoken more commonly at home than Lithuanian. Russian was a vestige of years of Russian occupation. Lithuania only became independent in 1918. There was, however, a strong nationalistic movement among the Lithuanians and a long history of Lithuanian duchies and kingdoms. During the middle-ages, Lithuania was a great power, extending from the Baltic Sea to the Black Sea. It subsequently became united with Poland, but in the third partition of Poland, in 1795, Lithuania was annexed to Russia. Between the two world wars it was an independent country, but not enough time had passed since its independence for the Jewish minority to appropriate the language.

Jews lived in Lithuania from the fourteenth century on, but it was from the seventeenth century that the country's yeshivas attained world wide fame. About 150,000 Jews lived in Lithuania at the time of its establishment after World War I. When Vilnius and its vicinity were returned to Lithuania in 1939, the Jewish population of the country grew to about 250,000, of whom 40,000 lived in Kaunas, nearly one quarter of the city's population. Less than ten percent of the Lithuanian Jewish population survived the Holocaust.

In my new Russian school every subject was conducted in Russian. This school, as most others that year, was hastily established by the Soviet authorities to meet the needs of the children whose schools were shut down. The Hebrew school I had attended was relatively small, intimate, with great emphasis on Zionism and Jewish content in general. Now, I had to learn to write and spell Russian, the language that I spoke but never had any formal instruction in, and all the subjects were taught by Russian teachers brought in from the Soviet Union, and focusing on Social Realism and Communism. I even became a Young Pioneer wearing a red tie and attended indoctrination meetings. This was one way to mitigate the effects of one's bourgeois background. Besides, there was tremendous social pressure on the children to join. As already mentioned, there was constant fear of being sent to Siberia as punishment for having been capitalists or nationalists, or both. Thousands of people were exiled to the depths of Russia, a large proportion of them were Jews. We were left alone. To this day I don't know what would have been preferable.

The year under the Soviet occupation was a difficult one but paradise compared to what came next. We were awakened at dawn on June 24, 1941, by the sounds of heavy bombardment. The non-aggression pact signed on August 23, 1939 between Ribbentrop and Molotov did not last. This time Lithuania was attacked brutally by the Germans on their way to Russia. Bridges were bombed. The Russians retreated.

During the Sovietization of Lithuania, underground extremist nationalist- fascist groups which strongly supported Nazi Germany were formed. While there always was much anti-Semitism in Lithuania, it now increased dramatically. During the short time of transition, even before the Germans set up their administration in Lithuania, the Lithuanians carried out pogroms against the Jews. The Lithuanians blamed the Jews for cooperating with the Russian Communists. While there were some Jews in the Communist Party, the majority of them were not, since many of them were owners of commercial establishments. Proportionally, more Jews than Lithuanians were exiled to Russia during the Soviet occupation of the country.

It is interesting to note that in the beginning of World War I before Germany seized Lithuania on its advance into Russia, the Russians blamed the Lithuanian Jews for being secretly supportive of Germany. The Cossacks staged devastating Pogroms killing thousands of Jews, and widespread looting of Jewish shops and homes occurred. The Russian government forced most of the remaining Jews to move into the interior of Russia. Anti-Semitism defies all logic.

The wave of murders and assaults grew with the entry of the German forces. On June 24, 100 Jews were killed and 10,000 arrested. On June 25, Lithuanian Fascists slaughtered 800 Jews. On June 26 and 27, several thousand Jews were shot. On July 5, Lithuanian Police shot 3,000 Jews during a systematic five day Action. The list goes on and on. In July and August of 1941 the majority of Jews in Lithuania were slaughtered in the most brutal way imaginable. Jews would be rounded up on the street or taken from their homes. Some were tortured, made to dig their own graves in the woods, and finally killed. Others were taken to the Seventh and Ninth Forts, a chain of fortifications constructed around Kaunas in the nineteenth century by one of the Czars to protect his western borders against Germany. There, they were first brutally mistreated by the Lithuanian guards and then shot to death. It was literally a reign of terror. It is estimated that over 10,000 Jews were killed in June, July, and August of 1941. No one knew who would be next.

Within a very short time of the German occupation we were made to wear a Yellow Star. Various restrictions were imposed on us. Curfews, limited shopping, and no employment. Since it was not safe for a Jew to be seen on the streets of Kaunas, and we needed food to survive, I used to remove the Yellow Star and go out with my Lithuanian friend, Birute, to shop for essentials. I looked upon it as both a challenge and a necessity. My family depended on me. I did not look Jewish and was able to pose as a gentile and get away with it. I was eleven.

On July 9, 1941, the Nazis ordered the erection of a ghetto, and the move had to be completed within four weeks. Thus, on August 15, the remaining Jews of Kaunas found themselves inside the ghetto located in Slobodka, a suburb of the city. A barbed wire fence, with posts manned by Lithuanian guards, was put up around it. When the ghetto was established in 1941, it contained 29,760 Jews.

This was the beginning of even a worse nightmare. Work brigades were organized. The lucky ones were picked to work. My father would work sporadically. Food was scarce. The workers were paid in food rations, which were at a starvation level. . We sold whatever belongings we still had in order to buy more food. At night there were curfews. Again we had to share a small house with another family, but worst of all were the periodic Actionen and Selections. Suddenly at dawn, a very loud alarm would sound that could be heard in every house in the ghetto. This meant that every man, woman, and child had to leave their home and assemble on a large field. The SS with their dogs, clubs, and bayonets would be there waiting for us. As soon as we were assembled the selection process would begin, ordering the people to go to the right or the left. We tried to look healthy by pinching our cheeks to get some color, to walk straight, and appear confident in order to make a good impression on the SS, but at five in the morning, cold and hungry, and scared to death of the fate that awaited us, it was a task at which few of us succeeded. I dreaded those Actionen, not only for myself, but for my family as well. My paternal grandparents were elderly, not well, and therefore at very high risk. Many families were split up by the Germans at these Selections. The SS very arbitrarily decided who was to live and who was to die. One often discerned some form of pattern, but with many exceptions. Usually the old, the weak, and the sick would be motioned to go to one side, but occasionally also some young ones who according to some twisted logic of the acting Germans, did not deserve to remain in the ghetto. There was also much brutality exercised by them. Persons who did not move quickly enough were beaten; others shot. We did not know for sure what the fate of those taken away was going to be, but we feared the worst. During the course of the Action of October 28, 1941, by order of Helmut Raucka, commander of the Kaunas Ghetto, 9,000 people were taken to the Ninth Fort and murdered there. Half of them were children. So far our luck was holding out. My parents, brother, and I were once again motioned to join the group that would remain in the ghetto, for the time being.

I dreaded those early morning wake up calls. How did I deal with such terror? I don't have all the answers, but I do know that since I felt totally powerless to change the situation, I assumed a fatalistic approach to life. Numbness set in. During the most critical times, I put my feelings on hold and became an observer, distancing myself from time and place, a Chagallesque image hovering in space, yet at the same time remaining very vigilant and aware of the precariousness of the situation we were facing. Each moment presented a new danger, a new challenge. One does not really know the extent of one's inner resources until they are called upon. It is also easier to face the possibility of death when you see people dying around you. It becomes the norm rather than the exception. It may not have been a rational approach, but it helped me deal with the hopelessness of the situation at hand.

Back to the ghetto. Life was harsh. You felt as if you lived at the edge of a precipice, with chunks of rocks constantly breaking away from underfoot. The solid ground shrinking with each passing day. There were public executions, shootings, torture, little food and a constant stream of frightening rumors'. It was there that I saw my first public hanging. I vividly remember a small puddle forming underneath the gallows. I asked why. My father explained. The future, if there was to be a future, was totally unpredictable and very bleak.

In the ghetto there were also politics. For the first two years there was an elected Jewish Council that represented the ghetto community. Forced labor and the maintenance of public order were the responsibility of the Jewish police. The Council also administered a department of health, welfare, and culture. Temporary schools were established for a while, but in 1942 they were ordered to close. In spite of the day to day very difficult conditions that existed, there were concerts, literary evenings, and other cultural events taking place. Life for the living continued. Attempts were also made to maintain contact with the anti-Nazi partisans in the forests. A small group of Jews had escaped from the ghetto and had joined the partisans. Connections were important. Favors could be obtained if you knew the right people. The Germans relied on the members of the Council to implement all kinds of orders, some of these orders presented terrible moral dilemmas such as providing the Germans with lists of people for punishments and executions.. While they had some power, their position was not an enviable one. The ghetto was a microcosm of society. It had its heroes as well as its villains.

Conditions changed drastically in the autumn of 1943. The ghetto became a concentration camp. On March 27, 1944, 1,800 persons consisting primarily of children, and elderly men and women, were dragged out of their home and murdered. Also killed were 40 officers of the Jewish police for having given aid to the Jewish underground in the ghetto. By the beginning of April only 17,412 Jews were left in the ghetto, most of them adults. Things went from bad to worse. The situation was truly hopeless, but by that time we were no longer there.

On October 26, 1943, the day finally arrived when a large part of the ghetto population was evacuated. Once more it started with an early morning assembly. Once more the difference between life and death was determined by either an almost imperceptible motion of a leather gloved hand or an impatient shout to hurry up accompanied by a shove, a blow on the head, or kick by a highly polished, black boot. Occasionally a shot would be heard that felled a laggard who could not keep up with the rest. Thousands of people were lined up, slowly advancing to their judgment. Facing the stream of humanity were a number of SS men who made sure that nothing would interfere with the efficiency in which they carried out their part towards the "Final Solution." Many German and Lithuanian guards were also on hand to help out.

This time, the selection was conducted more methodically. It was the most gut wrenching event that I have ever witnessed. The men were separated from the women, the old and the frail were grouped together, but worst of all, the children were separated from their parents.. The parents who clung to their children were forced to give them up, and the children who hung on to their parents were one by one plucked away like vermin and carried screaming to the waiting trucks. The parents who volunteered to accompany their children were beaten and shoved towards their assigned sections. There are some events for which there are no words. How do you describe the cries of a child being snatched away from his parents' embrace? The weeping and the wailing, and the screaming of the parents? These are the sounds and sights that will remain with me to the day I die.

As for me, I did not know until the last minute what my fate was going to be. Fortunately, at age thirteen, I looked older than my years, and when my turn came to face the SS, the one whom I approached, must have considered me to be a productive adult who could be put to work. My mother and I became part of a large group of women who were sent to a concentration camp in Estonia. My father and brother also stayed together. They too were sent to Estonia, but to a different camp. We never saw each other again. After the war we found out from people who were sent to the same camp as my father and brother, Port Kunda, that my father lost a lot of weight, looked very frail and on August 4, 1944, at a selection at his camp was motioned to go to the side which was obviously the undesirable one. My brother, who did not want to be separated from my father, pretended to suffer from a bad knee and begged to join him. His wish was granted. This group was taken to a nearby forest, Eredu, shot and then the bodies were burned on a heap of firewood.

The train ride to Estonia was a nightmare. We were herded into box cars and kept uninformed of our destination until we got there. The journey lasted a week. The sanitary conditions were indescribable; hardly any food, very little water, and no air. The grieving mothers who lost their children were inconsolable. It was hell.

Our destination was Camp Kurame in Estonia, a remote area in the middle of nowhere. The weather was deteriorating. There were heavy rains, and the mud was knee deep. Winter was approaching. We were given shoes with wooden soles. Our clothes was skimpy. After being two years in the ghetto, we had little clothes left, and we could only take with us what we could carry. No one wanted to be considered sick and not go to work since that meant you were no longer being productive, and therefore could be easily eliminated. Dysentery was common and a host of other diseases that even under much better conditions would occur during the course of time, let alone among a group of undernourished people living in unsanitary, substandard conditions. No matter how sick we were, we would go to work. Staying in the barracks during the day was a death sentence. From time to time we would return to camp after a day's work and people would be missing. They were never heard of again.

Our bunks were very primitive. No running water. No toilet facilities. An outhouse and a well were all we had. We did what we could to keep ourselves clean, but most of the time it was too cold to even want to undress and bathe. Looking for lice in the seams of our clothes was the most common evening recreational activity. Needless to say, the smell in the bunks, particularly at night, was odious. We slept on tiers of boards, one above the other, bundled up in our day clothes for warmth. Blankets were scarce. There was a wood stove in the center of the bunk that would burn dimly at night.

Mornings, or rather at dawn, we were made to line up in the square of the camp to be counted. A large kettle of very thin gruel would be ladled out into a bowl to each prisoner. After "breakfast" we would assemble into work crews and march off to our assignments. We built roads in the middle of nowhere. Ostensibly, these roads were going to provide the Germans with greater access to the Russian front. Trees had to be cleared, road beds dug, and gravel spread, all manually. The supervisors were mainly local Estonians recruited by the Germans. Some were quite decent; others were worse than the Germans. Lunch consisted of some nondescript cabbage soup with a few potatoes thrown in, and upon our return to our bunks, more of the same with a slice or two of bread. Work was a privilege, a hope to stay alive.

We stayed at that camp half way through the winter. Then, for some unknown reason, we were made to move to another camp, also in Estonia. It could not have been very far away since we were made to march there. Distance is relative, though. Forty- five or fifty kilometers by car is a short distance; the same distance walking in the depth of winter through non-- existing roads, poorly dressed, wearing wooden shoes, and half starved, seemed endless. We walked for three days. Those who stumbled and fell were shot. Those who could not take another step due to exhaustion and sat down, met the same fate. You could not afford to stop to help the fallen unless you were prepared to give up your own life. What did you do? You donned imaginary blinders, faced the front, put one foot in front of the other and became totally self-absorbed with your own survival. You became dehumanized. I was fourteen, in better shape than my mother. At one point my mother was prepared to give up. She lost her will and strength to continue. Upon my unrelenting urging, she mustered up enough strength to continue. Luckily, we were not far from our destination, Camp Goldfiels.

At this camp we stayed until September 1944, when we were evacuated to Germany. My memory of this camp would have been somewhat better if not for a very tragic incident. We arrived there at the end of winter. It was a smaller camp. The weather started to improve. Life became a little easier, the guards a little friendlier. We still worked on building roads, but the days were longer, brighter, and warmer. We were also beginning to hear rumors of the advancing Russian Army.

To this day I can't quite comprehend how this tragedy occurred. If it hadn't had such tragic consequences, I would refer to it as the theatre of the absurd. I met at that camp a girl my age. This was a rarity in itself since I was one of the youngest inmates in all the camps where I was. On a beautiful spring day, this girl whom I hardly knew, and I struck up a conversation with a young guard at the gate. We decided to ask him for permission to walk down the road, never thinking that he would say, yes. It was a country road inhabited by farmers. It looked very inviting. The guard was a young Estonian recruit who obviously took it upon himself to grant our request. No sooner did we walk five hundred feet along the road than a shot was fired either from a rifle or a revolver. My friend was hit in the stomach. I was walking beside her when it happened. I had the task of dragging her back to camp, bleeding profusely with her intestines visibly protruding. It seems that the shot was fired by a young boy. I never discovered why. The girl died within a couple of hours. The astonishing part was that no one asked me any questions about the incident. It was as if it had never occurred. Under the circumstances, the total disregard for the event, suited me fine since I feared punishment, but to this day it remains one of those very powerful memories that I have kept to myself all these years. This was one adventure I wish I had not undertaken.

In August of 1944, we were again on the move. The Russians were advancing. All that toil that we put into those forsaken roads did not do the Germans any good. Once again we were put into box cars, and once again we had no idea what our destination was going to be. This time we were taken to Germany. It was from this train that I observed the peaceful idyllic scenes of the German countryside whose contrast with my own condition at the time made such a lasting impression on me. To this day, I still taste the longing I felt for a life free of terror, squalor, and hunger. I got a glimpse of what life could be like.

My mother and I ended up in Stutthof in a camp. We stayed there for two months. My recollection of that camp is vague except that our heads were shaved there. From there we were taken to Oksenzolt a concentration camp near Hamburg. Again we were put to work. I don't remember what work my mother did, but I worked in a munitions factory. I was filing metal parts for guns. My supervisor was a young Belgian prisoner who was nice to me. The best part of the deal was that I was entitled to a glass of milk a day because of the work I was doing. It was felt that the filing dust was bad for me. It could affect my health, and therefore to make up for it, I was given milk. I suspect that it was the Belgian supervisor who was responsible for it. How else can it be explained? Surely, the Germans were not going to worry about one Jew dying when millions were being killed. It was also a warm place. I was working indoors. This place is one of the better memories of my camp experiences. We stayed there until February 1945.

World War II was coming to a close. The Germans were losing ground. The Allied armies continued to advance. Consequently, the SS transferred most of the prisoners from the concentration camps near the front to those further inside the Reich. Once again we were moved. This time it was going to be Bergen-Belsen. By now I had seventeen months of ghetto survival and twenty-eight months of concentration camp life behind me. I experienced the nadir of human degradation and German depravity. Surely things could not get any worse. I also thought nothing would ever shock me again. I was wrong on both counts.

We arrived in Bergen-Belsen in the dead of winter. After being deloused and hair shorn once again, we were given striped uniforms to wear. It was a huge camp, more and more transports were arriving. It was terribly overcrowded. We joined several other women's groups in the section to which we were assigned. I believe it was called the

Large Women's Camp. The camp was divided into units, each surrounded by barbed wire. Officially, there was no communication by prisoners from one section with those of another one, but people found a way. We discovered that there were other Lithuanian Jews in that camp, and through the grapevine we found out the fate of some of our relatives and friends. Of my father and brother, we had no word. In our section there were many nationalities speaking a multitude of languages. The enormous scope of Hitler's Final Solution was made very clear to us.

What shocked me most upon our arrival there was the appearance of the inmates. The majority of them were emaciated to the bone, literally, walking skeletons. They were the lucky ones because they could still walk. A large number of the prisoners were sick and dying. Typhus reached epidemic proportions. Starvation also took its toll. It was impossible to tell the difference between the living and the dead among those lying on the ground. Death was in the air. The bodies would remain scattered on the ground for days before they were removed. There were stacks of corpses waiting to be disposed. Many were not buried until after liberation.

Again every morning there were roll calls. Again people would disappear without a trace. Again there were public executions and floggings. Whatever food we were given was not fit for human consumption, but those who could eat, ate. I now know that there were prisoners there who spent several years under those dreadful conditions. How they survived, I don't know. What saved my mother and me was the relative short time that we were there before being freed by the British army. We arrived in Bergen-Belsen in February and were liberated on April 15th. In the first months of 1945, 35,000 men, women, and children perished there. Even weeks after the camp was liberated 13,000 more people died from disease, malnutrition, and torture.

My mother and I also contracted Typhus in the beginning of April. We were very sick, but gradually recovered. We were too sick and too weak to celebrate our long awaited freedom. There was no energy left to take in the true significance of the event. We felt spent. Our stomachs, too, found it difficult to adjust to their good fortune. It took weeks to get used to food again and to recover our strength. The British soldiers were very kind. They shared their rations with us and tried to clean up the camp. They made the German guards and officers who failed to escape, as well as some neighboring civilians, bury the dead. But in order to stop disease from spreading the British army units burnt the camp barracks to the ground.

We were finally free, but what now? Did my father and brother survive? What about the rest of the members of our family? My paternal grandparents? Aunts and uncles? Cousins? It took a while to get the news we were dreading to receive. Most of it was bad. My grandparents were taken away in one of the subsequent Selections and killed, and so were most of the members of our family. I already mentioned the fate of my father and brother.

The one place we knew we did not want to return to was home to Kaunas. It was no longer our home. It was under Russian occupation, and we had nothing to return to. So we remained in Germany in a Displaced Persons camp living in a converted school, waiting for news from our relatives from abroad. While there I attended a temporary school set up by members of the Jewish Brigade sent to Germany from Palestine. It was a makeshift school, but better than no school at all. The Hebrew language was taught, and we learned some Hebrew songs. It was more of a preparation for immigration to Palestine than formal education. We chose not to mix with the local German population, for good reasons. My mother and I got jobs distributing clothes that were sent by various Jewish agencies for the newly liberated Displaced Persons. We were biding time, waiting for a visa either to go to Palestine or to Canada. Again I was one of the youngest there. It was a rather lonely existence. Freedom from oppression did not result in instant happiness. So many feelings and thoughts had to be sorted out, dealt with. For me, it was the loss of a father and brother, numerous relatives, and my wasted years. My mother had her own grieving to deal with. The loss of a husband and son, on top of her own five years of suffering, did not leave her much energy to offer me significant emotional support. I, in turn, was anxious to get on with my life and was not willing to look back. We each coped as best as we could.

The one foray my mother and I made to Hamburg is difficult to forget. We had to go to some office there regarding our immigration papers to Sweden. Having had no money for a hotel and post-war Germany still in disarray, we had to stay in an underground shelter over-night. It was a very scary ten hours. People kept drifting in, men and women, with whom you would not have wanted to come face to face in broad daylight, let alone at night. There were drunks, prostitutes, and other unwholesome characters that gave me the creeps. I was sixteen and felt very vulnerable. It all ended well though. No one bothered us, and at the first sign of daylight we made our escape. It was a very long night.

The British soldiers tried to provide us with some semblance of a social life. They used to arrange dances for the soldiers and invited us, that is the young women, to join them. It would be an evening out, but communication was difficult because of language, I knew what they had on their mind, and it was not what I needed at that point to boost my morale. I tried the dances a couple of times but soon gave up on them.

In the meantime, my aunt and uncle in Israel Manassia and Joseph Muller, who were doing business with Sweden, were trying to arrange for us to go to Sweden and wait for our immigration papers there. It took a while to accomplish that, but on September 22, 1946, my mother and I arrived in Stockholm after spending over a year in post-war Germany.

Sweden had escaped the war. Life was normal there. I found it very difficult to adjust to yet another change in my life. While life in the Displaced Persons Camp was far from comfortable, it was familiar and predictable. We were surrounded by people who went through similar experiences to ours, and we were looking forward to emigrating and making a fresh start.

When we finally arrived in Sweden, the reality was very different. We were facing a new language, new customs, and people who did not know what to make of us. Sweden was not affected by the war. There was very little organized support from the tiny Jewish community there. The Jews who immigrated there before the war, took little interest in us. We were pretty much on our own.

Having arrived there in September, I started to attend school. It was a regular Swedish school, and I entered a year behind to compensate for the six years of formal education that I missed. It was not a happy experience. I did not understand a word the teachers were saying, I had nothing in common with the students there, and the six years of no math, science or history did not help either. Culturally, I could have landed on a different planet.

By the end of the school year I could communicate haltingly in Swedish. I also started taking private English lessons. Those I really liked. I started reading voraciously English books, looking up almost every word in a dictionary. I read most of the James Hilton books, a good number of the Daphne du Maurier books (these two authors must have been very popular then), and any other books I could lay my hands on. My English improved.

We lived in a Pension, a rather common European form of accommodations. My mother and I shared a room and we ate in a common dining-room. The people who lived there were mainly Swedish, mainly single, and mainly elderly. We knew that it was a temporary arrangement and were happy with the set up. I did make a few friends my age, eventually. We used to go to movies and to dances outdoors. It was a Swedish custom for girls and boys to go stag to these dances and for the girls to wait to be asked to dance. It was all very respectable and sometimes fun. The movies were another good source for improving my English since they were either British or American.

In the summer of 1947 I went to visit my uncle, Arno, in England. It was a wonderful visit. I spent some time in London with him, and the rest of the time in Manchester. When September rolled around, I returned to Sweden and to school. This time I felt like a veteran. I could understand some Swedish, I had absorbed some algebra and science the year before, and I could actually keep up with my school work. I also kept plugging away at my English with my dictionary always beside me. In the beginning of December our Visa to Canada materialized, and once again we were on the move. We crossed the Atlantic on the Batory, a Polish ocean liner. Both my mother and I were awfully seasick most of the time. The Statue of Liberty was a very welcome sight. We docked in New York in the beginning of December, and after spending there a few days, we arrived by train in Montreal on December 11, 1947.

There was one more major adjustment to be made on our arrival here. We stayed with my Aunt Sonia and her family. We received a very warm reception there. Again I started attending school. This time it was Grade 10 at the High School of Montreal for Girls. I started school in January, and by June I passed all my courses. The English I worked on in Sweden served me well in Montreal. The irony was that of all the languages that I spoke, there was not one language that I could write correctly or whose grammar I knew. The knowledge of Russian, Yiddish, Lithuanian, Hebrew, and some German that I picked up while in Germany, were all at a child's level of literacy. I had no knowledge of literature other than the fairy tales that I knew from childhood, and the novels that I read while in Sweden.

Upon my arrival in Canada, I made up my mind that there had to be one language that I would appropriate as my own, and it was going to be English. Language is more than a system of sound and meaning. It helps one to forge an identity. By age ten, I had not absorbed enough of the culture into which I was born, nor a language I could call my own. There was a void that needed to be filled. Looking back now, I wonder whether at a very deep level, even while in Sweden, I knew that a new language would serve as an entry to a new life. Hebrew would have been easier to improve, and we were not at all sure at that time that the Visa to Canada would materialize before that to Palestine. It was as if the languages of my childhood represented to me traces of my past that I preferred to ignore. After all that I had gone through, my happy early childhood years vanished with my home and my old world. I wanted a new beginning. I did not want to remain a refugee nor a displaced person forever. In fact, for the first few years in Canada, I chose not to associate with refugees. They brought me face to face with my own past, a period in my life I preferred not to be reminded of.

As for the fifty years it took to deal with the seven very painful years of my life, I suppose it took as long as it had to take. I have never denied my past, but neither did I dwell on it. I could not live both in the past, the present, and look forward to a future. I chose the latter two.

Until I sat down to write my story, I did not realize how powerful these memories still are. I am glad I finally was able to relate, as best as I could, my Holocaust experiences. The few pages that I have recorded obviously don't tell my whole story. My recollection of those years appears like a hazy seascape of icebergs of varying shapes and sizes as far as the eye can see, floating in an enormous body of water. There are clearings through which a late afternoon sun is breaking through. Some of these monuments to my past are dim, remote, and fuzzy; others are near, razor sharp, and menacing. The one property they all share is that much more of their mass is submerged than is visible. Many incidents I had to forget to survive. Others fell victim to the passage of time. The human psyche finds a way to protect itself. I owe a lasting debt to events forgotten.

Some made it; too many did not. Some lived to tell their story; too many did not. I wish there had been no story to tell. The rest you know. As it turned out, the best was yet to be.

The Family of Yakov and Bronnia Abramovich

Rebecca Abramovih who prrished in Stutthof Concentration Camp on January 21, 1945

Beno Abramovich, who was shot in August 1941 in Kaunas Fort VII 1935

Yakov (seated) with his brothers, Leon and Arno Abramovich,
before parting, Plombietrs-les-Bains, France

LETTER OF DR JACOB ABRAMOVICH TO HIS BROTHER ARNO IN ENGLAND, 1945

My dear Brother!

I wrote a few letters to you three months ago and I also wrote to Leo, and wonder if you have received them. I am writing to you again and hope that the sad news about the tragedy of our family will reach you.

In July, 1941, we were all locked up in the Ghetto in Slobodka with the exception of our brother Benno, who perished with 7,000 Jews in Kaunas on the 7th Fort.

On the 24th July[1] 1941, a few days after the Nazi attack on the Russians, I, Benno and my wife and her uncle were arrested without cause and locked up in the Yellow Prison. My wife, being pregnant, was released, and due to her efforts and those of the Director of the hospital where I used to work, I was also released. 7,000 Jews, including our brother Benno, were transferred on August 1st to the 7th Fort, and within a few weeks were all murderously killed. There they went through the worst horror and torments any human being could think of.

In the Ghetto the Nazis started a series of killings and acts of terrorism. The technique of the sadist murderers is impossible to describe in a letter. A few weeks after being locked up a part of the ghetto was surrounded and the people were driven on to the 9th Fort where they were thrown half alive into pits. The Jewish hospital was set on fire and the patients were all burned alive, amongst them our uncle Z.

225

Caplan, who was lying there after suffering a heart-attack while on forced labour. Our Auntie Goldie and their daughter Rebecca were visiting him there and they also perished.

We all lived next to each other in the ghetto. We used to exchange our clothes for bread with the Lithuanian workers on forced labour, but this did not last for long, as the Nazis confiscated all our clothes.

On 24th October 1941, the Nazis with the Lithuanian Fascist Police broke into my room and knocked out the windows. My wife had a shock and gave birth to a daughter. This happened at night without light and without food for her. On the 28th October 1941, the Nazis, with the help of heavily armed police, surrounded the ghetto, separated parents from children, old men and women, and eleven thousand Jews were sent on to the 9th Fort where they were all shot.[2] The majority of the children were thrown alive into pits. Our Mother came into this group with the old people, but I succeeded in prolonging her life until 26 March 1944. And so, with the exception of Benno, we all lived together in ghetto. Max, Anna and their daughter Rebecca, Ruvim and I used to go on forced labour. Our shirts, clothes, shoes, sheets and blankets we exchanged for bread. And every day we were tormented physically and morally by the threat of being killed.

On the 28th September 1943, 3,000 Jews were deported to Estonia. Our brother Ruvim, Bassia and their children were amongst them. A few people who were able to escape from Esthonia and were liberated by the Red Army have told us that they were all killed or burnt. This depended on which camp they fell into. The small children and old people were killed at the Kaunas Railway Station where the children were taken away from their parents. In any case our brother Ruvim and his family perished there.[3]

When the Red Army reached the Lithuanian Frontiers, we had messages as follows: that the ghetto in Vilno had been burned down, that the people of the ghetto in Schawel[4] were deported to Taurage and there killed.[5]

In our ghetto they had already started to separate us into groups. This was a preliminary to immediate extermination...

[Page missing]

...on the steps of a Lithuanian Orphanage under a Lithuanian name. The doctor who was Director of the Orphanage was a colleague of mine with whom I had worked in a hospital before the War. I left your address with him and Leo's and Bronia's family's, with the request that after the War they should contact you to tell you about my child. I contacted him on a dark night after crawling through the barbed wire of the ghetto. On the night of 14 December 1943, I smuggled Bronia and our child out of the ghetto, and left my child at the orphanage as arranged. There was nowhere for us to hide and the next day we smuggled ourselves back.

Meanwhile the Nazis had started to deport the people into camps. Our brother Max, Anna and their daughter, Rebecca, who had grown into a beautiful girl, were sent in December 1943 to Scanzer (Šančiai)[6] camp. In the ghetto there remained then our parents, Rebecca, Samuel,[7] Joseph,[8] Bronia and I. They also wanted to send my wife and I to Scanzer where Max was. Since our child was in the Lithuanian Orphanage we decided to run away instead of going to a camp. We knew that a camp or ghetto meant death. We also wanted to see our child for once. On 3 January 1944 we escaped. For a few days we were hiding in the cellars of Gentiles. Nobody wanted to keep us for long and we were destitute and homeless. I had got to know that our child was seriously ill and dying in the Orphanage. The Director advised me to take her away since they had got to know that she was a Jewess. It was winter and we were without money, clothes and food. At any moment the Nazis might get hold of us and shoot us.

Bronia and I set out into the villages in the hope of finding a good person who would be willing to take a dying Jewish child, and we could not find one. Wandering through the villages by night and through the woods by day we reached Kulautova. Not far from the woods was a peasant Kumpaitis (he used to help our parents to move in summer). We hid ourselves in a ditch beside his pig-sty. We used to get food at night. Meantime I also found a poor fishmonger who adopted my child from the Orphanage. For four weeks my child struggled for life. At night I used to go 15 kilometres to treat her and give her injections. She was in Rodondware.[9] At last she recovered and was there for another seven months.

On 26 March 1944, the Nazis took out a few thousand children and old people.[10] Among them were our parents. They led our Mother and Father with other old people to a horrible death with a few thousand children aged from 2 to 12 years. Before I ran away from the ghetto I said goodbye to them and I remember my father's words. He

227

has suffered a lot and he always used to say he would like to live to see the downfall of the Nazis. Mother has suffered too but she showed no trace of it. After the horrible murder of the children when they also took our parents, a few thousand Jews still remained in the ghetto, amongst them Rebecca, Samuel and Joseph.

As I have already told you my brother Ruwin and his family were in Esthonia, Max and his family in Šančiai, my wife and I were hiding in the woods. When the Red Army crossed the Lithuanian Frontier, our sister Rebecca and her family with a few thousand other Jews were sent to Danzig, where Max and his family were sent from his camp. The people who were hiding themselves in the cellars of the Slobodka Ghetto[11] were all burnt, and there are still some corpses lying about. In Lithuania about eight to nine hundred Jews have escaped, and the remainder have all met a horrible death.

On 3 August 1944 the Red Army saved us. We collected our daughter from the fisherman and found her a nice healthy child.

This is, in short, the tragedy of our family together with another few hundred thousand Jews. I will write to you again in the near future in detail.

I work in a hospital and earn relatively enough...

[A page is missing with the end of the letter]

Notes

1. Father mixed up July and June here.
2. According to the Karl Jäger Report, 9,200 Jews were massacred in the 9th Fort on 29 October 1941, including 2,007 men, 2,920 women and 4,273 children.
3. Ruvim and his son perished there, however Ruvim's wife and daughter were sent to the concentration camp and survived, and at the time of Liberation found themselves in the American Zone of Germany. When Father wrote the letter in 1945 he did not know that Ruvim's wife Basia and her daughter Miriam have survived.
4. Now Šiauliai.
5. During the liquidation of the Kaunas Ghetto (8–13 July 1944) about 6,000–7,000 people were transported to concentration camps. On 12 July 1944 Kaunas Ghetto was set on fire. Hundreds of people died in the fire or were shot and killed. About 7,000 Šiauliai Jews as well as Jews brought to the Šiauliai Ghetto

from Vilnius, Kaunas and Smurgainys labour camps were transported to Stut-thof concentration camp in four stages. From there, men were taken to Dachau concentration camp, while women and children were taken to Auschwitz.

6. In autumn of 1943, the Kaunas Ghetto was reorganised into an SS concentration camp. Around 4,000 prisoners of the ghetto were transferred to isolated labour camps in the neighbourhoods of Aleksotas and Šančiai.

7. The husband of my aunt Rebecca.

8. The son of my aunt Rebecca.

9. At the present time it is known as Raudondvaris and is near the village of Šilelis where I was living.

10. 27–28 March 1944 a cruel Children's Action took place in the Kaunas Ghetto: 1,700 children and old people were taken from the Ghetto in two days and transported to Auschwitz for annihilation.

11. Slobodka (also known by its Lithuanian name: Vilijampolé) was the district of Kaunas, in which the Ghetto was situated.

'Born in the Ghetto' is a personal testimony about the Abramovich - Prop family. Ariela's memoirs are played out against a background of some of the most momentous historical events of the twentieth century. She brings these events to life as she narrates her gripping stories of survival in the Ghetto in Lithuania, growing up in the Soviet Union during the Cold War and Thaw period, and migrating to the West.

The author of the book is unique by virtue not only because of her very birth, but also of the time and place of her birth. There are only a few people who had similar experiences because Ariela was born in the Kaunas Ghetto in Lithuania in 1941, just a few days prior to the Great Action when small children, the elderly and infirm were selected to the left side to die and others to the right side to prolong their life to work. She miraculously survived the Nazi manhunt when her parents smuggled her out of the Ghetto in a potato sack and left her on the doorsteps of an orphanage. From there she was taken in by a fisherman's family and, after the war, reunited with her parents who had also miraculously succeeded in escaping from the ghetto.

Ariela's family lived for generations in Lithuania and her father, Dr Yakov Abramovich, was born in Taurage which was on the border with what used to be East Prussia (from the area where the Prop family emanates). Immediately after the war, Father wrote a letter to his brothers, Aaron in England and Leon in the USA, in which he gave the news about the tragedy of those in the Abramovich-Prop family who had perished in the Holocaust. The letter was added into Ariela's book and a few notes at the end of his letter were made for clarification. The missing page of the letter is thought to describe some of the events of smuggling little Ariela from the Ghetto to the orphanage.

BORN IN THE GHETTO
My Triumph over Adversity
Ariela Abramovich Sef

First puplished in 2014 by Gainsborough House Press

ISBN 978 1 909719 00 2 (Hardback)
ISBN 978 1 909719 01 9 (Paperback)
ISBN 978 1 909719 03 3 (Ebook)

1908 Calumet, Michigan (Upper Peninsula Michigan) Propp Cousins
*Back Row: John Joseph (Wilburton, OK), William Kaplan, Samuel Jacobson (South
Africa), Leon Sachs (Chicago, Illinois), Arthur Jacobson (California)*
*Front Row: Louis Arne (Calumet, Michigan), Nathan Friedman (Chicago, Illinois),
Benjamin Arne(Hougton-Hancock, Michigan)*

Marjasha Prop Sachs Aronovich　　　　　　*Shaya-Mendel Aronovich*

*Shaya Medel married Sora Prop after she died and he married her younger sister Marjasha
is also the daughter of Betzalel. Originally she married Yankel Sachs.*

*Chaya Miriam Prop
in Shkudvil, 1930s*

*Skaudvil
Chaya Royaiza Halevy Prop*

Shkudvil, the tall gentleman in the is Leib Aryieh Prop

Reb Shimon Prop, son of Betzalel Prop, and his wife,
Gittel-Sora Prop, daughter of Avram Prop

Gaon Rabbi Michel Shlapobersky Grandson
of Reb Shimon and Gittel Prop

New York City, c: :1909
Marie Propp, Daughter of Marcus Propp
and Granddaughter of Shimon Propp

Baltimore 1913
Marie Propp Lebow and son,
Sylvan Lebow

Joseph and Marie Lebow

Marie and her youngest son, Alan

Johnston Island, 1962
Hank Propp

ר׳ צבי
כ״ה טודרוס
ינה תשרי תרע״ט
ת׳נ׳צ׳ב׳ה׳

מרת שרה
בת ר אליקום
יבא ארר תרע
ת׳נ׳צ׳ב׳ה׳

OUR BELOVED
MOTHER | FATHER
SARAH | HENRY
DIED
APR. 8, 1910 | SEP. 11, 1918.
AGE
48 YRS. | 59 YRS.

PROPP

Waldheim Cemetery, Chicago, IL
Of Blessed Memory

Relationship Chart

	0	1	2	3	4	5	6
0	CP	S	GS	GGS	2 GGS	3 GGS	4 GGS
1	S	B	N	GN	GGN	2 GGN	3 GGN
2	GS	N	1C	1C 1R	1C 2R	1C 3R	1C 4R
3	GGS	GN	1C 1R	2C	2C 1R	2C 2R	2C 3R
4	2 GGS	GGN	1C 2R	2C 1R	3C	3C 1R	3C 2R
5	3 GGS	2 GGN	1C 3R	2C 2R	3C 1R	4C	4C 1R
6	4 GGS	3 GGN	1C 4R	2C 3R	3C 2R	4C 1R	5C

CP = Common Progenitor

C = Cousin

B = Brother or Sister

R = Times Removed

N = Nephew or Niece

GS = Grandson or Granddaughter

GGS = Great-grandson or Great-granddaug

פּרָאפּ

Shimel Girshevich Probnovich
(Shimon Prop)

of

שקודוויל
Shkudvil, Vilna Guberniya
Russia Empire

Born 1765

Shimon is listed in the August 14th, 1816 reviskie shazki (Vital Document) for Jewish males and females located within the Litovsko-Vilenskaya Province, Town of Shkudvil (Skaudvile). He most likely was an Inn Keeper and one of the original settlers of the Jewish Community in Shkudvil which started in 1795, and was caused by partition and resettlement of Lithuanian by the Russia Empire.

Shimel Girshevich Probnovich

Shimel Girshevich Probnovich-1. He was born Abt. 1765 in Unknown. His residence on Aug 14, 1816 was in Skaudvile. He died Abt. 1837 in Shkudvil, Vilna, Russia. He was also known as Shimon Prop. Title was Rav. Hebrew Name in Shimon ben Tzvi (Hirsh).

Roch'l. She was born Abt.1759 in Unknown. She died 1840 in Shkudvil, Vilna, Russia. Shimel Girshevich Probnovich and Roch'l. They were married Abt. 1879 in Russia. They had eight children.

i.   **Leah Probnovich.** She was born Abt 1787 in Zemaitija Duchy, Grand Duchy of Lithuania-Poland. She died Abt. 1865. *No informanation is known.*

ii. **Marjasha Probnovich.** She was born 1789 in Zemaitija Duchy, Grand Duchy of Lithuania-Poland. She died Abt. 1844 *No informanation is known.*

iii. **Efraim Prop.** He was born 1791 in Zemaitija Duchy, Grand Duchy of Lithuania. He died Abt. 1850 in Russia. Census.shows he departed Shaudvile in 1812. *No informanation is known.*

iv. **Avram "Abel" Prop.** He was born 1790 in Zemaitija Duchy, Grand Duchy of Lithuania-Poland. He married Liba. They were married 1810 in Shkudvil, Kovno, Russia. Census 1847 in Merchant of the 3rd Guild. Information 1857 in Shkudvil, Kovno, Russia (Rents from Anton Burzhinsky, 600 rubles/Skaudvile, Taurage, Lithuania/). Occupation 1857 in Raseiniai Area (Tavern Keeper). He died Abt. 1860 in Shkudvil, Kovno, Russia. He was also known as Hirsh as a second name. Title was Rav. Burial in Shkudvil, Kovno, Russia (Skaudvile, Taurage, Lithuania/Skaudvile, Taurage, Lithuania). Title was Rav

v.   **Hirsh Zalman Prop.** He was born 1791 in Zemaitija Duchy, Grand Duchy of Lithuania. He married Chaya Berlowitz. They were married 1805 in Shkudvil, Kovno, Russia. He died 1856 in Jerusalem, Eretz Yisrael. Title was Rav.

vi. **Eliyahu Prop.** He was born 1795 in Zemaitija Duchy, Grand Duchy of Lithuania-Poland. He died Abt. 1826 in Gaure, Kovno, Russia. Title was Rav.

vii. **Rivka Prop.** She was born 1799 in Zemaitija Duchy, Grand Duchy of Lithuania. She died 1882 in Shkudvil, Kovno, Russia. She married Oral or "Ahron". They were married in Shkudvil, Kovno, Russia.

viii. **Sora Prop.** She was born 1810 in Zemaitija Duchy, Grand Duchy of Lithuania. She married Dovid Fridman-Muskin. They were married 1824 in Shkudvil, Kovno, Russia. She died 1844 in Shkudvil, Kovno, Russia

A Drawing depicting the Murders and Suffering of the Jews at 9th Fort, Kovno Ghett

פּרָאפּ

Avram ben Shimon Prop

of

שׁקודוויל

Shkudvil, Vilna Guberniya
Russia Empire

Born 1790

According to the 1816 Reviskie Shazki and 1847 Family List (Russian Census),
Avram remained in Shkudvil throughout his life.

Circa 1917
Tzvi-Hirsh "Henry" Propp
Chicago Illinios.

1 **Avram "Abel" Prop** (1790 - 1860) b: 1790 in Zemaitija Duchy, Grand Duchy of Lithuania-Poland,
    d: Abt.1860 in Shkudvil, Kovno, Russia
..... + Liba (1792 - 1832) b: 1792 in Zemaitija Duchy, Grand Duchy of Lithuania-Poland, m: 1810 in
    Shkudvil,
    Kovno, Russia, d: 1832 in Shkudvil, Kovno, Russia
.... 2 Yosel Prop (1810 - 1882) b: 1810 in Shkudvil, Kovno, Russia, d: 1882 in Shkudvil, Kovno,
    Russia
.... + Cherne (1812 - 1884) b: 1812 in Kovno, Russia, m: 1830 in Shkudvil, Kovno, Russia, d: 1884 in
    Shkudvil, Kovno, Russia
.... 3 Itzik Prop (1828 - 1904) b: 1828 in Shkudvil, Kovno, Russia, d: 1904 in Shkudvil, Kovno,
    Russia
.... + Eide m: in Shkudvil, Kovno, Russia
.... 4 Tzvi-Hirsh Prop (1855 - 1923) b: 1855 in Shkudvil, Kovno, Russia, d: 1923 in
    Shkudvil, Kovno, Russia
.... + Rivka Grodziensky (1863 - 1927) b: 1863 in Vilna, Vilna Guberniya, Russia, m: 1882 in
    Shkudvil, Kovno, Russia, d: 1927 in Shkudvil, Kovno, Russia
.... 5 Naftali "Naftl" Prop (1881 - 1941) b: May 22, 1881 in Birzai, Panevezys
    Guberniya, Lithuania, d: Jul 21, 1941 in Shkudvil, Lithuania, Holocaust
.... + Rifka (1899 - 1941) b: 1899 in Memel, East Prussia, d: Sep 19, 1941 in Batok,
    Lithuania, Holocaust
.... 6 Ari Prop (1931 - 1941) b: 1931 in Shkudvil, Kovno, Russia, d: Sep 19, 1941 in
    Batok, Lithuania, Holocaust
.... 5 Shmuel Prop (1884 -) b: 1884 in Shkudvil, Kovno, Russia
.... 5 Chana Prop (1885 -) b: 1885 in Shkudvil, Kovno, Russia, d: in Riga, Latvia,
    Holocaust
.... + Zalman Levine (1879 - 1941) b: 1879 in Riga, Riga, Latvia, m: 1901 in Riga, Riga,
    Latvia, d: 1941 in Riga Ghetto, Latvia, Holocaust
.... 6 Mark "Meir" Levine (1902 - 1965) b: 1902 in Riga, Riga, Latvia, d: 1965 in
    Riga, Riga, Latvia
.... + Rosa (1914 - 1980) b: 1914 in Riga, Riga, Latvia, d: 1980 in Riga, Riga, Latvia
.... 7 Nina Levine (1936 -) b: 1936 in Riga, Riga, Latvia
.... + Vladimir Polubelov (1933 -) b: 1933 in Riga, Riga, Latvia
.... 8 Elena Polubelov (1951 -) b: 1951 in Riga, Riga, Latvia
.... 6 Samuel "Shmuel" Levine (1906 - 1977) b: 1906 in Riga, Riga, Latvia, d: 1977 in
    Riga, Riga, Latvia
.... + Faina (1912 -) b: 1912 in Riga, Riga, Latvia
.... 7 Valentine Levine (1934 -) b: 1934 in Riga, Riga, Latvia
.... 7 Noemi Levine (1947 -) b: 1947
.... + Mark Davidson (1940 -) b: 1940
.... + Rivka (1919 - 1985) b: 1919 in Riga, Riga, Latvia, d: 1985 in Riga, Riga,
    Latvia
.... 6 Roza Levine (1908 - 1983) b: 1908 in Riga, Riga, Latvia, d: 1983 in Riga,
    Riga, Latvia
.... + Myron Berkovich (1906 - 1941) b: 1906 in Riga, Riga, Latvia, d: 1941 in
    Moscow, Russia
.... 7 Lucien Berkovich (1936 -) b: 1936 in Paris, Ile-de-France, France
.... + Rema (1936 -) b: 1936 in Leningrad, Russia
.... 8 Alexander Berkovich (1957 -) b: 1957 in Riga, Riga, Latvia
.... + Maya (1959 -) b: 1959 in Riga, Riga, Latvia
.... 9 Alisa Berkovich (1985 -) b: 1985 in Riga, Riga, Latvia
.... 9 Mark Berkovich (1988 -) b: 1988 in Riga, Riga, Latvia
.... + Hirsh Zilberman (1912 - 1949) b: 1912 in Riga, Riga, Latvia, d: 1949 in Riga,
    Riga, Latvia
.... 7 Aaron Zilberman (1947 -) b: 1947 in Riga, Riga, Latvia
.... + Lucy (1954 -) b: 1954 in Riga, Russia
.... 8 Leon Zilberman (1980 -) b: 1980 in Riga, Riga, Latvia
.... 8 Mark Zilberman (1980 -) b: 1980 in Riga, Riga, Latvia
.... 6 Wolf Levine (1910 - 1941) b: 1910 in Riga, Riga, Latvia, d: Jun 1941 in Riga,

Riga, Latvia
.... 5 Yechiel Moshe Prop (1886 - 1933) b: 1886 in Shkudvil, Kovno, Russia, d: 1933 in
Schwarzwald, Germany
.... + Frieda '"Fruma" Segal (1894 - 1932) b: 1894 in Raseiniai, Kovno Guberniya,
Russia, m: 1910 in Shkudvil, Kovno, Russia, d: 1932 in Shkudvil, Kovno, Russia
.... 6 Yaakov "Yankel" Prop (1912 -) b: Mar 15, 1912 in Raseiniai, Kovno
Guberniya, Russia
.... + Bela Segal (1915 - 1996) b: 1915 in Vilna, Vilna Guberniya, Russia, m: 1938 in
Kovno, Kovno Guberni, d: Apr 1996 in Jerusalem, Israel
.... 7 Ra'anna Propp (1941 - 1942) b: Nov 1941 in Ulyanovisk, Russia, d: 1942 in
Uzbekistan, Russia
.... 7 Aliza Prop (1951 -) b: 1951 in Uzbekistan, Russia
.... + Efi Shalev (1947 -) b: 1947 in Tel Aviv, Israel, m: in Tel Aviv, Israel
.... 8 Gali Shalev (1974 -) b: Sep 09, 1974 in Tel Aviv, Israel
.... 8 Tamar Shalev (1978 -) b: Jun 05, 1978 in Tel Aviv, Israel
.... 7 Victor "Propp" Ramon (1953 -) b: 1953 in Uzbekistan, Russia
.... + Ruth m: in Israel
.... 8 Tal Ramon (1974 -) b: Jan 03, 1974 in Jerusalem, Israel
.... 8 Dan Ramon (1976 -) b: Nov 15, 1976 in Jerusalem, Israel
.... 5 Sonya Prop (1888 - 1941) b: 1888 in Shkudvil, Kovno, Russia, d: Sep 19, 1941 in
Botak, Lithuania, Holocaust
.... + Yaakov "Yankel" Markov (1882 - 1941) b: 1882 in Shkudvil, Kovno, Russia, m: 1911 in
Shkudvil, Kovno, Russia, d: Jul 21, 1941 in Shkudvil, Lithuania, Holocaust
.... 6 Leib Markov (1913 - 1941) b: 1913 in Shkudvil, Kovno, Russia, d: Jul 21, 1941 in
Shkudvil, Lithuania, Holocaust
.... 6 Leah Markov (1915 - 1941) b: 1915 in Shkudvil, Kovno, Russia, d: Sep 19,
1941 in Botak, Lithuania, Holocaust
.... 5 Feiga Prop (1890 - 1960) b: 1890 in Shkudvil, Kovno, Russia, d: 1960 in Vilna,
Lithuania
.... + Boym (1874 - 1955) b: 1874 in Lithuania, d: 1955 in Gulag, Siberia, Russia
.... 6 Harry Harma Boym (1925 - 1993) b: Oct 08, 1925 in Gulag, Siberia, Russia, d: Sep
16, 1993 in Holon, Israel
.... + Dina Jadviga (1924 -) b: 1924 in Vilna, Lithuania, m: in Russia
.... 4 Sheine "Shayne" Prop (1858 - 1941) b: 1858 in Shkudvil, Kovno, Russia, d: Sep 19,
1941 in Shkudvil, Lithuania, Holocaust
.... + Menashe "Motel" Zaks (1868 - 1941) b: 1868 in Shkudvil, Kovno, Russia, d: in
Shkudvil, Kovno, Russia, d: Jul 21, 1941 in Shkudvil, Lithuania, Holocaust
.... 4 Chaya Prop (1864 -) b: 1864 in Shkudvil, Kovno, Russia, d: in Shkudvil, Kovno,
Russia
.... 4 Khone Prop (1867 - 1936) b: 1867 in Shkudvil, Kovno, Russia, d: 1936 in Shkudvil,
Kovno, Russia
.... 5 Aydeh Prop (1899 - 1941) b: 1899 in Shkudvil, Kovno, Russia, d: Jul 21, 1941 in
Shkudvil, Lithuania, Holocaust
.... 5 Yosef "Yosel" Prop (1902 - 1941) b: 1902 in Shkudvil, Kovno, Russia, d: Jul 21,
1941 in Shkudvil, Lithuania, Holocaust
.... 5 Ester Prop (1904 - 1941) b: 1904 in Shkudvil, Kovno, Russia, d: Sep 19, 1941 in
Batok, Lithuania, Holocaust
.... 5 Itzik Prop (1907 - 1994) b: 1907 in Shkudvil, Kovno, Russia, d: 1994 in Shkudvil,
Kovno,
.... 4 Chaim Prop (1867 -) b: 1867 in Shkudvil, Kovno, Russia
.... 3 Chaim Prop (1832 -) b: 1832 in Shkudvil, Kovno, Russia, d: in Königsberg, East Prussia
.... + Minnie Goldberg (1846 -) b: 1846 in Königsberg, East Prussia, d: in Königsberg, East
Prussia
.... 3 Bluma Prop (1833 - 1914) b: 1833 in Shkudvil, Kovno, Russia, d: 1914 in Shkudvil, Kovno,
Russia
.... + Shlomo-Yankel Epshtein (1830 - 1879) b: 1830 in Tavrig, Kovno Guberniya, Russia, m:
1855 in Shkudvil, Kovno, Russia, d: 1879 in Shkudvil, Kovno, Russia
1. Gershon Epshtein (1857 -) b: 1857, d: in Tavrig, Kovno, Russia
+Johanna Meirowitz b: in Tavrig, Kovno Guberniya, Russis

244

.... 5 Sholmo Yakov Epshtein (1880 -) b: 1880 in Tavrig, Kovno, Russia
.... 5 Fana Epshtein (1888 -) b: 1888
.... 4 Chana Epshtein (1859 -) b: 1859 in Shkudvil, Kovno, Russia
.... + Marcus Levin d: in Wilkes-Barre, Pennsylvaina
.... 4 Libe-Chaye Epshtein (1860 -) b: 1860 in Shkudvil, Kovno, Russia
.... + Libshitz b: in Kelm, Kovno Guberiya, Russia
.... 5 Libshitz
.... 5 Libshitz
.... 5 Gerson Libshitz
.... 5 Tevye Libshitz
.... 4 Teme Epshtein (1867 -) b: 1867 in Shkudvil, Kovno, Russia
.... + Josel Javich (1855 -) b: 1855 in Shkudvil, Kovno, Russia, m: 1884 in Shkudvil, Kovno,
                        Russia
.... 4 Moshe Epshtein (1876 -) b: 1876 in Shkudvil, Kovno, Russia
.... 4 Tzerne Epshtein (1877 -) b: 1877
.... 3 Raphal Shimel Prop (1845 -) b: 1845 in Shkudvil, Kovno, Russia
.... 2 Leib Prop (1812 - 1902) b: 1812 in Shkudvil, Kovno, Russia, d: 1902
.... 2 Todres Prop (1820 - 1888) b: 1820 in Shkudvil, Kovno, Russia, d: 1888 in Shkudvil, Kovno,
               Russia
.... + Leah (1822 - 1888) b: 1822 in Shkudvil, Kovno, Russia, m: 1839 in Shkudvil, Kovno, Russia, d:
             1888 in Shkudvil, Kovno, Russia
.... 3 Sora Prop (1840 -) b: 1840 in Shkudvil, Kovno, Russia
.... 3 Samuel "Shimon" Propp (1843 - 1918) b: Jan 1843 in Shkudvil, Kovno, Russia, d: Abt.
               1918 in New York, New York, USA
.... + Mary Luboshitz (1848 - 1880) b: 1848 in Shkudvil, Kovno, Russia, m: 1865 in Shkudvil,
             Kovno, Russia, d: Abt. 1880 in Shkudvil, Kovno, Russia
.... 4 Marcus Propp (1867 - 1935) b: 1867 in Shkudvil, Kovno, Russia, d: Dec 02, 1935 in New
                        York, New York, USA
.... + Fanny Zackman (1872 - 1943) b: 1872 in Kovno, Kovno Guberniya, Russia, m: 1889 in
                        New York, New York, d: 1943 in New York, New York, USA
.... 5 Marie Propp (1892 - 1966) b: Feb 03, 1892 in New York, New York, USA, d: 1966 in
                        Baltimore, Maryland, USA
.... + Joseph Lebow (1883 - 1964) b: Apr 28, 1883 in Tavrig, Kovno, Lithuania, m: 1910 in
                        New York, New York, USA, d: Jan 16, 1964 in Baltimore, Maryland, USA
.... 6 Sylvan Lebow (1912 - 2001) b: Jul 23, 1912 in Baltimore, Maryland, USA, d: Dec
                        25, 2001 in New York, New York, USA
.... + Ruth Lebowitz (1913 - 2003) b: 1913 in St. Michael,s Maryland, m: 1937 in New
                        York, New York, USA, d: 2003 in Los Angeles, Los Angeles, California, USA
.... 7 Mark Denis Lebow (1940 -) b: Apr 02, 1940 in Harrisberg, Pennsylvania
.... + Patricia E Harris (1952 -) b: 1952 in New York, New York, USA, m: Jan
                        1988 in
                        New York, New York, USA
.... 8 Michael Lebow (1975 -) b: 1975 in New York, New York, USA
.... 8 Jeffrey Lebow (1988 -) b: 1988 in New York, New York, USA
.... 8 Alexandra Lebow (1992 -) b: 1992 in New York, New York, USA
.... 7 Joy Lebow (1943 -) b: Apr 04, 1943 in Harrisburg, Pennsylvania
.... + William B. Cohen (1937 -) b: Apr 23, 1937 in Los Angeles, Los Angeles, California,
                        USA
.... 8 Lauren Cohen (1980 -) b: Apr 17, 1980 in Los Angeles, Los Angeles,
                        California,USA
.... 6 Stanleigh Lebow (1920 - 2002) b: Dec 03, 1920 in Baltimore, Maryland, USA, d:
                        May 02, 2002 in Los Angeles, Los Angeles, California, USA
.... + Isabelle Dorman (1916 - 1994) b: Feb 22, 1916 in Baltimore, Maryland, USA, m:
                        1939, d: Jan 01, 1994 in Baltimore, Maryland, USA
.... 7 Edward Lebow (1940 -) b: 1940 in Baltimore, Maryland, USA
.... 6 Alan J Lebow (1927 - 2009) b: Mar 31, 1927 in Baltimore, Baltimore, Maryland, USA,
                        d: Feb 03, 2009 in Palm Beach, Palm Beach, Florida, USA
.... + Patricia Susan Levey (1947 -) b: 1947 in New Hartford, Litchfield, Connecticut, USA,
                        m:

Jun 18, 1978 in Palm Beach, Palm Beach, Florida, USA

.... 7 Amanda Marie Lebow (1985 -) b: Jan 12, 1985 in Palm Beach, Palm Beach, Florida, USA

.... 5 Samuel Propp (1892 - 1963) b: Apr 06, 1892 in New York, New York, USA, d: Nov 1963 in New York, New York, USA

.... + Anna (1906 -) b: 1906 in Virginia, USA, m: 1926 in New York, New York, USA, d: in New York, New York, USA

.... 5 Ellis A. Propp (1894 - 1968) b: Jun 07, 1894 in New York, New York, USA, d: Feb 29, 1968 in Bronxville, Westchester County, New York

.... + Ethel Patricia Walsh (1902 - 1944) b: 1902 in Ohio, m: Aug 10, 1925 in New York, New York, USA, d: Oct 19, 1944 in Bronxville, Westchester County, New York

.... 5 Anna Propp (1895 - 1983) b: Dec 25, 1895 in New York, New York, USA, d: Dec 1983 in New York, New York, USA

.... + Nathan "Nat" Waldman (1895 - 1971) b: Dec 09, 1895 in New York, New York, USA, d: Jan 1971 in New York, New York, USA

.... 6 Sheila Waldman (1920 - 1984) b: Sep 27, 1920 in New York, New York, USA, d: Oct 1984 in New York, New York, USA

.... 5 Elizabeth Propp (1904 - 1977) b: May 31, 1904 in New York, New York, USA, d: May 1977 in New York, New York, USA

.... 4 Katie "Yetta" Propp (1876 - 1954) b: 1876 in Shkudvil, Kovno, Russia, d: Jan 22, 1954 in New York, New York, USA

.... + Joseph "Yael" Cantor (1876 - 1948) b: 1876 in Minsk, Minsk Gubernyia, Russia, m: 1905 in New York, New York, USA, d: Apr 08, 1948 in New York, New York, USA

.... 5 Etty Cantor (1902 - 1993) b: Mar 01, 1902 in Bronx, Bronx, New York, USA, d: Dec 14, 1993 in New York, New York, USA

.... + Jacob "Jack" Brand (1897 - 1987) b: Aug 09, 1897 in New York, New York, USA, m: Apr 27, 1930 in New York, New York, USA, d: Jun 27, 1987 in Miami, Florida

.... 6 Marcia Brand (1931 -) b: Aug 28, 1931 in Bronx, Bronx, New York, USA

.... 6 Arnold Joseph Brand (1938 -) b: Sep 23, 1938 in New York, New York, USA

.... + Barbara Distler (1941 -) b: Feb 28, 1941 in New York, New York, USA, m: Aug 14, 1960 in New York, New York, USA

.... 7 Laura Susan Brand (1963 -) b: Feb 28, 1963 in New York, New York, USA

.... + Mario Rainville (1963 -) b: Oct 08, 1963 in Quebec, Canada

.... 8 Sophia Rose Rainville (2002 -) b: Oct 16, 2002

.... 5 Harry Cantor (1905 - 1964) b: 1905 in New York, New York, USA, d: Apr 20, 1964 in New York, New York, USA

.... + Sophie (1907 - 1955) b: 1907 in New York, New York, USA, m: 1940 in New York, New York, USA, d: Jan 06, 1955 in New York, New York, USA

.... 6 Harriet Cantor (1939 -) b: 1939 in New York, New York, USA

.... 6 Daniel Cantor (1944 -) b: 1944 in New York, New York, USA

.... 6 Marilyn Cantor (1947 - 1952) b: 1947 in New York, New York, USA, d: Jul 31, 1952

.... 5 Irving Cantor (1911 - 1981) b: May 11, 1911 in New York, New York, USA, d: Feb 11, 1981 in New York, New York, USA

.... + Roslinde Tillman (1913 - 1998) b: 1913 in New York, New York, USA, d: Jun 15, 1998 in New York, New York, USA

.... 6 Isabel Cantor b: in Bronx, Bronx, New York, USA

.... 6 Richard Cantor b: in Bronx, Bronx, New York, USA

.... 6 Joel Cantor b: in Bronx, Bronx, New York, USA

.... 5 Sadie Cantor (1908 - 1992) b: Nov 08, 1908 in Bronx, Bronx, New York, USA, d: Oct 06, 1992 in Pompano Beach, Broward County, Florida

.... + Leon Elton (1907 - 2003) b: Jan 08, 1907 in New York, New York, USA, m: in New York, New York, USA, d: Apr 24, 2003 in Woodbridge, New Haven County, Connecticut

.... 6 Alan Elton b: in Woodbridge, New Haven County, Connecticut

.... + Winifred

.... 5 Morris Cantor (1910 - 1994) b: Sep 24, 1910 in New York, New York, USA, d: May 25, 1994 in Los Angeles, Los Angeles, California, USA

.... + Helen

.... 6 Jerome Cantor b: in New York, New York, USA

.... 6 Rita Cantor b: in New York, New York, USA

.... 5 Leah Cantor (1912 - 1988) b: May 18, 1912 in New York, New York, USA, d: Jun 01, 1988 in Delray Beach, Palm Beach County, Florida

.... + Arthur Resnick (1906 - 1988) b: Aug 16, 1906 in New York, New York, USA, d: Jun 01, 1988 in West Palm Beach, Palm Beach County, Florida

.... 6 Marvin Resnick b: in Bronx, Bronx, New York, USA

.... 6 Judith Resnick (1944 - 1981) b: Dec 07, 1944 in Bronx, Bronx, New York, USA, d: Jan 1981 in West Hartford, Hartford County, Connecticut

.... 5 Sidney Cantor (1917 - 1996) b: Jun 30, 1917 in Bronx, Bronx, New York, USA, d: Apr 26, 1996 in Pompano Beach, Broward County, Florida

.... + Mildred (1914 - 1998) b: Mar 29, 1914 in New York, New York, USA, m: Abt. 1940 in New York, d: Dec 10, 1998 in Pompano Beach, Broward County, Florida

.... 6 Jane Cantor b: in Bronx, Bronx, New York, USA

.... 4 Rosie "Riew" Propp (1877 - 1894) b: 1877 in Shkudvil, Kovno, Russia, d: Jun 23, 1894 in New York, New York, USA

.... 4 David Theodore Propp (1878 - 1924) b: Feb 03, 1878 in Shkudvil, Kovno, Russia, d: Mar 31, 1924 in New York, New York, USA

.... + Rebecca "Beckie" Pollack (1887 - 1926) b: 1887 in Grodno, Russia, m: Jan 1904 in New York, New York, USA, d: May 24, 1926 in New York, New York, USA

.... 5 Mary Propp (1904 - 1994) b: Nov 06, 1904 in New York, New York, USA, d: May 1994 in Miami, Dade, Florida, USA

.... + Abraham J Rose (1901 - 1987) b: Jun 27, 1901 in Bazzan, Hungery, m: 1927 in New York, New York, USA, d: Dec 09, 1987 in Miami, Dade, Florida, USA

.... 6 David Hillel Rose (1928 - 2002) b: Nov 09, 1928 in New York, New York, USA, d: Apr 29, 2002 in Kinston, Lenoir, North Carolina, USA

.... + Vivan Schwartz (1930 -) b: Jan 11, 1930 in Cincinnati, Ohio

.... 7 Judith Rose (1956 -) b: May 05, 1956 in Denver, Adams, Nebraska, USA

.... + Gordon

.... 8 Noaha Abraham Gordon (1992 -) b: Aug 03, 1992 in Florida

.... 7 Deborah Rose (1957 -) b: Jul 03, 1957 in Cincinnati, Ohio

.... + Richard Lally (1953 -) b: 1953 in Chicago, Cook, Illinois, USA

.... 8 Jessica Beth Lally (1985 -) b: Jul 17, 1985 in Kansas City, Kansas

.... 8 Ian Joseph Lally (1991 -) b: Jun 29, 1991 in Kansas City, Kansas

.... 7 Daniel Himan Rose (1960 -) b: Oct 06, 1960 in Cincinnati, Ohio

.... + Dianna White (1961 -) b: 1961 in Kinston, Lenoir, North Carolina, USA

.... 6 Emanuel Rose (1931 -) b: 1931 in New York, New York, USA

.... + Lorraine J Wilson (1938 -) b: 1938 in London, England, m: Mar 27, 1960 in New York, New York, USA

.... 7 Ruth Melanie Rose (1962 -) b: 1962 in Portland, Oregon

.... 7 Tanya Beth Rose (1964 -) b: 1964 in Portland, Oregon

.... 7 Lorrian Rachel Rose (1965 -) b: 1965 in Portland, Oregon

.... 7 Joshua Adam Rose (1970 -) b: 1970 in Portland, Oregon

.... 5 Lillian Propp (1910 - 1995) b: Sep 11, 1910 in New York, New York, USA, d: Dec 05, 1995 in Miami, Dade, Florida, USA

.... + Bernie Weinstein (1911 - 2001) b: Apr 07, 1911 in New York, New York, USA, m: Abt. 1936 in New York, New York, USA, d: Sep 07, 2001 in Miami, Dade, Florida, USA

.... 6 Ruth Weinstein (1939 -) b: 1939 in Brooklyn, Kings, New York, USA

.... + Richard Jaffe (1934 -) b: 1934 in New York, New York, USA

.... 7 Loren Jaffe (1963 -) b: 1963 in New York, New York, USA

.... + Michell Mirkin (1959 -) b: 1959 in Washington, DC, USA

.... 7 Steven Jaffe (1964 -) b: 1964 in New York, New York, USA

.... 7 Nina Jaffe (1969 -) b: 1969 in New York, New York, USA

.... 6 Hariet Weinstein (1941 -) b: Jul 06, 1941 in Brooklyn, Kings, New York, USA

.... + Walter Messcher (1940 -) b: 1940 in New York, New York, USA

.... 7 Daniel Jonathan Messcher (1964 -) b: May 26, 1964 in New York, New York,

.... + Janet Anne Mikulski (1963 -) b: Nov 06, 1963
.... 8 Deirdre Anne Messcher (1991 -) b: Jan 14, 1991
.... 8 Zachary Henry Messcher (1996 -) b: Aug 18, 1996
.... 8 Rebecca Lena Messcher (1998 -) b: Jan 08, 1998
.... 7 David Joel Messcher (1965 -) b: Nov 21, 1965 in New York, New York, USA
.... + Amy (1967 -) b: Mar 06, 1967
.... 8 Nocole Messcher (1994 -) b: May 16, 1994
.... 8 Ryan Messcher (1999 -) b: Feb 20, 1999
.... 4 Harry Propp (1879 - 1957) b: Mar 1879 in Minsk Russia, d: 1957 in New York, New
                York, USA
.... + Sarah Leritsky (1850 - 1923) b: Oct 03, 1850 in Minsk, Minsk Guberniya, Russia, m: Abt. 1883 in
                Minsk, Minsk Guberniya, Russia, d: Dec 05, 1923 in New York, New York, USA
.... 4 Jacob Samuel Propp (1884 - 1958) b: Feb 26, 1884 in Minsk, Minsk Gubernyia,
                Russia, d: Jul 17, 1958 in New York, New York, USA
.... + Dina Cantor (1886 - 1980) b: Jun 02, 1886 in Minsk, Minsk Gubernyia, Russia, m: Jan 08,
                1911 in New York, New York, USA, d: Dec 25, 1980 in New York, New York, USA
.... 5 Sidney Propp (1914 - 1958) b: Apr 21, 1914 in New York, New York, USA, d: Jun 19,
                1958 in New York, New York, USA
.... + Frances Sarney (1915 - 1981) b: 1915 in New York, New York, USA, d: May 21, 1981
                in New York, New York, USA
.... 6 Stanley Propp (1938 -) b: 1938 in New York, New York, USA
.... + Helen
.... 7 Michael Propp (1964 -) b: 1964 in New York, New York, USA
.... 7 Brian Propp (1967 -) b: 1967 in New York, New York, USA
.... 6 Barbara I. Propp (1946 -) b: 1946 in New York, New York, USA
.... 5 Seymour Propp (1916 - 2001) b: Jun 07, 1916 in New York, New York, USA, d: Jun
                28, 2001 in Long Beach, Nassau, New York, USA
.... + Elaine Eagle (1925 -) b: Jun 09, 1925 in Brooklyn, Kings, New York, USA, m:
                1946 in New York, New York, USA
.... 6 William Bennett Propp (1947 -) b: Aug 20, 1947 in New York, New York, USA
.... + Mary C. Deluca m: Aug 08, 1980 in Clark, Nevada
.... 6 Susan Jane Propp (1954 -) b: Jan 08, 1954 in New York, New York, USA
.... + Hal Teitelbaum (1948 -) b: 1948 in New York, New York, USA
.... 7 Robert Jason Teitelbaum (1977 -) b: May 09, 1977 in Los Angeles, Los
                Angeles, California, USA
.... 7 Danielle Leigh Teitelbaum (1988 -) b: Aug 12, 1988 in Orange County,
                California
.... 7 Jeffrey Scott Teitelbaum (1990 -) b: Mar 04, 1990 in Orange County,
                California
.... 6 Deborah L. Propp (1954 -) b: Oct 04, 1954 in New York, New York, USA
.... + Kenneth Ernstoff (1948 -) b: Dec 25, 1948 in New York, New York, USA
.... + Leonard Mintz m: 1999
.... 5 Josephine Propp (1918 -) b: 1918 in New York, New York, USA
.... + Milton "Micky" Laitman (1916 -) b: 1916 in New York, New York, USA
.... 6 Marcie Laitman (1941 -) b: 1941 in New York, New York, USA
.... + Morris Kotler (1937 -) b: 1937 in Johannesburg, South Africa, m: 1964
.... 7 Lawrence Kotler (1965 -) b: 1965 in Johannesburg, South Africa
.... + Rita Eichmann (1964 -) b: 1964 in Philadelphia, Philadelphia, Pennsylvania,
                USA, m: 1992
.... 8 Julia Renee Kotler (1995 -) b: Nov 01, 1995 in Gladwyne,
                Pennsylvania
.... 7 Lila Kotler (1967 -) b: 1967 in New York, New York, USA
.... + Ian Joffe (1965 -) b: 1965 in Johannesburg, South Africa
.... 8 Julia Rena Joffe (1995 -) b: 1995 in New York, New York, USA
.... 6 Lynn Laitman (1946 -) b: 1946 in New York, New York, USA
.... + Donald Siebert (1946 -) b: 1946 in Beacon, New York
.... 7 Areille Siebert (1975 -) b: 1975 in Morristown, New Jersey
.... 7 Asher Siebert (1980 -) b: 1980 in Morristown, New Jersey

.... 6   Lori Laitman (1955 -) b: 1955 in New York, New York, USA
.... + Bruce E. Rosenblum (1953 -) b: 1953 in Boston, Suffolk, Massachusetts,
                            USA
.... 7   James Rosenblum (1980 -) b: 1980 in Boston, Suffolk, Massachusetts, USA
.... 7   Diana Rosenblum (1983 -) b: 1983 in Washington, DC, USA
.... 7   Andrew Rosenblum (1986 -) b: 1986 in Washington, DC, USA
.... 5   Theodore Propp (1923 -) b: 1923 in New York, New York, USA
.... + Ellen Barbara Honig (1935 -) b: 1935 in New York, New York, USA, m: Jul 30,
                          1956 in New York, New York, USA
.... 6   William Henry Propp (1957 -) b: 1957 in New York, New York, USA
.... + Anna Covici (1958 -) b: 1958 in Dalles, Texas
.... 7   Saul Benjamin Propp (1993 -) b: May 08, 1993 in San Diego, California
.... 7   Jonah Pascall Propp (1997 -) b: Mar 05, 1997
.... 6   James Gary Propp (1960 -) b: Mar 05, 1960 in New York, New York, USA
.... + Alexandra "Sandi" Gubin
.... 6   Sharman Toby Propp (1961 -) b: Jun 09, 1961 in New York, New York, USA
.... + Richard Leslie Gans (1959 -) b: 1959 in New York, New York, USA, m: Sep 10,
                          1989 in Great Neck, New York
.... 7   Rebecca Danielle Gans (1992 -) b: 1992 in New York, New York, USA
.... 7   Ezra Samuel Gans (1997 -) b: Jul 31, 1997
.... 6   Donna Jane Propp (1966 -) b: Sep 01, 1966 in New York, New York, USA
.... 4   Dorothy "Dvora" Propp (1885 - 1970) b: Mar 14, 1885 in Minsk, Minsk Gubernyia,
                     Russia, d: Jan 17, 1970 in Manhattan, New York County, New York
.... + Benjamin Kantrowitz (1886 - 1957) b: Dec 31, 1886 in New York, New York, USA, m:
                     1907 in Manhattan, New York County, New York, d: Abt. 1957 in Bronx, Bronx County,
                     New York
.... 5   Harold Kantrowitz (1911 -) b: Abt. 1911 in New York, New York, USA
.... 5   Sidney Kantrowitz (1916 - 1975) b: Jul 28, 1916 in New York, New York, USA, d: Jun
                       21, 1975 in New York, New York, USA
.... 4   Leah Propp (1889 - 1977) b: Oct 18, 1889 in Minsk, Minsk Guberniya, Russia, d: May 09,
                     1977 in Los Angeles, Los Angeles, California, USA
.... + Randel Woodruff Baremore (1884 - 1960) b: Jul 20, 1884 in New York, New York,
                     USA, m: 1910 in Atlantic City, Atlantic, New Jersey, USA, d: Feb 01, 1960 in Los
                     Angeles, Los Angeles, California, USA
.... 5   Carolyn B. Baremore (1911 - 1993) b: Mar 27, 1911 in New York, New York, USA, d:
                       Mar 26, 1993 in Encino, Los Angeles, California, USA
.... + Alferd Schiff (1904 - 1980) b: Feb 04, 1904 in New York, New York, USA, m: 1934 in
                          New York, New York, USA, d: Oct 23, 1980 in Los Angeles, Los Angeles, California,
                          USA
.... 5   Beth Baremore (1916 -) b: Oct 08, 1916 in New York, New York, USA, d: in Los
                       Angeles, Los Angeles, California, USA
.... + Van Alexander (1915 -) b: May 02, 1915 in New York, New York, USA, m: Sep 22,
                          1938 in New York, New York, USA, d: in Los Angeles, Los Angeles, California, USA
.... 6   Lynn Alexander (1941 -) b: Jun 23, 1941 in New York, New York, USA
.... + Hyman H. Tobias (1905 - 1997) b: Apr 23, 1905 in Worcester, Massachusetts, m:
                              1965 in California, USA, d: Dec 05, 1997 in Los Angeles, Los Angeles, California,
                              USA
.... 7   Mitch Tobias (1969 -) b: Abt. 1969 in Los Angeles, Los Angeles,
                                  California, USA
.... 6   Joyce Alexander (1943 -) b: Oct 25, 1943 in New York, New York, USA
.... + Harris
.... 4   Anna I. Propp (1890 - 1971) b: Dec 25, 1890 in Minsk, Minsk Guberniya, Russia, d: May
                     09, 1971 in Los Angeles, Los Angeles, California, USA
.... + John E. McNamara (1885 - 1937) b: Abt. 1885 in New York, New York, USA, m: Jun 25,
                     1925 in Naples, Maine, d: 1937 in New York, New York, USA
.... 3   Vulf Ayzyk Prop (1845 - 1920) b: 1845 in Shkudvil, Kovno, Russia, d: Abt. 1920 in
               Shkudvil, Kovno, Russia
.... 3   Morris "Movshe" Propp (1848 - 1931) b: May 1848 in Shkudvil, Kovno, Russia, d: Jul 12,
               1931 in Newark, Essex, New Jersey, USA

249

.... + Hanna (1847 - 1927) b: Aug 1847 in Kovno Guberniya, Russia, m: 1880 in Russia, d: Dec 17, 1927 in Newark, Essex, New Jersey, USA

.... 3 Efraim Propp (1857 - 1932) b: May 08, 1857 in Shkudvil, Kovno, Russia, d: Sep 17, 1932 in Stockholm, Stockholms, Sweden

.... + Ernestine Grun (1856 - 1918) b: Jun 14, 1856 in Danzig, West Prussia, m: Sep 21, 1883 in Stockholm, Stockholms, Sweden, d: Aug 27, 1918 in Stockholm, Stockholms, Sweden

.... 3 Hirsh Propp (1859 - 1918) b: May 12, 1859 in Shkudvil, Kovno, Russia, d: Sep 11, 1918 in Chicago, Cook, Illinois, USA

.... + Sarah "Sora" Frum" (1862 - 1910) b: Mar 23, 1862 in Kovno Guberniya, Russia, m: 1884 in Memel, East Prussia, d: Apr 08, 1910 in Chicago, Cook, Illinois, USA

.... 4 Ella T Propp (1885 - 1964) b: Aug 17, 1885 in Memel, East Prussia, d: Oct 28, 1964 in Chicago, Cook, Illinois, USA

.... + Leon Aaron Sachs (1878 - 1954) b: 1878 in Shkudvil, Kovno, Russia, m: 1910 in Chicago, Cook, Illinois, USA, d: Feb 07, 1954 in Chicago, Cook, Illinois, USA

.... 5 Charlotte S. Sachs (1912 - 1993) b: May 29, 1912 in Chicago, Cook, Illinois, USA, d: Jan 09, 1993 in Portland, Multnomah County, Oregon

.... + Sam R. Lazerwith (1906 - 1973) b: Aug 31, 1906 in Cincinnati, Ohio, m: Nov 10, 1934 in Chicago, Cook County, Illinois, USA, d: Jan 09, 1973 in Chicago, Cook, Illinois, USA

.... 6 Mark Allen Lazerwith (1936 - 2007) b: Mar 06, 1936 in Chicago, Cook, Illinois, USA, d: May 25, 2007 in Glenview, Cook County, Illinois

.... + Fanchon Meyers (1941 -) b: 1941 in Chicago, Cook, Illinois, USA, m: 1969 in Chicago, Cook, Illinois, USA

.... 7 Cara Beth Lazerwith (1970 -) b: Sep 03, 1970 in Chicago, Cook, Illinois, USA

.... + Michael A. Shlau (1973 -) b: Aug 11, 1973 in Chicago, Cook, Illinois, USA

.... 8 Samuel Jacob Shlau (2005 -) b: Nov 29, 2005 in Park Ridge, Lake, Illinois, USA

.... 8 Evan Mark Shlau (2008 -) b: Jul 22, 2008 in Lake Forest, Lake, Illinois, USA

.... 7 Scott Edward Lazerwith (1973 -) b: Sep 18, 1973 in Chicago, Cook, Illinois, USA

.... + Emma "Holly" Herndon (1978 -) b: Abt. 1978, m: Mar 2002 in Chicago, Cook, Illinois, USA

.... 8 Nora Fay Herndon-Lazerwith (2004 -) b: Jul 15, 2004 in Ann Arbor, Michigan

.... 6 Myra Lazerwith (1945 -) b: Dec 02, 1945 in Chicago, Cook, Illinois, USA

.... + John H Gevurtz (1937 -) b: Mar 19, 1937 in Portland, Oregon, m: 1967 in Chicago, Cook, Illinois, USA

.... 7 Rayna E. Gevurtz (1973 -) b: Nov 14, 1973 in Stanford, California

.... + Gersh Zylberman (1972 -) b: Jun 18, 1972 in Melbourne, Victoria, Australia, m: Jun 18, 2000 in Portland, Clackamas, Oregon, USA

.... 8 Adira Rachel Zylberman (2005 -) b: Oct 13, 2005 in Melbourne, Victoria, Australia

.... 8 Noa Zylberman (2007 -) b: Abt. 2007 in Melbourne, Victoria, Australia

.... 7 Steven Gevurtz (1976 -) b: Apr 26, 1976 in Chicago, Cook, Illinois, USA

.... 5 Jerome Michael Sachs (1914 -) b: Oct 12, 1914 in Chicago, Cook, Illinois, USA

.... + Joan Frankenstein (1915 - 1978) b: Mar 18, 1915 in Chicago, Cook, Illinois, USA, m: Jun 08, 1939 in Chicago, Cook, Illinois, USA, d: Apr 24, 1978 in Chicago, Cook, Illinois, USA

.... 6 Jennifer Sachs (1942 -) b: Jul 15, 1942 in Chicago, Cook, Illinois, USA

.... + James Donovan (1948 -) b: Jan 15, 1948 in Lowell, Massachusetts, m: 1970

.... + Larry Bolch (1937 -) b: Jul 13, 1937 in Edmonton, Alberta, Canada, m: 1960

.... 7 Ayn Bolch (1962 -) b: Dec 28, 1962 in Edmonton, Alberta, Canada

.... + Patrick Swihart (1947 -) b: 1947 in Texas

.... 8 Es Louise Swihart (1983 -) b: 1983 in Dallas, Dallas County, Texas

.... + Eric Skjeie (1960 -) b: 1960 in Portland, Oregon

.... 8 Malachi Skjeie (1996 -) b: Jan 12, 1996 in Dallas, Dallas County, Texas

d: Jun 05, 1982 in New York, New York, USA

.... 6 Jonathan Sachs (1949 -) b: 1949 in Chicago, Cook, Illinois, USA
.... + Emily Sandblade m: 1978
.... + Irene Levin (1917 - 2004) b: Apr 21, 1917 in Chicago, Cook, Illinois, USA, m: 1981 in Chicago, Cook, Illinois, USA, d: Feb 21, 2004 in Chicago, Cook, Illinois, USA
.... 4 Lillian Propp (1889 - 1977) b: Jul 27, 1889 in Chicago, Cook, Illinois, USA, d: Jan 20, 1977 in Palm Springs, Riverside, California, USA
.... + Nathan Ruttenberg (1891 - 1980) b: Jun 27, 1891 in Ishpeming, Marquette, Michigan, USA, m: 1922 in Chicago, Cook, Illinois, USA, d: Feb 05, 1980 in Palm Springs, Riverside, California, USA
.... 4 Theodore Propp (1892 - 1974) b: Jul 19, 1892 in Chicago, Cook, Illinois, USA, d: Aug 21, 1974 in Philadelphia, Philadelphia, Pennsylvania, USA
.... + Jessie Elizabeth Amanda McCutcheon (1895 - 1987) b: Apr 11, 1895 in Princeton, Gibson County, Indiana, m: Jan 14, 1931 in Lucas County, Ohio, d: Mar 01, 1987 in Jamesville, Onondaga, New York, USA
.... 5 Henry William Propp (1933 -) b: Dec 08, 1933 in Chicago, Cook, Illinois, USA
.... + Patricia Margaret Gubbins (1934 -) b: Nov 27, 1934 in Rome, Oneida, New York, USA, m: Jan 08, 1955 in Rome, Oneida, New York, USA
.... 6 Jody Ann Propp (1955 -) b: Sep 27, 1955 in Rome, Oneida, New York, USA
.... + Tadeusz Fundalinski (1954 -) b: Aug 02, 1954 in Buffalo, Erie, New York, USA, m: Sep 01, 1979 in North Syracuse, New York
.... 7 Briana Kristine Fundalinski (1987 -) b: Mar 31, 1987 in Syracuse, Onondaga, New York, USA
.... 7 Jessica Ann Fundalinski (1990 -) b: Jan 22, 1990 in Syracuse, Onondaga, New York, USA
.... 6 Cindy Marie Propp (1957 -) b: May 11, 1957 in Hyannis Port, Barnstable, Massachusetts, USA
.... + David Winslow (1954 -) b: Aug 07, 1954 in Syracuse, Onondaga, New York, USA, m: Nov 05, 1977 in Syracuse, Onondaga, New York, USA
.... 7 Nikki S. Winslow (1986 -) b: Jun 25, 1986 in South Korea
.... + Joshua Rojeck (1981 -) b: Abt. 1981 in Syracuse, Onondaga, New York, USA
.... 8 Joshua Nathan Rojek (2007 -) b: Aug 16, 2007 in Syracuse, Onondaga, New York, USA
.... 6 Theodore Henry Propp (1960 -) b: Jul 16, 1960 in Mt. Airy, Surry, North Carolina
.... 7 Rachael Elizabeth Propp (1986 -) b: Sep 06, 1986 in Syracuse, Onondaga, New York, USA
.... 7 Amanda Leah Propp (1989 -) b: Aug 09, 1989 in Syracuse, Onondaga, New York, USA
.... 6 David Edward Propp (1966 -) b: Mar 12, 1966 in Biloxi, Jackson County, Mississippi
.... + Carol Ann Flanagan (1965 -) b: Jan 06, 1965 in Hamburg, Erie County, New York, m: Aug 05, 1989 in Hamburg, New York
.... 7 Dawson Flanagan Propp (1997 -) b: Oct 13, 1997 in Yaroslavl, Russia
.... 7 Morgan Gwyneth Propp (2000 -) b: Oct 23, 2000 in Buffalo, Erie, New York, USA
.... 5 Daniel Searle Propp (1936 -) b: Jun 09, 1936 in Chicago, Cook, Illinois, USA
.... + Dolores Wojtaszek (1938 -) b: Dec 02, 1938 in Chicago, Cook, Illinois, USA, m: Jun 30, 1962 in Chicago, Cook, Illinois, USA
.... 6 Deneen Propp (1963 -) b: 1963 in Chicago, Cook, Illinois, USA
.... + Michael Casey (1961 -) b: 1961 in Chicago, Cook, Illinois, USA, m: Sep 29, 1989 in Lakeland, Polk, Florida, USA
.... 7 Adam Michael Casey (1994 -) b: Dec 21, 1994 in Orlando, Florida
.... 4 Lydia Propp (1896 - 1992) b: Jun 20, 1896 in Chicago, Cook, Illinois, USA, d: Mar 27, 1992 in Skokie, Cook, Illinois, USA
.... + Louis A Imber (1897 - 1967) b: Abt. 1897 in Romania, m: 1926 in Chicago, Cook, Illinois, USA, d: Oct 09, 1967 in Chicago, Cook, Illinois, USA
.... 3 Hannah "Hinda" Prop (1863 - 1949) b: 1863 in Shkudvil, Kovno, Russia, d: 1949 in

Newark, Essex, New Jersey, USA
.... + Julius Horwitz (1862 - 1912) b: 1862 in Russia, m: Abt. 1889 in Newark, Essex, New Jersey, USA, d: 1912 in Newark, Essex, New Jersey, USA
.... 4 Leah Horwitz (1896 - 1949) b: 1896 in Newark, Essex, New Jersey, USA, d: 1949 in Newark, Essex, New Jersey, USA
.... 4 Marie Horwitz (1896 - 1967) b: Oct 20, 1896 in Newark, Essex, New Jersey, USA, d: Nov 12, 1967 in Hartford, Hartford, Connecticut, USA
.... + Harry Cantor (1895 - 1923) b: 1895 in Newark, New Jersey, m: in Newark, New Jersey, d: 1923 in Newark, New Jersey
.... 5 Myra Cantor (1924 - 1996) b: Sep 22, 1924 in Livingston, Essex County, New Jersey, d: Jul 13, 1996 in West Hartford, Hartford County, Connecticut
.... + Robert Winkler (1929 - 2000) b: Jul 22, 1929 in Hartford, Hartford, Connecticut, USA, d: May 17, 2000 in Orange, Essex, New Jersey, USA
.... + Albert Harris (1890 - 1948) b: 1890 in Newark, Essex, New Jersey, USA, m: Abt. 1916 in Newark, Essex, New Jersey, USA, d: 1948 in Hartford, Hartford, Connecticut, USA
.... 4 Selma Horwitz (1898 - 1971) b: Dec 25, 1898 in Newark, Essex, New Jersey, USA, d: 1971 in Orange, New Jersey
.... + Jacob "Jasper" Mandy (1896 - 1954) b: 1896 in Newark, New Jersey, d: 1954 in Newark, Newark
.... 5 Jewel Mandy (1924 - 1996) b: Dec 25, 1924 in Newark, Essex, New Jersey, USA, d: Jan 25, 1996 in Livingston, New Jersey
.... + John Folander (1915 - 2000) b: Dec 14, 1915 in Hartford, Hartford, Connecticut, USA, m: 1951 in Newark, New Jersey, d: May 17, 2000 in Florham Park, Morris County, New Jersey
.... 6 Hal Folander (1954 -) b: Mar 06, 1954 in Newark, Essex, New Jersey, USA
.... + Kimberly Scrimmer (1961 -) b: 1961 in Long Beach Island, Morris County, New Jersey
.... 6 Jamie Folander (1958 -) b: Aug 11, 1958 in Newark, Essex, New Jersey, USA
.... + Robert Merold (1954 -) b: 1954 in Orange, Connecticut, m: 1994
.... 7 Sabrina Skye Merold (1995 -) b: Apr 19, 1995 in Livingston, New Jersey
.... 4 Samuel Horwitz (1899 - 1983) b: Apr 12, 1899 in Newark, Essex, New Jersey, USA, d: 1983 in Miami Beach, Florida
.... + Anna Marsa (1904 - 1995) b: 1904 in Newark, New Jersey, d: 1995 in Miami Beach, Florida
.... 4 Rose Horwitz (1905 - 1954) b: Jul 28, 1905 in Newark, Essex, New Jersey, USA, d: Mar 11, 1954 in West Orange, Essex County, New Jersey
.... + Samual Garb (1902 - 1999) b: May 07, 1902 in Newark, Essex, New Jersey, USA, m: Aug 10, 1930 in Newark, Essex, New Jersey, USA, d: Sep 26, 1999 in Newark, Essex, New Jersey, USA
.... 5 Martin Garb (1932 -) b: Jul 20, 1932 in Newark, Essex, New Jersey, USA
.... + Sandra Warhaftig (1936 -) b: Jan 1936 in Newark, Essex, New Jersey, USA, m: Jan 24, 1956 in Newark, Essex, New Jersey, USA
.... 6 Randi Garb (1958 -) b: Mar 02, 1958 in Newark, Essex, New Jersey, USA
.... + Eliot Goldberg (1951 -) b: 1951 in Brooklyn, Kings, New York, USA
.... 7 Robert Andrew Goldberg (1996 -) b: 1996 in Bay Side, Queens, New Jersey
.... 6 Mindi Garb (1961 -) b: Jul 22, 1961 in Newark, Essex, New Jersey, USA
.... 6 Lawrence "Larry" Garb (1969 -) b: May 18, 1969 in Newark, Essex, New Jersey, USA
.... 5 Constance Garb (1935 -) b: Nov 25, 1935 in Newark, New Jersey
.... + Lee Cherenson (1929 -) b: Aug 09, 1929 in Lowell, Massachusetts, m: Sep 02, 1956 in Newark, New Jersey
.... 6 Robert Cherenson (1958 -) b: Oct 31, 1958 in Newark, New Jersey
.... + Lisa Fennell (1969 -) b: 1969 in Deerfield, Massachusetts
.... 7 Rachel Cherenson (1988 -) b: 1988 in Deerfield, Massachusetts
.... 7 Ryan Cherenson (1992 -) b: 1992 in Turlock, California
.... 6 Steven Cherenson (1961 - 1994) b: Jul 10, 1961 in Newark, New Jersey, d: 1994 in Newark, New Jersey

.... + Tamara Hosage (1963 -) b: 1963 in Philadelphia, Philadelphia, Pennsylvania, USA
.... 6 Linda Cherenson (1968 -) b: Mar 14, 1968 in Newark, New Jersey
.... 6 Michael Cherenson (1968 -) b: Mar 14, 1968 in Newark, New Jersey
.... + Gail Codiroli (1968 -) b: 1968 in Pompton Plains, New Jersey
.... 3 Pesa Sora Prop (1864 - 1920) b: 1864 in Shkudvil, Kovno, Russia, d: Abt. 1920 in
Shkudvil, Kovno, Russia
.... + Bencelis Lurie (1860 -) b: 1860 in Shkudvil, Kovno, Russia, m: Abt. 1887 in Shkudvil,
Kovno, Russia
.... 4 Todres Lurie (1889 -) b: 1889 in Shkudvil, Kovno, Russia
.... + Mere Sapiru (1898 -) b: 1898 in Raguva, m: 1929 in Kupishok, Lithuania
.... 2 Mirayam "Mira Liba" Prop (1823 - 1908) b: Sep 1823 in Shkudvil, Kovno, Russia, d: Oct 27, 1908
in Calumet, Hancock County, Michigan
.... + Beniash "Benjamin" Ruttenberg (1812 - 1906) b: Oct 1812 in Vainutas, Kovno Guberniya, Russia,
m: 1843 in Shkudvil, Kovno, Russia, d: Oct 13, 1906 in Calumet, Houghton, Michigan, USA
.... 3 Joseph "Josel" Ruttenberg (1844 - 1938) b: 1844 in Shkudvil, Kovno, Russia, d: 1938 in
Chicago, Cook, Illinois, USA
.... + Elizabeth (1857 -) b: Abt. 1857 in England, m: 1874
.... 4 Louis H Ruttenberg (1878 - 1967) b: Abt. 1878 in Chicago, Cook, Illinois, USA, d: Jan
1967 in Maimi Beach, Florida
.... + Lucille (1880 -) b: Abt. 1880
.... 5 Janet Ruttenberg (1910 -) b: Abt. 1910
.... 5 Elliot Ruttenberg b: in Chicago, Cook, Illinois, USA, d: in Melrose, Massachusetts
.... 6 Beth Ruttenberg (1939 -) b: 1939 in Melrose, Massachusetts
.... 6 Frank Ruttenberg (1945 -) b: 1945 in Melrose, Massachusetts
.... 5 Lewis W. Ruttenberg (1918 -) b: Jul 1918 in Chicago, Cook, Illinois, USA
.... 3 Herman "Hirsh" Ruttenberg (1846 - 1921) b: May 15, 1846 in Shkudvil, Kovno, Russia, d: Feb
14, 1921 in Oslo, Oslo, Norway
.... + Beda-Rebekka Brodovitch (1856 - 1927) b: Apr 14, 1856 in Russia, m: 1869 in Oslo,
Oslo, Norway, d: Apr 18, 1927 in Oslo, Oslo, Norway
.... 4 Abel Rothenberg (1871 - 1941) b: Jun 26, 1871 in Härnösand, Vasternorrlands,
Sweden, d: Aug 22, 1941 in Oslo, Oslo, Norway
.... + Matilde Rozenholtz (1891 - 1942) b: Jan 20, 1891 in Poland, d: 1942 in Auschwitz,
Poland, Holocaust
.... 4 Jacob Rothenberg (1876 - 1938) b: 1876 in Härnösand, Vasternorrlands, Sweden, d:
1938 in Chicago, Cook, Illinois, USA
.... 4 Cecile Bertha Rothenberg (1878 - 1961) b: Mar 19, 1878 in Härnösand,
Vasternorrlands, Sweden, d: Nov 21, 1961 in Oslo, Oslo, Norway
.... + Solomon David Selikowitz (1869 - 1940) b: Aug 10, 1869 in Seda, Shavl Guberniya,
Russia, m: 1897 in Oslo, Oslo, Norway, d: Feb 15, 1940 in Oslo, Oslo, Norway
.... 5 Julius Martin Selikowitz (1898 - 1964) b: Jun 03, 1898 in Oslo, Oslo, Norway, d:
1964 in Oslo, Oslo, Norway
.... + Esther Levensohn (1912 - 1938) b: Abt. 1912 in Oslo, Oslo, Norway, m: May 1938 in
Oslo, Oslo, Norway, d: Abt. 1938 in Oslo, Oslo, Norway
.... 5 Josef Rueben Selikowitz (1899 - 1962) b: Aug 10, 1899 in Oslo, Oslo, Norway, d:
1962 in Oslo, Oslo, Norway
.... + Olga Wilk (1902 -) b: 1902 in Oslo, Oslo, Norway
.... 6 Helen Liv Selikowitz (1943 -) b: Abt. 1943 in Oslo, Oslo, Norway
.... + Jean Claude Modini (1940 -) b: Abt. 1940 in France, m: Dec 17, 1977 in
France
.... 7 Josefa Modini (1980 -) b: Dec 15, 1980
.... 7 Cecilia Modini (1984 -) b: Dec 04, 1984
.... 5 Heiman Selikowitz (1900 - 1974) b: Aug 09, 1900 in Oslo, Oslo, Norway, d: 1974 in
Oslo, Oslo, Norway
.... 5 Jacob Selikowitz (1901 - 1979) b: Dec 13, 1901 in Oslo, Oslo, Norway, d: 1979 in
Oslo, Oslo, Norway
.... + Inge
.... 5 Rachel Selikowitz (1903 - 1980) b: Mar 15, 1903 in Oslo, Oslo, Norway, d: 1980 in
Oslo, Oslo, Norway

.... + Willy Alexander (1900 - 1976) b: 1900 in Berlin, Stadt Berlin, Berlin, Germany, m:
1923 in Oslo, Oslo, Norway, d: 1976 in Oslo, Oslo, Norway
.... 5   Rosa Selikowitz (1904 - 1967) b: Aug 07, 1904 in Oslo, Oslo, Norway, d: 1967 in
Oslo, Oslo, Norway
.... + Marcus Levin (1899 - 1965) b: 1899 in Christiania, Norway, m: 1933 in Oslo, Oslo,
Norway, d: 1965 in Oslo, Oslo, Norway
.... 6   Leif-Arild Levin (1935 -) b: 1935 in Oslo, Oslo, Norway
.... + Cathinka Qvenild (1936 -) b: Abt. 1936
.... 7   Anne Levin (1958 -) b: 1958
.... 7   Levin (1960 -) b: 1960
.... 6   Irene Levin (1938 -) b: 1938 in Oslo, Oslo, Norway
.... + Martin Berman (1936 -) b: 1936, m: in Oslo, Oslo, Norway
.... 7   Carry Beth Berman (1963 -) b: 1963
.... + Ron Apter
.... 8   Emely Apter (1995 -) b: 1995
.... 8   Marcus Apter (1996 -) b: Dec 25, 1996
.... 7   Adrienne Berman (1964 -) b: 1964
.... 7   Rosanne Berman (1968 -) b: 1968
.... 5   Charlotte Lotta Selikowitz (1906 - 1988) b: May 25, 1906 in Oslo, Oslo, Norway, d:
1988 in Oslo, Oslo, Norway
.... + Axsel Scheer (1904 - 1964) b: 1904 in Riga, Riga, Latvia, m: 1928 in Oslo, Oslo,
Norway, d: 1964 in Oslo, Oslo, Norway
.... 6   Markus "Frank" Scheer (1929 - 1995) b: 1929 in Paris, Ile-de-France, France, d:
1995 in Canada
.... + Freya
.... + Liv Asgjer (1929 -) b: Abt. 1929, m: 1955
.... 7   Eric Scheer (1957 - 1979) b: Abt. 1957, d: Abt. 1979
.... 7   William Billy Scheer (1962 -) b: Abt. 1962
.... 7   Donald Scheer (1964 -) b: Abt. 1964
.... + Eva Gunderson (1925 -) b: Abt. 1925
..........................7   Marianne Scheer (1951 -) b: Abt. 1951
.... + Gunner Gulbrandson
.... 8   Anita Gulbrandson (1973 -) b: Abt. 1973
.... 5   Amalie Makka Selikowitz (1908 - 1998) b: Dec 31, 1908 in Oslo, Oslo, Norway, d: Aug
07, 1998 in Oslo, Oslo, Norway
.... + Berdnard Goldberg m: 1937 in Oslo, Oslo, Norway, d: in Copenhagen, Norway
.... 5   Miriam Selikowitz (1910 - 1910) b: 1910 in Oslo, Oslo, Norway, d: 1910 in Oslo,
Oslo, Norway
.... 5   Arnold Koppel Nolt Selikowitz (1912 -) b: Mar 11, 1912 in Oslo, Oslo, Norway
.... + Rochel Jarner (1910 - 1982) b: Apr 11, 1910 in Kristiania, Norway, m: Sep 10, 1941
in Oslo, Oslo, Norway, d: Feb 19, 1982 in Oslo, Oslo, Norway
.... 6   Harry-Sam Selikowitz (1945 -) b: Jan 13, 1945 in Stockholm, Stockholms,
Sweden
.... 6   Ethel Liv Selikowitz (1950 -) b: Aug 01, 1950 in Oslo, Oslo, Norway
.... + Henning Rouchman (1949 -) b: 1949 in Oslo, Oslo, Norway, m: Nov 02, 1976 in
Oslo, Oslo, Norway
.... 7   Bo-Martin Rouchman (1978 -) b: Aug 05, 1978 in Copenhagen, Denmark
.... 4   Charlotte Rothenberg (1888 - 1973) b: Jan 02, 1888 in Härnösand, Vasternorrlands,
Sweden, d: Apr 11, 1973 in Oslo, Oslo, Norway
.... + Fillip Hirsh (1888 - 1962) b: Aug 28, 1888 in Oslo, Oslo, Norway, d: 1962 in Oslo,
Oslo, Norway
.... 5   Libali Hirsh (1922 - 1942) b: 1922 in Oslo, Oslo, Norway, d: 1942 in Auschwitz,
Poland, Holocaust
.... 4   Dora-Goldine Rothenberg (1890 - 1975) b: Oct 21, 1890 in Härnösand, Vasternorrlands,
Sweden, d: Feb 26, 1975 in Stockholm, Stockholms, Sweden
.... + Paltiel Jacobsen (1890 - 1970) b: Feb 26, 1890 in Trondheim, Sor-Trondelag,
Norway, m: Abt. 1923 in Trondheim, Sor-Trondelag, Norway, d: Sep 19, 1970 in
Stockholm, Stockholms, Sweden

.... 5 Leif-Herman Jacobsen (1925 - 2006) b: Jun 19, 1925 in Trondheim, Sor-
            Trondelag, Norway, d: Nov 24, 2006 in Stockholm, Stockholms, Sweden
.... + Birthe Litichevsky (1937 - 2005) b: Jan 17, 1937 in Copenhagen, Denmark, m: Abt.
            1969 in Stockholm, Stockholms, Sweden, d: 2005 in Stockholm, Stockholms, Sweden
.....................6 Per-Herman Jacobsen (1971-) b:Aug 15, 1971 in Stockholm, Stockholm, Sweden
.... + Sara Jacobsen b: Feb 08, 1976 in Stockholm, Stockholm, Sweden
.....................7 Rebecca Jacobsen b: Mar 15, 2014 in Stockholm, Stockholm, Sweden
.....................6 Anne-Solveig Leifsdatter Jacobsen (1972-) b:Oct 16, 1972 in Stockholm, Stockholm, Sweden
.... + Mats Bjorkestrand b:Abt. 1970 in Stockholm, Stockholm, Sweden
.....................7 Hugo Evert Herbert Bjorkestrand Apr 27, 2008 in Stockholm, Sweden
.....................7 Viggo Harald Peter Bjorkestrand b:Mar 09, 2011 in Stockholm, Sweden
.....................7 Thor Otto John Bjorkestrand b:Mar 09, 2011 in Stockholm, Sweden
.... 3   Simon "Shimon" Ruttenberg (1850 - 1910) b: Aug 15, 1850 in Shkudvil, Kovno, Russia, d: Apr
            05, 1910 in St Paul, Ramsey County, Minnesota
.... + Goldie Massevitch (1866 - 1952) b: Jul 01, 1866 in Odessa, Russia, m: 1885 in
            Ishpeming, Marquette, Michigan, USA, d: Dec 13, 1952 in St Paul, Ramsey County,
            Minnesota
.... 4   Abbot "Abraham" Ruttenberg (1886 - 1918) b: Aug 01, 1886 in St Paul, Dakota,
            Minnesota, USA, d: 1918 in France
.... 4   Sarah Ruttenberg (1886 - 1974) b: Dec 29, 1886 in St Paul, Dakota, Minnesota, USA, d:
            Sep 1974 in Los Angeles, Los Angeles, California, USA
.... + William Harris (1882 - 1968) b: Dec 08, 1882, d: Apr 1968 in Los Angeles, Los
            Angeles, California, United States of America
.... 5   Marcelle Harris (1911 - 1933) b: 1911 in St Paul, Dakota, Minnesota, USA, d:
            1933 in St Paul, Dakota, Minnesota, USA
.... 4   Frances Ruttenberg (1891 - 1981) b: Sep 15, 1891 in Ishpeming, Marquette,
            Michigan, USA, d: May 1981 in Los Angeles, Los Angeles, California, USA
.... + Arthur Brash (1885 - 1971) b: Nov 26, 1885 in Los Angeles, Los Angeles, California,
            USA, d: Sep 1971 in Chicago, Cook, Illinois, USA
.... 4   Bessie "Betty" Ruttenberg (1893 - 1996) b: Dec 27, 1893 in Ishpeming, Marquette,
            Michigan, USA, d: Jul 01, 1996 in Los Angels, California
.... + Daniel Hacker (1893 - 1984) b: Oct 25, 1893 in England, d: May 1984 in Los Angeles, Los
            Angeles, California, USA
.... 5   William S Hacker (1929 - 1996) b: Jan 01, 1929 in St Paul, Dakota, Minnesota,
            USA, d: Jun 21, 1996 in Fautibault, Minnesota
.... + Joy Levy m: Jan 18, 1948 in Fautibault, Minnesota
.... 6   James Hacker (1949 -) b: 1949 in St Paul, Dakota, Minnesota, USA
.... 6   Linda Hacker (1951 -) b: 1951 in St Paul, Dakota, Minnesota, USA
.... 6   Steven Hacker (1953 -) b: 1953 in St Paul, Dakota, Minnesota, USA
.... 5   Barbara Hacker (1930 - 1993) b: May 06, 1930 in St Paul, Dakota, Minnesota,
            USA, d: Oct 28, 1993 in Los Angeles, Los Angeles, California, USA
.... + David Shore (1926 -) b: 1926 in Los Angelus, California
.... 6   Jenny Shore (1953 -) b: 1953 in Los Angeles, Los Angeles, California, USA
.... 6   Duggan Shore (1954 -) b: 1954 in Los Angeles, Los Angeles, California, USA
.... 4   Arnold Ruttenberg (1896 - 1918) b: Mar 26, 1896 in Ishpeming, Marquette, Michigan,
            USA, d: 1918 in Canada
.... + Susan Waller (1897 -) b: 1897
.... 4   Edward Harold Ruttenberg (1899 - 1988) b: Feb 10, 1899 in Ishpeming, Marquette,
            Michigan, USA, d: Jan 1988 in Laguna Hills, California
.... + Goldene Hloss (1902 - 1993) b: Mar 07, 1902 in Pietra Namt, Romania, d: Apr 24,
            1993 in Boulder, Colarado
.... 5   Stanley Ruttenberg (1926 -) b: 1926 in St Paul, Dakota, Minnesota, USA
.... + Patricia (1931 -) b: 1931
.... 6   Alison Lee Ruttenberg (1959 -) b: 1959 in Washington, DC, USA
.... 6   Rebecca Ruttenberg (1962 -) b: Sep 1962 in Boulder, Boulder, Colorado,
            USA
.... 5   Herbert David Ruttenberg (1930 -) b: 1930 in Philadelphia, Philadelphia,
            Pennsylvania, USA
.... + Susanna (1938 -) b: Abt. 1938 in New York
.... 6   Julia A. Ruttenberg (1958 - 2002) b: 1958 in Los Angeles, Los Angeles,
            California, USA, d: Jun 05, 2002 in La Habra, Orange, California, United
            States of America
.... 6   Kathleen Ruttenberg (1960 -) b: 1960 in Myrtle Beach, North Carolina

```
........................... + Diane Kathleen Claire Hanson
.................................. 6  Carolyn Jeanne Ruttenberg (1962 - ) b: Aug 03, 1962 in Hennepin, Minnesota
.................................. + Spencer Steinberg (1958 - ) b: 1958 in New York, New York, USA
.................................... 7  Hillary Steinberg (1990 - ) b: 1990 in Los Angeles, Los Angeles, California,
                 USA
.................................. 6  Loretta L Ruttenberg (1963 - ) b: 1963 in Seattle, King, Washington, USA
.................... 4  Harold Edward Ruttenberg (1904 - ) b: 1904 in St Paul, Dakota, Minnesota, USA
.................... + Blanche Melunchick (1906 - 1998) b: 1906 in St Paul, Dakota, Minnesota, USA, d: Oct 21,
                 1998 in Los Angeles, Los Angeles, California, USA
.......................... 5  Marly Ruttenberg (1930 - ) b: 1930 in St Paul, Dakota, Minnesota, USA
.......................... + Morley Drucker (1927 - ) b: 1927 in St Paul, Dakota, Minnesota, USA, m: 1950
.......................... 6  Pamala Drucker (1953 - ) b: 1953 in St Paul, Dakota, USA
.......................... 6  Elana L Drucker (1960 - ) b: Jul 19, 1960 in Los Angeles, Los Angeles,
                 California, USA
.............. 3  Sam "Shmuel" Ruttenberg (1852 - ) b: 1852 in Shkudvil, Kovno, Russia, d: in New York,  New
                 York, USA
.............. 3  Albert "Efroim" Ruttenberg (1859 - 1936) b: 1859 in Shkudvil, Russia, d: Oct 17, 1936 in
                 Chicago Cook, Illinois, USA
.............. + Katherine Tresize (1870 - 1920) b: 1870 in Leeds, England, m: 1886 in St Paul,
                 Minnesota, d: Bef. 1920 in Chicago, Cook, Illinois, USA
.................... 4  Alphonse Ruttenberg (1893 - 1930) b: Jun 26, 1893 in Ishpeming, Marquette,
                 Michigan, USA, d: Bef. 1930 in Hancock, Houghton, Michigan, USA
.................... 4  Bertha Ruttenberg (1889 - 1982) b: Sep 14, 1889 in Hancock, Houghton, Michigan,
                 USA, d: Jan 1982 in Palm Springs, Riverside, California, USA
.................... + David Rice (1885 - 1965) b: Dec 27, 1885 in Milwaukee, Milwaukee, Wisconsin, USA,  m:
                 Apr 14, 1904 in Ishpeming, Marquette, Michigan, USA, d: Feb 1965 in Chicago,  Cook,
                 Illinois, USA
.......................... 5  Ethel Rice (1908 - 1987) b: May 05, 1908 in Ishpeming, Marquette, Michigan,
                 USA, d: Nov 1987 in Chicago, Cook, Illinois, USA
.......................... + Benjamin F. Gordon (1906 - 1993) b: Oct 06, 1906 in Chicago, Cook, Illinois,
                 USA, d: Jun 21, 1993 in Chicago, Cook, Illinois, USA
.......................... 5  Marianna "Marion" Rice (1910 - 1997) b: Mar 07, 1910 in Calumet, Houghton,
                 Michigan, USA, d: Jun 15, 1997 in Riverside County, California
.......................... + Harry E Balaban (1903 - 1985) b: Jul 21, 1903 in Chicago, Cook, Illinois, USA, m:  May
                 1928 in Chicago, Cook, Illinois, USA, d: Mar 08, 1985 in Chicago, Cook,  Illinois, USA
.................................. 6  Richard Lee Balaban (1929 - ) b: Jul 07, 1929 in Chicago, Cook, Illinois, USA
.................................. + Kathleen E "Kathi" (1943 - ) b: May 1943 in Minneapolis, Anoka, Minnesota,
                 USA
.......................... 6  Barbara J Balaban (1940 - ) b: Apr 1940 in Chicago, Cook, Illinois, USA
.......................... 5  Caroline E Rice (1915 - ) b: Nov 04, 1915 in Chicago, Cook, Illinois, USA
.......................... + Albert Jean Marks (1913 - ) b: Jun 03, 1913 in Chicago, Cook, Illinois, USA, m:  Aug
                 09, 1930 in Chicago, Cook, Illinois, USA
.................................. 6  Albert J Marks (1940 - 2001) b: Aug 25, 1940 in Chicago, Cook, Illinois, USA,  d:
                 Apr 07, 2001 in Chicago, Cook, Illinois, USA
.................................. 6  Jeffery Marks (1943 - ) b: 1943 in Chicago, Cook, Illinois, USA
.......................... 5  Shirley Rose Rice (1923 - ) b: 1923 in Chicago, Cook, Illinois, USA
.................... 4  Nathan Ruttenberg (1891 - 1980) b: Jun 27, 1891 in Ishpeming, Marquette, Michigan,
                 USA, d: Feb 05, 1980 in Palm Springs, Riverside, California, USA
.................... + Lillian Propp (1889 - 1977) b: Jul 27, 1889 in Chicago, Cook, Illinois, USA, m: 1922 in
                 Chicago, Cook, Illinois, USA, d: Jan 20, 1977 in Palm Springs, Riverside, California,  USA
.................... 4  Ruth G. Ruttenberg (1898 - 1994) b: Sep 19, 1898 in Hancock, Houghton, Michigan,
                 USA, d: May 31, 1994 in Chicago, Cook, Illinois, USA
.................... + Alfred Hart (1893 - 1968) b: Aug 29, 1893 in Chicago, Cook, Illinois, USA, m: Abt.
                 1921 in Chicago, Cook, Illinois, USA, d: Nov 1968 in Chicago, Cook, Illinois, USA
.......................... 5  Caroline Hart (1923 - ) b: 1923 in Chicago, Cook, Illinois, USA
.............. 3  Oscar "Chaim" Ruttenberg (1867 - 1931) b: 1867 in Shkudvil, Kovno, Russia, d: Abt. 1931  in
                 Calumet, Houghton, Michigan, USA
.............. + Celcia S Neimark (1879 - 1972) b: 1879 in New York, New York, USA, m: Abt. 1900 in
                 Calumet, Houghton, Michigan, USA, d: 1972 in Chicago, Cook, Illinois, USA
```

.... 4 Marion "Myron" Ruttenberg (1902 -) b: Dec 10, 1902 in Calumet, Houghton,
               Michigan, USA, d: in Miami, Florida
.... + Shirley (1914 - 1981) b: Mar 23, 1914, m: 1935, d: Aug 1981 in Miami, Florida
.... 5 David Ruttenberg (1937 -) b: 1937
.... 4 Jules "Butch" Ruttenberg (1904 - 1971) b: Nov 05, 1904 in Red Jacket, Michigan, d: Jan
               06, 1971 in Pasco, Florida, United States
.... + Leila Marie Tiffen (1900 - 1984) b: Jan 03, 1900 in Petrolia, Canada, d: Sep 1984 in
               Wayne County, Michigan
.... 5 John Jules Ruttenberg (1932 -) b: Jan 26, 1932 in Detroit, Wayne County,
               Michigan
.... + Marilyn Mason Genung (1938 -) b: Jun 19, 1938 in Summit, New Jersey
.... 6 Denise Ruttenberg (1959 -) b: Aug 20, 1959 in Lakehurst Navel Air Base, New
.... + William Porter Harben (1957 -) b: May 19, 1957 in Pomtiac, Michigan, m: 1990
               in Detroit, Wayne, Michigan, USA
.... 7 Stephanie Louise Harben (1992 -) b: Feb 24, 1992 in Auburn, California
.... 7 Aylssa Lee Harben (1994 -) b: Mar 16, 1994 in Fresno, California
.... 7 Tiffany Grace Harben (1998 -) b: Mar 02, 1998
.... 6 Bruce John Ruttenberg (1962 -) b: 1962 in Detroit, Wayne, Michigan, USA
.... + Terry Hotig (1965 -) b: 1965
.... 4 Miriam Gertrude Ruttenberg (1911 - 2000) b: Jan 15, 1911 in Calumet, Houghton,
               Michigan, USA, d: Apr 24, 2000 in Marquette, Mackinac, Michigan, USA
.... + Richmond W Boyd (1908 - 1988) b: Oct 07, 1908, m: 1933 in Marquette, Mackinac,
               Michigan, USA, d: Jan 16, 1988 in Marquette, Marquette, Michigan
.... 5 Mary Celia Boyd (1936 -) b: 1936 in Marquette, Mackinac, Michigan, USA
.... + David Mileski (1934 -) b: Abt. 1934
.... 6 James Mileski
.... + Sandy
.... 7 Cavey Lynn Mileski
.... 7 Nathan Mileski
.... 6 Stephen Mileski
.... + Jane
.... 5 David R. Boyd (1941 -) b: 1941 in Marquette, Mackinac, Michigan, USA
.... 6 David Boyd (1961 -) b: 1961 in Marquette, Mackinac, Michigan, USA
.... + Lisa Vetter
.... 7 Ransem Boyd (1992 -) b: 1992
.... 7 Zane Boyd (1994 -) b: 1994
.... 6 Terra Lynn Boyd (1963 -) b: 1963 in Marquette, Mackinac, Michigan, USA
.... + Steven Heyward
.... 6 Susan Boyd (1965 -) b: 1965 in Marquette, Mackinac, Michigan, USA
.... 3 Morris "Meir" Ruttenberg (1869 - 1937) b: 1869 in Shkudvil, Kovno, Russia, d: Jun 09, 1937
           in Chicago, Cook, Illinois, USA
.... + Bessie Bar (1874 - 1930) b: 1874 in Russia, d: Jan 11, 1930 in Chicago, Cook, Illinois, USA
.... 4 Albert M. Ruttenberg (1891 - 1976) b: Apr 22, 1891 in Malmö, Kalmar, Sweden, d: May
               1976 in Milwaukee, Milwaukee, Wisconsin, USA
.... + Henriette "Betty" (1899 - 1993) b: Mar 08, 1899 in Chicago, Cook, Illinois, USA, m: Bef.
               1920 in Chicago, Cook, Illinois, USA, d: Apr 27, 1993 in Milwaukee, Milwaukee,
               Wisconsin, USA
.... 4 Louis M. Ruttenberg (1895 - 1967) b: Oct 24, 1895 in New York, New York, USA, d: Jan
               1967 in Miami, Florida
.... + Florence (1855 -) b: Abt. 1855 in Missouri
.... 4 Samuel "Saul" Ruttenberg (1898 - 1966) b: Mar 10, 1898 in New York, New York, USA,
               d: Mar 1966 in Chicago, Cook, Illinois, USA
.... 4 Joseph Joshua Ruttenberg (1899 - 1978) b: Jun 19, 1899 in New York, New York, USA,
               d: Jul 30, 1978 in Riverside, California, USA
.... 4 Clara Ruttenberg (1902 -) b: 1902 in New York, New York, USA
.... 4 Ida Ruttenberg (1903 -) b: 1903 in New York, New York, USA
.... 4 Bertha Ruttenberg (1906 - 1997) b: 1906 in Chicago, Cook, Illinois, USA, d: Feb 06, 1997
               in Chicago, Cook, Illinois, United States of America

.... + Diver

.... 4 Jerome Ruttenberg (1908 - 1986) b: Feb 11, 1908 in Chicago, Cook, Illinois, USA, d: Jun 05, 1986 in Los Angeles, California

.... + Harriett B Burkson (1901 - 1991) b: Jun 24, 1901 in Illinois, d: Oct 08, 1991 in Los Angeles, California

.... 4 Dudley C Ruttenberg (1914 - 1966) b: Jul 26, 1914 in Chicago, Cook, Illinois, USA, d: Oct 1966 in Chicago, Cook, Illinois, USA

.... 3 Celia Ruttenberg (1870 - 1957) b: 1870 in Shkudvil, Kovno, Russia, d: Oct 29, 1957 in Chicago, Cook, Illinois, USA

.... + Louis "Lazer Aronovich" Arne (1867 - 1939) b: Feb 11, 1867 in Shkudvil, Kovno, Russia, m: 1894 in Calumet, Houghton, Michigan, USA, d: Sep 18, 1939 in Milwaukee, Milwaukee, Wisconsin, USA

.... 4 Sarah Arne (1895 - 1977) b: Jul 02, 1895 in Ishpeming, Marquette, Michigan, USA, d: Oct 1977 in Chicago, Cook, Illinois, USA

.... + George Leviton (1890 - 1963) b: Sep 27, 1890 in Kovno, Lithuania, d: Jan 1963 in Chicago, Cook, Illinois, USA

.... 5 Theodore Leviton (1929 - 1980) b: Oct 01, 1929 in Milwaukee, Milwaukee, Wisconsin, USA, d: Feb 1980 in Chicago, Cook, Illinois, USA

.... + Harriet Joyce Franklin (1945 -) b: May 22, 1945 in Chicago, Cook, Illinois, USA, m: 1967 in Chicago, Cook, Illinois, USA

...........................6 Brook Jennifer Leviton b:Dec 19, 1972 in Chicago, Cook, Illinois, USA

.... + Michael Mandie

...........................7 ? Mandie

...........................7 ? Mandie

...........................6 Alison Lee Leviton b:Oct 1, 1975 in Chicago, Cook, Illinois, USA

.... + Vitaly Rindner b:Sep 17, 1975, Minsk, Minsk, Belarus

...........................7 Theodora Rindner

.... 5 Joyce Leviton (1933 -) b: 1933 in Chicago, Cook, Illinois, USA

.... + Gershon Hammer (1930 -) b: 1930 in Chicago, Cook, Illinois, USA

.... 6 Lori Hammer (1968 - 1997) b: Jan 02, 1968 in Chicago, Cook, Illinois, d: Jan 01, 1997 in Chicago, Cook, Illinois

.... + David Charles Recupero (1961 -) b: 1961, m: Jul 22, 1989 in Racine, Racine, Wisconsin, USA

.... + Alan Zelinsky (1933 -) b: 1933 in Chicago, Cook, Illinois, USA

.... 6 Deborah Gail Zelinsky (1960 -) b: Jan 17, 1960 in Chicago, Cook, Illinois, USA

.... 4 Phillip A. Arne (1898 - 1972) b: Sep 05, 1898 in Calumet, Houghton, Michigan, USA, d: Jun 1972 in Milwaukee, Milwaukee, Wisconsin, USA

.... + Bertha Levin (1911 -) b: 1911 in Racine, Racine, Wisconsin, USA

.... 5 Annette Rachele Arne (1936 - 1986) b: Feb 13, 1936 in Milwaukee, Milwaukee, Wisconsin, USA, d: Jul 1986 in Milwaukee, Milwaukee, Wisconsin, USA

.... + Ronald Irving Pachefsky (1935 -) b: 1935 in Milwaukee, Milwaukee, Wisconsin, USA

.... 6 Larry Pachefsky (1960 -) b: 1960 in Milwaukee, Milwaukee, Wisconsin, USA

.... + Ronna Bromberg (1960 -) b: 1960 in Pittsburgh, Allegheny, Pennsylvania, USA

.... 7 Joel Pachefsky (1990 -) b: 1990 in Milwaukee, Milwaukee, Wisconsin, USA

.... 7 David Pachefsky (1991 -) b: 1991 in Milwaukee, Milwaukee, Wisconsin, USA

.... 7 Michel Pachefsky (1993 -) b: 1993 in Milwaukee, Milwaukee, Wisconsin, USA

.... 6 Mark Pachefsky (1961 -) b: 1961 in Milwaukee, Milwaukee, Wisconsin, USA

.... + Lori Goldner (1962 -) b: 1962 in Milwaukee, Milwaukee, Wisconsin, USA

.... 7 Braley Pachefsky (1985 -) b: 1985 in Milwaukee, Milwaukee, Wisconsin, USA

.... 7 Cory Pachefsky (1987 -) b: 1987 in Milwaukee, Milwaukee, Wisconsin,

.... 7 Andrew Pachefsky (1989 -) b: 1989 in Milwaukee, Milwaukee, Wisconsin, USA

.... + Max Streitman (1929 -) b: 1929 in Minneapolis, Anoka, Minnesota, USA

.... 4 Charles B. Arne (1901 - 1965) b: Jan 01, 1901 in Hancock, Houghton, Michigan, USA, d: Oct 1965 in Milwaukee, Milwaukee, Wisconsin, USA

.... + Mary Sagle (1912 - 1983) b: 1912 in Milwaukee, Milwaukee, Wisconsin, USA, d: 1983 in Los Angeles, Los Angeles, California, USA

.... 5 Janice Arne (1929 - 1986) b: 1929 in Milwaukee, Milwaukee, Wisconsin, USA, d: 1986 in Boston, Suffolk, Massachusetts, USA

.... + Robert Gold (1927 -) b: 1927 in Milwaukee, Milwaukee, Wisconsin, USA

.... 6 Michael Gold (1951 -) b: 1951 in West Medford, Massachusetts

.... + Ricki Tanger (1953 -) b: 1953

.... 7 Taylor Gold (1974 -) b: 1974

.... 6   Peter Gold (1953 -) b: 1953 in West Medford, Massachusetts
.... + Candy Kosow (1954 -) b: 1954
.... 7   Carly Gold (1975 -) b: 1975
.... 7   David Gold (1977 -) b: 1977
.... 6   James Elieger Gold (1955 -) b: 1955 in West Medford, Massachusetts
.... + Basya Bookfinder (1957 -) b: 1957 in Massachusetts, USA
.... 7   Menachem Gold (1980 -) b: 1980
.... 7   Levi Gold (1982 -) b: 1982
.... 7   Hunnah Gold (1985 -) b: 1985
.... 7   Chaya Gold (1988 -) b: 1988
.... 5   Elinor "Ellie" Arne (1942 -) b: May 12, 1942 in Milwaukee, Milwaukee, Wisconsin,
            USA
.... + Arthur Pirelli (1940 -) b: 1940
.... 6   Lisa Ann Pirelli (1965 -) b: Jun 23, 1965 in Novato, California
.... 6   Arthur Allen Pirelli (1966 -) b: Oct 28, 1966 in Novato, California
.... + Sarah "Rose" Bromovitz (1905 - 1987) b: 1905 in Milwaukee, Milwaukee, Wisconsin,
            USA, d: 1987 in Milwaukee, Milwaukee, Wisconsin, USA
.... 4   Lillian Arne (1902 - 1980) b: May 11, 1902 in Calumet, Houghton, Michigan, USA, d:
            Aug 1980 in Milwaukee, Milwaukee, Wisconsin, USA
.... 4   Rosalye Arne (1904 - 1986) b: 1904 in Calumet, Houghton, Michigan, USA, d: 1986 in
            Milwaukee, Milwaukee, Wisconsin, USA
.... + John Schwartz (1901 - 1981) b: Sep 13, 1901 in Milwaukee, Milwaukee, Wisconsin,
            USA, m: 1934 in Milwaukee, Milwaukee, Wisconsin, USA, d: Jun 1981 in Milwaukee,
            Milwaukee, Wisconsin, USA
.... 5   Hershel Schwartz (1936 -) b: 1936 in Milwaukee, Milwaukee, Wisconsin, USA
.... + Arlene (1936 -) b: 1936 in Milwaukee, Milwaukee, Wisconsin, USA
.... 5   Lois Schwartz (1938 -) b: 1938 in Milwaukee, Milwaukee, Wisconsin, USA
.... + Martin Shickman (1927 - 1995) b: May 27, 1927 in Milwaukee, Milwaukee,
            Wisconsin, USA, d: Apr 21, 1995 in Los Angeles, Los Angeles, California, USA
.... 6   Steven Shickman (1958 -) b: 1958 in Los Angeles, Los Angeles, California,
            USA
.... 6   David Shickman (1962 -) b: 1962 in Los Angeles, Los Angeles, California,
            USA
.... + Kathryn (1964 -) b: 1964
.... 7   Ryan Shickman (1991 -) b: 1991 in Los Angeles, Los Angeles, California,
            USA
.... 7   Jordan William Shickman (1995 -) b: Feb 10, 1995 in Los Angeles, Los
            Angeles, California, USA
.... 6   Trevor Shickman (1970 -) b: 1970 in Los Angeles, Los Angeles, California, USA
.... 3   Nathan "Nokhum" Ruttenberg (1873 - 1935) b: 1873 in Shkudvil, Kovno, Russia, d: Mar 13,
            1935 in Chicago, Cook, Illinois, USA
.... + Esther Rosenblum (1870 - 1947) b: 1870 in Russia, d: Jan 12, 1947 in Chicago, Cook,
            Illinois, USA
.... 4   Robert Ruttenberg (1909 -) b: 1909
.... + Beatrice (1910 - 1990) b: Apr 07, 1910 in Chicago, Cook, Illinois, USA, d: May 27,
            1990 in Winter Park, Orange, Florida
.... 5   Edward Ruttenberg (1941 -) b: 1941 in Chicago, Cook, Illinois, USA
.... 5   Ronald Ruttenberg (1944 -) b: 1944 in Chicago, Cook, Illinois, USA
.... 5   Nancy Ruttenberg (1950 -) b: 1950 in Chicago, Cook, Illinois, USA
.... 4   Ruth C. Ruttenberg (1910 -) b: 1910
.... 4   Edwin Ruttenberg (1911 -) b: 1911
.... 4   Lyle C Ruttenberg (1911 -) b: 1911
.... + Sidney Marschak
.... 5   Joan Marschak (1927 -) b: 1927
.... + Yeli Blanc
.... 6   Susan Blanc (1949 -) b: 1949
.... 6   Denise Blanc (1951 -) b: 1951
.... 6   Robin Blanc (1953 -) b: 1953

259

.... 3 Rosalie Ruttenberg (1875 -) b: 1875 in Shkudvil, Kovno, Russia, d: in Sweden
.... + Marcus Kohn (1871 -) b: 1871 in Härnösand, Vasternorrlands, Sweden, m: in Sweden, d: in
           Sweden
.... 4 Lena Kohn (1894 -) b: 1894 in Härnösand, Vasternorrlands, Sweden
.... + Alfred Torner (1891 -) b: 1891 in Härnösand, Vasternorrlands, Sweden, d: in
           Holocaust, Hero

.... 5 Styrbjoir Torner (1915 -) b: 1915 in Härnösand, Vasternorrlands, Sweden
.... + Ines
.... 6 Torner b: in Sweden
.... 6 Torner
.... 6 Torner (1944 -) b: 1944 in Sweden
.... 5 Trygve Torner (1919 -) b: 1919 in Härnösand, Vasternorrlands, Sweden
.... 4 Julius Rothenberg (1896 -) b: 1896 in Gothenbourg, Sweden
.... + Dagmar b: in Sweden
.... 5 Rothenberg b: in Sweden
.... 5 Rothenberg b: in Sweden
.... 5 Rothenberg (1920 -) b: 1920 in Sweden
.... 2 Elje "Eliyahu" Prop (1827 - 1891) b: 1827 in Shkudvil, Kovno, Russia, d: 1891 in Shkudvil,
           Kovno, Russia
.... + Chazel Stern (1832 - 1898) b: 1832 in Kovno Guberniya, Lithuania, m: 1853 in Shkudvil,
           Kovno, Russia, d: 1898 in Shkudvil, Kovno, Russia
.... 3 Libe Prop (1853 - 1925) b: 1853 in Shkudvil, Kovno, Russia, d: 1925
.... + Mordechai "Mot'l" Krom (1847 - 1909) b: 1847 in Shkudvil, Kovno, Russia, m: 1881 in
           Shkudvil, Kovno, Russia, d: 1909
.... 4 Elje "Eliyahu" Krom (1882 - 1941) b: 1882 in Shkudvil, Kovno, Russia, d: Jul 21, 1941 in
           Shkudvil, Lithuania, Holocaust
.... 4 Pesa Rochel Krom (1888 -) b: 1888 in Shkudvil, Kovno, Russia
.... + Moshe Ber Ziv (1872 -) b: May 08, 1872 in Sveksne, Kovno Guberniya, Russia, m:
           1907 in Sveksne, Kovno Guberniya, Russia
.... 5 Mordechai Ziv (1909 -) b: 1909 in Sveksna, Kovno Guberniya, Russia
.... 5 Luba Ziv (1911 -) b: 1911 in Sveksne, Kovno Guberniya, Russia
.... + Moshe Todres (1907 - 1979) b: 1907 in Sveksna, Kovno Guberniya, Russia, m:
           1937 in Lithuania, d: 1979 in Hertzlia, Israel
.... 5 Miriam Ziv (1912 - 1941) b: 1912 in Sveksna, Kovno Guberniya, Russia, d: 1941 in
           Sveksne, Lithuania, Holocaust
.... 5 Minda Ziv (1914 -) b: 1914 in Sveksna, Kovno Guberniya, Russia, d: in Holocaust
.... 5 Naftali Ziv (1918 -) b: 1918 in Sveksna, Lithuania
.... + Hannah
.... 3 Barnett "Ber" Propp (1856 - 1911) b: Feb 14, 1856 in Shkudvil, Kovno, Russia, d: 1911 in
           Tupper Lake, Franklin, New York, USA
.... + Betsy "Pese-Rochel" Singer (1856 - 1924) b: Mar 17, 1856 in Shkudvil, Kovno, Russia, m: Abt. 1875
           in Shkudvil, Kovno, Russia, d: 1924 in Tupper Lake, Franklin, New York, USA
.... 4 Louis Alexander Propp (1876 - 1941) b: Sep 20, 1876 in Vilna, Vilna Guberniya,
           Russia, d: Dec 08, 1941 in New York, New York, USA
.... + Rebecca Siff (1880 - 1948) b: 1880 in Kovno Guberniya, Russia, m: Apr 10, 1902 in New
           York, New York, USA, d: Nov 03, 1948 in New York, New York, USA
.... 5 Perry S. Propp (1904 - 1974) b: Aug 02, 1904 in New York, New York, USA, d: Mar
           06, 1974 in Pittsfield, Berkshire, Massachusetts, USA
.... + Rosalie Lepow (1903 - 1985) b: Mar 28, 1903 in Brooklyn, Kings, New York, USA, m:
           Abt. 1935 in Brooklyn, Kings, New York, USA, d: Jun 21, 1985 in Pittsfield, Berkshire,
           Massachusetts, USA
.... 6 Norma Propp (1937 -) b: May 19, 1937 in Brooklyn, Kings, New York, USA
.... + Henry Tulgan (1933 -) b: Aug 02, 1933 in Brooklyn, Kings, New York, USA, m:
           May 08, 1954 in Brooklyn, Kings, New York, USA
.... 7 James Propp Tulgan (1959 -) b: Dec 31, 1959 in Albany, Albany, New
           York, USA
.... + Terri Lee Reder (1965 -) b: 1965 in Pittsfield, Massachusetts, m: Jun 16,

260

1988 in Pittsfield, Massachusetts
.... 8   Elisa Rose Tulgan (1988 -) b: 1988 in Pittsfield, Massachusetts
.... 8   Joseph Perry Tulgan (1991 -) b: 1991 in Springfield, Massachusetts
.... 7   Ronna Lynn Tulgan (1961 -) b: Jan 01, 1961 Albany, Albany, New York,
USA
.... + Thomas W. Ostheimer (1992 -) b: 1992 in Pittsfield, Massachusetts, m: Aug
13, 1988
.... 8   Perry Elizabeth Ostheimer (1992 -) b: 1992 in Pittsfield,
Massachusetts
.... 8   Erin Rosalie Ostheimer (1993 -) b: 1993 in North Adams,
Massachusetts
.... 8   Ganet Elias Ostheimer (2000 -) b: 2000 in North Adams,
Massachusetts
.... 7   Bruce Lorin Tulgan (1967 -) b: Jun 27, 1967 in Pittsfield, Berkshire,
Massachusetts, USA
....   + Deborah Mari Applegate (1968 -) b: Feb 01, 1968 in Pittsfield, Berkshire,
Massachusetts, USA
.... 5   Helene G. Propp (1909 - 1995) b: Mar 15, 1909 in New York, New York, USA, d: Feb
1995 in Chicago, Illinois, 60615
.... + Oscar Weissman (1908 - 1966) b: Oct 13, 1908 in Brooklyn, Kings, New York,
USA, m: Abt. 1939 in New York, New York, USA, d: Dec 1966 in Lakewood,
Cuyahoga, Ohio, USA
.... 6   Andrew Weissman (1941 -) b: 1941 in Brooklyn, Kings, New York, USA
....   + Marian Bates
.... 7   Dana Propp Weissman (1965 -) b: Abt. 1965
....   + Christoper Spurling
.... 8   Jackson Spurling
.... 7   Joshue Weissman (1967 -) b: Abt. 1967
....   + Karen Balog m: Abt. 1990
.... 6   Judy Weissman (1944 -) b: 1944 in St Louis, St Louis, Missouri, USA
....   + John Williams (1939 -) b: 1939 in Michigan, USA, m: Abt. 1964
.... 7   Tanya Williams (1966 -) b: 1966 in Michigan, USA
....   + Kiam Meachan
.... 8   Dese Williams
.... 8   Erich Williams
....   + Rufus Griffin m: Abt. 1975
.... 4   Elizabeth Propp (1886 - 1978) b: Aug 10, 1886 in Tupper Lake, Franklin, New York,
USA, d: Dec 1978 in Schenectady, Schenectady, New York, USA
....   + Samuel Levy (1881 - 1960) b: 1881 in Malone, New York, m: 1909 in Tupper Lake,
Franklin, New York, USA, d: 1960 in Schenectady, Schenectady, New York, USA
.... 5   Richard A. Levy (1909 - 1989) b: May 19, 1909 in Schenectady, Schenectady, New
York, USA, d: Jul 17, 1989 in Osprey, Sarasota, Florida, USA
....   + Ruth Hirschon (1915 -) b: 1915 in Schenectady, Schenectady County, New York, m: in
Schenectady, Schenectady, New York, USA, d: in Sarasota County, Florida
.... 5   Barbara M. Levy (1918 - 1996) b: Jan 28, 1918 in Schenectady, Schenectady, New
York, USA, d: Jul 12, 1996 in Sarasota, Flordia
....   + Lester Kornblith (1917 - 1992) b: Apr 27, 1917 in Ohio, d: Jan 12, 1992 in
Sarasota, Flordia
.... 4   Nathan A. Propp (1888 - 1957) b: Nov 15, 1888 in Tupper Lake, Franklin, New York,
USA, d: Oct 06, 1957 in Palm Beach, Dade County, Florida
....   + Meriam L Magner (1897 - 1976) b: Jan 04, 1897 in Tupper, Lake, Franklin County, New
York, m: Jun 01, 1915 in New York, New York, USA, d: Mar 06, 1976 in Palm Beach,
Dade County, Florida
.... 5   George Barnett Propp (1917 - 1972) b: Feb 22, 1917 in Tupper Lake, Franklin, New
York, USA, d: Jan 1972 in New York, New York, USA
.... 5   Beatrice Magner Propp (1918 - 1975) b: Apr 09, 1918 in Tupper Lake, Franklin, New
York, USA, d: Mar 14, 1975 in Palm Beach, Florida
....   + Fitterer
.... 3   Todres Prop (1854 - 1915) b: 1854 in Shkudvil, Kovno, Russia, d: Aug 02, 1915 in

Shkudvil, Kovno, Russia
.... + Chayna Royaiza Halevy (1866 - 1968) b: 1866 in Shkudvil, Kovno, Russia, m: 1886 in
Shkudvil, Kovno, Russia, d: 1968 in Kfar Saba, Israel
.... 4 Moshe Prop (1887 - 1966) b: 1887 in Shkudvil, Kovno, Russia, d: May 11, 1966 in Tel Aviv,
Israel
.... + Manja (1904 - 1963) b: 1904 in Sklov, Byelorussia, m: 1918 in Shkudvil, Kovno,
Russia, d: 1963 in Tel Aviv, Israel
.... 5 Theodore "Teddy" Propp (1921 - 1991) b: Jul 17, 1921 in Shkudvil, Kovno,
Russia, d: Jan 06, 1991 in Tel Aviv, Israel
.... + Esther (1924 -) b: Mar 13, 1924 in Jerusalem, Eretz Yisrael, m: in Israel
.... 6 Dalia Prop (1947 -) b: Jun 13, 1947 in Tel Aviv, Eretz Yisrael
.... + Gideon Regev (1941 -) b: Jan 22, 1941 in Jerusalem, Eretz Yisrael, m: 1970 in
Israel
.... 7 Moshe Regev (1971 -) b: Jan 21, 1971 in Tel Aviv, Israel
.... 7 Guy Regev (1975 -) b: Mar 25, 1975 in Tel Aviv, Israel
.... 6 Ronny Prop (1952 -) b: Mar 02, 1952 in Tel Aviv, Israel
.... + Etty (1956 -) b: Jun 22, 1956 in Tel Aviv, Israel, m: 1984 in Tel Aviv, Israel
.... 7 Miri Propp (1985 -) b: Aug 27, 1985 in Tel Aviv, Israel
.... 7 Dori Propp (1986 -) b: Jul 17, 1986 in Tel Aviv, Israel
.... 7 Tali Prop (1989 -) b: Dec 10, 1989 in Tel Aviv, Israel
.... 5 Baby Prop (1922 - 1924) b: 1922 in Shkudvil, Kovno, Russia, d: 1924 in Shkudvil,
Kovno, Russia
.... 4 Chaya Miriam Prop (1888 - 1968) b: 1888 in Shkudvil, Kovno, Russia, d: Jan 11, 1968 in
Herzliyya, Israel
.... + Mishel A "Plo" Plokst (1892 - 1984) b: 1892 in Russia, m: 1924 in Shkudvil, Kovno,
Russia, d: Feb 08, 1984 in Herzliyya, Israel
.... 5 Matityau Todi Todres Peli (1926 -) b: Jul 22, 1926 in Tel Aviv, Eretz Yisrael
.... + Sarah Liba Melomad (1928 -) b: Aug 24, 1928 in Jerusalem, Eretz Yisrael, m: in
Herzelia, Eretz Yisr
.... 6 Moriya Peli (1948 -) b: Jul 30, 1948 in Herzliyya, Israel
.... + Raphael Stern (1951 -) b: Jan 07, 1951 in Israel, m: in Israel
.... 7 Ruth Esther Stern (1974 -) b: Oct 29, 1974 in Herzliyya, Israel
.... + Noam Bolvik (1972 -) b: 1972 in Israel
.... 8 Zohar Bolvik (1994 -) b: Sep 29, 1994 in Israel
.... 7 Elad Stern (1976 -) b: Apr 24, 1976 in Herzliyya, Israel
.... 7 Geolit Stern (1978 -) b: Aug 13, 1978 in Herzliyya, Israel
.... 7 Nili Stern (1981 -) b: Feb 16, 1981 in Herzliyya, Israel
.... 7 Ronnie Stern (1984 -) b: Aug 23, 1984 in Herzliyya, Israel
.... 6 Gilead Aaron Peli (1953 -) b: Jan 06, 1953 in Herzliyya, Israel
.... + Yehudit Judith Aviva Lenzer (1957 -) b: Apr 07, 1957 in Israel, m: in Israel
.... 7 Elazer Sholmo Peli (1978 -) b: Aug 03, 1978 in Herzliyya, Israel
.... 7 Yair Peli (1980 -) b: Feb 23, 1980 in Herzliyya, Israel
.... 7 Amishav Sinai Peli (1981 -) b: Sep 21, 1981 in Herzliyya, Israel
.... 7 Achiya Chaim Yosef Peli (1987 -) b: May 11, 1987 in Herzliyya, Israel
.... 6 Arnon Peli (1955 - 1982) b: Sep 03, 1955 in Herzliyya, Israel, d: Apr 23, 1982 in
Israel
.... + Batya Pins (1958 -) b: Jun 12, 1958 in Israel, m: in Israel
.... 5 Yaffa Plokst (1930 -) b: 1930 in Kfar Saba, Eretz Yisrael
.... + Avraham Mintz (1929 -) b: Nov 29, 1929 in Warsaw, Poland, m: in Israel
.... 6 Yehuda Arieh "Mintz" Etzion (1951 -) b: Dec 28, 1951 in Kibutz Ein Murim,
Israel
.... + Haya Montag (1955 -) b: Jun 20, 1955 in Poland, m: in Israel
.... 7 Pinhas Matiyahu Etzion (1976 -) b: Jan 22, 1976 in Ofra, Israel
.... 7 Yaakov Shalem Etzion (1977 -) b: Oct 05, 1977 in Ofra, Israel
.... 7 Shulamit Etzion (1979 -) b: Mar 24, 1979 in Ofra, Israel
.... 7 Levona Etzion (1981 -) b: Oct 05, 1981 in Ofra, Israel
.... 7 Shabtai Moshe Etzion (1983 -) b: Oct 05, 1983 in Ofra, Israel
.... 7 Amatzia Benyamin Etzion (1988 -) b: Jun 21, 1988 in Ofra, Israel

.... 7 Raaya Etzion (1988 -) b: Jun 21, 1988 in Ofra, Israel
.... 6 Orit Mintz (1953 -) b: Oct 13, 1953 in Kibutz Ein Surim, Israel
.... + Ira Rappaport (1945 -) b: Apr 05, 1945 in New York, New York, USA, m: in Israel
.... 7 Moriya Haya Rappaport (1976 -) b: Dec 24, 1976 in Ofra, Israel
.... 7 David Shimon Rappaport (1978 -) b: Apr 15, 1978 in Shilo, Israel
.... 7 Atara Sarah Rappaport (1979 -) b: Dec 29, 1979 in Shilo, Israel
.... 7 Yitzchak Yehuda Rappaport (1983 -) b: Apr 15, 1983 in Shilo, Israel
.... 7 Tsofia Geula Rappaport (1985 -) b: Mar 27, 1985 in New York, New York, USA
.... 7 Dvir Mishel Rappaport (1987 -) b: Feb 09, 1987 in Shilo, Israel
.... 7 Yisrael Shalem Rappaport (1989 -) b: Jul 13, 1989 in Shilo, Israel
.... 6 Avner "Mintz" Etzion (1955 -) b: Oct 18, 1955 in Kibutz Ein Zurim, Israel
.... + Neama (1955 -) b: Oct 17, 1955 in Jerusalem, Israel, m: in Israel
.... 7 Yehonadav Yihiel Etzion (1978 -) b: Sep 21, 1978 in Jerusalem, Israel
.... 7 Elyashiv Ami Etzion (1979 -) b: Sep 17, 1979 in Yatir, Israel
.... 7 Reut Etzion (1981 -) b: Mar 12, 1981 in Yatir, Israel
.... 7 Ahinoam Etzion (1983 -) b: Aug 10, 1983 in Yatir, Israel
.... 7 Tamar Etzion (1987 -) b: Dec 20, 1987 in Yatir, Israel
.... 7 Roni Etzion (1992 -) b: Apr 12, 1992 in Yatir, Israel
.... 4 Leib Aryieh Propp (1890 - 1959) b: 1890 in Shkudvil, Kovno, Russia, d: Jan 01, 1959 in Johannesburg, South Africa
.... + Roch'l Zippa Taub (1901 - 1984) b: 1901 in Shkudvil, Kovno, Russia, m: 1928 in Shkudvil, Kovno, Russia, d: 1984 in Tele Aviv, Israel
.... 5 Aviva Prop (1928 -) b: Dec 28, 1928 in Tel Aviv, Eretz Yisrael
.... + Hillel Matityahu Daleski (1925 -) b: 1925 in Eretz Yisrael, m: 1950 in Israel
.... 6 Deborah Vered Daleski (1951 -) b: Nov 24, 1951 in Johannesburg, South Africa
.... + Menashe Weinstein (1951 -) b: Dec 19, 1951 in Jerusalem, Israel, m: 1985 in Israel
.... 7 Roni Weinstein (1986 -) b: Dec 13, 1986 in Jerusalem, Israel
.... 7 Ori Weinstein (1992 -) b: Mar 28, 1992 in Jerusalem, Israel
.... 6 Gil Daleski (1954 -) b: Oct 18, 1954 in Jerusalem, Israel
.... + Arnona Zahavi (1956 -) b: 1956 in Israel, m: 1985 in Israel
.... 7 Tara Daleski (1987 -) b: Mar 01, 1987 in Jerusalem, Israel
.... 7 Mihal Daleski (1992 -) b: May 09, 1992 in Jerusalem, Israel
.... 7 Ruth Daleski (1995 -) b: Oct 16, 1995 in Abirim, Israel
.... + Irit Aba (1968 -) b: 1968 in Jerusalem, Israel, m: 1991 in Israel
.... + Orna Nakar (1963 -) b: 1963 in Jerusalem, Israel, m: 1994 in Jerusalem, Israel
.... 6 Arit Talia Daleski (1960 -) b: Oct 26, 1960 in Jerusalem, Israel
.... + Adi Lak (1958 -) b: Jan 06, 1958 in Kibutz Merhavia, Israel, m: 1988 in Israel
.... 7 Yehonatan Lak (1990 -) b: Oct 03, 1990 in Tel Aviv, Israel
.... 7 Shulamit Lak (1994 -) b: May 09, 1994 in Tel Aviv, Israel
.... 6 Yonat Ariela Daleski (1963 -) b: May 29, 1963 in Jerusalem, Israel
.... + Yaron Cohen (1964 -) b: Apr 25, 1964 in Tel Aviv, Israel, m: 1993 in Israel
.... 7 Itamar Cohen (1995 -) b: May 09, 1995 in Tel Aviv, Israel
.... + Michael Gross (1920 -) b: Apr 13, 1920 in Tiberius, Eretz Yisrael, m: 1975 in Israel
.... 5 Theodore "Ted" Prop (1934 -) b: Aug 24, 1934 in Johannesburg, South Africa
.... + Anneke Verdoner (1935 - 1973) b: Jul 21, 1935 in Den Haag, Amsterdam, Netherlands, m: 1961 in Israel, d: Aug 27, 1973 in Jerusalem, Israel
.... 6 Meira Livia Propp (1962 -) b: Feb 07, 1962 in Jerusalem, Israel
.... + Hagai Pizem (1962 -) b: Sep 01, 1962 in Tiberius, Israel, m: 1990 in Israel
.... 7 Dor Pizem (1991 -) b: May 20, 1991 in Tel Aviv, Israel
.... 7 Omer Pizem (1993 -) b: Jan 20, 1993 in Moshav Gealya, Israel
.... 7 Yael Pizem (1997 -) b: May 30, 1997 in Israel

.... 6 Yehuda Prop (1964 -) b: Jul 27, 1964 in Jerusalem, Israel
.... + Dana b: in Israel
.... 7 Yanai Prop (1997 -) b: Jul 15, 1997 in Moshav Galiya, Israel
.... 6 David Propp (1967 -) b: Jun 16, 1967 in Jerusalem, Israel
.... + Sharon Rashbaum (1967 -) b: Feb 25, 1967 in Kibutz Givat, Haim, Israel, m: 1993 in
   Israel
.... 7 Eitan Prop (1994 -) b: Nov 19, 1994 in Tel Aviv, Israel
.... 7 Roy Propp (1996 -) b: Mar 10, 1996 in Moshav Galiya, Israel
.... + Mazal Mutseri (1942 -) b: Jan 06, 1942 in Tel Aviv, Eretz Yisrael, m: 1974 in Tel Aviv, Israel
.... 6 Oded Propp (1975 -) b: May 10, 1975 in Jerusalem, Israel
.... 6 Dana Propp (1976 -) b: Aug 23, 1976 in Jerusalem, Israel
.... 3 Peter "Pesach" Propp (1865 - 1939) b: Apr 17, 1865 in Minsk, Minsk Guberniya, Russia, d:
   Sep 17, 1939 in Tupper Lake, Franklin, New York, USA
.... + Anna R. Rockoff (1874 - 1961) b: Oct 09, 1874 in Tilsit, East Prussia, m: 1885 in Baltimore,
   Maryland, USA, d: Oct 07, 1961 in Tupper Lake, Franklin, New York, USA
.... 4 Elihu Propp (1893 - 1981) b: Apr 27, 1893 in Baltimore, Maryland, USA, d: Dec 1981 in
   Albany, Albany, New York, USA
.... + Sara Rockovitz (1904 - 1999) b: Dec 18, 1904 in Gloversville, Fulton, New York, USA, m:
   1929 in New York, New York, USA, d: Apr 24, 1999 in Albany, Albany, New York, USA
.... 5 Lawrence A. Propp (1931 -) b: 1931 in Albany, Albany, New York, USA
.... + Mancia E. Schwartz (1934 -) b: 1934 in Brooklyn, Kings, New York, USA, m: Abt.
   1960 in Albany, Albany, New York, USA
.... 6 David Richard Propp (1962 -) b: 1962 in Albany, Albany, New York, USA
.... + Susan Kolodkin (1964 -) b: 1964 in Boston, Suffolk, Massachusetts, USA
.... 7 Zachary Morris Propp (1999 -) b: Dec 05, 1999 in Atlantia Georgia
.... 6 Jonathan Propp (1964 -) b: 1964 in Albany, Albany, New York, USA
.... + Tina Susanna Sarrinen (1967 -) b: 1967 in Espoo, Finland
.... 7 Maxwell Elias Propp (1995 -) b: Apr 23, 1995 in Helsinki, Finland
.... 7 Daniel Propp (1997 -) b: Jul 21, 1997 in Helsinki, Finland
.... 6 Laura Propp (1966 -) b: 1966 in Albany, Albany, New York, USA
.... + Michael C Postell (1967 -) b: Sep 1967 in Atlanta, De Kalb, Georgia, USA
.... 7 Benjamin Michael Propp (2004 -) b: Mar 04, 2004 in Atlanta, De Kalb,
   Georgia, USA
.... 7 Samantha Lindsey Postell (2004 -) b: Mar 04, 2004 in Atlanta, De Kalb, Georgia,
   USA
.... 5 Richard Paul Propp (1934 -) b: Jan 01, 1934 in Albany, Albany, New York, USA
.... + Vera Weichman (1935 -) b: 1935 in Germany, m: Abt. 1961
.... 6 Peter A. Propp (1963 -) b: Jan 04, 1963 in Los Angeles, California
.... + Susan Sherman (1963 -) b: 1963 in Needham, Massachusetts
.... 7 Rose Alice Propp (1995 -) b: May 19, 1995 in Albany, Albany, New York, USA
.... 7 Bennett Elihu Propp (1997 -) b: Apr 10, 1997 in Albany, Albany, New York,
   USA
.... 6 Elizabeth T Propp (1964 -) b: 1964 in Albany, Albany, New York, USA
.... 4 Leah Propp (1894 - 1992) b: Oct 29, 1894 in Baltimore, Maryland, USA, d: Aug 23,
   1992 in New York, New York, USA
.... + Frank R. Siegal (1892 - 1993) b: 1892 in Tupper Lake, Franklin, New York, USA, d:
   1993 in Atlanta, De Kalb, Georgia, USA
.... 5 Theodore Siegal (1927 - 1994) b: 1927 in Tupper Lake, Franklin, New York, USA, d:
   1994 in Atlanta, De Kalb, Georgia, USA
.... + Naomi (1929 - 1978) b: 1929 in New York, d: 1978 in Atlanta, De Kalb, Georgia, USA
.... 6 Peter Siegal (1963 - 1994) b: 1963 in Atlanta, De Kalb, Georgia, USA, d: 1994 in
   Atlanta, De Kalb, Georgia, USA
.... 6 Frank Siegal (1965 -) b: 1965 in Atlanta, De Kalb, Georgia, USA
.... 5 Adele Siegal (1932 - 1995) b: 1932 in Tupper Lake, Franklin, New York, USA, d:
   1995 in Los Angeles, Los Angeles, California, USA
.... + Samual Reiter (1930 -) b: 1930 in Atlanta, De Kalb, Georgia, USA
.... 4 Jesse Propp (1897 - 1976) b: Jul 08, 1897 in Baltimore, Maryland, USA, d: Jul 26,

Santa Monica, Los Angeles County, California

.... + Shirley Jean Wallock (1910 - 1994) b: Jan 30, 1910 in Tupper Lake, Franklin, New York, USA, m: Jul 1931 in Tupper Lake, Franklin, New York, USA, d: Dec 30, 1994 in Santa Monica, Los Angeles County, California

.... 5 Joan Propp (1932 -) b: 1932 in Tupper Lake, Franklin, New York, USA, d: in Mount Kisco, New York

.... + Royal F Potter (1929 -) b: Oct 1929, d: in Mount Kisco, New York

.... 6 Alison Potter (1956 -) b: 1956 in Brooklyn, Kings, New York, USA

.... + Munoz

.... 6 Katherine Potter (1958 -) b: 1958 in New York, New York, USA

.... + Richardson

.... 6 Jonathan Potter (1962 -) b: 1962 in Mount Kisco, New York

.... 6 Stephen Potter (1966 -) b: 1966 in Mount Kisco, New York

.... 5 Abby Propp (1934 -) b: 1934 in Tupper Lake, Franklin, New York, USA, d: in Grass Valley, California

.... + Joseph Schlesinger (1932 -) b: 1932, d: in Grass Valley, California

.... 6 Joseph E Schlesinger (1961 -) b: Aug 20, 1961 in Los Angeles, Los Angeles, California, USA

.... 6 Lauren M Schlesinger (1963 -) b: Jun 27, 1963 in Los Angeles, Los Angeles, California, USA

.... 6 Juliane K Schlesinger (1966 - 1999) b: Apr 19, 1966 in Orange, California, USA, d: Feb 18, 1999 in Orange, California, USA

.... 6 Nicholas J Schlesinger (1970 -) b: Jan 08, 1970 in Ventura, California

.... 5 Linda Ann Propp (1938 -) b: May 29, 1938 in Tupper Lake, Franklin, New York, USA

.... + Andrew K. Alper (1933 -) b: 1933 in New York, m: 1960 in New York

.... 6 David M Alper (1962 -) b: Jan 13, 1962 in Orange, California, USA

.... + Elaine

.... 7 Nicole Marie Alper b: in California, USA

.... 7 Brandon David (2001 -) b: Nov 02, 2001 in Orange, California, USA

.... 6 Todd B. Alper (1963 - 1963) b: Apr 14, 1963 in Orange, California, USA, d: Dec 10, 1963 in Orange, California, USA

.... 6 Leslie D. Alper (1965 - 2008) b: Mar 13, 1965 in Orange, California, USA, d: Jan 16, 2008 in Orange, California, USA

.... + Ronald Walter Votaw (1943 -) b: Aug 09, 1943 in Beaverton, Oregon, m: 1969 in California, USA

.... 6 Kirsten Elena Votaw (1970 -) b: Apr 24, 1970 in Morgan Hill, Santa Clara, California, USA

.... 4 Hazel B. Propp (1900 - 2000) b: 1900 in Flemingsburg, Fleming, Kentucky, USA, d: 2000 in New York, New York, USA

.... + Victor W. Sohmer (1894 - 1970) b: 1894 in Tupper Lake, Franklin, New York, USA, m: Dec 21, 1947 in Albany, Albany, New York, USA, d: 1970 in New York, New York, USA

.... 4 Abram Propp (1904 - 1925) b: Nov 15, 1904 in Tupper Lake, Franklin, New York, USA, d: Jun 08, 1925 in Tupper Lake, Franklin, New York, USA

.... 4 Simon Propp (1907 - 1998) b: Oct 25, 1907 in Tupper Lake, Franklin, New York, USA, d: Mar 08, 1998 in Long Boat Key, Florid

.... + Mary Frances Stern (1917 - 1990) b: Jul 08, 1917 in Tupper Lake, Franklin, New York, USA, m: 1942 in Tupper Lake, Franklin, New York, USA, d: Jul 08, 1990 in Long Boat Key,

.... 5 Paula Propp (1943 -) b: 1943 in Tupper Lake, Franklin, New York, USA

.... + Irving Goldsmith (1940 -) b: 1940 in Albany, Albany, New York, USA

.... 6 Jeffery Goldsmith (1964 -) b: 1964 in Woodstock, New York

.... 6 Bruce Goldsmith (1968 -) b: 1968 in Woodstock, New York

.... 5 Julie Propp (1946 -) b: 1946 in Tupper Lake, Franklin, New York, USA

.... + Eric Martin (1941 -) b: 1941 in Albany, Albany, New York, USA

.... 6 Meg Martin (1978 -) b: 1978 in New Jersey

.... 6 Drew Martin (1980 -) b: 1980 in New Jersey

.... + Gardinier

.... 6 Meg Gardinier (1978 -) b: 1978
.... 6 Drew Gardinier (1980 -) b: 1980
.... 5 Marilyn Propp (1950 -) b: 1950 in Tupper Lake, Franklin, New York, USA
.... + David Jones (1948 -) b: 1948 in Chicago, Cook, Illinois, USA
.... 2 Tauba Prop (1831 -) b: 1831 in Shkudvil, Kovno, Russia
.... 2 Meyer "Greenberg" Prop (1837 - 1916) b: 1837 in Shkudvil, Kovno, Russia, d: Jan 28, 1916 in
              Boston, Suffolk, Massachusetts, USA
.... + Rochel "Rose" Pikin (1842 - 1913) b: 1842 in Upina, Kovno Guberniya, Russia, m: 1860 in
              Shkudvil, Kovno, Russia, d: Feb 01, 1913 in Boston, Suffolk, Massachusetts, USA
.... 3 Simon "Shimon" Greenberg (1865 -) b: Abt. 1865 in Sweden
                   + Tamara (1805 - 1876) b: 1805 in Shkudvil, Kovno, Russia, m: 1836 in Shkudvil, Kovno, Russia,
                     d: 1876 in Shkudvil, Kovno, Russia
.... 3 Fredrick P Green (1867 - 1939) b: 1867 in Malmö, Kalmar, Sweden, d: Dec 08, 1939 in
                     Boston, Suffolk, Massachusetts, USA
.... + Sarah L. Cohen (1870 - 1953) b: 1870 in New York, New York, USA, m: Abt. 1890 in
                     Boston, Suffolk, Massachusetts, USA, d: Jun 22, 1953 in Boston, Suffolk, Massachusetts,
                     USA
.... 4 Anna Green (1891 - 1970) b: Nov 08, 1891 in Boston, Suffolk, Massachusetts, USA, d:
                         Jul 07, 1970 in Boston, Suffolk, Massachusetts, USA
.... + Samuel Pinanski (1893 - 1972) b: Jun 07, 1893 in Boston, Suffolk, Massachusetts,
                         USA, m: Abt. 1914 in Boston, Suffolk, Massachusetts, USA, d: Feb 1972 in Boston,
                         Suffolk, Massachusetts, USA
.... 5 Ruth Pinanski (1916 - 1983) b: Sep 04, 1916 in Boston, Suffolk, Massachusetts,
                              USA, d: Jan 14, 1983 in Boston, Suffolk, Massachusetts, USA
.... + Milton G. Green (1913 - 1989) b: Sep 30, 1913 in Boston, Suffolk, Massachusetts, USA,
                         m: Abt. 1938 in Boston, Suffolk, Massachusetts, USA, d: Aug 27, 1989 in Boston,
                         Suffolk, Massachusetts, USA
.... 6 Patricia Green (1939 -) b: Abt. 1939 in Boston, Suffolk, Massachusetts, USA
.... + Stephen Dunn (1937 -) b: Abt. 1937 in Boston, Suffolk, Massachusetts, USA, m:
                              Jun 15, 1978 in Boston, Suffolk, Massachusetts, USA
.... 7 Melissa Ann Dunn (1980 -) b: Abt. 1980 in Boston, Suffolk,
                                        Massachusetts, USA
.... 6 Charles Green (1946 -) b: Abt. 1946 in Boston, Suffolk, Massachusetts, USA
.... + Marion
.... 6 Kathy Lee Green (1949 -) b: Abt. 1949 in Boston, Suffolk, Massachusetts,
                              USA
.... + Scheff m: Abt. 1972
.... 5 Doris Nathalie Pinanski (1928 -) b: Abt. 1928 in Boston, Suffolk, Massachusetts,
                              USA
.... 6 Priscilla Dunne (1952 -) b: Abt. 1952 in Boston, Suffolk, Massachusetts, USA
.... 4 Irving Isadore Green (1894 - 1983) b: Oct 19, 1894 in Boston, Suffolk, Massachusetts,
                         USA, d:
                       Aug 03, 1983 in Boston, Suffolk, Massachusetts, USA
.... + Lillian Hootstein (1909 - 1966) b: Abt. 1909 in Boston, Suffolk, Massachusetts, USA, m:
                         1929 in Boston, Suffolk, Massachusetts, USA, d: Jan 1966 in Boston, Suffolk,
                         Massachusetts, USA
.... 5 Lawrence Roy Green (1929 - 1986) b: Dec 27, 1929 in Boston, Suffolk, Massachusetts,
                              USA, d: Feb 04, 1986 in Boston, Suffolk, Massachusetts, USA
.... 5 Constance Green (1932 -) b: Abt. 1932 in Boston, Suffolk, Massachusetts, USA
.... + Marc S. Jacobson (1933 -) b: 1933
.... 6 Steven A Jacobson (1958 -) b: 1958
.... + Dale
.... 6 Susan Jacobson (1960 -) b: 1960
.... + Gordon Coburn
.... 4 Meyer "Maurice" M. Green (1896 - 1978) b: Jun 10, 1896 in Boston, Suffolk,
                         Massachusetts, USA, d: Sep 05, 1978 in Dade, Florida, United States
.... + Gladys Marion Green (1903 - 1988) b: Jul 27, 1903 in Alston, Suffolk County,
                         Massachusetts, m: Jun 05, 1924 in Boston, Suffolk, Massachusetts, USA, d: Mar 22,
                         1988 in Dade, Florida, United States

.... 5 Roberta Green (1926 -) b: Sep 14, 1926
.... 3 Greenberg (1868 -) b: Abt. 1868
.... 3 Philip "Feivel" Greenberg (1870 - 1923) b: Abt. 1870 in Sweden, d: Dec 13, 1923 in
             Boston, Suffolk, Massachusetts, USA
.... 3 Greenberg (1871 -) b: Abt. 1871
.... 3 Thomas Green (1873 -) b: Abt. 1873 in Sweden
.... 3 Simon Greenberg
.... 3 Peter J. Greenberg
.... 3 Greenberg
.... 2 Shimon Prop (1842 - 1905) b: 1842 in Shkudvil, Vilna, Russia, d: 1905 in Shkudvil, Kovno,
             Russia
.... + Rivka (1837 -) b: 1837 in Shkudvil, Vilna, Russia, m: 1853 in Shkudvil, Kovno, Russia, d: in
             Shkudvil, Kovno, Russia
.... 3 Chaya Prop (1855 -) b: 1855 in Shkudvil, Kovno, Russia
.... 3 Chaim Prop (1856 -) b: 1856 in Shkudvil, Kovno, Russia
.... + Tode (1860 -) b: 1860
.... 3 Leah Prop (1859 -) b: 1859 in Shkudvil, Kovno, Russia
.... 3 Shmuel Prop (1864 -) b: 1864 in Shkudvil, Kovno, Russia
.... 2 Gita Sora Prop (1843 - 1915) b: 1843 in Shkudvil, Kovno, Russia, d: 1915 in Shkudvil, Kovno,
             Russia
.... + Shimon "Shimel" Prop (1839 - 1912) b: 1839 in Shkudvil, Kovno, Russia, m: Abt. 1863 in
             Shkudvil, Kovno, Russia, d: 1912 in Shkudvil, Kovno, Russia
.... 3 Hasha Leah Prop (1864 -) b: Abt. 1864 in Shkudvil, Kovno, Russia
.... 3 Leah Prop (1865 -) b: Abt. 1865 in Shkudvil, Kovno, Russia
.... 3 Tamara Prop (1868 -) b: Abt. 1868 in Shkudvil, Kovno, Russia
.... 3 Hinda Rivka Prop (1871 - 1933) b: 1871 in Shkudvil, Kovno, Russia, d: 1933 in
             Naumiestis,
             Kovno Guberniya, Russia
.... + Moshe Yisrael "Gurland" Shlapobersky (1862 - 1926) b: 1862 in Vilna, Vilna Guberniya,
             Russia, m: 1890 in Shkudvil, Kovno, Russia, d: 1926 in Naumiestis, Kovno Guberniya,
             Russia
.... 4 Eta Shlapobersky (1893 - 1944) b: 1893 in Shkudvil, Kovno, Russia, d: 1944 in Telz,
             Lithuania Holocaust
.... + Ephraim Helphan (1891 - 1944) b: 1891 in Russia, d: 1944 in Telz, Lithuania
             Holocaust
.... 5 Hinda Rivka Helphan (1925 -) b: 1925 in Shkudvil, Kovno, Russia
.... 5 Sarah Helphan (1927 -) b: 1927 in Shkudvil, Kovno, Russia
.... 5 Moshe Yitzchak Helphan (1929 -) b: 1929 in Shkudvil, Kovno, Russia
.... 5 Yankel Helphan (1931 -) b: 1931
.... 4 Tamara Shlapobersky (1894 - 1941) b: 1894 in Shkudvil, Kovno, Russia, d: 1941 in
             Chavdian, Holocaust
.... + Moshe Aron (1893 - 1941) b: 1893 in Russia, d: 1941 in Chavdian, Holocaust
.... 5 Sarah Ettel Arian (1926 - 1941) b: 1926 in Shkudvil, Kovno, Russia, d: 1941 in
             Chavdian, Holocaust
.... 5 Yerachmiel Arian (1928 - 1941) b: 1928 in Shkudvil, Kovno, Russia, d: 1941 in
             Chavdian, Holocaust
.... 5 Tzerel Arian (1930 - 1941) b: 1930 in Shkudvil, Kovno, Russia, d: 1941 in
             Chavdian, Holocaust
.... 4 Betzalel Shlapobersky (1896 - 1967) b: 1896 in Shkudvil, Kovno, Russia, d: Sep 08,
             1967 in Zeerust, South Africa
.... + Golda Lab (1894 - 1978) b: 1894 in RaguvaLithuania, d: 1978 in Zeerust, South Africa
.... 4 Yosef Reuven Shlapobersky (1898 - 1979) b: 1898 in Shkudvil, Kovno, Russia, d: Dec 28,
             1979 in Jerusalem, Israel
.... + Eta Fayet (1899 - 1986) b: 1899 in Neishtot-Tavrig, Kovno Guberniya, Russia, d: 1986 in
             Jerusalem, Israel
.... 5 Yitzchak Shlapobersky (1926 -) b: 1926 in Jerusalem, Israel
.... + Meira b: in Jerusalem, Israel
.... 4 Mikhel Dovid Shlapobersky (1900 - 1995) b: 1900 in Shkudvil, Kovno, Russia, d: Sep 13,

1995 in Jerusalem, Israel
.... + Nechama Blumenthal (1905 - 1994) b: 1905 in Jerusalem, Israel, m: 1927 in Hebron,
Eretz Yisrael, d: 1994 in Jerusalem, Israel
.... 5 Rivka Shlapobersky (1930 -) b: 1930 in Jerusalem, Eretz Yisrael
.... + Eliezer Rakovsky (1927 - 1996) b: 1927 in Jerusalem, Eretz Yisrael, m: 1951 in
Jerusalem, Israel, d: Jul 28, 1996 in Jerusalem, Israel
.... 6 Tamar Rakovsky (1953 -) b: 1953 in Jerusalem, Israel
.... + Yeshayaahu Moshe Hurvitz (1951 -) b: 1951 in Israel
.... 7 Rachel Hurvitz (1973 -) b: 1973 in Jerusalem, Israel
.... + Yecheskel Weinbach (1971 -) b: 1971 in Israel, m: Abt. 1994 in
Jeusalem, Israel
.... 8 Yosef Weinbach (1996 -) b: Abt. 1996 in Jerusalem, Israel
.... 8 Nechama Weinbach (1998 -) b: Abt. 1998 in Jerusalem, Israel
.... 8 Michael David Weinbach (1997 -) b: Abt. 1997 in Jerusalem, Israel
.... 7 Chana Sheina Hurvitz (1975 -) b: 1975 in Jerusalem, Israel
.... + Menachem Rozovski (1972 -) b: 1972 in Israel, m: Abt. 1995 in Jeusalem,
Israel
.... 8 Eliezer Rozovski (1997 -) b: Abt. 1997 in Jerusalem, Israel
.... 8 Zvi Pesach Rozovski (1998 -) b: Abt. 1998 in Jerusalem, Israel
.... 7 Yosef Hurvitz (1978 -) b: Abt. 1978 in Jerusalem, Israel
.... + Mira Shub
.... 7 Chaya Basha Hurvitz (1980 -) b: Abt. 1980 in Jerusalem, Israel
.... + Yakov Genut m: in Jerusalem, Israel
.... 7 Goldy Hurvitz (1982 -) b: Abt. 1982 in Jerusalem, Israel
.... + Baruch Yehuda Munk m: in Jeusalem, Israel
.... 7 Miri Hurvitz (1985 -) b: Abt. 1985 in Jerusalem, Israel
.... 7 Asher Hurvitz (1988 -) b: Abt. 1988 in Jerusalem, Israel
.... 7 Ruth Hurvitz (1990 -) b: Abt. 1990 in Jerusalem, Israel
.... 6 Sarah Rakovsky (1955 -) b: 1955 in Jerusalem, Israel
.... + Dov Freund (1951 -) b: 1951 in Israel, m: 1974 in Jerusalem, Israel
.... 7 Chaya Basha Freund (1975 -) b: Abt. 1975 in Jerusalem, Israel
.... 7 Avraham Yochanan Freund (1977 -) b: Abt. 1977 in Jerusalem, Israel
.... 7 Rachael Freund b: in Jerusalem, Israel
.... 7 Zvi Freund b: in Jerusalem, Israel
.... 7 Naomi Freund b: in Jerusalem, Israel
.... 7 Shaul Zev Freund b: in Jerusalem, Israel
.... 7 Chana Sheina Freund b: in Jerusalem, Israel
.... 7 Goldy Freund b: in Jerusalem, Israel
.... 7 Baruch Abba Freund b: in Jerusalem, Israel
.... 7 Yocheved Freund b: in Jerusalem, Israel
.... 7 Modechai Freund b: in Jerusalem, Israel
.... 6 Bracha Rakovsky (1957 -) b: 1957 in Jerusalem, Israel
.... + Aharon Zvi Tauber (1955 -) b: 1955 in Israel, m: 1974 in Jerusalem, Israel
.... 7 Shlomo Tauber (1977 -) b: Abt. 1977 in Jerusalem, Israel
.... + Rachel Katz
.... 7 Sara Tauber (1979 -) b: Abt. 1979 in Jerusalem, Israel
.... + Rafael Siomcha Breines (1975 -) b: Abt. 1975 in Israel
.... 7 Chaya Basha Tauber b: in Jerusalem, Israel
.... 7 Esther Tauber b: in Jerusalem, Israel
.... 7 Yehudit Tauber b: in Jerusalem, Israel
.... 7 Meir Tauber b: in Jerusalem, Israel
.... 7 Naomi Tauber b: in Jerusalem, Israel
.... 7 Leah Tauber b: in Jerusalem, Israel
.... 6 Tzivia Rakovsky (1958 -) b: 1958 in Jerusalem, Israel
.... + Araham Segal (1955 -) b: 1955 in Jerusalem, Israel, m: Abt. 1979
Jeusalem, Israel
.... 7 Tamar Segal b: in Jerusalem, Israel

..............................7   Moshe Meir Segal b: in Jerusalem, Israel
..............................7   Chaim Segal b: in Jerusalem, Israel
..............................7   Bracha Segal b: in Jerusalem, Israel
..............................7   Baruch Michel Segal b: in Jerusalem, Israel
..............................7   Nechama Segal b: in Jerusalem, Israel
..........................6 Avraham Baruch Abba Rakovsky (1962 -) b: 1962 in Haifa District, Israel
                + Leah Mendelson (1966 -) b: 1966 in Israel
..............................7   Yehudit Rakovsky (1988 -) b: Abt. 1988 in Jerusalem, Israel
..............................7   Chaim Rakovsky (1990 -) b: Abt. 1990 in Jerusalem, Israel
..............................7   Shmuel Rakovsky (1992 -) b: Abt. 1992 in Jerusalem, Israel
..............................7   Yakov Rakovsky (1994 -) b: Abt. 1994 in Jerusalem, Israel
..............................7   Eliezer Rakovsky (1996 -) b: Abt. 1996 in Jerusalem, Israel
..............................7   Michael David Rakovsky (1997 -) b: Abt. 1997 in Jerusalem, Israel
..................5 Mirah Shlapobersky (1931 -) b: 1931 in Jerusalem, Eretz Yisrael
                + Rafael Reichman (1929 -) b: 1929 in Bronx, Bronx, New York, USA
.... 6   Devora Reichman (1952 -) b: Feb 12, 1952 in Jerusalem, Israel
.... + Zvi Braverman (1950 -) b: 1950 in Jerusalem, Israel, m: 1980 in Jerusalem, Israel
.... 7   Hinda Rivka Braverman (1981 -) b: 1981 in Jerusalem, Israel
.... 7   Shlomo Braverman (1982 -) b: 1982 in Jerusalem, Israel
.... 7   Nathan Braverman (1985 -) b: 1985 in Jerusalem, Israel
.... 7   Hannah Sheine Braverman (1986 -) b: 1986 in Jerusalem, Israel
.... 7   Shnei'or Zalman Braverman (1988 -) b: 1988 in Jerusalem, Israel
.... 7   Avorhom Mordechai Braverman (1992 -) b: 1992 in Jerusalem, Israel
.... 7   Miriam Braverman (1993 -) b: 1993 in Jerusalem, Israel
.... 7   Moshe Braverman (1994 -) b: 1994 in Jerusalem, Israel
.... 7   Yehuda Leib Braverman (1995 -) b: 1995 in Jerusalem, Israel
.... 7   Nechama Braverman (1996 -) b: 1996 in Jerusalem, Israel
.... 7   Pnina Braverman (1996 -) b: 1996 in Jerusalem, Israel
.... 6   Hannah Sheine Reichman (1967 -) b: 1967 in Jerusalem, Israel
.... + Yehuda ben Shlomo (1962 -) b: 1962 in Jerusalem, Israel, m: 1986 in
                Jerusalem, Israel
.... 7   Devora bat Yehuda (1987 -) b: 1987 in Jerusalem, Israel
.... 7   Hannah bat Yehuda (1988 -) b: 1988 in Jerusalem, Israel
.... 7   Shne'ior Zalman Yehuda (1989 -) b: 1989 in Jerusalem, Israel
.... 7   Tzvi ben Yehuda (1991 -) b: 1991 in Jerusalem, Israel
.... 7   Avorhom ben Yehuda (1992 -) b: 1992 in Jerusalem, Israel
.... 7   Ella bat Yehuda (1993 -) b: 1993 in Jerusalem, Israel
.... 7   Nechama Yehuda (1995 -) b: 1995 in Jerusalem, Israel
.... 7   Mikhel Dovid ben Yehuda (1996 -) b: 1996 in Jerusalem, Israel
.... 6   Chava Reichman (1969 -) b: 1969 in Jerusalem, Israel
.... + Benjamin Dryfess (1966 -) b: 1966 in Jerusalem, Israel
.... 7   Shne'ior Dryfess (1990 -) b: 1990 in Jerusalem, Israel
.... 7   Eliezer Dryfess (1991 -) b: 1991 in Jerusalem, Israel
.... 7   Miriam Dryfess (1993 -) b: 1993 in Jerusalem, Israel
.... 7   Hinda Rivka Dryfess (1994 -) b: 1994 in Jerusalem, Israel
.... 7   Nechama Dryfess (1995 -) b: 1995 in Jerusalem, Israel
.... 7   Hannah Dryfess (1996 -) b: 1996 in Jerusalem, Israel
..........................5 Moshe Yisrael Shlapobersky (1933 -) b: 1933 in Jerusalem, Eretz Yisrael
.... + Esther Deutch
.... 6   Pnina Shlapobersky (1968 -) b: 1968 in Jerusalem, Israel
.... + Ittamar Muskat (1965 -) b: 1965 in Jerusalem, Israel
.... 7   Avorhom Muskat (1988 -) b: Jun 25, 1988 in Jerusalem, Israel
.... 7   Bracha Muskat (1989 -) b: 1989 in Jerusalem, Israel
.... 7   Yisrael Arieh Muskat (1991 -) b: 1991 in Jerusalem, Israel
.... 7   Yechiel Muskat (1992 -) b: 1992 in Jerusalem, Israel
.... 7   Shlomo Muskat (1995 -) b: 1995 in Jerusalem, Israel
.... 7   Mikhel David Muskat (1996 -) b: 1996 in Jerusalem, Israel
.... 6   Mordechai Shlapobersky (1969 -) b: 1969 in Jerusalem, Israel

.... + Kali (1970 -) b: 1970 in Jerusalem, Israel
.... 7 Arron Shlapobersky (1990 -) b: 1990 in Jerusalem, Israel
.... 7 Leah Shlapobersky (1991 -) b: 1991 in Jerusalem, Israel
.... 7 Chaya Shlapobersky (1992 -) b: 1992 in Jerusalem, Israel
.... 7 Shimon Shlapobersky (1994 -) b: 1994 in Jerusalem, Israel
.... 7 Nechama Shlapobersky (1996 -) b: 1996 in Jerusalem, Israel
.... 7 Pnina Shlapobersky (1996 -) b: 1996 in Jerusalem, Israel
.... 6 Hannah Shlapobersky (1972 -) b: 1972 in Jerusalem, Israel
.... + Yehuda Vanervalde (1967 -) b: 1967 in Jerusalem, Israel
.... 7 Avorhom Yochanan Vanervalde (1990 -) b: 1990 in Jerusalem, Israel
.... 7 Baruch Vanervalde (1992 -) b: 1992 in Jerusalem, Israel
.... 7 Shmuel Vanervalde (1993 -) b: 1993 in Jerusalem, Israel
.... 7 Mikhel Dovid Vanervalde (1995 -) b: Nov 1995 in Jerusalem, Israel
.... 6 Gitel Shlapobersky (1974 -) b: 1974 in Jerusalem, Israel
.... + Leib Layush (1962 -) b: 1962 in Jerusalem, Israel
.... 7 Chava Layush (1996 -) b: 1996 in Jerusalem, Israel
.... 6 Hinda Rivka Shlapobersky (1976 -) b: 1976 in Jerusalem, Israel
.... 6 Chava Shlapobersky (1980 -) b: 1980 in Jerusalem, Israel
.... 4 Yehoshua Arieh Leib Shlapobersky (1901 - 1961) b: 1901 in Shkudvil, Kovno, Russia, d:
           Jan 15, 1961 in Petach Tikvah, Israel
.... + Rach'l Pese Shapira (1904 - 1989) b: 1904 in Neishtot-Tavrig , Kovno Guberniya,
           Russia, m: 1935 in Kvedarna, Kovno Guberinya, Lithuania, d: Mar 16, 1989 in Petach
           Tikvah, Israel
.... 4 Mordechai Shlapobersky (1905 - 1967) b: 1905 in Shkudvil, Kovno, Russia, d: Nov 04,
           1967 in Jerusalem, Israel
.... + Rivka Gutman (1912 - 1944) b: 1912 in Kovno, Kovno Guberniya, Russia, d: Aug
           1944 in Auschwitz, Poland, Holocaust
.... 5 Hinda Rivka Shlapobersky (1937 - 1943) b: 1937 in Kovno, Lithuania, d: 1943 in
           Kovno Ghetto, Lithuania
.... 5 Roch'l Shlapobersky (1940 - 1944) b: 1940 in Kovno, Lithuania, d: 1944 in Kovno
           Ghetto, Lithuania, Holocaust
.... 5 Leiba Shlapobersky (1941 - 1944) b: 1941 in Kovno, Lithuania, d: 1944 in Kovno
           Ghetto, Lithuania, Holocaust
.... 3 Roch'l Prop (1873 - 1937) b: 1873 in Shkudvil, Kovno, Russia, d: 1937 in Shkudvil,
           Kovno, Russia
.... + Moshe Baruch Braude (1871 - 1941) b: 1871 in Kelm, Kovno Guberniya, Russia, m: 1910 in
           Shkudvil, Kovno, Russia, d: Jul 04, 1941 in Shkudvil, Lithuania, Holocaust
.... 4 himon Braude (1911 - 1941) b: 1911 in Shkudvil, Kovno, Russia, d: Jul 21, 1941 in
           Shkudvil, Lithuania, Holocaust
.... 5 Israel Braude (1937 - 1941) b: 1937 in Shkudvil, Kovno, Russia, d: Sep 19, 1941 in
           Batok, Lithuania, Holocaust
.... 5 Unknown Braude (1941 - 1941) b: Jul 23, 1941 in Batok, Lithuania, d: Sep 19,
           1941 in Batok, Lithuania, Holocaust
.... 4 Yisrael Betzalel Braude (1914 - 1941) b: 1914 in Shkudvil, Kovno, Russia, d: Jul 21,
           1941 in Shkudvil, Lithuania, Holocaust
.... + Leah (1918 - 1941) b: 1918 in Lithuania, m: 1940 in Shkudvil, Kovno, Russia, d: Sep 19,
           1941 in Botak, Lithuania, Holocaust
.... 3 Chaya Prop (1875 - 1938) b: Abt. 1875 in Shkudvil, Kovno, Russia, d: 1938 in Shkudvil,
           Kovno, Russia
.... + Mordechai Yosef Shapira (1860 - 1923) b: 1860 in Shkudvil, Kovno, Russia, m: 1903 in
           Kvedarna ,Kovno Guberniya, Russia, d: 1923 in Shkudvil, Kovno, Russia
.... 4 Rach'l Pese Shapira (1904 - 1989) b: 1904 in Neishtot-Tavrig , Kovno Guberniya,
           Russia, d: Mar 6, 1989 in Petach Tikvah, Israel
.... + Yehoshua Arieh Leib Shlapobersky (1901 - 1961) b: 1901 in Shkudvil, Kovno, Russia, m: 1935 in
           Kvedarna, Kovno Guberinya, Lithuania, d: Jan 15, 1961 in Petach Tikvah, Israel

פּרָאפּ

Hirsh ben Shimon Prop

of

שקודוויל
Shkudvil, Vilna Guberniya
Russia Empire

1790 - 1856

1 Hirsh Zalman Prop b:1791 in Zemaitija Duchy, Grand Duchy of Lithuania-Poland, d: 1852 in Jerusalem, Eretz Yisrael

... + Chaya Berlowitz b: 1808 in Zemaitija Duchy, Grand Duchy of Lithuania, m: 1805 in Skaudvile, Kovno, Russia, d: 1880 in Jerusalem, Eretz Yisrael

......2 Leib "Leibzik" Prop b: 1813 in Skaudvile, Kovno, Russia, d: 1894 in Smalininkai, Jurbarkas, Russia

.........3 Adolph Prop b: 1846 in Smalininkai, East Prussia

.........3 Fritze Prop b: 1851 in Smalininkai, East Prussia, d: 1910 in Tilsit, Gumbinnen, East Prussia, Germany

.... + Franz Dobriner b: 1840 in Tilsit, Gumbinnen, East Prussia, Germany, d: Tilsit, East Prussia

............4 Joseph Dobriner b: 1874 in Tilsit, Gumbinnen, East Prussia, Germany

............4 Theodore Dobriner b: 1876 in Tilsit, Gumbinnen, East Prussia, Germany

............4 Wanda Dobriner b: May 28, 1878 in Tilsit, Gumbinnen, East Prussia, Germany, d: May 28, 1940 in Peoria, Peoria, Illinois, USA; Age at Death: 60

.... + Julius "Yudl" Propp b: Oct 18, 1872 in Tavrig, Kovno, Russia, m: Jun 19, 1909 in Laporte, Indiana, USA, d: 1977 in Peoria, Peoria, Illinois, USA

...............5 Leo Isaac Propp b: Jul 29, 1909 in Peoria, Peoria, Illinois, USA, d: May 22, 2008 in Schaumburg, Cook, Illinois, USA

.... + Janet Rosen b: Jan 06, 1912 in Toronto, Ontario, Canada, m: 1944, d: Oct 1984 in Peoria Heights, Peoria, Illinois, USA

..................6 Lawrence Propp b: Mar 24, 1945 in Peror, d: Jul 28, 1983 in Cook, Illinois, USA

..................6 Gail Susan Propp b: Oct 10, 1947 in Peoria, Peoria, Illinois, USA

.... + Stephen Heckmyer b: 1947 in Chicago, Cook, Illinois, USA, d: May 11, 2003 in Chicago, Cook, Illinois, USA

......................7 Joseph Heckmyer b: Dec 07, 1973 in Skokie, Cook, Illinois, USA

......................7 Daniel Heckmyer b: Nov 22, 1976 in Skokie, Cook, Illinois, USA

.... + Marion Brown b: Apr 18, 1916 in Washington City, District Of Columbia, District of Columbia, USA, m: Abt. 1996 in Los Angeles, Los Angeles, California, USA, d: May 29, 2002 in Yorba Linda, Orange, California, USA

...............5 Fred J. Propp b: Jun 19, 1910 in Farmington, Fulton, Illinois, USA, d: Dec 1983 in Peoria, Peoria, Illinois,

...............5 Roy T. Propp b: Jun 26, 1916 in Farmington, Fulton, Illinois, USA, d: Mar 02, 2002 in Peoria, Peoria, Illinois, USA

.... + Marilyn Zvi b: 1928 in Chicago, Cook, Illinois, USA, m: 1950 in Peoria, Peoria, Illinois, USA

..................6 Sharon L Propp b: 1952 in Peoria, Peoria, Illinois, USA

.... + Michael Stein b: 1951 in Chicago, Cook, Illinois, USA

......................7 Lesile Stein b: Aug 1986 in Chicago, Cook, Illinois, USA

......................7 Anna Stein b: Aug 1988 in Highland Park, Lake, Illinois, USA

......................7 Peter Stein b: Aug 1992 in Highland Park, Lake, Illinois, USA

..................6 Wanda Propp b: 1954 in Peoria, Peoria, Illinois, USA

.... + Larry Brunell b: 1953 in Chicago, Cook, Illinois, USA

......................7 Rebecca Brunell b: Aug 1986 in Jackson, Hinds, Mississippi, USA

......................7 Adam Brunell b: Jul 1988 in Jackson, Hinds, Mississippi, USA

..................6 Judith J. Propp b: Feb 03, 1957 in Peoria, Peoria, Illinois, USA

......2 Velvel "Vulf" Prop b: 1814 in Shkudvil, Kovno Guberniya, Russia

...... + Chaya Kuna b: 1812 in Kovno, Kovno, Russia; Same location as Kaunas, Lithuania, m: 1936

.........3 Girsh Prop b: Abt. 1830, d: May 07, 1875

......2 Sora Prop b: 1814 in Skaudvile, Kovno, Russia

...... + Eizikowitz b: 1802 in Smalininkai, East Prussia

.........3 Eizikowitz b: 1829 in Kovno, Kovno, Russia

......2 Meyer "Prop" Fayn b: 1816 in Skaudvile, Kovno, Russia, d: 1854 in Libau, Courland, Russia

...... + Zlata b: Abt. 1814, m: 1837 in Skaudvile, Kovno, Russia, d: Libau, Courland, Russia

.........3 Aron "Orel" Fayn b: 1838 in Skaudvile, Kovno, Russia

.........3 Elka Fayn b: 1845 in Skaudvile, Kovno, Russia

.........3 Roch"l Fayn b: 1846 in Skaudvile, Kovno, Russia, d: 1913 in Smalininkai, East Prussia

.... + David Shmuel Berlowitz b: Dec 18, 1836 in Smalininkai, Jurbarkas, Russia, m: Abt. 1865, d: 1907 in Smalininkai, East Prussia

............4 Martha "Marta" Berlowitz b: Jun 23, 1866 in Smalininkai, East Prussia, d: Feb 23, 1940 in Memphis, Shelby, Tennessee, USA

.... + Max "Meyer' Propp b: Dec 23, 1857 in Skaudvile, Kovno, Russia, m: Sep 28, 1887 in Chicago, Cook, Illinois, USA, d: Mar 29, 1943 in Memphis, Shelby, Tennessee, USA

...............5 Clara P. Propp b: Aug 15, 1888 in Chicago, Cook, Illinois, USA, d: Jul 01, 1977 in Memphis, Shelby, Tennessee, USA

.... + George Washington. Meyer b: Feb 22, 1880 in Chicago, Cook, Illinois, USA, m: Dec 30, 1912 in Michigan City, La Porte, Indiana, USA, d: Feb 24, 1954 in Memphis, Shelby, Tennessee, USA

.................6 Myron P Meyer b: Jun 28, 1915 in Michigan City, La Porte, Indiana, USA, d: Jan 17, 1948 in Memphis, Shelby, Tennessee, USA

.... + Mary Dean Nix b: Jun 28, 1915 in Michigan City, La Porte, Indiana, USA, d: Jan 17, 1948 in Memphis, Shelby, Tennessee, USA

.................6 Robert "Bobby" Meyer b: Mar 01, 1920 in Michigan City, La Porte, Indiana, USA, d: Mar 05, 1997 in Memphis, Shelby, Tennessee, USA

...............5 Anna Propp b: Jun 24, 1895 in Chicago, Cook, Illinois, USA, d: Mar 1977 in Chicago, Cook, Illinois, USA

.... + Louis David Smith b: Jul 10, 1889 in Chicago, Cook, Illinois, USA, m: 1916 in Chicago, Cook, Illinois, USA, d: Jul 1968 in Chicago, Cook, Illinois, USA

.................6 Lester H. Smith b: Oct 27, 1917 in Chicago, Cook, Illinois, USA, d: Mar 23, 2000 in Highland Park, Lake, Illinois, USA

.... + Nancy Joy Heyman b: Sep 04, 1924 in Fayette, Kentucky

...................7 Edwin "Eric" Smith b: Sep 29, 1946 in Jefferson, Kentucky

.... + Katharine "Kitty" Thomson b: 1951 in Boston, Suffolk, Massachusetts, USA, m: 1974 in Weston, Middlesex, Massachusetts, USA

.......................8 Benjamin Clark Smith b: 1976 in Boston, Suffolk, Massachusetts, USA

.......................8 George Louis Smith b: 1978 in New York, New York, USA

.......................8 Andrew Laurence Smith b: 1980 in Boston, Suffolk, Massachusetts, USA

...................7 Louis David Smith II b: 1949 in Highland Park, Lake, Illinois, USA

...................7 Laurel Anne Smith b: 1951 in Highland Park, Lake, Illinois, USA

...............5 Bertha "Berdie" Propp b: Apr 1897 in Michigan City, La Porte, Indiana, USA, d: Aug 02, 1965 in Milwaukee, Milwaukee, Wisconsin, USA

...............5 Grace Propp b: Jan 28, 1900 in Michigan City, La Porte, Indiana, USA, d: Sep 17, 1988 in New York,

.... + Maurice Julius b: Apr 27 in New York, New York, USA, d: Aug 1977 in New York, New York, USA

.... + Frederick Eugene Alexander b: Mar 14, 1885 in Jersey City, New Jersey, m: Jul 15, 1920 in Michigan City, La Porte, Indiana, USA, d: Jan 17, 1958 in Contra Costa, California

.................6 Arthur E. Alexander b: Abt. 1924 in Michigan City

.... + Joan b: California, USA

...................7 Jill Alexander b: 1946 in New York, New York, USA

.... + Kenneth Sprague b: 1947 in New York, New York, USA

.......................8 Heather Sprague b: 1977 in New York, New York, USA

.... + Ian Wilson

...................7 Michael Alexander b: 1951 in New York, New York, USA

.... + Heather Sprague

.... + Greta Hoda b: California, USA, m: 1994

...............5 Ruth D. Propp b: Aug 13, 1904 in Michigan City, La Porte, Indiana, USA, d: Nov 1993 in Memphis, Shelby, Tennessee, USA

.... + Jefferson Davis Marks b: Sep 19, 1902 in New Orleans, Orleans, Louisiana, USA, m: Abt. 1939 in Chicago, Cook, Illinois, USA, d: Sep 28, 1987 in Memphis, Shelby, Tennessee, USA

...........4 Hugo Berlowitz b: Aug 22, 1867 in Smalininkai, East Prussia, d: Nov 09, 1868 in Smalininkai, East Prussia

...........4 Max Louis Berlowitz b: Mar 12, 1869 in Smalininkai, East Prussia, d: 1932 in Deutsche Strasse, East Prussia

.... + Herta Jacobi

...........4 Arno Berlowitz b: Aug 09, 1870 in Smalininkai, East Prussia, d: Nov 28, 1942 in Theresienstadt, Germany; Holocaust

...........4 Johanna Sofia Berlowitz b: Mar 24, 1872 in Smalininkai, East Prussia, d: Apr 27, 1972 in Smalininkai, East Prussia

...........4 Adolf Berlowitz b: Mar 12, 1873 in Smalininkai, East Prussia, d: 1927 in Tilsit, Gumbinnen, East Prussia, Germany

.... + Elisabeth Epstein b: Jul 10, 1884 in Germany, m: Tilsit, Gumbinnen, East Prussia, Germany, d: 1942 in Poland; Trawnicki Camp

...............5 Kurt "Ze'ev" Berlowitz b: Apr 27, 1921 in Tilsit, Gumbinnen, East Prussia, Germany

.... + Aliza Freud b: 1924 in Israel, d: 1980 in Holon, Tel Aviv, Israel

.................6 Yael Berlowitz b: Sep 06, 1946 in Holon, Tel Aviv, Israel

.... + Yair Ehrenstreich b: Feb 08, 1946 in Kraków, Lodzkie, Poland
...................7 Jonathan Ehrenstreich b: Sep 14, 1967 in Kiriath, Bialik, Israel
...................7 Dana Ehrenstreich b: Feb 05, 1975 in Kiriath, Bialik, Israel
...................7 Ido Ehrenstreich b: Aug 06, 1982 in Kiriath, Bialik, Israel
...............6 Ilan Berlowitz b: Mar 14, 1952 in Holon, Tel Aviv, Israel
.... + Idit b: Mar 16, 1957
...................7 Ella Berlowitz b: Dec 02, 1983 in Bat Yam, Tel Aviv, Israel
...................7 Tal Berlowitz b: Dec 07, 1990 in Bat Yam, Tel Aviv, Israel
.............5 Ilse Berlowitz b: Apr 27, 1921 in Tilsit, Gumbinnen, East Prussia, Germany
.... + Martin Michel b: 1918 in Kansas City, Wyandotte, Kansas, USA, m: Kansas City, Wyandotte, Kansas, USA
..............6 Marion Elizabeth Michel b: 1949 in Kansas City, Wyandotte, Kansas, USA
.... + Tenney
...................7 Trevor Tenney
..........4 Joseph Berlowitz b: 1874 in Smalininkai, East Prussia
..........4 Selma Berlowitz b: 1875 in Smalininkai, East Prussia, d: New York, New York, USA
.... + Solomon M. Maltenfort b: Feb 23, 1882 in East Prussia, m: Abt. 1910 in Smalininkai, East Prussia, d: Dec 1966 in New York, New York, USA
.............5 Vera Maltenfort b: Nov 06, 1911 in Smalininkai, East Prussia, d: Jan 22, 2001 in New York, New York, USA; Age at Death: 89
.... + Eric Briess b: Nov 13, 1898 in Moravská Nová Ves, South Moravia, Czech Republic, d: Aug 1968 in New York, New York, USA
...............6 Roger C. Briess b: Nov 02, 1937 in Paris, France, d: 2001 in Curacao Ant.
.... + Monica Gerst b: 1952 in New York, New York, USA, m: Abt. 1974 in New York, New York, USA, d: Age: 64
...................7 Colin Briess b: Aug 13, 1976 in New York, New York, USA
...................7 Craig Briess b: Jul 15, 1978 in New York, New York, USA
.... + Koelner b: 1910 in Buenos Aires, Acre, Brazil
..........4 Benjamin "Bensel" Berlowitz b: 1877 in Smalininkai, East Prussia, d: 1941 in Smalininkai, East Prussia, Holocaust
.... + Gertrud Czerninski m: Smalininkai, East Prussia
.............5 Margot Berlowitz b: 1917 in Smalininkai, East Prussia
.... + Avraham Feuer b: Jun 08, 1916 in Romania, m: Israel
...............6 Benjamin Feuer b: 1949 in Holon, Tel Aviv, Israel
.... + Anna b: 1954 in Israel, m: 1982 in Israel
...................7 Noah Feuer b: 1988 in Israel
...................7 Tom Feuer b: 1989 in Israel
...............6 Ilan Yoram Feuer b: 1954 in Holon, Tel Aviv, Israel
.... + Miriam
...................7 Yael Feuer b: 1882 in Australia
...................7 Hana Feuer b: 1984 in Australia
...................7 Deborah Feuer b: 1988 in Australia
...................7 Yonatan Feuer b: 1988 in Australia
.............5 Siegfried Berlowitz b: Dec 30, 1920 in Smalininkai, East Prussia, d: 1941 in Smalininkai, East Prussia, Holocaust
..........4 Anna Berlowitz b: 1879 in Smalininkai, East Prussia, d: 1933 in Elblag, Warminsko-Mazurskie, Poland
.... + Herman Feinstein b: Mar 17, 1876 in Meldiglanken, East Prussia, m: 1906 in Smalininkai, East Prussia, d: 1944 in Switzerland; Holocaust
.............5 Ruth Feinstein b: Jun 10, 1908 in Elblag, Warminsko-Mazurskie, Poland
.... + Leo "Brody" Ostrobrod b: Dec 13, 1898 in Jívoví, South Moravia, Czech Republic, m: Dec 25, 1928 in Berlin, Stadt Berlin, Berlin, Germany, d: Sep 12, 1959 in New York, New York, USA
.........3 Izrael Peysakh Fayn b: 1849 in Skaudvile, Kovno, Russia
.........3 Ente Fayn b: Abt. 1850
......2 Betsalel Tzalel Prop b: 1816 in Skaudvile, Kovno, Russia, d: 1880 in Skaudvile, Kovno, Russia
...... + Hinda "Hannah" b: 1820 in Skaudvile, Kovno, Russia, m: 1837 in Skaudvile, Kovno, Russia; Skaudvile, Taurage, Lithuania, d: 1874 in Skaudvile, Kovno, Russia; Skaudvile, Taurage, Lithuania/
.........3 Sora Prop b: 1838 in Skaudvile, Kovno, Russia, d: 1891 in Skaudvile, Kovno, Russia
.... + Shaya Mendel Aronovich b: 1839 in Vainutas, Kovno, Russia, m: Abt. 1862 in Kovno, Kovno, Russia;

............4 Chaye-Rivka Aronovich b: 1864 in Skaudvile, Kovno, Russia; Skaudvile, Taurage, Lithuainia/Skaudvile, Taurage, Lithuania/
.... + Itzig Seif b: 1860 in Skaudvile, Kovno, Russia; Skaudvile, Taurage, Lithuainia/Skaudvile, Taurage, Lithuania/
...............5 Charles Seif
...............5 Hinde Seif
...............5 John Seif
...............5 Pere Seif
...............5 Philip Seif
............4 Roch"l Aronovich b: 1864 in Skaudvile, Kovno, Russia, d: Dec 07, 1923 in Chicago, Cook, Illinois, USA
.... + Joseph "Yosef Propp" Berlow b: Dec 15, 1858 in Skaudvile, Kovno, Russia, m: 1884 in Philadelphia, Philadelphia, Pennsylvania, USA, d: Jun 14, 1927 in Chicago, Cook, Illinois, USA
...............5 Charles Berlow b: Aug 02, 1883 in Wilkes-Barre, Luzerne, Pennsylvania, USA, d: Mar 03, 1947 in South Bend, St Joseph, Indiana, USA
.... + Celia Gershman b: Sep 18, 1885 in Chicago, Cook, Illinois, USA, d: May 1974 in South Bend, St Joseph, Indiana, USA
...............5 Abraham L. Berlow b: 1887 in Philadelphia, Philadelphia, Pennsylvania, USA, d: Aug 19, 1958 in Hollywood, Broward, Florida, USA
.... + Mae Minsky b: Feb 11, 1893 in South Bend, St Joseph, Indiana, USA, m: Abt. 1915 in Chicago, Cook, Illinois, USA, d: Jun 1966 in Hollywood, Broward, Florida, USA
...............5 Harry Berlow b: 1889 in St Paul, Dakota, Minnesota, USA, d: Sep 22, 1952 in Chicago, Cook, Illinois, USA
.... + Jennie Chalem b: Jan 10, 1899 in Chicago, Cook, Illinois, USA, m: 1923, d: Dec 25, 1950 in Chicago, Cook, Illinois, USA
..................6 Ralph Richard Berlow b: 1927 in Chicago, Cook, Illinois, USA, d: 1984 in Virginia, USA
.... + Patricia b: 1927
....................7 James Richard Berlow b: 1952 in Chicago, Cook, Illinois, USA
.... + Nancy Willis b: 1956
........................8 Anne Berlow b: 1986 in Vienna, Fairfax, Virginia, USA
........................8 Scott Richard Berlow b: 1988 in Vienna, Fairfax, Virginia, USA
....................7 Cathy Lynn Berlow b: 1955 in Chicago, Cook, Illinois, USA
.... + Ella Tecotsky b: 1891 in Chicago, Cook, Illinois, USA, m: 1916 in Chicago, Cook, Illinois, USA, d: 1917 in Chicago, Cook, Illinois, USA
...............5 Irving E. Berlow b: Oct 23, 1892 in Ishpeming, Marquette, Michigan, USA, d: Jan 01, 1965 in Phoenix, Maricopa, Arizona, USA
.... + Florence Horowitz b: 1897 in Detroit, Wayne, Michigan, USA, d: 1970 in Phoenix, Maricopa, Arizona, USA
..................6 Shirley Berlow b: Jul 14, 1922 in Detroit, Wayne, Michigan, USA, d: Feb 07, 2002 in San Antonio,
.... + Robert Joseph Simon b: 1920 in Chicago, Cook, Illinois, USA, m: 1943 in Chicago, Cook, Illinois, USA, d: Bef. 1954
....................7 Roger Simon b: May 12, 1945 in Los Angeles, Los Angeles, California, USA, d: 1984
.... + Irving Simon b: 1922 in Chicago, Cook, Illinois, USA, d: Unknown in Chicago, Cook, Illinois, USA
....................7 Randy Simon b: Oct 10, 1954 in Phoenix, Maricopa, Arizona, USA
.... + John Lady b: 1918, d: Unknown
..................6 Eleanor Berlow b: Sep 12, 1927 in Chicago, Cook, Illinois, USA
.... + Sidney H Wolfson b: Jan 24, 1919 in Gaffney, Cherokee, South Carolina, USA, m: Abt. 1948, d: Dec 09, 2004 in San Antonio, Bexar, Texas, USA
....................7 Sheri Lynn Wolfson b: Jun 12, 1949 in Point Eustis, Virginia
....................7 Daniel Wolfson b: 1953 in Memphis, Shelby, Tennessee, USA
.... + Chery Lamb b: 1955
........................8 Susan Taylor Wolfson b: Dec 25, 1986 in Nashue, New Hampshire
........................8 Austin Wolfson b: Jan 06, 1988
........................8 Kendell Wolfson b: Jan 06, 1988
...............5 Peter R. Berlow b: Feb 12, 1894 in Ishpeming, Marquette, Michigan, USA, d: Jan 14, 1967 in Los Angeles, Los Angeles, California, USA
.... + Dora Goldstein b: Jul 10, 1894 in Chicago, Cook, Illinois, USA, d: Nov 08, 1994 in Los Angeles, Los Angeles, California, USA
...............5 Rose Anna "Hinda" Berlow b: 1897 in St Paul, Dakota, Minnesota, USA, d: 1982 in Chicago, Cook, Illinois, USA
.... + Benjamin Isaac Twery b: 1897 in Chicago, Cook, Illinois, USA, d: 1972 in Florida, USA

...............6 Raymond Twery b: 1930 in Chicago, Cook, Illinois, USA
.... + Maxine Norma Rudman b: 1934 in St Louis, Missouri, USA, m: 1954 in Evanston, Cook, Illinois, USA
...................7 Michael Jay Twery b: 1956 in Champaign, Champaign, Illinois, USA
              2. Linda Ai Kheng Wong b: 1960, m: 1989 in Charlotte, Mecklenburg, North Carolina, USA 7
            Scott Craig Twery b: 1958 in St Louis, Missouri, USA
              3. Deborah Carol Theissen b: 1955 in Connecticut, USA, m: 1990 in Atlanta, De Kalb, Georgia, USA
.................8 Hanna Rose Twery b: 1992 in Atlanta, De Kalb, Georgia, USA
...................7 Seth Aaron Twery b: 1961 in Carmel, Monterey, California, USA
.... + Marrene Del Pierce b: 1963 in Charlotte, Mecklenburg, North Carolina, USA
......................8 Nicole Twery b: Jan 31, 1997 in Charlotte, Mecklenburg, North Carolina, USA
...................7 Bruce Hugh Twery b: 1963 in Charlotte, Mecklenburg, North Carolina, USA
.... + Teresa "Tina" Sicher b: 1961 in Kane, McKean, Pennsylvania, USA, m: 1990 in Kane, McKean, Pennsylvania, USA
......................8 Alexander Twery b: 1991 in Baltimore, Maryland, USA
......................8 Joshua Keller Twery b: 1992 in Baltimore, Maryland, USA
......................8 Benjamin Louis Twery b: 1994 in Baltimore, Maryland, USA
......................8 Twery b: Jan 2000
.............5 Maurice P "Moshe" Berlow b: Mar 22, 1899 in Sault Sainte Marie, Chippewa, Michigan, USA, d: Mar 1983 in Miami, Dade, Florida, USA
.... + Evelyn Feuereisen b: May 31, 1909 in New York, New York, USA, m: Feb 02, 1933 in Chicago, Cook, Illinois, USA, d: Aug 26, 1997 in Los Angeles, Los Angeles, California, USA
.................6 Irene Bunny Berlow b: 1936 in Chicago, Cook, Illinois, USA, d: 1967 in Chicago, Cook, Illinois, USA
.................6 Linda Rachael Berlow b: 1938 in Chicago, Cook, Illinois, USA
.... + Dennis Kluk b: Apr 15, 1946 in Racine, Racine, Wisconsin, USA, m: Nov 25, 2002 in Skokie, Cook, Illinois, USA
.... + Rose b: 1910 in Chicago, Cook, Illinois, USA, m: 1982 in Miami Beach, Dade, Florida, USA
.............5 Sarah Berlow b: 1900 in Calumet, Houghton, Michigan, USA, d: 1983 in California, USA
.... + William Romain b: 1898 in Chicago, Cook, Illinois, USA, d: 1988 in California, USA
.................6 Joseph R "Jerry" Romain b: 1930 in Chicago, Cook, Illinois, USA
.... + Gail b: 1945 in Chicago, Cook, Illinois, USA
...................7 Matthew Romain b: 1972 in Chicago, Cook, Illinois, USA
.... + Sheila b: 1938 in Chicago, Cook, Illinois, USA, m: 1986 in Chicago, Cook, Illinois, USA
.............5 Gordon P Berlow b: 1907 in Calumet, Houghton, Michigan, USA, d: Feb 27, 1967 in Chicago, Cook, Illinois, USA
.... + Esther Wigodski b: May 19, 1911 in Chicago, Cook, Illinois, USA, d: Sep 1984 in Chicago, Cook, Illinois, USA
.................6 Bruce Berlow b: 1941 in Chicago, Cook, Illinois, USA
.................6 Susan Berlow b: 1946 in Chicago, Cook, Illinois, USA
...........4 Louis "Lazer Aronovich" Arne b: Feb 11, 1867 in Skaudvile, Kovno, Russia, d: Sep 18, 1939 in Milwaukee, Milwaukee, Wisconsin, USA
.... + Celia Ruttenberg b: 1872 in Skaudvile, Kovno, Russia, m: Aug 16, 1893 in Ishpeming, Marquette, Michigan, USA, d: Oct 29, 1957 in Chicago, Cook, Illinois, USA
.............5 Sarah Arne b: Jul 02, 1895 in Ishpeming, Marquette, Michigan, USA, d: Oct 1977 in Chicago, Illinois, USA
.... + George Leviton b: Sep 27, 1890 in Kovno, Kovno, Russia, d: Jan 1963 in Chicago, Cook, Illinois, USA
.................6 Theodore Leviton b: Oct 01, 1929 in Milwaukee, Milwaukee, Wisconsin, USA, d: Feb 1980 in Chicago, Cook, Illinois, USA
.... + Harriet Joyce Franklin b: May 22, 1945 in Chicago, Cook, Illinois, USA, m: 1967 in Chicago, Cook, Illinois, USA
...................7 Brook Jennifer Leviton b:Dec 19, 1972 in Chicago, Cook, Illinois, USA
.... + Michael Mandie
......................8   ?   Mandie
......................8   ?   Mandie
...................7 Alison Lee Leviton b:Oct 1, 1975 in Chicago, Cook, Illinois, USA
.... + Vitaly Rindner b:Sep 17, 1975, Minsk, Minsk, Belarus
......................8 Theodora Rindner
.................6 Joyce Leviton b: 1933 in Chicago, Cook, Illinois, USA
.... + Gershon Hammer b: Sep 19, 1934 in Chicago, Cook, Illinois, USA
...................7 Lori Hammer b: Jan 02, 1968 in Chicago, Cook, Illinois, USA, d: Jan 01, 1997 in Chicago, Cook, Illinois, USA
.... + David Charles Recupero b: 1961, m: Jul 22, 1989 in Racine, Racine, Wisconsin, USA
.... + Alan Zelinsky b: Feb 18, 1933 in Chicago, Cook, Illinois, USA, m: Aug 27, 1956 in Chicago, Cook, Illinois, USA
...................7 Deborah Gail Zelinsky b: Jan 05, 1960 in Chicago, Cook, Illinois, USA

...............5 Phillip A. Arne b: Sep 05, 1898 in Calumet, Houghton, Michigan, USA, d: Jun 1972 in Milwaukee, Milwaukee, Wisconsin, USA
.... + Bertha Levin b: May 14, 1910 in Racine, Racine, Wisconsin, USA, d: Jun 16, 2007 in Slinger, Washington, Wisconsin, USA; Age at Death: 97
.................6 Annette Rachele Arne b: Feb 13, 1936 in Milwaukee, Milwaukee, Wisconsin, USA, d: Jul 11, 1986 in Milwaukee, Milwaukee, Wisconsin
.... + Ronald Irving Pachefsky b: Nov 23, 1932 in Milwaukee, Milwaukee, Wisconsin, USA
...................7 Mark Robert Pachefsky b: Aug 21, 1958 in Milwaukee, Milwaukee, Wisconsin, USA
.... + Lori Goldner b: Mar 21, 1962 in Milwaukee, Milwaukee, Wisconsin, USA, m: Jun 13, 1982 in Milwaukee, Milwaukee, Wisconsin, USA
.......................8 Braley Pachefsky b: 1985 in Milwaukee, Milwaukee, Wisconsin, USA
.......................8 Cory Pachefsky b: 1987 in Milwaukee, Milwaukee, Wisconsin, USA
.......................8 Andrew Pachefsky b: 1989 in Milwaukee, Milwaukee, Wisconsin, USA
...................7 Larry A Pachefsky b: Jul 22, 1960 in Milwaukee, Milwaukee, Wisconsin, USA
.... + Ronna M Bromberg b: Nov 23, 1963 in Pittsburgh, Allegheny, Pennsylvania, USA
.......................8 Joel Pachefsky b: 1990 in Milwaukee, Milwaukee, Wisconsin, USA
.......................8 David Pachefsky b: 1991 in Milwaukee, Milwaukee, Wisconsin, USA
.......................8 Michel Pachefsky b: 1993 in Milwaukee, Milwaukee, Wisconsin, USA
.... + Max Streitman b: 1929 in Minneapolis, Anoka, Minnesota, USA
..............5 Charles B. Arne b: Jan 01, 1901 in Hancock, Houghton, Michigan, USA, d: Oct 19, 1965 in Milwaukee, Milwaukee County, Wisconsin; Wisconsin Death Index, 1959-1997 and Social Security Death Index
.... + Mary Sagle b: 1912 in Milwaukee, Milwaukee, Wisconsin, USA, d: Aug 12, 1983 in Marin County,California; California, Death Index, 1940-1997
.................6 Janice Arne b: 1929 in Milwaukee, Milwaukee, Wisconsin, USA, d: 1986 in Boston, MA
.... + Robert Gold b: 1927 in Milwaukee, Milwaukee, Wisconsin, USA
...................7 Michael Gold b: 1951 in West Medford, Middlesex, Massachusetts, USA
.... + Ricki Tanger b: 1953
.......................8 Taylor Gold b: 1974
...................7 Peter Gold b: 1953 in West Medford, Middlesex, Massachusetts, USA
.... + Candy Kosow b: 1954
.......................8 Carly Gold b: 1975
.......................8 David Gold b: 1977
...................7 James Elieger Gold b: 1955 in West Medford, Middlesex, Massachusetts, USA
.... + Basya Bookfinder b: 1957 in Massachusetts, USA
.......................8 Menachem Gold b: 1980
.......................8 Levi Gold b: 1982
.......................8 Hunnah Gold b: 1985
.......................8 Chaya Gold b: 1988
.................6 Eleanor Claire Arne b: May 12, 1942 in Milwaukee, Milwaukee County, Wisconsin, d: Oct 27, 2000 in Greenbrae,Marin County, California; Social Security Death Index
.... + Elmer Arthur Pirelli b: Oct 19, 1942 in Milwaukee, Milwaukee County, Wisconsin
...................7 Lisa Ann Pirelli b: Jun 23, 1965 in Novato, Marin, California, USA
...................7 Arthur Allen Pirelli b: Oct 28, 1966 in Novato, Marin, California, USA
.... + Patricia
.... + Sarah "Rose" Bromovitz b: 1905 in Milwaukee, Milwaukee, Wisconsin, USA, d: 1987 in Milwaukee, Milwaukee, Wisconsin, USA
..............5 Lillian Arne b: May 11, 1902 in Calumet, Houghton, Michigan, USA, d: Aug 04, 1980 in Wisconsin, Milwaukee
..............5 Rosalye Arne b: 1904 in Calumet, Houghton, Michigan, USA, d: 1986 in Milwaukee, Milwaukee, Wisconsin, USA
.... + John Schwartz b: Sep 13, 1901 in Milwaukee, Milwaukee, Wisconsin, USA, m: 1934 in Milwaukee, Milwaukee, Wisconsin, USA, d: Jun 1981 in Milwaukee, Milwaukee, Wisconsin, USA
.................6 Hershel Schwartz b: 1936 in Milwaukee, Milwaukee, Wisconsin, USA
.... + Arlene b: 1936 in Milwaukee, Milwaukee, Wisconsin, USA
.................6 Lois Schwartz b: 1938 in Milwaukee, Milwaukee, Wisconsin, USA
.... + Martin Shickman b: May 27, 1927 in Milwaukee, Milwaukee, Wisconsin, USA, d: Apr 21, 1995 in Los Angeles, Los Angeles, California, USA
...................7 Steven Shickman b: 1958 in Los Angeles, Los Angeles, California, USA
...................7 David Shickman b: 1962 in Los Angeles, Los Angeles, California, USA

.... + Kathryn b: 1964
.......................8 Ryan Shickman b: 1991 in Los Angeles, Los Angeles, California, USA
.......................8 Jordan William Shickman b: Feb 10, 1995 in Los Angeles, Los Angeles, California, USA
.....................7 Trevor Shickman b: 1970 in Los Angeles, Los Angeles, California, USA
...........4 Benjamin "Bentzion Aronovich" Arne b: Mar 04, 1873 in Skaudvile, Kovno, Russia, d: Bef. 1930 in
          Milwaukee, Milwaukee, Wisconsin, USA
...........+ Fannie Steier b: 1880 in Austria, m: 1901 in Hancock, Houghton, Michigan, USA
...............5 Cecile Arne b: Aug 06, 1901 in Hancock, Houghton, Michigan, USA, d: Aug 09, 1954 in Chicago, Cook,
          Illinois, USA
...............5 Earl Arne b: Nov 01, 1904 in Calumet, Houghton, Michigan, USA, d: Feb 01, 1905 in Calumet, Michigan,
...............5 Preston Samuel Arne b: Mar 28, 1907 in Hancock, Houghton, Michigan, USA, d: Jun 29, 1987 in Palm
          Springs, Riverside, California, USA
.... + Phyllis Mandel b: Dec 08, 1909 in Chicago, Cook, Illinois, USA, d: May 27, 1995 in Palm Springs,
          Riverside, California, USA
.........3 Shimon "Shimel" Prop b: 1839 in Skaudvile, Kovno, Russia, d: 1912 in Skaudvile, Kovno, Russia
.... + Sora Gita Prop b: 1843 in Skaudvile, Kovno, Russia, m: Abt. 1863 in Skaudvile, Kovno, Russia, d: Aug 26, 1924
          in Skaudvile, Kovno, Russia
...........4 Hasha Leah Prop b: Abt. 1864 in Skaudvile, Kovno, Russia
...........4 Leah Prop b: Abt. 1865 in Skaudvile, Kovno, Russia
...........4 Tamara Prop b: Abt. 1868 in Skaudvile, Kovno, Russia
...........4 Hinda Rivka Prop b: 1871 in Skaudvile, Kovno, Russia, d: May 26, 1930 in Skaudvile, Taurage, Lithuania
.... + Moshe Yisrael "Gurland" Shlapobersky b: 1862 in Vilna, Vilna, Russia, m: 1890 in Skaudvile, Kovno,
          Russia, d: 1926 in Naumiestis, Kovno, Russia
...............5 Eta Shlapobersky b: 1893 in Skaudvile, Kovno, Russia; Skaudvile, Taurage, Lithuania/, d: 1944 in
          Telšiai, Telsiai, Lithuania
.... + Efriom Gelfan b: 1891 in Telsiai, Telsiai, Russia, m: Mar 20, 1930 in Skaudvile, Taurage, Lithuania, d: 1944
          in Telšiai, Telsiai, Lithuania
.................6 Hinda Rivka Helfan b: 1925 in Skaudvile, Kovno, Russia; Skaudvile, Taurage, Lithuania/
.................6 Sarah Helfan b: 1927 in Skaudvile, Kovno, Russia; Skaudvile, Taurage, Lithuania/
.................6 Moshe Yitzchak Helfan b: 1929 in Skaudvile, Kovno, Russia; Skaudvile, Taurage, Lithuania/
.................6 Yankel Helfan b: 1931
...............5 Tamara Shlapobersky b: 1894 in Skaudvile, Kovno, Russia, d: 1941 in Kvedarna, Silale, Lithuania;
          Holocaust
.... + Moshe Aron b: 1893 in Kvedarna, Silale, Lithuania, m: Abt. 1924, d: 1941 in Kvedarna, Silale,
          Lithuania; Holocaust
.................6 Sarah Ettel Aron b: 1925 in Skaudvile, Kovno, Russia, d: 1941 in Kvedarna, Silale, Lithuania;
          Holocaust
.................6 Jerachmiel Sabse Aron b: 1926 in Kvedarna, Silale, Lithuania, d: 1941 in Kvedarna, Silale, Lithuania;
          Holocaust
.................6 Tzira Jehudis Aron b: 1928 in Kvedarna, Silale, Lithuania, d: 1941 in Kvedarna, Silale, Lithuania;
          Holocaust
.................6 Meier Itzik Aron b: 1935 in Kvedarna, Silale, Lithuania, d: 1941 in Kvedarna, Silale, Lithuania;
          Holocaust
...............5 Betzalel Shlapobersky b: 1896 in Skaudvile, Kovno, Russia; Skaudvile, Taurage, Lithuainia/Skaudvile,
          Taurage, Lithuania/, d: Sep 08, 1967 in Zeerust, North West South Africa, South Africa
.... + Golda Lab b: 1894 in Raguva, Panevezio, Lithuania, d: 1978 in Zeerust, North West South Africa,
          South Africa
...............5 Yosef Reuven Shlapobersky b: 1898 in Skaudvile, Kovno, Russia; Skaudvile, Taurage,
          Lithuainia/Skaudvile, Taurage, Lithuania/, d: Dec 28, 1979 in Jerusalem, Israel
.... + Eta Fayet b: 1899 in Neishtot-Tavrig, Kovno Guberniya, Russia, d: 1986 in Jerusalem, Israel
.................6 Yitzchak Shlapobersky b: 1926 in Jerusalem, Israel
.... + Meira b: Jerusalem, Israel
...............5 Mikhel Dovid Shlapobersky b: 1900 in Skaudvile, Kovno, Russia; Skaudvile, Taurage,
          Lithuainia/Skaudvile, Taurage, Lithuania/, d: Sep 13, 1995 in Jerusalem, Israel
.... + Nechama Blumenthal b: 1905 in Jerusalem, Israel, m: 1927 in Hebron, Eretz Yisrael, d: 1994 in
          Jerusalem, Israel
.................6 Rivka Shlapobersky b: 1930 in Jerusalem, Eretz Yisrael
.... + Eliezer Rakovsky b: 1927 in Jerusalem, Eretz Yisrael, m: 1951 in Jerusalem, Israel, d: Jul 28, 1996 in
          Jerusalem, Israel
.....................7 Tamar Rakovsky b: 1953 in Jerusalem, Israel

.... + Yeshayaahu Moshe Hurvitz b: 1951 in Israel
....................8 Rachel Hurvitz b: 1973 in Jerusalem, Israel
.... + Yecheskel Weinbach b: 1971 in Israel, m: Abt. 1994 in Jerusalem, Israel
........................9 Yosef Weinbach b: Abt. 1996 in Jerusalem, Israel
........................9 Michael David Weinbach b: Abt. 1997 in Jerusalem, Israel
........................9 Nechama Weinbach b: Abt. 1998 in Jerusalem, Israel
....................8 Chana Sheina Hurvitz b: 1975 in Jerusalem, Israel
.... + Menachem Rozovski b: 1972 in Israel, m: Abt. 1995 in Jerusalem, Israel
........................9 Eliezer Rozovski b: Abt. 1997 in Jerusalem, Israel
........................9 Zvi Pesach Rozovski b: Abt. 1998 in Jerusalem, Israel
....................8 Yosef Hurvitz b: Abt. 1978 in Jerusalem, Israel
.... + Mira Shub
....................8 Chaya Basha Hurvitz b: Abt. 1980 in Jerusalem, Israel
.... + Yakov Genut m: Jeusalem, Israel
....................8 Goldy Hurvitz b: Abt. 1982 in Jerusalem, Israel
.... + Baruch Yehuda Munk m: Jeusalem, Israel
....................8 Miri Hurvitz b: Abt. 1985 in Jerusalem, Israel
....................8 Asher Hurvitz b: Abt. 1988 in Jerusalem, Israel
....................8 Ruth Hurvitz b: Abt. 1990 in Jerusalem, Israel
................7 Sarah Rakovsky b: 1955 in Jerusalem, Israel
.... + Dov Freund b: 1951 in Israel, m: 1974 in Jerusalem, Israel
....................8 Chaya Basha Freund b: Abt. 1975 in Jerusalem, Israel
....................8 Avraham Yochanan Freund b: Abt. 1977 in Jerusalem, Israel
....................8 Chana Sheina Freund b: Jerusalem, Israel
....................8 Shaul Zev Freund b: Jerusalem, Israel
....................8 Naomi Freund b: Jerusalem, Israel
....................8 Zvi Freund b: Jerusalem, Israel
....................8 Rachael Freund b: Jerusalem, Israel
....................8 Baruch Abba Freund b: Jerusalem, Israel
....................8 Goldy Freund b: Jerusalem, Israel
....................8 Modechai Freund b: Jerusalem, Israel
....................8 Yocheved Freund b: Jerusalem, Israel
................7 Bracha Rakovsky b: 1957 in Jerusalem, Israel
.... + Aharon Zvi Tauber b: 1955 in Israel, m: 1974 in Jerusalem, Israel
....................8 Shlomo Tauber b: Abt. 1977 in Jerusalem, Israel
.... + Rachel Katz
....................8 Sara Tauber b: Abt. 1979 in Jerusalem, Israel
.... + Rafael Siomcha Breines b: Abt. 1975 in Israel
....................8 Leah Tauber b: Jerusalem, Israel
....................8 Naomi Tauber b: Jerusalem, Israel
....................8 Esther Tauber b: Jerusalem, Israel
....................8 Chaya Basha Tauber b: Jerusalem, Israel
....................8 Meir Tauber b: Jerusalem, Israel
....................8 Yehudit Tauber b: Jerusalem, Israel
................7 Tzivia Rakovsky b: 1958 in Jerusalem, Israel
.... + Avraham Segal b: 1955 in Jerusalem, Israel, m: Abt. 1979 in Jeusalem, Israel
....................8 Nechama Segal b: Jerusalem, Israel
....................8 Baruch Michel Segal b: Jerusalem, Israel
....................8 Bracha Segal b: Jerusalem, Israel
....................8 Chaim Segal b: Jerusalem, Israel
....................8 Moshe Meir Segal b: Jerusalem, Israel
....................8 Tamar Segal b: Jerusalem, Israel
................7 Avraham Baruch Abba Rakovsky b: 1962 in Haifa, Israel
.... + Leah Mendelson b: 1966 in Israel
....................8 Yehudit Rakovsky b: Abt. 1988 in Jerusalem, Israel
.... + Yissachar Dov Rotlevy b: Abt. 1984 in Jerusalem, Israel, m: Dec 29, 2009 in Jerusalem, Israel
....................8 Chaim Rakovsky b: Abt. 1990 in Jerusalem, Israel

........................8 Shmuel Rakovsky b: Abt. 1992 in Jerusalem, Israel
........................8 Yakov Rakovsky b: Abt. 1994 in Jerusalem, Israel
........................8 Eliezer Rakovsky b: Abt. 1996 in Jerusalem, Israel
........................8 Michael David Rakovsky b: Abt. 1997 in Jerusalem, Israel
..................6 Mirah Shlapobersky b: 1931 in Jerusalem, Eretz Yisrael
.... + Rafael Reichman b: 1929 in Bronx, Bronx, New York, USA
..................7 Devora Reichman b: Feb 12, 1952 in Jerusalem, Israel
.... + Zvi Braverman b: 1950 in Jerusalem, Israel, m: 1980 in Jerusalem, Israel
........................8 Hinda Rivka Braverman b: 1981 in Jerusalem, Israel
........................8 Shlomo Braverman b: 1982 in Jerusalem, Israel
........................8 Nathan Braverman b: 1985 in Jerusalem, Israel
........................8 Hannah Sheine Braverman b: 1986 in Jerusalem, Israel
........................8 Shnei'or Zalman Braverman b: 1988 in Jerusalem, Israel
........................8 Avraham Mordechai Braverman b: 1992 in Jerusalem, Israel
........................8 Miriam Braverman b: 1993 in Jerusalem, Israel
........................8 Moshe Braverman b: 1994 in Jerusalem, Israel
........................8 Yehuda Leib Braverman b: 1995 in Jerusalem, Israel
........................8 Pnina Braverman b: 1996 in Jerusalem, Israel
........................8 Nechama Braverman b: 1996 in Jerusalem, Israel
..................7 Hannah Sheine Reichman b: 1967 in Jerusalem, Israel
.... + Yehuda Ben Shlomo b: 1962 in Jerusalem, Israel, m: 1986 in Jerusalem, Israel
........................8 Devora Bat Yehuda b: 1987 in Jerusalem, Israel
........................8 Hannah Bat Yehuda b: 1988 in Jerusalem, Israel
........................8 Shne'ior Zalman Yehuda b: 1989 in Jerusalem, Israel
........................8 Tzvi Ben Yehuda b: 1991 in Jerusalem, Israel
........................8 Avorhom Ben Yehuda b: 1992 in Jerusalem, Israel
........................8 Ella Bat Yehuda b: 1993 in Jerusalem, Israel
........................8 Nechama Yehuda b: 1995 in Jerusalem, Israel
........................8 Mikhel Dovid Ben Yehuda b: 1996 in Jerusalem, Israel
..................7 Chava Reichman b: 1969 in Jerusalem, Israel
.... + Benjamin Dryfess b: 1966 in Jerusalem, Israel
........................8 Shne'ior Dryfess b: 1990 in Jerusalem, Israel
........................8 Eliezer Dryfess b: 1991 in Jerusalem, Israel
........................8 Miriam Dryfess b: 1993 in Jerusalem, Israel
........................8 Hinda Rivka Dryfess b: 1994 in Jerusalem, Israel
........................8 Nechama Dryfess b: 1995 in Jerusalem, Israel
........................8 Hannah Dryfess b: 1996 in Jerusalem, Israel
..................6 Moshe Yisrael Shlapobersky b: 1933 in Jerusalem, Eretz Yisrael
.... + Esther Deutch
..................7 Pnina Shlapobersky b: 1968 in Jerusalem, Israel
.... + Ittamar Muskat b: 1965 in Jerusalem, Israel
........................8 Avorhom Muskat b: Jun 25, 1988 in Jerusalem, Israel
........................8 Bracha Muskat b: 1989 in Jerusalem, Israel
........................8 Yisrael Arieh Muskat b: 1991 in Jerusalem, Israel
........................8 Yechiel Muskat b: 1992 in Jerusalem, Israel
........................8 Shlomo Muskat b: 1995 in Jerusalem, Israel
........................8 Mikhel David Muskat b: 1996 in Jerusalem, Israel
..................7 Mordechai Shlapobersky b: 1969 in Jerusalem, Israel
.... + Kali b: 1970 in Jerusalem, Israel
........................8 Arron Shlapobersky b: 1990 in Jerusalem, Israel
........................8 Leah Shlapobersky b: 1991 in Jerusalem, Israel
........................8 Chaya Shlapobersky b: 1992 in Jerusalem, Israel
........................8 Shimon Shlapobersky b: 1994 in Jerusalem, Israel
........................8 Pnina Shlapobersky b: 1996 in Jerusalem, Israel
........................8 Nechama Shlapobersky b: 1996 in Jerusalem, Israel
..................7 Hannah Shlapobersky b: 1972 in Jerusalem, Israel
.... + Yehuda Vanervalde b: 1967 in Jerusalem, Israel

........................8 Avorhom Yochanan Vanervalde b: 1990 in Jerusalem, Israel
........................8 Baruch Vanervalde b: 1992 in Jerusalem, Israel
........................8 Shmuel Vanervalde b: 1993 in Jerusalem, Israel
........................8 Mikhel Dovid Vanervalde b: Nov 1995 in Jerusalem, Israel
....................7 Gitel Shlapobersky b: 1974 in Jerusalem, Israel
.... + Leib Layush b: 1962 in Jerusalem, Israel
........................8 Chava Layush b: 1996 in Jerusalem, Israel
....................7 Hinda Rivka Shlapobersky b: 1976 in Jerusalem, Israel
....................7 Chava Shlapobersky b: 1980 in Jerusalem, Israel
...............5 Yehoshua Ovsa Leib Shlapobersky b: 1901 in Skaudvile, Kovno, Russia; Skaudvile, Taurage, Lithuainia, d: Jan
            15, 1961 in Petach Tikvah, Israel
            + Rach'l Pese Shapiro b: 1904 in Neishtot-Tavrig , Kovno, Russia, m: 1935 in Kvedarna, Kovno, Russia, d:
            Mar 16, 1989 in Petach Tikvah, Israel
...............5 Mordechai Shlapobersky b: 1905 in Skaudvile, Kovno, Russia; Skaudvile, Taurage, Lithuainia/Skaudvile,
            Taurage, Lithuania/, d: Nov 04, 1967 in Jerusalem, Israel
            + Rivka Gutman b: 1912 in Kovno, Kovno, Russia, d: Aug 1944 in Auschwitz, Poland; Holocaust
.................6 Hinda Rivka Shlapobersky b: 1937 in Kovno, Kovno, Russia, d: 1943 in Kovno, Kovno, Lithuania
.................6 Roch"l Shlapobersky b: 1940 in Kovno, Kovno, Russia, d: 1944 in Kovno, Kovno, Lithuania
.................6 Leiba Shlapobersky b: 1941 in Kovno, Kovno, Russia, d: 1944 in Kovno, Kovno, Lithuania
...........4 Roch"l Prop b: 1873 in Skaudvile, Kovno, Russia, d: Apr 06, 1937 in Taurage, Taurage, Lithuania
            + Moshe Baruch Braude b: 1871 in Kelm, Kovno, Russia, m: 1910 in Skaudvile, Kovno, Russia, d: Jul 04, 1941
            in Skaudvile, Lithuania, Holocaust
...............5 Yisrael Betzalel Braude b: 1910 in Skaudvile, Kovno, Lithuania, d: Jul 21, 1941 in Skaudvile, Lithuania,
            Holocaust
            + Feige Faktor b: 1913 in Skaudvile, Kovno, Lithuania, m: Feb 06, 1938 in Suodas. Telsiai, Lithuania, d: Sep
            19, 1941 in Batakiai, Taurage, Lithuania
...............5 Shimon Braude b: 1911 in Skaudvile, Kovno, Russia; Skaudvile, Taurage, Lithuainia/Skaudvile, Taurage,
            Lithuania/, d: Jul 21, 1941 in Skaudvile, Lithuania, Holocaust
.................6 Israel Braude b: 1937 in Skaudvile, Kovno, Russia, d: Sep 19, 1941 in Batakiai, Taurage, Lithuania;
            Holocaust
.................6 Unknown Braude b: Jul 23, 1941 in Batakiai, Taurage, Lithuania, d: Sep 19, 1941 in Batakiai, Taurage,
            Lithuania
...........4 Chaya Prop b: Abt. 1875 in Skaudvile, Kovno, Russia, d: 1938 in Skaudvile, Kovno, Russia
            + Mordechai Yosef Shapiro b: 1860 in Skaudvile, Kovno, Russia; Skaudvile, Taurage District, Lithuania/Skaudvile,
            Taurage, Lithuania/, m: 1903 in Kvedarna, Kovno, Russia; Rabbi Faivelis Gavreb, d: 1923 in Skaudvile, Kovno,
            Russia; Skaudvile, Taurage District, Lithuania/Skaudvile, Taurage, Lithuania/
...............5 Rach'l Pese Shapiro b: 1904 in Neishtot-Tavrig , Kovno, Russia, d: Mar 16, 1989 in Petach Tikvah, Israel
            + Yehoshua Ovsa Leib Shlapobersky b: 1901 in Skaudvile, Kovno, Russia; Skaudvile, Taurage, Lithuainia,
            m: 1935 in Kvedarna, Kovno, Russia, d: Jan 15, 1961 in Petach Tikvah, Israel
.........3 Moshe "Berlow" Prop b: 1839 in Skaudvile, Kovno, Russia, d: Wilkes-Barre, Luzerne, Pennsylvania, USA
....   + Pearl b: 1852 in Skaudvile, Kovno, Russia; Skaudvile, Taurage, Lithuania/, d: Wilkes-Barre, Luzerne,
            Pennsylvania, USA
...........4 Ekel Prop b: Abt. 1860 in Skaudvile, Kovno, Russia; Skaudvile, Taurage, Lithuania/
...........4 Rivka Berlow
....   + Plessit
...........4 Avram Berlow
...........4 Itzig Berlow
...........4 Ethel Berlow
....   + Plessit
...........4 Pesa Berlow
.........3 Marjasha Prop b: Abt. 1839 in Skaudvile, Kovno, Russia, d: 1918 in Jerusalem, Eretz Yisrael
....   + Yankel Zaks b: 1850 in Skaudvile, Kovno, Russia; Skaudvile, Taurage, Lithuania/, m: 1876 in Skaudvile,
            Kovno, Russia, d: 1885 in Skaudvile, Kovno, Russia; Skaudvile, Taurage, Lithuainia/Skaudvile, Taurage,
            Lithuania/
...........4 Hinde Zaks b: Abt. 1878 in Skaudvile, Kovno, Russia, d: 1963 in New York, New York, USA
....   + Morris "Moshe" Gordon b: 1873 in Keidan, Kovno, Russia, d: Jul 08, 1932 in Brooklyn, Kings, New York, USA
...............5 Edith Gordon b: May 08, 1906 in Keidan, Kovno, Russia, d: May 1983 in Brooklyn, Kings, New York, USA

281

.... + Moe Melman b: Sep 15, 1906, m: 1936 in Brooklyn, Kings, New York, USA, d: Jan 1986 in Brooklyn, Kings, New York, USA

............5 Louis "Lazer" Gordon b: Jun 13, 1907 in Kedainiai, Kovno, Russia, d: May 1991 in Brick, Ocean, New Jersey, USA

............5 Jack "Yacob" Gordon b: Aug 07, 1916 in Astrakhan', Kirov, Russia, d: Nov 22, 2000 in New York, New York, USA; Age at Death: 84

.... + Edith Bashist b: 1923 in New York, New York, USA, m: Abt. 1951 in New York, New York, USA

...............6 Mark Gordon b: Mar 15, 1954 in New York, New York, USA

.........4 Lieb "Leon" Aaron Sachs b: May 20, 1879 in Skaudvile, Kovno, Russia, d: Feb 07, 1954 in Chicago, Cook, Illinois, USA

.... + Ella T Propp b: Aug 17, 1885 in Memel, East Prussia, m: Jan 22, 1911 in Chicago, Cook, Illinois, USA, d: Oct 28, 1964 in Chicago, Cook, Illinois, USA

............5 Charlotte S. Sachs b: May 29, 1912 in Chicago, Cook, Illinois, USA, d: Jan 09, 1993 in Portland, Multnomah, Oregon, USA

.... + Samual R. Lazerwith b: Aug 31, 1906 in Cincinnati, Clermont, Ohio, USA, m: Nov 10, 1934 in Chicago, Cook, Illinois, USA, d: Jan 09, 1973 in Chicago, Cook, Illinois, USA

............6 Mark Allen Lazerwith b: Mar 06, 1936 in Cincinnati, Clermont, Ohio, USA, d: May 25, 2007 in Glenview, Cook, Illinois, USA

.... + Fanchon H Lazerwith b: Apr 07, 1941 in Chicago, Cook, Illinois, USA, m: 1969 in Chicago, Cook, Illinois, USA

.................7 Cara Beth Lazerwith b: Sep 03, 1970 in Chicago, Cook, Illinois, USA

.... + Michael A. Shlau b: Aug 11, 1973 in Chicago, Cook, Illinois, USA

...................8 Samuel Jacob Shlau b: Nov 29, 2005 in Park Ridge, Cook, Illinois, USA

...................8 Evan Mark Shlau b: Jul 22, 2008 in Lake Forest, Lake, Illinois, USA; born at 342 AM

.................7 Scott Edward Lazerwith b: Sep 18, 1973 in Chicago, Cook, Illinois, USA

.... + Emma "Holly" Herndon b: Abt. 1978, m: Mar 2002 in Chicago, Cook, Illinois, USA

...................8 Nora Fay Herndon-Lazerwith b: Jul 15, 2004 in Ann Arbor, Washtenaw, Michigan, USA

...............6 Myra J Lazerwith b: Dec 02, 1945 in Chicago, Cook, Illinois, USA

.... + John H Gevurtz b: Mar 19, 1937 in Portland, Clackamas, Oregon, USA, m: 1967 in Chicago, Cook, Illinois, USA

.................7 Rayna Ellen Gevurtz b: Nov 14, 1973 in Stanford, Santa Clara, California, USA

.... + Gershon Jeremy Zylberman b: Jun 18, 1972 in Melbourne, Victoria, Australia, m: Jun 18, 2000 in Portland, Clackamas, Oregon, USA

...................8 Adira Rachel Zylberman b: Oct 13, 2005 in Melbourne, Victoria, Australia

...................8 Noa Zylberman b: Abt. 2007 in Melbourne, Victoria, Australia

...................8 Mira Chana Zylberman b: Apr 03, 2012 in Melbourne, Victoria, Australia

.................7 Steven Gevurtz b: Apr 26, 1976 in Chicago, Cook, Illinois, USA

............5 Jerome Michael Sachs b: Oct 12, 1914 in Chicago, Cook, Illinois, USA, d: Oct 12, 2012 in Chicago, Cook, Illinois, USA

.... + Joan Frankenstein b: Mar 18, 1915 in Chicago, Cook, Illinois, USA, m: Jun 08, 1939 in Chicago, Cook, Illinois, USA, d: Apr 24, 1978 in Chicago, Cook, Illinois, USA

...............6 Jennifer Sachs b: Jul 15, 1942 in Chicago, Cook, Illinois, USA

.... + Richard Boeth b: Feb 10, 1933 in New York, New York, USA, m: 1965, d: Jun 05, 1982 in New York, New York, USA

.... + Larry Bolch b: Jul 13, 1937 in Edmonton, Alberta, Canada, m: 1960

.................7 Ayn Bolch b: Dec 28, 1962 in Edmonton, Alberta, Canada

.... + Eric Skjeie b: 1960 in Portland, Clackamas, Oregon, USA

...................8 Malachi Skjeie b: Jan 12, 1996 in Dallas, Dallas, Texas, USA

.... + Patrick Swihart b: 1947 in Texas, USA

...................8 Es Louise Swihart b: 1983 in Dallas, Dallas, Texas, USA

.... + James Donovan b: Jan 15, 1948 in Lowell, Middlesex, Massachusetts, USA, m: 1970

...............6 Jonathan Sachs b: 1949 in Chicago, Cook, Illinois, USA

.... + Emily Sandblade m: 1978

.... + Irene Levin b: Apr 21, 1917 in Chicago, Cook, Illinois, USA, m: 1981 in Chicago, Cook, Illinois, USA, d: Feb 21, 2004 in Chicago, Cook, Illinois, USA

.........4 Charley Sachs b: Abt. 1880 in Skaudvile, Kovno, Russia, d: 1893 in Wilkes-Barre, Luzerne, Pennsylvania, USA

.... + Shaya Mendel Aronovich b: 1839 in Vainutas, Kovno, Russia, d: 1919 in Jerusalem, Eretz Yisrael, Israel

.........3 Liba Prop b: 1840 in Skaudvile, Kovno, Russia, d: 1927 in Wilkes-Barre, Luzerne, Pennsylvania, USA

.... + Avram Friedman b: 1834 in Skaudvile, Kovno, Russia, m: 1872 in Skaudvile, Kovno, Russia, d: 1915 in
Wilkes-Barre, Luzerne, Pennsylvania, USA
............4 Hinda "Annie" Friedman b: 1873 in Skaudvile, Kovno, Russia, d: 1931 in Wilkes-Barre, Luzerne,
Pennsylvania, USA
.... + Max L Fainberg b: 1875 in Russia, m: 1891 in Kovno, Kovno, Russia, d: Feb 25, 1950 in Wilkes-Barre,
Luzerne, Pennsylvania, USA
.............5 Eva Fainberg b: Nov 1895 in Wilkes-Barre, Luzerne, Pennsylvania, USA, d: Nov 05, 1961 in Wilkes-Barre,
Luzerne, Pennsylvania, USA
.... + Abram Mangel b: Oct 1893 in Luzerne, Pennsylvania, USA, m: 1915 in Wilkes-Barre, Luzerne,
Pennsylvania, USA, d: Nov 1953 in Wilkes-Barre, Luzerne, Pennsylvania, USA
.................6 Florence Mangel b: Jul 28, 1920 in Wilkes-Barre, Luzerne, Pennsylvania, USA, d: 1997 in
Massachusetts, USA
.... + Allan Isadore Recht b: 1918 in Aliquippa, Beaver, Pennsylvania, USA, m: 1946
.................7 James Charles Recht b: Feb 1947 in Wilkes-Barre, Luzerne, Pennsylvania, USA
.... + Judith Heaton b: 1947
.....................8 Marc Recht b: 1973
.....................8 Tracy Recht b: 1976
.................7 Keith Recht b: 1949 in Wilkes-Barre, Luzerne, Pennsylvania, USA
.... + Mary Ellen Blankenship b: Abt. 1952
.....................8 Zachary Recht b: Abt. 1975
.....................8 Adam Recht b: Abt. 1977
.....................8 Allison Recht b: Abt. 1981
.................6 Zelda Mangel b: Jul 28, 1920 in Wilkes-Barre, Luzerne, Pennsylvania, USA, d: Sep 14, 1994 in
Needham, Norfolk, Massachusetts, USA
.... + Melvin Lowe b: 1921 in New York, New York, USA, d: 1980 in Needham, Norfolk, Massachusetts, USA
.................7 Howard Lowe b: 1948
.... + Sandy
.....................8 Jenna Lowe b: 1976
.................7 Michael Lowe b: 1950
.... + Bettina
.....................8 Melanie Lowe b: Abt. 1978
.....................8 Lowe b: Abt. 1980
.................6 Lois Mangel b: Jun 15, 1928 in Wilkes-Barre, Luzerne, Pennsylvania, USA
.... + Allan Hyman b: Jan 1929 in Wilkes-Barre, Luzerne, Pennsylvania, USA, d: Jan 1997 in Pittsburgh,
Allegheny, Pennsylvania, USA
.................7 Robert Hyman b: 1952 in Wilkes-Barre, Luzerne, Pennsylvania, USA
.... + Jessie Brynan b: Abt. 1953, m: 1980
.....................8 Rebecca Hyman b: 1983
.....................8 Bryan Hyman b: 1990
.................7 Abby Hyman b: 1956 in Wilkes-Barre, Luzerne, Pennsylvania, USA
.... + Keith Kutner b: Abt. 1955
.....................8 Robert Kutner b: 1982
.....................8 Sarah Kutner b: 1983
.............5 Samuel Fainberg b: Apr 04, 1896 in Wilkes-Barre, Luzerne, Pennsylvania, USA, d: May 29, 1990 in
Wilkes-Barre, Luzerne, Pennsylvania, USA
.... + Claire Karfunckle b: Dec 11, 1900 in Olyphant, Lackawanna, Pennsylvania, USA, m: 1927 in Wilkes-Barre,
Luzerne, Pennsylvania, USA, d: Apr 12, 1993 in Wilkes-Barre, Luzerne, Pennsylvania, USA
.................6 Stanley R. Fainberg b: Sep 07, 1928 in Wilkes-Barre, Luzerne, Pennsylvania, USA
.... + Jeane Fortinsky b: 1929 in Wilkes-Barre, Luzerne, Pennsylvania, USA, m: Abt. 1951 in Wilkes-Barre,
Luzerne, Pennsylvania, USA
.................7 Jack Harold Fainberg b: Dec 20, 1952 in Wilkes-Barre, Luzerne, Pennsylvania, USA
.... + Jennifer Peck b: Sep 25, 1957 in New York, New York, USA
.....................8 Jonathan Fainberg b: Jun 08, 1986 in Boston, Suffolk, Massachusetts, USA
.....................8 Rebbecca Fainberg b: Oct 27, 1990 in Boston, Suffolk, Massachusetts, USA
.................7 Debbie Ann Fainberg b: Dec 06, 1955 in Kingston, Luzerne, Pennsylvania, USA
.... + Alan Hollander b: Mar 01, 1951 in New York, New York, USA
.....................8 Andrew Hollander b: Oct 29, 1980 in Wilkes-Barre, Luzerne, Pennsylvania, USA
.....................8 Sara Hollander b: Feb 14, 1983 in Wilkes-Barre, Luzerne, Pennsylvania, USA

........................8 Daniel Hollander b: Jun 14, 1986 in Wilkes-Barre, Luzerne, Pennsylvania, USA
..................6 Barbara Fainberg b: Apr 06, 1936 in Wilkes-Barre, Luzerne, Pennsylvania, USA
...............5 Lillian Fainberg b: 1899 in Wilkes-Barre, Luzerne, Pennsylvania, USA, d: 1904 in Wilkes-Barre, Luzerne,
        Pennsylvania, USA
.........3 Ephraim "Efraim" Propp b: 1845 in Skaudvile, Kovno, Russia, d: Feb 27, 1919 in New York, New York, New York,
        United States of America
.... + Rivka Raizel Nachenson b: Aug 1849 in Kovno, Kovno, Russia, m: 1866 in Skaudvile, Kovno, Russia, d: Dec
        01, 1927 in New York, New York, USA
.........4 Mary "Manja" Propp b: Aug 1868 in Shavel, Kovno Guberniya, Russia, d: 1950 in New York, New York, USA
.... + Israel Littwin b: Aug 1853 in Russia, m: 1890 in Russia, d: 1958 in New York, New York, USA
...............5 Hyman Littwin b: Abt. 1882 in Russia
...............5 Sarah Littwin b: Abt. 1891 in Russia
...............5 Charles Littwin b: Oct 02, 1893 in Silesia, Siberia, Russia, d: 1983
.... + Caroline b: 1900 in New York, New York, USA, m: 1922, d: Abt. 1946 in New York, New York, USA
..................6 Stuart Littwin b: 1923 in Tenafly, Bergen, New Jersey, USA
.... + Ruth Helene Wieder m: 1951 in New York, New York, USA
...............5 Anna Littwin b: Sep 25, 1894 in New York, New York, USA, d: Mar 1975 in East Orange, Essex, New
        Jersey, USA
.... + Solomen "Rodale" Cohen b: 1896 in New York, New York, USA, m: 1916 in New York, New York, USA,
        d: 1988 in New York, New York, USA
..................6 Milton Rodale b: 1918 in New York, New York, USA
..................6 Irving Rodale b: 1920 in New York, New York, USA
..................6 Rosaline Rodale b: 1924 in New York, New York, USA
...............5 Harry Littwin b: Oct 06, 1896 in New York, New York, USA, d: Jan 1973 in New York, New York, USA
.... + Esther b: Sep 01, 1902 in New York, New York, USA, d: Apr 1987 in New York, New York, USA
...............5 Fany Littwin b: Abt. 1898 in New York
...............5 Samual Littwin b: Feb 02, 1900 in New York, New York, USA, d: Dec 1981 in New York, New York, USA
.... + Hariet Golding b: 1907 in New York, New York, USA
..................6 Florence "Cookie" Littwin b: 1931 in New York, New York, USA, d: 1988 in New York, New York, USA
..................6 Ruth Littwin b: 1934 in New York, New York, USA
..................6 Steven Littwin b: 1939 in New York, New York, USA
.... + Florence Stern b: 1942 in New York, New York, USA
.....................7 Mark Littwin b: 1966 in New York, New York, USA
.... + Jody Goldberg b: 1967 in New York, New York, USA
.....................7 Michael Littwin b: 1969 in New York, New York, USA
.....................7 Anne Littwin b: 1976 in New York, New York, USA
...............5 Florence Littwin b: Jan 24, 1903 in New York, New York, USA, d: Nov 1988 in New York, New York, USA
.... + Frank Adler b: Mar 12, 1902 in New York, New York, USA, m: 1923 in New York, New York, USA, d: Aug
        1972 in New York, New York, USA
..................6 Roy Adler b: 1924 in New York, New York, USA, d: 1973 in New York, New York, USA
..................6 Evertt Adler b: 1927 in New York, New York, USA
...............5 Libbie Littwin b: Jun 23, 1905 in New York, New York, USA, d: May 14, 1987 in Hallandale, Broward,
        Florida, USA
.... + Joseph Wise b: Dec 14, 1903 in New York, New York, USA, m: 1936 in New York, New York, USA, d: Jun
        1973 in Hallandale, Broward, Florida, USA
..................6 Edwin Martin Wise b: 1938 in New York, New York, USA
..................6 Norman Wise b: 1940 in New York, New York, USA
.........4 Isaac Leopold Propp b: Aug 22, 1873 in Shavel, Kovno Guberniya, Russia, d: Jan 15, 1955 in New York, New
        York, USA
.... + Ida L. Berger b: 1877 in Kovno, Kovno, Russia, m: 1900 in New York, New York, USA, d: Dec 26, 1934 in
        New York, New York, USA
...............5 Samuel Propp b: 1902 in Newark, Essex, New Jersey, USA, d: Dec 19, 1944 in New York, New York,
.... + Anna Leah Gordon b: Jan 09, 1901 in New York, New York, USA, d: Mar 1985 in New York, New York, USA;
        Age at Death: 84
..................6 Emily Propp b: 1934 in New York, New York, USA, d: Dec 16, 1996 in New York, New York, USA
.... + Edward Leibowitz b: 1933 in New York, New York, USA, m: Nov 12, 1961 in New York, New York, USA,
        d: Feb 15, 2013 in New York, New York, USA
.....................7 Samuel Leibowitz b: 1962 in New York, New York, USA

...................7 Jonathan Leibowitz b: 1964 in New York, New York, USA
...................7 Eric Leibowitz b: 1965 in New York, New York, USA
.................6 Audrey "Chaya" Propp b: Apr 11, 1937 in Baltimore, Maryland, USA, d: Dec 16, 1996 in New York, New
               York, USA
.... + Samual Maurice Ward b: Mar 12, 1932 in New York, New York, USA, m: Jun 24, 1963 in New York, New
               York, USA, d: Feb 15, 2013 in New York, New York, USA
...................7 Elise Ward b: Mar 02, 1959 in New York, New York, USA
.... + Pulitzer m: Abt. 1983 in New York, New York, USA
......................8 Joshua Pulitzer b: Aug 01, 1985 in New York, New York, USA
...................7 Rachel Ward b: Apr 03, 1966 in New York, New York, USA
.... + Hershel Herskowitz b: Aug 18, 1965 in Los Angeles, Los Angeles, California, USA, m: Mar 19, 1989
              in New York, New York, USA
......................8 Malya Herskowitz b: May 30, 1995 in New York, New York, USA
......................8 Isaac L. Herskowitz b: Apr 03, 1997 in New York, New York, USA
......................8 Audrey "Chaya" Herskowitz b: Apr 03, 1997 in New York, New York, USA
......................8 Meyer Herskowitz b: Apr 03, 1997 in New York, New York, USA
......................8 Lena "Leah" Herskowitz b: Apr 03, 1997 in New York, New York, USA
......................8 Henya Herskowitz b: Feb 02, 2006 in New York, New York, USA
...................7 Jennifer Ward b: Apr 20, 1969 in New York, New York, USA
.... + Alan Friedman b: 1952 in Cape Town, Western Cape, South Africa
.... + Bennett Rothenberg b: Abt. 1927 in New York, New York, USA, m: Jun 1956 in New York, New York, USA
.............5 Julius Propp b: Oct 29, 1903 in New York, New York, USA, d: Dec 1981 in Miami, Dade, Florida, USA
.... + Nancy E. Sheinwold b: Sep 15, 1903 in England, d: Nov 13, 1997 in Miami, Dade, Florida, USA
.................6 Bernice Propp b: 1925 in New York, New York, USA
.... + Raymond "Milzitzky" Mills b: 1922, m: Jun 08, 1947 in New York, New York, USA
...................7 Henry L Mills b: Abt. 1949
...................7 Richard A Mills b: Abt. 1951
......................8 Michael A Mills b: 1984
.............5 Benjamin Propp b: Feb 18, 1905 in Wilkes-Barre, Luzerne, Pennsylvania, USA, d: Jul 03, 1987 in West Palm
             Beach, Palm Beach, Florida, USA
.... + Helen Stern b: Sep 03, 1907 in Pittsburgh, Allegheny, Pennsylvania, USA, m: Abt. 1931 in New York, New
             York, USA, d: Apr 1990 in Royal Palm Beach, Palm Beach, Florida, USA
.................6 Frank Propp b: Jan 16, 1928 in New York, New York, USA
.... + Edith Hirsh b: Jul 04, 1931 in Vienna, Austria
...................7 Karen Propp b: Jul 14, 1957 in New York, New York, USA
.... + Roger Hurwitz b: Abt. 1955 in Chicago, Cook, Illinois, USA
......................8 Zohar Hurwitz b: Sep 13, 1997 in Cambridge, Middlesex, Massachusetts, USA
...................7 Leslie Propp b: Aug 09, 1960 in New Rochelle, Westchester, New York, USA
.... + Scott Pearson b: Feb 1961 in Ann Arbor, Washtenaw, Michigan, USA
......................8 Linnea Propp Pearson b: Sep 02, 1995 in Olympia, Thurston, Washington, USA
...................7 Kenneth Tio Propp b: Jun 01, 1964 in Niger, Nigeria
.... + Patricia McGarry b: Jan 01, 1963 in New York, New York, USA
......................8 Greta Maeve Propp b: Nov 06, 1999 in Beverly, Essex, Massachusetts, USA
.................6 Sandra Propp b: Nov 20, 1933 in New York, New York, USA
.... + Jerome Schwartz b: Feb 10, 1932 in New York, New York, USA
...................7 Madeline "Lena" Bennet Schwartz b: Dec 26, 1964 in New York, New York, USA
.... + Jon Wasserman b: Oct 08, 1968 in Chicago, Cook, Illinois, USA
...................7 Monika L Schwartz b: Aug 15, 1970 in Pittsburgh, Allegheny, Pennsylvania, USA
.............5 Charles Propp b: Dec 1908 in Wilkes-Barre, Luzerne, Pennsylvania, USA, d: Apr 1961 in New York,
.... + Celia b: Sep 01, 1910 in New York, New York, USA, m: 1932 in New York, New York, USA, d: Aug 29, 1995
             in New York, New York, USA
.................6 Gloria S Propp b: Jan 18, 1932 in New York, New York, USA
.... + Shaw
.................6 Marvin L Propp b: Mar 1933 in New York, New York, USA
.... + Marjorie b: 1932
...................7 Timothy M. Propp b: 1957 in Brooklyn, Kings, New York, USA
...................7 Pamela K. Propp b: 1964 in Brooklyn, Kings, New York, USA

.... + Gentry

...............5 Morris Propp b: Apr 22, 1910 in Wilkes-Barre, Luzerne, Pennsylvania, USA, d: Feb 1967 in New York, New York, USA

.... + Betty Adams b: Mar 26, 1912 in New York, New York, USA, d: Nov 15, 1994 in Westchester, New York, USA

..................6 Robert Rapheal Samuel Propp b: Jan 16, 1947 in New York, New York, USA

.... + Melante b: Abt. 1950 in New York, New York, USA, m: Abt. 1974 in New York, New York, USA

.....................7 David Propp b: Jan 21, 1975

.....................7 Jason N. Propp b: Mar 31, 1977

.... + Almazan b: Abt. 1954 in Los Angeles, Los Angeles, California, USA, m: Abt. 1984 in Los Angeles, Los Angeles, California, USA

.....................7 Steven Propp b: May 07, 1987 in Los Angeles, Los Angeles, California, USA

.... + Frieda Reiss b: 1905 in New York, New York, USA, m: Abt. 1939, d: 1986 in New York, New York, USA

............4 Morris Propp b: May 22, 1884 in Ishim, Tobolsk Guberniy, Russia, d: Feb 22, 1933 in New York, New York, USA

.... + Anna Cohen b: Jun 05, 1889 in New York, m: 1907 in New York, New York, USA, d: Dec 01, 1935 in New York, New York, USA

...............5 Mortimer J. Propp b: Jul 06, 1912 in New York, New York, USA, d: Apr 24, 2008 in New York, New York, USA

.... + Eugenie "Enia" Alter b: Feb 22, 1922 in Moscow, Russia, m: Aug 02, 1942 in New York, New York, USA, d: Aug 12, 2009 in New York, New York, USA

..................6 Helen Ann Propp b: May 21, 1943 in New York, New York, USA

.... + Melvin S. Heller b: 1938 in New York, New York, USA, m: Abt. 1980 in New York, New York, USA

.....................7 Jack W. Heller b: 1982 in New York, New York, USA

..................6 Morris S. Propp b: Mar 01, 1945 in New York, New York, USA

.... + Martha "Marni" Morrell b: 1950 in New York, New York, USA, m: Sep 04, 1997 in Essex, Middlesex, Connecticut, USA

.....................7 Adrienne Margaret Propp b: Jul 02, 1995 in Essex, Middlesex, Connecticut, USA

..................6 Adrienne L. Propp b: Jun 08, 1947 in New York, New York, USA, d: Apr 09, 1948 in New York, New York, USA

...............5 Seymour Propp b: Dec 30, 1916 in New York, New York, USA, d: Oct 27, 1993 in New York, New York, USA

.... + Eve T. Grunenbaum b: 1934 in New York, New York, USA, m: 1959 in New York, New York, USA

..................6 Douglas Alfred Propp b: Aug 03, 1961 in New York, New York, USA

.... + Dina Elisabeth Stein b: Jun 12, 1967 in New York, New York, USA, m: Nov 24, 2002 in New York, New York, USA

..................6 Rodney Michael Propp b: Dec 23, 1964 in New York, New York, USA

.... + Eleanor Sarah Heyman b: Dec 21, 1974 in New York, New York, USA, m: Sep 30, 2001 in Fairfield, Connecticut, USA; Greens Farm

.....................7 Stella Sabine Propp b: Dec 12, 2002 in New York, New York, USA

.....................7 Juliette Seymour Propp b: Mar 24, 2004 in New York, New York, USA

.....................7 Clara Arden Propp b: Dec 28, 2006 in New York, New York, USA

..................6 James Samuel Propp b: Feb 17, 1970 in New York, New York, USA

.... + Sang A Yim b: Feb 25, 1973 in Seoul, South Korea, m: Abt. 2001 in New York, New York, USA

.....................7 Olivia Im Propp b: Abt. 2006 in New York, New York, USA

.... + Gabrielle Gail Riback b: 1941 in New York, New York, USA, m: 1978 in New York, New York, USA

..................6 Amory Benjamin Propp b: Apr 14, 1979 in New York, New York, USA

...............5 Ephraim. Propp b: Dec 22, 1923 in New York, New York, USA, d: Aug 07, 2010 in New York, New York, USA; Age at Death: 86

.... + Gail G Dane b: Mar 22, 1944 in New York, New York, USA, m: 1984 in New York, New York, USA

..................6 Eric Gomberg b: Abt. 1983 in New York, New York, USA

..................6 David Gomberg b: Abt. 1983 in New York, New York, USA

..................6 Anna Michelle Propp b: Jun 16, 1984 in New York, New York, USA

.... + Gedaliah Riesnberg b: Abt. 1980 in New South Wales, Australia, m: Apr 09, 2014 in New York

............4 Anna Propp b: Jun 1886 in Ishim, Kemerovo, Russia, d: 1913 in New York, New York, USA

.... + Morris Glasgow b: 1880 in Russia, d: 1963 in New York, New York, USA

...............5 Belle Glasgow b: 1908 in New York, New York, USA, d: 1987 in New York, New York, USA

...............5 Sidney Glasgow b: 1913 in New York, New York, USA

.... + May Polskin b: 1917 in New York, New York, USA

..................6 Kenneth Glasgow b: 1940 in New York, New York, USA
.... + Linda b: 1945 in New York, New York, USA
....................7 Heather Glasgow b: 1970 in Florida, USA
.... + Diamond b: 1967 in Rochester, Monroe, New York, USA
....................7 Scott Glasgow b: 1972 in Florida, USA
....................7 Stacey Glasgow b: 1976 in Rochester, Monroe, New York, USA
..................6 Ronney Glasgow b: 1944 in New York, New York, USA
.... + Melvin Poplock b: 1942 in Rochester, Monroe, New York, USA
....................7 Randy Poplock b: 1970 in Rochester, Monroe, New York, USA
....................7 Darell Poplock b: 1974 in Rochester, Monroe, New York, USA
..................6 Edward Glasgow b: 1948 in New York, New York, USA
.... + Laurie b: 1953 in Rochester, Monroe, New York, USA
....................7 Jake Glasgow b: 1977 in Rochester, Monroe, New York, USA
....................7 Adam Glasgow b: 1980 in Rochester, Monroe, New York, USA
....................7 Benjamin Glasgow b: 1984 in Rochester, Monroe, New York, USA
............4 Iida "Chaya Golda' Propp b: Dec 09, 1889 in Irkutsk, Irkutsk, Russia, d: Jun 15, 1951 in New York, New York, USA
.... + Max "Mordechai" Brilliant b: 1887 in Devart, Poland, m: 1913 in Brooklyn, Kings, New York, USA, d: Sep 05, 1968 in New York, New York, USA
...............5 Moshe David Brilliant b: Apr 26, 1915 in Hoboken, Hudson, New Jersey, USA, d: Mar 17, 1995 in Ramat Gan, Tel Aviv, Israel
.... + Sylvia Rebecca Abrams b: Jan 25, 1918 in New York, m: 1941 in Tel Aviv, Eretz Yisrael
..................6 Joshua Zeev Brilliant b: 1943 in Tel Aviv, Israel
.... + Gina Schiby b: Sep 09, 1950 in Thessaloniki, Greece
....................7 Jonathan Baruch Brilliant b: Nov 26, 1986 in Palo Alto, San Mateo, California, USA
....................7 Dafria Rachel Brilliant b: Mar 18, 1991 in Hashomer-Rauiat, Israel
..................6 Hedva Judith Brilliant b: 1946 in Brooklyn, Kings, New York, USA
.... + Aryeh Wayne Stark b: 1949 in Montréal, Quebec, Canada
....................7 Yo'av Shmuel Stark b: 1984 in Tel Aviv, Israel
....................7 Omri Mordechai Elazar Stark b: 1987 in Tel Aviv, Israel
....................7 Noa Michal Stark b: 1989 in Tel Aviv, Israel
....................7 Daniel Gil Benjamin Stark b: Jan 1995 in Tel Aviv, Israel
...............5 Leslie Brilliant b: Nov 14, 1917 in New York, New York, USA, d: Sep 16, 2000 in Flushing, Queens, New York, USA
.... + Mina Tarshish b: Jul 24, 1920 in Odessa, Russia, d: Feb 04, 2003 in Flushing, Queens, New York, USA
..................6 Shalom Brilliant b: 1947 in Brooklyn, Kings, New York, USA
.... + Cynthia Gittlman b: 1954 in New York, New York, USA
....................7 Yitzchak Brilliant b: 1979 in New York, New York, USA
....................7 Chanie Brilliant b: 1981 in New York, New York, USA
..................6 Judith Brilliant b: 1949 in Brooklyn, Kings, New York, USA
..................6 Ephraim Brilliant b: 1955 in Brooklyn, Kings, New York, USA
.... + Dina Stein b: Oct 03, 1957 in New York, New York, USA
....................7 Shira Brilliant b: Jan 23, 1977 in New York, New York, USA
....................7 Uri Brilliant b: Apr 25, 1979 in New York, New York, USA
....................7 Michal Brilliant b: Apr 30, 1983 in Israel
....................7 Daniel Brilliant b: Jan 1986 in Kfar Saba, Israel
....................7 Talia Brilliant b: Oct 25, 1991 in Kfar Saba, Israel
...............5 Rivka Brilliant b: 1928 in Brooklyn, Kings, New York, USA
.... + Moe Moshe Behar b: May 02, 1928 in Istanbul, Istanbul, Turkey, m: 1951 in New York, New York, USA
..................6 Manny Behar b: 1953 in New York, New York, USA
.... + Evelyn Weissman b: 1954 in New York, New York, USA
....................7 Moshe David Behar b: 1988 in New York, New York, USA
....................7 Nathan Behar b: 1990 in New York, New York, USA
..................6 Daniel Behar b: Dec 31, 1955 in New York, New York, USA
.... + Esther Gross b: Dec 05, 1958 in Cleveland, Cuyahoga, Ohio, USA, m: May 19, 1980 in New York, New York, USA
....................7 Moshe Behar b: Jun 30, 1981 in New York, New York, USA

...............7 Mordechai Behar b: Feb 13, 1985 in New York, New York, USA
...............7 Ephraim Behar b: Apr 30, 1987 in Albany, Albany, New York, USA
...............7 Miriam Behar b: May 04, 1990 in Washington City, District Of Columbia, District of Columbia, USA
...............7 Yael Behar b: Jul 04, 1993 in Washington City, District Of Columbia, District of Columbia, USA
.............6 Eda Behar b: Jun 18, 1958 in New York, New York, USA
.... + Moshe Nulman b: Sep 30, 1955 in Montréal, Quebec, Canada
...............7 Rachel Elisheva Nulman b: Nov 12, 1989 in New York, New York, USA
...............7 Avigayil Sarah Nulman b: Apr 18, 1994 in New Jersey, USA
.........4 Louis Propp b: May 26, 1891 in Skaudvile, Kovno, Russia,, d: Mar 24, 1933 in New York, New York, USA
.... + Pansy Lunitz b: Jun 05, 1900 in New York, New York, USA, m: Mar 01, 1920 in New York, New York, USA, d: Aug 1967 in Kingston, Ulster, New York, USA
............5 Florence Propp b: May 19, 1922 in New York, New York, USA, d: Aug 03, 2003 in Kingston, Ulster, New York, USA
.... + Aaron E. Klein b: May 19, 1912 in New York, New York, USA, m: 1941 in New York, New York, USA, d: Nov 08, 1999 in Kingston, Ulster, New York, USA
.............6 Louis Klein b: Jun 30, 1942 in Kingston, Ulster, New York, USA
.... + Mary Jane Cappozzi b: Apr 22, 1949 in Kingston, Ulster, New York, USA
...............7 Andrea Klein b: Jan 31, 1967 in Kingston, Ulster, New York, USA
...............7 Steven Klein b: Oct 09, 1967 in Kingston, Ulster, New York, USA
.... + Deborah Sonnenstein b: Sep 03, 1966 in Kingston, Ulster, New York, USA
...............7 Nicole Klein b: Jan 31, 1969 in Kingston, Ulster, New York, USA
...............7 David Klein b: Jan 08, 1970 in Kingston, Ulster, New York, USA
.... + Christina Rask b: Sep 18, 1967 in Columbus, Fairfield, Ohio, USA
...............7 Robert Klein b: Mar 30, 1971 in Kingston, Ulster, New York, USA
.............6 Phyllis Klein b: May 24, 1946 in Kingston, Ulster, New York, USA
.... + Lon Glassbrook b: Sep 02, 1946 in New York, New York, USA
...............7 Daryn Glassbrook b: Sep 06, 1972 in Kingston, Ulster, New York, USA
...............7 Jarret Glassbrook b: Sep 06, 1979 in Kingston, Ulster, New York, USA
.... + Lawrence Reer b: Apr 01, 1957 in Kingston, Ulster, New York, USA 6
Brenda Klein b: Apr 03, 1950 in Kingston, Ulster, New York, USA
.... + Stewart Ross b: Kingston, Ulster, New York, USA, m: Abt. 1977 in Kingston, Ulster, New York, USA
...............7 Jason Ross b: May 19, 1978 in Kingston, Ulster, New York, USA
...............7 Zachary Ross b: Sep 18, 1981 in Kingston, Ulster, New York, USA
...............7 Alexandria Ross b: Feb 15, 1986 in Kingston, Ulster, New York, USA
...............7 Ariana Ross b: Dec 19, 1989 in Kingston, Ulster, New York, USA·
...........5 Ephraim Propp b: Oct 21, 1923 in New York, New York, USA, d: Feb 13, 1998 in Kingston, Ulster, NY
.... + Madeline Tepper b: Apr 14, 1922 in New York, New York, USA, d: Mar 22, 2001 in Kingston, Ulster, New York, USA
.............6 Louis Propp b: 1949 in Kingston, Ulster, New York, USA
.... + Kristen Williams b: 1953 in Hanover, Grafton, New Hampshire, USA, m: May 23, 1979 in Annandale On Hudson, Dutchess, New York, USA
...............7 Jascha Propp b: Jun 21, 1980 in Catskill, Greene, New York, USA
...............7 Hannah Propp b: May 24, 1983 in North Adams, Berkshire, Massachusetts, USA
.............6 Andrea Propp b: Feb 10, 1953 in Kingston, Ulster, New York, USA
.... + Walter Ten Eyek b: May 21, 1952 in Kingston, Ulster, New York, USA
...............7 Wyatt Ten Eyek b: Apr 05, 1980 in Kingston, Ulster, New York, USA
...............7 Wesley Ten Eyek b: Jun 04, 1981 in Kingston, Ulster, New York, USA
...........5 Samuel Propp b: Dec 22, 1926 in New York, New York, USA; Montrepose Cemetery, d: Apr 22, 1997 in Kingston, Ulster, New York, USA
.......3 Prejdel Prop b: 1847 in Skaudvile, Kovno, Russia, d: 1903 in Skaudvile, Kovno, Russia
.... + Slova b: 1838 in Kovno, Russia, m: 1858 in Skaudvile, Kovno, Russia, d: 1901 in Skaudvile, Kovno, Russia; Skaudvile, Taurage District, Lithuania/Skaudvile, Taurage, Lithuania/
.........4 Avrahom "Ahron" Prop b: 1863 in Skaudvile, Kovno, Russia
.... + Beila
............5 Simon "Shimon" Propp b: Jun 16, 1878 in Skaudvile, Kovno, Russia, d: Aug 28, 1948 in Lancaster, Lancaster, Pennsylvania, USA
.........4 Roch"l Propp b: May 1872 in Skaudvile, Kovno, Russia, d: Abt. 1914 in Calumet, Houghton, Michigan, USA

.... + Yisrael Epstein b: Jun 1859 in Tavrig, Kovno, Russia, m: 1884 in Skaudvile, Kovno, Russia, d: Mar 20, 1932 in Duluth, St Louis, Minnesota, USA
...............5 Lena E. Epstein b: Jun 29, 1885 in Kovno, Kovno, Russia, d: Jul 24, 1962 in Duluth, St Louis, Minnesota, USA
.... + Sigmond S Slonim b: Apr 25, 1883 in Russia, m: 1914 in Chicago, Cook, Illinois, USA, d: May 14, 1981 in Duluth, St Louis, Minnesota, USA
.................6 Ruth Slonim b: Jan 30, 1918 in Chicago, Cook, Illinois, USA, d: Feb 16, 2005 in Lewiston, Nez Perce, Idaho
.................6 Edward Epstein Slonim b: Jun 18, 1921 in Duluth, St Louis, Minnesota, USA
.... + Dorothy Marian Hoffman b: 1925 in Duluth, St Louis, Minnesota, USA, m: 1946 in Duluth, St Louis, Minnesota, USA
.....................7 Alan C Slonim b: Jul 29, 1947
.... + Kim E Dunlap b: Aug 07, 1958, m: Oct 16, 1974 in Hennepin, Minnesota, USA
.....................7 Marc Hoffman Slonim b: Dec 30, 1948 in Saint Louis, Minnesota
.....................7 Lynn Curtis Slonim b: Sep 26, 1950 in Saint Louis, Minnesota
.....................7 John Slonim b: 1953 in Duluth, St Louis, Minnesota, USA
...............5 Nathan Henry Epstein b: Aug 13, 1897 in Hancock, Houghton, Michigan, USA, d: Mar 20, 1976 in St Paul, Dakota, Minnesota, USA
.... + Jean Goldberg b: Oct 28, 1901 in Russia, m: Jun 19, 1934 in Chicago, Cook, Illinois, USA, d: Jan 1974 in St Paul, Dakota, Minnesota, USA
.................6 Laurel Irene Epstein b: Mar 28, 1935 in Ramsey, Minnesota, USA
.... + Donald Brandon Ray b: Jun 07, 1926 in Santa Maria, Santa Barbara, California, USA, m: Jun 28, 1958 in Los Angeles, California, USA
.....................7 David C. Ray b: Jul 31, 1961 in Los Angeles, Los Angeles, California, USA
.........3 Chaya Prop b: 1848 in Skaudvile, Kovno, Russia
.... + Leyzer Borukh b: Abt. 1833, d: Jan 12, 1926 ; Age: 84
............4 Dveyra Levinson b: Abt. 1866
............4 Leyb Levinson b: Abt. 1873
............4 Levinson
............4 Levinson
.........3 Leah Propp b: 1853 in Skaudvile, Kovno, Russia, d: 1862 in Skaudvile, Kovno, Russia
.........3 Samuel "Sleime Propp" Berlow b: 1854 in Skaudvile, Kovno, Russia, d: Oct 10, 1920 in Boston, Suffolk, Massachusetts, USA
.... + Maryann "Chana Miryam" Sternberg b: 1852 in Kovno, Kovno, Russia, m: 1873 in New York, New York, USA, d: Apr 12, 1923 in Boston, Suffolk, Massachusetts, USA
............4 Katherine "Chaya Gitel" Berlow b: 1870 in Skaudvile, Kovno, Russia, d: Boston, Suffolk, Massachusetts, USA
.... + Israel Ginsburg b: 1863 in Russia, m: 1888 in Boston, Suffolk, Massachusetts, USA, d: Feb 04, 1947 in Boston, Suffolk, Massachusetts, USA
...............5 Myer Ginsburg b: Jul 14, 1884 in Boston, Suffolk, Massachusetts, USA, d: Mar 07, 1952 in Boston, Suffolk, Massachusetts, USA
.... + Helen Alberts b: 1897 in Boston, Suffolk, Massachusetts, USA, m: 1919 in Boston, Suffolk, Massachusetts, USA, d: Boston, Suffolk, Massachusetts, USA
.................6 Evelyn Ginsburg b: 1922
.... + Harvey Edlin b: 1919
.....................7 Gary Edlin
.....................7 David Edlin
.....................7 Richard Edlin
.....................7 Robert Edlin
.................6 Arnold Ginsburg b: 1925
.... + Jane Martin b: 1927
.....................7 Lauren Ginsburg
.... + Steven Leboyer
.......................8 Henry Leboyer
.......................8 Donnain Leboyer
.......................8 Charlotte Leboyer
.......................8 Martin Leboyer
.....................7 Donna Ginsburg
.....................7 Martin Ginsburg

...............5 Goldie Ginsburg b: 1889 in Boston, Suffolk, Massachusetts, USA, d: 1918 in Boston, Suffolk, Massachusetts, USA
.... + Harry "Kaiser" King b: 1885 in Boston, Suffolk, Massachusetts, USA, m: 1913 in Boston, Suffolk, Massachusetts, USA, d: Boston, Suffolk, Massachusetts, USA
..................6 Paul J. King b: 1916 in Boston, Suffolk, Massachusetts, USA
.... + Naomi Rosenfeld b: 1919 in Boston, Suffolk, Massachusetts, USA, m: 1947 in Boston, Suffolk, Massachusetts, USA
.....................7 Isabel King b: 1949
.... + David Bradshaw b: 1946
.....................8 Hazel Bradshaw
.....................8 James Bradshaw
.....................7 William King b: 1951
.....................7 Tamar King b: 1955
.... + Richard Citron b: 1952
.....................8 Raffi Citron
.....................8 Yemima Citron
.....................8 Zvi Citron
.....................7 Allen King b: 1963
...............5 Martha Ginsburg b: Dec 05, 1892 in Boston, Suffolk, Massachusetts, USA, d: Jan 15, 1966
.... + Charles Perkins b: 1887 in Boston, Suffolk, Massachusetts, USA, m: 1913 in Boston, Suffolk, Massachusetts, USA
..................6 Irving J Perkins b: 1915, d: Oct 12, 1944 in Boston, Suffolk, Massachusetts, USA
..................6 Lawrence Perkins b: Jun 07, 1916 in Boston, Suffolk, Massachusetts, USA, d: Sep 16, 1996 in Boston, Suffolk, Massachusetts, USA
.....................7 Patricia Perkins b: 1946
.... + Calvin Andinga
.....................8 Katherine Andinga
.....................8 Deborah Andinga
.....................8 Gordon Andinga
.....................7 Jane Perkins b: 1948
.... + Edward Stein
.....................8 Andrew Stein
.....................8 Stephine Stein
.....................7 Harry Perkins b: 1952
.... + Stacey Jackson
.....................8 Nicholas Jackson
.....................8 James Jackson
.....................8 Mathew Jackson
.....................8 Elizabeth Jackson
...............5 Albert H. Ginsburg b: Sep 16, 1899 in Boston, Suffolk, Massachusetts, USA, d: Jun 1978 in Brockton, Plymouth, Massachusetts, USA
.... + Rose Hurwitz b: May 28, 1903 in Boston, Suffolk, Massachusetts, USA, m: 1921 in Boston, Suffolk, Massachusetts, USA, d: Feb 1970 in Brockton, Plymouth, Massachusetts, USA
..................6 Louise Ginsburg b: 1923
.... + Hyman Eiseman b: 1920, m: 1947
.....................7 Phillip Eiseman b: 1950
.....................7 Ellen Eiseman b: 1952
..................6 Brenda Ginsburg b: 1926
...............5 Elise Ginsburg b: 1900 in Boston, Suffolk, Massachusetts, USA, d: Boston, Suffolk, Massachusetts, USA
.... + Harry King b: 1896 in Boston, Suffolk, Massachusetts, USA, m: 1919 in Boston, Suffolk, Massachusetts, USA
..................6 Gloria King b: 1921
.... + Milton Elkin b: 1918, m: 1947
.....................7 Karen Elkin
.... + Mark Segal
.....................8 Michael Segal
.....................8 Steven Segal
.....................7 Laura Elkin

.... + James Freidman
.....................8 Jessica Freidman
.....................8 Craig Freidman
....................7 Phillip Elkin
.... + Sandy Phoenix
.....................8 David Elkin
.....................8 Susana Elkin
.................6 Alferd "Buddy" King b: 1925
..............5 Frances Ginsburg b: 1903 in Boston, Suffolk, Massachusetts, USA, d: Boston, Suffolk, Massachusetts, USA
.... + Robert Rogers b: Apr 28, 1895 in Boston, Suffolk, Massachusetts, USA, m: 1927 in Boston, Suffolk,
        Massachusetts, USA, d: Aug 1987 in West Newbury, Essex, Massachusetts, USA
..............5 Sadye Ginsburg b: Jun 02, 1904 in Boston, Suffolk, Massachusetts, USA
.... + Leo Flax b: Apr 09, 1901 in Boston, Suffolk, Massachusetts, USA, m: 1930 in Boston, Suffolk,
        Massachusetts, USA, d: Apr 11, 1974 in Boston, Suffolk, Massachusetts, USA
.................6 Susan Flax b: 1932
.... + Richard Smith b: 1930
.................6 Caroline Flax b: 1936
.... + Samuel Freda b: 1933
..............5 Lilla Ginsburg b: Jul 24, 1906 in Boston, Suffolk, Massachusetts, USA, d: Aug 1979 in Cranbury,
        Middlesex, New Jersey, USA
.... + Joseph Simberg b: Mar 16, 1904 in Boston, Suffolk, Massachusetts, USA, m: 1934 in Boston, Suffolk,
        Massachusetts, USA, d: Jul 1987 in Cranbury, Middlesex, New Jersey, USA
.................6 Charles Simberg b: 1936
.... + Saralee Drubner b: 1939, m: 1963
....................7 Michael Simberg
....................7 Joel Simberg
....................7 Stephen Simberg
.................6 Irma Simberg b: 1938
.... + William Turtle b: 1936
..............5 Estelle S. Ginsburg b: 1914 in Boston, Suffolk, Massachusetts, USA
.... + Howard Rubin b: 1913 in Boston, Suffolk, Massachusetts, USA, m: 1937 in Boston, Suffolk,
        Massachusetts, USA, d: 1982 in Boston, Suffolk, Massachusetts, USA
.................6 Mathew Rubin b: 1939 in Boston, Suffolk, Massachusetts, USA
.................6 Richard Rubin b: 1941 in Boston, Suffolk, Massachusetts, USA
.... + Scotty m: 1965
....................7 Samuel Rubin b: 1967
....................7 Nicholas Rubin b: 1971
............4 Hannah Annie Berlow b: 1878 in New York, New York, USA, d: 1947 in Boston, Suffolk, Massachusetts,
.... + Nathan Ginsburg b: 1878 in Boston, Suffolk, Massachusetts, USA, m: 1899 in Boston, Suffolk,
        Massachusetts, USA, d: 1944 in Boston, Suffolk, Massachusetts, USA
..............5 Edith Ginsburg b: Feb 01, 1900 in Boston, Suffolk, Massachusetts, USA, d: Dec 18, 1976 in Boston,
        Suffolk, Massachusetts, USA
.... + Harry L. Michaels b: 1896 in Boston, Suffolk, Massachusetts, USA, m: 1920 in Boston, Suffolk,
        Massachusetts, USA, d: Dec 07, 1947 in Boston, Suffolk, Massachusetts, USA
.................6 Alan Michaels b: Oct 29, 1922 in Boston, Suffolk, Massachusetts, USA
.... + Janet Glotzer b: Jan 05, 1930 in Hartford, Hartford, Connecticut, USA, m: 1951
....................7 Steven Michaels b: 1953 in Boston, Suffolk, Massachusetts, USA
....................7 James Michaels b: 1955 in Boston, Suffolk, Massachusetts, USA
.... + Colleen b: 1957 in Tampa, Hillsborough, Florida, USA, m: 1985
.....................8 Aaron Michaels b: 1989 in San Francisco, San Francisco, California, USA
.....................8 Andrew Michaels b: 1991 in Newark, Essex, New Jersey, USA
.................6 Richard Michaels b: 1926 in Boston, Suffolk, Massachusetts, USA
.... + Penny b: 1927 in Chicago, Cook, Illinois, USA
....................7 Glenn Michaels b: 1953 in Brunswick, Cumberland, Maine, USA
.... + Alice b: 1962 in Wellesley, Maine
.....................8 Allen Micheals b: 1987 in Maine, USA
....................7 David Micheals b: 1964

....................7 Daniel Micheals b: 1966

.... + Eleanor b: 1924 in Portland, Cumberland, Maine, USA, d: Sep 14, 1997 in Maine, USA

..............5 Alfred Ginsburg b: Oct 26, 1901 in Boston, Suffolk, Massachusetts, USA, d: Dec 1983 in Newton, Middlesex, Massachusetts, USA

.... + Portia Goldman b: Jun 20, 1901 in Boston, Suffolk, Massachusetts, USA, m: 1931 in Boston, Suffolk, Massachusetts, USA, d: Apr 1988 in Brookline, Norfolk, Massachusetts, USA

..................6 David Ginsburg b: 1933

..................6 Daniel Ginsburg b: 1936

..............5 Joseph Ginsburg b: 1909

..............5 Lester Ginsburg b: Jul 15, 1915 in Boston, Suffolk, Massachusetts, USA, d: Jul 18, 1975 in Fort Lauderdale, Broward, Florida, USA

.... + Rosalind Gorney b: 1915 in Boston, Suffolk, Massachusetts, USA, m: 1932

..................6 Paula Ginsburg b: 1936 in Boston, Suffolk, Massachusetts, USA

.... + Eric Terrel

....................7 Eric Terrel b: 1969

............4 Fanny Berlow b: Aug 1879 in New York, New York, USA, d: 1959 in Boston, Suffolk, Massachusetts, USA

.... + Albert Rosenthal b: 1874 in Boston, Suffolk, Massachusetts, USA, m: 1905 in Boston, Suffolk, Massachusetts, USA, d: Sep 26, 1921 in Boston, Suffolk, Massachusetts, USA

..............5 Sylvia Rosenthal b: Dec 26, 1909 in Boston, Suffolk, Massachusetts, USA

.... + George Alberts b: Sep 19, 1904 in Boston, Suffolk, Massachusetts, USA, m: 1934 in Boston, Suffolk, Massachusetts, USA, d: Dec 26, 1975 in Newton, Middlesex, Massachusetts, USA

..................6 Alan Alberts b: May 20, 1936 in Newton, Middlesex, Massachusetts, USA

..................6 Annie Alberts b: May 04, 1944 in Newton, Middlesex, Massachusetts, USA

.... + Lee

..............5 Mildred Rosenthal b: Mar 11, 1910 in Boston, Suffolk, Massachusetts, USA, d: Aug 1988 in Jaffrey, Cheshire, New Hampshire, USA

.... + Milton Morse b: Sep 30, 1902 in Boston, Suffolk, Massachusetts, USA, m: 1926, d: Jan 1980 in Jaffrey, Cheshire, New Hampshire, USA

..............5 Margaret Peggy Rosenthal b: 1912 in Boston, Suffolk, Massachusetts, USA, d: 1986 in Boston, Suffolk, Massachusetts, USA

.... + Royal "Roy" Beal b: Mar 11, 1910 in Boston, Suffolk, Massachusetts, USA

..................6 Ronald Beal b: Jun 11, 1926

............4 Charles Berlow b: Feb 27, 1882 in New York, New York, USA, d: Oct 1980 in West Orange, Essex, New Jersey, USA

.... + Florence Oppenheimer b: 1886 in New York, New York, USA, m: 1905 in Boston, Suffolk, Massachusetts, USA, d: 1923 in New York, New York, USA

..............5 Leona Berlow b: May 15, 1910 in New York, New York, USA, d: Sep 1973 in Boston, Suffolk, Massachusetts, USA

.... + Fredrick Kaiser b: Jan 07, 1902 in Boston, Suffolk, Massachusetts, USA, m: 1930 in Boston, Suffolk, Massachusetts, USA, d: Mar 1977 in Boston, Suffolk, Massachusetts, USA

..............5 Norma H. Berlow b: Mar 20, 1913 in New York, New York, USA, d: May 28, 1997 in Boston, Suffolk, Massachusetts, USA

............4 Bessie Berlow b: Apr 1882 in New York

.... + Max Cohan b: Abt. 1888 in Germany, d: Feb 1976 in Miami, Miami-dade, Florida, USA; Age at Death: 87

..............5 Avery Cohan b: Abt. 1915 in Massachusetts

.... + Margaret Kelly

..................6 Bess Cohan

..................6 Kevin Cohan

..............5 Charlotte Cohan b: Abt. 1917 in Massachusetts

............4 Harry Berlow b: Abt. 1885 in New York, New York, USA

.... + Betty Levine b: 1884 in New York, New York, USA

..............5 Jack Berlow b: 1906 in New York, New York, USA, d: 1944 in New York, New York, USA

............4 Myer Berlow b: Apr 25, 1890 in New York, New York, USA, d: 1935 in New York, New York, USA

.... + Mae Finkelstein b: 1896 in New York, New York, USA, m: 1919 in New York, New York, USA, d: 1972

..............5 Stanley Berlow b: Jun 16, 1921, d: Dec 16, 2005 in Vineyard Haven, Dukes, Massachusetts

.... + Marjorie Ettenheim b: Apr 19, 1925

..................6 Myer Berlow b: Apr 25, 1950 in New York, New York, USA

.... + Marlene Soifer b: 1954 in Chicago, Cook, Illinois, USA, m: 1978

....................7 Benjamin Berlow b: May 27, 1980

....................7 Aaron Berlow b: May 22, 1984

.... + Deborah B. Barr b: 1962
................6 Lisa Berlow b: Feb 15, 1952 in New York, New York, USA
.... + Robert Lehner b: 1950 in Miami, Dade, Florida, USA, m: 1988
...................7 Isabelle Lehner b: May 11, 1992
................6 David Adam Berlow b: Apr 09, 1954 in Boston, Suffolk, Massachusetts, USA
................6 Rustin Ralph Berlow b: Jul 25, 1957 in Milwaukee, Milwaukee, Wisconsin, USA
.... + Julie Seversin b: Nov 24, 1961 in Madison, Dane, Wisconsin, USA, m: Oct 25, 1980 in Madison,
             Dane, Wisconsin, USA
...................7 Rose Berlow b: Nov 03, 1984 in Madison, Dane, Wisconsin, USA
...................7 Jacob Thomas Berlow b: Jan 07, 1987 in Madison, Dane, Wisconsin, USA
...................7 Mae Lisa Berlow b: Dec 10, 1990 in Chicago, Cook, Illinois, USA
................6 Rebecca Ann Berlow b: Aug 12, 1959 in Milwaukee, Milwaukee, Wisconsin, USA
.... + Andrzej Rapaczynski b: 1948, m: Jun 15, 1986 in Dane, Wisconsin
...................7 Tessa Rapaczynski b: Sep 1988 in New York, New York, USA
................6 Samuel Berlow b: Apr 21, 1962 in Boston, Suffolk, Massachusetts, USA
.... + Alice Gartzke b: 1966, m: 1990
...................7 Max Coulter Berlow b: 1993 in Edgartown, Dukes, Massachusetts, USA
...................7 Eli Berlow b: 1995 in Edgartown, Dukes, Massachusetts, USA
.............5 Ralph Berlow b: Mar 16, 1923 in New York, New York, USA, d: Nov 16, 1972 in Bethesda, Montgomery,
             Maryland, USA
.... + Ellen Jane Rosenbloom b: Feb 28, 1933 in Baltimore, Maryland, USA, m: Jun 14, 1958 in Washington City,
             District Of Columbia, District of Columbia, USA
................6 Jenifer Miriam Berlow b: Sep 13, 1948
.... + David Tartakover
...................7 Alexandera Rose "Aly" Tartakover b: May 10, 1987
................6 Joshua Daniel Berlow b: May 26, 1959 in Washington City, District Of Columbia, District of Columbia, USA
................6 Liza "Eleiza" Berlow b: May 11, 1961 in Washington City, District Of Columbia, District of Columbia, USA
.... + Greg Voight b: 1959 in Washington City, District Of Columbia, District of Columbia, USA, m: Oct 04, 1992
             in Chevy Chase, Montgomery, Maryland, USA
...................7 Daniel Voight b: May 26, 1994
...................7 David Voight b: Dec 06, 1996
.... + Grace Freudberg b: Feb 16, 1923 in Washington City, District Of Columbia, District of Columbia, USA,
..........4 Florence "Flora" Berlow b: 1893 in New York, New York, USA, d: Jul 10, 1959 in Boston, Suffolk,
             Massachusetts, USA; [This came from the family research of "rberlow".]
.... + J. Leonard Michelson b: Jul 11, 1896 in New York, New York, USA, m: 1919 in Boston, Suffolk,
             Massachusetts, USA, d: Dec 1978 in Boston, Suffolk, Massachusetts, USA
.............5 Semah Michelson b: Mar 03, 1920 in Boston, Suffolk, Massachusetts, USA
.... + Herbert Klein b: Apr 11, 1920 in Woodbridge, Middlesex, New Jersey, USA, m: 1946 in Boston,
             Suffolk, Massachusetts, USA
................6 Robert Ellis Klein b: Mar 17, 1947
.... + Charlotte Hermens b: Oct 03, 1950, m: 1975
...................7 Jonathan Klein b: Nov 26, 1976
...................7 Michael Klein b: Apr 07, 1978
................6 Jane Klein b: Jun 28, 1951
.... + Michael S. Brown b: Nov 20, 1950, m: 1981
...................7 Abigail Brown b: Jul 12, 1986
...................7 Emily Brown b: Oct 03, 1987
.............5 Marjorie Michelson b: 1927 in Boston, Suffolk, Massachusetts, USA
.... + Feinberg
................6 Ellen Ann Freinberg b: Jun 28, 1951
................6 Susan Harriet Feinberg b: 1953
.........3 Joseph "Yosef Propp" Berlow b: Dec 15, 1858 in Skaudvile, Kovno, Russia, d: Jun 14, 1927 in Chicago, Cook,
         Illinois, USA
.... + Roch"l Aronovich b: 1864 in Skaudvile, Kovno, Russia, m: 1884 in Philadelphia, Philadelphia,
         Pennsylvania, USA, d: Dec 07, 1923 in Chicago, Cook, Illinois, USA
.............4 Charles Berlow b: Aug 02, 1883 in Wilkes-Barre, Luzerne, Pennsylvania, USA, d: Mar 03, 1947 in South Bend,
             St Joseph, Indiana, USA

.... + Celia Gershman b: Sep 18, 1885 in Chicago, Cook, Illinois, USA, d: May 1974 in South Bend, St Joseph, Indiana, USA

...........4 Abraham L. Berlow b: 1887 in Philadelphia, Philadelphia, Pennsylvania, USA, d: Aug 19, 1958 in Hollywood, Broward, Florida, USA

.... + Mae Minsky b: Feb 11, 1893 in South Bend, St Joseph, Indiana, USA, m: Abt. 1915 in Chicago, Cook, Illinois, USA, d: Jun 1966 in Hollywood, Broward, Florida, USA

...........4 Harry Berlow b: 1889 in St Paul, Dakota, Minnesota, USA, d: Sep 22, 1952 in Chicago, Cook, Illinois, USA

.... + Jennie Chalem b: Jan 10, 1899 in Chicago, Cook, Illinois, USA, m: 1923, d: Dec 25, 1950 in Chicago, Cook, Illinois, USA

...............5 Ralph Richard Berlow b: 1927 in Chicago, Cook, Illinois, USA, d: 1984 in Virginia, USA

.... + Patricia b: 1927

..................6 James Richard Berlow b: 1952 in Chicago, Cook, Illinois, USA

.... + Nancy Willis b: 1956

....................7 Anne Berlow b: 1986 in Vienna, Fairfax, Virginia, USA

....................7 Scott Richard Berlow b: 1988 in Vienna, Fairfax, Virginia, USA

..................6 Cathy Lynn Berlow b: 1955 in Chicago, Cook, Illinois, USA

.... + Ella Tecotsky b: 1891 in Chicago, Cook, Illinois, USA, m: 1916 in Chicago, Cook, Illinois, USA, d: 1917 in Chicago, Cook, Illinois, USA

...........4 Irving E. Berlow b: Oct 23, 1892 in Ishpeming, Marquette, Michigan, USA, d: Jan 01, 1965 in Phoenix, Maricopa, Arizona, USA

.... + Florence Horowitz b: 1897 in Detroit, Wayne, Michigan, USA, d: 1970 in Phoenix, Maricopa, Arizona, USA

...............5 Shirley Berlow b: Jul 14, 1922 in Detroit, Wayne, Michigan, USA, d: Feb 07, 2002 in San Antonio, Bexar, Texas, USA

.... + Robert Joseph Simon b: 1920 in Chicago, Cook, Illinois, USA, m: 1943 in Chicago, Cook, Illinois, USA, d: Bef. 1954

..................6 Roger Simon b: May 12, 1945 in Los Angeles, Los Angeles, California, USA, d: 1984

.... + Irving Simon b: 1922 in Chicago, Cook, Illinois, USA, d: Unknown in Chicago, Cook, Illinois, USA

..................6 Randy Simon b: Oct 10, 1954 in Phoenix, Maricopa, Arizona, USA

.... + John Lady b: 1918, d: Unknown

...............5 Eleanor Berlow b: Sep 12, 1927 in Chicago, Cook, Illinois, USA

.... + Sidney H Wolfson b: Jan 24, 1919 in Gaffney, Cherokee, South Carolina, USA, m: Abt. 1948, d: Dec 09, 2004 in San Antonio, Bexar, Texas, USA

..................6 Sheri Lynn Wolfson b: Jun 12, 1949 in Point Eustis, Virginia

..................6 Daniel Wolfson b: 1953 in Memphis, Shelby, Tennessee, USA

.... + Chery Lamb b: 1955

....................7 Susan Taylor Wolfson b: Dec 25, 1986 in Nashue, New Hampshire

....................7 Austin Wolfson b: Jan 06, 1988

....................7 Kendell Wolfson b: Jan 06, 1988

...........4 Peter R. Berlow b: Feb 12, 1894 in Ishpeming, Marquette, Michigan, USA, d: Jan 14, 1967 in Los Angeles, Los Angeles, California, USA

.... + Dora Goldstein b: Jul 10, 1894 in Chicago, Cook, Illinois, USA, d: Nov 08, 1994 in Los Angeles, Los Angeles, California, USA

...........4 Rose Anna "Hinda" Berlow b: 1897 in St Paul, Dakota, Minnesota, USA, d: 1982 in Chicago, Cook,

.... + Benjamin Isaac Twery b: 1897 in Chicago, Cook, Illinois, USA, d: 1972 in Florida, USA

...............5 Raymond Twery b: 1930 in Chicago, Cook, Illinois, USA

.... + Maxine Norma Rudman b: 1934 in St Louis, Missouri, USA, m: 1954 in Evanston, Cook, Illinois, USA

..................6 Michael Jay Twery b: 1956 in Champaign, Champaign, Illinois, USA

.... + Linda Ai Kheng Wong b: 1960, m: 1989 in Charlotte, Mecklenburg, North Carolina, USA 6 Scott Craig Twery b: 1958 in St Louis, Missouri, USA

.... + Deborah Carol Theissen b: 1955 in Connecticut, USA, m: 1990 in Atlanta, De Kalb, Georgia, USA

....................7 Hanna Rose Twery b: 1992 in Atlanta, De Kalb, Georgia, USA

..................6 Seth Aaron Twery b: 1961 in Carmel, Monterey, California, USA

.... + Marrene Del Pierce b: 1963 in Charlotte, Mecklenburg, North Carolina, USA

....................7 Nicole Twery b: Jan 31, 1997 in Charlotte, Mecklenburg, North Carolina, USA

..................6 Bruce Hugh Twery b: 1963 in Charlotte, Mecklenburg, North Carolina, USA

.... + Teresa "Tina" Sicher b: 1961 in Kane, McKean, Pennsylvania, USA, m: 1990 in Kane, McKean, Pennsylvania, USA

....................7 Alexander Twery b: 1991 in Baltimore, Maryland, USA

.................7 Joshua Keller Twery b: 1992 in Baltimore, Maryland, USA
.................7 Benjamin Louis Twery b: 1994 in Baltimore, Maryland, USA
.................7 Twery b: Jan 2000
...........4 Maurice P "Moshe" Berlow b: Mar 22, 1899 in Sault Sainte Marie, Chippewa, Michigan, USA, d: Mar 1983 in Miami, Dade, Florida, USA
.... + Evelyn Feuereisen b: May 31, 1909 in New York, New York, USA, m: Feb 02, 1933 in Chicago, Cook, Illinois, USA, d: Aug 26, 1997 in Los Angeles, Los Angeles, California, USA
.............5 Irene Bunny Berlow b: 1936 in Chicago, Cook, Illinois, USA, d: 1967 in Chicago, Cook, Illinois, USA
.............5 Linda Rachael Berlow b: 1938 in Chicago, Cook, Illinois, USA
.... + Dennis Kluk b: Apr 15, 1946 in Racine, Racine, Wisconsin, USA, m: Nov 25, 2002 in Skokie, Cook, Illinois, USA
.... + Rose b: 1910 in Chicago, Cook, Illinois, USA, m: 1982 in Miami Beach, Dade, Florida, USA
...........4 Sarah Berlow b: 1900 in Calumet, Houghton, Michigan, USA, d: 1983 in California, USA
.... + William Romain b: 1898 in Chicago, Cook, Illinois, USA, d: 1988 in California, USA
.............5 Joseph R "Jerry" Romain b: 1930 in Chicago, Cook, Illinois, USA
.... + Gail b: 1945 in Chicago, Cook, Illinois, USA
...............6 Matthew Romain b: 1972 in Chicago, Cook, Illinois, USA
.... + Sheila b: 1938 in Chicago, Cook, Illinois, USA, m: 1986 in Chicago, Cook, Illinois, USA
...........4 Gordon P Berlow b: 1907 in Calumet, Houghton, Michigan, USA, d: Feb 27, 1967 in Chicago, Cook, Illinois, USA
.... + Esther Wigodski b: May 19, 1911 in Chicago, Cook, Illinois, USA, d: Sep 1984 in Chicago, Cook, Illinois, USA
.............5 Bruce Berlow b: 1941 in Chicago, Cook, Illinois, USA
.............5 Susan Berlow b: 1946 in Chicago, Cook, Illinois, USA
......2 Itzik Prop b: 1818 in Skaudvile, Kovno, Russia, d: 1893 in Skaudvile, Kovno, Russia
...... + Tzerna Chaya Rosenzweig b: 1823 in Kovno, Kovno, Russia; Same location as Kaunas, Lithuania, m: 1836 in Skaudvile, Kovno, Russia, d: 1911 in Skaudvile, Kovno, Russia; Skaudvile, Taurage, Lithuainia/Skaudvile, Taurage, Lithuania/
.........3 Dov-Ber "Bertzik" Prop b: Apr 1844 in Skaudvile, Kovno, Russia, d: 1923 in Taurage, Taurage, Lithuania
.... + (first sister Shraga) b: 1852 in Tavrig, Kovno, Russia, m: 1870 in Tavrig, Kovno, Russia, d: 1879 in Tavrig, Kovno, Russia
...........4 Sira Prop b: Mar 1871 in Tavrig, Kovno, Russia, d: Mar 26, 1944 in Kovno, Kovno, Lithuania,; Ninth Fort, Holocaust
.... + Shlomo Yitzchak Abramovich b: Jun 02, 1866 in Kovno, Kovno, Russia, m: Abt. 1893 in Tavrig, Kovno, Russia, d: Mar 26, 1944 in Kovno, Kovno, Lithuania; Kovno Ghetto, Ninth Fort
.............5 Max "Mordechai" Abramovich b: 1894 in Tavrig, Kovno, Russia, d: 1944 in Auschwitz, Poland; Holocaust
.... + Anna Chana Heyman b: Dec 1902 in Kelm, Kovno, Russia, m: Abt. 1925, d: 1992 in Israel
...............6 Boris Abramovich b: 1926 in Tavrig, Kovno, Lithuania, d: Mar 26, 1944 in Kovno, Kovno, Lithuania; Kovno Ghetto, Holocaust
...............6 Rivka " Rivochka" Abramovich b: 1929 in Kovno, Kovno, Russia
.... + Ronald Theodore Garrel b: 1925 in New York, New York, USA
.................7 Maxine Garrel b: Apr 14, 1958 in New York, New York, USA
.................7 Arie Lawrence "Aharon" Garrel b: Jul 21, 1960 in New York, New York, USA
.... + Rosemary Belgrader b: 1962 in New York, New York, USA
...................8 Joseph Garrel b: Jan 02, 1999 in New York, New York, USA
...................8 Shmuel Garrel b: Jan 02, 1999 in New York, New York, USA
.................7 Stuart "Shimon" Garrel b: Jan 1962 in New York, New York, USA, d: 1987 in New York, New York, USA
.................7 Michelle Ellen Garrel b: Dec 19, 1962 in New York, New York, USA
.... + Andrew Barnet Hona Freedland b: 1959 in Toronto, Ontario, Canada
...................8 Avraham Yonaton Freedland b: Sep 01, 1984 in Jerusalem, Israel
...................8 David Elihu Freedland b: May 16, 1989 in Jerusalem, Israel
...................8 Mordechai Shalom Freedland b: Feb 25, 1992 in Jerusalem, Israel
...................8 Chana Yochevet Edel Freeland b: Dec 20, 1993 in Jerusalem, Israel
...................8 Sara Feigie Freedland b: Aug 27, 1995 in Jerusalem, Israel
...................8 Shimon Elazar Freedland b: Dec 27, 1996 in Jerusalem, Israel
...................8 Nachman Freedland b: Jul 26, 1998 in Jerusalem, Israel
.................7 Barry David "Baruch" Garrel b: Feb 22, 1964 in New York, New York, USA
.... + Linda Gitlin

...................8 Justin Garrel b: Mar 1995 in Livingston, Essex, New Jersey, USA
...................8 Gershon Aron Garrel b: May 1998 in New York, New York, USA
...................7 Daniel Sheldon Garrel b: May 22, 1966 in New York, New York, USA
...................7 Gary Ira "Gershon" Garrel b: Sep 11, 1968 in New York, New York, USA
...................7 Jonathan Steven "Jay" Garrel b: Sep 17, 1970 in New York, New York, USA
.... + Elisheva Sangilovsky
...................8 Simcha Eliyahu Chain Garrel b: Apr 1997 in New York, New York, USA
..............5 Reuven Abramovich b: 1895 in Tavrig, Kovno, Russia, d: Aug 04, 1944 in Port Kunda Labor-Camp, Estonia
.... + Basia Strassburg b: May 26, 1903 in Kovno, Kovno, Russia, d: Dec 30, 1979 in Montréal, Quebec, Canada
..................6 Boria "Boris" Abramovich b: Feb 02, 1928 in Kovno, Kovno, Russia, d: Aug 04, 1944 in Port Kunda Labor-Camp, Estonia; Holocaust
..................6 Miriam Mussie "Brahms" Abramovich b: Jun 18, 1930 in Kovno, Kovno, Russia, d: Jul 08, 2008 in Montréal, Quebec, Canada
.... + Herman Reich b: Jan 04, 1914 in Jablonka, Podkarpackie, Poland, m: Aug 29, 1948 in Montréal, Quebec, Canada, d: Aug 23, 2005 in Montréal, Quebec, Canada
...................7 Robert Irving Reich b: Nov 21, 1949 in Montréal, Quebec, Canada
.... + Ann Edwards b: May 24, 1950 in Montréal, Quebec, Canada, m: Jun 08, 1970 in Montréal, Quebec, Canada
...................8 Jessica Danielle Reich b: Sep 20, 1972 in Cleveland, Cuyahoga, Ohio, USA
...................8 Jamey Bradley Reich b: Jul 01, 1974 in Cleveland, Cuyahoga, Ohio, USA
...................7 Celia Reich b: May 20, 1953 in Montréal, Quebec, Canada
.... + Stanley Nattel b: Sep 25, 1951 in Haifa, Israel, m: Sep 25, 1973 in Montréal, Quebec, Canada
...................8 Jonathan Dov Nattel b: Apr 25, 1980 in Indianapolis, Marion, Indiana, USA
...................8 Ilana Batya Nattel b: Oct 17, 1983 in Montréal, Quebec, Canada
.... + Yehunda "Hooie" Turetsky m: Nov 22, 2007 in Montréal, Quebec, Canada
...................9 Chaim Turetsky b: Aug 28, 2008 in New York, New York, USA
...................9 Shira Turetsky b: Aug 17, 2010 in New York, New York, USA
...................8 Daniel Yehuda Nattel b: May 27, 1986 in Montréal, Quebec, Canada
...................8 Sarah Naomi Nattel b: Feb 05, 1991 in Montréal, Quebec, Canada
...................7 Mark Edward Reich b: Nov 17, 1954 in Montréal, Quebec, Canada
.... + Sharon Miriam Wildstein b: Dec 05, 1960 in New York, New York, USA, m: Nov 25, 1990
...................8 Jacob Michael Reich b: 1996 in Atlanta, Fulton, Georgia, USA
...................8 Benjamin David Reich b: Apr 20, 1999 in Atlanta, Fulton, Georgia, USA
...................8 Micah Reich b: 2002 in Atlanta, Fulton, Georgia, USA
..............5 Leo "Brahm" Abramovich b: Apr 1897 in Tavrig, Kovno, Russia, d: Aug 24, 1994 in Worcester, Worcester, Massachusetts, USA
.... + Clara "Kisiuta" Margolin b: Aug 16, 1903 in Kovno, Kovno, Russia, m: 1930 in Tavrig, Kovno, Lithuania, d: Jan 10, 1957 in Worcester, Worcester, Massachusetts, USA
..................6 Alexander Emanuel Brahm b: 1932 in Berlin, Stadt Berlin, Berlin, Germany, d: 1951 in New York, New York, USA
..................6 Gabriel Noah Brahm b: Dec 24, 1934, d: Jul 11, 1993 ; Age: 58
.... + Carol Louise Walters b: Aug 09, 1942 in Gloucester, Essex, Massachusetts, USA, m: 1962 in Massachusetts, USA
...................7 Gabriel Noah Brahm b: May 29, 1963 in Worcester, Worcester, Massachusetts, USA
...................7 Laura Clare Brahm b: Jul 28, 1964 in Valley City, Barnes, North Dakota, USA
...................7 Nancy Sheara Brahm b: Sep 18, 1966 in Haverhill, Essex, Massachusetts, USA
.... + Paul Price b: Feb 11, 1962 in Walnut Creek, Contra Costa, California, USA
..............5 Rivka Leah Abramovich b: 1898 in Tavrig, Kovno, Russia, d: Jan 21, 1945 in Danzig, West Prussia; Stutthof Camp, Holocaust
.... + Samuel Griliches b: Aug 29, 1890, m: Dec 1919 in Kovno, Kovno, Russia, d: Jun 23, 1965 in New York, New York, USA
..................6 Josef Griliches b: Jun 04, 1923 in Köenigsberg, East Prussia
..............5 Arno "Abrams" Abramovich b: Aug 11, 1899 in Tavrig, Kovno, Russia, d: Jan 04, 2003 in London,
.... + Marjorie b: 1918 in New York, New York, USA, d: 1994 in New York, New York, USA
..................6 Louise Abrams b: 1950 in New York, New York, USA
.... + George Browning b: 1946 in New York, New York, USA
...................7 Simon Browning b: Dec 27, 2000 in New York, New York, USA

...................7 Leora Browning b: Dec 27, 2000 in New York, New York, USA
...............5 Benno Abramovich b: 1905 in Tavrig, Kovno, Russia, d: Aug 1941 in Kovno, Kovno, Lithuania; Shot in the
        Seventh Fort, Kovno
...............5 Yankel "Jolubas" Abramovich b: 1907 in Tavrig, Kovno, Russia, d: 1977 in Tel Aviv, Israel
.... + Bronnia "Brocha" Mazsel b: 1915 in Iekaterinoslav, Lithuania, m: Dec 12, 1939 in Kovno, Kovno,
        Russia, d: 1984 in New York, New York, USA
...................6 Ariela Abramovich b;Oct 24, 1941 in Kovno, Lithuania; Kovno Ghetto, d:23 Dec, 2008 in Paris, France
.... + Roman Sef b:Oct 06, 1931 in Moscow, Russia, d:Feb 20, 2009 in Paris, France
...................6 Solomon I 'Manya' Abramovich b: Dec 18, 1946 in Kovno, Kovno, Russia
.... + Gillian Armstrong b:1956 in New York, New York, USA, m:1989 in New York, New York, USA
.......................7 Alexander Abramovich b: Jan 05, 1992 in New York, New York, USA
.......................7 Natasha Abramovich b: Jan 06, 1996 in New York, New York, USA

.......................7 Jacob Abramovich b: 2001 in New York, New York, USA
...................6 Benjamin "Abramovich" Brahms b: Nov 11, 1948 in Kovno, Kovno, Russia
.... + Lena Mironova b: 1952 in New York, New York, USA, m: 1990 in New York, New York, USA
.......................7 Yacol Brahms b: Jan 01, 1992 in New York, New York, USA
...........4 Julius "Yudl" Propp b: Oct 18, 1872 in Tavrig, Kovno, Russia, d: 1977 in Peoria, Peoria, Illinois, USA
.... + Wanda Dobriner b: May 28, 1878 in Tilsit, Gumbinnen, East Prussia, Germany, m: Jun 19, 1909 in
        Laporte, Indiana, USA, d: May 28, 1940 in Peoria, Peoria, Illinois, USA; Age at Death: 60
...............5 Leo Isaac Propp b: Jul 29, 1909 in Peoria, Peoria, Illinois, USA, d: May 22, 2008 in Schaumburg, Cook,
        Illinois, USA
.... + Janet Rosen b: Jan 06, 1912 in Toronto, Ontario, Canada, m: 1944, d: Oct 1984 in Peoria Heights,
        Peoria, Illinois, USA
...................6 Lawrence Propp b: Mar 24, 1945 in Peror, d: Jul 28, 1983 in Cook, Illinois, USA
...................6 Gail Susan Propp b: Oct 10, 1947 in Peoria, Peoria, Illinois, USA
.... + Stephen Heckmyer b: 1947 in Chicago, Cook, Illinois, USA, d: May 11, 2003 in Chicago, Cook,
        Illinois, USA
.......................7 Joseph Heckmyer b: Dec 07, 1973 in Skokie, Cook, Illinois, USA
.......................7 Daniel Heckmyer b: Nov 22, 1976 in Skokie, Cook, Illinois, USA
.... + Marion Brown b: Apr 18, 1916 in Washington City, District Of Columbia, District of Columbia, USA, m: Abt.
        1996 in Los Angeles, Los Angeles, California, USA, d: May 29, 2002 in Yorba Linda, Orange, California, USA
...............5 Fred J. Propp b: Jun 19, 1910 in Farmington, Fulton, Illinois, USA, d: Dec 1983 in Peoria, Peoria, Illinois, USA;
        Age at Death: 72
...............5 Roy T. Propp b: Jun 26, 1916 in Farmington, Fulton, Illinois, USA, d: Mar 02, 2002 in Peoria, Peoria,
        Illinois, USA
.... + Marilyn Zvi b: 1928 in Chicago, Cook, Illinois, USA, m: 1950 in Peoria, Peoria, Illinois, USA
...................6 Sharon L Propp b: 1952 in Peoria, Peoria, Illinois, USA
.... + Michael Stein b: 1951 in Chicago, Cook, Illinois, USA
.......................7 Lesile Stein b: Aug 1986 in Chicago, Cook, Illinois, USA
.......................7 Anna Stein b: Aug 1988 in Highland Park, Lake, Illinois, USA
.......................7 Peter Stein b: Aug 1992 in Highland Park, Lake, Illinois, USA
...................6 Wanda Propp b: 1954 in Peoria, Peoria, Illinois, USA
.... + Larry Brunell b: 1953 in Chicago, Cook, Illinois, USA
.......................7 Rebecca Brunell b: Aug 1986 in Jackson, Hinds, Mississippi, USA
.......................7 Adam Brunell b: Jul 1988 in Jackson, Hinds, Mississippi, USA
...................6 Judith J. Propp b: Feb 03, 1957 in Peoria, Peoria, Illinois, USA
...........4 Dvora Propp b: Dec 05, 1872 in Tavrig, Kovno, Russia, d: Jan 12, 1942 in Moscow, Russia; Holocaust
.... + Notel Stolov b: 1875 in Tavrig, Kovno, Russia, m: Jul 14, 1934 in Kovno, Kovno, Lithuania, d: Oct 04, 1941
        in Siauliai Ghetto, Kovno, Lithuania
...............5 Rivka Stolov b: 1907 in Tavrig, Kovno, Russia, d: 1976 in Moscow, Russia
.... + Chaim David Rabinovich b: 1906 in Ukmerge, Lithuania, m: Jul 24, 1934 in Tavrig, Kovno, Russia, d: 1969
        in Moscow, Russia
...................6 Genia Rabinovitz b: 1936 in Kovno, Kovno, Lithuania
.... + Efim Pinsky b: 1925 in Gomel, Russia, m: 1961 in Moscow, Russia
.......................7 Anatoly "Tolya" Pinsky b: 1963 in Moscow, Russia
.... + Irina b: 1967 in Moscow, Russia, m: 1986 in Moscow, Russia
...........................8 David "Dima" Pinsky b: 1988 in New York, New York, USA
...........................8 Elizabeth Liza Pinsky b: 1995 in New York, New York, USA

...................7 Leonid Pinsky b: 1969 in Moscow, Russia
...............5 Sheva Stolov b: 1908 in Tavrig, Kovno, Russia, d: 1983 in Moscow, Russia
...........4 Golda O. Prop b: Aug 14, 1877 in Tavrig, Kovno, Russia, d: Oct 04, 1941 in Kovno, Kovno, Lithuania
....   + Zalman Kaplan b: 1873 in Kovno, Kovno, Russia, m: Abt. 1911 in Tavrig, Kovno, Russia, d: Oct 04, 1941 in Kovno, Kovno, Lithuania
...............5 Riva Kaplan b: 1913 in Tavrig, Kovno, Russia, d: Oct 04, 1941 in Kovno, Kovno, Lithuania; Holocaust
....   + (second sister Shraga) b: 1855 in Tavrig, Kovno, Russia, m: 1881 in Tavrig, Kovno, Russia, d: 1884 in Tavrig, Kovno, Russia
...........4 Lena "Tzerna-Elke" Propp b: Jun 1864 in Tavrig, Kovno, Russia, d: Feb 10, 1946 in Chicago, Cook, Illinois, USA
....   + Joseph Leviton b: Feb 1858 in Tavrig, Kovno, Russia, m: Jun 1901 in Tavrig, Kovno, Russia, d: Oct 14, 1942 in Chicago, Cook, Illinois, USA
...............5 Isadore Leviton b: Abt. 1881 in Lithuania
....   + Ella Propp b: Abt. 1883 in Lithuania
...................6 Sydney Leviton b: Sep 11, 1905 in Chicago, Cook, Illinois, USA
...................6 Thelma Leviton b: Dec 15, 1907 in Chicago, Cook, Illinois, USA
...................6 Max Leviton b: Oct 08, 1912 in Chicago, Cook, Illinois, USA
...................6 Ruth Leviton b: Mar 21, 1916 in Chicago, Cook, Ilinois, USA, d: Feb 15, 2005 in Asbury Park, Monmouth, New Jersey; SelfDeathAge: 88
...................6 William Leviton b: Mar 24, 1917 in Chicago, Cook, Illinois, USA
...................6 Leo Leviton b: Mar 24, 1917 in Chicago, Cook, Illinois, USA, d: Sep 15, 1995 in Syracuse, Onondaga, New York, USA; Age at Death: 78
...................6 Blanche Leviton b: Feb 27, 1920 in Chicago, Cook, Illinois, USA
....   + John Edward Brock m: Jun 04, 1960 in Cook, Illinois, USA
...............5 Sara Leviton b: Jul 1888 in Chicago, Cook, Illinois, USA, d: Sep 06, 1984 in Chicago, Cook, Illinois, USA
...............5 Nathan Leviton b: May 1890 in Chicago, Cook, Illinois, USA, d: May 1974 in Los Angeles, Los Angeles, California, USA
...............5 Theodore J. Leviton b: Aug 1892 in Chicago, Cook, Illinois, USA
...............5 Frank Leviton b: Apr 1894 in Chicago, Cook, Illinois, USA, d: Dec 06, 1995 in Chicago, Cook, Illinois, USA
....   + (third sister Shraga) b: 1852 in Tavrig, Kovno, Russia, m: 1886 in Tavrig, Kovno, Russia, d: 1905 in Tavrig, Kovno, Russia
...........4 Max "Motl" Propp b: Dec 15, 1888 in Tavrig, Kovno, Russia, d: Nov 24, 1970 in Los Angeles, Los Angeles, California, USA
...........4 Solomon "Selig" Propp b: Jan 15, 1890 in Tavrig, Kovno, Russia, d: Mar 18, 1941 in Los Angeles, Los Angeles, California, USA
....   + Rose Horn b: Aug 25, 1895 in Lithuania, m: Abt. 1923 in United Kingdom, d: Nov 29, 1985 in Los Angeles, Los Angeles, California, USA
...............5 Daniel Berle Propp b: Nov 06, 1925 in Los Angeles, Los Angeles, California, USA, d: May 01, 2006 in Marcola, Lane, Oregon, USA
....   + Gloria "Cohan" Abbott b: 1933 in Los Angeles, Los Angeles, California, USA, m: 1954 in Los Angeles, Los Angeles, California, USA
...............5 Norma Hermein Propp b: Jul 15, 1932 in Los Angeles, Los Angeles, California, USA
....   + Lionel Freeman b: 1929 in Los Angeles, Los Angeles, California, USA, m: 1952 in Los Angeles, Los Angeles, California, USA
...................6 Scott Alan Freeman b: Dec 27, 1952 in Los Angeles, Los Angeles, California, USA
...................6 Gale Allison Freeman b: Feb 23, 1955 in Los Angeles, Los Angeles, California, USA
...........4 Isadore "Itzik" B. Propp b: Jan 25, 1894 in Tavrig, Kovno, Russia, d: Feb 20, 1981 in Oakland, Alameda, California, USA
....   + Cecilia Levy b: Oct 29, 1901 in Baltimore, Maryland, USA, m: 1925, d: Aug 05, 1985 in Oakland, Alameda, California, USA
...............5 Burton Monroe Propp b: Dec 24, 1926 in Hannibal, Marion, Missouri, USA
....   + Joan Elise Kistler b: Oct 12, 1930 in San Leandro, Alameda, California, USA
...........4 Chaim Propp b: Aug 12, 1894 in Tavrig, Kovno, Russia, d: 1941 in Zhaleznovodsk, Caucuses, Russia, Holocaust
...........4 Sarah Propp b: 1898 in Tavrig, Kovno, Russia, d: 1944 in Camp Stutthof, Poland; Holocaust
....   + Elija Flaks b: 1891 in Tavrig, Kovno, Russia, m: Feb 28, 1926 in Radviliškiai, Kauno, Lithuania, d: 1943 in Shavel Ghetto
...........4 Jenny "Genia" Propp b: Apr 20, 1898 in Tavrig, Kovno, Russia, d: Dec 12, 1996 in Charlotte, Mecklenburg, North Carolina, USA

.... + Jacob David "Yankel" Baicovitz b: Sep 29, 1895 in Kovno, Kovno, Russia, m: Abt. 1930 in Tavrig, Kovno, Lithuania, d: May 10, 1970 in Charlotte, Mecklenburg, North Carolina, USA
..............5 Leib Baicovitz b: 1931 in Tavrig, Kovno, Russia, d: 1936 in Tavrig, Kovno, Russia
..............5 Zahava "Zava" Baicovitz b: 1932 in Tavrig, Kovno, Russia, d: Charlotte, Mecklenburg, North Carolina,
.... + Thomas Rosenberg b: 1931 in Habana, Ciego de Avila, Cuba, m: 1955 in Habana, Ciego de Avila, Cuba, d: Charlotte, Mecklenburg, North Carolina, USA
................6 Leora Marian Rosenberg b: 1957 in Habana, Ciego de Avila, Cuba
.... + Steven Mark Levy b: 1954 in New York, New York, USA
...................7 Michael Philip Levy b: Jun 30, 1989 in New York, New York, USA
...................7 David Abraham Levy b: Jun 30, 1989 in New York, New York, USA
...................7 Benjamin Zalman Levy b: May 17, 1993 in New York, New York, USA
................6 Sarah Rose Rosenberg b: 1959 in Habana, Ciego de Avila, Cuba
.... + Shmuel Weinstein b: 1960 in Richmond, Wise, Virginia, USA
...................7 Chana Sima Weinstein b: Sep 26, 1986 in Charlotte, Mecklenburg, North Carolina, USA
...................7 Chaya Mushka Weinstein b: Feb 26, 1988 in Newark, New Castle, Delaware, USA
...................7 Golda Miriam Weinstein b: Feb 14, 1990 in Pittsburgh, Allegheny, Pennsylvania, USA
...................7 Chasia Shoshana Weinstein b: Sep 08, 1991 in Pittsburgh, Allegheny, Pennsylvania, USA
...................7 Nechama Aviva Weinstein b: Jun 10, 1993 in Pittsburgh, Allegheny, Pennsylvania, USA
...................7 Avram Yitzchak Weinstein b: Jan 29, 1995 in Pittsburgh, Allegheny, Pennsylvania, USA
...................7 Menachem Mendel Weinstein b: Sep 10, 1996
...................7 Shira Malka Weinstein b: Oct 12, 1998 in Pittsburgh, Allegheny, Pennsylvania, USA
...................7 Yisrael Arie Lieb Weinstein b: Jul 2000 in Pittsburgh, Allegheny, Pennsylvania, USA
...................7 Meir Levi Weinstein b: Aug 2002 in Pittsburgh, Allegheny, Pennsylvania, USA
................6 Cynthia Ann Rosenberg b: 1961 in Miami Beach, Dade, Florida, USA
.... + Carlus Felipe Jaramillo b: Aug 20, 1962 in Bogotá, Bolivar, Colombia
...................7 Daniel Isaac Jaramillo b: Aug 14, 1996 in Charlotte, Mecklenburg, North Carolina, USA
...................7 Alexander Jacob Jaramillo b: Jan 03, 1999 in Bogotá, Bolivar, Colombia
.........3 Leib Propp b: 1853 in Skaudvile, Kovno, Russia
.........3 Ida "Chaya" Propp b: Aug 03, 1856 in Skaudvile, Kovno, Russia, d: Jan 14, 1936 in Chicago, Cook, Illinois, USA
.... + Aronson m: Chicago, Cook, Illinois, USA
.... + Louis "Aryeh Leib" Blumenthal b: Apr 20, 1844 in Iloki, Kovno, Russia, m: 1878 in Königsberg, East Prussia, d: Dec 1917 in Malmö, Kalmar, Sweden
.............4 Theodore "Noak" Blumenthal b: Dec 15, 1879 in Königsberg, East Prussia, d: Feb 22, 1927 in Chicago, Cook, Illinois, USA
.... + Mary Furlett b: 1888 in Chicago, Cook, Illinois, USA, d: Sep 07, 1957 in Chicago, Cook, Illinois, USA
..............5 Ruth L Blumenthal b: 1909 in Chicago, Cook, Illinois, USA, d: Jan 1992 in Chicago, Cook, Illinois, USA
.... + Edward Gradman b: Jul 14, 1911 in Chicago, Cook, Illinois, USA, m: Sep 10, 1939 in Chicago, Cook, Illinois, USA, d: Mar 1979 in Chicago, Cook, Illinois, USA
..................6 Tanisse Gradman b: 1948 in Chicago, Cook, Illinois, USA
..................6 Sidney Gradman b: 1950 in Chicago, Cook, Illinois, USA
..............5 Ceil Blumenthal b: 1911 in Chicago, Cook, Illinois, USA
.... + Leo Jaffee b: May 13, 1913 in Chicago, Cook, Illinois, USA, m: 1941 in Chicago, Cook, Illinois, USA, d: Sep 1972 in Chicago, Cook, Illinois, USA
..............5 Arthur Blumenthal b: 1915 in Chicago, Cook, Illinois, USA, d: 1991 in Chicago, Cook, Illinois, USA
.............4 Samuel "Shimon" Blumenthal b: Jul 26, 1882 in Königsburg, East Prussia, d: Apr 1973 in Chicago, Cook, Illinois, USA
.... + Gertrude Givens b: Jul 01, 1899 in Poland, d: Oct 1973 in Chicago, Cook, Illinois, USA
..............5 Lucyle H. "Lucy" Blumenthal b: May 16, 1923 in Gary, Lake, Indiana, USA, d: Aug 11, 1999 in Portland, Cumberland, Maine, USA
.... + Jack Fein b: Feb 22, 1922 in Chicago, Cook, Illinois, USA, m: Abt. 1947 in Chicago, Cook, Illinois, USA
..................6 David Allen Fein b: May 15, 1949 in Chicago, Cook, Illinois, USA
.... + Rita May Leonard b: Jul 31, 1949 in New Hanover, North Carolina, USA
...................7 Aaron Leonard Gabriel Fein b: Jun 29, 1977 in Guilford, North Carolina
...................7 Dana Catherine Fein b: Mar 11, 1981 in Guilford, North Carolina
...................7 Margot Fein b: 1986 in Durham, Durham, North Carolina, USA
..................6 Judith Gale Fein b: Feb 23, 1951 in Chicago, Cook, Illinois, USA
..................6 Joanna Maria Fein b: Jun 28, 1959 in Durham, Durham, North Carolina, USA

.................7 Jacob Jack b: Nov 28, 1989 in Durham, Durham, North Carolina, USA
...............6 Laura Jean Fein b: Jun 14, 1961 in Durham, Durham, North Carolina, USA
.... + David Hesselink
.............5 Harold Sidney Blumenthal b: Dec 08, 1925 in Chicago, Cook, Illinois, USA, d: Abt. 1999
.............5 Isadore M Blumenthal b: 1907
..........4 Herman Blumenthal b: Jul 20, 1887 in Malmö, Kalmar, Sweden, d: Nov 18, 1887 in Malmö, Kalmar, Sweden
..........4 Dora Judith Blumenthal b: Jul 12, 1888 in Malmö, Kalmar, Sweden, d: Sep 13, 1888 in Malmö, Kalmar, Sweden
..........4 Charles "Betzalel Moshe" Blumenthal b: Aug 26, 1889 in Malmö, Kalmar, Sweden, d: Dec 18, 1960
.... + Bertha Gelb b: Oct 26, 1890 in Chicago, Cook, Illinois, USA, m: 1911 in Chicago, Cook, Illinois, USA, d: Mar 1982 in Highland Park, Lake, Illinois, USA
.............5 Sunoll Allen Blumenthal b: Jan 31, 1913 in Chicago, Cook, Illinois, USA, d: Jun 01, 1996 in Northbrook, Cook, Illinois, USA
.... + Frema Horwitch b: 1917 in Chicago, Cook, Illinois, USA, m: Jun 27, 1945, d: 1981 in Chicago, Cook, Illinois, USA
................6 Lyn Blumenthal b: 1942 in Chicago, Cook, Illinois, USA, d: 1987 in Chicago, Cook, Illinois, USA
................6 Alan D Blumenthal b: Aug 07, 1947 in Chicago, Cook, Illinois, USA
..........4 Unnamed Blumenthal b: Jan 07, 1891 in Malmö, Kalmar, Sweden, d: Jan 07, 1891 in Malmö, Kalmar, Sweden
..........4 Henrietta "Gerda Judith" Blumenthal b: Sep 18, 1892 in Malmö, Kalmar, Sweden, d: Sep 13, 1966 in Chicago, Cook, Illinois, USA
.... + Miller b: 1891 in Chicago, Cook, Illinois, USA, m: 1912 in Chicago, Cook, Illinois, USA, d: 1915 in Chicago, Cook, Illinois, USA
.... + Ivan Charnoff b: Jun 05, 1893 in Byalistock, Russia, m: 1921 in Chicago, Cook, Illinois, USA, d: Jan 18, 1953 in Chicago, Cook, Illinois, USA
.............5 Esther Charnoff b: 1916 in Chicago, Cook, Illinois, USA, d: 1991 in Chicago, Cook, Illinois, USA
.... + Armin Maag b: Jun 26, 1895 in Chicago, Cook, Illinois, USA, d: Oct 1981 in East Hampton, Suffolk, New York, USA
.... + Harold Lewis Nimz b: 1909 in Chicago, Cook, Illinois, USA, m: 1928 in Chicago, Cook, Illinois, USA, d: 1956 in Chicago, Cook, Illinois, USA
................6 David L. Nimz b: Oct 03, 1935 in Chicago, Cook, Illinois, USA
.... + Sally J. Lucks m: Feb 27, 1960 in Chicago, Cook, Illinois, USA
................6 Linda Nimz b: 1941 in Chicago, Cook, Illinois, USA
.... + Donald Ryan b: 1940 in New York, New York, USA
.................7 David Ryan b: 1971 in New York, New York, USA
.................7 Gail Ryan b: 1973 in New York, New York, USA
.................7 Nora Ryan b: 1983 in New York, New York, USA
.............5 Irving Charnoff b: 1918 in Chicago, Cook, Illinois, USA, d: 1985 in New York, New York, USA
.... + Helen
........3 Bluma Sora Propp b: Sep 1856 in Skaudvile, Kovno, Russia, d: May 11, 1917 in Chicago, Cook, Illinois, USA
.... + Philip (Feivel Yitzhak) Propp b: May 14, 1855 in Gaure, Kovno, Russia, m: 1879 in Skaudvile, Kovno, Russia, d: Dec 18, 1920 in Chicago, Cook, Illinois, USA
..........4 Devorah "Dora" Propp b: Sep 27, 1881 in Gaure, Kovno, Russia, d: Aug 18, 1933 in Chicago, Cook, Illinois, USA
..........4 Anna Propp b: Apr 19, 1883 in Tavrig, Kovno, Russia, d: Oct 14, 1958 in Chicago, Cook, Illinois, USA
..........4 Charles H. "Solomon" Propp b: May 1884 in Tavrig, Kovno, Russia, d: Jun 07, 1940 in South Bend, St Joseph, Indiana, USA
.... + Sophia Brooks b: England, m: Jan 25, 1910 in Chicago, Cook, Illinois, USA, d: 1984 in South Bend, St Joseph, Indiana, USA
.............5 Elliott Stanley Propp b: Nov 10, 1910 in Michigan City, La Porte, Indiana, USA, d: Aug 10, 1979 in Los Angeles, Los Angeles, California, USA
.... + Joan Muriel Zapolen b: Jun 01, 1912 in Chicago, Cook, Illinois, USA, m: 1939 in Chicago, Cook, Illinois, USA, d: May 24, 1991 in Los Angeles, Los Angeles, California, USA
................6 Virginia C. "Dina" Propp b: Mar 16, 1941 in Chicago, Cook, Illinois, USA
.... + James L. Divine m: Jan 10, 1958 in Cook, Illinois, USA
.................7 Michael James Devine b: Oct 06, 1958 in Los Angeles, Los Angeles, California, USA
.... + Gwendlen "Wendy" Sladen b: Mar 05, 1961 in Los Angeles, Los Angeles, California, USA
.....................8 Rebecca Angela Devine b: Mar 05, 1992 in Los Angeles, Los Angeles, California, USA
.....................8 Emily Alexandra Devine b: Apr 15, 1994 in Los Angeles, Los Angeles, California, USA

....................7 Constance Ann Devine b: Jun 09, 1961 in Los Angeles, Los Angeles, California, USA
.... + Melvin Gallaway b: 1961 in Los Angeles, Los Angeles, California, USA
........................8 Melvin Gallaway b: Aug 1990 in Los Angeles, Los Angeles, California, USA
........................8 Brooklyn Gallaway b: May 1992 in Los Angeles, Los Angeles, California, USA
.... + Robert L Melville b: 1938 in Los Angeles, Los Angeles, California, USA
...............5 Earle Brooks Propp b: Jun 02, 1915 in Decatur, Van Buren, Michigan, USA, d: Aug 19, 2004 in
         Bradenton, Manatee, Florida, USA
.... + Ruth C. Lentzer b: 1918 in Detroit, Wayne, Michigan, USA
.................6 Carla Diane Propp b: 1945 in Chicago, Cook, Illinois, USA
.... + Gilbert Bernard Ceifetz b: 1942 in Detroit, Wayne, Michigan, USA, m: Abt. 1964
....................7 Glenn Ceifetz b: 1966 in Westland, Wayne, Michigan, USA
....................7 Dean Ceifetz b: 1969 in Westland, Wayne, Michigan, USA
.................6 Charles H Propp b: May 16, 1948 in Chicago, Cook, Illinois, USA
...............5 Barbara "Bobby" Propp b: Abt. 1925 in South Bend, St Joseph, Indiana, USA, d: 2014 in Houston, Texas
.... + Arthur Wachtel b: May 01, 1918 in Chicago, Cook, Ilinois, USA, m: 1944 in Dade, Florida, d: Oct 22, 2003
         in Palm Desert, Riverside, California, USA; Age at Death: 85
.................6 Arthur Brooks Wachtel b: Sep 09, 1949 in Washington, DC, USA
.................6 Steven J Wachtel b: Sep 21, 1952 in Trinidad, Cartago, Costa Rica,d: 2014 in Los Angeles, California
         + Ronda Burns b: Sep 01, 1947 in Los Angeles, Los Angeles, California, USA
....................7 Melodie Wachtel
.................6 Sharon L Wachtel b: Aug 09, 1960 in San Diego, California
         + Sunil L Chada b: Feb 26, 1960, m: Los Angeles, Los Angeles, California, USA
....................7 Sasha Chada b: Jan 07, 1992 in Los Angeles, Los Angeles, California, USA
....................7 Misha Chada b: Sep 09, 1996 in Los Angeles, Los Angeles, California, USA
............4 Lillian Propp b: Jan 1888 in Chicago, Cook, Illinois, USA, d: Nov 15, 1970 in Chicago, Cook, Illinois, USA
.... + Bert Ruben b: Oct 11, 1887 in Grimsby, Lincolnshire, England, m: Dec 25, 1910 in Chicago Ward 19,
         Cook, Illinois, USA, d: Mar 05, 1978 in Chicago, Cook, Illinois, USA
...............5 Zerna "Tzerna Chaya" Ruben b: Nov 02, 1911 in Chicago, Cook, Illinois, USA, d: Apr 13, 1996 in
         Boynton, Palm Beach, Florida, USA
...............5 Blair "Buddy" S. Ruben b: May 05, 1918 in Chicago, Cook, Illinois, USA, d: Jan 16, 2003 in Casper,
         Natrona, Wyoming, USA
.... + Sylvia Ginsberg b: May 09, 1920 in Dalton, Whitfield, Georgia, USA, m: 1942 in Chicago, Cook, Illinois, USA,
         d: Aug 04, 1997 in Boynton, Palm Beach, Florida, USA
.................6 David Hillel Ruben b: Jul 25, 1943 in Chicago, Cook, Illinois, USA
.... + Eira Karlinsky b: 1945 in Wales, m: 1968 in New York, New York, USA
....................7 Anna Lilian Ruben b: Jun 04, 1972 in Glasgow, Lanarkshire, Scotland
.... + David Spivac b: Jul 28, 1970 in Paris, Ile-de-France, France, m: Jul 2000 in Paris, Ile-de-France,
         France
........................8 Arielle Leora Spivac b: Jul 20, 2004 in London, London, England
....................7 Sophie Rachel Ruben b: Aug 16, 1977 in London, London, England
.... + Adam Silverstein b: Oct 20, 1976 in New York, New York, USA, m: Jul 1999 in Cambridge,
         Cambridgeshire, England
........................8 Ella Zoe Silverstein b: Feb 18, 2006 in London, London, England
........................8 Zara Eva Silverstein b: Jun 09, 2008 in London, London, England
........................8 Theo Silverstein b: Jan. 4, 2011 in London, London, England
....................7 Simon Daniel Ruben b: May 04, 1980 in London, London, England
.... + Natasha Simon b: Oct 14, 1980 in Caracas, Distrito Federal, Venezuela, m: 2008 in Caesarea,
         Israel
........................8 Asher Brian Ruben b: Jan. 11, 2012 in London England
........................8 Gabriella Sylvia Ruben b: Nov. 12, 2014 in London, England
.................6 Stuart J. Ruben b: Dec 09, 1945 in Chicago, Cook, Illinois, USA
.... + Estelle S. Schlager b: 1945 in Cincinnati, Clermont, Ohio, USA
....................7 Andrew Bruce Ruben b: 1969 in Columbus, Fairfield, Ohio, USA
.... + Kristi Bahr b: 1970 in Fairfax Station, Fairfax, Virginia, USA, m: 1995 in Fairfax Station, Fairfax,
         Virginia, USA
....................7 Brenda Ruben b: 1974 in Melbourne, Brevard, Florida, USA
........................8 Allison Ruben
.................6 Kenneth Louis Ruben b: Mar 03, 1949 in Birmingham, Jefferson, Alabama, USA
............4 Michael Herman Propp b: Dec 11, 1892 in Chicago, Cook, Illinois, USA, d: Jul 14, 1949 in Chicago, Cook,
         Illinois, USA

.... + Cecliah Mendelsohn b: 1893 in Philadelphia, Philadelphia, Pennsylvania, USA, m: 1918 in Chicago, Cook, Illinois, USA, d: 1975 in Philadelphia, Philadelphia, Pennsylvania, USA

...............5 Phyllis E Propp b: Jan 04, 1924 in Chicago, Cook, Illinois, USA, d: Jan 23, 2002 in Daytona Beach, Volusia, Florida, USA

.... + Milton D. Greenberg b: 1919 in Philadelphia, Philadelphia, Pennsylvania, USA, m: Abt. 1968

.........3 Devorah "Dora" Propp b: 1857 in Skaudvile, Kovno, Russia, d: Aug 18, 1933 in Chicago, Cook, Illinois, USA

.... + Isaac Chaim Gershman b: Dec 15, 1852 in Germany, m: 1882 in Chicago, Cook, Illinois, USA, d: 1921 in Chicago, Cook, Illinois, USA

............4 Celia Gershman b: Sep 18, 1885 in Chicago, Cook, Illinois, USA, d: May 1974 in South Bend, St Joseph, Indiana, USA

.... + Charles Berlow b: Aug 02, 1883 in Wilkes-Barre, Luzerne, Pennsylvania, USA, d: Mar 03, 1947 in South Bend, St Joseph, Indiana, USA

............4 Abraham L Gershman b: Dec 23, 1887 in Skaudvile, Kovno, Russia, d: Jan 01, 1944 in Chicago, Cook, Illinois, USA

.... + Mary Abraham b: Abt. 1888 in Russia

...............5 Jacob Gershman b: Nov 30, 1914, d: May 14, 1931 in Chicago, Cook, Illinois, USA

...............5 David Gershman b: Abt. 1916 in Russia

.... + Fannie b: Abt. 1910

...............5 Issie Gershman b: Abt. 1919 in Russia

...............5 Samuel Gershman b: Abt. 1921 in Russia

...............5 Francis Gershman b: Abt. 1924 in Chicago, Cook, Illinois, USA

...............5 Ida Gershman b: Sep 02, 1925 in Chicago, Cook, Illinois, USA, d: Apr 1985 in Munster, Lake, Indiana, USA

............4 Isaac C. "Ike" Gershman b: Jun 20, 1894 in Chicago, Cook, Illinois, USA, d: Dec 1976 in Miami, Miami-dade, Florida, USA; Age at Death: 82

.... + Agnhild L b: Jul 02, 1899 in Malmö, Kalmar, Sweden, m: 1922 in Chicago, Cook, Illinois, USA, d: Sep 1983 in New York, New York, USA

...............5 David C. Gershman b: Apr 19, 1927 in Chicago, Cook, Illinois, USA

...............5 Richard K. Gershman b: Mar 01, 1929 in Chicago, Cook, Illinois, USA, d: Aug 26, 1998 in New Milford, CT

.........3 Max "Meyer' Propp b: Dec 23, 1857 in Skaudvile, Kovno, Russia, d: Mar 29, 1943 in Memphis, Shelby, Tennessee, USA

.... + Martha "Marta" Berlowitz b: Jun 23, 1866 in Smalininkai, East Prussia, m: Sep 28, 1887 in Chicago, Cook, Illinois, USA, d: Feb 23, 1940 in Memphis, Shelby, Tennessee, USA

............4 Clara P. Propp b: Aug 15, 1888 in Chicago, Cook, Illinois, USA, d: Jul 01, 1977 in Memphis, Shelby, Tennessee, USA

.... + George Washington. Meyer b: Feb 22, 1880 in Chicago, Cook, Illinois, USA, m: Dec 30, 1912 in Michigan City, La Porte, Indiana, USA, d: Feb 24, 1954 in Memphis, Shelby, Tennessee, USA

...............5 Myron P Meyer b: Jun 28, 1915 in Michigan City, La Porte, Indiana, USA, d: Jan 17, 1948 in Memphis, Shelby, Tennessee, USA

.... + Mary Dean Nix b: Jun 28, 1915 in Michigan City, La Porte, Indiana, USA, d: Jan 17, 1948 in Memphis, Shelby, Tennessee, USA

...............5 Robert "Bobby" Meyer b: Mar 01, 1920 in Michigan City, La Porte, Indiana, USA, d: Mar 05, 1997 in Memphis, Shelby, Tennessee, USA

............4 Anna Propp b: Jun 24, 1895 in Chicago, Cook, Illinois, USA, d: Mar 1977 in Chicago, Cook, Illinois, USA

.... + Louis David Smith b: Jul 10, 1889 in Chicago, Cook, Illinois, USA, m: 1916 in Chicago, Cook, Illinois, USA, d: Jul 1968 in Chicago, Cook, Illinois, USA

...............5 Lester H. Smith b: Oct 27, 1917 in Chicago, Cook, Illinois, USA, d: Mar 23, 2000 in Highland Park, Lake, Illinois, USA

.... + Nancy Joy Heyman b: Sep 04, 1924 in Fayette, Kentucky

..................6 Edwin "Eric" Smith b: Sep 29, 1946 in Jefferson, Kentucky

.... + Katharine "Kitty" Thomson b: 1951 in Boston, Suffolk, Massachusetts, USA, m: 1974 in Weston, Middlesex, Massachusetts, USA

....................7 Benjamin Clark Smith b: 1976 in Boston, Suffolk, Massachusetts, USA

....................7 George Louis Smith b: 1978 in New York, New York, USA

....................7 Andrew Laurence Smith b: 1980 in Boston, Suffolk, Massachusetts, USA

..................6 Louis David Smith II b: 1949 in Highland Park, Lake, Illinois, USA

..................6 Laurel Anne Smith b: 1951 in Highland Park, Lake, Illinois, USA

............4 Bertha "Berdie" Propp b: Apr 1897 in Michigan City, La Porte, Indiana, USA, d: Aug 02, 1965 in Milwaukee, Milwaukee, Wisconsin, USA

...........4 Grace Propp b: Jan 28, 1900 in Michigan City, La Porte, Indiana, USA, d: Sep 17, 1988 in New York, New York, USA
....   + Maurice Julius b: Apr 27 in New York, New York, USA, d: Aug 1977 in New York, New York, USA
....   + Frederick Eugene Alexander b: Mar 14, 1885 in Jersey City, New Jersey, m: Jul 15, 1920 in Michigan City, La Porte, Indiana, USA, d: Jan 17, 1958 in Contra Costa, California
..............5 Arthur E. Alexander b: Abt. 1924 in Michigan City
....   + Joan b: California, USA
................6 Jill Alexander b: 1946 in New York, New York, USA
....   + Kenneth Sprague b: 1947 in New York, New York, USA
...................7 Heather Sprague b: 1977 in New York, New York, USA
....   + Ian Wilson
................6 Michael Alexander b: 1951 in New York, New York, USA
....   + Heather Sprague
....   + Greta Hoda b: California, USA, m: 1994
...........4 Ruth D. Propp b: Aug 13, 1904 in Michigan City, La Porte, Indiana, USA, d: Nov 1993 in Memphis, Shelby, Tennessee, USA
....   + Jefferson Davis Marks b: Sep 19, 1902 in New Orleans, Orleans, Louisiana, USA, m: Abt. 1939 in Chicago, Cook, Illinois, USA, d: Sep 28, 1987 in Memphis, Shelby, Tennessee, USA
.........3 Sigmond Propp b: Apr 25, 1858 in Smalininkai, East Prussia, d: Sep 04, 1948 in Hollywood, Los Angeles, California, USA
....   + Sarah Florence Ringer b: Sep 1866 in Vilna, Vilna, Russia, m: May 21, 1885 in Chicago, Cook, Illinois, USA, d: 1934 in Chicago, Cook, Illinois, USA
...........4 Charles H. Propp b: Dec 17, 1887 in Chicago, Cook, Illinois, USA, d: Aug 23, 1963 in North Hollywood, Los Angeles, California, USA
...........4 Anna Dora Propp b: Oct 20, 1888 in Chicago, Cook, Illinois, USA, d: Mar 1965 in North Hollywood, Los Angeles, California, USA
....   + Mendel Frank Levin b: Nov 16, 1880 in Penza, Russia, m: Jun 1910 in Chicago, Cook, Illinois, USA, d: Jun 1923 in Los Angeles, Los Angeles, California, USA
..............5 Arthur Irving Levin b: May 29, 1911 in Los Angeles, Los Angeles, California, USA, d: Sep 25, 1999 in Los Angeles, Los Angeles, California, USA
....   + Dora Diane Melman b: Sep 27, 1907 in Los Angeles, Los Angeles, California, USA, m: 1942 in Los Angeles, Los Angeles, California, USA, d: Jan 13, 2003 in North Hollywood, Los Angeles, California, USA
................6 Ronna Adelyn Levin b: Aug 23, 1945 in Kings, California
....   + Robert F. Katz b: Abt. 1941, m: Aug 10, 1969 in Los Angeles City, California
................6 Melanie Frances Levin b: Feb 09, 1949 in Los Angeles, Los Angeles, California, USA
....   + Thomas C Montague b: May 23, 1950, m: Sep 03, 1976 in Los Angeles, California
..............5 Sidney F. Levine b: Jun 18, 1916 in Los Angeles, Los Angeles, California, USA, d: Oct 23, 1986 in North Hollywood, Los Angeles, California, USA
....   + Marion Goldie Schwartz b: Apr 17, 1912 in Los Angeles, Los Angeles, California, USA, m: Abt. 1944 in Los Angeles, Los Angeles, California, USA, d: Aug 19, 1996 in Orange, California
................6 Marsha Brona Levine b: Jul 13, 1945 in Los Angeles, Los Angeles, California, USA
....   + Lawrence N Krieger m: Aug 26, 1979 in Los Angeles, California
....   + Gary H Carmona b: Mar 14, 1940 in Los Angeles, Los Angeles, California, USA, m: 1967 in Los
...................7 Johsua Carmona
....   + Angelo A Segarra m: Mar 23, 1983 in Ventura, California
................6 Jerry Steven Levine b: Feb 10, 1949 in Los Angeles, Los Angeles, California, USA
...........4 Lillian "Nellie" Propp b: May 28, 1891 in Chicago, Cook, Illinois, USA, d: Feb 24, 1991 in Los Angeles, Los Angeles, California, USA
....   + David Julius Siskin b: Nov 03, 1891 in Chicago, Cook, Illinois, USA, m: Feb 02, 1918 in Chicago, Cook, d: Nov 30, 1932 in Chicago, Cook, Illinois, USA
..............5 Milton Sherwood Siskin b: Jan 30, 1922 in Chicago, Cook, Illinois, USA, d: Feb 22, 1991 in Pinellas Park, Pinellas, Florida, USA
..............5 Howard Leonard Siskin b: Aug 02, 1925 in Chicago, Cook, Illinois, USA, d: Aug 15, 2000 in Albuquerque, Bernalillo, New Mexico, USA
....   + Florence Dora Pitt b: Jul 08, 1924 in New York, USA, m: Abt. 1950, d: Oct 24, 2009 in Cape Coral, Lee, Florida; Self-DeathAge: 85
................6 David L Siskin b: Jul 03, 1952 in Chicago, Cook, Illinois, USA
...........4 Edyth Propp b: Jun 15, 1897 in Chicago, Cook, Illinois, USA

.... + Herman Earl Morton b: Jan 15, 1897 in Chicago, Cook, Illinois, USA, m: Bef. 1920 in Chicago, Cook, Illinois, USA, d: Nov 10, 1964 in Allegheny, PA, USA
..............5 Lester S Morton b: Dec 11, 1922, d: Oct 15, 1987 in St Louis, St Louis, Missouri, USA
.... + Mes Morton m: Abt. 1949 in Illinois, USA
................6 Ronald Morton b: 1950
................6 Candice Morton b: 1951
................6 Melody Morton b: 1952
............4 Max Aaron "Macarthur" Propp b: Feb 10, 1900 in Jasper, Indiana, USA, d: Sep 30, 1973 in Temple City, Los Angeles, California, USA
.... + Frances Christine Tingleff b: Aug 13, 1896 in Clinton, Iowa, USA, d: Apr 06, 1987 in Temple City, Los Angeles, California, USA
..............5 Paul Macarther Propp b: Nov 16, 1936 in Los Angeles, Los Angeles, California, USA
.... + Frances D Gasper m: Apr 03, 1960 in Los Angeles, California
......2 Moshe "Moshel" Prop b: 1819 in Skaudvile, Kovno, Russia, d: 1895 in Jurbarkas, Kovno, Russia
...... + Chaya b: 1814 in Russia, m: 1838 in Russia, d: 1905 in Jurbarkas, Kovno, Russia
........3 Yaakov "Yekel" Prop b: 1840 in Skaudvile, Kovno, Russia, d: 1912 in Kovno, Kovno, Russia
.... + Rivka Posin b: 1847 in Lithuania, m: 1870, d: 1920 in Lithuania
............4 Minna Propp b: 1872 in Skaudvile, Kovno, Russia; Taurage, Lithuania/, d: 1960 in Russia
.... + Witposky d: Russia
............4 Joseph "Zevel" Zevulun Propp b: Dec 10, 1878 in Skaudvile, Kovno, Russia, d: 1950 in New York, New York, USA
.... + Annie Wilenski b: 1883 in Russia, m: Aug 28, 1904 in New York, New York, USA, d: 1946 in New York, New York, USA
..............5 Nettie Propp b: 1905 in New York, New York, USA, d: 1962 in New York, New York, USA
..............5 Betsy Propp b: Apr 21, 1908, d: May 10, 1994 in Brooklyn, Kings, New York, USA; Age at Death: 86
.... + Ralph Lazarus b: 1912 in New York, New York, USA, m: 1939 in New York, New York, USA, d: 1972 in New York, New York, USA
................6 Shirley Lazarus b: 1941 in New York, New York, USA
.... + Bernard Flashman b: 1935 in New York, New York, USA, m: New York, New York, USA
.... 7 Jermey Flashman b: 1963 in New York, New York, USA
.... + Debbie Harvey b: 1966 in New York, New York, USA
........................8 Jack Flashman b: 1990 in New York, New York, USA
........................8 Rosie Flashman b: 1991 in New York, New York, USA
.... 7 Karen Flashman b: 1965 in New York, New York, USA
................6 Roslyn "Roz" Lazarus b: 1945 in Portsmouth, Hampshire, England
.... + Michael Flashman b: 1937 in New York, New York, USA
.... 7 Simon Flashman b: 1965 in New York, New York, USA
.... 7 Richard Flashman b: 1968 in New York, New York, USA
................6 Anne Lazarus b: 1947 in Portsmouth, Hampshire, England
.... + Raymond Mendlessohn b: 1949 in New York, New York, USA, m: New York, New York, USA
.... 7 Ruth Mendlessohn b: 1976 in New York, New York, USA
..............5 Morris Efraim Moshe Propp b: Aug 24, 1908 in New York, New York, USA, d: May 23, 1979 in New York, New York, USA
.... + Leah "Lily" Levenstain b: Aug 20, 1910 in New York, New York, USA, m: Aug 29, 1937 in New York, New York, USA, d: Jan 11, 2009 in Tel Aviv, Israel; Segulah Cemetery, Petach Tikvah, Israel
................6 Jason Stanley Propp b: 1938 in New York, New York, USA, d: Israel
.... + Marian Fay Fox b: 1942 in Derbyshire, England, m: Oct 27, 1963 in New York, New York, USA, d:
.... 7 Adam Emanuel Propp b: Jan 09, 1965 in Montréal, Quebec, Canada
.... + Iris "Yehudit Chava" Ben Amitai b: Dec 27, 1964 in Jerusalem, Israel, m: Aug 27, 1987 in Israel
.... 7 Daniel Nathan Propp b: Jul 06, 1966 in Montréal, Quebec, Canada
.... + Nurit Avtabi b: Jul 17, 1969 in Jerusalem, Israel, m: Sep 11, 1990 in Israel
........................8 Eyal Propp b: Jul 22, 1991 in Jerusalem, Israel
........................8 Tehila Propp b: Mar 29, 1995 in Jerusalem, Israel
........................8 Amir Yossef Propp b: Jan 16, 1998
.... 7 Ariyeh Zevulun Propp b: Mar 25, 1969 in Montréal, Quebec, Canada, d: Dec 13, 1980 in Petach Tikvah, Israel; Segulah Cemetery
.... 7 Sarit Ilana Propp b: Jul 11, 1973 in Tel Aviv, Israel
.... + Chanoch Haimovitch b: Jun 02, 1973 in Jerusalem, Israel, m: Aug 18, 1994 in Israel

........................8 Ode'ya Devora Haimovitch b: Apr 19, 1996 in Jerusalem, Israel

........................8 Emunah Haimovitch b: Dec 09, 1997

.....................7 Yehonatan Lev "Yonni" Propp b: Jun 08, 1978 in Tel Aviv, Israel

..........3 Arhon "Ortzig" Propp b: 1845 in Skaudvile, Kovno, Russia, d: Nov 27, 1885 in New York, New York, USA

.... + Bessie "Beile" Rozenblum b: Mar 1845 in Kovno, Kovno, Russia; Same location as Kaunas, Lithuania, m: 1863 in Kovno, Kovno, Russia, d: Feb 14, 1908 in New York, New York, USA

............4 Robert Max "Israel" Propp b: Dec 25, 1861 in Skaudvile, Kovno, Russia,, d: May 26, 1932 in Des Moines, Polk, Iowa, United States of America

.... + Celia Michalson b: Apr 18, 1868 in Jurbarkas, Kovno, Russia, m: 1894 in Chicago, Cook, Illinois, USA, d: Jun 28, 1928 in Des Moines, Polk, Iowa, USA

...............5 Marian Propp b: Dec 16, 1889 in Des Moines, Polk, Iowa, USA, d: Feb 03, 1965 in Chicago, Cook, Illinois, USA

.... + Nathaniel I. Baskind b: Dec 24, 1890 in Libau, Russia, m: 1929 in Chicago, Cook, Illinois, USA, d: Jun 28, 1961 in Chicago, Cook, Illinois, United States

...................6 Myron Baskind b: Jan 01, 1920 in Chicago, Cook, Illinois, USA, d: Jan 17, 1961 in Chicago, Cook, Illinois, USA

...............5 Harry H "Aaron" Propp b: Apr 05, 1892 in Des Moines, Polk, Iowa, USA, d: 1948 in Des Moines, Polk, Iowa, USA

...............5 Moses Herman "Moe" Propp b: Mar 18, 1896 in Des Moines, Polk, Iowa, USA, d: Oct 1951 in Miami Beach, Dade, Florida, USA

.... + Miriam "Mimi" Rubel b: Dec 29, 1908 in Corinth, Alcorn, Mississippi, USA, m: 1933 in Chicago, Cook, Illinois, USA, d: Dec 28, 2003 in Corinth, Alcorn, Mississippi, USA

...................6 Robert Rubel Propp b: Jan 02, 1935 in Corinth, Alcorn, Mississippi, USA

.... + Maxine M. Propp b: Sep 30, 1937 in Atlanta, De Kalb, Georgia, USA, m: 1958 in Atlanta, De Kalb, Georgia, USA, d: Jun 25, 2004 in Corona Del Mar, Orange, California, USA

...................7 Robert Rubel Propp b: Feb 19, 1961 in Huntsville, Madison, Alabama, USA

.... + Catherine Kalfus b: May 07, 1963 in New York, New York, USA, m: Nov 1990

........................8 Brandon Robert Propp b: Jan 15, 1993 in Pomona, Los Angeles, California, USA

........................8 Alec Taylor Propp b: May 13, 1995 in Pomona, Los Angeles, California, USA

...................7 Kenneth Morris Propp b: Sep 09, 1964 in Morristown, Middlesex, New Jersey, USA

...................7 David Michael Propp b: Dec 30, 1965 in Morristown, Middlesex, New Jersey, USA

.... + Susan Sauter b: Dec 07, 1967 in Biminton, Alabama

............4 Joseph "Yosef" Propp b: Feb 18, 1867 in Jurbarkas, Kovno, Russia, d: Dec 24, 1906 in New York, New York, USA

.... + Carrie Rosenstock b: Jan 1873 in Russia, m: 1893 in New York, New York, USA, d: 1934 in New York, New York, USA

...............5 Harry Archibald "Joshua" Propp b: Feb 16, 1894 in New York, New York, USA, d: Jul 12, 1966 in Brooklyn, Kings, New York, USA

.... + Bessie Sadye Saftler b: Sep 11, 1899 in Brooklyn, Kings, New York, USA, m: 1929 in New York, New York, USA, d: Oct 27, 1988 in New York, New York, USA

...................6 Allen Jay Propp b: Nov 30, 1927 in Brooklyn, Kings, New York, USA, d: Jan 02, 2006 in Lakeland, Polk, Florida, USA

.... + Johanne Walker b: Sep 22, 1927 in Bainbridge, Decatur, Georgia, USA, d: Nov 28, 2007 in Lakeland, Polk, Florida, USA

...................7 William Walker Propp b: Jan 05, 1956 in Louisville, Jefferson, Kentucky, USA

...................7 James Lee Propp b: Oct 22, 1957 in Louisville, Jefferson, Kentucky, USA

.... + Paula Hargroves b: Jun 09, 1958, m: Abt. 1989

........................8 Melissa Diane Propp b: Mar 22, 1990

...................7 Nancy Ann Propp b: Mar 14, 1961 in Louisville, Jefferson, Kentucky, USA

...................7 Richard Michael Propp b: Jan 20, 1969 in Lakeland, Polk, Florida, USA

.................6 Martin Budd Propp b: May 30, 1930 in Brooklyn, Kings, New York, USA

.... + Patricia Lally b: Abt. 1933 in New York, New York, USA, m: 1978

.... + Ruth Jean Sugerman b: Jan 11, 1933 in Brooklyn, Kings, New York, USA, m: Mar 15, 1954 in New York, New York, USA

...................7 Kenneth Ray Propp b: Sep 25, 1956 in Stanford, Connecticut

.... + Kelly Diane Lukins b: Jul 05, 1956 in Frankfurt, Frankfurt am Main, Hessen, Germany, m: 1986

........................8 Andrew Lukins Propp b: Mar 18, 1988 in Bonn, Bonn, North Rhine-Westphalia, Germany

........................8 Alexander Bernard Propp b: Feb 08, 1991 in Arlington, Arlington, Virginia, USA

...................7 Jonathan Bruce Propp b: Oct 30, 1958 in Stanford, Connecticut

.... + Peggy Stern b: Apr 09, 1959 in New York, New York, USA

........................8 Alan Isaac Propp b: Nov 01, 1993 in Santa Clara, Santander, Colombia
........................8 Daniel Joshua Propp b: Feb 12, 1996 in Menlo Park, San Mateo, California, USA
........................8 Jeffery Stem Propp b: Sep 17, 1998 in Palo Alto, San Mateo, California, USA
................5 Rosie Propp b: Jan 1897 in New York, New York, USA, d: 1945 in New York, New York, USA
................5 Sidney H Propp b: Jul 12, 1899 in New York, New York, USA, d: Apr 01, 1962 in White Plains,
        Westchester, New York, USA
.... + Katherine Djula b: Dec 05, 1909 in Brooklyn, Kings, New York, USA, m: 1944 in New York, New York, USA,
        d: Dec 02, 2000 in Greenwich, Fairfield, Connecticut, USA
....................6 David Propp b: 1945 in White Plains, Westchester, New York, USA
.... + Pearl W. b: Oct 10, 1902 in New York, New York, USA, m: Bef. 1930 in New York, New York, USA
............4 Henrietta "Yette" Propp b: Dec 1875 in Jurbarkas, Kovno, Russia, d: New York, New York, USA
............4 Ella Propp b: Nov 1876 in Jurbarkas, Kovno, Russia, d: New York, New York, USA
.... + Harry Golvberg
............4 Rosalie "Rose" Propp b: 1877 in Hamburg, Germany, d: Jun 23, 1894 in New York, New York, USA
............4 Roch"l "Rae" Propp b: Apr 1880 in Hamburg, Germany
............4 Ruth Propp b: Jan 01, 1890 in New York, New York, USA, d: Mar 1971 in Caldwell, Essex, New Jersey,
        United States of America
.... + Edwin A Starn b: Sep 17, 1884 in New York, New York, USA, m: Sep 14, 1913 in Manhattan, Kings, New York,
        USA, d: May 21, 1959 in New York, New York, USA
........3 Sheyna Rochel Prop b: 1847 in Skaudvile, Kovno, Russia, d: 1914 in Jurbarkas, Kovno, Russia
.... + Elij "Eliyahu" Michelson b: 1843 in Jurbarkas, Kovno, Russia, m: 1869 in Skaudvile, Kovno, Russia, d:
............4 Celia Michalson b: Apr 18, 1868 in Jurbarkas, Kovno, Russia, d: Jun 28, 1928 in Des Moines, Polk, Iowa, USA
.... + Robert Max "Israel" Propp b: Dec 25, 1861 in Skaudvile, Kovno, Russia,, m: 1894 in Chicago, Cook,
        Illinois, USA, d: May 26, 1932 in Des Moines, Polk, Iowa, United States of America
................5 Marian Propp b: Dec 16, 1889 in Des Moines, Polk, Iowa, USA, d: Feb 03, 1965 in Chicago, Cook,
        Illinois, USA
.... + Nathaniel I. Baskind b: Dec 24, 1890 in Libau, Russia, m: 1929 in Chicago, Cook, Illinois, USA, d: Jun 28,
        1961 in Chicago, Cook, Illinois, United States
....................6 Myron Baskind b: Jan 01, 1920 in Chicago, Cook, Illinois, USA, d: Jan 17, 1961 in Chicago, Cook,
        Illinois, USA
................5 Harry H "Aaron" Propp b: Apr 05, 1892 in Des Moines, Polk, Iowa, USA, d: 1948 in Des Moines, Polk, Iowa,
        USA
................5 Moses Herman "Moe" Propp b: Mar 18, 1896 in Des Moines, Polk, Iowa, USA, d: Oct 1951 in Miami
        Beach, Dade, Florida, USA
.... + Miriam "Mimi" Rubel b: Dec 29, 1908 in Corinth, Alcorn, Mississippi, USA, m: 1933 in Chicago, Cook,
        Illinois, USA, d: Dec 28, 2003 in Corinth, Alcorn, Mississippi, USA
....................6 Robert Rubel Propp b: Jan 02, 1935 in Corinth, Alcorn, Mississippi, USA
.... + Maxine M. Propp b: Sep 30, 1937 in Atlanta, De Kalb, Georgia, USA, m: 1958 in Atlanta, De Kalb,
        Georgia, USA, d: Jun 25, 2004 in Corona Del Mar, Orange, California, USA
........................7 Robert Rubel Propp b: Feb 19, 1961 in Huntsville, Madison, Alabama, USA
.... + Catherine Kalfus b: May 07, 1963 in New York, New York, USA, m: Nov 1990
............................8 Brandon Robert Propp b: Jan 15, 1993 in Pomona, Los Angeles, California, USA
............................8 Alec Taylor Propp b: May 13, 1995 in Pomona, Los Angeles, California, USA
........................7 Kenneth Morris Propp b: Sep 09, 1964 in Morristown, Middlesex, New Jersey, USA
........................7 David Michael Propp b: Dec 30, 1965 in Morristown, Middlesex, New Jersey, USA
.... + Susan Sauter b: Dec 07, 1967 in Biminton, Alabama
............4 Herman Michelson b: 1874 in Jurbarkas, Kovno, Russia
................5 Kolja Michelson b: 1897 in Kovno, Kovno, Russia
................5 Nussa Michelson b: 1903 in Kovno, Kovno, Russia
................5 Issa Michelson b: 1905 in Kovno, Kovno, Russia
.... + Jan Frankal b: 1906 in Austrian Hungary Empire, m: Abt. 1924 ; Lithuania or Russia, d: 1984 in New York,
        New York, USA
........3 Max "Moshe" Propp b: 1851 in Skaudvile, Kovno, Russia, d: 1908 in Königsberg, East Prussia
.... + Sophia Sammel b: 1867 in Tavrig, Kovno, Lithuania, m: Abt. 1885 in Königsberg, East Prussia, d: 1922 in
        Königsberg, East Prussia
............4 Benno Moritz Propp b: Jan 20, 1886 in Königsberg, East Prussia, d: May 31, 1952 in Los Angeles, Los
        Angeles, California, USA
.... + Margarete Levinsohn b: May 11, 1883 in Kühstein, Rottal-Inn, Bavaria, Germany, d: 1943 in Auschwitz,
        Poland

..............5 Dorothy K. Propp b: Aug 18, 1921 in Königsberg, East Prussia, d: Apr 06, 2001 in Sonoma, Sonoma, California, USA

.... + Jean Fendulli b: Dec 24, 1903 in Connecticut, USA, m: Abt. 1941 in Chicago, Cook, Illinois, USA, d: Sep 1994 in Chicago, Cook, Illinois, USA

.... + Joseph Kane Blonder b: Jun 21, 1908 in New York, New York, USA, m: 1951 in Los Angeles, Los Angeles, California, USA, d: Nov 29, 1985 in San Francisco, San Francisco, California, USA

..............6 Nicholas George Blonder b: Oct 04, 1949 in Los Angeles, Los Angeles, California, USA

.... + Ellen Leong b: Jan 06, 1950 in Sacramento, Sacramento, California, USA, m: Jul 18, 1974 in Marin, California

...........4 Hans Josef Propp b: 1889 in Königsberg, East Prussia, d: 1962 in London, London, England

.... + Edith b: 1894 in Königsberg, East Prussia, m: 1919 in Königsberg, East Prussia, d: 1974 in London, London, England

..............5 Heinz "Henry" Propp b: 1921 in Königsberg, East Prussia, d: 1972 in New York, New York, USA

..............5 Alice Sophie "Lissi" Propp b: 1924 in Königsberg, East Prussia

.... + Henry Rodwell b: 1921 in Berlin, Stadt Berlin, Berlin, Germany, m: 1948 in New York, New York, USA

..............6 Nichols Rodwell b: May 1950 in London, London, England

..............6 Mark Rodwell b: Jun 1953 in London, London, England

....................7 Jessica Rodwell b: 1976 in New York, New York, USA

....................7 Mark Rodwell b: 1978 in New York, New York, USA

...........4 Arthur Propp b: Jun 02, 1890 in Königsberg, East Prussia, d: Dec 31, 1965 in Sechelt, British Columbia, Canada

.... + Else Laaser b: Nov 14, 1891 in Tilsit, Gumbinnen, East Prussia, Germany, m: 1922 in Königsberg, East Prussia, d: 1945 in Riga, Riga, Latvia

..............5 Max Propp b: 1923 in Königsberg, East Prussia

.... + Edith "Yehudit" b: Jun 18, 1924 in Canada, m: 1950, d: Mar 07, 2010 in Toronto, Ontario, Canada

..................6 Michael B. Propp b: Sep 14, 1956 in Vancouver, British Columbia, Canada

.... + Tamar B Babila b: Sep 01, 1974 in Israel, m: 1998

....................7 Gilbert "Gil" Propp b: Dec 04, 1994 in Boston, Suffolk, Massachusetts, USA

....................7 Oron Propp b: Feb 23, 1997 in Boston, Suffolk, Massachusetts, USA

....................7 Hodaya Propp b: Apr 30, 1999 in Boston, Suffolk, Massachusetts, USA

....................7 Yakir Propp b: Jul 19, 2007 in Boston, Suffolk, Massachusetts, USA

..................6 David L Propp b: Nov 22, 1958 in Vancouver, British Columbia, Canada

.... + Debra Anne Shapero b: Nov 26, 1959

....................7 Roni Propp b: May 24, 1991 in Toronto, Ontario, Canada

....................7 Lee Propp b: Apr 11, 1993 in Toronto, Ontario, Canada

.... + Elsa Kopetzky b: 1914 in Prague, Czech Republic, m: 1942 in Sucre, Chuquisaca, Bolivia, d: Jun 27, 1973 in Sechelt, British Columbia, Canada

..............5 Daniel Propp b: Oct 16, 1944 in Sucre, Chuquisaca, Bolivia, d: Ricmond, Canada

.... + Rita b: 1951 in Philippines

..................6 Adam J. Propp b: 1977 in Richmond, British Columbia, Canada

..................6 Jennifer Propp b: 1979 in Richmond, British Columbia, Canada

...........4 Helene Propp b: 1892 in Königsberg, East Prussia, d: 1958 in Paris, Ile-de-France, France

......2 Jenta "Johana" Prop b: Dec 10, 1821 in Skaudvile, Kovno, Russia, d: Jan 07, 1903 in or East Prussia; Elbing (Elbag) Poland and

...... + Israel Pincus Berlowitz b: Dec 27, 1819 in Smalininkai, Jurbarkas, Russia, m: Mar 20, 1837 in Skaudvile, Kovno, Russia, d: Feb 15, 1881 in Memel, East Prussia

.........3 Simon Ber Berlowitz b: Dec 09, 1838 in Smalininkai, Jurbarkas, Russia, d: Memel, East Prussia

.... + Taube Schagebewski

.........3 Feivel "Phoebus" Berlowitz b: Jul 09, 1840 in Smalininkai, Jurbarkas, Russia, d: Memel, East Prussia

.........3 Roch"l Michke "Minna" Berlowitz b: Mar 04, 1843 in Smalininkai, Jurbarkas, Russia

.... + Nathan "Erdreich" Erdreych b: 1839 in Suvalkai, Vilkaviskis, Lithuania, m: Jun 11, 1864 in Suvalkai, Vilkaviskis, Lithuania

...........4 Paul "Pinchas" Erdreych b: 1864

...........4 Zelman Erdreych b: Jan 01, 1866

...........4 Abraham Meyer Erdreych b: Jun 1867

...........4 Aizik Erdreych b: 1871, d: 1872

...........4 Hirsz Erdreych b: 1872, d: 1873

...........4 Golda Erdreych b: 1875

...........4 Hinda Erdreych b: 1876

............4 Tauba Erdreych b: 1878

............4 Zennia Erdreych b: 1882

........3 Jette Gitel Pittel Berlowitz b: Dec 28, 1843 in Smalininkai, Jurbarkas, Russia

.... + M Markson b: Suvalkai, Vilkaviskis, Lithuania

........3 Ephraim Chaim Berlowitz b: Nov 02, 1845 in Smalininkai, Jurbarkas, Russia, d: Jan 22, 1913 in New York, New York, USA

.... + Lena Lina b: 1846, d: Aug 02, 1937 in New York, New York, USA

........3 Frederika "Rivka" Berlowitz b: Jun 25, 1848 in Smalininkai, Jurbarkas, Russia

.... + Meyer Feinstein b: 1851 in Libau, Courtland

........3 Wolf "Wilhelm" Berlowitz b: Jul 11, 1850 in Smalininkai, Jurbarkas, Russia, d: Dec 21, 1875 in New York, New York, USA

.... + Feige "Fanny" Finkelstein b: Jan 11, 1855 in Smalininkai, East Prussia, m: 1872 in Smalininkai, East Prussia

............4 Julius Berlowitz b: Dec 21, 1875 in Insterburg, East Prussia, d: Apr 22, 1943 in Theresienstadt, Germany; Holocaust

.... + Hinde-Esther Else Kupferberg b: Jan 02, 1892 in Drohobycz, Austria; Holocaust, m: 1919 in Berlin, Stadt Berlin, Berlin, Germany, d: Jan 30, 1944 in Theresienstadt, Germany

...............5 William Wolf Berton b: Aug 08, 1920 in Berlin, Stadt Berlin, Berlin, Germany, d: Saginaw, Saginaw, Michigan, USA

.... + Shirley Weinberg b: 1926 in Milwaukee, Milwaukee, Wisconsin, USA, m: Feb 15, 1948 in Milwaukee, Milwaukee, Wisconsin, USA, d: Saginaw, Saginaw, Michigan, USA

..................6 Bruce Jay Berton b: Mar 04, 1952 in Milwaukee, Milwaukee, Wisconsin, USA

.... + Kathleen August b: Mar 02, 1962, m: Mar 03, 2002 in Saginaw, Saginaw, Michigan, USA

..................6 Elliot Scott Berton b: Feb 04, 1954 in Milwaukee, Milwaukee, Wisconsin, USA

.... + Lori A Rombalski b: Feb 09, 1956 in Carrollton, Saginaw, Michigan, USA, m: Oct 23, 1981 in Saginaw, Saginaw, Michigan, USA

.....................7 Aaron Mathew Berton b: Aug 16, 1984 in Saginaw, Saginaw, Michigan, USA

.....................7 Amy Maire Berton b: May 30, 1987 in Saginaw, Saginaw, Michigan, USA

..................6 Robert Michael Berton b: Aug 07, 1956 in Jackson, Jackson, Michigan, USA

.... + Julie Wazny b: Dec 15, 1956 in Saginaw, Saginaw, Michigan, USA, m: Oct 23, 1981 in Saginaw, Saginaw, Michigan, USA

.....................7 Dayna Rochelle Berton b: Aug 07, 1979 in Jackson, Jackson, Michigan, USA

.... + Chad Michael Carey b: Nov 13, 1977, m: Sep 05, 2004 in Michigan, USA

.....................7 Gheric Allen Berton b: Sep 05, 1981 in Charlotte, Mecklenburg, North Carolina, USA

.....................7 Nathan Scott Berton b: Apr 10, 1984 in Charlotte, Mecklenburg, North Carolina, USA

.... + Renee Dixon b: Jul 03, 1984

.....................8 Hayden Berton b: Mar 28, 2003 in Wisconsin, USA

.....................7 Jacob Alexander Berton b: May 08, 1986 in Charlotte, Mecklenburg, North Carolina, USA

.....................7 Jordan Alysa Berton b: Nov 02, 1989 in Charlotte, Mecklenburg, North Carolina, USA

..................6 Tamara Jo Berton b: Oct 11, 1959 in Beloit, Rock, Wisconsin, USA

.... + Thomas R Benkert b: Apr 04, 1953 in Saginaw, Saginaw, Michigan, USA, m: Aug 28, 1981 in Saginaw, Saginaw, Michigan, USA

.....................7 Thomas Ryan Benkert b: Dec 15, 1984 in Saginaw, Saginaw, Michigan, USA

.....................7 Megan Jo Benkert b: Dec 15, 1984 in Saginaw, Saginaw, Michigan, USA

...............5 Gerda-Ruth Dina Berlowitz b: Jun 29, 1923 in Berlin, Stadt Berlin, Berlin, Germany

.... + Joachim Marcuse b: 1917 in Treptow, Demmin, Mecklenburg-Vorpommern, Germany, m: 1940

.... + Ernst "Joseph" Weil b: Feb 07, 1915 in Frankfurt, Frankfurt am Main, Hessen, Germany, m: 1949 in Israel, d: Jun 21, 1985 in Kiriath, Bialik, Israel

..................6 Nava Weil b: Nov 02, 1952 in Israel

.... + Ze'ev Effroni b: Sep 15, 1949 in Tel Aviv, Israel

.....................7 Maya Effroni b: 1974 in Israel

.... + Shalom Aftar b: Sep 30, 1969 in Israel, m: Jun 2001 in Israel

.....................8 Allay Aftar b: Sep 11, 2002

.....................7 Amit Effroni b: 1980 in Israel

.....................7 Itai Josef Effroni b: Dec 1987 in Israel

.....................7 Mor Effroni b: Dec 1987 in Israel

..................6 Rona Weil b: Mar 28, 1955 in Israel

.... + Eres Taoz b: Oct 27, 1954 in Hedera, Israel, m: 1979 in Israel

.....................7 Noam Taoz b: Feb 01, 1981 in Kiriath, Bialik, Israel

....................7 Lior Taoz b: Oct 19, 1982 in Kiriath, Bialik, Israel

....................7 Li-Hi Taoz b: Sep 1988 in Kiriath, Bialik, Israel

................6 Shlomith Weil b: Jan 18, 1958 in Israel

.... + Haim Cohen b: Jan 13, 1958 in Israel, m: Aug 1982 in Israel

....................7 Ro'ee Avraham Cohen b: Apr 15, 1984 in Tel Aviv, Israel

....................7 Assaf Cohen b: Nov 1986 in Israel

....................7 Eran Cohen b: Nov 1986 in Israel

...........4 Paul Berlowitz b: Jan 05, 1877 in Insterburg, East Prussia, d: Sep 02, 1941 in Berlin, Stadt Berlin, Berlin, Germany

...........4 Martha Berlowitz b: Apr 11, 1878 in Preussisch, Netherlands, d: Jun 18, 1953 in Atlantic City, Atlantic, New Jersey, USA

.... + Jacques Hamburger b: May 31, 1872 in St Louis, St Louis, Missouri, USA, d: Mar 30, 1937 in Germany

..............5 Werner Hamburger b: Aug 10, 1910 in Straußberg, Kyffhauserkreis, Thüringen, Germany, d: Mar 18, 1998 in Hemet, Riverside, California, USA

.... + Margot Engel b: Apr 04, 1912 in Straußberg, Kyffhauserkreis, Thüringen, Germany, m: Oct 1936 in Germany

................6 Evelyn Engel Hamburger b: Jul 14, 1938 in Utica, Oneida, New York, USA, d: Feb 26, 1979 in Atlantic City, Atlantic, New Jersey, USA

.... + Dennis Allee b: 1935 in New York, New York, USA

....................7 Elena Allee b: Mar 01, 1963 in New York, New York, USA

....................7 Glenna Allee b: Apr 20, 1965 in New York, New York, USA

.... + Kerry Krater m: Oct 2000 in New York, New York, USA

...........4 Irma Berlowitz b: Dec 27, 1884 in Preußnitz, Potsdam-Mittelmark, Brandenburg, Germany

.... + Ferdinand Schaal b: Dec 27, 1872, d: Minsk, Minsk, Russia

..............5 Walter Abraham Schaal b: Mar 12, 1908 in Berlin, Stadt Berlin, Berlin, Germany

..............5 Gerhard Israel Schaal b: Dec 15, 1910 in Berlin, Stadt Berlin, Berlin, Germany, d: Mar 25, 1997

.... + Rachel Dora b: Aug 13, 1920 in Bamberg, Bavaria, Germany, d: Dec 29, 1967 in Israel

................6 Michael Schaal b: Aug 10, 1941 in Eretz Yisrael

.... + Nina Penski b: May 20, 1944 in Tel Josef, Eretz Yisrael, m: Mar 03, 1965 in Israel, d: Aug 1990 in Kiriath, Bialik, Israel

....................7 Rinath Schaal b: Apr 1975 in Haifa, Israel

.... + Eitan Fwniger b: Jul 27, 1971 in Haifa, Israel, m: Oct 03, 1999 in New York, New York, USA

....................8 Tahel Fwniger b: May 25, 2003 in New York, New York, USA

....................7 Naor Schaal b: Israel

.... + Shlomit Gonen

....................8 Noy Schaal b: Jul 22, 1992 in Israel

....................8 Yuval Schaal b: Nov 05, 1995 in Israel

....................8 Yam "Twin" Schaal b: Apr 29, 1998 in Israel

....................8 Hilla "Twin" Schaal b: Apr 29, 1998

................6 Yael Schaal b: Jan 19, 1946 in Eretz Yisrael

.... + Yair Lichter b: Mar 23, 1945 in Tel Aviv, Eretz Yisrael, m: Israel

....................7 Ido Lichter b: Apr 15, 1972 in Haifa, Israel

....................7 Uri Lichter b: Sep 22, 1975 in Haifa, Israel

................6 Haggith Schaal b: Feb 01, 1952 in Israel

.... + Alberto Spilka b: Nov 19, 1949 in Montevideo, Uruguay, m: Kaf Hamaakkabi, Israel

....................7 Ariel Spilka b: Jul 28, 1979 in Haifa, Israel

....................7 Gabriela Spilka b: Sep 22, 1992 in Haifa, Israel

.... + Eva Taitza b: Mar 14, 1915 in Merseburg, Merseburg-Querfurt, Saxony-Anhalt, Germany, d: 1997

..............5 Hildegard Schaal b: Oct 17, 1917 in Berlin, Stadt Berlin, Berlin, Germany

.... + Mordechai Lachmann b: Poland, m: Eretz Yisrael

................6 Gabriel Lachmann b: Aug 07, 1943 in Tel Aviv, Eretz Yisrael

.... + Dalia Tamarlin m: Germany

....................7 Michael Lachmann b: May 15, 1966 in Germany

....................7 Karin Lachmann b: May 17, 1970 in Germany

...........4 Gertrud Berlowitz b: Jul 26, 1890 in Preussisch, Netherlands, d: Budapest, Budapest, Hungary

.... + Herman Berlowitz b: Jan 26, 1882 in Thorn, East Prussia, d: 1960 in Budapest, Budapest, Hungary

..............5 Anna Maria Cuni Berlowitz b: May 19, 1923 in Budapest, Budapest, Hungary

.... + Zoltan Olcsai Kiss b: Nov 04, 1895 in Szalafo, Vas, Hungary

................6 Anna Maria Kiss b: Nov 04, 1953 in Budapest, Budapest, Hungary, d: Nov 03, 1997
.... + Peter Erzberger
....................7 Sarah Julia Erzberger b: Apr 30, 1979 in New York, New York, USA
.............5 Elizabeth Berlowitz b: Nov 1927 in Budapest, Budapest, Hungary, d: Dec 31, 1981 in Budapest,
.... Budapest, Hungary
.... + Molnar m: 1979 in Budapest, Budapest, Hungary
........3 Abraham Meyer Berlowitz b: Aug 08, 1852 in Smalininkai, Jurbarkas, Russia, d: Dec 19, 1916 in Thorn,
.... West Prussia
.... + Rosa Horwitz b: Jul 26, 1842 in Margonin, East Prussia, m: Mar 10, 1880, d: Nov 27, 1937 in Eretz Yisrael
............4 Iwan Berlowitz b: Jan 06, 1881 in Thorn, West Prussia, d: 1952 in Karkur, Haifa, Israel
.... + Elise Simon b: Jastrowie West Prussia
.............5 Gerda Berlowitz b: 1913 in East Prussia, d: Jul 2001
.... + Ishu Kleinmann b: Eretz Yisrael, m: 1936 in Eretz Yisrael
................6 Daniel "Dekel" Kleinmann b: Jul 14, 1938 in Eretz Yisrael
.... + Nili b: Jun 09, 1942, m: Israel
....................7 Tamir Dekel b: Sep 07, 1966 in Israel
....................7 Ishai Dekel b: Aug 29, 1969 in Israel
....................7 Jaron Dekel b: Nov 30, 1973 in Israel
....................7 Tal Dekel b: Jun 19, 1977 in Israel
................6 Levia Kleinmann b: Sep 24, 1943 in Eretz Yisrael
.... + Josef Hershkowitz b: Sep 20, 1939, m: 1975 in Israel
....................7 Keren Hershkowitz b: Aug 06, 1977 in Israel
....................7 Gil Hershkowitz b: Jun 07, 1978 in Israel
................6 Shlomit Kleinmann b: Oct 18, 1948 in Israel
.... + Moshe Hason m: 1971 in Israel
....................7 Adi Hason b: Sep 23, 1973 in Israel
....................7 Ofer Hason b: Feb 06, 1977 in Israel
....................7 Oz Hason b: Aug 24, 1986 in Israel
.............5 Heinz Berlowitz b: East Prussia, d: 1954 in Israel
.............5 Margot Berlowitz b: East Prussia, d: Elblag, Warminsko-Mazurskie, Poland
............4 Herman Berlowitz b: Jan 26, 1882 in Thorn, East Prussia, d: 1960 in Budapest, Budapest, Hungary
.... + Gertrud Berlowitz b: Jul 26, 1890 in Preussisch, Netherlands, d: Budapest, Budapest, Hungary
.............5 Anna Maria Cuni Berlowitz b: May 19, 1923 in Budapest, Budapest, Hungary
.... + Zoltan Olcsai Kiss b: Nov 04, 1895 in Szalafo, Vas, Hungary
................6 Anna Maria Kiss b: Nov 04, 1953 in Budapest, Budapest, Hungary, d: Nov 03, 1997
.... + Peter Erzberger
....................7 Sarah Julia Erzberger b: Apr 30, 1979 in New York, New York, USA
.............5 Elizabeth Berlowitz b: Nov 1927 in Budapest, Budapest, Hungary, d: Dec 31, 1981 in Budapest,
.... Budapest, Hungary
.... + Molnar m: 1979 in Budapest, Budapest, Hungary
............4 Betty Berlowitz b: Mar 24, 1884 in Thorn, East Prussia, d: Jan 24, 1947 in Jerusalem, Eretz Yisrael
.... + Isaak Keiwe b: Abt. 1881, m: Mar 13, 1904 in Golub-Dobrzyn, Kujawsko-Pomorskie, West Prussia, d: Oct
.... 19, 1935 in Danzig, West Prussia
.............5 Moritz "Mor" Abraham Keiwe b: Sep 09, 1906 in Golub-Dobrzyn, Kujawsko-Pomorskie, West Prussia, d: Aug
.... 07, 1943 in Tel Aviv, Eretz Yisrael
.... + Chana Lipinska b: 1906 in Conin, Poland, m: Jul 1935 in Tel Aviv, Eretz Yisrael
................6 Ariela Keiwe b: Jul 06, 1942 in Tel Aviv, Eretz Yisrael
.... + Asher Aisenberg m: Jul 29, 1968 in Israel
....................7 Michal Aisenberg b: Apr 13, 1971 in Haifa, Israel
....................7 Gabi Aisenberg b: May 24, 1972 in Haifa, Israel
....................7 Mor Aisenberg b: Jun 04, 1976 in Tel Aviv, Israel
....................7 Roi Aisenberg b: Oct 05, 1978 in Tel Aviv, Israel
.............5 Charlotte Keiwe b: Feb 13, 1908 in Golub-Dobrzyn, Kujawsko-Pomorskie, West Prussia, d: Sep 02, 1920 in
.... Neidenberga, Saalfeld-Rudolstadt, Thuringia, Germany
.............5 Norbert Keiwe b: Jul 16, 1909 in Golub-Dobrzyn, Kujawsko-Pomorskie, West Prussia
.............5 Kurt Keiwe b: May 29, 1911 in Golub-Dobrzyn, Kujawsko-Pomorskie, West Prussia, d: May 26, 1920 in
.... Danzig, West Prussia
.............5 Hanna Keiwe b: May 1919 in Golub-Dobrzyn, Kujawsko-Pomorskie, West Prussia, d: 1988 in Tel Aviv,
.... + Armin Hoffmann b: Jun 19, 1903 in Maramaros Sziget, Hungary, m: Jan 04, 1944 in Tel Aviv, Eretz
.... Yisrael, d: 1988 in Tel Aviv, Israel
................6 Ruth Hoffmann b: Mar 30, 1946 in Tel Aviv, Eretz Yisrael

310

................6 Daniel Bar-Tikvah Hoffmann b: Oct 08, 1948 in Tel Aviv, Israel
.... + Rachel Gruenfeld b: Jan 04, 1948 in Hungary, m: Aug 30, 1970 in Tel Aviv, Israel
....................7 Ran Bar-Tikvah b: Jul 15, 1976 in Tel Aviv, Israel
....................7 Shachar Bar-Tikvah b: Feb 15, 1983 in Tel Aviv, Israel
....................7 Amir Bar-Tikvah b: Tel Aviv, Israel
............4 Meta Berlowitz b: Mar 24, 1884 in Thorn, East Prussia, d: 1944 in Estonia; Holocaust
.... + Simon Feinstein
...............5 Feinstein b: Russia
...............5 Feinstein b: Russia
............4 Emma Emmy Berlowitz b: Apr 12, 1885 in Thorn, East Prussia
.... + Arthur Heymann b: Köenigsberg, East Prussia, m: 1910 in Soldau, West Prussia, d: 1950 in Karkur,
.... Haifa, Israel
...............5 Gerhard Heymann b: 1912 in Soldau, West Prussia
............4 Leo Berlowitz b: Dec 14, 1890 in Thorn, East Prussia
.........3 Chaya Henchen Rose Berlowitz b: Oct 10, 1854 in Smalininkai, Jurbarkas, Russia, d: Sep 23, 1923 in Tilsit,
.... Gumbinnen, East Prussia, Germany
.... + Leibe Feinstein b: 1851 in Laursargen, East Prussia, d: Dec 1918 in Tilsit, Gumbinnen, East Prussia,
............4 Herman Feinstein b: Mar 17, 1876 in Meldiglanken, East Prussia, d: 1944 in Switzerland; Holocaust
.... + Anna Berlowitz b: 1879 in Smalininkai, East Prussia, m: 1906 in Smalininkai, East Prussia, d: 1933 in
.... Elblag, Warminsko-Mazurskie, Poland
...............5 Ruth Feinstein b: Jun 10, 1908 in Elblag, Warminsko-Mazurskie, Poland
.... + Leo "Brody" Ostrobrod b: Dec 13, 1898 in Jívoví, South Moravia, Czech Republic, m: Dec 25, 1928 in
.... Berlin, Stadt Berlin, Berlin, Germany, d: Sep 12, 1959 in New York, New York, USA
............4 Wanda Feinstein b: Dec 05, 1879 in Laursargen, East Prussia
.... + Adolf Morgenstern b: Aug 15, 1869 in Stallupoenen, East Prussia, d: Tel Aviv, Israel
...............5 Paul Morgenstern d: 1973 in Tel Aviv, Israel
.... + Kate
................6 Ina Morgenstern b: Israel
.... + Harlev
...............5 Bernhard Morgenstern d: 1949 in Venezuela, Piaui, Brazil
............4 Isidor "Hans" Feinstein b: Oct 05, 1880 in Meldiglanken, East Prussia
.... + Selma Bollag
...............5 Kurt Feinstein b: Sep 19, 1909, d: Feb 05, 1992 in Basel, Basel-City, Switzerland
.... + Clara Rosenberg
................6 Sylvia Feinstein b: Feb 07, 1945 in Switzerland
.... + Raymond Guggenheim b: Feb 07, 1945
....................7 Alain Hans Guggenheim b: Apr 08, 1978
....................7 Dennis Guggenheim b: 1980
....................7 Carol Guggenheim b: 1983
................6 Richard Feinstein b: Feb 10, 1946 in Switzerland
.... + Marianne Heymann b: East Prussia, m: Switzerland
....................7 Simone Feinstein b: Mar 20, 1973 in Switzerland
....................7 Danielle Feinstein b: Oct 08, 1975 in Switzerland
....................7 Nadine Feinstein b: Aug 23, 1977 in Switzerland
....................7 David Feinstein b: 1983 in Switzerland
................6 Marianne Feinstein b: Jan 01, 1948 in Switzerland
............4 Max Feinstein b: Jan 26, 1882 in Laursargen, East Prussia
.... + Lucie Walter d: 1935
.... + Suzanne Tessier b: 1900, m: 1936 in New York, New York, USA 4 Hertha
.... Herta Feinstein b: Sep 26, 1892 in Laursargen, East Prussia
.... + Leo Dembinsky b: Apr 11, 1882, d: Feb 1969 in Ontario, Canada
...............5 Eva Dembinsky b: Abt. 1911
.... + Harry Michelson b: Jun 19, 1904, d: Nov 20, 1987 in Northhampton, Massachusetts
................6 David Michelson

.... + Carmin
....................7 Michelson
.................6 Vera Michelson
..............5 Heinz Dembinsky d: 1945 in Ontario, Canada
..............5 Hans Dembinsky
.... + Celia Sandler
.................6 Alan Dembinsky b: 1958 in Ontario, Canada, d: 1962 in Ontario, Canada
...........4 Arthur Feinstein b: 1893 in Laursargen, East Prussia, d: Feb 1918 in Pittsburgh, Allegheny, Pennsylvania, USA
........3 Blume "Bertha" Berlowitz b: May 19, 1858 in Smalininkai, Jurbarkas, Russia, d: 1940
.... + Ivan Herzberg
...........4 Hermine Herzberg b: 1898, d: 1968 in Naarden, Noord-Holland, Netherlands
.... + Adolf Herz
..............5 Edith Herz b: Naarden, Noord-Holland, Netherlands, d: Naarden, Noord-Holland, Netherlands
.... + Walter Gluecksmann
.................6 Ralph Gluecksmann b: 1932 in Naarden, Noord-Holland, Netherlands, d: 1946 in Naarden, Noord-Holland, Netherlands
.... + Richard Wijnhujsen d: 1968 in Naarden, Noord-Holland, Netherlands
...........4 Else Herzberg
...........4 Ivan Herzberg
........3 Markus Aron Berlowitz b: Nov 17, 1860 in Goldup, Poland, d: Apr 1935 in Milwaukee, Milwaukee, Wisconsin, USA
.... + Miriam Mae "Maggie" Rolfe b: Jul 28, 1869 in Rome, Oneida, New York, USA, m: 1890, d: 1956 in New York, New York, USA
...........4 Esther Berlowitz b: Mar 30, 1892 in Michigan, USA, d: Mar 1983 in Rochester, Monroe, New York, USA
.... + Harold Shrier m: 1920 in Milwaukee, Milwaukee, Wisconsin, USA, d: 1956 in New York, New York, USA
..............5 Joseph Shrier b: 1923
.... + Dorothy Taylor b: 1933, m: 1950
.................6 Tracy Shrier b: 1955 in Cleveland, Cuyahoga, Ohio, USA
.................6 Robin Shrier b: 1958 in Cleveland, Cuyahoga, Ohio, USA
.................6 Harry Shrier b: 1961 in Cleveland, Cuyahoga, Ohio, USA
..............5 Harry Shrier b: 1928
.... + Joan Mason b: Rochester, Monroe, New York, USA, m: 1950
.................6 Todd Shrier b: 1953 in Rochester, Monroe, New York, USA
.................6 Steven Shrier b: 1955 in Rochester, Monroe, New York, USA
.................6 Elizabeth Shrier b: 1959 in Rochester, Monroe, New York, USA
...........4 Paul "Berton" Berlowitz b: Dec 25, 1893 in Michigan, USA, d: 1962 in New York, New York, USA
.... + Madelyn Frank b: 1899 in New York, New York, USA, m: 1919 in New York, New York, USA, d: 1972 in New York, New York, USA
..............5 Dorothy Berton b: 1924 in New York, New York, USA
.... + Shapiro
.................6 Margaret Shapiro b: 1948 in New York, New York, USA
.... + Alex Rose m: 1950
....................7 Joel Rose b: 1970
.................6 Carol Shapiro b: 1951 in New York, New York, USA
...........4 Harry R. Berlowitz b: Mar 15, 1896, d: Mar 1922 in Milwaukee, Milwaukee, Wisconsin, USA
........3 Felix Berlowitz b: Dec 30, 1862 in Goldap, Poland, d: Feb 16, 1939 in Dresden, Stadt Dresden, Saxony, Germany
.... + Franziska Freidlaender b: Dec 19, 1867 in Rudersdorf, Brandenburg, Germany, d: Nov 14, 1937 in Dresden, Stadt Dresden, Saxony, Germany
...........4 Hertha Berlowitz b: Apr 12, 1894 in Elblag, Warminsko-Mazurskie, Poland, d: Auschwitz, Poland; Holocaust
.... + Sigmund Basch b: Jun 13, 1883 in Wollstein, West Prussia, m: 1914 in Posen, West Prussia, d: Auschwitz, Poland; Holocaust
..............5 Hilde Basch b: Nov 11, 1915 in Posen, West Prussia
.... + Michael Joseph Loftus b: May 13, 1915 in Leigh, Dorset, England, m: Jan 31, 1942 in England
.................6 Brian Thomas Loftus b: Jun 15, 1943 in New York, New York, USA
.................6 Barbara Ann Loftus b: Jan 29, 1946 in New York, New York, USA

.... + Brian Costal b: Jun 15, 1943 in New York, New York, USA, m: Oct 08, 1968 in New York, New York, USA
..............5 Heinz Basch b: Apr 05, 1920 in Poznan, Wielkopolskie, Poland, d: Auschwitz, Poland; Holocaust
...........4 Lotte Berlowitz b: May 18, 1896 in Elblag, Warminsko-Mazurskie, Poland, d: Riga, Latvia, Holocaust
.... + George Cohn b: Jul 08, 1885 in Berlin, Stadt Berlin, Berlin, Germany, m: 1920 in Berlin, Stadt Berlin, Berlin,
            Germany, d: Riga, Riga, Latvia
..............5 Roy "Hans Cohn" Calder b: Apr 10, 1921 in Berlin, Stadt Berlin, Berlin, Germany
.... + Alice Baruch b: Sep 08, 1920 in Hamburg, Germany, m: Sep 08, 1942 in Edinburgh Tolbooth, Midlothian,
            Scotland
.................6 Michael Allen Calder b: Feb 22, 1944 in New York, New York, USA
.... + Judith Ann Hackett b: Dec 13, 1946, m: Sep 01, 1968 in San Francisco, San Francisco, California, USA
....................7 Brian Calder b: May 11, 1970 in San Francisco, San Francisco, California, USA
....................7 Deborah Anette Calder b: Mar 15, 1973 in San Francisco, San Francisco, California, USA
....................7 Naomi Calder b: 1979 in San Francisco, San Francisco, California, USA
.................6 Jacqueline Calder b: Jan 17, 1950 in New York, New York, USA
..............5 Steffie Cohn b: Mar 23, 1923 in Berlin, Stadt Berlin, Berlin, Germany, d: Holocaust
...........4 Gertrud Berlowitz b: Sep 17, 1897 in Elblag, Warminsko-Mazurskie, Poland, d: Sep 1943 in
            Theresienstadt, Germany; Holocaust
.... + Izidore Kann b: Abt. 1888 in Konitz, West Prussia, m: Apr 27, 1930 in Berlin, Stadt Berlin, Berlin, Germany,
            d: Theresienstadt, Germany; , Holocaust
.... + Max Podschubski m: Apr 28, 1919 in Germany
..............5 Fritz Podschubski b: Sep 21, 1921 in Landsberg, Landsberg am Lech, Bavaria, Germany, d: Auschwitz, Poland;
            Holocaust
...........4 Ilse Berlowitz b: May 21, 1904 in Elblag, Warminsko-Mazurskie, Poland, d: May 12, 1977 in Wiesbaden, Hesse,
            Germany
.... + Kurt Klinkowstein b: Apr 25, 1899 in Seeburg, West Prussia, m: Jun 14, 1927 in Elblag, Warminsko-Mazurskie,
            Poland, d: Jun 06, 1936 in Köenigsberg, East Prussia
..............5 Peter Hans Stone b: Sep 1928 in Köenigsberg, East Prussia
...........4 Lucie Berlowitz b: Mar 29, 1908 in Elblag, Warminsko-Mazurskie, Poland, d: Apr 19, 1993 in São Paulo, Bahia, Brazil
.... + Nathan Oberndoerfer b: Jul 15, 1902 ; Rothenberg Ob, Der, m: Jul 29, 1947 in Brazil, d: Aug 18, 1972 in São Paulo,
            Bahia, Brazil
.... + Alfred Steinecke b: May 13, 1901 in Angermund, Dusseldorf, North Rhine-Westphalia, Germany, m: Jun 23, 1929 in
            Elblag, Warminsko-Mazurskie, Poland, d: 1975 in Germany
..............5 Klaus Steinecke b: Mar 29, 1930 in Angermund, Dusseldorf, North Rhine-Westphalia, Germany
.... + Aurora Kleinmann b: Apr 02, 1929 in São Paulo, Bahia, Brazil, m: Jan 31, 1954 in São Paulo, Bahia, Brazil
.................6 Carlos Roberto Steinecke b: Feb 08, 1955 in São Paulo, Bahia, Brazil
.... + Denise Smelstein b: Mar 10, 1959 in São Paulo, Bahia, Brazil, m: Jun 24, 1959 in São Paulo, Bahia, Brazil
....................7 Fabio Steinecke b: Apr 18, 1985 in São Paulo, Bahia, Brazil
....................7 Michel Steinecke b: Feb 03, 1988 in São Paulo, Bahia, Brazil
.................6 Luis Sergio Steinecke b: Jan 31, 1958 in São Paulo, Bahia, Brazil
.... + Simone Priest b: Feb 10, 1959 in São Paulo, Bahia, Brazil, m: Dec 07, 1980 in São Paulo, Bahia, Brazil
....................7 Ursula Steinecke b: Apr 01, 1981 in São Paulo, Bahia, Brazil
..............5 Ursula Steinecke b: Oct 21, 1932 in Angermund, Dusseldorf, North Rhine-Westphalia, Germany
.... + Paul Lichtenstein b: Jun 06, 1922 in Saar Louis, Brazil, m: Feb 28, 1957 in São Paulo, Bahia, Brazil
.................6 Andre Max Lichtenstein b: Dec 09, 1957 in São Paulo, Bahia, Brazil
.... + Jussara Helene Correa b: Apr 18, 1951 in São Paulo, Bahia, Brazil, m: Dec 1981 in São Paulo, Bahia,
            Brazil
....................7 Marcello Lichtenstein b: Mar 14, 1989 in São Paulo, Bahia, Brazil
....................7 Ricardo Lichtenstein b: Apr 05, 1991 in São Paulo, Bahia, Brazil
.................6 Flavio Lichtenstein b: Jan 14, 1959 in São Paulo, Bahia, Brazil
.... + Regina Casseb Lima b: Nov 29, 1959 in São Paulo, Bahia, Brazil, m: 1984 in São Paulo, Bahia, Brazil
....................7 Paul Lichtenstein b: Apr 30, 1986 in São Paulo, Bahia, Brazil
....................7 Gabriela Lichtenstein b: Nov 04, 1988 in São Paulo, Bahia, Brazil

פראפ

Eliyahu Ben Shimon Prop

of

שקודוויל

Shkudvil, Vilna Guberniya
Russia Empire

1795 - Abt. 1826

He was born in Zemaitija Duchy, Grand Duchy of Lithuania-Poland He died in Gaure or Tavrig, Kovno, Russia.

*Dora and Anna Propp, daughters of Philip (Feivel Yitzchak) and Bluma
Propp - Chicago, Illinois*

Chicago, Illinois, 1939
Julius Propp, Sam Blumenthal, Lillian Propp, Michael Propp, Anna Propp

Mr. & Mrs. P. Propp
request the pleasure of your presence
at the wedding reception of their daughter

Lillian

and

Mr. Bert Ruben

Sunday evening, the twenty-fifth of December
One thousand nine hundred and ten
at half past seven o'clock
1016 South Marshfield Avenue
Chicago, Illinois

Bert Ruben

Blair 'Buddy' Ruben

Zerna Ruben

Lillian Propp Ruben

Bert Ruben Family of Chicago, Illinois

Lillian Propp Ruben
daughter of Philip (Feivel Yitzchak) and Bluma Propp

Zerna Ruben

1 Eliyahu Prop b: 1792 in Zemaitija Duchy, Grand Duchy of Lithuania-Poland, d: Abt. 1826 in Gaure, Kovno, Russia
... + Unknown
......2 Lozer Ben Eliyahu Prop b: 1820 in Gaure, Kovno, Russia, d: 1906 in Kovno, Kovno, Russia
...... + Pese b: 1820 in Tavrig, Kovno, Russia, m: 1845 in Kovno, Kovno, Russia; Same location as Kaunas, Lithuania,
     d: 1912 in Gaure, Kovno, Russia
.........3 Sora Prop b: Abt. 1840 in Gaure, Kovno, Russia, d: Dec 19, 1930 in Skaudvile, Taurage, Lithuania
.........3 Tauba Prop b: 1848 in Gaure, Kovno, Russia
.........3 Barnett (Shumel Ber) Propp b: May 1849 in Gaure, Kovno, Russia, d: Mar 18, 1923 in Chicago, Cook, Illinois,
     USA
.... + Hinda (Annie) Z. Rossenzwieg b: Mar 1857 in Gaure, Kovno Guberniya, Russia, m: 1877 in Kovno, Kovno, Russia;
     Same location as Kaunas, Lituania, d: Feb 16, 1910 in Chicago, Cook, Illinois, United States of America
............4 Isaac "Ike" Propp b: May 04, 1879 in Gaure, Kovno Guberniya, Russia, d: May 03, 1931 in Chicago, Cook, Illinois, USA
.... + Lillian Silverstein b: Dec 25, 1881 in Russia, m: 1903 in Chicago, Cook, Illinois, USA, d: Nov 15, 1970 in Chicago,
     Cook, Illinois, USA
...............5 Selma Propp b: Feb 14, 1905 in Peoria, Peoria, Illinois, USA, d: Nov 02, 1968 in Chicago, Cook, Illinois, USA
...............5 Corinine Propp b: Apr 30, 1907 in Chicago, Cook, Illinois, USA, d: Nov 16, 1937 in Chicago, Cook, Illinois,
     USA
.... + Edwin Nutter b: 1905 in Chicago, Cook, Illinois, USA, d: 1975 in Chicago, Cook, Illinois, USA
...............5 Melba Propp b: Aug 28, 1909 in Chicago, Cook, Illinois, USA, d: Nov 27, 1978 in Chicago, Cook, Illinois, USA
.... + Lloyd Biggs b: Dec 20, 1903 in Chicago, Cook, Illinois, USA, m: Chicago, Cook, Illinois, USA, d: Jul 25, 1989 in
     Chicago, Cook, Illinois, USA
.... + Meyer Patur b: May 04, 1893 in Chicago, Cook, Illinois, USA, m: 1925 in Chicago, Cook, Illinois, USA, d: Jan
     1985 in Chicago, Cook, Illinois, USA
..................6 Blair L. Patur b: Nov 02, 1926 in Chicago, Cook, Illinois, USA
.... + Phyllis Selma Cohen b: May 16, 1928 in Chicago, Cook, Illinois, USA, m: Jun 18, 1949 in Chicago, Cook,
     Illinois, USA
.....................7 Steven Ian Patur b: Jun 28, 1950 in Chicago, Cook, Illinois, USA
.... + Laurita Cruz b: 1952 in Chicago, Cook, Illinois, USA
........................8 Mary Elizabeth Remington b: Oct 13, 1983 in Chicago, Cook, Illinois, USA
.....................7 Laura Dine Patur b: Jan 23, 1953 in Chicago, Cook, Illinois, USA
.....................7 Sandra Jean Patur b: Dec 10, 1955 in Chicago, Cook, Illinois, USA
.... + Ronald J. Weiser b: Dec 13, 1954 in Chicago, Cook, Illinois, USA, m: Aug 15, 1982 in Chicago, Cook,
     Illinois, USA
........................8 Melissa Lynn Weiser b: Jan 24, 1984 in Chicago, Cook, Illinois, USA
........................8 Eric Zoltan Weiser b: Aug 31, 1993 in Chicago, Cook, Illinois, USA
..................6 Myrette Patur b: Nov 03, 1928 in Chicago, Cook, Illinois, USA, d: Dec 06, 1997 in Boulder, Boulder, Colorado,
     USA
.... + Alan Katz b: Nov 02, 1928 in Chicago, Cook, Illinois, USA, m: Abt. 1954 in Chicago, Cook, Illinois,
.....................7 Suzanne Katz b: Mar 28, 1956 in Chicago, Cook, Illinois, USA
.....................7 Clarissa Katz b: Jun 23, 1960 in Chicago, Cook, Illinois, USA
.... + Paul D. King b: 1948, m: 1983
........................8 Benjamin King b: 1986
........................8 Megan King b: 1990
...............5 Hinda Harvina Propp b: Dec 30, 1911 in Chicago, Cook, Illinois, USA, d: Dec 10, 1975 in Chicago, Cook, Illinois, USA
...............5 Lesile Boyd. Propp b: Oct 21, 1918 in Chicago, Cook, Illinois, USA, d: Nov 21, 1978 in Northbrook, Cook, Illinois, USA
.... + Eileen Barkan b: 1928 in Chicago, Cook, Illinois, USA, m: Jan 02, 1947 in Chicago, Cook, Illinois, USA, d:
     Northbrook, Cook, Illinois, USA
..................6 Carole Lesile Propp b: Dec 26, 1949 in Skokie, Cook, Illinois, USA
..................6 Douglas Alan "Twin" Propp b: May 31, 1953 in Skokie, Cook, Illinois, USA
.... + Rhonda Konarski b: Feb 02, 1956 in Chicago, Cook, Illinois, USA, m: 1985 in Chicago, Cook, Illinois, USA
.....................7 Jordon Leslie Propp b: May 05, 1988 in Chicago, Cook, Illinois, USA

....................7 Joshua Maxwell Propp b: Feb 04, 1991 in Chicago, Cook, Illinois, USA
.................6 Dennis Brian "Twin" Propp b: May 31, 1953 in Skokie, Cook, Illinois, USA
.... + Phyllis Boyd b: 1955 in Chicago, Cook, Illinois, USA, m: 1981 in Chicago, Cook, Illinois, USA
....................7 Lesile Boyd Propp b: Mar 30, 1983 in Chicago, Cook, Illinois, USA
....................7 Stacy B Propp b: Jan 30, 1986 in Chicago, Cook, Illinois, USA
....................7 J. Dillon Propp b: Apr 29, 1991 in Chicago, Cook, Illinois, USA
.............5 Eugene Arthur Propp b: Mar 13, 1921 in Canal Zone, Panama
.... + Guita Liane Rosbac b: Sep 01, 1928 in Brussels, Brussels (Bruxelles), Belgium, m: Abt. 1955 in Chicago, Cook, Illinois, USA, d: Mar 17, 2003 in Chicago, Cook, Illinois, USA
.................6 Winston E. Propp b: Oct 26, 1956 in Chicago, Cook, Illinois, USA, d: 2002 in Chicago, Cook, Illinois, USA
.................6 Gina Alexis Propp b: Jun 23, 1959 in Chicago, Cook, Illinois, USA
.... + Bradley S. Schmarak b: 1956 in Chicago, Cook, Illinois, USA, m: Abt. 1993 in Chicago, Cook, Illinois, USA
....................7 Tyler Schmarak b: Sep 18, 1994 in Chicago, Cook, Illinois, USA
....................7 Grant Schmarak b: Nov 17, 1997 in Chicago, Cook, Illinois, USA
...........4 Rebecca Beatrice Propp b: Apr 14, 1889 in Gaure, Kovno, Russia, d: Oct 27, 1925 in Chicago, Cook, Illinois, USA
.... + Louis Silberman b: 1884 in Pennsylvania, m: Aug 21, 1912 in Chicago, Cook, Illinois, USA, d: Chicago, Cook, Illinois, USA
.............5 Harriette Rochelle Silberman b: Jul 15, 1912 in Chicago, Cook, Illinois, USA, d: Nov 23, 2003 in Hallandale, Broward, Florida, USA
.... + Jack Lipsitz b: Jul 15, 1911 in Pittsburgh, Pennsylvania, USA, m: Jun 23, 1937 in Chicago, Cook, Illinois, USA, d: Oct 23, 1987 in Hallandale, Broward, Florida, USA
.............5 Stanley Bert Silberman b: May 08, 1917 in Jasper, Indiana, USA, d: Aug 1965 in Chicago, Cook, Illinois, USA
.............5 James Silberman b: 1919 in Chicago, Cook, Illinois, USA
.............5 Beck Garson Silberman Silbe b: Oct 27, 1925 in Cook County, IL, d: Apr 24, 2011 in Palm Springs, Riverside, California, USA
.... + Esther Louise Fultz b: Apr 14, 1918 in Indianapolis, Marion, Indiana, USA, m: Oct 23, 1993 in Garden Grove, Orange, California, USA, d: Mar 04, 2010 in Palm Desert, Riverside, California, USA; burial Crystal Cath, Los Angeles, California
...........4 Ida "Leah" Propp b: Apr 14, 1889 in Gaure, Kovno Guberniya, Russia, d: Dec 1970 in Chicago, Cook, Illinois, USA
.... + Abraham Singer b: Jan 19, 1889 in Chicago, Cook, Illinois, USA, m: 1913 in Chicago, Cook, Illinois, USA, d: Jun 1978 in Chicago, Cook, Illinois, USA
.............5 Harold P. Singer b: Sep 17, 1911 in Chicago, Cook, Illinois, USA, d: Sep 25, 1991 in Chicago, Cook, Illinois, USA
.... + Ruth b: 1917 in Chicago, Cook, Illinois, USA
.............5 Sylvia Singer b: Sep 10, 1916 in Chicago, Cook, Illinois, USA, d: Jan 12, 1993 in Chicago, Cook, Illinois, USA
...........4 Sarah "Sally" Propp b: Apr 02, 1895 in Chicago, Cook, Illinois, USA, d: Dec 1983 in Bronx, Bronx, New York, USA
.... + Isadore "Izzy" Fabian b: Feb 06, 1894 in Hungary, m: Aft. 1920 in Chicago, Cook, Illinois, USA, d: Jul 1967 in New York, New York, USA; Age at Death: 73
.............5 Shaldon B Fabian b: Abt. 1924 in Chicago, Cook, Illinois, USA, d: Jun 04, 1944 in Normandy, France
.............5 Harvey J. Fabian b: May 28, 1931 in Chicago, Cook, Illinois, USA, d: Jan 15, 1999 in Chicago, Cook, Illinois, USA
.... + Rebecca Shapiro b: Abt. 1855, m: Aft. 1911 in Chicago, Cook, Illinois, USA, d: Jan 06, 1929 in Chicago, Cook, Illinois, USA
.........3 Philip (Feivel Yitzhak) Propp b: May 14, 1855 in Gaure, Kovno, Russia, d: Dec 18, 1920 in Chicago, Cook, Illinois, USA
.... + Bluma Sora Propp b: Sep 1856 in Skaudvile, Kovno, Russia, m: 1879 in Skaudvile, Kovno, Russia, d: May 11, 1917 in Chicago, Cook, Illinois, USA
...........4 Devorah "Dora" Propp b: Sep 27, 1881 in Gaure, Kovno, Russia, d: Aug 18, 1933 in Chicago, Cook, Illinois, USA
...........4 Anna Propp b: Apr 19, 1883 in Tavrig, Kovno, Russia, d: Oct 14, 1958 in Chicago, Cook, Illinois, USA
...........4 Charles H. "Solomon" Propp b: May 1884 in Tavrig, Kovno, Russia, d: Jun 07, 1940 in South Bend, St Joseph, Indiana, USA
.... + Sophia Brooks b: England, m: Jan 25, 1910 in Chicago, Cook, Illinois, USA, d: 1984 in South Bend, St Joseph, Indiana, USA

...........5 Elliott Stanley Propp b: Nov 10, 1910 in Michigan City, La Porte, Indiana, USA, d: Aug 10, 1979 in Los Angeles, Los Angeles, California, USA
.... + Joan Muriel Zapolen b: Jun 01, 1912 in Chicago, Cook, Illinois, USA, m: 1939 in Chicago, Cook, Illinois, USA, d: May 24, 1991 in Los Angeles, Los Angeles, California, USA
...........6 Virginia C. "Dina" Propp b: Mar 16, 1941 in Chicago, Cook, Illinois, USA
.... + James L. Divine m: Jan 10, 1958 in Cook, Illinois, USA
.............7 Michael James Devine b: Oct 06, 1958 in Los Angeles, Los Angeles, California, USA
.... + Gwendlen "Wendy" Sladen b: Mar 05, 1961 in Los Angeles, Los Angeles, California, USA
.............8 Rebecca Angela Devine b: Mar 05, 1992 in Los Angeles, Los Angeles, California, USA
.............8 Emily Alexandra Devine b: Apr 15, 1994 in Los Angeles, Los Angeles, California, USA
.............7 Constance Ann Devine b: Jun 09, 1961 in Los Angeles, Los Angeles, California, USA
.... + Melvin Gallaway b: 1961 in Los Angeles, Los Angeles, California, USA
.............8 Melvin Gallaway b: Aug 1990 in Los Angeles, Los Angeles, California, USA
.............8 Brooklyn Gallaway b: May 1992 in Los Angeles, Los Angeles, California, USA
.... + Robert L Melville b: 1938 in Los Angeles, Los Angeles, California, USA
...........5 Earle Brooks Propp b: Jun 02, 1915 in Decatur, Van Buren, Michigan, USA, d: Aug 19, 2004 in Bradenton, Manatee, Florida, USA
.... + Ruth C. Lentzer b: 1918 in Detroit, Wayne, Michigan, USA
...........6 Carla Diane Propp b: 1945 in Chicago, Cook, Illinois, USA
.... + Gilbert Bernard Ceifetz b: 1942 in Detroit, Wayne, Michigan, USA, m: Abt. 1964
.............7 Glenn Ceifetz b: 1966 in Westland, Wayne, Michigan, USA
.............7 Dean Ceifetz b: 1969 in Westland, Wayne, Michigan, USA
...........6 Charles H Propp b: May 16, 1948 in Chicago, Cook, Illinois, USA
...........5 Barbara "Bobby" Propp b: Abt. 1925 in South Bend, St Joseph, Indiana, USA, d: 2014 in Houston, Texas
.... + Arthur Wachtel b: May 01, 1918 in Chicago, Cook, Ilinois, USA, m: 1944 in Dade, Florida, d: Oct 22, 2003 in Palm Desert, Riverside, California, USA; Age at Death: 85
...........6 Arthur Brooks Wachtel b: Sep 09, 1949 in Washington, DC, USA
...........6 Steven J Wachtel b: Sep 21, 1952 in Trinidad, Cartago, Costa Rica, d: 2014 in Los Angelis, California
.... + Ronda Burns b:Sep 01, 1947 in Los Angelis, Los Angelis, California, USA
.............7 Melodie Wachtel
...........6 Sharon L Wachtel b:Aug 09, 1960 in San Diego, California
.... + Sunil L Chada b:Feb 26, 1960, m: Los Angelis, Los Angelis, California, USA
.............7 Sasha Chada b:Jan 27, 1992 in Los Angelis, Los Angelis, California, USA
.............7 Misha Chada b:Sep 09, 1996 in Los Angelis, Los Angelis, California, USA
.........4 Lillian Propp b: Jan 1888 in Chicago, Cook, Illinois, USA, d: Nov 15, 1970 in Chicago, Cook, Illinois, USA
.... + Bert Ruben b: Oct 11, 1887 in Grimsby, Lincolnshire, England, m: Dec 25, 1910 in Chicago Ward 19, Cook, Illinois, USA, d: Mar 05, 1978 in Chicago, Cook, Illinois, USA
...........5 Zerna "Tzerna Chaya" Ruben b: Nov 02, 1911 in Chicago, Cook, Illinois, USA, d: Apr 13, 1996 in Boynton, Palm Beach, Florida, USA
...........5 Blair "Buddy" S. Ruben b: May 05, 1918 in Chicago, Cook, Illinois, USA, d: Jan 16, 2003 in Casper, Natrona, Wyoming, USA
.... + Sylvia Ginsberg b: May 09, 1920 in Dalton, Whitfield, Georgia, USA, m: 1942 in Chicago, Cook, Illinois, USA, d: Aug 04, 1997 in Boynton, Palm Beach, Florida, USA
...........6 David Hillel (Donald) Ruben b: Jul 25, 1943 in Chicago, Cook, Illinois, USA
.... + Eira Karlinsky b: Nov. 21 1945 in Wales, m: 1968 in New York, New York, USA
.............7 Anna Lilian Ruben b: Jun 04, 1972 in Glasgow, Lanarkshire, Scotland
.... + David Spivac b: Jul 28, 1970 in Paris, Ile-de-France, France, m: Jul 2000 in Paris, Ile-de-France, France
.............8 Arielle Leora Spivac b: Jul 20, 2004 in London, London, England
.............7 Sophie Rachel Ruben b: Aug 16, 1977 in London, London, England
.... + Adam Silverstein b: Oct 20, 1976 in New York, New York, USA, m: Jul 1999 in Cambridge, Cambridgeshire, England
.............8 Ella Zoe Silverstein b: Feb 18, 2006 in London, London, England
.............8 Zara Eva Silverstein b: Jun 09, 2008 in London, London, England
.............8 Theodore Silverstein b: Jan. 04 2011 in London, London, England
.............7 Simon Daniel Ruben b: May 04, 1980 in London, London, England
.... + Natasha Simon b: Oct 14, 1980 in Caracas, Distrito Federal, Venezuela, m: 2008 in Caesarea, Israel
.............8 Asher Brian Ruben b: Jan. 11 2012 in London England
.............8 Gabriella Sylvia Ruben b: Nov. 12 2014
...........6 Stuart J. Ruben b: Dec 09, 1945 in Chicago, Cook, Illinois, USA

.... + Estelle S. Schlager b: 1945 in Cincinnati, Clermont, Ohio, USA

.....................7 Andrew Bruce Ruben b: 1969 in Columbus, Fairfield, Ohio, USA

.... + Kristi Bahr b: 1970 in Fairfax Station, Fairfax, Virginia, USA, m: 1995 in Fairfax Station, Fairfax, Virginia, USA

.....................8 Sawyer Ruben b: Jan. 28, 1999 in Loiusville, Colorado

.....................8 Reece Ruben b.March 21, 2001 in Ft. Collins, Colorado

.....................7 Brenda Ruben b: 1974 in Melbourne, Brevard, Florida, USA

.........................8 Allison Ruben

.................6 Kenneth Louis Ruben b: Mar 03, 1949 in Birmingham, Jefferson, Alabama, USA

............4 Michael Herman Propp b: Dec 11, 1892 in Chicago, Cook, Illinois, USA, d: Jul 14, 1949 in Chicago, Cook, Illinois, USA

.... + Cecliah Mendelsohn b: 1893 in Philadelphia, Philadelphia, Pennsylvania, USA, m: 1918 in Chicago, Cook, Illinois, USA, d: 1975 in Philadelphia, Philadelphia, Pennsylvania, USA

...............5 Phyllis E Propp b: Jan 04, 1924 in Chicago, Cook, Illinois, USA, d: Jan 23, 2002 in Daytona Beach, Volusia, Florida, USA

.... + Milton D. Greenberg b: 1919 in Philadelphia, Philadelphia, Pennsylvania, USA, m: Abt. 1968

פְּרָאפ

Rivka bat Shimon Prop

of

שקודוויל

Shkudvil, Vilna Guberniya
Russia Empire

1799 - 1882

Rivka married Aaron and the family remained in Shkudvil for the couple of generations then many immigrated to the United States and elsewhere in the world. All of their children seemed to take different surnames; Fishman, Arnovitz, Friedman and Leah married Yosef Perez and their family took the name Joseph when entering the United States.

1 Rivka Prop b: 1799 in Skaudvile, Kovno, Russia, d: 1882 in Skaudvile, Kovno, Russia

... + Oral "Ahron" b: 1790 in Zemaitija Duchy, Grand Duchy of Lithuania, m: Skaudvile, Kovno, Russia, d: 1863 in Kovno, Kovno, Russia; Same location as the area surrounding Kaunas, Lithuania

......2 Peretz Ovsey Davidzon b: 1819 in Vainutas, Kovno, Russia, d: Vainutas, Kovno, Russia

...... + Roch"'l "Reyza" b: 1816 in Vainutas, Kovno, Russia, m: Abt. 1837 in Kovno, Kovno, Russia; Same location as Kaunas, Lithuania, d: Vainutas, Kovno, Russia

.........3 Gita Ester Davidzon b: 1838 in Vainutas, Kovno, Russia, d: Skaudvile, Kovno, Russia; Skaudvile, Taurage, Lithuainia/Skaudvile, Taurage, Lithuania/

.... + Kalman Kaplan b: 1840 in Skaudvile, Kovno, Russia; Skaudvile, Taurage, Lithuainia/Skaudvile, Taurage, Lithuania/, d: 1913 in Skaudvile, Kovno, Russia; Skaudvile, Taurage, Lithuainia/Skaudvile, Taurage, Lithuania/

............4 Ber Yudel Kaplan b: May 09, 1879 in Jonava, Kaunas, Kaunas

................5 Henry Kaplan b: 1901

................5 Frank Kaplan b: 1903

................5 Fred Kaplan b: 1907

............4 William Kaplan b: 1880 in Skaudvile, Kovno, Russia; Skaudvile, Taurage District, Lithuania/Skaudvile, Taurage, Lithuania/

.........3 Shaya Mendel Aronovich b: 1839 in Vainutas, Kovno, Russia, d: 1919 in Jerusalem, Eretz Yisrael, Israel

.... + Sora Prop b: 1838 in Skaudvile, Kovno, Russia, m: Abt. 1862 in Kovno, Kovno, Russia; Same location as Kaunas, Lithuania, d: 1891 in Skaudvile, Kovno, Russia

............4 Chaye-Rivka Aronovich b: 1864 in Skaudvile, Kovno, Russia; Skaudvile, Taurage, Lithuainia/Skaudvile, Taurage, Lithuania/

.... + Itzig Seif b: 1860 in Skaudvile, Kovno, Russia; Skaudvile, Taurage, Lithuainia/Skaudvile, Taurage, Lithuania/

................5 Charles Seif

................5 Hinde Seif

................5 John Seif

................5 Pere Seif

................5 Philip Seif

............4 Roch"l Aronovich b: 1864 in Skaudvile, Kovno, Russia, d: Dec 07, 1923 in Chicago, Cook, Illinois, USA

.... + Joseph "Yosef Propp" Berlow b: Dec 15, 1858 in Skaudvile, Kovno, Russia, m: 1884 in Philadelphia, Philadelphia, Pennsylvania, USA, d: Jun 14, 1927 in Chicago, Cook, Illinois, USA

................5 Charles Berlow b: Aug 02, 1883 in Wilkes-Barre, Luzerne, Pennsylvania, USA, d: Mar 03, 1947 in South Bend, St Joseph, Indiana, USA

.... + Celia Gershman b: Sep 18, 1885 in Chicago, Cook, Illinois, USA, d: May 1974 in South Bend, St Joseph, Indiana, USA

................5 Abraham L. Berlow b: 1887 in Philadelphia, Philadelphia, Pennsylvania, USA, d: Aug 19, 1958 in Hollywood, Broward, Florida, USA

.... + Mae Minsky b: Feb 11, 1893 in South Bend, St Joseph, Indiana, USA, m: Abt. 1915 in Chicago, Cook, Illinois, USA, d: Jun 1966 in Hollywood, Broward, Florida, USA

................5 Harry Berlow b: 1889 in St Paul, Dakota, Minnesota, USA, d: Sep 22, 1952 in Chicago, Cook, Illinois,

.... + Jennie Chalem b: Jan 10, 1899 in Chicago, Cook, Illinois, USA, m: 1923, d: Dec 25, 1950 in Chicago, Cook, Illinois, USA

...................6 Ralph Richard Berlow b: 1927 in Chicago, Cook, Illinois, USA, d: 1984 in Virginia, USA

.... + Patricia b: 1927

......................7 James Richard Berlow b: 1952 in Chicago, Cook, Illinois, USA

.... + Nancy Willis b: 1956

..........................8 Anne Berlow b: 1986 in Vienna, Fairfax, Virginia, USA

..........................8 Scott Richard Berlow b: 1988 in Vienna, Fairfax, Virginia, USA

......................7 Cathy Lynn Berlow b: 1955 in Chicago, Cook, Illinois, USA

.... + Ella Tecotsky b: 1891 in Chicago, Cook, Illinois, USA, m: 1916 in Chicago, Cook, Illinois, USA, d: 1917 in Chicago, Cook, Illinois, USA

................5 Irving E. Berlow b: Oct 23, 1892 in Ishpeming, Marquette, Michigan, USA, d: Jan 01, 1965 in Phoenix, Maricopa, Arizona, USA

.... + Florence Horowitz b: 1897 in Detroit, Wayne, Michigan, USA, d: 1970 in Phoenix, Maricopa, Arizona, USA

...................6 Shirley Berlow b: Jul 14, 1922 in Detroit, Wayne, Michigan, USA, d: Feb 07, 2002 in San Antonio, Bexar, Texas, USA

.... + Robert Joseph Simon b: 1920 in Chicago, Cook, Illinois, USA, m: 1943 in Chicago, Cook, Illinois, USA, d: Bef. 1954
....................7 Roger Simon b: May 12, 1945 in Los Angeles, Los Angeles, California, USA, d: 1984
.... + Irving Simon b: 1922 in Chicago, Cook, Illinois, USA, d: Unknown in Chicago, Cook, Illinois, USA
....................7 Randy Simon b: Oct 10, 1954 in Phoenix, Maricopa, Arizona, USA
.... + John Lady b: 1918, d: Unknown
................6 Eleanor Berlow b: Sep 12, 1927 in Chicago, Cook, Illinois, USA
.... + Sidney H Wolfson b: Jan 24, 1919 in Gaffney, Cherokee, South Carolina, USA, m: Abt. 1948, d: Dec 09, 2004 in San Antonio, Bexar, Texas, USA
....................7 Sheri Lynn Wolfson b: Jun 12, 1949 in Point Eustis, Virginia
....................7 Daniel Wolfson b: 1953 in Memphis, Shelby, Tennessee, USA
.... + Chery Lamb b: 1955
........................8 Susan Taylor Wolfson b: Dec 25, 1986 in Nashue, New Hampshire
........................8 Austin Wolfson b: Jan 06, 1988
........................8 Kendell Wolfson b: Jan 06, 1988
..............5 Peter R. Berlow b: Feb 12, 1894 in Ishpeming, Marquette, Michigan, USA, d: Jan 14, 1967 in Los Angeles, Los Angeles, California, USA
.... + Dora Goldstein b: Jul 10, 1894 in Chicago, Cook, Illinois, USA, d: Nov 08, 1994 in Los Angeles, Los Angeles, California, USA
..............5 Rose Anna "Hinda" Berlow b: 1897 in St Paul, Dakota, Minnesota, USA, d: 1982 in Chicago, Cook, Illinois, USA
.... + Benjamin Isaac Twery b: 1897 in Chicago, Cook, Illinois, USA, d: 1972 in Florida, USA
................6 Raymond Twery b: 1930 in Chicago, Cook, Illinois, USA
.... + Maxine Norma Rudman b: 1934 in St Louis, Missouri, USA, m: 1954 in Evanston, Cook, Illinois, USA
....................7 Michael Jay Twery b: 1956 in Champaign, Champaign, Illinois, USA
.... + Linda Ai Kheng Wong b: 1960, m: 1989 in Charlotte, Mecklenburg, North Carolina, USA
....................7 Scott Craig Twery b: 1958 in St Louis, Missouri, USA
.... + Deborah Carol Theissen b: 1955 in Connecticut, USA, m: 1990 in Atlanta, De Kalb, Georgia, USA
........................8 Hanna Rose Twery b: 1992 in Atlanta, De Kalb, Georgia, USA
....................7 Seth Aaron Twery b: 1961 in Carmel, Monterey, California, USA
.... + Marrene Del Pierce b: 1963 in Charlotte, Mecklenburg, North Carolina, USA
........................8 Nicole Twery b: Jan 31, 1997 in Charlotte, Mecklenburg, North Carolina, USA
....................7 Bruce Hugh Twery b: 1963 in Charlotte, Mecklenburg, North Carolina, USA
.... + Teresa "Tina" Sicher b: 1961 in Kane, McKean, Pennsylvania, USA, m: 1990 in Kane, McKean, Pennsylvania, USA
........................8 Alexander Twery b: 1991 in Baltimore, Maryland, USA
........................8 Joshua Keller Twery b: 1992 in Baltimore, Maryland, USA
........................8 Benjamin Louis Twery b: 1994 in Baltimore, Maryland, USA
........................8 Twery b: Jan 2000
..............5 Maurice P "Moshe" Berlow b: Mar 22, 1899 in Sault Sainte Marie, Chippewa, Michigan, USA, d: Mar 1983 in Miami, Dade, Florida, USA
.... + Evelyn Feuereisen b: May 31, 1909 in New York, New York, USA, m: Feb 02, 1933 in Chicago, Cook, Illinois, USA, d: Aug 26, 1997 in Los Angeles, Los Angeles, California, USA
................6 Irene Bunny Berlow b: 1936 in Chicago, Cook, Illinois, USA, d: 1967 in Chicago, Cook, Illinois, USA
................6 Linda Rachael Berlow b: 1938 in Chicago, Cook, Illinois, USA
.... + Dennis Kluk b: Apr 15, 1946 in Racine, Racine, Wisconsin, USA, m: Nov 25, 2002 in Skokie, Cook, Illinois, USA
.... + Rose b: 1910 in Chicago, Cook, Illinois, USA, m: 1982 in Miami Beach, Dade, Florida, USA
..............5 Sarah Berlow b: 1900 in Calumet, Houghton, Michigan, USA, d: 1983 in California, USA
.... + William Romain b: 1898 in Chicago, Cook, Illinois, USA, d: 1988 in California, USA
................6 Joseph R "Jerry" Romain b: 1930 in Chicago, Cook, Illinois, USA
.... + Gail b: 1945 in Chicago, Cook, Illinois, USA
....................7 Matthew Romain b: 1972 in Chicago, Cook, Illinois, USA
.... + Sheila b: 1938 in Chicago, Cook, Illinois, USA, m: 1986 in Chicago, Cook, Illinois, USA
..............5 Gordon P Berlow b: 1907 in Calumet, Houghton, Michigan, USA, d: Feb 27, 1967 in Chicago, Cook, Illinois, USA
.... + Esther Wigodski b: May 19, 1911 in Chicago, Cook, Illinois, USA, d: Sep 1984 in Chicago, Cook, Illinois, USA
................6 Bruce Berlow b: 1941 in Chicago, Cook, Illinois, USA

................6 Susan Berlow b: 1946 in Chicago, Cook, Illinois, USA

............4 Louis "Lazer Aronovich" Arne b: Feb 11, 1867 in Skaudvile, Kovno, Russia, d: Sep 18, 1939 in Milwaukee, Milwaukee, Wisconsin, USA

.... + Celia Ruttenberg b: 1872 in Skaudvile, Kovno, Russia, m: Aug 16, 1893 in Ishpeming, Marquette, Michigan, USA, d: Oct 29, 1957 in Chicago, Cook, Illinois, USA

................5 Sarah Arne b: Jul 02, 1895 in Ishpeming, Marquette, Michigan, USA, d: Oct 1977 in Chicago, Cook, Illinois, USA

.... + George Leviton b: Sep 27, 1890 in Kovno, Kovno, Russia, d: Jan 1963 in Chicago, Cook, Illinois, USA

................6 Theodore Leviton b: Oct 01, 1929 in Milwaukee, Milwaukee, Wisconsin, USA, d: Feb 1980 in Chicago, Cook, Illinois, USA

.... + Harriet Joyce Franklin b: May 22, 1945 in Chicago, Cook, Illinois, USA, m: 1967 in Chicago, Cook, Illinois, USA

....................7 Brook Jennifer Leviton b:Dec 19, 1972 in Chicago, Cook, Illinois, USA

.... + Michael Mandie

....................8   ?   Mandie

....................8   ?   Mandie

....................7 Alison Lee Leviton b:Oct 1, 1975 in Chicago, Cook, Illinois, USA

.... + Vitaly Rindner b:Sep 17, 1975, Minsk, Minsk, Belarus

....................8 Theodora Rindner

................6 Joyce Leviton b: 1933 in Chicago, Cook, Illinois, USA

.... + Gershon Hammer b: Sep 19, 1934 in Chicago, Cook, Illinois, USA

....................7 Lori Hammer b: Jan 02, 1968 in Chicago, Cook, Illinois, USA, d: Jan 01, 1997 in Chicago, Cook, Illinois, USA

.... + David Charles Recupero b: 1961, m: Jul 22, 1989 in Racine, Racine, Wisconsin, USA

.... + Alan Zelinsky b: Feb 18, 1933 in Chicago, Cook, Illinois, USA, m: Aug 27, 1956 in Chicago, Cook, Illinois, USA

....................7 Deborah Gail Zelinsky b: Jan 05, 1960 in Chicago, Cook, Illinois, USA

................5 Phillip A. Arne b: Sep 05, 1898 in Calumet, Houghton, Michigan, USA, d: Jun 1972 in Milwaukee, Milwaukee, Wisconsin, USA

.... + Bertha Levin b: May 14, 1910 in Racine, Racine, Wisconsin, USA, d: Jun 16, 2007 in Slinger, Washington, Wisconsin, USA; Age at Death: 97

................6 Annette Rachele Arne b: Feb 13, 1936 in Milwaukee, Milwaukee, Wisconsin, USA, d: Jul 11, 1986 in Milwaukee, Milwaukee, Wisconsin

.... + Ronald Irving Pachefsky b: Nov 23, 1932 in Milwaukee, Milwaukee, Wisconsin, USA

....................7 Mark Robert Pachefsky b: Aug 21, 1958 in Milwaukee, Milwaukee, Wisconsin, USA

.... + Lori Goldner b: Mar 21, 1962 in Milwaukee, Milwaukee, Wisconsin, USA, m: Jun 13, 1982 in Milwaukee, Milwaukee, Wisconsin, USA

....................8 Braley Pachefsky b: 1985 in Milwaukee, Milwaukee, Wisconsin, USA

....................8 Cory Pachefsky b: 1987 in Milwaukee, Milwaukee, Wisconsin, USA

....................8 Andrew Pachefsky b: 1989 in Milwaukee, Milwaukee, Wisconsin, USA

....................7 Larry A Pachefsky b: Jul 22, 1960 in Milwaukee, Milwaukee, Wisconsin, USA

.... + Ronna M Bromberg b: Nov 23, 1963 in Pittsburgh, Allegheny, Pennsylvania, USA

....................8 Joel Pachefsky b: 1990 in Milwaukee, Milwaukee, Wisconsin, USA

....................8 David Pachefsky b: 1991 in Milwaukee, Milwaukee, Wisconsin, USA

....................8 Michel Pachefsky b: 1993 in Milwaukee, Milwaukee, Wisconsin, USA

.... + Max Streitman b: 1929 in Minneapolis, Anoka, Minnesota, USA

................5 Charles B. Arne b: Jan 01, 1901 in Hancock, Houghton, Michigan, USA, d: Oct 19, 1965 in Milwaukee, Milwaukee County, Wisconsin; Wisconsin Death Index, 1959-1997 and Social Security Death Index

.... + Mary Sagle b: 1912 in Milwaukee, Milwaukee, Wisconsin, USA, d: Aug 12, 1983 in Marin County,California; California, Death Index, 1940-1997

................6 Janice Arne b: 1929 in Milwaukee, Milwaukee, Wisconsin, USA, d: 1986 in Boston, Suffolk,

.... + Robert Gold b: 1927 in Milwaukee, Milwaukee, Wisconsin, USA

....................7 Michael Gold b: 1951 in West Medford, Middlesex, Massachusetts, USA

.... + Ricki Tanger b: 1953

....................8 Taylor Gold b: 1974

....................7 Peter Gold b: 1953 in West Medford, Middlesex, Massachusetts, USA

.... + Candy Kosow b: 1954

....................8 Carly Gold b: 1975

....................8 David Gold b: 1977

....................7 James Elieger Gold b: 1955 in West Medford, Middlesex, Massachusetts, USA

.... + Basya Bookfinder b: 1957 in Massachusetts, USA

....................8 Menachem Gold b: 1980

....................8 Levi Gold b: 1982

....................8 Hunnah Gold b: 1985

...................8 Chaya Gold b: 1988
.................6 Eleanor Claire Arne b: May 12, 1942 in Milwaukee, Milwaukee County, Wisconsin, d: Oct 27, 2000 in Greenbrae,Marin County, California; Social Security Death Index
.... + Elmer Arthur Pirelli b: Oct 19, 1942 in Milwaukee, Milwaukee County, Wisconsin
.....................7 Lisa Ann Pirelli b: Jun 23, 1965 in Novato, Marin, California, USA
.....................7 Arthur Allen Pirelli b: Oct 28, 1966 in Novato, Marin, California, USA
.... + Patricia
.... + Sarah "Rose" Bromovitz b: 1905 in Milwaukee, Milwaukee, Wisconsin, USA, d: 1987 in Milwaukee, Milwaukee, Wisconsin, USA
..............5 Lillian Arne b: May 11, 1902 in Calumet, Houghton, Michigan, USA, d: Aug 04, 1980 in Wisconsin, Milwaukee
..............5 Rosalye Arne b: 1904 in Calumet, Houghton, Michigan, USA, d: 1986 in Milwaukee, Milwaukee, Wisconsin, USA
.... + John Schwartz b: Sep 13, 1901 in Milwaukee, Milwaukee, Wisconsin, USA, m: 1934 in Milwaukee, Milwaukee, Wisconsin, USA, d: Jun 1981 in Milwaukee, Milwaukee, Wisconsin, USA
.................6 Hershel Schwartz b: 1936 in Milwaukee, Milwaukee, Wisconsin, USA
.... + Arlene b: 1936 in Milwaukee, Milwaukee, Wisconsin, USA
.................6 Lois Schwartz b: 1938 in Milwaukee, Milwaukee, Wisconsin, USA
.... + Martin Shickman b: May 27, 1927 in Milwaukee, Milwaukee, Wisconsin, USA, d: Apr 21, 1995 in Los Angeles, Los Angeles, California, USA
.....................7 Steven Shickman b: 1958 in Los Angeles, Los Angeles, California, USA
.....................7 David Shickman b: 1962 in Los Angeles, Los Angeles, California, USA
.... + Kathryn b: 1964
........................8 Ryan Shickman b: 1991 in Los Angeles, Los Angeles, California, USA
........................8 Jordan William Shickman b: Feb 10, 1995 in Los Angeles, Los Angeles, California, USA
.....................7 Trevor Shickman b: 1970 in Los Angeles, Los Angeles, California, USA
...........4 Benjamin "Bentzion Aronovich" Arne b: Mar 04, 1873 in Skaudvile, Kovno, Russia, d: Bef. 1930 in Milwaukee, Milwaukee, Wisconsin, USA
.... + Fannie Steier b: 1880 in Austria, m: 1901 in Hancock, Houghton, Michigan, USA
..............5 Cecile Arne b: Aug 06, 1901 in Hancock, Houghton, Michigan, USA, d: Aug 09, 1954 in Chicago, Cook, Illinois, USA
..............5 Earl Arne b: Nov 01, 1904 in Calumet, Houghton, Michigan, USA, d: Feb 01, 1905 in Calumet, Houghton, Michigan, USA
..............5 Preston Samuel Arne b: Mar 28, 1907 in Hancock, Houghton, Michigan, USA, d: Jun 29, 1987 in Palm Springs, Riverside, California, USA
.... + Phyllis Mandel b: Dec 08, 1909 in Chicago, Cook, Illinois, USA, d: May 27, 1995 in Palm Springs, Riverside, California, USA
.... + Marjasha Prop b: Abt. 1839 in Skaudvile, Kovno, Russia, d: 1918 in Jerusalem, Eretz Yisrael
.........3 Moshe Davidzon b: Abt. 1846
.........3 Sheyna Sora Davidzon b: 1848 in Vainutas, Kovno, Russia
.........3 Kalman Meyer Davidson b: Aug 15, 1860 in Vainutas, Kovno, Russia, d: Jul 22, 1938 in West Roxbury, Suffolk, Massachusetts, USA
.... + Margaret E. "Gitel" Lipschitz b: Oct 25, 1867 in Skaudvile, Kovno, Russia, m: 1887 in Skaudvile, Kovno, Russia, d: Nov 07, 1911 in West Roxbury, Suffolk, Massachusetts, USA
...........4 Anna E Davidson b: Oct 17, 1888 in Skaudvile, Kovno, Russia, d: Jan 10, 1970 in Roxbury, Suffolk, Massachusetts, USA
.... + Mark Linenthal b: Nov 02, 1886 in Boston, Suffolk, Massachusetts, USA, m: 1911 in Boston, Suffolk, Massachusetts, USA, d: Feb 07, 1976 in Boston, Suffolk, Massachusetts, USA
..............5 Margaret Linenthal b: Oct 15, 1912 in Boston, Suffolk, Massachusetts, USA, d: Mar 21, 1989 in
.... + Paul Kervin Goldman b: Apr 19, 1906 in Boston, Suffolk, Massachusetts, USA, m: 1936 in Boston, Suffolk, Massachusetts, USA, d: Jan 02, 1980 in Boston, Suffolk, Massachusetts, USA
.................6 Paula Goldman b: Jun 01, 1938 in Boston, Suffolk, Massachusetts, USA
.... + Philip Friend b: Oct 27, 1938 in Boston, Suffolk, Massachusetts, USA, m: Jun 12, 1960 in Boston, Suffolk, Massachusetts, USA, d: Mar 24, 1994 in Palo Alto, San Mateo, California, USA
.....................7 Robert Charles Friend b: Mar 25, 1962 in Los Angeles, Los Angeles, California, USA
.... + Laurie Grant b: 1962 in Iowa, USA
.....................7 Marc Allen Friend b: Apr 21, 1964 in Los Angeles, Los Angeles, California, USA
.....................7 Susan Phylis Friend b: Dec 13, 1967 in Los Angeles, Los Angeles, California, USA
.... + Daniel Anthony Vorhess b: Feb 04, 1938 in Los Angeles, Los Angeles, California, USA, m: Aug 11, 1985 in Los Angeles, Los Angeles, California, USA

................6 Carol May Goldman b: May 10, 1946 in Boston, Suffolk, Massachusetts, USA

.... + Mark Edward Haltom b: Mar 21, 1948 in Boston, Suffolk, Massachusetts, USA, m: 1985

.... + Richard Neil Braude b: Nov 05, 1945 in Cambridge, Middlesex, Massachusetts, USA, m: 1970 in Boston, Suffolk, Massachusetts, USA, d: Sep 09, 1983 in Paris, Ile-de-France, France

....................7 Nicholas Palais Braude b: Nov 22, 1972 in Boston, Suffolk, Massachusetts, USA

...............5 Michael Linenthal b: Aug 17, 1916 in Boston, Suffolk, Massachusetts, USA, d: Jan 18, 1974 in San Francisco, San Francisco, California, USA

...............5 Mark Linenthal b: Nov 12, 1921 in Boston, Suffolk, Massachusetts, USA

.... + Alice Adams b: Aug 14, 1926 in Fredericksburg, Stafford, Virginia, USA, m: 1949

................6 Peter A. Linenthal b: Mar 20, 1951 in Redwood City, Alameda, California, USA

.... + Anasovich b: May 04, 1950 in Seymour, New Haven, Connecticut, USA

.... + Frances E. Jaffer b: Mar 13, 1921 in Hartford, Hartford, Connecticut, USA, m: 1973

............4 Percy B Davidson b: Jul 1893 in Boston, Suffolk, Massachusetts, USA, d: Apr 29, 1932 in West Roxbury, Suffolk, Massachusetts, USA

.... + Christina Affeld b: 1896 in Boston, Suffolk, Massachusetts, USA, m: 1922 in Boston, Suffolk, Massachusetts, USA

...............5 Judith Davidson b: 1924 in Boston, Suffolk, Massachusetts, USA

.... + Chaffee

......2 Mende Davidzon b: 1831 in Skaudvile, Kovno, Russia

...... + Fridman b: Russia

.........3 Rivka Fridman b: 1857 in Tavrig, Kovno, Russia

.... + Itzig Jacobson b: 1856 in Kros (Kraziai), Kovno, Russia

............4 Arthur Jacobson b: 1882 in Skaudvile, Kovno, Russia; Skaudvile, Taurage District, Lithuania/Skaudvile, Taurage, Lithuania/

.........3 Feige Fridman b: 1858 in Tavrig, Kovno, Lithuania

.........3 Nathan Friedman b: May 10, 1868 in Tavrig, Kovno, Russia, d: 1945 in Chicago, Cook, Illinois, USA

.... + Sarah "Sora" Jacobson b: 1865 in Upina, Kovno, Russia, m: 1907 in Kovno, Kovno, Russia; Same location as Kaunas, Lithuania, d: 1953 in Chicago, Cook, Illinois, USA

............4 Abraham Friedman b: Aug 1892 in Russia

.... + Ida Friedman b: 1897

...............5 Burton D Friedman b: Aug 22, 1924, d: Dec 29, 1994 in Springfield, Fairfax, Virginia, USA

............4 Peter Freedman b: Mar 1896 in Chicago, Cook, Illinois, USA

............4 Arthur Friedman b: 1901 in Chicago, Cook, Illinois, USA

.... + Kate Friedman b: 1902 in Chicago, Cook, Illinois, USA

......2 Shmuel Fishman b: 1837 in Skaudvile, Kovno, Russia, d: 1922 in Shavel, Kovno Guberniya, Russia

...... + Jenta Meltzer b: 1831 in Skaudvile, Kovno, Russia, m: 1861 in Skaudvile, Kovno, Russia, d: 1913 in Skaudvile, Kovno, Russia

.........3 Rivka Fishman b: 1863 in Skaudvile, Kovno, Russia, d: 1940 in Skaudvile, Kovno, Russia; Skaudvile, Taurage District, Lithuania/Skaudvile, Taurage, Lithuania/

.... + Ora "Ahron" Beker b: 1844 in Skaudvile, Kovno, Russia, m: 1884 in Skaudvile, Kovno, Russia, d: 1916 in Skaudvile, Kovno, Russia

............4 Edie Baker b: 1882 in Skaudvile, Kovno, Russia; Skaudvile, Taurage, Lithuania/Skaudvile, Taurage, Lithuania/, d: Johannesberg, South Africa

.... + Hirsh Taub b: 1880, d: Johannesberg, South Africa

............4 Kuna Belia Beker b: 1885 in Skaudvile, Kovno, Russia; Skaudvile, Taurage, Lithuainia/Skaudvile, Taurage, Lithuania/, d: Sep 19, 1941 in Lithuania

............4 Morris "Moshe" Baker b: Jul 04, 1887 in Skaudvile, Kovno, Russia, d: Sep 24, 1952 in Clarksdale, Coahoma, Mississippi, USA

.... + Ida Frank b: Jan 15, 1891 in Louisville, Jefferson, Kentucky, USA, m: 1913 in Clarksdale, Coahoma, Mississippi, USA, d: May 06, 1942 in Clarksdale, Coahoma, Mississippi, USA

...............5 Alma Baker b: Sep 08, 1916 in Clarksdale, Coahoma, Mississippi, USA, d: Nov 13, 1958 in Memphis, Shelby, Tennessee, USA

.... + Herman Lerner b: Jun 17, 1912 in Germany, m: 1946 in Memphis, Shelby, Tennessee, USA, d: May 03, 2000 in Germantown, Shelby, Tennessee, USA

................6 Joseph Irving Lerner b: Mar 28, 1951 in Memphis, Shelby, Tennessee, USA

.... + Linda m: 1982 in Memphis, Shelby, Tennessee, USA

....................7 Bradley Lerner b: Mar 30, 1984 in Memphis, Shelby, Tennessee, USA

................6 Marshall Bert Lerner b: Jun 28, 1954 in Memphis, Shelby, Tennessee, USA

.... + Doreen b: Dec 19 in Glasgow, Lanarkshire, Scotland

...............5 Julia Belle Baker b: Jun 02, 1919 in Clarksdale, Coahoma, Mississippi, USA, d: Memphis, Shelby, Tennessee, USA

.... + Julius Glassman b: Mar 31, 1918 in Memphis, Shelby, Tennessee, USA, m: 1941 in Memphis, Shelby, Tennessee, USA, d: Feb 1985 in Memphis, Shelby, Tennessee, USA

................6 Irene Michelle Glassman b: Jan 29, 1943 in Memphis, Shelby, Tennessee, USA

.... + William R. Lippe b: Sep 05, 1944 in Ohio, USA

....................7 Tanya Lippe b: Oct 24, 1971 in Costa Mesa, Orange, California, USA, d: Aug 16, 1995 in Seattle, King, Washington, USA

....................7 Eric Lippe b: Jun 01, 1975 in Youngstown, Mahoning, Ohio, USA

................6 Nathan Richard Glassman b: Nov 11, 1946 in Memphis, Shelby, Tennessee, USA

.... + Susan Lawless b: May 28, 1953 in Riverhead, Suffolk, New York, USA, m: 1972 in Memphis, Shelby, Tennessee, USA

....................7 Samantha Nicole Glassman b: Oct 15, 1973 in Memphis, Shelby, Tennessee, USA

....................7 Lauran Elizabeth Glassman b: Nov 28, 1981 in Memphis, Shelby, Tennessee, USA

....................7 Kathryn Bailey Glassman b: Nov 17, 1983 in Memphis, Shelby, Tennessee, USA

....................7 Julian Zoe Glassman b: Jul 19, 1990 in Memphis, Shelby, Tennessee, USA

....................6.Helen Cohen b: Jan 01, 1947 in Sparta, Alleghany, North Carolina, USA

.... 6.Alan Neil Glassman b: Aug 22, 1950 in Memphis, Shelby, Tennessee, USA Michael Mandie

...................+ Jill Rasco Glassman b:Abt. 1962 in Houston, Texas, USA, m:Jul 19, 1992 in Houston, Texas, USA

....................7 Brian Rasco Glassman b:Mar 01, 1994 in Houston, Texas, USA

...............5 Leonard Samuel Baker b: Aug 26, 1922 in Clarksdale, Coahoma, Mississippi, USA

.... + Janet b: Jul 14, 1923, m: 1955

................6 Sallie Elene Baker b: Apr 18, 1957 in Washington City, District Of Columbia, District of Columbia, USA

................6 Michael David Baker b: Jan 06, 1959 in Washington City, District Of Columbia, District of Columbia, USA

.... + Beth

....................7 David Baker b: Russia

....................7 Allyson Baker b: Washington City, District Of Columbia, District of Columbia, USA

...............5 Harriet Shirley Baker b: Oct 03, 1929 in Clarksdale, Coahoma, Mississippi, USA

.... + Robert I. Greenberg b: Jul 13, 1924 in Tallahassee, Leon, Florida, USA, m: 1950

................6 Margo Ida Greenberg b: Jul 30, 1952 in Tallahassee, Leon, Florida, USA

.... + James M. Tavess b: Jul 26, 1940 in New York, New York, USA, m: 1980 in Tallahassee, Leon, Florida, USA

....................7 Lisa Tavess b: Sep 01, 1969 in Miami, Dade, Florida, USA

....................7 Stephaine Elizabeth Tavess b: Jan 08, 1983 in Hollywood, Broward, Florida, USA

....................7 Michelle Leigh Tavess b: Nov 01, 1984 in Hollywood, Broward, Florida, USA

................6 Amy Marsha Greenberg b: Nov 29, 1954 in Tallahassee, Leon, Florida, USA

.... + Christopher Robison b: 1950 in Seattle, King, Washington, USA, m: Oct 25, 1998 in Seattle, King, Washington, USA

................6 Susan Roberta Greenberg b: Oct 11, 1956 in Tallahassee, Leon, Florida, USA

.... + William L. Stabile b: Aug 20, 1956 in New York, New York, USA, m: 1984 in Tallahassee, Leon, Florida, USA

....................7 Brian Jeffrey Stabile b: Apr 22, 1985 in Hollywood, Broward, Florida, USA

....................7 Kevin Michael Stabile b: Jul 17, 1987 in Overland Park, Johnson, Kansas, USA

................6 Richard Adam Greenberg b: Feb 26, 1958 in Tallahassee, Leon, Florida, USA

.... + Leigh Ann Ziff b: Jul 12, 1961 in Birmingham, Jefferson, Alabama, USA, m: 1987 in Tallahassee, Leon, Florida, USA

....................7 Jeffery Alan Greenberg b: May 10, 1989 in Tampa, Hillsborough, Florida, USA

....................7 Julie Barrye Greenberg b: Mar 09, 1993 in Tallahassee, Leon, Florida, USA

................6 Sharon Beth Greenberg b: Aug 09, 1960 in Tallahassee, Leon, Florida, USA

.... + David Alan Goren b: Jul 09, 1961 in New Jersey, USA, m: 1989 in Tallahassee, Leon, Florida, USA

....................7 Samuel Abe Goren b: Dec 16, 1992 in Orlando, Brevard, Florida, USA

....................7 Benjamin Scott Goren b: Sep 09, 1996 in Atlanta, De Kalb, Georgia, USA

............4 Chana Beker b: 1889 in Skaudvile, Kovno, Russia; Holocaust, d: Sep 19, 1941 in Skaudvile, Lithuania, Holocaust

.... + Greener b: 1881 in Skaudvile, Kovno, Russia; Skaudvile, Taurage District, Lithuania/Skaudvile, Taurage, Lithuania/

............4 David Beker b: 1890 in Skaudvile, Kovno, Russia; Skaudvile, Taurage, Lithuainia/Skaudvile, Taurage, Lithuania/, d: 1910 in Skaudvile, Kovno, Russia; Skaudvile, Taurage, Lithuainia/Skaudvile, Taurage,

.........3 Max "Meyer" Fishman b: Aug 20, 1865 in Skaudvile, Kovno, Russia, d: Mar 04, 1929 in Trenton, Gibson, Tennessee, USA
.... + Jennie Katz b: 1876 in Russia, m: 1895 in Trenton, Gibson, Tennessee, USA, d: Nov 29, 1932 in Denver, Adams, Colorado, USA
...........4 Hattie Mae Fishman b: Jan 28, 1897 in Trenton, Gibson, Tennessee, USA, d: Nov 1979 in St Louis, St Louis, Missouri, USA
...........4 Philip Fishman b: Apr 08, 1897 in Wilburton, Latimer, Oklahoma, USA, d: Apr 1985 in Denver, Denver, Colorado, USA
.... + Dorothy Opplyn b: May 20, 1900 in Oklahoma, USA, d: Apr 1987 in Denver, Adams, Colorado, USA
...........4 Sadie Fishman b: Sep 19, 1898 in Trenton, Gibson, Tennessee, USA, d: Jan 1986 in Denver, Adams, Colorado, USA
.... + Maurice Myer Epstein b: Apr 17, 1897 in Denver, Adams, Nebraska, USA, d: Aug 1976 in Denver, Adams, Colorado, USA
...............5 Ruth Epstein b: 1922 in Denver, Adams, Colorado, USA
.... + Marvin I Malk b: 1921 in Denver, Adams, Colorado, USA
.................6 Diane Malk b: 1950 in Denver, Adams, Colorado, USA
.... + Jon Dietz b: 1950 in Denver, Adams, Colorado, USA
.................6 Janice Malk b: 1952 in Denver, Adams, Colorado, USA
.... + Warren Dennis b: 1949
....................7 Lindsay Dennis
....................7 Lauren Dennis
...............5 Max Epstein b: 1924 in Denver, Adams, Colorado, USA
.... + Annette b: 1927
.................6 Laura Epstein b: 1950
.................6 David Epstein b: 1952
.................6 Stephen Epstein b: 1956
.... + Jennifer
.... + Judy
...............5 Jayne Epstein b: 1927 in Denver, Adams, Colorado, USA
.... + Sidney Schetina b: 1925 in Denver, Adams, Colorado, USA, m: 1960
.................6 Ari Schetina b: Denver, Adams, Colorado, USA
.................6 Saul Schetina b: Denver, Adams, Colorado, USA
.... + Stanley Schwartz b: 1924 in Denver, Adams, Colorado, USA, m: 1950 in Denver, Denver, Colorado, USA
.................6 Mark Schwartz b: 1952 in Denver, Adams, Colorado, USA
.... + Debbie
.................6 Karen Schwartz b: 1954 in Denver, Adams, Colorado, USA
.... + Evan R. Harolds b: 1950 in Denver, Adams, Nebraska, USA
...........4 Leon Fishman b: Oct 08, 1905 in Trenton, Gibson, Tennessee, USA, d: Dec 1972 in Denver, Denver, Colorado, USA
.... + Florence Tobias b: 1909 in Denver, Adams, Colorado, USA, m: 1935 in Denver, Adams, Nebraska, USA, d: Jul 21, 1963 in Denver, Adams, Colorado, USA
...........4 Mabel Fishman b: Nov 15, 1907 in Trenton, Gibson, Tennessee, USA, d: Aug 28, 1985 in Denver, Denver, Colorado, USA
.... + Herman "Chaim" Berman b: Aug 09, 1902 in Philadelphia, Philadelphia, Pennsylvania, USA, m: Sep 11, 1930 in Denver, Denver, Colorado, USA, d: Oct 30, 1988 in Denver, Denver, Colorado, USA
...............5 Jeanne Berman b: Aug 05, 1935 in Denver, Adams, Colorado, USA
.... + Irman "Dean" Pepper b: Jun 18, 1932 in Salt Lake City, Salt Lake, Utah, USA
.................6 Caryn Jo Pepper b: Jul 16, 1958 in Detroit, Wayne, Michigan, USA
.... + Shaul Zadik b: 1958 in Israel, m: 1986
....................7 Timor Jacob Zadik b: Jul 30, 1987
....................7 Oren Haim Zadik b: Oct 09, 1991
.................6 Lawrence Aaron Pepper b: Aug 20, 1960 in Denver, Adams, Colorado, USA
.... + Dana Yogend b: 1963 in Minneapolis, Anoka, Minnesota, USA, m: 1986
....................7 Micah David Pepper b: Oct 14, 1987
....................7 Sophie Mae Pepper b: Jul 20, 1990
....................7 Ari Louis Pepper b: Jun 06, 1995
.................6 Bryan Jacob Pepper b: Jan 29, 1965 in Chicago, Cook, Illinois, USA
.... + Laura Golaski b: 1970 in Chicago, Cook, Illinois, USA, m: 1991 in Chicago, Cook, Illinois, USA

....................7 Matthew Bryan Pepper b: Dec 22, 1994 in Chicago, Cook, Illinois, USA
....................7 Benjamin Michael Pepper b: Jan 01, 1997 in Chicago, Cook, Illinois, USA
..............5 Barbara Berman b: Feb 28, 1938 in Denver, Adams, Colorado, USA
.... + Edward Tonningsen b: 1933
...........4 Evelyn Fishman b: 1911 in Trenton, Gibson, Tennessee, USA, d: 1953 in Denver, Adams, Colorado, USA
.... + Michael Ginsburg b: Mar 02, 1887 in Denver, Adams, Colorado, USA, m: 1936 in Denver, Adams,
           Nebraska, USA, d: Jun 1974 in Denver, Adams, Colorado, USA
..............5 Myron "Mickey" Ginsburg b: 1938 in Denver, Adams, Colorado, USA
.... + Bryna b: 1940, m: 1969
.................6 Deborah Ginsburg b: 1963
.... + Jessica
..............5 Sara Ginsburg b: 1940 in Denver, Adams, Colorado, USA
.... + Thomas Stoen b: 1938 in Denver, Adams, Colorado, USA, m: 1967 in Denver, Denver, Colorado, USA
.................6 Eric Stoen b: 1968 in Colorado Springs, El Paso, Colorado, USA
.................6 Erin Stoen b: 1971 in Colorado Springs, El Paso, Colorado, USA
...........4 Harold S. Fishman b: Dec 19, 1919 in Trenton North, Gibson, Tennessee, USA, d: Jan 26, 2000 in Denver,
           Adams, Colorado, USA
........3 Sora Fishman b: 1867 in Skaudvile, Kovno, Russia, d: 1935 in Skaudvile, Kovno, Russia
........3 Malka "Mannie" Fishman b: 1875 in Skaudvile, Kovno, Russia, d: Feb 27, 1938 in Los Angeles, Los Angeles,
           California, USA
.... + Lewis Lyon b: Abt. 1872 in Russia, m: 1895 in Denver, Denver, Colorado, USA, d: 1934 in Denver, Adams,
           Colorado, USA
...........4 Rebecca "Becky" R. Lyon b: Aug 01, 1897 in Trenton, Gibson, Tennessee, USA, d: Jan 26, 1975 in
           Denver, Adams, Colorado, USA
...........4 Sophie Lyons b: Aug 15, 1901 in Trenton, Gibson, Tennessee, USA, d: Jun 08, 1943 in Los Angeles, Los
           Angeles, California, USA
.... + Dickman
...........4 Maurice Lyon b: Jun 13, 1905 in Trenton, Gibson, Tennessee, USA, d: Apr 19, 1976 in Aliso Viejo,
           Orange, California, USA
.... + Mary b: Jun 03, 1905 in California, USA, d: Jan 16, 1998 in Aliso Viejo, Orange, California, USA
........3 Simon "Shimon" Fishman b: Aug 14, 1879 in Skaudvile, Kovno, Russia; Skaudvile, Taurage,
           Lithuainia/Skaudvile, Taurage, Lithuania/, d: May 20, 1956 in Denver, Adams, Colorado, USA
.... + Mary Fine b: Oct 21, 1881 in Skaudvile, Kovno, Russia; Skaudvile, Taurage, Lithuainia/Skaudvile, Taurage,
           Lithuania/, m: 1899 in Sterling, Logan, Colorado, USA, d: Jan 1972 in Denver, Adams, Colorado, USA
...........4 Myrtle Fishman b: 1901 in Denver, Adams, Colorado, USA, d: 1934 in Tribune, Greeley, Kansas, USA
...........4 Naomi Fishman b: 1907 in Sidney, Cheyenne, Nebraska, USA, d: 1927 in Sidney, Cheyenne, Nebraska, USA
...........4 Irving L. "Boy" Fishman b: Sep 07, 1914 in Sidney, Cheyenne, Nebraska, USA, d: Dec 04, 2005 in Denver,
           Adams, Nebraska, USA
.... + Phebe Cohen b: 1922 in Denver, Colorado, USA, m: Abt. 1946 in Denver, Adams, Nebraska, USA, d: 1956
           in Denver, Adams, Nebraska, USA
..............5 Gary S. Fishman b: Jun 28, 1948 in Denver, Adams, Nebraska, USA
.... + Jenny b: 1949
.................6 Benjamin Fishman b: 1969 in Denver, Adams, Nebraska, USA
..............5 Stephen Fishman b: Nov 27, 1949 in Denver, Adams, Nebraska, USA
.................6 Emma Fishman b: 1968 in Denver, Colorado, USA
.................6 Eric Fishman b: 1970 in Denver, Colorado, USA
..............5 Myrna Fishman b: Dec 21, 1952 in Denver, Adams, Nebraska, USA
.... + Mikko A. Koski b: Mar 22, 1948 in Finland, m: 1973 in Denver, Denver, Colorado, USA
.................6 Ezra Koski b: May 02, 1975 in Denver, Adams, Nebraska, USA
.................6 Simon Koski b: Jul 25, 1978 in Denver, Adams, Nebraska, USA
.................6 Hannah Koski b: Jul 29, 1981 in Calcutta Settlement, Caroni, Trinidad and Tobago
.................6 Zac Koski b: Oct 11, 1989 in Denver, Adams, Nebraska, USA
......2 Leah Davidzon b: 1839 in Vainutas, Kovno, Russia
...... + Yosef Perez b: 1835 in Skaudvile, Kovno, Russia; Skaudvile, Taurage District, Lithuania/Skaudvile, Taurage,
           Lithuania/, m: 1889, d: 1915 in Skaudvile, Kovno, Russia; Skaudvile, Taurage District, Lithuania/Skaudvile, Taurage,
           Lithuania/
.........3 Mendel Joseph b: Mar 09, 1865 in Skaudvile, Kovno, Russia, d: Jul 31, 1940 in Adams, Colorado, USA

.... + Bell Charney b: 1873 in Russia, m: 1891 in Sidney, Cheyenne, Nebraska, USA, d: 1924 in Denver, Adams, Colorado, USA
............4 Rebecca Joseph b: Nov 13, 1890 in Sidney, Cheyenne, Nebraska, USA
............4 Bessie Joseph b: Feb 05, 1894 in Arkansas, USA, d: Mar 08, 1938 in Denver, Adams, Colorado, USA
.... + Leon Fine b: 1883 in Russia (Lithuania), m: 1916, d: Aug 11, 1956 in Mt Nebo Cemetery, Denver, Adams, Colorado, USA
................5 Leonard J. Fine b: Sep 09, 1919 in Sidney, Cheyenne, Nebraska, USA, d: Jul 1984 in Denver, Adams, Nebraska, USA
.... + Betty Jane b: 1925 in Denver, Adams, Nebraska, USA, m: 1948 in Denver, Adams, Nebraska, USA
................6 Jill Fine b: 1949 in Denver, Adams, Colorado, USA
.... + Duane A. Gill b: 1946 in Denver, Adams, Colorado, USA, m: 1973 in Denver, Denver, Colorado, USA
...................7 Joel Gill b: 1975 in Denver, Adams, Colorado, USA
...................7 Joshua Gill b: 1978 in Denver, Adams, Colorado, USA
...................7 Jordan Gill b: 1982 in Denver, Adams, Colorado, USA
................6 Melissa Fine b: 1951
............4 Lillian Joseph b: Aug 17, 1897 ; Indian Territory (Oklahoma), d: Jan 1988 in Deer Park, Suffolk, New York, USA
.... + A. John Hepner b: Sep 01, 1892 in New York, New York, USA, m: 1919 in Sidney, Cheyenne, Nebraska, USA, d: Mar 1972 in Deer Park, Suffolk, New York, USA
................5 Theresa Henper b: Nov 06, 1920 in Deer Park, Suffolk, New York, USA, d: Dec 1980 in Deer Park, Suffolk, New York, USA
............4 Leon Ralph Joseph b: Jul 17, 1901 in McAlester, Pittsburg, Oklahoma, USA; Indian Territory, Oklahoma, d: Aug 26, 1981 in Sacramento, Sacramento, California, USA
........3 Rivka Perez b: 1866 in Skaudvile, Kovno, Russia; Skaudvile, Taurage District, Lithuania/Skaudvile, Taurage, Lithuania/, d: 1887 in Skaudvile, Kovno, Russia
.... + Furman b: 1860 in Skaudvile, Kovno, Russia; Skaudvile, Taurage, Lithuainia/Skaudvile, Taurage, Lithuania/
........3 John Aaron Joseph b: Sep 15, 1875 in Skaudvile, Kovno, Russia; Skaudvile, Taurage, Lithuainia/Skaudvile, Taurage, Lithuania/, d: Nov 11, 1944 in Tulsa, Tulsa, Oklahoma, USA
.... + Anna Rubinstein b: Jun 01, 1879 in New York, New York, USA, m: Feb 11, 1902 in St Louis, St Louis, Missouri, USA, d: Sep 09, 1964 in Tulsa, Tulsa, Oklahoma, USA
............4 Julien Joseph b: Nov 01, 1904 in Wilburton, Latimer, Oklahoma, USA, d: Sep 12, 1977 in Tucson, Pima, Arizona, USA
.... + Ruth b: Feb 01, 1906, m: 1941, d: Feb 1972 in Tucson, Pima, Arizona, USA
................5 Lawrence Larry Joseph b: Feb 03, 1943
..................6 Randy Joseph b: Dec 01, 1970
............4 Sylvia Joseph b: Jul 02, 1908 in Wilburton, Latimer, Oklahoma, USA, d: Feb 19, 2005 in Oklahoma City, Oklahoma, Oklahoma, USA
.... + Samuel E. Goldberg b: Dec 27, 1902 in Hartshorne, Pittsburg, Oklahoma, USA, m: Jun 07, 1936 in McAlester, Pittsburg, Oklahoma, USA, d: Apr 07, 1975 in Oklahoma City, Oklahoma, Oklahoma, USA
................5 Harriet L. Goldberg b: Mar 08, 1937 in McAlester, Pittsburg, Oklahoma, USA
.... + Joel L Carson b: Jul 05, 1937 in Houston, Texas, USA, m: Dec 28, 1958 in Oklahoma City, Oklahoma, Oklahoma, USA
..................6 Melanie Joanie Carson b: Sep 27, 1961 in Norman, Cleveland, Oklahoma, USA
.... + Bart Raff b: Sep 16, 1960 in Fort Worth, Johnson, Texas, USA, m: Sep 04, 1983 in Oklahoma City,
...................7 Natalie Suzanne Raff b: Jun 07, 1988 in Oklahoma City, Canadian, Oklahoma, USA
...................7 Alex Mitchell Raff b: Jan 14, 1992 in Oklahoma City, Canadian, Oklahoma, USA
..................6 Laura Sue Carson b: Feb 08, 1963 in George AFB, San Bernardino, California, USA
.... + Jon A Epstein b: Jun 17, 1963 in Massachusetts, USA, m: Jun 15, 1985 in Oklahoma City, Oklahoma, Oklahoma, USA
...................7 Adam Carson Epstein b: Apr 22, 1989 in Oklahoma City, Canadian, Oklahoma, USA
...................7 Anna Rachel Epstein b: Mar 20, 1992 in Oklahoma City, Canadian, Oklahoma, USA
................5 Sally Goldberg b: 1939 in McAlester, Pittsburg, Oklahoma, USA
.... + Mark L Siegel b: Apr 14, 1938 in Milwaukee, Milwaukee, Wisconsin, USA
..................6 Lisa A Siegel b: Aug 19, 1963 in Phoenix, Maricopa, Arizona, USA
.... + Steven Klipin b: Jan 10, 1964 in Johannesburg, Gauteng, South Africa, m: Oct 14, 1993 in Kibbutz Lotan, Israel
..................6 Andrea Lynn Siegel b: Apr 19, 1965 in Phoenix, Maricopa, Arizona, USA
..................6 Loren Shara Siegel b: Aug 04, 1968 in San Jose, Los Angeles, California, USA
.... + David Levin b: Aug 07, 1963 in San Francisco, San Francisco, California, USA

....................7 Sophia Siegel Levin b: Mar 22, 1995 in San Francisco, San Francisco, California, USA
...............5 Michael Mende Goldberg b: Jan 25, 1943 in McAlester, Pittsburg, Oklahoma, USA
.... + Joanne L.s Scott b: Mar 06, 1943 in Christchurch, Canterbury, New Zealand, m: Mar 01, 1974 in
               Christchurch, Canterbury, New Zealand
..................6 Andrew Zachary Scott Goldberg b: Mar 06, 1975 in Christchurch, Canterbury, New Zealand
..................6 Sarah Rachel Goldberg b: Aug 26, 1977 in Virginia, USA
............4 Leonard Joseph b: Feb 16, 1910 in Wilburton, Latimer, Oklahoma, USA, d: Nov 21, 1986 in Denver,
               Adams, Nebraska, USA
.... + Harriet Schibel b: Jun 06, 1914 in Montana, USA, m: Mar 01, 1943, d: Denver, Adams, Colorado, USA
...............5 Judy A. Joseph b: Oct 21, 1946 in Denver, Adams, Colorado, USA
.... + Arlan Crane m: Jan 1995
.... + Allan Striker b: 1940 in Denver, Adams, Colorado, USA, m: 1968
..................6 Douglas Striker b: Jul 19, 1974 in Denver, Adams, Colorado, USA
...............5 Nancy Joseph b: May 11, 1950 in Denver, Adams, Colorado, USA
.... + Thomas Gould b: 1947 in Denver, Adams, Colorado, USA, m: 1973 in Denver, Adams, Nebraska, USA
............4 Dorothy Joseph b: May 14, 1914 in Wilburton, Latimer, Oklahoma, USA, d: Jan 13, 2008 in Denver,
               Adams, Nebraska, USA
.... + Nathan L. Koin b: Jun 09, 1902 in United Kingdom, d: Aug 03, 1990 in Denver, Adams, Nebraska, USA
...............5 Diana Koin b: Dec 06, 1943 in Denver, Adams, Nebraska, USA
.... + Richard A. Silverberg m: 1963 in Denver, Adams, Nebraska, USA
..................6 Katherine Anne Silverberg b: Oct 12, 1964 in Denver, Adams, Nebraska, USA, d: May 15, 2010 in
               Chicago, Cook, Illinois, USA
.... + Robert "Rob" Levin
....................7 Isbel Levin
....................7 Clair Levin
..................6 Helen Silverberg b: Feb 10, 1969 in Denver, Adams, Nebraska, USA
.... + William Bill Vermeere m: Dec 15, 1987
...............5 Janet Koin b: Jul 21, 1947 in Denver, Adams, Nebraska, USA
.... + John Dampeer
..................6 Nicole Dampeer b: Jun 14, 1980 in Denver, Adams, Nebraska, USA

פּרָאפּ

Sora bat Shimon Prop

of

שקודוויל

Shkudvil, Vilna Guberniya
Russia Empire

1806 - 1875

Sora married Dovid Muskin and the family Lived in Upina a few miles from Shkudvil for the couple of generations then many immigrated to the United States and elsewhere in the world.

1 Sora Prop b: 1810 in Zemaitija Duchy, Grand Duchy of Lithuania, d: 1844 in Skaudvile, Kovno, Russia
... + Dovid Fridman-Muskin b: 1805 in Skaudvile, Kovno, Russia, m: 1824 in Skaudvile, Kovno, Russia, d: 1884 in
    Skaudvile, Kovno, Russia
......2 Tisa Muskin b: 1832 in Skaudvile, Kovno, Russia
...... + Prejdel Jacobson b: 1830 in Kros, Kovno, Russia, m: 1855 in Skaudvile, Kovno, Russia
.........3 Itzig Jacobson b: 1856 in Kros (Kraziai), Kovno, Russia
.... + Rivka Fridman b: 1857 in Tavrig, Kovno, Russia
............4 Arthur Jacobson b: 1882 in Skaudvile, Kovno, Russia; Skaudvile, Taurage District, Lithuania/Skaudvile,
            Taurage, Lithuania/
.........3 Shmuel Jacobson b: 1858 in Kros (Kraziai), Kovno, Russia
............4 Moshe Jacobson b: 1891 in Chicago, Cook, Illinois, USA
.........3 Todres Jacobson b: 1860 in Upina, Kovno, Russia, d: 1934 in Chicago, Cook, Illinois, USA
............4 Louis Jacobson b: 1895 in Upina, Kovno, Russia
.........3 Abram Jacobson b: 1864 in Upina, Kovno, Russia, d: Chicago, Cook, Illinois, USA
.........3 Shimon Jacobson b: 1864 in Upina, Kovno, Russia
.........3 Sarah "Sora" Jacobson b: 1865 in Upina, Kovno, Russia, d: 1953 in Chicago, Cook, Illinois, USA
.... + Nathan Friedman b: May 10, 1868 in Tavrig, Kovno, Russia, m: 1907 in Kovno, Kovno, Russia; Same
            location as Kaunas, Lithuania, d: 1945 in Chicago, Cook, Illinois, USA
............4 Abraham Friedman b: Aug 1892 in Russia
.... + Ida Friedman b: 1897
...............5 Burton D Friedman b: Aug 22, 1924, d: Dec 29, 1994 in Springfield, Fairfax, Virginia, USA
............4 Peter Freedman b: Mar 1896 in Chicago, Cook, Illinois, USA
............4 Arthur Friedman b: 1901 in Chicago, Cook, Illinois, USA
.... + Kate Friedman b: 1902 in Chicago, Cook, Illinois, USA
......2 Basa Muskin b: 1833 in Skaudvile, Kovno, Russia
......2 Elazar Reuven Muskin b: 1834 in Skaudvile, Kovno, Russia, d: 1884 in Skaudvile, Kovno, Russia
...... + Rivka b: 1835 in Kovno, Kovno, Russia; Same location as Kaunas, Lithuania, m: 1847 in Skaudvile, Kovno,
            Russia, d: Abt. 1922 in Skaudvile, Kovno, Russia; Skaudvile, Taurage, Lithuainia/Skaudvile, Taurage, Lithuania/
.........3 Tuvia Muskin b: 1852 in Skaudvile, Kovno, Russia, d: May 30, 1920 in Chicago, Cook, Illinois, USA
.... + Sarah Rapaport b: 1855 in Upina, Kovno, Russia, m: Abt. 1886 in Skaudvile, Kovno, Russia, d: Mar 20, 1935
            in Chicago, Cook, Illinois, USA
............4 Ella Muskin b: Mar 20, 1887 in Upina, Kovno, Russia, d: Aug 17, 1982 in Chicago, Cook, Illinois, USA
.... + Isidore Greenberg b: Apr 24, 1887 in Kovno, Kovno, Russia, m: Abt. 1905 in Upina, Kovno, Russia, d: May
            01, 1949 in Chicago, Cook, Illinois, USA
...............5 Jerome "Jerry" Greenberg b: Apr 26, 1905 in Upina, Kovno, Lithuania, d: Jun 29, 1987 in Chicago, Cook,
            Illinois, USA
.... + Faye Drucker b: Jun 28, 1913 in Chicago, Cook, Illinois, USA, d: Feb 14, 1996 in Ozona, Pinellas,
            Florida, USA
...................6 Fred Greenberg b: 1934
.... + Susan M Fogelson b: Feb 1943
......................7 Justin Greenberg b: 1964
......................7 Jordan Greenberg b: 1967
......................7 Yair Greenberg b: 1971
...................6 Marcy Greenberg b: 1936
.... + James Edelstein
...............5 Beatrice Greenberg b: Jul 08, 1912 in Upina, Kovno Gubernia Lithuania, d: May 20, 1988 in Broward,
            Duval, Florida, USA
.... + Gilbert Siegel b: 1912 in Chicago, Cook, Illinois, USA
...................6 Arthur Siegel b: 1938
......................7 Jonathan Siegel b: 1963
...................6 James Siegel b: 1940
.... + Gabriela Dula b: 1946
......................7 Jordana Siegel b: 1970
......................7 Erica Siegel b: 1972
...............5 Esther R. Greenberg b: Oct 06, 1913 in Chicago, Cook, Illinois, USA
.... + Charles Levin b: May 25, 1909 in Chicago, Cook, Illinois, USA, d: Aug 1985 in Chicago, Cook, Illinois, USA
...................6 Civia Levin b: 1947 in Chicago, Cook, Illinois, USA
.... + Robert Tamarkin b: 1935
......................7 Elisa Tamarkin

................6 Ira Levin b: 1950 in Chicago, Cook, Illinois, USA
.... + Michele Padrovski b: 1947
..............5 Edythe Greenberg b: Sep 05, 1915 in Chicago, Cook, Illinois, USA, d: Mar 20, 1967 in Dade, Florida, USA
.... + Solomon Futterman b: Jan 11, 1915 in Chicago, Cook, Illinois, USA, d: Oct 22, 1974 in Dade, Florida, USA
................6 Ronald L Futterman b: Mar 05, 1943 in Chicago, Cook, Illinois, USA
.... + Pamela A. Hayes b: Bet. Sep 1945–1949
...................7 Elizabeth Futterman b: Abt. 1973
...................7 Samantha Futterman b: Abt. 1975
................6 Joel Futterman b: 1947
.... + Nancy b: 1951
...................7 Demian Futterman b: 1973
...................7 Euphany Futterman b: 1976
..............5 Allen "Abraham" Greenberg b: Aug 09, 1917 in Chicago, Cook, Illinois, USA, d: Feb 04, 2004 in
            Shawnee Mission, Johnson, Kansas, USA
.... + Lillian Sweet b: Aug 24, 1921 in Kansas City, Clay, Missouri, USA, m: Abt. 1942 in Kansas City, Clay,
            Missouri, USA
................6 Jackye Sue Greenberg b: Nov 02, 1944 in Kansas City, Clay, Missouri, USA
.... + Alan Goldberg b: Jan 09, 1945 in Highland Park, Wayne, Michigan, USA, m: Abt. 1965, d: Feb 1980
...................7 Rebeka Grace "Rivka" Goldberg b: Aug 30, 1967 in Sycamore, De Kalb, Illinois, USA
.... + Joel Philip Krigsman b: Jul 12, 1967 in Brooklyn, Kings, New York, USA
.......................8 Simcha Netanel Krigsman b: Jun 19, 1997 in Baltimore, Maryland, USA
.......................8 Leeba Tova Krigsman b: Oct 12, 1998 in Baltimore, Maryland, USA
.......................8 Chayim Yisroel Krigsman b: Jun 04, 2001 in Baltimore, Maryland, USA
...................7 Amy Goldberg b: May 24, 1970 in Royal Oak, Oakland, Michigan, USA
.... + David Rasmussen
...................7 Katharine Goldberg b: Dec 14, 1972 in Royal Oak, Oakland, Michigan, USA
.... + Michael Rosell
...................7 Margaret "Maggie" Goldberg b: Feb 01, 1976 in Warren, Macomb, Michigan, USA
................6 Jerry "Tov" Greenberg b: May 17, 1945 in Kansas City, Clay, Missouri, USA
................6 Debra Joy "Dvora" Greenberg b: Jan 09, 1949 in Kansas City, Clay, Missouri, USA
.... + Perry Krevat b: Sep 07, 1945 in St Louis, St Louis, Missouri, USA
...................7 Elie Krevat b: Mar 28, 1980 in St Louis, St Louis, Missouri, USA
...................7 Ariela Krevat b: Oct 19, 1983 in Greenbrae, Marin, California, USA
...................7 Rina Krevat b: Dec 30, 1991 in Greenbrae, Marin, California, USA
................6 Terry Lee "Esther Liba" Greenberg b: May 05, 1952 in Kansas City, Clay, Missouri, USA
.... + Samuel "Simcha Leib" Krause b: Aug 25, 1950 in Tel Aviv, Israel
...................7 Adina Krause b: May 16, 1984 in New York, New York, USA
...................7 Rochel Krause b: Nov 09, 1986 in Greenbrae, Marin, California, USA
...................7 Eliyahu Krause b: Jun 21, 1990 in Greenbrae, Marin, California, USA
...................7 Zalman Krause b: Feb 17, 1992 in Greenbrae, Marin, California, USA
...................7 Moshe Krause b: May 19, 1994 in Morristown, Middlesex, New Jersey, USA
...................7 Sosha Krause b: Feb 09, 1996 in Morristown, Middlesex, New Jersey, USA
..............5 Eli Greenberg b: Mar 12, 1919 in Chicago, Cook, Illinois, USA, d: Jan 20, 1978 in Chicago, Cook, Illinois, USA
.... + Harriett Skolnik b: 1923, d: Chicago, Cook, Illinois, USA
................6 Ivy Greenberg b: 1943 in Chicago, Cook, Illinois, USA
.... + Gary Levinson b: 1941
...................7 Julie Levinson b: 1978
...................7 Jennifer Levinson b: 1983
...................7 Chad Levinson b: 1984
................6 Murray Greenberg b: 1946 in Chicago, Cook, Illinois, USA

.... + Anita b: 1950

.................6 Judy Greenberg b: 1952 in Chicago, Cook, Illinois, USA

.... + James Gumbiner b: 1948

.....................7 Brandon Gumbiner b: 1978

.....................7 Bradley Gumbiner b: 1981

............4 Elazar Reuven Muskin b: Jul 26, 1888 in Upina, Kovno, Russia, d: Aug 02, 1950 in New York, New York, USA

.... + Rose Celia. Grad b: Apr 03, 1894 in Riga, Russia, m: Jun 1916 in Chicago, Cook, Illinois, USA, d: Mar 29, 1995 in Brookline, Norfolk, Massachusetts, USA

...............5 Jacob "Yaakov" Muskin b: Feb 27, 1918 in Chicago, Cook, Illinois, USA, d: Jan 08, 1990 in Cleveland, Cuyahoga, Ohio, USA

.... + Miriam Greenberg b: Jan 24, 1925, m: 1947 in New York, New York, USA, d: May 09, 2006 in Boynton Beach, Palm Beach, Florida, USA

.................6 Yosef Yitzchak Muskin b: Jun 02, 1950 in New York, New York, USA

.... + Barbara Beiss b: Oct 11, 1950 in Montréal, Quebec, Canada

.....................7 Hana Malka Muskin b: May 18, 1983 in New York, New York, USA

.....................7 Eliana Tova Muskin b: Mar 07, 1985 in New York, New York, USA

.....................7 Dorit Yedida Muskin b: Jun 15, 1990 in New York, New York, USA

.................6 Aliza Reena Muskin b: Nov 08, 1952 in Cleveland, Cuyahoga, Ohio, USA

.... + Efrem Lifschitz b: May 19, 1950 in New York, New York, USA

.....................7 Eliyahu Yitzchak Lifschitz b: Dec 14, 1977 in Rochester, Monroe, New York, USA

.....................7 Yonaton Dov Lifschitz b: Oct 07, 1979 in Highland Park, Camden, New Jersey, USA

.....................7 Shira Ilana Lifschitz b: Aug 19, 1982 in Highland Park, Camden, New Jersey, USA

.....................7 Avi Don Lifschitz b: May 12, 1984 in Dayton, Greene, Ohio, USA

.................6 Elazar Reuven Muskin b: Aug 09, 1955 in Cleveland, Cuyahoga, Ohio, USA

.... + Ruhama Helpern b: Nov 30, 1958 in New York, New York, USA, m: Abt. 1986 in New York, New York, USA

.....................7 Gila Sara Muskin b: Feb 11, 1988 in Los Angeles, Los Angeles, California, USA

.....................7 Dina Haya Muskin b: Jan 12, 1990 in Los Angeles, Los Angeles, California, USA

.................6 Refhel Maier Muskin b: May 03, 1960 in Cleveland, Cuyahoga, Ohio, USA

.... + Sharon Jacoby b: Mar 10, 1963 in Cleveland, Cuyahoga, Ohio, USA

.....................7 Adena Lyla Muskin b: Nov 29, 1989 in Washington City, District Of Columbia, District of Columbia, USA

.....................7 Yaakov Yeoshua Muskin b: Jul 07, 1991 in Washington City, District Of Columbia, District of Columbia, USA

.....................7 Carmi Nadav Muskin b: Nov 17, 1992 in Washington City, District Of Columbia, District of Columbia, USA

...............5 Edith "Etta-Peena" Muskin b: Sep 30, 1919 in Chicago, Cook, Illinois, USA, d: Feb 03, 1991 in Lynn, Essex, Massachusetts, USA

.... + Samuel J Fox b: Feb 25, 1919 in Rochester, Monroe, New York, USA, d: Dec 26, 1994 in Lynn, Essex, Massachusetts, USA

.................6 Joseph M Fox b: Abt. 1948 in Lynn, Essex, Massachusetts, USA

...............5 Tobey Muskin b: Apr 16, 1924 in Chicago, Cook, Illinois, USA, d: Dec 09, 2002 in New Bedford, Bristol, Massachusetts, USA

.... + Charles S. Weinstein b: Jun 16, 1924 in Worcester, Worcester, Massachusetts, USA, m: Abt. 1951 in Chicago, Cook, Illinois, USA, d: Sep 04, 2009 in New Bedford, Bristol, Massachusetts, USA

.................6 Ellie Weinstein b: 1952 in Brookline, Norfolk, Massachusetts, USA

.................6 Reuben Weinstein b: Feb 1954 in Brookline, Norfolk, Massachusetts, USA

.................6 Judith Weinstein b: 1958 in Brookline, Norfolk, Massachusetts, USA

.................6 Jonathan Weinstein b: 1961 in Brookline, Norfolk, Massachusetts, USA

...............5 Esther Shullamith Muskin b: Dec 18, 1926 in Chicago, Cook, Illinois, USA, d: Feb 10, 2003 in Brookline, Norfolk, Massachusetts, USA

.... + Julian Edelman b: Dec 18, 1928 in Boston, Suffolk, Massachusetts, USA, d: Feb 10, 2003 in Brookline, Norfolk, Massachusetts, USA

.................6 Elazer R. Edelman b: 1957 in Brookline, Norfolk, Massachusetts, USA

.... + Cheryl A. m: Brookline, Norfolk, Massachusetts, USA

.................6 Raymond H. Edelman b: 1963 in Brookline, Norfolk, Massachusetts, USA

.... + Linda "Altha"

.....................7 Raymond Edelman b: Abt. 1988

..................6 Daniel Edelman b: Feb 28, 1969 in Brookline, Norfolk, Massachusetts, USA
.... + Nancy
..................6 Kenneth Edelman b: Brookline, Norfolk, Massachusetts, USA
.... + Denise M
...............5 Tuvia Muskin b: Oct 02, 1931 in Chicago, Cook, Illinois, USA, d: Israel; Living in 2010 in Israel
.... + Adele d: Israel; Living in Israel 2010
..................6 Rena Muskin
.... + Yair Chamudot m: 2002 in Israel
....................7 Chamudot b: Jul 2003 in Israel
...............5 Hadassah Ruth Muskin b: Oct 02, 1931 in Chicago, Cook, Illinois, USA, d: Feb 14, 1932 in Chicago, Cook, Illinois, USA
............4 Alter "Albert" Muskin b: 1890 in Upyna, Silale, Lithuania, d: May 07, 1925 in Chicago, Cook, Illinois, USA
.... + Bertha b: Jan 15, 1899 in Austria, d: California, USA
...............5 Toby Muskin b: Jun 14, 1920 in Chicago, Cook, Illinois, USA, d: 1949 in Chicago, Cook, Illinois, USA
...............5 Edith Muskin b: Jan 14, 1922 in Chicago, Cook, Illinois, USA, d: 1947
...............5 Theodore B. "Tuvia" Muskin b: Sep 02, 1924 in Chicago, Cook, Illinois, USA, d: Feb 22, 1995 in Nokomis, Sarasota, Florida, USA
.... + Del Rudolph
..................6 Toby Muskin b: Aug 02, 1951 in Chicago, Cook, Illinois, USA, d: Apr 04, 1997 in Nokomis, Sarasota, Florida, USA
..................6 Theodore Muskin b: Abt. 1953 in Chicago, Cook, Illinois, USA
.........3 Chaja-Tene Muskin b: 1859 in Skaudvile, Kovno, Russia; Skaudvile, Taurage, Lithuainia/Skaudvile, Taurage, Lithuania/
......2 Shmuylo Itzig Muskin b: 1837 in Skaudvile, Kovno, Russia
...... + Sora b: 1832
.........3 Muskin b: 1854 in Upina, Kovno, Russia, d: Minneapolis, Anoka, Minnesota, USA
.... + Lurie b: Skaudvile, Kovno, Russia; Skaudvile, Taurage, Lithuainia/Skaudvile, Taurage, Lithuania/, d: Minneapolis, Anoka, Minnesota, USA
......2 Shimon Shilel Muskin b: 1844 in Skaudvile, Kovno, Russia

פְּרָאפּ

Efraim ben Shimon Prop

of

שקודוויל

Shkudvil, Vilna Guberniya
Russia Empire

Born 1786

According to the 1816 Reviskie Shazki (Russian Census) Efraim departed Shkudvil in 1812 for places unknown. No further record of him has been found.

פּרָפּ

Leah bat Shimon Prop

of

שׁקודוויל

Shkudvil, Vilna Guberniya
Russia Empire

Born circa 1786

Currently there has been no record of Leah bat Shimon, other than the family oral history passed down from Louis Arne's family tree.

פּרָאפּ

Marjasha bat Shimon Prop

of

שקודוויל

Shkudvil, Vilna Guberniya
Russia Empire

Born circa 1789

Currently there is no information concerning Marjasha bat Shimon.

www.ingramcontent.com/pod-product-compliance
Lightning Source LLC
Chambersburg PA
CBHW060423100426
42812CB00030B/3285/J